Rough Draft

Rough Draft

The Modernist Diaries of Emily Holmes Coleman, 1929–1937

Edited by

Elizabeth Podnieks

UNIVERSITY OF DELAWARE PRESS
Newark

Published by University of Delaware Press
Co-published with The Rowman & Littlefield Publishing Group, Inc.
4501 Forbes Boulevard, Suite 200, Lanham, Maryland 20706
http://www.rowman.com

Estover Road, Plymouth PL6 7PY, United Kingdom

Copyright © 2012 by Elizabeth Podnieks

All rights reserved. No part of this book may be reproduced in any form or by any electronic or mechanical means, including information storage and retrieval systems, without written permission from the publisher, except by a reviewer who may quote passages in a review.

All quotes by Emily Holmes Coleman are Copyright © 2012 by Estate of Emily Holmes Coleman.

All quotes by John Holmes Coleman are Copyright © 2012 by Marie Claire Coleman.

British Library Cataloguing in Publication Information Available

Library of Congress Cataloging-in-Publication Data

Coleman, Emily Holmes, 1899-1974.
  Rough draft : the modernist diaries of Emily Holmes Coleman, 1929-1937 / edited by Elizabeth Podnieks.
     p. cm.
  Includes bibliographical references and index.
  ISBN 978-1-61149-376-4 (cloth : alk. paper) — ISBN 978-1-61149-377-1 (electronic)
  1. Coleman, Emily Holmes, 1899-1974. I. Podnieks, Elizabeth, 1964- II. Title.
PS3505.O2783Z46 2012
813'.52—dc23
                                                                          2011041029

∞™ The paper used in this publication meets the minimum requirements of American National Standard for Information Sciences—Permanence of Paper for Printed Library Materials, ANSI/NISO Z39.48-1992.

Printed in the United States of America

Contents

Acknowledgments vii

Introduction xi

The Diary

PART I

Section 1 Paris: October 30–December 17, 1929   3

Section 2 St. Tropez: December 18, 1929–February 15, 1930   45

PART II

Section 1 Gloucestershire: August 9–August 25, 1932   77

Section 2 Devonshire: August 26–September 9, 1932   93

Section 3 Gloucestershire: September 23–October 9, 1932   125

Section 4 London: October 11–October 29, 1932   131

Section 5 Paris: November 30–December 23, 1932   143

Part III

Section 1 London and Devonshire: March 22–July 24, 1933   165

Section 2 Yorkshire: June 8–July 3, 1934   173

Section 3 London: July 5–September 1, 1934   183

PART IV

Section 1	London: January 16–March 13, 1936	215
Section 2	London and Petersfield: March 16–May 28, 1936	247
Section 3	London: May 29–June 12, 1936	287
Section 4	Glyndebourne, London, and Yorkshire: June 23–July 21, 1936	307

PART V

| Section 1 | London: November 14–December 31, 1936 | 323 |
| Section 2 | London, Winchcombe, and Petersfield: June 10–October 5, 1937 | 341 |

Coleman Diary Entries Omitted	359
Bibliography	361
Index	367
About the Editor	383

Acknowledgments

Having been immersed in Emily Coleman's diary for many years, I have become indebted to numerous people who have assisted in bringing this text to light.

My first and most profound thanks are to Emily Coleman for keeping her remarkable diary and for taking the necessary steps to preserve her life's record for posterity. Coleman clearly intended that her private words would one day reach a broad readership, and it has been a professional and personal privilege to serve as her editor in this regard.

While I never knew Coleman, I have benefited from the ongoing support of her literary executor, Joseph Geraci, an American rare books and photographs dealer living in Amsterdam. In addition to granting permission to begin this project, Mr. Geraci has, over the years, been unfailing with his patience, his insights into Coleman's life, his feedback on my progress, and his commitment to bringing his dear friend's work to her much-deserved audience. This book is predicated on Mr. Geraci's prescient recognition of Coleman's talent. In arranging for her papers to be preserved at the University of Delaware Library, Special Collections, he has provided many scholars with access to a compelling and valuable literary history.

Mr. Geraci put me in touch with Marie Claire Coleman, Emily Coleman's daughter-in-law, to whom I extend my deepest gratitude for her support of my work. In the first stages of editing, Marie Claire Coleman opened her home to me in France, sharing her memories of her husband and illuminating Emily Coleman's biography from her personal perspective. An early meeting with Mr. Geraci in Amsterdam was similarly inspiring and enlightening. I am deeply grateful to Mr. Geraci and Ms. Coleman for their time, encouragement, and friendship. They have made this edition feasible through their generous approval of the material published here.

One of the great pleasures of this project has been the opportunity to work with Rebecca Johnson Melvin, superb librarian with the University of Delaware's Special Collections department. From the moment I met Rebecca during my first research trip to Delaware I have been well served by her knowledge of the archive, her eagerness to locate and prepare documents, and her enthusiasm in promoting scholarship. Our countless e-mails over these years have been informative as well as energizing for me, and it is my hope that together we will pursue future endeavors related to Coleman's archive.

I would also like to extend my continuing gratitude to the family of Antonia White, specifically White's daughter and executor, Lady Susan Chitty, and Chitty's husband, Sir Thomas Chitty. Their openness, sense of humor, and unsparing hospitality have been a gift; on several occasions they invited me to their home in England, where they shared stories about White and her circle and where I was able to read unpublished letters between Coleman and White.

Thanks are due to Bonnie Kime Scott, who served as my supervisor on my Post-Doctoral Fellowship studies on Coleman and whose modernist scholarship continues to inspire; Mary Lynn Broe, whose early research on Coleman's Hayford Hall group first alerted me to the presence of Coleman's diary at Delaware; Sandra Chait, for her insights into Coleman as we co-edited our collection on Hayford Hall; and Beth Alvarez, Curator of Literary Manuscripts at the University of Maryland at College Park Libraries and Isabel Howe of the Authors League Fund for their assistance with and permission to quote from the Djuna Barnes Papers.

I wish to acknowledge, moreover, all the members of the press who have made possible the publication of this book. At the University of Delaware Press, Dr. Donald C. Mell, Chair, Board of Editors for his early and sustained commitment to the project; Karen G. Druliner, Managing Editor, for her wonderful assistance during the various stages of completion; and the Readers for the press, whose astute comments guided the final shaping of the material. At Rowman & Littlefield Publishing Group, my thanks go to Brooke Bascietto, Associate Editor, for her superb skills organizing the production of the book; and to Dane Torbeck, project manager with Adept Content Solutions, for producing the book.

Closer to home I am buoyed and vitalized by my colleagues in the Department of English at Ryerson University. I note with gratitude that the preparation of the index was supported with a grant provided by the office of the Dean of Arts, Ryerson University. I wish also to recognize the talented efforts of my Research Assistants at Ryerson, Sacha Staples and Sarah Lambert, who came on board in the final stages of manuscript preparation, Sacha to help in identifying some last minute footnotes and Sarah to copy edit the diary manuscript before its final submission to the press.

I am most grateful to Professor François Paré in the Department of French Studies at the University of Waterloo, Ontario, for his translations of Coleman's French phrases.

I have been with Coleman's diary for many years, just as my family has been with me. This edited version would not exist, and neither would the rewards of seeing it in print register, without my family by my side. To Elizabeth Podnieks (Sr), Andrew Podnicks, Mary-Jane Podnieks, Mairi Macdonald, Zachary Smith, and Emily Smith, immense thanks for your tolerance, stimulation, and sustenance. A special thanks to my husband, Ian Smith, for driving me all over England and France on an Emily Coleman "tour" and for everything else as well along this long and fruitful road.

Introduction

By Elizabeth Podnieks

"Emily is one of the people I love and value most—unique and irreplaceable. Her passionate *interest* in literature, her wonderful eye for the best in any work, her marvelous vitality, her honesty, her generosity, her glorious humour, her intense loyal devotion to her friends. She's the most *loyal* person I know." So British author Antonia White described her long-time friend Emily Coleman who was, White believed, "built on the heroic scale . . . faults, virtues and all!" Learning of Coleman's death on June 13, 1974, White affirmed: "She was somehow more than life size, with enough vitality for at least half-a-dozen people. Right to the last she attracted people."[1] Born in 1899 in California and raised on the east coast of the United States, Emily Holmes Coleman joined the exodus of Americans expatriating to Europe in the nineteen-twenties where she developed as a surrealist writer, publishing a novel, *The Shutter of Snow*, and poems in little magazines like *transition*. She also began her life's work, her diary, which was sustained for over four decades. In making the rounds of the literary circuit in France and England during the heyday of Anglo-American modernism, Coleman told her journal, "I live abroad because I need it vitally."[2] The edited selection of her diary, published here for the first time, compellingly preserves her sojourn in Europe and reveals just how dramatic, engaging, and larger-than-life a figure Coleman could be.

---

[1] White, *Diaries 1958–1979* Vol. 2, 76; 74; 244. Emphasis in the original.
[2] November 26, 1929, F. 625. All references to Emily Coleman's unpublished material in this introduction and in the notes to the diary are from The Emily Holmes Coleman Papers housed at the University of Delaware Library, Special Collections, cited according to the date (where possible) as well as file (F) number.

Introduction

The diary also presents us with a multitude of literary, artistic, and intellectual figures of the period with whom Coleman interacted. She documented the lively and complex social networks in which the personal and professional encouragements, jealousies, and ambitions of her friends unfolded within a world of limitless sexual longing, supplies of alcohol, and aesthetic discussions. With Coleman at the centre, the diary swirls around three of her closest female friends: Djuna Barnes, one of modernism's most iconic bisexual representatives and author of experimental texts like *Ryder* and *Nightwood*; Peggy Guggenheim, the American heiress who served as a modernist patron and who became a prominent modern art collector; and Antonia White, whose autobiographical novel *Frost in May*, which provides a young female counterpart to James Joyce's protagonist in *A Portrait of the Artist as a Young Man*, became a "legend."[3] Other major participants include Coleman's long-time lover (Sir) Samuel "Peter" Hoare, a literary-minded member of London's Home Office; Guggenheim's partner, the charismatic British intellect John Ferrar Holms, a burned-out, one-time critic with whom Coleman was also in love; and the bisexual poet George Barker, twenty years Coleman's junior, whom Coleman financially supported while he preoccupied her both artistically and erotically.

Added to this cast are a host of others in recurring roles such as Edwin Muir, Scottish critic, poet, and translator; Phyllis Jones, who wrote an advice column for London's *Daily Mirror*; Cyril Connolly, *New Statesman and Nation* columnist and author of the supposedly "obscene" novel *The Rock Pool*; Arthur Waley, translator of *The Tale of Genji*; Thelma Wood, the silverpoint artist and infamously promiscuous partner of Barnes; Humphrey Jennings, who made documentary films; Dylan Thomas, as noted for his pub crawling as for his verse; and T. S. Eliot, whom Coleman convinced to publish *Nightwood* when he was director of Faber & Faber.

While visiting Guggenheim at her summer estate in 1934, Coleman told her diary: "Very witty conversation going on the whole time [. . .] I long for a dictaphone in the livingroom."[4] Coleman's diary in fact became that dictaphone, for she turned it "on" to record conversations between, impressions of, and experiences with anyone and everyone with whom she crossed paths. For this reason her diary is relevant to readers eager for intimate, first-hand accounts of the era's personalities, including Coleman's own.

Coleman started to keep her personal record some time after her arrival in Paris in October 1926; but, unfortunately for scholars, she burned this early material. The first extant diary begins on October 30, 1929. She continued to

---

[3] Reflecting on her first novel in 1954, White twice noted that it had become a "legend" (*Diaries 1926–1957* Vol. 1, 276, 281).
[4] July 15, 16, 17 (single entry), 1934, F. 633.

update it until 1970, preserving in total about 19,000 pages for posterity. The sheer length of the manuscript precludes the possibility of publishing it in its entirety. The selection here is limited to a period spanning only eight years: from the diary's opening scenes on the Left Bank to its closing description of Coleman setting sail for her return to the United States in 1937. My decision to focus on this section is an obvious one in both chronological and aesthetic terms, for the time frames her experiences as an expatriate and illuminates the period during which she most fully engaged with and pursued modernist art and life.

While I subsequently discuss my editing practices in detail, it is important to note now that the selection presented here is itself heavily excised, culled as it is from over 1,300 leaves of largely typed, single-spaced manuscript pages—it was her habit to type two columns, or leaves, per horizontal letter-sized page. Coleman wrote by hand in general only if her ribbon was used up or if she could not access a typewriter when travelling. Her method of composition signals her public aspirations for the work, for she came to view it artistically and believed it was deserving of an audience. This abridged version testifies to her belief that "Life is the rough draft of art," as readers will discover how she transformed the rough draft of her life into an enduring literary text.[5]

Coleman's journal is a kaleidoscope of the early twentieth century in the throes of industrialization, commercialization, and modernization. In particular, it is a product of, and a tribute to, modernism, a term referring to the aesthetic, cultural, and political movements spreading across the western world from roughly 1890 to 1940. Modernism embodies critical, theoretical, and imaginative responses to the inventions and developments that helped define this era, such as the railroad, telephone, airplane, automobile, radio, film, and photography and an attendant mass and popular culture of consumerism. Modernism was the context within which developed Freudian psychology with its focus on subjectivity, sexuality, and the unconscious; the privileging of science over religion that went hand in hand with the secularization of society; the battles for Empire; and the rise of Fascism and Communism, the First World War, and the Spanish Civil War. Driven by issues of gender and the so-called "sex wars" at the turn of the century, modernism also attends to how roles of women were being contested and debated in political, intellectual, and artistic circles and texts, whose rhetoric registered the increasingly militant suffrage movement; challenges to heteronormative identities by lesbians, bisexuals, and anti-conventional heterosexuals; and the growing presence of women in institutions of higher learning and in the labor market.

As scholars like Bonnie Kime Scott and Peter Nicholls define it as a series or network of modernisms, modernism was articulated in diverse expressions

---
[5]September 18, 1937, F. 639.

of and manifestoes promoting impressionism, surrealism, symbolism, imagism, primitivism, and futurism, for example. "Isms" such as these testify to Ezra Pound's mandate to "make it new," which was taken up by writers, artists, musicians, and architects who drew on and simultaneously rejected the conservative ideologies, styles, and materials of their Victorian and Edwardian predecessors.[6] Within the field of literature specifically, writers reflected seismic shifts as they confronted taboo or radical subject matter concomitant with democratizing notions of what constitutes appropriate literary content. As Virginia Woolf advocated in her 1925 essay "Modern Fiction," authors must attend to "an ordinary mind on an ordinary day" because "'The proper stuff of fiction' does not exist; everything is the proper stuff of fiction, every feeling, every thought; every quality of brain and spirit is drawn upon; no perception comes amiss."[7] Preoccupied with rendering a character's interiority and personality as fully and authentically as possible, modernists experimented with techniques like free indirect discourse and stream of consciousness monologues, just as they privileged time as measured by one's internal or private rhythms over artificial or mechanized clock systems. The self-conscious construction of a text *as* text is often evident, while fragmented or discontinuous plots, genre blending, typographical play, and lack of closure mirror narrative themes like alienation, psychic trauma, and the difficulty communicating in a foreboding and changing world. In many ways, these points also speak to the structure and composition of diaries, which inscribe the autobiographer's "ordinary" personhood and life in a series of daily, self-reflexive reports, and in which "no perception comes amiss." And although a diary is chronologically ordered, calendrical dates exist in tension with the emotional or psychological time flowing through the entries, just as formal stylistic considerations like paragraphing and punctuation may give way to the immediacy and spontaneity of the writing moment.

"ALL FAMOUS PEOPLE KEPT THEM IN THEIR YOUTH"

A look at Coleman's biography and her development as a creative writer sets the scene for our immersion in her modernist milieu as well as for our understanding of her diary's contribution to modernism. In 1963, Coleman was working on a document entitled "The Story of My Childhood," and although it was never finished this extant autobiographical fragment, along with passages from her

---

[6] See Nicolls' *Modernisms: A Literary Guide*, and Scott's introduction to *The Gender of Modernism*, 1–18.
[7] 189; 194–195.

diary, provides us with information about her early years.[8] She was born Emily Tyler Holmes on January 22, 1899, in Oakland, California, to parents whom she described as "Americans, Protestants, of the middle class." Her father, John Milton Holmes, sold insurance and was often away from home on business. Her mother, Lucy Adams Coaney, was mentally unstable, and the children were supervised by a "nurse." Coleman would soon have two younger brothers, John and William, but she was singled out for attention: "My mother loved me especially and made much of me, at the expense of my brothers, whom she neglected."[9] In February 1906, the family moved east to live with Coaney's parents in Wyoming, New Jersey, a move likely motivated by Coaney's increasingly erratic behavior, which included hitting the child living next door and deliberately breaking the neighbours' window. Soon after arriving in Wyoming, Coaney was admitted to a facility in Summit, New Jersey.[10] In a 1937 diary entry, while "trying to take a birds-eye view" of herself by writing in third person, Coleman explained: "Born when her mother was just beginning to show signs of the mental trouble which finally made her permanently insane, she was in close relation to this mother until the age of 7; and her early life must have been saturated with strange images, in those impressionable fatal years.[11]

Coleman was certainly affected by "strange images." In the summer of 1908, when she was only nine years old she was sent to Dr. Combes' Sanitarium in Corona, Long Island, for observation.[12] Her family considered her to be a "nervous" child and worried she may have inherited her mother's illness, while her Aunt Eleanor accused her of masturbating and therefore being in need of help. Coleman was the only child patient there, and the experience was clearly a haunting one. She recalled in "The Story" how she suffered the worst fright of her life one night when a woman was brought to Combes': "I was awakened by groans, that seemed to come from Hell. . . . It sounded like a demon." Years later, Coleman descended into her own hell. On January 6, 1924, she gave birth to John (Johnny) Milton Holmes Coleman in a parturition so difficult that she developed toxic exhaustive psychosis, which led to her being institutionalized in the Rochester (New York) State

---

[8] "The Story of My Childhood" (F. 1075, Second Draft). In her diary entries for November 5 and 9, 1937 (F. 641, not transcribed), she offers a detailed review of her life, narrated in third person.
[9] "The Story." Coleman rarely mentioned her brothers in the diary; she was not close with either one.
[10] "The Story." Coaney spent the rest of her life in the institution, dying in 1918 when Coleman was nineteen.
[11] November 5, 1937, F. 641.
[12] Coleman misspelled the name, referring to it as "Dr Coombes' Nursing Home"—she has written "Nursing Home" in pen, atop the original typed word "Sanitarium," which remains legible despite being crossed out.

Hospital for two months. Exposure to the Combes sanitarium as a child and to her mother's psychiatric history, along with her own experiences of postpartum depression, fostered Coleman's preoccupation with "madness," a theme that informed her writing. She translated the birth trauma into her only published novel, *The Shutter of Snow* (1930), and she documented and analyzed her frequent mood swings, bouts of depression, and ongoing suicidal longings throughout her diary, as readers will see in many of the entries which follow.

Coleman reported in "The Story" that while life in California had been dominated by her mother, in the east, when her mother "was taken away [her] father became all-important." Mr. Holmes, though, was not long at the Wyoming house: within the year he moved to Pittsburgh to work for the Hartford Fire Insurance Company. He was transferred to Philadelphia in 1913, and then again to Hartford, Connecticut, in 1918, where he spent the remainder of his life, and where he became a close friend of his poet-colleague Wallace Stevens.[13] In her parents' absence, Coleman was cared for by her grandparents, by her great Aunt Lottie, and by her Aunt Eleanor who seemed to the girl to be an "old maid" and a religious fanatic. She also made occasional visits to New York to see her Uncle Charlie (the "Chief"), a bachelor who worked on Wall Street. Coleman described the family in "The Story" as being odd, and asserted, "It is no wonder my poor mother went insane, coming from that collection." She elaborated: "The Coaneys were not a loving family, and I desperately needed to be loved (I was, by my father)." Coleman's craving for love was likely exacerbated by the fact that not long after her arrival in Wyoming—with her mother gone and her father about to move to another state—she was sent in the fall of 1906, at age seven, to St. Mary's on Mount-St. Gabriel boarding school in Peekskill, New York. She acknowledged, however, that she was a "cocky" student and after her second year the school told her father not to bring her back.

Following her stint at Combes' nursing home in the summer of 1908, that fall Coleman attended the School of Good Shepherd in Asbury Park, New Jersey, where she remained for eight years. It was where she "grew up," though she would also refer to it as a "prison."[14] In her diary, she commented that "the incessant discipline" of the school "drove her mad, and laid the foundations for a sort of insane rebellion against organized society which became one of the keystones" of her personality.[15] The letters she sent to her father in Pittsburgh shed light on her adolescent experiences there and offer

---

[13]Coleman noted: "Mr. Wallace Stevens is Father's friend, he loves my father, sits next to him at luncheon, a businessman's luncheon, every day" (October 20, 1937, F. 641).
[14]August 24, 1932, F. 629.
[15]November 9, 1937, F. 641.

us a portrait of a young girl discovering literature. For instance, when she was 12, she was studying *Julius Caesar* and proud to report that her teacher "Miss Jenckes has put me in the same class with the big girls, who are all about 15 or 16. Isn't that fine? That is, only in English Classics."[16] She would receive the highest mark in the class. As she matured, she became a fanatic reader of anything and everything she could get her hands on.

Coleman also became a writer. In April 1908, when she was nine years old her poem "The Stars" appeared in *St. Nicholas*, the popular and prestigious American children's magazine (1873–1940) which published works by authors such as Louisa May Alcott and Mark Twain. At the Good Shepherd school her literary passion further bloomed. She noted in "The Story" that her teacher, Frances Buchan, was the first to encourage her to write: "'Put down your thoughts,' she shouted," and Coleman did. In a letter sent to her father in February 1914, she referred to the book she had begun drafting the previous summer and stated her intentions to revise it; however, she did not mention it again and there is no extant manuscript. In a self-assessment of an English assignment the next year, Coleman wrote: "My composition this month is the hardest I ever did. The title is 'Ruskin as Compared with Carlyle' (sounds learned, doesn't it?) and I assure you it is a work of art, not to say genius."[17] Her use of the term genius is prescient, for as an adult Coleman would become preoccupied with both striving to develop genius and believing she already possessed it.

Coleman was honing her skills as an author of poems and short stories, two very public genres. Just as importantly, she was developing her talent as a private writer of letters and diaries. On January 29, 1912, she interrupted an account of her activities with this observation: "I suppose you think I'm writing you a book, but you're glad of it, aren't you? Every once in a while one of the girls comes in this school room, inquiring, 'How many pages have you written now, Emily?' To which I reply triumphantly 'Fifteen!'" She soon added, "(Mary has just said, 'How many pages now?' I say 'Sixteen!' upon which Mary groans.)"[18] This portrait of a prolific autobiographer from early on foreshadows the older Coleman who continued to produce not only detailed letters to her father and friends but also lengthy diary entries: composed almost entirely by typewriter, entries could be more than ten pages for a single day. The passage also shows that she viewed her epistle as a "book" and presages how she would later conceive her diary as a literary product.

A few months later, on April 27, Coleman noted that her father had returned to her some of the letters she had earlier written to him, and she

---

[16]October 7, 1911, F. 1589.
[17]February 28, 1914, F. 1592; February 20, 1915, F. 1593.
[18]F. 1590.

asked, "Won't you please send me some more, if you have time, Father dear? I wish you would, as I love to read them, and the girls are always asking to do the same."[19] Coleman had previously suggested that she was writing a "book" out of her letters to her father. Her notion of audience here further emphasizes the association of letters with literary work. We generally think a letter has only its addressee as its audience, but even at this young age Coleman was disrupting genre assumptions, as she made clear that her epistles were read by many of her classmates. In like spirit, an older Coleman would view and use her diary as a source of entertainment for herself and for her friends.

As a child, she had been keeping a diary concomitant with letter-writing, making the first reference to such an activity on July 14, 1915: "I must tell you how gay I have been this week. My journal tells all my doings since I left Asbury Park." She concluded her report: "There, Father, is what I have done this week, as my journal tells it." John Holmes had likely inquired about her journaling habit, for in her letter of July 20, she followed: "In regard to keeping a journal, I do it for two reasons. First, because so many things happen that I can't remember them, and when I want to tell you what I have been doing, all I have to do is to read the account I have written. And second, because it is so interesting to read after the summer is over. All famous people kept them in their youth; and mine may prove useful when they want to compile my biography!"[20] As with the book she referred to revising in 1914, she did not comment on the fate of this diary, but its short life anticipates the massive journal penned by Coleman as an adult.

We might extend Coleman's "two reasons" for keeping a diary to at least a third, one predicated on gender. That is, in keeping a journal as a young girl she was participating in one of the most traditional activities of female expression, a feature of life writing noted by a plethora of scholars who trace the history of women's diarizing from the sixteenth to the twentieth century.[21] Adrienne Rich, for instance, names the diary "that profoundly female, and feminist, genre," and Harriet Blodgett studies it as a "characteristic" female form.[22] It is not surprising that Coleman wrote her diary in tandem with letters throughout her life, for as Cinthia Gannett underscores, "Women's journals were often practiced, indeed, as part of a continuum of domestic discourse that included letter writing."[23] While men have

---

[19] F. 1590.
[20] F. 1593.
[21] See for instance Blodgett *Centuries of Female Days*, Rich *On Lies, Secrets, and Silence*, Hogan "Engendered Autobiographies," Gannett *Gender and the Journal*, and Bunkers and Huff *Inscribing the Daily*.
[22] Rich 217; Blodgett 5.
[23] Gannett 133.

created their own diary traditions, the content of their texts has typically focused on the public spheres in which men have functioned. By contrast, historically relegated to the private spheres, women turn to their diaries to inscribe "the home, the hearth, the family, the sexual, the emotional" details of women's lives.[24]

In our western patriarchal culture in which girls and women have been encouraged to mute or even deny their public voices, then, the diary, the seemingly quintessential secret text, emerged over the past four centuries as a safe and legitimized forum for female expression. Blodgett contends that "diary keeping has been practiced so extensively by women because it has been possible for them and gratifying to them"; "A diary is an act of language that, by speaking of one's self, sustains one's sense of being a self, with an autonomous and significant identity."[25] Functioning as such a crucial outlet, coupled with the fact that from the early twentieth century on blank diaries have been marketed mainly to girls and women, the diary was an acceptable venue to which the young Coleman, seeking self-definition in a world in which she often felt alone, could turn to express and to comfort herself. In my own study of the genre, *Daily Modernism: The Literary Diaries of Virginia Woolf, Antonia White, Elizabeth Smart, and Anaïs Nin*, I suggest that modernist authors in particular used their diaries in subversive ways. They both fulfilled and challenged prescribed stereotypes for respectable feminine conduct within these private and domesticated spaces, while also undermining societal expectations of female silence by conceiving of their life texts as works of art intended for public consumption and for posterity, as an adult Coleman did.

Coleman yearned as a child for recognition, and she regarded her journal as one means to a celebrated end. Her conception of her English assignment as a work of "genius" resonates nicely with her sense of kinship with "All famous people" who kept journals "in their youth." She was so convinced of success that she regarded her diary as being "useful" to her future biographer. She was just sixteen years old when she revealed these sentiments, so her words must be understood within the context of her youth and naiveté. And yet, Coleman would continue to write through her sense of self as genius throughout her adulthood, displaying a staggering self-confidence that was on one hand authentic and on the other designed to compensate for what she justly perceived to be a male-led denigration of the female artist.

---

[24] Rich 214.
[25] Blodgett 5.

Introduction

"CORRIDORS OF LIBERTY"

Eager to advance her formal studies of literature, Coleman majored in English at Wellesley College from 1916–20. Reflecting in her diary on this experience (again from the third-person "birds-eye view" seen earlier) she described how at Wellesley "she emerged into what seemed to her for four unbelievable years, a paradise. In later life she dreamed constantly of this paradise. What was an ordinary American upper-class finishing school became to her the symbol of life, and freedom; she never got over it." She added that "the memory of Wellesley College haunted her all through her life—that first emerging into the corridors of liberty" which signaled her "first escape." Coleman had already spent years away from home at boarding school, but Wellesley marked a profound break—or "escape"—from the controlling forces of her high-school teachers and family for, as she noted of herself, "her whole youth was poisoned by the sincere, well-meaning but utterly misguided notions entertained by those who brought her up for her spiritual welfare," including Mr. Holmes who had "co-operated whole-heartedly with the school system."[26] At Wellesley, she cultivated her interests in poetry while dedicating herself to an active social life, one in which she began to define herself in terms of her relationships with men, as she would do throughout the diary years included in this selection.

When she was 17 she became engaged, but soon after the fiancé in question went "overseas" for two years and when he returned she learned he had not been faithful to her and "had changed horribly," so she left him.[27] She began to "egg" on other men to forget this first love, and she became "hard" and "disillusioned" about men as a result, but she continued to enjoy the fact that many of her college suitors could nonetheless fall in love with her.[28] She recorded these vague details in a letter to her future husband, Loyd (*sic*) (Deak) Coleman, warning him as to why she needed to be careful in proceeding with their flirtations.[29] These points also prepare us for the Emily

---

[26]November 9, 1937, F. 641.
[27]The fiancé may have been a soldier. Coleman had been involved in the war effort when she spent the summer of 1918 working as a volunteer at the All College War Farm organized by Wellesley (Letter to Deak Coleman, July 9, 1920, F. 99).
[28]Emily Coleman to Deak Coleman, July 16, 1920, F. 99.
[29]In one of his first letters to Emily, Deak stated that his "real name" is "Deac, short for Deacon" (June 8, 1920, F. 91). However, he also went by the name Loyd Ring, as he explained: "If I were disposed to be facetious, I should say that in my early youth my father beat the 'L' out of me. Being, as I am, perfectly frank and straightforward, I will state for your information that my family, sensing the advertising value in an original name, wished Loyd onto me. I am not called that, however, except by sarcastic persons. 'R' is the initial letter of Ring. In detail, the Ring name came here from Salisbury, Massachusetts" (F. 91, undated). He signed his letters

Coleman we meet in the diaries, one who is constantly craving and buoyed by, yet also endlessly disappointed in, romantic and sexual relations.

Toward the end of her senior year in June 1920, a mutual friend had put Emily, then twenty-one, in epistolary contact with Deak, a twenty-three-year-old from Brockport, New York, who was a graduate of Rochester University. Deak was working in the merchandising and advertising department of the Rochester Bureau of Printing, though he was soon to take a new job as an advertising manager at the General Railway Signal Works.[30] Emily was finishing at Wellesley and then spent the summer as a drama counselor and song leader at Camp Pinecliffe in Harrison, Maine, at which point she moved to Hartford to "settle down to the domestic life" with her father.[31] Having never met, the two began a courtship wholly through their correspondence.

Although Deak had turned to the practical pursuits of an advertising career, he shared Emily's love for poetry, and it was on this foundation that she set the terms for their connection in her first extant letter, just two weeks before her graduation in June: "I don't see any particular point in our corresponding unless we do it poetically. I have too many to write to now in ordinary form, so that I hesitate to take on another unless he looks extremely interesting. But you know a man who can really write clever poetry as a diversion is rare in this day and age—and I am perfectly willing to admit that I have never met my equal before!"[32] Premised on the literary, their letters were in part dedicated to the topic of poetry and often included their own verses.

The letters were also entertaining. At college Emily had garnered a reputation as a popular young woman with a sense of humor. Writing about graduation festivities she told Deak that she "had the pleasant job of being toast-mistress at class supper" and "had to think up jokes for 350 place cards." She was also able to look at herself with deprecation—a quality which permeates the diary—as she laughed to Deak: "the fact that you are quiet appeals strongly to me, for I could never in the very millennium be said to be that myself!"[33] Deak appreciated her linguistic skill, noting of her epistles: "your unusually brilliant and scintillating sarcasm provides the one bright spot in my otherwise drab and colorless existence."[34]

---

variously as "Deac" "LR Coleman," "Loyd R Coleman," or "LR." In 1926, Emily would begin to spell Deac (the name she generally called him) "Deak," though in letters of the 1930s she addressed him as "Duku."

[30] At some point in late 1920 or 1921 he returned to the Bureau of Printing.
[31] Emily Coleman to Deak Coleman, June 18, 1920, F. 98.
[32] Emily Coleman to Deak Coleman, June 2, 1920, F. 98.
[33] Emily Coleman to Deak Coleman, June 18; June 2, 1920, F. 98.
[34] Deak Coleman to Emily Coleman, June 8, 1920, F. 91.

The couple's bond strengthened over the next few months, but they had yet to meet in person and so, not surprisingly, they became increasingly curious about one another's physical appearances. Deak cautioned her that "One of us will certainly be surprised when we meet. It will probably be I (get that grammar) because if you can imagine the funniest looking, freckled faced redhead that you ever saw, you can imagine me."[35] She described herself in turn: "I am tall, but not so very—I am five feet, six-and-a half. And I am 'slender.' I have blue eyes and I have a good complexion and dimples and a frightfully wide mouth and a turned-up nose and a few freckles and 'an engaging smile.' And I have a temper." She went on: "I dare say that, like all men, you are very anxious to know if I am goodlooking. (That's all they care about.) I think it depends on how much a person likes me whether I am or not. So, you see, you'll have to judge for yourself." In reply to another letter, she was "offended" that a mutual acquaintance relayed to him that she was "popular rather than goodlooking" for "I always thought I was both."[36] After they met in person—there are no extant descriptions of the event—and just before they were to be married, Deak reported on her new bob hair cut: "I knew you would look like twelve; you never did look like more than fourteen."[37] Peggy Guggenheim would later note that in 1928 "Emily looked like a little boy, although she was twenty-nine."[38] Portraits such as these are complimented by friend and writer Mary Siepmann, who describes her in the introduction to the Virago edition of *The Shutter of Snow*: "In appearance Emily has been described as 'a traffic stopper': not strictly beautiful but unforgettable: widely spaced blue eyes, yellow hair, golden complexion, a lovely figure. She had twice the high spirits and vitality of any of her compatriots, was highly intelligent and very funny: marvellous company."

Deak and Emily probably came face to face for the first time at Camp Pinecliffe, as he had been asking to visit her there. They clearly liked what they saw for by the end of August she was writing to him about their engagement. There are only a few extant letters by Deak to Emily for the period leading up to their wedding on May 28, 1921, and their tone has markedly shifted to the sexual as he became increasingly aroused by the prospect of their honeymoon. He told her, for instance, "Wanna put one hand on each it [*sic*] and love 'em pashy-like and hard. I do. Oh, Babe, wanna lie beside yuh and love." Deak was specifically looking forward to sex that was uninterrupted, for the letters reveal that the pair had had premarital intercourse:

---

[35]Deak Coleman to Emily Coleman, July 13, 1920, F. 91.
[36]Emily Coleman to Deak Coleman, June 22, 1920, F. 98; July 1, 1920, F. 99.
[37]Deak Coleman to Emily Coleman, May 21, 1921, F. 92.
[38]Guggenheim 78.

"We have never really done it before without a slight modicum of worry." He justified their activities: "We have been married most certainly before this. Marriage, some one says, it just a compromise with immorality. I have never felt, with us, that there was the slightest trace of anything immoral."[39]

Within the diary, however, we witness Emily struggling to reconcile her sexual practices with the dictates of so-called respectable or moral society. Mr. Holmes, for instance, exerted such a psychological hold over her that she was terrified throughout her adulthood that if he knew about her promiscuous behavior after her divorce, "He would kill himself."[40] Ironically, her later lover Hoare, a bachelor, was often rendered impotent because he was so horrified by the prospect of being discovered post-coitus by his housekeeper and hotel clerks. His inhibitions contributed to Coleman's emotional—and sexual—distress and to the failure of the relationship.

After a few years of marriage, in January 1924, the Colemans had their first and only child, John, in a delivery that was so traumatic Emily suffered from post-partum "insanity" which "came from excessive pain (not taking gas oxygen), and an infection."[41] Following her hospitalization in Rochester she admitted in a letter to her father, "You know, I've been terribly depressed since I've been home [. . .] I fight it all the time, but it's been very hard."[42] She found some solace in writing, and the next year the Colemans moved to New York where Emily, still recovering, wrote poems while Deak pursued a Ph.D. in psychology at Columbia.[43]

It was during this period that the couple determined to move to Europe, believing that Emily's weak health would benefit from a life abroad and the cultural stimulation that would accompany such a change of scene. Like many Anglo-American writers and artists of the time, Emily felt she had to give up the conservatism of her homeland in order to realize her literary potential. As Shari Benstock explains in *Women of the Left Bank*, these eponymous women fled from the United States to France to find "the necessary cultural, sexual, and personal freedom to explore their creative intuitions."[44] Because Emily's illness had shattered the Colemans' finances it was decided that Deak would remain in New York to work while Emily and John went on ahead.

---

[39] Deak Coleman to Emily Coleman, May 19, 1921, F. 92; Undated, F. 92; May 24, 1921, F. 92.
[40] Diary, August 30, 1932, F. 629.
[41] October 9, 1932, F. 630.
[42] April, 1924, F. 1595.
[43] Though Deak stayed only one year at Columbia, he co-authored with Saxe Commins *Psychology: A Simplification* (1927). Commins (1892–1958) was the nephew of revolutionary Emma Goldman, and a highly respected literary editor.
[44] Benstock 10.

"I WANT THE GREAT FLARE OF GENIUS"

Sailing to Paris in October 1926, Coleman and her son settled, appropriately, on the Left Bank, moving first into a flat on the Boulevard du Montparnasse and then into one on the rue Bonaparte. They thus took up residence in one of modernism's preeminent expatriate neighborhoods for, as Benstock so engagingly details, this bohemian district was a major arena of modernist fashioning, serving as both a home and an inspiration to the artists who gathered and produced there. Reflecting in 1937 on her experiences a decade earlier, Coleman showed a clear sense of their significance: "In Paris at this time was occurring a kind of life which will take its place in American history."[45] She began attending classes at the Sorbonne and, more importantly, secured a much-needed job as a society editor for the Paris edition of the Chicago *Tribune*. As described by Hugh Ford, the *Tribune* (which ran from 1917 to 1934) "began reporting the activities of the cultural adventurists from America, as well as Europe, who were turning the old Latin Quarter of Montparnasse into an artistic and social *pied-à-terre*"; the contributing journalists "erected in the pages" of the paper "the one most comprehensive documentary history we possess of the Left Bank."[46] Coleman's professional start was certainly auspicious.

Deak joined his family in September 1927, but he was unemployed and they were financially strained. Having tried to find work with the prestigious advertising firm of J. Walter Thompson when he had been in New York, he was finally successful on March 3, 1928. However, the job for which he was hired by Thompson was in London.[47] Emily had by that time become involved in a lawsuit she had filed against the *Tribune*, which had fired her "for insisting upon extra money for double work" and so she stayed in France, as did John—though he was by now living more or less apart from his parents.[48] Shortly upon arriving in Europe, Emily had confronted her limitations as a mother. Plagued by her now-familiar mood swings and a tendency to hit John when he was naughty, she also resented the time and energy child rearing took away from her writing. In the interests of both John's and her own well-being, she and Deak arranged for John to live permanently with his governess, Madame Donn, who with her husband effectively raised John along with their own two children in Ivry, a suburb of Paris. Emily and Deak made sporadic trips to see him there

---

[45] November 9, 1937, F. 641.
[46] Ford 1; 6.
[47] Emily Coleman to John Milton Holmes, March 3, 1928, F. 1595.
[48] Coleman wrote to her father about the lawsuit on March 3, 1928 (F. 1595). She recounted in her diary that upon being fired, she attacked her boss, Paris *Tribune* publisher Jack Hummel: "On the Chicago *Tribune*—one year—and then I went wild and socked the Director with a beaded bag, in an evening dress" (October 20, 1937, F. 641).

and also took him to their respective homes for short visits. This plan decimated the Colemans' finances, for they not only paid John's expenses but also helped to support the Donns, who were impoverished Russian exiles.

Thus, although Emily had considered joining Deak in London as soon as the *Tribune* suit was settled—which it was in May 1928, in her favour—she instead leaped at the opportunity to move to St. Tropez at the end of that month to help the revolutionary Emma Goldman write her autobiography, for which she would receive room and board and thus alleviate some of their economic strain.[49] Goldman's friend Peggy Guggenheim had encouraged Goldman to write her life story, and had provided her with both funds and a villa in the south of France where she could work in solitude. Goldman in turn invited Coleman, who had sent Goldman a "fan letter" in 1925 and with whom she had continued to correspond, to serve as her assistant.[50] Through Goldman, Coleman met Guggenheim who was vacationing in the south. Guggenheim reflected on their first encounter, "Even though I liked her at once it never occurred to me what a role she was to assume in my life."[51] Coleman's diary brings this major role to centre stage, highlighting the intensity of their mutual devotion and the complex ways in which they had an impact on each other's artistic drives.

Deak and Emily would never live together for any considerable time after this St. Tropez interlude. She joined him for a few months in London in mid-1929 and again in the fall of 1929 when he was transferred to Thompson's Belgian office in Antwerp. However, she spent this period shifting about between London, Paris, the south of France, and Italy, in part looking for the best climate to accommodate her weak health and in part seeking independence while she developed herself as a writer. Although Deak could have supported her if she remained with him, and if they did not have the enormous expenses of childcare, he believed so strongly in her talent that he encouraged her to live wherever her artistic nature took her. While their letters to each other are loving and reciprocally supportive, neither party had remained monogamous and Emily had come to realize that she was no longer *in* love with him. She officially left him at the start of 1931, and their divorce was finalized on May 17, 1932.[52]

---

[49]Despite winning the suit, Coleman did not want to continue working at the paper (Emily Coleman to John Holmes, May 11, 1928, F. 1595). During this period in St. Tropez, John Coleman came to visit twice: once with the Donns from July to September 1928 and once on his own (accompanied on the train by a friend of Emily) in April 1929.
[50]See Mary V. Dearborn, *Mistress of Modernism: The Life of Peggy Guggenheim*, 63–64.
[51]See Guggenheim, *Out of This Century*, 78.
[52]Coleman wrote to her father that she "was not afraid of the consequences of leaving Deak"; and "The truth is that the actual step of leaving Deak has done a great deal for me. This has been hanging over me for four years" (August 25, 1931, F. 1597). In 1941, Deak became the

Mr. Holmes had given financial aid to his daughter while she was married, and after her divorce he provided her with a monthly income so that she did not have to seek further employment. As he worked his way up through the Hartford Insurance Company, becoming a director in 1936, he increased her allowance accordingly. Coleman's economic situation illuminates crucial intersections of gender, class, and modernism. In her letters to her father from Wellesley, for instance, we learn that she had drained his financial resources, and the subject of money is a refrain in the majority of letters she sent to him during her expatriate period just as it is within the diary. Her job with the *Tribune* between 1927 and 1928 was one of the only times she earned a regular salary during his lifetime.

Unofficially acknowledging her father's own calling as a patron of modernism, Coleman consistently offered thanks to him, as in this letter from St. Tropez: "Never think I forget that it is due to you that I am here at this moment, that I have this lovely country and this solitude, instead of having to look for a job somewhere that would take up my energies where they should not be allowed to go. Think how many people of real talent have been frustrated by the economic problem."[53] Coleman thus exemplifies the modernism of the American expatriate women like Gertrude Stein, Alice B. Toklas, and Maria Jolas who came, Benstock tells us, "from solidly middle-class circumstances" and who "experienced greater financial freedom" than their male counterparts, "having arrived in Paris with small annuities or inheritances with which they purchased their freedom from America."[54] Coleman's diary possibly owes its existence to this freedom, for had she been forced to work at a steady job it seems unlikely that she would have been able to write in it as she did for upwards of several hours each day.

Coleman herself was an active patron of modernism. Financially supported by her father, she took it as a given that she would delve liberally into those funds to support others in turn. She often denied herself material goods and

---

managing director of the Thompson's branch in Sydney, Australia, where he lived with his second wife, Henriette Louise Jamme, for nineteen years after which they returned to France.

[53] January 8, 1930, F. 1596. Mr. Holmes also often sent enormous sums of money, at Coleman's request, to the Donns. Moreover, he generously approved of the fact that Coleman gave away large portions of his money to her artist friends like Barnes and Barker, as Holmes told her in one letter, "I hope I shall be able to give more myself in order that you, in turn, may give" (December 17, 1936). Following her work for the *Tribune*, eighteen years would pass before she took another position, in January 1946, this time as a grade three teacher in a Catholic school in Connecticut. Her students included thirty-two boys and girls between the ages of seven and nine. She had been reluctant to find a job, but was compelled to because her father retired in January 1946 (unpublished letter from Coleman to Antonia White, January 27, 1946, courtesy of Lady Susan Chitty and Sir Thomas Chitty).

[54] Benstock, *Women*, 9.

pleasures, and she frequently strained her relationship with the wealthy Guggenheim by harping on her to provide patronage to their friends, seeing to it that writers like Barnes, White, and Barker always had something to live on. Moreover, she spent months working without a salary helping to shape Goldman's autobiography *Living My Life* (1931)—a life described by Theodore Dreiser as "the richest of any woman's of our century"—and over a year to help edit, and then convince T. S. Eliot to publish, Barnes' masterpiece *Nightwood* (1936).[55] Coleman would presciently predict, "When all is known, and we know even as also we are known, the story of Coleman and Barnes over the ms. of *Nightwood* in NY in 1935 will become a saga, a unique thing in literature, as indeed it was."[56] These are just a few examples that make clear the lengths to which she went to help her fellow artists and the extent to which she contributed to the modernisms of her day.

As a society editor at the *Tribune* immersed in the goings-on of her largely expatriate community, Coleman was a cultural cartographer who participated in the immediate mapping of the Left Bank. In like manner her diary, which she began at some point upon arriving in Paris, is itself a valuable archive of modernism as it preserves her observations about the historical, social, artistic, and political milieu in which she was then living. She marked parts of France and England—where she moved in 1932—with precision, leading us on a journey with the same skill which Virginia Woolf and James Joyce use to take their respective readers through the London of *Mrs. Dalloway* and the Dublin of *Ulysses*. Coleman invites us to eat and drink at the most popular cafés, restaurants, and nightclubs such as the Deux Magots, the Select, Brick Tops, Monico's, and the Ivy. She takes us to art galleries to see shows such as Wyndham Lewis' *Thirty Personalities* exhibit and the London Group's 30th Exhibition. As an avid filmgoer Coleman enjoyed herself in the increasingly industrialized and commercialized world of mass-mediated culture and entertainment, and her diary consequently offers viewers a filmography of movie releases for the 1930s with stars like Greta Garbo, Jack Hurlbut, Harold Lloyd, Charlie Chaplin, the Marx Brothers, Ginger Rogers, and Fred Astaire. The diary also recaps some of the current affairs during this vital inter-war period in history as she reports on the death of King George V and the abdication crisis of King Edward the VIII, for example; the topics of Communism, the Spanish Civil War, and Hitler and Mussolini intermingle with her private and domestic narratives.

---

[55] Quoted in *Living My Life* Vol. 2, 986. See Goldman's "In Appreciation" in *Living My Life* Vol. 1 for her thanks to Coleman; and Cheryl J. Plumb's introduction to Djuna Barnes *Nightwood, The Original Version and Related Drafts*, vii–xxvi.
[56] October 21, 1937, F. 641.

Coleman positioned her friends, lovers, colleagues, and acquaintances within and against this broad cultural backdrop. In addition to those mentioned earlier, figures who make appearances or are referenced include Wambly Bald, Kay Boyle, Mary Butts, Marcel Duchamp, Jacob Epstein, Douglas Garman, David Gascoyne, Virgil Geddes, Emma Goldman, Ernest Hemingway, Eugene and Maria Jolas, Giorgio and Helen Joyce, Mina Loy, Alex Small, and Gertrude Stein, to name just a few more in an expansive list. Such a varied artistic assemblage provided Coleman with fodder for her diary, which she used to bring this vibrant cast of players to light and life. Her observations about the personalities, appearances, and accomplishments of her subjects are unique, raw, and skilled, often sharpened by her barbed pen, as in the following examples. Hemingway: "His mind is slow and ambles through words like a rhinoceros in the mud." French painter André Dunoyer de Segonzac: "I did not like him at all, flabby and the remains of good looks, gone stale because there was nothing to support it." Comparing Joyce and Rabelais: "Joyce makes me think of a little boy writing Annie Jones Fucks on the wall. Rabelais would shit on the wall and say nothing at all." And a passage from D. H. Lawrence's *Women in Love*: "Reading this last night made me roar with laughter, but I went to bed and had an orgasm in a dream, so I suppose he can be said to have been successful."[57]

The humor of others is also consistently repeated for our amusement. Coleman believed that Guggenheim, for instance, possessed a "surrealist wit" as indicated when Guggenheim's lover Holms was flirting with Barnes: "Djuna threw herself on John and kept hugging him. Peggy said, 'He'll assert his lump.' Then she made a comprehensive survey of her person and said, 'It's all right.' She said, 'If you rise, the dollar will fall.'" Barnes was equally clever, evidenced in this line from Coleman: "I told her she said at Hayford Hall that her mother thought her father was 'Shelley on horseback' when she saw him. Djuna said 'yes but he dismounted.'"[58] Coleman and her friends became well aware of the diary's comedic status after she relieved their boredom by reading aloud from the text on September 2, 1932: "From this opening sentence, until I stopped exhausted, at time for dinner, they sat and roared, and screamed, and howled with laughter, they doubled up and shrieked, until I was worn and Peggy had to go to the lavatory, because it had made her bowels work." Like these Hayford Hallions, present readers will similarly be entertained by the diary's wit, humor, and irreverence.

---

[57]December 4, 1929, F. 625; December 25, 1929, F. 626; October 30, 1929, F. 625; October 7, 1932, F. 630.
[58] July 23, 1933, F. 631; June 2, 1936, F. 636.

Introduction xxix

Coleman used her journal as a writer's notebook where she could register her discovery of other authors, and while she was raucous and sarcastic she was just as often serious, delivering sustained examinations of texts by such writers as Dante, Henry Handel Richardson, Herman Melville, and William Wordsworth. At times she was overwhelmed by the beauty or success of the work in question and at other times she would offer passionate critiques followed by astonishing suggestions for how a writer like Shakespeare could improve his writing. Either way she would copy down pages and pages of quotations interspersed with her commentary to prove her points. Her analyses of these other texts would more often than not lead her to take stock of her own work, which could be praised or rejected just as eagerly, just as ruthlessly. She longed to be part of a tradition that included not only classic greats such as Chaucer, Shakespeare, Rabelais, Rimbaud, and Emily Brontë, but also her contemporaries like Lawrence, Eliot, and Joyce. She felt these latter three were "the three strong spirits of this time," and announced: "I want the great flare of genius, genius of the highest order that has been in the world [. . .] I want enormous energies, devastating intellects, imaginations that have no limits, passion of the eternal sweep of earth."[59] In order to tap this genius, she embarked on a rigorous, self-directed education in Europe where she read voraciously and wrote voluminously, and where for a time her talent and reputation showed promise of flourishing.

"I HAVE ONLY TO PRACTISE, TO WRITE, TO PRUNE, TO WRITE"

When we first meet Coleman as the diary opens in 1929, she had already become a fixture on the Left Bank scene. Her stint at the *Tribune* had led to her involvement with *transition*, one of the most innovative little magazines in the city, referred to by Coleman as "the literary gospel of that era."[60] *Tribune* editor and fellow American Eugene Jolas launched the magazine in April 1927, with Elliot Paul, a colleague from the paper, and together they outlined their mandate in their introduction to the first issue: "TRANSITION wishes to offer American writers an opportunity to express themselves freely, to experiment, if they are so minded, and to avail themselves of a ready, alert and critical audience."[61] Coleman responded to the invitation "to experiment" and by the fifth issue was publishing her own stories and poems there. With

---
[59] June 21, 1934, F. 632; December 25, 1929, F. 626.
[60] November 9, 1937, F. 641.
[61] Quoted in Fitch, *In transition*, 21.

transition she had her "first recognition. Jolas said I was 'a real poet'" and "Elliot Paul said I 'could write anything I wanted to.' This made me walk on air and I produced perpetually."[62]

Coleman kept impressive company within the pages of *transition*. In addition to Americans such as Boyle, Hart Crane, H. D., Hemingway (also a *Tribune* colleague), and Stein, it published Europeans such as André Gide, Carl Jung, Franz Kafka, Rainer Maria Rilke, Dylan Thomas, and Tristan Tzara. Work from artists such as Giorgio de Chirico, Max Ernst, Paul Klee, Picasso, Man Ray, and Yves Tanguy adorned the pages. Despite this extensive list of gifted contributors, Noël Riley Fitch states in the introduction to her anthology *In transition*, "The main star of *transition* was of course James Joyce, who, though forty-five years old in 1927, was the quintessential modern revolutionary artist on the Paris scene." She suggests that "*transition* earned a place in literary history for publishing eighteen segments of James Joyce's *Finnegan's Wake* (called at the time simply *Work in Progress*)."[63]

Coleman's surrealist poems and stories appeared in eight of the issues, often alongside Joyce's *Work*, signaling her successful venture into a niche market.[64] Some of her *transition* material was taken directly from her own work in progress, the manuscript which would become *The Shutter of Snow*, groundbreaking for being one of the first literary works to depict postpartum depression. As she described the book to her father, "It is the first time anyone has written an account of life in an insane hospital in any other way than to make propaganda—no one has ever treated a subject of this kind in an imaginative, poetic way. Obviously such a subject lends itself gorgeously to the opportunities of modern writing—extravagant imagery and the dream forms that the Freud era has released for poetry and poetic prose."[65] The novel was praised by London's *Times Literary Supplement* in the issue for Thursday, July 2, 1931, in the "New Books and Reprints" section. Affirming that "there is a sustained note of convincing genuineness," the reviewer stated: "Everyone who has had much to do with the victims of disordered mind will recognize the essential truth of the picture here set out with a skill unsurpassed in this peculiar branch of literature." The novel was again reviewed in that paper on Thursday, September 17, 1931, in an article entitled "Lives of the Insane," in which the critic complimented Coleman for "the poetic gift of creating vivid and immediately convincing images"; "She is describing an

---

[62]October 28, 1937, F. 641.
[63]Fitch 14; 11.
[64]Coleman's work appeared in the following issues: August 1927, October 1927, November 1927, January 1928, Summer 1928, February 1929, November 1929, and March 1932.
[65]September 16, 1929, F. 1595.

insane fantasy" "but the cadences fall with a controlled and graceful rhythm and the images are, as often throughout the book, singularly beautiful."

In honing her craft, Coleman was galvanized by many writers of the day with whom she circulated. Hemingway, for instance, was so impressed with her *transition* pieces that he wrote a note to his publisher, Maxwell Perkins, urging him to accept her *Shutter of Snow* manuscript[66]; experimental playwright Virgil Geddes reassured her that she was capable of producing dramatic verse[67]; and fellow novelist Kay Boyle commended her fiction.[68] Peter Neagoe fortified her literary standing when he included her with, among others, Barnes, Boyle, e. e. Cummings, Hemingway, Henry Miller, and Stein in his anthology *Americans Abroad* (1932), a collection showcasing expatriate excellence.

Coleman was particularly championed by Guggenheim's lover Holms, who had contributed to *The Calendar of Modern Letters* from 1925–27 and who shared *Calendar* space with many of the people who appear in Coleman's diary such as Douglas Garman, William Gerhardi, Hoare, Muir, Peter Quennell, and Edgell Rickword.[69] Coleman had met Holms while in St. Tropez in 1928, and, though she fell in love with him, he fell for Guggenheim instead. Coleman, however, remained magnetized by him, and he encouraged her to nourish a sense of herself as a potential poetic genius, which she happily did. The first part of the diary is particularly dedicated to Holms' teaching and wisdom: she showed him everything she wrote, and his word-for-word critiques, which she dutifully replicated, contribute to the substantial length of the original diary.

Coleman eventually realized that she was suffocating under the weight of Holms, Joyce, *et al*, and that she needed to get out of what she called her "*transition*-Joyce haze."[70] Sadly for us, she felt that even her diary had become imitative. When in 1932 she was re-reading the journal she kept in 1928, she became embarrassed by its apparent lack of originality and she destroyed it. Concluding that this portion of the diary made her "sick," she recounted how one day she "went down and fed the entire thick manuscript to the flames in

---

[66] Emily Coleman to John Holmes, March 3, 1928, F. 1595. See also the note for Hemingway in the diary entry for December 4, 1929.

[67] See her entry for February 11, 1930, F. 626. Her archive contains several drafts and manuscripts of plays such as "The Death of Jesus Christ" (Box 113, F. 996) and "The Death of Samson (a Dramatic Poem in 3 Acts)" (Box 113, F. 997).

[68] September 6, 1932, F. 629.

[69] Malcolm Bradbury contends that *The Calendar* was "in many ways much the best" of "the three great literary reviews of the 1920s," the other two being *The Criterion* and *The Adelphi* (37).

[70] April 10, 1930, F. 628.

the house furnace. It gave me a slight pang." We may thank Holms for possibly preventing further destruction, as she conceded: "John said I shouldn't have thrown away my diary, that one should keep all records."[71] And from then on she did just that, leaving upon her death in 1974 an archive bursting with four decades of carefully preserved life writings.

Hoping to liberate her own voice, Coleman assessed her imaginative powers: "I have only to practise, to write, to prune, to write. The best will not come soon."[72] The question we might ask, however, is if the best came at all? In the period of Holms, which covers approximately three years or the first third of the diary selected here, we see Coleman as a writer who spent her days absorbed in composing sonnets and dramatic poetry. But in the remaining portion she frequently appears unable and even unwilling to tend to her art and bring her talent to fruition. She received emotional, intellectual, and creative reinforcement from her literary network, regularly sharing her drafts and manuscripts with best friends like White, whose critiques she valued above all else; and with Barnes, who pushed her to be more focused and productive. Moreover, in addition to Holms, Scottish writer Edwin Muir offered her praise and editorial commentary. In all these years, however, she polished only two significant poems, "Melville on Land" and "The Cremation." She struggled with the manuscript of her second novel, "The Tygon," based in part on her tempestuous and violent relationship with Italian translator Lelletto Bianchetti, with whom she was involved between 1931 and 1932; and in part on her longest post-marital relationship, with Hoare, from 1929–1937.[73] She began the narrative some time shortly after the affair with Bianchetti ended and completed the first version in 1936, but was unable to place it with a publisher. Undaunted, she returned to this project off and on for the next three decades: there are seven versions of it in her archive, the last one dated April 1963, but not one has ever seen the shelf of a bookstore. The bulk of the diary for these crucial years of Coleman's immersion in modernism would seem to record, then, the creative process not as steadily realized but rather as slowly undermined for Coleman by herself as well as by those around her.

---

[71] December 8, 1932, F. 631.
[72] December 23, 1929, F. 626.
[73] Throughout her life she produced multiple versions of this work, in each case revising it slightly. She initially titled the manuscript "Five Years" and "Four Years," but in 1936 she took the advice of Barnes, who was helping her to edit it, and changed the title to "The Tigon." She then modified the spelling to "The Tygon," telling Barnes in a letter: "What I want is to see the Tygon published (my spelling for fear they'll [publishers] say Tiggon)" (July 9, 1938). Series 2, Box 3, Folder 12, Djuna Barnes Papers, Archives and Manuscripts Department, University of Maryland Libraries, College Park.

Specifically, Coleman's approach to a literary life was determined by her status as a woman in a traditionally male-dominated domain. She felt the pressures to follow stereotypical models that women could and should find fulfillment through marriage and children, and through private as opposed to public experiences. Her recorded attempts to infiltrate the realm of art and intellect reveal how she often had to regulate her behaviour with men so as not to offend their masculine sensibilities. For example, although she was energized by her exchanges with Barker—"poetry with him becomes a universe"—she deplored the fact that during their literary debates, "I've had to call halt several times with Barker: he doesn't like it at all when I hold forth. (He says 'sh')."[74] She likewise described an evening with Hoare: "I was docile at first, sewing; but he got into literature and I expressed myself. [. . .] He hates me so when I'm opinionated."[75] Misogyny also permeated the more public art world, as when the editor Edward Titus touched her hair while asking about her short stories or when poet Hart Crane "pinched my bottom and wouldn't talk to me about poetry."[76]

Coleman recognized that society's expectations that a woman be angelic, unobtrusive, and ready to serve others were in direct opposition to art's demands that a writer be aggressive and willing to serve only oneself and one's craft: "I must try to make some fusion between the two halves of my nature; nothing could be more split in two [. . .] The artist part of me loathes the female—it seems to stand for every weakness. The feminine hates the artist because it thwarts its functioning."[77] In this divisive state Coleman found it difficult to complete her artistic endeavors.

The "artist part" of Coleman did, however, manifest itself through an egotism that is certainly staggering at times, for she brazenly touted her poetic gifts and self-worth. "My vanity is Colossal!" she shouts from the rooftop of her diary, her barbaric yawp reverberating as she emerges from the pages of her text singing, like Walt Whitman before her, the song of her self.[78] Readers of her diary may castigate or dislike her for her arrogance but as she defended, "A woman has to get twice as much confidence as a man if she wants to do anything because no one expects it of her."[79] Certainly her power-wielding contemporaries like T. S. Eliot and Ezra Pound expected nothing. In 1917 Eliot wrote as editor of the London-based *Egoist*: "I struggle to keep the writing as much as possible in Male hands, as I distrust the Feminine in

---

[74] April 15, 1936, F. 636; April 20, 1936, F. 636.
[75] August 15, 1934, F. 633.
[76] November 11, 1929, F. 625; September 25, 1937, F. 639.
[77] June 21, 1934, F. 632.
[78] May 15, 1936, F. 636.
[79] January 5, 1930, F. 626.

literature," while in 1918 Pound wrote of the staff at the British *New Age* journal: "Not wildly anti-feminist we are yet to be convinced that any woman ever invented anything in the arts."[80] Given such publicly promoted views that women could not produce important art, Coleman's need to aggrandize herself seems reasonably justified.

"SEXUAL LOVE IS A GIFT OF GOD"

As an affront to stereotypical femininity, Coleman's unabashed egoism went hand in hand with what Gillian Hanscombe and Virginia Smyers call the "anti-conventional" life led by modernist women, emphasizing that they often lived unconventional *sexual* lives: "some were lesbian, some were bisexual, some promiscuous, some seemingly asexual."[81] Benstock similarly asserts that for many expatriate American women, "the flight to freedom often meant a flight from the implicit expectation of marriage and motherhood"; from this liberated position "[h]eterosexual and homosexual expatriates . . . discovered sexualized writing identities in expatriation—and in doing so they changed the history of modern women's writing, charting the terrain of female sexuality from female perspectives."[82] To this end the diary inscribes themes and topics such as menstruation, gynecological exams, abortion, and incest, so that the diary itself emerges as an "anti-conventional" and taboo-breaking text. More pointedly, Coleman resisted the "implicit expectation" that because she had a child she had to remain married and monogamous, and she embarked on a series of love-affairs both during and after her marriage which she duly recorded; in this way she lived as well as wrote through a sexualized sensibility.

In 1932 Coleman confided to Barnes, "To tell you the truth I don't live on anything now but passionate sexual hope," and while she was at that moment referring to her dreams of a permanent relationship with Hoare this admission could well articulate her *modus operandi*.[83] Coleman was, quite simply, obsessed with sex—as were the women and men closest to her, according to the diary—but she regarded sex as the means to ends beyond erotic stimulation. She believed that "sex is, at first, the only way to know anyone" and that it was necessary to finding the "truth" in human relations.[84]

---

[80]Eliot quoted in Hermione Lee, *Virginia Woolf*, 439; Pound quoted in Scott, *The Women of 1928*, 79.
[81]Hanscombe and Smyers, 12; xvii.
[82]Benstock, "Expatriate Modernism" 28.
[83]August 29, 1932, F. 629.
[84]January 5, 1930, F 626; August 14, 1934, F. 633.

Though primarily drawn to men, Coleman infused her diary with homoerotic, lesbian, and bisexual narratives as well as heterosexual ones. This fact is especially significant given that she was writing the diary at the time of the 1928 trial against English author Radclyffe Hall, whose novel *The Well of Loneliness* was charged with being obscene for its depiction of the lesbian protagonist Stephen Gordon—a charge which was upheld on appeal. Although the 1928 diary is among the portion Coleman destroyed, in 1930 she commented on this journal: "My old diary (1928–9) is not honest. Not a word about the violent homosexual feelings I had all that summer, and the winter too, whenever I was alone."[85] Perhaps Coleman felt compelled to censor her own text in light of the trial. In contrast, the extant diary, which opens in 1929, features Coleman reflecting in the second entry on those "violent homosexual feelings" which were directed at her lesbian lover, referred to only as "Judith," whom she had been with in St. Tropez in 1928: "She I made love to, her body is pear-like and full. I found her body perfect, so I poured passion into her. I was a flame on which oil is spent, I ate up my indifference." Years later, she noted that her "Lesbian affair" was one of the "only genuine sexual feelings I have ever had."[86] Entries such as these signal the tension created by her taboo emotions.

Indeed, in "Queer Conjunctions in Modernism" Colleen Lamos introduces us to "same-sex passion in modernist works in terms of *both* its avowal and disavowal," for as she states: "Homophobia and homophilia are equally constitutive of Anglo-American modernist literature, a literature that is charged by the split between same- and other-sex love, energized and riven by the homo/hetero binary division. In short, there is not, on the one hand, a 'homosexual' modernism and, on the other hand, a 'heterosexual' modernism, but a single literary corpus that is torn in various ways by the scission between these (supposedly) incongruent longings. 'Queer' describes this uneasy conjunction." She concludes that "Known for their avant-garde daring, modernist writers queered the literary tradition that they inherited."[87]

We can read Coleman's diary as contributing to this literature of both "avowal and disavowal" in the ways she documented and constructed not only her own sexual identities but also those of her friends and lovers. While Guggenheim "just wanted fucking" with Holms, Coleman recounted how Guggenheim "said I had always attracted her, that she loved my face and wanted to touch my hair," and vacationing together at the Hayford Hall estate

---

[85]January 5, 1930, F 626; August 14, 1934, F. 633.
[86]November 3, 1929, F. 625; March 11, 1936, F. 635.
[87]336–337; 341.

Gugeheim, Coleman, and Holms frequently shared the same bed.[88] Moreover, Coleman not only was sexually drawn to Barnes' ex, Thelma Wood, but she enjoyed it when Barnes, always on hand to give a massage, "pounded" Coleman's bottom to an orgasm.[89] Barnes pined for Wood while also moving on to relationships with men like Peter Neagoe and Eric Siepmann. Further, Coleman felt Antonia ("Tony") White, married three times, "needs primarily SEX" with a stable man, while Coleman also described how "Djuna went over, very tight, and began embracing [White], and Tony snuggled up to Djuna's bosom like a real little blonde woman, sensual."[90] White regarded Coleman as a "gay blade"; we learn that Holms "loves to get tight and feel gay, and how much he wants a man," and that Hoare would "love to be a woman."[91] Coleman summarized in a conversation with friends, "We all said whom we liked, some said they liked men, some women. Peggy said, 'I met someone I liked the other day—I forget which sex it was.'"[92] Such comments underscore the extent to which the diary queers modernism.

Coleman's sexual being was both reflected in and opposed by her spiritual sensibilities. She desired to be looked at by lovers "in passion for [her] soul," and in her longing for "paradise on earth" she felt "Paradise approaching" after intercourse with Hoare.[93] Sex was for her, though, the key to spiritual knowledge, as articulated by her protagonist Frieda to lover Donato in her novel "The Tygon": "Sexual love is a gift of God; it is only through that that some people see God."[94] Coleman also looked for God in nature, responding to it with an ecstasy that was sexualized as she recalled, for instance, "lying on a moor hearing skylarks and smelling heather, one's heart fit to burst with rapture of nature getting into one's blood and bones."[95]

On her many pilgrimages to Devonshire, Gloucestershire, and Yorkshire, she roamed fields and moors for hours, looking at birds and flowers, or she rode horses, a favorite hobby. She read extensively on these subjects and passionately transcribed what she deemed relevant or striking information about them into her diary. She found the natural world to be a representation of

---

[88] July 25, 1934, F. 633; November 11, 1929, F. 625.
[89] July 23, 1933, F. 631.
[90] February 27, 1936, F. 635; September 22, 1937, F. 639.
[91] January 17, 1936, F. 635; September 3, 1932, F. 629; August 14, 1934, F. 633.
[92] July 14, 1934, F. 633.
[93] December 24, 1929, F. 626; July 4, 1936, F. 637; February 14, 1936, F. 635.
[94] "Tygon" 174, F. 980. For a more detailed discussion of the relationship between sexual and religious knowledge in "The Tygon," see "Site Also of Angst and Spiritual Search" by Sandra Chait (150–169).
[95] March 6, 1936, F. 635.

spiritual goodness on a physical level, and she sought it out as an antidote for urban life as often as she could, pitting Paris and London against the uncomplicated and "uncivilized" countryside.

The diary thus traces not only her participation in a modernist milieu but also her concurrent withdrawal from its cosmopolitan, atheistic atmosphere. Early on we find her preparing to go off alone to St. Tropez to write, for she needed, "Not people for me, nor cities, but my own soul, and the solitude to know it in," and this thought filled her with "spiritual excitement." Once there she confirmed, "There is much that is sensible in the Catholic Church. The practise of 'retreat'—that is exactly what I am doing now."[96] But strains between a sexual and spiritual life threatened her equilibrium, as she confessed to White in 1936: "I want either to make love from morning till night for 5 years; or else retire to a convent; anything short of that is killing me."[97] In a related sense, she would write to White in 1942, "The conflict between artist and the good life, between artist and woman, has nearly killed me."[98]

These multiple divisions rendered her perpetually depressed and frequently suicidal. Too preoccupied with her romances, she was unable to apply herself fully enough to the rigorous discipline that a literary career required and her creative output was produced with much effort and procrastination. Her sexual experiences did not bring her the fulfillment she was seeking either, as her choices in partners seemed misguided. Barker and Humphrey Jennings were married men; Barker told her he preferred male lovers; Dylan Thomas was a heavy-drinking flirt; she found each of Jennings, Bianchetti, and Hoare "sadistic"; and all her years with Hoare involved the battle between her relentless "sexual mania" for him and what she considered his pathological or neurotic reluctance to engage in intercourse. Her psyche was further unbalanced by the fact that despite her willingness to embrace casual or "free" love with Hoare and others, she wanted more than anything else the heteronormative stability that comes from a committed and monogamous union.

Coleman lived as an anti-conventional modernist but like many women she was never able to resolve fully the gendered pressures inherent even in such a supposedly unfettered life.[99] This point is further appreciated when

---

[96] November 9, 1929, F. 625; December 6, 1929, F. 625; January 15, 1930, F. 626.
[97] Diary June 12, 1936, F. 636.
[98] Unpublished letter from Coleman to Antonia White, August 21, 1942. Courtesy of Lady Susan Chitty and Sir Thomas Chitty.
[99] Many modernist women experienced difficult relationships with their children, such as Rebecca West, Mary Butts, Zelda Fitzgerald, Hilda Doolittle, Antonia White, Mina Loy, and Frieda Lawrence.

we consider that in handing her son over to Nina Donn, Coleman radically challenged assumptions about maternity, especially about what constitutes the role of the "good" mother. This decision, however, was agonizing and plagued her for years, for while she did not want to raise him she also wanted him with her. By her accounts, Deak felt no such remorse. In order to resolve conflicts such as these, she visited a psychoanalyst briefly in 1936. However, the diary itself was her more general laboratory for self-directed analysis, serving for Coleman the way the genre has always served its practitioners: as a forum for confession and as the means to catharsis. She recognized, "The fact that I can write a diary is some relief."[100]

The spiritual increasingly took precedence over the sexual and worldly life and Coleman found "relief" in religion. The diary transcribed here ends at the point of Coleman's departure in late 1937 to visit her father in Hartford and, although she returned to Europe in early 1938, she was back in the United States by June, where she decided to remain in light of the threat of war abroad.[101] Having gone to see her friend Sonia Himmel in Arizona in early 1939, Coleman fell with her characteristic sexual hunger for the ranch-hand "cowboy" Jake Scarborough who worked at Coleman's guesthouse, and they were soon living together. But over the next few years her fascination with Catholicism intensified, strengthened by her readings of the leftist Catholic philosophers Jacques and Raïssa Maritain, and as she reflected on her past and present life in light of the Church she was filled with agony. By 1942, she had renounced her relationship with Scarborough, moved to New York, converted to Catholicism, and committed herself to a life of celibacy and holy poverty. In 1953, Coleman made her way back to England and in 1957 settled into retreat at Stanbrook Abbey near Worcester in the West Midlands. She underwent surgery for a brain tumor in 1964, and in 1968 she joined the Catholic Worker Farm in Tivoli, New York, one of a series of communities created by Dorothy Day and Peter Maurin in 1933, whose members attempt to put into practice the social teachings of the gospels. She died in Tivoli on June 13, 1974.

---

[100] February 17, 1936.

[101] In London in March 1938, Coleman became involved with a man named Henry who was in his fifties and broke, having lost money in stocks. Coleman joined him in Canada where he went to work on various investments and where, under her tutelage, he tried his hand as a writer. She spent the second half of 1938 moving with him to cities such as Ottawa, Montreal, and Toronto, but the relationship deteriorated quickly as Henry became increasingly physically violent. It was to escape him that she fled to Arizona. See, for instance, the letter to her father dated November 11, 1939, F. 1598.

"IT'S ALL IN THE RAW"

It is a long way from 1930, the year *The Shutter of Snow* appeared, to 1974, but in that time Coleman published very little. She wrestled endlessly with how to reconcile her personal and professional quests, desires, and ambitions. And yet, while she both fought and ceded to debilitating stereotypes of gender, certainly many of her female contemporaries were able to produce and manage successful literary careers. How then do we account for her limited public presence? White suggested that Coleman resisted sending out her work in order to avoid public criticism: Coleman was afraid of "exposing herself to the rough world where writers aren't taken entirely on their own valuation"—Coleman's "own valuation" being that she was a genius.[102]

At the same time, Coleman's commitment to the spiritual, anti-material world was a wholly genuine and extended one. Factors informing her decision to enter the Church were registered in the diary all along, especially her seeking solace in solitude and nature; her conviction that it was her duty to provide financial support to her less fortunate artist-friends and lovers; her engagement with individuals and groups experimenting with or drawn to socialist and communist beliefs and activities; and her extensive use of biblical references throughout her poetry. Her relationship with the marketplace was thus to some degree always tempered by her rejection of the world which that market served.

Coleman's son furthers our understanding of her approach to art. As a teenager, John eventually followed his mother back to the United States, enrolling at Columbia University in the fall of 1940. Three years later, he and Emily joined the Catholic Church and as they aged, their mother-son bond was fortified by their shared faith in God.[103] In a detailed letter he wrote to Guggenheim in 1945, he makes it clear how his mother's spirituality affected her professional aspirations. He explained that a religious life "means keeping down one's ego and selfish desires, it means avoiding to seek power, influence, fame or even the good opinion of men [. . .]." He entered the Church just as he himself "was beginning to do what so many moderns do, which is spend a life in adoring

---

[102] White, *Diaries 1958–1979* Vol. 2, 74.

[103] John was baptised on August 28, 1943; Emily on October 22, 1943. After performing a series of odd jobs such as journalist, secretary, and book editor, later in life John (fluent in English, French, and Russian) became an interpreter. At the age of twenty-two he married a woman named Gloria, whom he had met at Columbia, and they had two children, Dunstan and Charlotte. After Gloria left him for another man, John eventually married Marie Claire, with whom he had a son, Thomas Maritain Coleman. John suffered from prostate and then bone cancer in the final four years of his life, dying at sixty-five. Interview with Marie Claire Coleman at her home in France, May 30, 1999.

and giving honor to myself."[104] John here addressed in spiritual terms many of the issues that have historically defined the artist in gendered ones: namely, that to be successful one has to be selfish, egoistic, and committed to one's self above all else, tensions Coleman grappled with throughout her adulthood.

White further wondered in 1964, "I don't know . . . [that] [Emily] is *really* a writer: I can't help feeling she ought to have done a bit better by now considering she's been writing endlessly for over 30 years." White explained, "She never seems to get anything properly shaped and finished—it's all in the raw."[105] This last phrase speaks to our need to redefine what we mean when we talk about artistic production. White was basing her evaluation of Coleman's achievements as a writer on Coleman's publication record, but when we look at her literary output in and of itself we cannot help but be impressed: the massive body of work that constitutes the Emily Holmes Coleman Papers at the University of Delaware contains the more than 19,000 pages of her diary; the manuscript *The Shutter of Snow*; multiple versions of "The Tygon"; dozens of short stories; drafts of essays, plays, and literary criticism; around 4,100 leaves of poetry; and over 31,000 pages of correspondence both to and from Coleman. By traditional standards, which measure success against the marketplace, Coleman indeed, as White put it, might "have done better." But if we position Coleman, as I believe we should, as a writer whose initial obsession with fame gave way to a view that art was an expression of life—of a lifetime—then we must conclude that she has done quite well.

After her conversion Coleman went on to produce hundreds of religious poems, took up painting equally zealous religious pictures, and continued to revise "The Tygon." She called herself "a mystic; and certainly a barbarian; and a fanatic" and felt, "I need to struggle, to live, being not only an artist but a woman and a saint."[106] Holms had told her she needed to suffer to write, "and known the suffering that comes through passion."[107] Her diary is the product and conflation of her life as a sexual, literary, spiritual woman, the text that most fully and consistently allowed her to dramatize and probe the tensions of her being. Throughout its pages she emphasized that she kept the diary because it concentrated her thoughts, made things clear to her, and served as a record of her development. Its purpose is illuminated in her statement, "Nothing seems real to me until I've written it down. I don't exist at all until I read what I've done."[108] More than any of her writings, then,

---

[104]Unpublished letter from John Coleman to Peggy Guggenheim, March 4, 1945. Courtesy of Marie Claire Coleman.
[105]White *Diaries 1958–1979* Vol. 2, 107.
[106]August 14, 1934, F. 633; June 11, 1936, F. 636.
[107]November 9, 1929, F. 625.
[108]March 8, 1936, F. 635.

her diary persistently reaffirmed her ontological status. It is the liberating space where she could unabashedly dwell on her ego while simultaneously "keeping it down"—to borrow John Coleman's phrase—due to the supposedly secret and private nature of the genre. The diary is her monument to her ongoing conviction that "Life is the rough draft of art."[109]

Appropriately, Coleman told her diary in 1937, "Djuna said it would turn out at my death that I was a diarist and not a poet," and she herself admitted that year, "I would so much rather write a diary—or talk—than read Dante, or do my book."[110] Barnes further suggested to Coleman: "Well, possibly you will go down to posterity as a Pepys and nothing else, but isnt [sic] that good enough?"[111] Coleman deserves recognition as a writer of fiction and poetry; however, like that of her predecessor Samuel Pepys (1633–1703), the British naval administrator and parliamentarian, her reputation is secured on the basis of her diary.

Barnes' reference to Pepys has particularly profound implications for thinking about the diary as a literary genre. His journal about his private and public life during the years 1660–1669 (published 1825) had been commended as both the first and best example of a tradition of unconsciously and thus "genuinely" produced diaries until scholar William Matthews examined the manuscript and demonstrated that Pepys often wrote up his entries for several days in one sitting, relied on his own notes and newspaper clippings for detail, and reread past entries with an aim to ensuring narrative continuity. Exposing what Lawrence Rosenwald calls the myths of a diary's artlessness and secrecy, Matthews proves that Pepys' "great diary is no simple product of nature, thrown together at the end of each succeeding day. In part, at least, it is a product fashioned with some care, both in its matter and its style."[112] Pepys, moreover, deposited this manuscript at his alma mater, Magdalene College, Cambridge, where it was, as he hoped, poured over by scholars, edited, and released to a posthumous glory.[113]

Like Pepys, Coleman "fashioned" her journal "with some care" in that she assembled it at times from hastily scrawled notes, reread entries with aesthetic criticism, and typed the text as if preparing it for submission. She was well aware of the diary's potential commercial viability for she

---

[109]September 18, 1937, F. 639.
[110]October 19, 1937, F. 641; October 25, 1937, F. 641.
[111]Barnes to Coleman, October 13, 1938. The Emily Holmes Coleman Papers, Box 4, F. 39.
[112]Rosenwald, *Emerson and the Art of the Diary*, 4, 10–12; Matthews, "The Diary as Literature," cii–ciii. For a more detailed discussion of the diary as a self-consciously crafted and audience directed genre, see *Daily Modernism*, as well as the work of, for example, Bunkers, Huff, and Fothergill *Private Chronicles*.
[113]See Gannett, *Gender and the Journal*, 13–24.

read published journals by authors like Goethe, Dorothy Wordsworth, and Katherine Mansfield. She admitted that after reading her own diary aloud to her friends at Hayford Hall in 1932, "I knew it was really funny, and should be published"; and in 1937 she suggested—in the spirit of Pepys—a postdated recognition: "But no human being shall see this record, until after I am dead.[114] We can thus regard the diary manuscript as an accomplished, long running literary performance in which various tenets of modernism are enacted. Her project contributes to expanding the definition and theorizing of modernism according to gendered, sexual, and maternal disruptions of identity, and as an innovative aesthetic practice informed by and inflected with the personal, the domestic, the daily, the interior, and the ordinary.[115]

This edited selection of Coleman's diary takes it place within the growing modernist canon of life writings of both female and male participants whose autobiographies, memoirs, and diaries offer diverse accounts of the period, especially as played out in the hubs of Paris and London, like Ernest Hemingway's *A Moveable Feast*, Gertrude Stein's *The Autobiography of Alice B. Toklas*, Sylvia Beach's *Shakespeare and Company*, Robert McAlmon and Kay Boyle's *Being Geniuses Together*, Vera Brittain's *Testament of Youth*, and Virginia Woolf's posthumously assembled *Moments of Being*. Books such as these, as well as diaries by, among others, Woolf, Brittain, Neith Boyce, Dora Carrington, Harry Crosby, Christopher Isherwood, Alice James, Katherine Mansfield, Anaïs Nin, Alice Dunbar-Nelson, Elizabeth Smart, and White provide the context of a modernist life writing tradition within which Coleman's diary can be viewed and valued.

Over the past few decades a body of auto/biographical and scholarly work has been formed around almost every key personage in Coleman's diary. Barnes is the subject of biographies by Andrew Field and Phillip Herring, while *Collected Poems with Notes Toward the Memoirs* by Djuna Barnes follows the scholarly edition of *Nightwood: The Original Version and Related Drafts*, edited by Cheryl J. Plumb. Guggenheim penned her memoir, *Out of This Century: Confessions of an Art Addict*, which has been complimented by biographies by Anton Gill and Mary V. Dearborn. White is revealed to us in numerous books: the two-volume *Antonia White Diaries 1926–1957* and *Antonia White Diaries 1958–1979*, edited by her elder daughter Susan Chitty; memoirs about White by Chitty (*Now to*

---

[114]September 6, 1932, F. 629; December 21, 1937, F. 642.
[115]For intersections of modernism, life writing, and daily life see, for example, Felber *Literary Liaisons*, Martinson *In the Presence of Audience*, Monk *Writing the Lost Generation*, Olson *Modernism and the Ordinary*, Rosner *Modernism and the Architecture of Private Life*, and Podnieks *Daily Modernism*.

My Mother) and White's younger daughter, Lyndall Hopkinson (*Nothing to Forgive*); and a biography by Jane Dunn. The relationships between Coleman, Barnes, Guggenheim, and White are explored in the collection of essays *Hayford Hall: Hangovers, Erotics, and Modernist Aesthetics* co-edited by Sandra Chait and me.

In addition, there are biographies of Barker (by Robert Fraser), Jennings (by Kevin Jackson), and Thomas (by George Tremlett). Thomas' love letters, including those to Coleman, were recently published, and the *Collected Journals 1936–42* by her friend, poet David Gascoyne, was reissued in 1991. Significantly, all of these texts reference Coleman, and many of the studies draw on and indeed are indebted to her unpublished diary manuscript, a fact that underscores her ongoing presence in a network of modernisms. Coleman's own novel, *The Shutter of Snow*, was reissued by Virago Press in 1981 and by Dalkey Archive Press in 1997. Now, with the publication of *Rough Draft: The Modernist Diaries of Emily Holmes Coleman,* her contributions to modernism as manifested in and by her diary are given a formal audience.

EDITING THE DIARY: "THAT'S MY GARGANTUAN ENERGY"

I first encountered Coleman while I was writing a chapter on the journals of White for my book *Daily Modernism*. The numerous references to Coleman in White's diary—such as the one about her being "built on the heroic scale"—ignited my interest in her. Further, my research on White led me to Mary Lynn Broe's chapter in *Women's Writing in Exile* entitled "My Art Belongs to Daddy: Incest as Exile, The Textual Economics of Hayford Hall," in which Broe discusses the lives and works of White, Barnes, and Coleman. In particular, in the notes to the piece Broe mentions that the Emily Coleman Papers, which include a diary, had been acquired by the University of Delaware Special Collections.[116] Because White was a fascinating, complex figure and because, according to White, so were her best friends like Coleman, I felt certain that Coleman's diary would prove to be a compelling one.

By way of the University of Delaware Library I contacted Coleman's executor, Joseph Geraci, and asked him if he thought the diary warranted publication. He did. An American rare books and photographs dealer living in Amsterdam, Geraci had met Coleman when he was a young man at the Catholic Worker Farm. At that time, she had been storing her entire archive at her friend Phyllis Jones' home in Devon, England. In 1973, a year before

---
[116] Broe 77, note # 4.

her death, Coleman asked Geraci to become her executor; after Jones' death in 1986, Coleman's papers were shipped to Geraci in Amsterdam so that he could catalogue them and sell them to an institution as the best means of preserving what he was convinced was a cultural trove. Indeed, his recognition of her place in literary history is summed up in his obituary of her in which he affirms: "She was remarkable, reasonable and quite simply the most important influence on the lives of those who knew her."[117]

Geraci suggested I go to Delaware to read the diary myself and then get back to him with my impressions, which I did. From the opening lines of the diary—"Last night we dined and went dancing [. . .] I love to let myself into the sweep of a dance"—I was drawn into the narrative of Coleman's life, and into the linguistic rendering of that life. I notified Geraci that I believed the diary must indeed be published and he generously gave me permission to proceed with this edited selection. With the assistance of Rebecca Johnson Melvin, a librarian with the Delaware Special Collections department, I was able to obtain a photocopy of the portion to be prepared and I got down to work.

Coleman was, to be sure, the first editor of her diary, frequently making intrusions into her own text by blacking out with lines of Xs countless words, sentences, and whole passages that perhaps did not measure up to her aesthetic standards or that she did not want deciphered. At the same time, during her favorite pastime of rereading her journal she has in many places copied over faint or unclear letters to make them legible, dutifully made grammatical corrections, and added hand-written detail and commentary in the text and margins. I have in places noted where Coleman has made insertions such as these.

For my part, I have tampered stylistically with the material transcribed in a number of ways. Coleman almost never used apostrophes when writing contractions and I have added them to make reading easier, just as I have added proper quotation marks around her dialogues, and typed out "and" to replace her frequent use of the ampersand. I have corrected her spelling—for example, changed her misspelling of Lawrence to Laurence Vail—and cleaned up the text by eliminating what are certainly basic typographical errors. Where she sometimes began sentences with lower case letters, I have altered them to capital ones. I have placed any words or letters that I have added in square brackets; all unbracketed ellipses in the text are hers.

Coleman's self-reflexive observation of her diary in 1937, "I am really unique—I've not stopped typing, except to read what I've written, for 7 hours. Well that's my Gargantuan energy," gives readers a sense of what

---

[117]Quoted in Minna Besser Geddes, "Emily Holmes Coleman," *Dictionary of Literary Biography*.

my task as editor required and explains why even the portion offered here is itself abridged.[118] In reducing the length of this Gargantuan text, I wrestled with how to give Coleman's voice as much unimpeded articulation as possible, while also registering my presence as one who intrudes upon and (re)shapes the narrative in the interests of both scholarship and the feasibility of the book. I considered indicating with ellipses in square brackets [. . .] every time I interrupted the story—both between and within entries—and to provide brief notes on what material was taken out. However, given the number of entries with which I was dealing, and given that each one runs, not untypically, from five to ten letter-sized sheets, I was faced with delivering a patchwork of hundreds if not thousands of bracketed deletions, making for unsightly and choppy reading. In the end I chose to privilege the accessibility of the diary by offering a fluid and absorbing life in which the reader is caught up by the narrative itself and not by the editorial cuts and distractions.

Some of my decisions came easily. In the frequent instances where she repeated herself from one entry to the next, I have often eliminated the duplicated information. While repetition can certainly signal significant preoccupations and even obsessions, there remains so much continuity between entries that I do not feel I have compromised the emotional or thematic patterns of the text. As well, Coleman had a penchant for quoting extensive portions of the books she was reading but I have not recopied most of the lengthy and extraneous material. In making more detailed excisions I have tried to maintain the breadth and breath of Coleman's exuberant pace, guided by my own sense of the text's merit firstly as an aesthetic rendering of a remarkable life and secondly as a resource for literary historians.

I have divided the diary into five parts, with each part further subdivided into sections identified by place and date. This structure was determined both by the available entries for a given period and by my desire to control the mass of material by creating a series of balanced "chapters." I introduce each section with an italicized summary of key narrative points and then, where relevant, fill in the gaps between the sections.

I tried to model my efforts in part on the impressive example of Anne Olivier Bell, editor of the complete five volumes of *The Diary of Virginia Woolf*, who comments, "I found the most difficult part of my work, after deciding what in Virginia Woolf's Diary required explanation, and gathering the material, was the actual writing of the annotations. I pinned up before my desk a notice with the words: accuracy/relevance/concision/interest; and these were my objectives."[119] Living with Coleman's journal has been like being immersed in

---

[118]October 25, 1937, F. 641.
[119]Bell 22.

a pre-Facebook world of networks and connections, where one friend links to countless others and where one biography or anecdote about one person, place, or thing opens up or completes intriguing facts about others, which I have tried to convey in my own annotations.[120] Further, as Bell concedes, "[t]he justification for burdening Virginia Woolf's swift and lovely flight of words with such a heavy load of annotation is that different readers need different things," a point which echoes my own wrangling with who and what to assume Coleman's readers will "know" and who or what needs to be explained.[121] I have erred, I believe, on the side of caution, so that the text may be apprehended and comprehended by as wide an audience as possible. In a different sense, in delivering here a truncated text I have followed the example of Mary Rubio and Elizabeth Waterston, who edited the five volumes of *The Selected Journals of L. M. Montgomery*, by providing an appendix of "omissions" in which I indicate by year, date, and archive file which entries have been wholly excised, for the benefit of readers who have more scholarly uses for the material and want to consult the archival sources in question.

Coleman is obviously not nearly as famous or accomplished a published author as Woolf, but Coleman's diary is, I believe, at least equal in literary craft and value to that of her British contemporary. Set in the cultural, social, and political atmosphere of modernist Europe, the diary is important to readers for its unique, eclectic, and often iconoclastic depiction of this vibrant period. Moreover, the diary appeals to those interested in Coleman's individual selfhood and consciousness while in more general and crucial ways it speaks to women who have grappled with how to define and realize themselves as artistic, intellectual, maternal, sexual, and spiritual beings within and against the scripted and often limiting roles imposed on them by western societies, including Coleman's twentieth and our own twenty-first century cultures.

My reading and shaping of the diary has been motivated by my sense that it is, throughout, a story of passion: passion for self, family, friends, and lovers; for writing, aesthetics, and literature; for spiritual and natural worlds; and for place, performance, and community. Coleman's intense emotions seem epic in scope, yielding anticipation, desire, agony, suffering, despair, and defeat, as well as inspiration, stimulation, illumination, ecstasy, energy, and hope. In 1932 Coleman wrote of her mentor Holms after he read part of her diary: "John said that some of these sentences were as good as anything he had ever heard in his life."[122] It is my conviction that new readers of her diary will agree.

---

[120] In like manner, see the "Tangled Mesh of Modernists" diagram in Scott's *The Gender of Modernism*, 10.
[121] Bell 22–23.
[122] September 2, 1932, F. 629.

Part I

Section 1

Paris

October 30–December 17, 1929

The exact date Emily Coleman began her diary is unclear, but in 1932 she made reference to the fact that she burned her volume for 1928. In the summer of 1928, with her marriage to Deak Coleman ostensibly over, she had gone alone to live in St. Tropez where she assisted the anarchist Emma Goldman in shaping her autobiography. There, she fell in love with the literary critic John Holms who was vacationing in the south of France with his common-law wife, the writer Dorothy Holms. It was at this time that Coleman met, through Goldman, the American heiress Peggy Guggenheim. Though Guggenheim was married to novelist Laurence Vail, she too fell in love with Holms. By the end of the year, Holms and Guggenheim had left their respective partners for each other, and had become two of the greatest influences on Coleman's life—and diary.

    The first extant diary is the one beginning on October 30, 1929. In the fall of 1929, Deak had been transferred from London to the Antwerp branch of J. Walter Thompson, at that time the largest advertising agency in the world. Emily had spent the summer in London with him, living in their flat at 1 Brunswick Square in Bloomsbury. Although she accompanied him to Belgium for the month of September she then went to Paris for the rest of the year, residing at the Hotel St. Germain des Prés, 36, rue Bonaparte, in the 6ᵉ arrondissement of the Left Bank. This area, lined by boulevards such as St. Germain and rue Bonaparte, was famous for cafés like the Café de Flore and Deux Magots. Also on the Left Bank are the Latin Quarter (5ᵉ arrondissement), which takes in the Sorbonne near the intersection of St. Germain and St. Michel, as well as Montparnasse (14ᵉ arrondissement), which by the early 1920s had become the hub of expatriate artistic and intellectual life, and where cafés like the Coupole, Dôme, Sélect, and Rotonde meet at the boulevards Raspail and du Montparnasse.

The diary opens with Coleman circulating between these Left Bank bars and cafés with Holms and Guggenheim, even though she had begun to fuel tensions between her friends as Guggenheim tried to prevent Holms from drinking and discussing literature with Coleman until all hours of the night. While Coleman still carried a torch for Holms, she had been living a promiscuous life; we find her reflecting on her one female and several male lovers, and anticipating the start of a new relationship with Philip Jordan, an aspiring British novelist who worked for Knopf publishers in London. Professionally, she was enjoying a small literary reputation as her novel, The Shutter of Snow, *had recently been accepted for publication, and she was continuing to produce poems and short stories for little magazines like* transition *and* This Quarter. *She was negotiating these sexual and literary identities with her maternal one, confronting both the strengths and the limits of her love for her only child, John Coleman, who was at the time five years old.*

As will be seen, she used nicknames or created pseudonyms to refer to many of her relatives, friends, and lovers, a habit kept up almost until the end of this first diary, which ends in April 1930. Her employment of pseudonyms is likely driven by three imperatives: her desire to protect the names of some figures from a possible public audience; the concern to conceal the identities of others—especially lovers—even from within her own intimate circle; and her literary interests in conceiving of the text's personages in dramatic, symbolic light.

PARIS, OCTOBER 1929

Wednesday, October 30

Last night we dined and went dancing. Karen, Panurge and an Englishman.[1] I danced all the time. The Englishman taught me the Argentine tango. He dances like a streak of snow. I am a prima donna, I cannot dance unless things are right. I came home with worn feet. I love to let myself into the sweep of a dance.

---

[1] "Karen" was Coleman's husband, Loyd (*sic*) Ring Coleman, who went by the name "Deak" (1896–1970); see the introduction. "Panurge" was a businessman and colleague (from the Antwerp office) of Deak Coleman, as well as lover of Emily Coleman; "Panurge" is one of the main characters in François Rabelais' *Pantagruel*, which Coleman was reading. The "Englishman" is later referred to as "that young Englishman who danced so well—Champion—who was in Karen's office" (F. 626, January 17, 1930, not transcribed). Emily had just arrived in Paris from Antwerp, having spent time there with her husband. For details on her living arrangements, see the introduction.

There is nothing so stimulating as Goethe's life. Goethe is I and I am he. He had a greater mind, he had a better education, he was master of himself at 16, I shall not be till 60. He was more mature at 15 than I am now.[2] But his character is my character, and his disposition and responses mine. There is no one else I wish to read about. When I was plowing through Emil Ludwig last winter I wish I had seen this ahead. This biography is not only the best of Goethe I have read, it is the best of anyone. Lewes was not a man of genius, but he understood the temperament of genius.[3]

Panurge is profoundly in love with me, it is like Lysander.[4] I do not want to break his commandments.

I will tell about my summer in London.[5] I found the English people more to my liking than any other. I found Agamemnon's Edwin Muir better than I for him.[6] He is not so brilliant as Ag[amemnon]. but he knows what he has thought. He knows that there is no absolute, Agamemnon and I do not. I read four things that surrounded me completely. Two of them I had read before. *Paradise Lost* I finished, and put every word of it I loved on paper to remember. There is no poem which has carried me so high. Then Plato, deep into his heart I dug. Then the sonnets of Shakespeare. I had read them, now I know

---

[2]Coleman, born on January 22, 1899, was thirty years old here. She went on to refer to Emil Ludwig's biography of Johann Wolfgang von Goethe, *Goethe*, translated by E. C. Mayne and first published in England in 1928; and George Henry Lewes' biography *Life of Goethe* (1855).
[3]Coleman spent the next three pages copying out quotations from Lewes' text.
[3]Coleman had travelled from St. Tropez to London in May 1929, spending the summer with Deak at their flat in Bloomsbury.
[4]The pseudonymous "Lysander," named after Hermia's beloved in Shakespeare's *A Midsummer Night's Dream*, was Alex Small, a Harvard graduate working, as Coleman had, on the Paris *Tribune*—he wrote for columns such as "Latin Quarter Notes," "Notes of Montparnasse," "Left Bank Notes," and his own "Of Fleeting Things," among other contributions. They had been lovers during her 1927–1928 tenure at the paper.
[5]Coleman had travelled from St. Tropez to London in May 1929, spending the summer with Deak at their flat in Bloomsbury.
[6]"Agamemnon," the lover of "Wendy"/Peggy Guggenheim (see note below), was John Ferrar Holms (1897–1934). Educated at the prestigious Rugby boarding school and the Sandhurst Military Academy in England, he became a literary critic for the leftist the *New Statesman* (renamed *New Statesman and Nation* in 1931) a weekly journal of art, politics and letters; and the literary periodical *The Calendar of Modern Letters* from 1925–1927, as well as a frustrated writer. Guggenheim notes in her memoir *Out of This Century* that "He loved his mother, a beautiful Irishwoman descended from Nicholas Ferrar, the founder of Little Gidding"(79)—the seventeenth century Anglican-based religious community on an estate in Huntingdonshire, and which T. S. Eliot would pay tribute to in the fourth chapter of *Four Quartets* (1942). Coleman had elevated Holms to mythic importance in her life, signaled by his code name of Agamemnon, the king of Mycenae who successfully led the Greeks in the Trojan War. In Glasgow in 1919, his friend Hugh Kingsmill (see August 2, 1934) had introduced him to Edwin Muir (1887–1959), Scottish critic, poet, and translator, and the two had become close friends.

them. And Coleridge again, more stirring than ever before.[7] Next to these I was excited by Rabelais, later Dostoyevsky. For English prose, Thomas Urquhart's Rabelais.[8] For an English writer to acquire style he should read and reread this. I love vigorously the matter, it grows close to my spirit. I am composed of this and of Milton.

It was Antony who showed me Dostoyevsky.[9] I gave him my Aristotle (after reading it once more) and he let me take *The Possessed*, precious to him. He loves it deeply because he is Nicolas Stavrogin. We became much to each other, then lost much. He has genius, it will never flower. He has not the maturity of Agamemnon, but he is more exciting as a person than either he or Muir. He is the most exciting man I have ever met. The most beautiful, he is beautiful like a thunderstorm. I read *The Possessed*. First for him. Then for itself. I found things in Dostoyevsky which I had not dreamed were there. He knows the human mind, he knows every cranny of it. He is a massive thinker, his people do everything from intricate motives. A great canvas, spread out all of human life. There is no novelist I enjoy so much, no English nor no French. Dostoyevsky's characters are not insane, they behave as people would behave if they dared. This is his secret, this is how he ennobles.

Panurge has more passion in him than anyone I have known. It is not complicated by genius, it is free and wholesome. He is tempestuous, and trembles when he thinks.

I sat and read Rabelais one afternoon. It is in the depths of my being. I love its richness, crisp vigorous shouting. It is lusty, it is earth, it is life. Joyce makes me think of a little boy writing Annie Jones Fucks on the wall.[10] Rabelais would shit on the wall and say nothing at all. He is

---

[7]In addition to John Milton's epic poem (1667), Coleman was reading Coleridge's *Table Talk* (1835), a document recording his conversations, *Notes on Shakespeare* (1849), and *Biographia Literaria* (1817), an autobiographical critique of poetry.

[8]Sir Thomas Urquhart (1611-1660), translator from French to English of Rabelais' epic romance *Gargantua and Pantagruel*, Books I and II (1653) and Book III (1693-4); Books IV and V were completed by Peter Anthony Motteux (1660-1718).

[9]"Antony" was Eric Siepmann (1903–1970), playwright, author, and journalist, who had briefly worked alongside Deak in the London office of J. Walter Thompson before being fired. At this time he was a member of the foreign staff of the *Manchester Guardian*. Coleman had had a brief affair with him in London in 1928. He was married to Benita Hume (1906–1967), a classmate from the Royal Academy of Dramatic Art in London, but she left him in 1929 for Ronald Colman, and together they established successful film and television careers. Siepmann's third wife, novelist Mary Wesley (1912–2002), would become a great friend of Coleman, co-authoring the introduction to the Virago reissue of *The Shutter of Snow* (1981). In this entry, Coleman went on to reference Stavrogin, the protagonist of Dostoyevsky's *The Possessed* (1871–72), who is a young, debauched, nihilistic nobleman.

[10]Coleman had been reading James Joyce's *Ulysses* (1922).

life. Chapter eleven in *Gargantua*.[11] A child of three. He has never been described before. "He wallowed and rolled himself up and down in the mire and dirt: he blurred and sullied his nose with filth; he blotted and smutched his face with any kind of scurvy stuff; Oftentimes he did spit in the basin, and fart for fatness, piss against the sun, and hide himself in the water for fear of rain."

November 3

Here I am in Paris and do not want it. I am confused, there is talk going on. I had Kay for two days, and liked that well.[12] I have seen Hero, she knows me.[13] We talked like mother and son. Kay's face is delicate. His face sheds light over me. I bought him a balloon. We were in the Luxembourg with Antony.[14]

If I should write of last summer I might write of many errors, but they came to nothing.

---

[11] The chapter is called "Of the Youthful Age of Gargantua."

[12] "Kay" was Coleman's son, John (Johnny) (1924–1990), whom she also referred to as "Na." He had been living in the suburb of Ivry with his governess, the Russian émigré Madame Donn (named in the first part of the diary "Mamotchka") and her family for two and a half years, with Coleman taking him for brief periods of time during her visits to Paris. He spoke Russian with the Donns, and more French than English with Coleman, who lamented the weakening of his mother tongue. For more on their relationship, see the introduction.

[13] "Hero" was Emma Goldman (1869–1940), Jewish Lithuanian-born anarchist labeled by the U.S. government "Red Emma." She emigrated to the U.S. in 1885 and eventually became the lover of Polish-born anarchist Alexander Berkman (1870–1936). In 1892, Berkman attempted to assassinate industrialist Henry Clay Frick and was imprisoned until 1906, while Goldman, a suspected accomplice, was put under constant governmental surveillance. Goldman spent years lecturing across the United States on topics ranging from Socialism and labour unrest to sexuality and birth control; published her *Social Significance of the Modern Drama* (1914); and was the editor and publisher from New York of the leftist magazine *Mother Earth* (1906–1917). Periodically imprisoned, she and Berkman were eventually deported from the U.S. in 1919. She spent two years in Russia and then moved throughout Europe and Canada, publishing *My Disillusionment in Russia* (1923). She and Berkman rented a cottage in St. Tropez in 1926, where they first met Peggy Guggenheim (see note below), who was one of a number of people to encourage her to pen her autobiography. In 1928, Guggenheim helped pay the rent on the St. Tropez cottage, called Bon Espirit, and helped to purchase it for her in 1929. Coleman joined Goldman in the south of France from June 1928-May 1929, acting as her secretary and helping to edit the autobiography, which was published as the 2-volume *Living My Life* (1931) by Knopf. Goldman had moved to Paris for the winter in October 1929. In Greek mythology, "Hero," priestess of Aphrodite, drowns herself after her lover Leander is drowned.

[14] The Luxembourg Gardens is a large park on the Left Bank in Paris.

The greatest thing was Karen, and the *Shutter of Snow* was taken. It will be published by Routledge.[15] It is due entirely to Tommy.[16] He saw my talent and made them take the book. Tommy loved me for a day, then angered because I am unfaithful. I did not give him my heart. His heart belongs to a Poplar. She is tall and has firm breasts. They have been married ten years and are subtle together. I love to be with them. But nothing like Kurn and Agamemnon.[17] Hero says Kurn is in the south of France, making trouble for Wendy. Now she is in London and did not look for me. She bears many things against me in her heart, I am a fool that I mingled with her at the end. My lusty Agamemnon came back from Sweden with Wendy fat and strong. One day in London the maid said "There is a gentleman to see you." I went to the door and there was Agamemnon. I embraced him and he came into the flat. He stalked around and said "How much do you pay for it?" He said, "I have just married Kurn." We went to a pub and he said keen things, more than ever, about painting. There is no one with his spirit. He said much about Giotto, he said "You like him because he cut a larger slice out of life than others." He said "Have you seen the Piero della Francescas in the National Gallery?"[18] All summer I went to the National Gallery. He said, "You are right, it is better than the Louvre." I said, "I love our Edwin Muir," he said "I thought you would." I said, "You do not know his wife, she is fine and strong, she is a person."[19] He said, "Perhaps she is changed since

---

[15]In her 1929 bio blurb for her Class of 1920 Wellesley Record Book, Coleman noted that she had begun the *Shutter of Snow* in Paris in the winter of 1927, and that before being accepted by Routledge, "It had previously been turned down by every American publisher and even by the Hogarth Press, London (Virginia Woolf)"—Woolf and her husband, Leonard, owned the press (Wellesley College Archives). For more on this novel, see the introduction.

[16]"Tommy" and his wife "Poplar" were the English Colonel Clement Egerton, a Chinese translator who worked for Routledge, and his American wife, Kay Egerton.

[17] "Kurn" was Dorothy Holms, writer. "Wendy" was Peggy (Marguerite) Guggenheim (1898–1979), American millionaire and patron of the arts. She later became a celebrated collector of modern art. Coleman may have named her "Wendy" after the child in J. M. Barrie's *Peter Pan*. Dorothy had been living with John Holms for nine years when he left her for Guggenheim. According to Guggenheim's memoir, though Dorothy accepted that their relationship was over and made plans to settle alone in her native England, she demanded that Holms marry her because everyone had assumed they had been married, and she did not want to face further shame. Holms reluctantly married her in Paris in 1929; she returned to England, and he continued his new life with Guggenheim (91–92). Guggenheim and Holms were living in a flat (which came with a studio) in the rue Campagne Première, a street on the Left Bank now famous for the many artists who lived there, such as Marcel Duchamp, Picabia, Man Ray, and Tristan Tzara.

[18]Coleman would have seen Piero della Francesca's *Saint Michael*, *The Baptism*, and *The Nativity of Christ* at London's National Gallery.

[19]Willa/Wilhelmina (Anderson) Muir (1890–1970), Scottish translator, poet, novelist, wife of Edwin Muir. Her work often appeared under the pseudonym "Agnes Neill Scott." Their son, Gavin, was born in 1927.

she had her child." We walked along the street to Tottenham Court Road.[20] We talked very fast. I am young with him, but how he responds to every thought. There is no one like him. Hippocra has more, but she has not his mind.[21] I would give up anything at any time to go to talk with Agamemnon. He does not write.[22]

Now I sit here in this room, I have taken out my books and put them up before me. I want nothing of life but solitude. I cannot hold myself until that time when I shall go back down to my little town and out into its country with the stallion sky.[23]

Of the people I have known in London are Edwin and Willa Muir, Tommy and the Poplar, the Redheaded Girl (who typed succinctly my mss. and became an admiration to me because of her habits), Arthur Waley (clear and uncertain), Judith.[24] She I made love to, her body is pear-like and full. I found her body perfect, so I poured passion into her. I was a flame on which oil is spent, I ate up my indifference. Now I see that I am a two-fold planet, I sing before men and crunch women in my fingers. Besides these there were Antony, and in the fullness of love, David.[25]

---

[20] A major street in London's Bloomsbury neighbourhood.
[21] "Hippocra" was Coleman's Russian-American friend, Sonia Ginsberg Himmel. They had both worked for *transition*, Himmel as a translator of Russian texts.
[22] Coleman was lamenting that Holms failed to realize his literary talents.
[23] Coleman was referring to St. Tropez, where she lived from the summer of 1928 to the spring of 1929, working on Emma Goldman's manuscript and socializing with Guggenheim and Holms, among others. She stayed for a time in Goldman's house, Bon Espirit, and also down the road at the Maison Mussier, on the chemin St. Antoine. She was planning to return to St. Tropez in December 1929.
[24] "The Redheaded Girl" was Phyllis Jones, one of Coleman's best friends, who typed Coleman's manuscripts. Under the pseudonym "Dorothy Disc," Jones wrote an advice column for London's *Daily Mirror*. Arthur Waley (1889–1966), English scholar who translated Chinese and Japanese literature, such as *The Tale of Genji* (1925–33), Lady Murasaki's 6-volume novel. He was also on staff at the British Museum as an Oriental print specialist. Coleman had met him in London through Colonel Clement Egerton in September 1929. "Judith," unidentified, was Coleman's one-time lover; she had been with Coleman in St. Tropez in 1928. Coleman would later note: "My old diary (1928–9) is not honest. Not a word about the violent homosexual feelings I had all that summer, and the winter too, whenever I was alone" (April 11, 1930, F. 628, not transcribed).
[25] "David," who was Philip Jordan, had been responsible for acquiring Emma Goldman's autobiography for Knopf, though at this point he was unemployed. Goldman had encouraged Coleman to look him up in London; when she did, she discovered that she had met him and his wife, Ruth, two years earlier at the Deux Magots in Paris. Though Coleman and Jordan were both married at the time of meeting again in London, he informed her after only a few evenings out that he wanted to have a love affair with her, to which she readily agreed. She went to Paris soon after and waited for his promised visit (which never came) and their passion remained unconsummated. In later years he became a novelist, critic, and war correspondent for the London *News Chronicle*.

I have sent my old Milton to Hippocra. I found when I had read again the last four books there was much that I had not marked. I had not even marked the speeches of Adam on death.[26] This I cannot understand. She will care for this more and more.

Judith is with me and I am not the same. Last summer her body stirred me, now I am cold. I do not want anyone to depend upon me, because I am only for myself. She is sweet like a little breeze, I am afraid to dominate her but I cannot help it. My opinions silence her. She chatters like a child learning to talk—I turn my face to the wall and strain my hands. I cannot listen to this chattering—she says everything in an ordinary way. I would not hurt her for a king's ransom. We were with Antony, who never says a dull word.

Now today David is coming. I do not dare to think of him. His hair is soft and flying, his face like Beethoven. We talked through endless lunches, we said very little. Forever will his eyes be in mine. We have touched our fingers, we could do no more. Now we are free, and when he will come there will be light.

November 9

I talked with Agamemnon for sixteen hours and it has shaken me to my foundations. Never did we come so close, I know his heart. He has said that I cannot write anything until I have suffered, and known the suffering that comes through passion. He says I have never known it, and until I do I am not a woman and cannot write. The tears stood in his eyes, and fell upon his face. He turned his head away. It was when he spoke of Kurn, he cannot think of Kurn. He said I could not go on identifying myself with Goethe, he said Goethe was a coward and had never lived his life, and for that he never wrote one complete thing. He said he had not lived, as Shakespeare lived, as Dante lived. Agamemnon sees neither to right nor to left, he sees the path ahead.

He said I am a child, a child of genius, but I have known passion only as an adolescent knows it, which is not at all. It is true that I do not know what life is. I have built up my wall, and a good wall, for such as do not count. But against life in the strength and heat of fire there cannot be a wall. There can nothing happen to me that could go more deeply into me than to break up Karen's life. Karen is my love, my deep and only love. I have never loved anyone but him.

---

[26]Coleman was notorious for writing in the books she read. Her friend Antonia White, for instance, noted in her own diary: "If you borrow Emily's Wordsworth you will not read Wordsworth but Emily's Wordsworth. She will fearlessly correct and alter passages. She does not read; she flings herself upon and passionately possesses a work" (*Diaries* Vol. 1, 79).

Agamemnon and I talked and drank, and as the hours passed we came to know companionship that comes through common understanding. I know him now, I know his heart. There is no one whom I have ever known who has so formed my life. Karen formed me, and that is done, that was through love. And now Agamemnon, through his genius, has formed my genius. My genius is myself, and until I am a grown woman, with woman's passions, my genius is a pretty thing. I am not Emily Brontë, I am a child.

We talked of Edwin Muir, whom Agamemnon loves. There is no other person with whom I can say my say but Agamemnon. He is the only human being to whom I can tell the truth. And it is because he knows me for what I am, and is not in love with me. Conversation with others less than this is futile, I feel this more and more. It is not futile with this man.

I wrote a letter to Antony before this and said I did not want to see him again. He expects too much of me, and is too young to comprehend my spirit. He is hard, his hardness no longer does me good. He is a beautiful thing, but he is mixed, and his chaos is irremediable.

David did not come, because he was prevented. He will come Saturday in an airplane. If he does not come then he will come to St. Tropez. But he will come. I said to Agamemnon, "I do not know the end of this, but I am going to the end."

Hero and I worked together, she is heavy with this city. We sat when Agamemnon and Wendy quarreled, and remembered the days long ago.[27] This upset Hero, she could not sleep, it did not bother me. But when Agamemnon dropped tears upon his dear face for Kurn, I could not stand it.

He said that all my life had been a reaction to my Puritan background, and that my poetry was filled with the Biblical phrases of my upbringing.[28] He said the bad part of me was the part that did not bear children, and that made me able to put my writing before my child or my love. He said that was good because it gave me the impetus and the chance to write, but that in the writing it hindered me because I am not a whole woman.

He said, "You have never suffered, and if you knew what adult passion was just once your writing would show it," he said it would be intensified. He said that I say in twenty lines what I would say in one if I had suffered through it, and not merely imagined it. What he says is true, I know it deeply, and what am I to do?

---

[27]"The days" being in St. Tropez in 1928.
[28]In "The Story of my Childhood" (F. 1075) Coleman registered that her paternal grandfather had been a Congregational minister, her maternal grandmother was "a devout Presbyterian," while her father became a Unitarian. She commented on herself: "I was a Puritan prig until I met my husband."

We remembered

> Fall, leaves, fall; die, flowers away;
> Lengthen night and shorten day:
> Every leaf speaks bliss to me,
> Fluttering from the autumn tree;
>
> I shall smile when wreaths of snow
> Blossom where the rose should grow:
> I shall sing when night's decay
> Ushers in the drearier day.[29]

There was a woman with adult passions, he said, and what she felt came out like that, cold and succinct, not hot and diffused. He said when a woman felt like that deeply enough she brought out things a man could not feel. He said no woman who led a happy life could write poetry.

He said he came away from London on the eve of his success because he could not stand the people.[30] They are the most intelligent there are, he said, and the most sensitive, but that is not enough. One cannot talk about things, one must do them. He feels as I do, he came to that before me. I did not want to go away from London, yet when I shook the dust off my feet I would not turn again. Not people for me, nor cities, but my own soul, and the solitude to know it in. I cannot know any more new people except for love.

Agamemnon and I talked about the people in London. I loved them so much, and they stimulated me, yet I could not go on with them. I came away from the Muirs not wishing ever to talk to them again, after three [ ] days of approaching intimacy, and talk of the things I loved.[31] I could not stand to talk to Arthur Waley, he knows poetry, but his way is not my way. I listened to Beryl de Zoete read Milton until it filled my eyes, but I wanted no more of it.[32] I cannot be with these people, I said, "They are not my people. I want never to talk of poetry to these people." I thought of this when Agamemnon came. I can talk to him endlessly, he is the only person that excites me as much as some that are dead. He is the only person I have known who lives only in the fundamental chrysalis, and not in the windings of the cocoon. He has a brain of steel, and he has built life from within his brain. He feels with a passion that storms his soul.

---

[29]"Fall, leaves, fall," by Emily Brontë (1818–1848).

[30]Holms had been, for instance, a literary critic in London for *The Calendar of Modern Letters* from 1925–1927.

[31]Coleman had spent three days with the Muirs at their home The Nook, Blackness Road, in the East Sussex town of Crowborough.

[32]Beryl de Zoete (1879–1962), teacher and writer of dance, as well as a translator of authors such as Italo Svevo—Coleman would become an ardent admirer of his *Confessions of Zeno* (1923). Zoete had been the companion of Waley since 1918.

Agamemnon admitted that Muir does not have vitality—none to spare—and that he has only a very good intelligence, not one of the best. He said Muir did not know enough about himself, and that is not intelligent. He represses himself and instead of letting his talent out he keeps it checked. This comes from lack of vitality for resistance. His wife swallows him, and what good she has done him is past. He said that Muir's genius was not great, but it was genuine, of the romantic type. He said many of his opinions in *Transition* and in his book on the novel were his Agamemnon's opinions.[33] I believe that this is so.

The next time I was with him and Wendy together. Wendy is a courageous little person, she is direct and childish. They seem very happy together. She loves him because he is a ghost (which means to her honest) and he loves her because she has an overwhelming sex attraction for him, and because she is receptive to him. He needs her more than he does Kurn.

The next time Antony telephoned me at midnight. I had just got to bed. He said, "I am here with Agamemnon." He has always wanted to know him. I thinking it would be an evening, redressed and went to the café. There were they, with Judith and Wendy. The evening was terrible. Agamemnon prodding Antony and me to make us fight, which we did not do, and Wendy very drunk and telling me truths. She likes me, she wants me to know that she will let me talk to Agamemnon. I understood, but her voice was rasping because she had a cold. Truth was under discussion and Agamemnon as usual held himself up as a pattern of it. I said he was a liar part of the time. He said I spent most of my time in romantic lies. I said I told myself the truth, which was more than he did. I said I would always lie to others, unless they were strong enough to hear the truth. He listened entranced to Wendy voicing his opinions. I said "A woman of genius must have a man of genius, but the contrary is not so." Agamemnon said, "Now you are speaking truth." "It is because," I said, "a woman cannot depend upon herself, she is not yet sure." Judith said this too. Wendy wept, and I was forced into sympathy with her. I have always liked her. She said I had contempt for all women who are not intellectual. This may have been so until recently. She said that was not a woman's job. Goddamn it, so it is not. He has told her all of these things, and smiles fatuously when she says them. That is the dull side of the coin.

November 11

Now I am wretchedly unhappy because of Panurge. He wired me he was coming, and he came. He is an unleashed torrent, and I have no right to bathe

---

[33] Muir's *Transition: Essays on Contemporary Literature* (1926), and *The Structure of the Novel* (1928).

in it. I must be a torrent too, and I cannot, except for play. I said to him, "A love like this can have only one response, and that is a complete one. I cannot give that, I am divided." I said, "You thrill me, I want you physically, but I cannot have you because that could not be the end, and it would have to be the end." He broke down and cried all the day. I have not been through this except when I sent Lysander away. I wish I were hard, I am not, it withers me to a drop of dust to see this. I have caused this — I did not stop his love. I wanted his love, it is so beautiful and so strong, it is simple and very true.

I have sent Hippocra the "Lysias" poem.[34] The Redhead typed it. She writes joyful letters, they are succinct and dry. I sent Hippocra the poem, but it is not done. I gave it to Agamemnon, now I will see what he says. I said, "All you will find will be some lovely passages that are remarkable for the sensuousness of the words. The rest is shit," I said. I have not shown him what I did in Antwerp. Nothing that I write is good. What I wish to say comes out wrong. Whereas I used to feel that I could say everything, now I can say nothing. There is not one thing I have written that suits me. If I cannot write the truth of the great I do not want to write at all.

I am happy with Kay, my little boy who hops in the street. In the Luxembourg with Antony, they lost their balloons. Antony was happy that day — all he wants is to be a child and not molested. I said, "O why do you not write a good poem?" He said, "Because I do not want to." I wonder what Agamemnon will say of Antony's genius when I ask him. Genius thrown to cats in the street. When I first knew him he was conscious of this, now he does not care. I said to Agamemnon, "Antony hates me because I write and he doesn't."

I finally found a jar of peanut butter for Kay. I had promised it, and it is hard to find. I went out of one place and saw tears coming down Kay's face. I cannot bear it, I kissed them passionately. I can stand any tears better than those of his disappointment. He made me 17 drawings for the walls of my room. I took him to the dentist to have a tooth out Saturday. It was quick, but he screamed. It was soon over. He was proud of the hole and showed the tooth suddenly at the Deux Magots before everybody.[35] He had it in his pocket. I bought him *Zig et Puce*, and read it to him.[36] I love little Kay when his face is sweet. When he is the devil I could skin him. In London for two weeks he

---

[34]This poem, not extant, was likely inspired by Coleman's reading of Plato's Dialogue *Phaedrus*, about philosophy and love, featuring the figure of Lysias, famous 4th century (B.C.) rhetorician. Another poem, called "The Phaedrus," is extant.

[35]Trendy Left Bank café at 170 blvd, St. Germain, Les Deux Magots was frequented by artists and intelligentsia, especially expatriates, during the 1920s–1950s, and is now a major tourist stop.

[36]*Zig et Puce* is a weekly comic strip created in 1925 by Alain Saint-Ogan for the Sunday children's paper *Dimanche Illustré*.

was a horror. It was like New York, he drove me to it, I finally struck him then I wept from despair. As soon as Mamotchka got back I rushed him back to Paris.[37]

Karen could not stand it either, he said it would break us apart. People who are close do not find themselves drawn together by a child.

Now for what Agamemnon said on the fourth evening, with Wendy there, and part of the time Hero. I said to Wendy, "I want to be among the English poets" and she said, "You mean the American." I said, "But there aren't any." Then I thought, This is wrong, I should want to be among the American and I do not. I said to Agamemnon, "Is my poetry American?" He said it was, but so influenced now by Keats and Milton that it could not come out. I said "I am going to the country for four months so that I can think," Agamemnon said, "That is too long." He wants to hold Wendy, to keep himself before her as an idol, and he will admit nothing against this. I see through this, I know when he is a liar. I hate it the more because I want more from him. When he talks free and without personal thought he is a god.[38]

He said to Antony when Antony said I wanted to know Bloomsbury—"Of course she does and it is good for her—because it is always good for a person of talent to know as many groups as possible."[39] (And then pass beyond them of course.) He said my "Lysias" poem had passage after passage which showed an extraordinary genius for words, but that there was hardly a line where I had concentrated enough to make it poetry. Hard words, but they are true. I hate them, there is my six months' work, what can I do? I have to be what I am, and it is evident that I am nothing.

Wendy said that I looked down on her because she was not intellectual, I was angry, I said I looked down on no one who had no pretensions, that that was

---

[37]Coleman had been living with her husband and son in New York prior to their departure for Europe. In August 1929, John, residing with the Donns, had been sent to London to stay with his parents while the Donns were out of town. In her 1929 entry for her Wellesley Class of 1920 Record Book, she explained: "If it is thought that I am an unfaithful mother let me say that his father, who is noted for dignity and patience, said he just could not stand him another minute in London!" (Wellesley College Archives). She revisited this episode in January 15, 1930.

[38]Holms not only spoke like but also resembled a "god," as Guggenheim explains: "He was very tall, over six feet in height. He had a magnificent physique, enormous broad shoulders and small hips and a fine chest. He wore a small red beard and looked very much like Jesus Christ. His hair was wavy, thick and auburn red. His skin was white, but from the southern sun it had turned pink. His eyes were deep brown and he wore glasses; he had a classical straight nose. His mouth was small and sensuous and seemed to be pursed up under his moustache" (79).

[39]The Bloomsbury Group, so called because its members circulated within this London district, included some of the most impressive writers, artists, and intellectuals of the early twentieth century, such as Virginia (Stephen) Woolf, Leonard Woolf, Vanessa (Stephen) Bell, Lytton Strachey, Clive Bell, Roger Fry, and John Maynard Keynes.

what I could not stand. I said, "If Agamemnon had fallen in love with me I might have felt differently about him." She said, "How honest that is, and I admire you for it." It did not hurt me to say that. I said, "If you had seen that poem ("Lysias") and had not known the writer, would you have been interested to know her?" He said, "Of course—talent like this is very rare," and that was all I could get out of him. I will have to believe in myself alone, he will not tell me. I said, "I am not in the romantic haze I once was in," he said, "I know." Wendy said she could not tackle abstract ideas, that she was a little jealous when we talked intellectually. He said a man of talent does not want an intellectual woman, he wants to give way to his instinct. But O Lord, I do want an intelligent man, one who does not bore me to the very death. I can not love physically a man who is not intelligent, and Agamemnon says that is what is the matter with me.

A letter from Karen from Antwerp. He says he will not read, that no one can follow my reading now, that he will only work. It depresses me to think of Karen, I wonder if he had no economic problem if he would keep at an idea and write about it.[40]

A cablegram from my father from California says "Conditions unchanged. Don't come. Doctor says you can do nothing."[41] My poor father, I wrote him I knew his sorrows and he replied that he did not have any more than anyone else, and that he had put them behind. I cannot keep from thinking that if I should die it would end every joy his life depends on. Karen would recover, but my father I think not.

Little Kay said, "*Au revoir, mon ange,*" and trudged off alone.[42] I think that some day he will be the only one whose opinion I will fear. It is not because he is my son—it is because of his intelligence, sensitiveness and independence. He has all the things that I want—and passion unconfined, and beauty. I hope I do not make him my inverted love. It is not likely to come until others have turned from me, and I have only fame to cheer my hardened heart. I hope I will have my genius—I hope it is one that will last the years. I know damn well it will.

Judith chatters, but she is quick to see, and she understands. I will forgive her the rest, even though she provokes me to things not of my best. I found her body lovely again, but not as it was before. I am too divided now, I want David and he does not come.

---

[40] Deak Coleman had aspired to being a poet.
[41] For Coleman's father, John Milton Holmes, see the introduction. On November 4 (F. 625, not transcribed) she mentioned that her younger brother William (1903–1930)—renamed "Don" in the diary—was dying from tuberculosis in California.
[42] "Goodbye, my angel."

When we were sitting in the café old Titus came in (he gave me 500 francs last summer for a story "The Fugitives" which Agamemnon said was not good, it is to come out in his dull magazine next week) and asked for more of my writings.[43] Then he put his hand on my hair and said it was pretty. I shrank but gave no sign. When he had gone I said, "Why is it I cannot bear to be touched?" and Agamemnon got very angry and said, "Of course you don't want to be touched—you are sensitive and sensitive people don't want to be touched by riff-raff." I said, "None of your snobbery," he said, "You cannot want to be touched except by someone who is a pleasure to you."

I said, "Why is it that if fifteen people tell you you have more sex attraction than any woman they have ever seen, and one says you have none you believe the one?" "Because" said Wendy, "you too must have an inferiority notion." Agamemnon said if fifteen people told him he was ugly and one said he was beautiful he would believe the one. I said to Wendy, "You have no pretensions," she said, "I have pretensions to inferiority." I told Agamemnon that I felt in an artistic way about Wendy as he did. I see her shape, and her movements, her gestures and her face as he does. She is a quick sprite, she moves suddenly and like a bird she looks about. She is shaped perfectly, thinly, her bones might break. She turns her head upon her neck and snaps her hand. Her shoulders are narrow and she walks with assurance which she has not, but so she walks. She said I had always attracted her, that she loved my face and wanted to touch my hair. I said I like my hair touched and would prefer to have my body looked at than invaded.

November 14

Now my Agamemnon again, this time Judith and I sitting in the Deux Magots, I bored through and through (though I love her), and he coming past. His presence does not thrill me like one I love, it is like seeing a long-wanted

---

[43]Edward Titus, American owner of the bookshop At the Sign of the Black Manikin, and of The Black Manikin Press. He took over the job of editing and publishing *This Quarter* (1929–1932), an avant-garde periodical first put out in Paris in 1925 by Ernest Walsh and Ethel Moorhead. Contributors included Paul Valéry, Arthur Rimbaud, Allan Tate, Robert Penn Warren, Thomas Mann, Herman Hesse, e. e. cummings, Harold Loeb, André Breton, Salvador Dali, and Marcel Duchamp. "The Fugitives" is a surrealistic account of a girl's visit, with her father, to her mother who is incarcerated in what appears to be an asylum. The theme of psychosis coupled with frequent references to snow—including the phrase "shutter of snow"—suggests both a rendering of the visits Coleman paid as a child to her institutionalized mother as well as Coleman's own experiences at the Rochester State Hospital (fictionalized in *The Shutter of Snow*). See the introduction.

book on the shelf, a book of wisdom and deep findings. It is like going to a sibyl who has once told you all the truth.

I said, "What about philosophy?" and Judith laughed, and so did he. I have formed this habit with Agamemnon since he has left St. Tropez. Because I never know how long the time will be. "Why have I such a passion now to read philosophy?" I said. He said "Because your chaos is so great that you are desperately reaching out for anything that will give you an illusion of order. People who think in groups may be very intelligent—as the people of Bloomsbury are—but they are not important. The only people of importance are those who think alone." He said Arthur Waley was as intelligent as it is possible for a person without talent to be. He said he thought in the manner of the Cambridge of his day. He said "If he really thought by himself he could not spend all his time translating." I remember Waley's saying that poetry did not have to contain ideas (or thought) and that a painting of a tree was as important as a painting of people and trees. "T.S. Eliot," he said, "Is not Bloomsbury—he thinks alone—but there are bad gaps in his thinking." I said, "He is nevertheless the greatest mind in England today," and Agamemnon said, "That may be true but he has gaps."[44]

Then we got down to the main point which was my poem ["Lysias"]. He did not have it with him, but Judith had a copy of it, which she had asked for. He said, "There is hardly a line where you have concentrated enough to make it come out pure. For instance," he said, "'The lines of frost grow fine before the sun,' which means spring, directly contradicts the first line, 'When falls the leaf upon the hardening ground.'" "I can see," I said, "that the influences of *transition* and the Surrealistes is not dead yet, for when I wrote those lines I left them because they had come out unconsciously.[45] The trouble is," I said, "that I cannot find the medium between what is in my unconscious mind and what I am saturated with from other minds. As soon as I write consciously it sounds like someone else." Then for my favourite

---

[44]T. S. Eliot (1888–1965), Anglo-American poet, critic, and dramatist. Coleman was referring to his critical works *Dante* (1929), and *For Lancelot Andrewes: Essays on Style and Order* (1928).
[45]*transition* (1927–1938), avant-garde magazine founded in Paris by Maria and Eugène Jolas, edited by Eugène Jolas and Elliot Paul. Jolas had been a literary critic and city editor of the Paris edition of the Chicago *Tribune*. Paul was a colleague from the *Tribune*, as was Coleman. For more on Coleman and *transition*, see the introduction. *transition* was especially devoted to publishing work by artists who in some manner ascribed to the dictates of surrealism as laid down by André Breton and Philippe Soupault in *The Magnetic Fields* (1920), and by Breton in his surrealist manifestos (1924, 1930). Breton propounded automatic writing which tapped in to the creative sources of the unconscious, rendering an experience which does not distinguish between dream and reality.

words—glittering, churned, turning (of the hand), shine, gleam, share, prod, cold, light, gold, eyes, prismic, burst, fold, sun, maze, seed, soft, doom, swift, content, withered, lean, mock, swell, rhythms, dream,—these words, he said, I had better psycho-analyze myself on, because there was some reason, probably sexual, why I used them so much. I will do this, I will think about these words.

"Now," said Agamemnon, "What you need is to write some prose. Have you?" "I have," said I, "But Hippocra said it was a waste of time, because anyone could write prose of that kind, and she said anyone could not write poetry as I can." "That is wrong," he said. "It is true that your talent is for poetry, but it will do you no harm to discipline yourself with prose." I told him about my novel, which I had begun before he left St. Tropez, and which he remembered.[46] I had written about 30, 000 words and then had left it because it seemed so ordinary. I said that I had written a third of a story in Antwerp and had stopped because it seemed so good and I knew it could not be as good as it seemed to me then, so I wanted to wait until I had gotten cold about it. I said, "Shall I get it?" and he said yes, so I left the café and went home to get the story. Agamemnon took it, and then I must say he did shame me. "After all, it is true," I said to him, "You might as well know the truth." "My God," he said, after reading some, "You know if you will finish this I really believe you could make some money out of it." I snatched it from him and tried to put it in the brasero but the coals were not hot enough.[47] I brought also the two sections of the "Life and Death of Jesus Christ," both of which I intended to destroy. The one on the "Woman of Samaria," which I knew to be the Bible and not myself, he said I might as well destroy.[48] The other he said he would read later, he could not do it then in the café, for the first time. With the "Woman of Samaria" one I had been inspired by the account in John IV, which is a beautiful and perfect narrative.[49] What I wanted to try to improve on it for I don't know—I succeeded in doing nothing but a dry and unoriginal paraphrase. That I did manage to burn up in the brasero, it was smaller. Thus all my work in Antwerp gone to the dogs.

---

[46]In her entry for December 21, 1929, Coleman described tearing up this manuscript.
[47]A brasero is a heater placed under tables.
[48]Despite Coleman's later admission that she burned this poem, her archive contains four versions of "The Woman of Samaria," as well as a poem entitled "The Life of Jesus and Mary" and a dramatic poem entitled "The Death of Jesus Christ."
[49]The Gospel according to St. John, 4: 1–42.

After Judith went Kristians Tonny came and sat with us.[50] He came the other time and if he comes again I shall kill him. He is said to be a great genius, and Gertrude Stein collects him, but I do not believe he can have much to say. I was so bored I nearly screamed—it was Agamemnon who asked him to sit down.

I walked along the street with him, as he went home to Wendy.

In the evening I continued with Hero's manuscript. I only want it to be clear and simple, and sometimes she does make it that, when she knows what she is saying and is not rushed. But sometimes it is just awful. I can handle it better this way, away from her. I can keep cool. I do love Hero, but damn her soul, she cannot write the English language, and sometimes it is more than I can bear.

Judith said she wanted to be a man, I said I did not. I never did, except when a child. I would not change my sex for all the world. It is because I feel that if I ever get out of this bog it will be an advantage to my writing that I am a woman.

Today when I got a request from Harriet Sampson, a member of my class (who sent me a little poem she had written) to write something about what I have been doing for the class paper, I wrote at length.[51] Then when I had mailed it to America I went and ate alone and pondered why I had done that. It is further evidence of what I am—I want these people to recognize me. I am not satisfied that I am cut off from them, I want them to know it. It interested me to know this—that I could write what I have done, and where I have been, for these dull and speechless tribes. I cannot forget that when I was in college I was the court jester. I must have it known that I am now above the earth.

November 16

Agamemnon came into my room this afternoon. I was playing with Kay, getting him ready for bed. Agamemnon later said he had never seen anyone less

---

[50]Kristians Tonny (1907–1977), Dutch surrealist artist whose work had appeared in *transition*. In 1930, he became the second painter (after Pablo Picasso) to paint Gertrude Stein's portrait. Stein (1874–1946), American expatriate avant-garde writer and art collector, hosted a literary and artistic salon at her Left Bank apartment at 27, rue de Fleurus, which Coleman once visited; it attracted some of the most celebrated modernists of the twentieth century, such as Picasso and Ernest Hemingway.

[51]Coleman wrote a detailed bio blurb for this 1929 Record Book for her Wellesley Class of 1920. Retracing much of the content recorded in the diary to this point, she summarized her past year, describing being in St. Tropez with Goldman through 1928, London and Antwerp with Deak in 1929, the forthcoming publication of her novel, publishing in *transition* and *This Quarter*, her brother dying of tuberculosis, and her son's living arrangements (Wellesley College Archives).

maternal and I didn't like that. I went over "The Photograph" and gave it to him to read later.[52] I said I agreed with what Muir said about Lawrence in his essay—that he has a sensuousness about the earth and the things of the earth, and sees man in relation to that—that he is all instincts and no mind—that he does people well physically but does not distinguish them from each other inside.[53] Agamemnon said he was interested in Lawrence because he had a bit of talent. I told him I was reading *Measure for Measure* and he read aloud "Be absolute for death," and then the other one, beginning, "Ay, but to die and go we know not where."[54]

Then I had Kay in bed and we went out to a café.[55] Agamemnon had looked at Kay's drawings and said as usual that they were good. At the Deux Magots before a brasero Agamemnon started to talk about himself. He said all he knew about life he found out in 18 months, the first months he was with Kurn, and all he had learned since was simply an elaboration of that. Before that he had gone around for years with a gun in his hand, partly a result of his two years of prison during the war, when he lost all sense of responsibility for life or for death.[56] He said it put him in such a state of exaltation to get right to the point of suicide that he would find himself doing things deliberately to get himself to that point, and this involved other people often and was very bad. He had no sense of money nor of anything practical. I said "I loathe now the slightest responsibility for anything practical and after I have been in St. Tropez for a few months writing, I cannot bring myself to it at all, I can only do these things when I have forced myself into the habit of them." "Now," he said, "I have the feeling I am going to live forever." "Yes," I said, "Edwin says that is bad for your writing. As for me,"

---

[52]Coleman's unpublished story "The Photograph" is about a widowed father's resistance to his daughter's impending marriage. In her entry for February 8, 1930, she noted that the story offers a portrait of her father.
[53]Coleman was citing the chapter on D. H. Lawrence in Muir's *Transition: Essays on Contemporary Literature*.
[54]The two passages Holms read from Shakespeare's comedy are Vincentio's speech to Claudio (III: i, l. 5–40), and Claudio's speech to Isabella (III: i, l. 117–130).
[55]Coleman often left her young son alone in bed while she went out at night.
[56]Muir tells us that Holms, having trained at Sandhurst, "had been intended for the Army, and had joined a battalion of the Highland Light Infantry at the end of 1915, when he was seventeen"; "He was captured by the Germans in 1917, and spent the rest of the War as a prisoner, a year at Karlsruhe and seven months at Mainz" (177). For more on Holms in the war, see Coleman's entry for December 6, 1929. Writing about John and Dorothy Holms, Guggenheim describes: "They had led a very stormy existence. He had taken her away from a man called Peacock and had gone through months of hell, while she wavered between them. He had carried a pistol constantly, with the idea of killing himself if she did not remain with him." She did stay; it was Holms who would leave her, nine years later, for Guggenheim (81).

I said, "I think constantly I am going to die tomorrow, and it is that makes me so impatient with myself, I fear dying before I have said my say, before I have learned enough to enable me to say it." He said his feeling of living forever was directly connected with an intense fear of death which he knew he had.

At noon Hero made me a salad of old. It was sweet to see her bending over a kitchen table with an onion in one hand and a knife in the other, nipping with her mouth the onion. Hero rushing an omelette on the table at the last moment, made of nothing, with Jewish sausages. I crying "Hero there you are, you always did that." She liked that, she is my mother and that is why I love her.

In the afternoon of this day I had taken Kay and Rostik to see Charlot.[57] I love this comedian because he is life, and it is burlesque on truth and I shout with laughter. I had my finger nail in my mouth and Kay said loudly at the cinema, "O Mimi, *une belle dame comme ça ne doit pas mettre le doigt dans la bouche!*" His eyes were large when he said it. He also corrected my saying the dog had "*gueuler*"—ed—he said women did not use that word.[58]

I know now why I want so much another genius, less than I, to inspire. Karen thinks it is because I am not sure of my own. It is because I want a sense of power, I want someone on whom to impress myself, someone finely sensitive who will snatch each word, as I do from Agamemnon. I wonder if this will be David. He wrote Hero today he cannot come before December 5th. He said, "Tell Emily I shall come direct to see her when I arrive, then I shall come to you." He set out last Saturday in the airplane and they were lost in the fog, and crashed, breaking the machine. I could only think how glad I was he was not dead. Now I must remain until the 5th, I would not do this if I did not think there would be much in his coming.[59] A letter from my Father from California saying "the sands of my brother's life are slowly ebbing away." He has to stay there until the end.

That night Agamemnon telephoned me and I met him and Wendy at the Café de Versailles.[60] We talked about vanity first, I said I was inconceivably vain and that no one knew it. Agamemnon said, "I know it," and Wendy said, "So do I." I said to Wendy, "How do you know it?" She wouldn't say, she

---

[57]Rostislaw (referred to by nickname and spelled variously as Rostik or Rostique), age ten, was the Donns' son; their daughter, Olga, was twelve, while John Coleman was nearly six. "Charlot" is the persona of the Little Tramp adopted by Charlie Chaplin (1889–1977) in many of his silent films. Coleman may have been watching the latest release, *The Circus* (1928).
[58]"O Mimi, a lovely lady like yourself should not put her finger in her mouth." "*Dégueuler*"—to vomit or barf.
[59]Coleman was eager to leave Paris for St. Tropez, where she planned to live in isolation in order to write.
[60]The Café de Versailles was located in Montparnasse, on the Left Bank.

said it was too personal. So I spiked her guns, I said, "Because you think I wanted Agamemnon and because he did not want me I will not show I wanted him." She said, "I swear it is not that," and he said, "That would be pride anyway." I said, "It is because I want so many men in love with me." She smiled at that and that was what it was. I said, "I did want every man in love with me." Agamemnon said, "You were surprised if one was not," I said, "No, if you want the truth, I am always surprised when one is." (This is truth.) Later Agamemnon said, "People who have inferiority complexes are such masochists." I said, "Nothing is so lustful as hearing bad things someone has said, eavesdropping preferably." Wendy said, "I get it by reading Kurn's letters when he [Agamemnon] is not there." She told about her father, who went down in the Titanic.[61] At ten she knew he had mistresses. At twenty I had never heard of a mistress. I said I had had a delayed adolescence after marriage because when I was in college and should have had men in love with me I was cold and prudish with them and they walked away.

Then I said suddenly to Wendy, "I wish you would let Agamemnon get drunk again and talk to me all night." I said it simply to get her to discuss that with him, I knew she would not like it. She was honest as usual, she said, "I hate that because I am without him for 24 hours after and it is besides not good for his health." Agamemnon said, "My God Wendy, I don't live like this." I didn't give a damn what either of them thought—like when Kurn was jealous and I would talk to him anyway, because my life was more important than my feelings just then. I need what he has to say and I will have it, even if there are always women in the way. He wants to talk to me now, I can see that sex is not enough. She wants to go to bed at nine and he begins feeling set up at midnight. The result of their discussion, which was personal and in which I did not join, was that Wendy did not mind how many hours I talk to Ag. if it would be in the daytime. He said, "I won't talk to anyone before six o'clock at night." He needs to get drunk, it is release for him. He said Wendy liked being drunk because she is repressed and that I did not really like it at all (which is true) because I really wanted to do nothing but talk about poetry and my genius. All else than this I consider so much waste. She is of course jealous, and I do not blame her, but she must not be a fool. I hope she does not go to London, that poor man should be allowed to see Kurn alone.[62]

---

[61]Benjamin Guggenheim (1865-1912) inherited, along with his six brothers, the smelting fortune built up by their father, Meyer Guggenheim, who had immigrated to New York from German Switzerland. He married the wealthy Florette Seligman, and they had three daughters: Benita (1895-1927), Peggy, and Hazel (1903-1995). A passenger on board the *Titanic*, he died when the ship, en route to New York, sank off the coast of Newfoundland.

[62]Holms was going to visit his wife, Dorothy, in England.

November 17

Kay all night and I took him to the Gare Montparnasse to see the trains.[63] I went to a concert with Judith, the Pasdeloup Orchestra, vilely performing Beethoven. Walter Gieseking on the piano, not so bad, first Beethoven concerto, then trash of Debussy.[64] I cannot endure this composer, nor Ravel, which followed. The drums were out of proportion and the violins ill geared. All I got was the feeling more than ever that I must, I must, have a victrola and play for hours alone. At Christmas I will have Karen buy one and I will send him records, then when I am in Antwerp I will have that.

At dinner showed Judith a little story "The Visit" which I found today.[65] Found it rather good, relieved my fury over the other story. Judith got excited over it, said it was a "little masterpiece." Said why, very intelligently. Went over it with me, suggested change in the short paragraph I had added. She was right and I excited at this. Must show this to Agamemnon, it is something. I know why too, it is because it is about a simple childhood experience which I know through and through. I wrote this the summer in St. Tropez, right in the middle of "the Wasted Earth." Showed it to Lysander, who was there then, and he liked [it] very much. No one else has seen it, it has been buried.

November 18

Karen's birthday, he is thirty-three.

I have wanted men who did not care for women, ones who were hard to get. I knew it was my vanity, that this made me feel more important, because they were not easily won. Now I know that too, that it was my desire for power. I must feel power over all that I know. Then when I got a man thoroughly in love with me I did not want him. I have always noted this, and was ashamed, and being tender I kept on after I did not longer care, because I had started.

---

[63]Train station in the Montparnasse district.
[64]The Pasdeloup Orchestra was formed in 1861 by Jules Pasdeloup to deliver "popular concerts." Though it ceased performing in 1886, the company started up again in 1918 (under the directorship of Serge Sandberg), and continues to perform today.
[65]"The Visit," written during her summer in St. Tropez in 1928, deals with a girl at a boarding-school who receives a visit from her mother, who lives in a sanitarium; as Coleman went on to suggest, the story is in part autobiographical. Coleman also mentioned her story "The Wasted Earth," an experimental poem/short-story which consists of three sections—Part I: The Poet Awakes and Finds the Earth. The Enchantment; Part II: The Poet Grapples with Life and is Vanquished. The Reckoning; Part III: The Poets Sleeps. The Desolation. Part I was published as "The Wasted Earth (Fragment)" in the November 1929 issue of *transition*.

Antony helped greatly my sense of power, he made me feel someone. "Promise me to wear a beret," things like this helped me on. I walked the streets gay and superior because Antony found me lovely.

I know I am jealous of Wendy. I am shut out of this, I am too proud to take her leavings. She says he [Agamemnon] must not stay up late drinking and he agrees. I want him to drink, then he is himself, he gets out of his moorings. She does not care for this, she says, "He is a lover, I do not care about his genius, I have seen no evidences of anything but intelligence." She has changed, she is more intense and more serious, he has made her this and must bear the brunt of it. I said, "My weakness is wanting people to recognize me. But a little recognition from the right people," I said, "would soon send my flying. I could not bear it!" "Yes," he said. "You need a little. It is quite natural." When I confessed, darkly, that I liked someone's saying "That's Emily Coleman" and was ashamed of it, they howled with laughter. "What a baby she is!" cried Wendy. "A sweet baby." She said she liked having inferior people talk about her even when they said mean things. "I like to see them talking," she said, "and know it is about me." It was Agamemnon's birthday today (the same as Karen's) and we ate at Prunier's.[66] They were having some kind of a row, she sulking or trying to, he amiable. He has a good disposition, she takes advantage of it. I do the same with Karen. They said I was wrong to tell Kay that it cost me much pain when he was born and that I did not want it again.[67] I did not believe them, thinking Kay to have been interested but not impressed. However the next day I said to Kay, "I was happy to have the pain because I wanted you." They said a child cannot know the truth until he is ready and that I would embitter him. I do not believe this but it bothered me so I said this to Kay. I could not get his attention, he was thinking of a balloon. I told him I wanted him terribly (true) and that for that I was glad of the pain (not true). I was angry when I left because Agamemnon wanted to go to Les Halles and Wendy did not, and she does not dare to leave him alone with me.[68] She is wrong (though she cannot know it) because he is an old woman to me, or an oracle, not a man. He is very

---

[66]Prunier's was and continues to be a famous seafood brasserie opened on the avenue Victor Hugo in 1924 by Emile Prunier, son of Alfred and Catherine Prunier, who had launched the first restaurant in 1872. Writers like Hemingway and Fitzgerald frequented Emile's place. See *Madame Prunier's Fish Cookery Book* (1938).

[67]Coleman suffered from puerperal fever following the birth of John, which led to her breakdown and subsequent treatment at the Rochester State Hospital. She wrote about her "infection" in October 9, 1932. See the introduction.

[68]Les Halles (now Forum des Halles) is a major market centre in the first arrondissement of Paris. Humphrey Carpenter tells us in *Geniuses Together* that "Les Halles was the traditional place to end an all-night binge, with a bowl of onion soup at one of the market cafés" (108).

like a woman sometimes, he gossips and when he gets mad he is catty. He has no guts, he has passion and independence, but he has no energy.

I spoke of Arthur Waley and how much I wanted his respect and how I would have it. Then I did not care, I found him inferior. If I had not known Agamemnon I would not have seen his shortcomings. I showed "The Visit" to Agamemnon and he was not deeply impressed. He said it was good, but it was full of my romantic ideas about people and things. I said to them both, "I am not interested in your relationship, I am interested in myself. I cannot help it," I said, "I have spent most of my life in other people's lives, I have begun to live alone." Wendy did not like this, but I said, "You do not know how fond I am of you." This is very true.

I go daily to the dentist, he kills me with pain. I cannot stand the least pain. He says, "*Mon pauvre petit*," and puts his hand against my cheek.[69] That I detest, I wish I had a stack of dynamite to drop burning beneath him. I will not be touched, especially by the French. Agamemnon said I was not a woman, I was a little boy. I said, "Some men think me the most feminine creature they have ever met," (Panurge), Agamemnon said, "But they are wrong," and I said, "They are indeed wrong!" I cannot sustain sexual passion; I can only feel it once in a fortnight and then it is gone again. I put all my sex into my work, I was sexual enough when I first met Karen. Now when next I fall in love it will have to be with my body as well as with my head.

November 19

I said, "I will no longer suffer this humiliation" because I wanted to stay up with Agamemnon and go to Les Halles, or anywhere, and Wendy wanted him to go to bed. I said, "I had enough of that with Kurn, he will always be dominated by women." Then I said I wished to be let out at my door. The trouble is I have preconceived ideas as to how a woman should treat a man, I cannot stand seeing someone try to keep someone else from drinking. But why not? It is silly of me and comes from my reaction against the dependence of woman.

The next day Wendy phoned and asked me to bring Kay and we took the two children to the Champs-Élysées to hear the Guignol and to ride on the donkeys and goats.[70] They had balloons and enjoyed everything, but the Guignol

---

[69]"My poor little one."
[70]Guignol is a character in puppet shows in France, similar to the Punch and Judy shows in England. The Champs-Élysées is the most famous promenade in Paris.

bored them. Kay behaved well with the little girl, and put the victrola records on alone.[71] When this child is sweet and has not the devil in him I love him tenderly.

November 20[72]

Agamemnon said that most people in the world are underdogs and that those of us who are not should be kind to them. I have felt this for some time, ever since I realized I was not an underdog. This holds for most of the people who are considered superior by the mob, and it certainly holds for people who have reached a certain age, whatever their attainments. This started by the presence in one party of Hero and an Englishwoman called Mina Loy who is supposed to be a poet.[73] She is very pretty and considers herself superior to Hero, about whom she laughs. I told her she wanted admiration just as much as Hero, only she had finesse while Hero has not. I told her she was superficial and that she had no brains. She did not like this. Agamemnon told her she was a fool several times but he said it as a man talks to a pretty woman and she did not mind. Wendy got independent with Hero at the wrong time—she has no sensitiveness about these things—and Hero left crying. I went after her and put her in the taxi. She cried, "You are all cynics!" It is the only way she can protest against an attitude of mind which she cannot understand. But I cannot bear to hurt Hero, only when she has drunk something she becomes so horrible I cannot bear it.

Later Agamemnon said things to Wendy which she protested. She said, "I admire your superiority complex, but you go too far." He does indeed. It is hard to know as much as he does, and if he had more sense he would adapt himself to the human animal. He cannot, and it comes out when he is drunk. I cannot say I do not admire this, but it is damned hard sledding. He told Wendy things that hurt her pride—he told her she knew nothing when she

---

[71]The "little girl" was Guggenheim and Laurence Vail's daughter, Pegeen (1925–1967). Guggenheim and Vail (1891–1968) married in 1922, separated in 1928, and divorced in 1930. An American expatriate avant-garde novelist, poet, playwright, and artist, Vail was a famous Left Bank fixture known as the King of Bohemia or the King of Montparnasse. They also had a son, Michael Cedric Sindbad (called Sindbad) (1923–1986). After their divorce, Guggenheim retained custody of Pegeen, Vail of Sindbad.

[72]Coleman dated this typed entry by hand; however, she also typed the next entry with the same date.

[73]Mina Loy (Mina Gertrude Lowy) (1882–1966), English poet and artist, was acquainted with Guggenheim, Gertrude Stein, and other Left Bank writers and artists, and was a lifelong friend of Djuna Barnes.

met him and that he was trying to teach her something about life. He said she lived in other people's opinions and thought nothing of herself, that she lived in reactions, like all Americans. Now she is living in the reaction against her former adulation of Hero, which he has punctured. Hero loathes Agamemnon, she cannot understand his mind or character. It is magnanimous of him to like her, but he does not overrate her.

My greatest fight is against my romantic tendency to view people and things through the eyes of those whom I admire. It has always been so, and what I have achieved has been slow and at heavy price. I can see that I have not gone far. I have succeeded in lifting myself above the opinions of the mob—it was not long ago that these completely dominated me. But since I got out of that I have from time to time seen everything through the eyes of someone whom I admired. I am at this moment completely under the sway of Agamemnon. It disgusts me. I am a medium, I come out of it only to go into it again. I have come out from Agamemnon several times, now I am in it again more intensely than ever. I thought like Antony, I was even in Tommy's mind for a brief interval. I have not yet been swayed by David. It must not be. I have got to think alone.

Edwin Muir and Arthur Waley—I believed everything through them too. Arthur Waley confused me, he upset all my tenets. I revolted from this—there is that consolation, I always revolt. But I have got to have a thorough and final revolt from Agamemnon. It is so hard because he is the only person I have ever known who was so near to what I feel is an Absolute.

As for the things I read, it is far worse. Only Agamemnon has dominated me as have Keats, Milton, and Goethe. And now it is Shakespeare. I am he, I live in his mind, I think his thoughts, I am not myself at all, I am this day Agamemnon and Shakespeare. I think this is good for me, but it has got to have its end. I must be myself, I must live my own mind. Spenser, Coleridge, Plato, the same. I am a medium for these people's thoughts. This disgusts me and I am eager for the time when it shall stop.

I have a better mind than Agamemnon, it is quicker and more sensitive. But I am less intelligent because I have not thought or read or suffered. When I have thought enough, and gone through passion that is not adolescent, I shall pass beyond him. I have the drive that he cannot feel, the push of the strongest genius. I feel in myself the push of genius greater than any living person, but I cannot be sure of it because it is only a feeling. When I have done something to show this, then I will be more certain. I feel myself with the very greatest—I feel the power to pass beyond all my present limitations. If only I live, if only that I live!

November 20

A devastating headache, I came up to see Hero, found her up and well (she now has the studio to herself) and scornful of Mina Loy last evening.[74] "I felt like an old whore," said Hero, "Sitting there. It was no place for me, I have work to do." I said with all my heart, "You are right." I sleeping in the bed at Hero's because my head ached so. I wish I did not so much want to hear what Agamemnon says—but what shall I do—there is no one else now who does me any good? And I don't know enough yet by myself.

Walter Lowenfels asked me to lunch on Thursday.[75] He said he had a book of poems out, *Finale of Seem*. When I was there last year he maddened me by his incoherence. It was just after I had begun to know Agamemnon and I was in Paris to meet my father.[76] Now I will be more tolerant, I will only expect from him what he has. He has sounds of words and skill in their arrangement, he has no thoughts or passion. I do not like his wife, I cannot bear wives except Kurn. This one should never have got in at all, I remember how she bored Karen. I am trying to hurry up Karen's coming.

I dream about David. That is not fair because I am trying not to think of him and to be calm. I wait intensely his coming, with clear eyes. If it is not so it shall not be so. This long wait has intensified a situation that was at first only piquant.

Another letter from father from California. My little brother Don is dying, he is growing weaker and weaker. Father has got to stay there till the end. He is "philosophical" about it.

November 21

This morning went out to American hospital and had gynocological examination for leucorrhea.[77] I hate so horribly to go through this, I can never grow used to it. I said, "You will be very gentle?" to the thick-skinned imbecile who was to make the examination. To my surprise he was. In the middle he said to me, "How long have you had this?" "Fifteen years." "How old are you

---

[74]In her memoir, Guggenheim explains that at this time in Montparnasse she and Holms "had rented a furnished flat with a studio in the Rue Campagne Première" (99).
[75]Walter Lowenfels (1897–1976), American expatriate poet, editor, and left-wing activist who would become a close friend of Henry Miller in 1931. His work appeared, like Coleman's, in publications such as *transition* and *This Quarter*. His book *Finale of Seem: A Lyrical Narrative*, was published in London in 1929. He was married to Lillian Apotheker, with whom he had three daughters.
[76]Coleman's father made annual trips to Europe to see his daughter.
[77]The American Hospital is located in Neuilly, about five miles from central Paris. Leucorrhea is vaginal discharge.

30   Section I

now?" "Thirty-one," I said. "I don't believe it," said he, "You look sixteen." He said it with American verity and I being as vain as I am was pleased, though in the same moment he was piercing my womb with his thumb. Judith went with me, and coming home I said to her, "Please my child get yourself into another state of mind." She is so depressed and I have tried to cheer her and it irritates me, though I know her and am sorry. She has suffered much and thinks little of herself, her life is not what she wants and she jumps from one thing to another. She depresses and does not stimulate me, but I am ashamed because I have everything she should have.

Then I had luncheon with the Walter Lowenfels, wife pretty and hanging on his words, baby changed to look like its father. It was a farce, a man there named McGreevy who decried Shakespeare.[78] At first I laughed, then he was so set I took him up. He made impossible statements, he is supposed to be a critic, mentioning all the people prominent. He knows Agamemnon, said he was "very intelligent, not so supercilious as he used to be." This man is Irish, living in American reactions. An imbecile of the first order. Walter on the other hand I like, he is innocent, though full of Quarter prune juice and thinking with other people.[79] He crumbles before the least onset. He has a little thing, I hope he keeps it clean. He showed me a letter from Ford Madox Ford saying rot, and I (who had been most controlled up to that) burst out, "Why do you show your poems to such a god-damned fool as that?"[80] I was ashamed, I should save my rages for the thick-skinned. I am a celebrity here, I hate it, they do not know what I say. My name, only my name, nothing that I think matters. Samuel Putnam was there, whom I remembered as the friend of Virgil Geddes.[81] I like him, he is true. He has just finished a biography of Rabelais. I want to read that. He is thin and worn, he studies hard. This was

---

[78]Thomas McGreevy (1893–1967), influential Irish critic and poet. A good friend and supporter of James Joyce, he wrote favorably about Joyce's *Work in Progress* (*Finnegan's Wake*) in the Fall 1928 issue of *transition*.

[79]In *Geniuses Together*, Carpenter explains that by the early 1920s Montparnasse had come to be called "the Quarter," as distinct from the Latin Quarter (90). Titus' little magazine, *This Quarter*, was named for Montparnasse.

[80]Ford Madox Ford (Ford Madox Hueffer) (1873–1939), English novelist. He was one of the founders of *The English Review* in 1908, and after moving to Paris in 1922, he founded and edited the *Transatlantic Review* (January 1924-January 1925).

[81]Samuel Putnam (1892–1950), American writer, translator, and editor. He was an associate editor of *This Quarter*, and he founded the *New Review* (January 1931-April 1932), published in Paris. His *François Rabelais, Man of the Renaissance: A Spiritual Biography* appeared in 1930. Virgil Geddes (1897- 1989), American poet, playwright, and director, who published like Coleman in little magazines such as *transition*. Geddes had been the finance editor for the Chicago *Tribune* in Paris (1924–28), where Coleman worked from 1927–28. See also note on Geddes for January 10, 1929.

all typical Quarter business, and I am glad to see myself out of it. No passion, and no mind. No independence above groups, and no groups above Joyce.

November 22

To American Hospital again, examination by Dr. Bruno, gynocologist, have to have electrical cauterization. He said "When do you wish to come to the hospital?" I said "Tomorrow." Judith was with me, drove me crazy by crabbing about little things. She is neurotic, has no courage, poor child, I am not the person to be with her now. Took Kay to play with Wendy's child [Pegeen] in afternoon, Agamemnon said he had been to my hotel and there was a telegram. Called M. Dore and had him read it to me as best he could. As I thought, it was from Karen, arriving at Gare du Nord in the evening.[82]

To the Gare de Nord with Kay to meet Karen. He came gayly, he is a sweet devil. I said, "You dare not talk to me about business." I said, "I am better alone, I cannot think when you are around, I chatter." I loved this sweet adolescent boy, who does not have any illusions, except that I am wonderful. He is intelligent, and it is falling into disuse. He has no taste and is not sensitive except to rebuff. He is in love with me and I cannot feel as I did. I have outgrown him, and this is not the last of this. It will be something more deep and painful than this. But I love him, I will love him to my death.

I talked so much to Karen about Agamemnon that he got tired of it. He is right, I am a fool to do this, and yet I cannot help it, I must always talk to him of what excites me. They are going to meet tonight (the 23rd).[83] That is something I have wanted for eighteen months.

When Karen met Agamemnon I watched with interest. Agamemnon behaved well, was not supercilious, was very young, afraid Karen would think him serious when he (Karen) was frivolous. Karen found himself at home (which I think he did not expect) and at ease. It was a charming evening, light laughter and quick sallies. Later Wendy went home (after we were intruded by Titus in the Select) and Agamemnon coming back from that had an accident (he drives like a madman) and had to go to the police station.[84] He returned finally and because of people all about we got away to another café. There he and Karen sparred on psychology and other things, each undermining the other's defenses, so that they had continually to begin again. This interested me, I know Karen's limitations but I know that in some ways he

---

[82] Gare du Nord is a major train station in Paris.
[83] Coleman dated this entry November 22.
[84] According to Humphrey Carpenter, the "chief attraction" of Montparnasse's Café Select "was that it stayed open all night" (91).

is a match for Agamemnon. Agamemnon was very drunk, Karen sleepy, but they liked each other and respected what the other said. I said, "Please talk about me," so Agamemnon said, "What do you think of your wife's poetry?" Karen replied, "I don't know about her poetry, but I think *she's* wonderful." It was amusing for them to see me with a husband, I am different, as I told them. They said I was younger, I said, "Yes, I am a baby, and it is he that keeps me so. What little I am of grown up I have achieved away from him."

November 26[85]

Now I am in the American Hospital, a room with another female ([please?]) (God exterminate) looking out on villas and trees, with a huge sweep of western sky. The clouds are gentle and cluster in colours that I love. I am quiet now. I silenced her by talking more than she did. She gave out finally and now I can read. I finished Lewes' *Goethe*. I was given three enemas in preparation for my cauterization. I cannot bear one enema, I cannot bear physical pain and <u>everything</u> pains me. I cannot be touched lightly—it hurts. A young girl shaved away my hair—I could not bear that either. Now there is nothing left—a prickly nymph. She did not hurt me—I gave way to pleasant, almost sexual, sensations. Wondered why they were not sexual—I thought they might have been if she had been conscious of me, or if I had been doing the same thing to her.

My lovely Karen gone. Last evening dined with Agamemnon and Wendy.

I live abroad because I need it vitally. It will be many years before I am strong enough to go back. I must make a citadel for myself before I do.

What a beastly little hypocrite I was at 19. I remember kissing a boy and liking it, then when I heard of someone else's doing it I sat high and admonishing. I was a real American prude. I hid behind safe platitudes until Karen forced me out.

I had the operation. Going under ether was like the second time—not like the first when I snatched the hood and clamped it on my nose because of the horror.[86] Two breaths, deep and sickeningly sweet, slight struggle, then down, press, press, whenever I am pressed it presses to the bone (like the dentist with gas), through me, oblivion. I came out crying that I hated America and

---

[85]Coleman typed the diary whenever she could. When she was away from her typewriter, as in this case hospitalized, she wrote entirely by hand.
[86]Coleman was referring to John's birth. In her autobiographical story "Interlude," published in *transition* (November 1927), she gives a searing account of the pain experienced during labour. At one point her persona, Mrs. Temple, begs for ether: "The cart rolled melodiously in on caressing rubber wheels. She clutched at the ether bay and thrust it violently to her face, breathing in the cool cessation of horror in tremendous gulps."

must have Karen. I was a little sick from ether, no pain in my belly. I love hospitals, I have always loved their order, regularity and efficiency. It is the only place in the world where housekeeping is done properly. The order and the whiteness spreads over me.

Tried to go over some of Hero's mss. It is more and more disgusting to me how sloppily that woman writes. I feel I just cannot go through another page of her clichés and mis-wrought words and sentences. She brims with sentimentality, her style is like the villain writers of the Victorian age. Only a deep love for her (which she does not in the least appreciate since it does not lie in her possibilities to know how violently bad writing can be loathed) keeps me at this. Some of what she writes is good, and when I see her I emphasize this. It is the only way I can make her see anything.

Telegram from Karen asking for my health. I have begun *Wilhelm Meister*.[87]

December 1

I remembered trying to read Virginia Woolf's *Mrs. Dalloway* which I found in Hero's studio. It was silly, and long-drawn-out, and purposeless. It was like a little girl in a garden with rose colored glasses on. She doesn't know any more about life, or people, than a puppy dog. Her style is so silly—it exasperated me. I worked at it for an hour, but could not get on. I can't remember what was happening when I stopped. For whom does this woman write? I suppose for people in hospitals, and for servant girls. Now I see why they called *Orlando* her best book.[88] That is bad enough, but there is more to it than this.

I am reading *Othello*. I feel I must read through the third act. I am consumed with jealousy when I see how Shakespeare does this. I am consumed with an overwhelming ambition to rival him. I wonder why I am not content to try to get what I can from him, instead of being devoured with a passion to do the same thing. In this case it seems really silly. It will take me years of thinking, observing and suffering to learn enough to write *one good tragedy*. And yet I feel in myself such powers. I am certainly going to write tragedy. It is in me to do—my whole soul is drawn towards it.

This ambition has me in its grip. I shall not be content until I am writing again.

David is coming in four days. I will not think of it at all. I will think of *Othello*, that Karen has so often read to me.

---

[87]Coleman had been reading, among other things, *Hamlet* as well as Thomas Carlyle's translations of Goethe's *Wilhelm Meister's Apprenticeship* (1795–96) (which contains commentary on *Hamlet*) and *Wilhelm Meister's Travels, or the Renunciants* (1829).
[88]Woolf's *Mrs. Dalloway* (1925) and *Orlando* (1928) are experimental works of fiction and biography, respectively.

34   Section I

December 4

Wendy came two days ago to the hospital and got me. I had had a raging toothache for several days, so now to another and more expensive dentist (American) who found much wrong. He is in the Champs-Élysées, very swank. I had just paid my bill to the other. God punish the French for their stupidity about health.

I had Kay this afternoon and read him *Mother Goose*, translating into French. What a lovely little boy—his wide eager eyes, his sensitive, sensitive face! But he is like a burst of storm, and I am weak. I cannot stand his roughness, when he is gentle I am close to him. Hero for dinner in the evening. I know how to handle her and can teach Wendy.[89] Wendy is good to me, spoils me and lets me read. Wendy's child is a mouse, blue and fragile, a yellow head thrust down. Wendy played music to me while I was in bed, Chopin, Beethoven and Bach. It was beautiful to my ears, and I went in and out of sleep. She is alone without Agamemnon, he telephoned it was "dreadful" and that he would return tonight. No doubt Kurn is not eager to let him go. Kurn has lost her husband, her lover, and her child.

I dreamed last night that Joyce and I were at a party and that he patronized me. This is easy to comprehend. I read at Wendy's request Hemingway's book, *A Farewell to Arms*.[90] I could not read it all. I skipped a lot. He has not the slightest imagination, no claims whatever that I can see. He sees nothing except what a camera could record. His mind is slow and ambles through

---

[89]Coleman was convalescing at Guggenheim's apartment; Holms had gone to London for three days to see Dorothy/"Kurn."

[90]Ernest Hemingway had been acquainted with Coleman in the late 1920s when they were colleagues on the *Tribune*. His novel *A Farewell to Arms* was published in 1929. Coleman reported in a 1928 letter to her father how Hemingway had tried to help her publish *The Shutter of Snow*: "About two weeks ago we [Emily and Deak] were sitting at the café des Deux Magots, which is around the corner here, when Ernest Hemingway came along. Deak had never met him and so I asked him to have a drink with us and he sat and talked for about an hour. We both enjoyed him immensely—he is very charming and has a fine native intelligence—and what do you think he did? He wrote a note to Mr. Maxwell Perkins, president of Charles Scribner's Sons (Hemingway's publishers) telling him that he was asking me to send them my book and recommending it highly on the strength of things of mine which he had seen in *Transition* and had liked, and telling him that this was an original piece of work, never, so far as he had known, done before in literature. He wrote the note right there on the café table and the next day the book was dispatched to New York with the note (March 3, 1928, F. 1595). Coleman then reported to her father that her friend Sonia Himmel had spoken to Perkins in New York, who "praised the book very highly but said it was too 'advanced' for a publishing house like Scribner's to risk money on" (June 14, 1928, F. 1595). Perkins had sent a note to Himmel stating: "I think Mrs. Coleman has very extraordinary abilities in writing. I wish intrinsic quality was the only question an editor had to consider" (Himmel to Coleman, May 25, 1928, F. 150).

words like a rhinoceros in the mud. Anyone who would want him for a lover should read this book and see how he has dullified love.

December 5

This is the day David is to arrive. I do not believe he will come. I left Wendy's in the afternoon. I barely saw Agamemnon, who returned from London very miserable. I could see in his face that he had not slept. I went home, toothache raging. I rested. David did not come.

December 6

I went to the dentist and he took out a nerve. Walking down the rue de Rennes I was full of spiritual excitement. I thought of St. Tropez and what I would do there.[91]

Suddenly Agamemnon telephoned me. His voice was strained. He said, "Can you take dinner with me?"

We went to Montparnasse, to the Vikings, then to the Coupole.[92] My back began to ache, and my belly. I did not know what to do. At the Vikings I was able to put my feet up. I hated myself, worrying about my health in this moment. I was afraid I would get an inflammation in my womb because the doctor said I must lie down all the time. He said, "Wendy is my opposite and it is good for me to live with her." He was angry with her now because she would not understand Kurn, nor would she give money to Kurn. He said, "If I had a lot of money I would give it all to my friends, but Wendy does not see this—she wants to give it away to people she does not know. She cannot conceive of friends," he said, "As anything but people who want her money. That comes from this dreadful Quarter life." Laurence was the cause, he said, (her husband), he cared for splurge. Agamemnon said you could tell it from his first novel, all about a young man who had a great deal of money and spent it lavishly.[93]

He grew more and more unhappy, and the tears flowed out of his eyes.[94]

He said <u>he was far less interested in writing than in finding out what is the good life</u>. He said he feared death terribly. I said, "Why?" and he would not

---

[91]Coleman would leave for her self-imposed writer's retreat to St. Tropez on December 17, 1929.
[92]Trendy brasseries on the Left Bank.
[93]Vail's first novel is *Piri and I* (1923).
[94]Holms was continually caught between his feelings for his wife, Dorothy, and his lover, Guggenheim. This entry goes on at length to document Holms' emotional pain. At one point, he informed Coleman that he was considering leaving Guggenheim.

go into it. I said "I write from ambition, and from a sense of rivalry. I feel it," I said, "Whenever I read good poetry. That stimulates me to write far more than my own experiences." I said, "I want immortality, I cannot bear the thought that my soul is not going to leave any impress on this world. That is really why I write." He said he used to feel that way, but no longer. He said he felt now as if he were going to live forever. I said I was constantly afraid of death, because I have done nothing.

Agamemnon said, "I am not weak in important things. I do not give a damn what anyone thinks." He was in love with Vera Meynell, but he did nothing about it. Wendy reminded him of her, that was why he loved her. That was three years ago and he came away from England to forget her.[95] He said that at that time he told Kurn he was not sure that he wanted to marry her.

Then in the Coupole he talked about the war. I made him. He did not want to, then he could not stop. He was put in command of a company at 18. The Germans made an attack, and came into his trench. Out of absolute terror he ran down the trench, killing six of them. He killed them by hitting them on the head with an iron stick. "I just hit them," he said, "As hard as I could as I went by. I must have hit them very hard. I am very strong. Later I found they were all dead. I broke down and cried then," he said. They gave him the Military Cross for that. "It was the first time my father was ever proud of me." He said he found out after the Germans were dead that a machine gun sector of his own men had been sent out without his orders and all of them had been killed. He was so angry about that that he could think of nothing else. He said he was so furious with all of them for allowing it that they would not forgive him. Then they marched 30 hours without food or rest. Some of them fell and they left them. He believed in the army then, although he could not bear it. Then he was taken prisoner by the Germans and put in a prison camp. He was there two years. He said the merchant marines were the most human. He climbed to the top of the enclosure one day because he could not stand it in the coop. The guards began to shoot at him but they missed, and one of his friends got him down. He read every minute of the two years. It was so cold they were in bed most of the time. He sent to England for books, and educated himself during that time. He read all philosophy then. Food was so scarce that when a crust of bread was found they had to divide it into as many pieces as there were people. Or chocolate was the same. Everyone was homosexual. He said he was not. He

---

[95]Vera Mendel Meynell (1896–1997) was the wife of (Sir) Frances Meynell (1891–1975), English book designer and publisher. In 1922 they founded, together with David Garnett, The Nonesuch Press whose mandate was to publish inexpensive but good quality books.

did not want it. He said he has not any of it, that he likes the most feminine of women. That is why, of course, he has never been sexually attracted to me. That in me which Panurge thinks is feminine Agamemnon is penetrating enough to see is a boy.

I could not stay up any longer, I ached so much. I said he could come to my place and I would lie down on the bed and he could sit up and we could talk. We did this. I could not keep awake. I was disgusted with myself. I could not help it, I was so tired. He took the third act of *Othello* and began reading it to me. He finally said he must go and get more drink. (He was very drunk.) I could not go with him, I did not know what he would do. I longed to put my arms around him, especially when he sat there with Shakespeare in his hand talking of Kurn and the tears again in his eyes. But I dared not. I did not want to show him tenderness now. I did not know what he was going to do, but he promised me he would go to Wendy.

In the morning, after only a little sleep, I got out of bed and ran up to Montparnasse to see if he was in any of the cafés. He was not, and so I telephoned Wendy and she said, "The young man is here." It took lead from my heart. I went back to sleep again. I had told him I must write a dramatic poem now, and he said, "It will be bad." I said, "I know, but I must try it anyway." He is right of course, but I must try my hand. I want so much to do it that I must.

December 9

I took Kay to the American Hospital this morning, to the clinic. He considered himself important. Dr. Helie gave him a thorough examination and found him in perfect condition. When I saw that child lying on the table, white and naked, his sweet little face smiling, he looked so small and lovely that I felt tears in my eyes. The doctor said he breathes better than the others. He has gained two and a half kilos and grown enormously. Kay was dignified, but smiled at the doctor. I liked this doctor. I fell to wondering why, and realized that he would not be a pediatrician if he did not like children. That is why gynocologists are such swine.

I then took Kay to the Louvre for a while. He was attentive, and there is no doubt that he has a flair for painting. I showed him only good things, but of course let him look at anything that attracted him. He was very much interested in the painters who were copying things. He likes the moderns best, I suppose because they are brighter. I love this child, I shall love him more and more.

When we came out I went into a shop on the rue Bonaparte to buy a few reproductions. As soon as we got to Mamotchka's he showed them to her and to the children. This has given me more pleasure than anything connected with him since he was born.

December 12[96]

In the afternoon took Kay to play with Wendy's little girl. He frightened her, he is very rough. One of them broke a glass, they both denied it. I took him in a room apart and on my knee. I was angry, because he had been doing everything to annoy me. I wanted to wallop him, but held back my hand. I held him there and talked earnestly to him. I said, "Obviously you do not love me." He screwed up his face a good deal, then I saw tears in his eyes. He hates to cry. He will not cry when he is hurt. I was impressed by this, and said I knew he would be better. We kissed fervently, he swearing that it was not he who broke the glass. Wendy said it was her child, that she had found out. I talked with W[endy]. and Agamemnon. He told about a sadistic nurse who used to beat his sister and him. His parents were in India, he and his sister were sent to England.[97] When he left that place at six he used to put up his arm to save his face every time anyone spoke to him. He had to write to his parents once a week at school. He got into a neurosis about it, he could not write. He put in a blank paper and sent that. The first time it was thought to be a mistake, then when it happened twice there was hell. I told about St. Gabriel's school and how I had to tell my sins at night, and all the children would point at me.[98] I lived in terror. We said the principal thing to do with a child is to have him happy. This I believe to the utmost. His character is of secondary importance. Childhood is a horror for a sensitive child, and all children are sensitive. Every little thing that can happen makes them afraid and miserable. That is why I am happy with Kay in the care of Mamotchka. I know first of all that he is full of joy.

---

[96]On December 10, not transcribed, Coleman noted that she was waiting for Jordan but feared his wife has found Coleman's letters to him and was preventing him from coming to see her; and she was working on Goldman's manuscript.

[97]Beatrix Holms, poet. Her poem "The Zodiac" was published in the July 1926 issue (3: 2) of *The Calendar*, and collected in *The Zodiac and other poems* (1980). Guggenheim reports in her memoir that Holms was born in India, as his father, whom he hated, "had been governor-general of the United Provinces of India" (79). The United Provinces of Agra and Oudh, formed in 1902, was a province in British India (1858–1947).

[98]For more on her childhood education, see the introduction.

December 14

I detest talking French all day. I want to speak English with my child.[99]

Today I took him to the school and left him.[100] Went with Mamotchka at three to get him. I had had another nerve taken out in the morning. This dentist is good, but I do not like pain.

Wendy and Agamemnon took Hero and me to dinner at the Trianon.[101] We had a swell dinner. Agamemon and I divided a lark. When we were in the Select afterwards Wendy's husband came in suddenly.[102] He is a fool and a jackass, but he loves Wendy underneath. Agamemnon had not seen him since they tried to kill each other in Pramousquier.[103] It was tense. The other was courteous, spoke pleasantly, sweetly to Hero, and went out. Wendy, who never feels such situations, insisted that he kiss her. We were all sitting there listening to the babble of an American painter and a high-bred English lady somewhat on the down grade, when in came Wendy's husband again.[104] Agamemnon did not see him. He passed by and went and sat in the back. Wendy, who was tight, got up and went and sat with him. She is just as irresponsible as that. Agamemnon thought she had gone downstairs, and sat talking. Sometime later I saw his face and said quickly, "What's the matter?"

"I've just seen where Wendy is," he said. I did not know what he was going to do. I remembered what they did the last time. I had thought that Wendy had told him she was going to sit with her husband. I found out afterwards that they had been quarreling all the week and that she did this to pique him. She is like a child playing with dynamite. I said, "I think you had better go out." He said he would go if I would go too. Hero, tight, and oblivious as she

---

[99] Recall that the Donns did not speak English and would raise John to be fluent in both French and Russian.

[100] John went for a trial day to an English-only kindergarten, and although he was disruptive, the head of the school agreed to sign him on, beginning January 6 (his sixth birthday).

[101] Left Bank brasserie.

[102] Laurence Vail.

[103] Guggenheim and Vail owned a villa in Pramousquier, in the south of France. In the summer of 1928, having met the Holms' through Coleman, Guggenheim invited them to Pramousquier, at which point Guggenheim began her affair with John. On another of the Holms' visits, with the affair in full swing, Vail walked in on the lovers. As Guggenheim recounts in her memoir, "Laurence followed me and caught us, which I suppose was what I wanted, but what I had not foreseen took place: a terrible battle from which a death might easily have resulted." Eventually, after the gardener intervened and the Holms' retreated, "Laurence went back to their house and told John that he would kill him on sight if he ever met him again" (84). This was the last night Guggenheim would spend with Vail. They were formally divorced in 1930.

[104] Coleman did not identify this painter and woman.

always gets, was next to me. I told her we had to go out. We went out into the cold street.

We walked to the boulevard Raspail. He kept clenching his hands and crying out, "I have made a mess of my life!" He kept talking about Kurn. He said he was going after Wendy's husband. I held him there, and would not let him go. I kept him walking up and down.

Finally he promised me to stay outside while I went in and got our coats. It was cold, and had begun to rain. I went in. Wendy and her husband had gone. I tried to say something to Hero but she wouldn't pay the least attention to me. I left her with the American painter. Then I went out again and told Agamemnon they had gone. "He has taken her home," I said. I knew she had no idea of going back to her husband. So we got into a taxi and drove to their hotel. He made me wait in the taxi. He came out again and said they were not there. Then we drove back again to Montparnasse, because there was nowhere else to go. It was about four o'clock in the morning. We went to the Vikings and sat on stools. We talked about Kurn and about Wendy and his relation to them. He kept repeating that he had irrevocably messed his life. I had never seen him down, it was like a giant falling. We were kicked out of the Vikings when it closed and we went to the Coupole. There we sat and went on with it. I said finally that he ought to telephone, and inasmuch as he hates telephoning I went and did it for him. They said she was not in. He was terribly upset by now, and getting drunker and drunker. He never shows it, except his eyes. He walks straight and seems about the same. He repeats a little. In half an hour I went again. I took him with me. She was in. I left him while he talked with her.

He insisted that I go with him in the taxi. He said he was not going to stay, that he was only going to talk to her. I stayed outside in the taxi and he went in. Their rooms are in the front and I heard voices raised. He came out again. I said I would have to go home, and he besought me with such piteousness not to leave him that I could not. We told the driver to go to Les Halles and then to the Bois.[105] It was beautiful driving up the Champs-Élysées in the rain. The lights were gleaming. It was five-thirty in the morning. The way seemed endless, between the lights. The Bois was very dark, with the grey morning coming over the hedge. At the end of this I succeeded in persuading him to go home. I said, "You can sneak into the living room and sleep on the couch." He wanted to come to my room and sleep on Kay's bed but I did not think that

---

[105] The Bois (wood) de Boulogne is the massive park on the west side of Paris designed by Baron Haussman and developed in the mid-to-late nineteenth century in the style of London's Hyde and Regent parks.

would do.[106] I told him he would absolutely have to stick to Wendy, because if this failed he would have to go through the whole thing again. "You have to have sex," I said. "And you cannot have it casually. You will be spending the rest of your life like this if you don't make this go." I dropped him at his hotel and went home. It was about seven.

    I slept a little and then went to Wendy's under pretext of getting a story Agamemnon had which I needed for Titus. She was in bed. I talked to her seriously for the first time. I said, "If you do not try to understand him he will leave you. It is not a joke. He loves you," I said, "And it will kill him to leave you. But he will do it." I said no matter who was in the wrong, and no doubt he was greatly to blame, that she must be sweet and tender with him, and not hard. She must not show him hate. Only that she must not do. There is much on her side—she is pregnant again and has already had two abortions, and he is so indifferent to physical things—and then she has no social life with him and she wants that.[107] But it is truer than earth that if she wants to keep him she will have to give in some. She will have to try first of all to understand him and his situation with Kurn. The pregnancy she admitted was her own fault. I know he is very selfish in love. Wendy said she would be sweet to him, she promised me. She went off on a tangent every moment I was talking. I wanted to drown her. She looked very cunning under the bedclothes with nothing but her eyes and hair showing. She has character, but she is a baby. I said to her, "For God's sake don't fool with Agamemnon." She seemed somewhat impressed by what I said.

December 15

Yesterday I bought two books for Kay. Unfortunately they were in French, but I hope he will read them in English sometime. *Robinson Crusoe* and Kipling's *Just So Stories*. I love the illustrations (Kipling's) in the *Just So Stories*. I would not let Kay see them before Christmas. I ordered toys for the children, and got them books.[108] Kay is to have an auto and a garage (which he requested) from Hero. I gave him colored crayons. Mamotchka is

---

[106] John Coleman had returned to the Donns.
[107] The only mention of this fact by Guggenheim, in her memoir, is the following: "I had had an operation performed in a convent by a wonderful Russian doctor called Popoff. The nuns were strict and dirty and had no idea why I was there" (97). According to her biographer Mary Dearborn, the abortion took place in Berlin in early 1929 (76–77); Dearborn finds no evidence of a second one by this time, or of the supposedly six Guggenheim claimed to have had by 1935 (111–12).
[108] The "children" included her son, John, and the Donn children, Rostik and Olga.

going to get him cubes for building. My story, "The Fugitives," came out in *This Quarter*. I didn't succeed in lifting any money off Titus this time. He is too full of other things. He did not have time to read the two I let him take ("The Vicar's Pants" and "The Photograph") and I took them away.[109] I am going to get paid for these or else not at all. "The Fugitives" is obscure, but it has atmosphere. It suggests a good deal. I think it has merit. I went to the Cluny.[110]

December 17

Last night with Agamemnon and Wendy. Judith took me to dinner, wanting my understanding, I could not give it. She is not sensitive in the right ways, she chatters and I clench my hands. After dinner we met A[gamemnon]. and W[endy]. A. suggested that I call Antony. I did so and found him sitting alone. He came, looking so sweet. I cried out, "How beautiful he is!" and continued in that vein. Wendy dragged A[gamemnon]. away, he could not bear to go, and I was drunk with *fines*.[111] I said dreadful things to Judith, she irritated me. Then I hated saying them. She said, "I do not mind what you say, I tolerate you for what there is in you." I said, "My God, do not tolerate me," but she did not understand. When she was away a few minutes I said to Antony, "This is all sex, and my fault." He said, "I foresaw it." Last summer when I was in Paris and loved Judith physically he knew it. He was in Paris, and I loved him with my soul, her with my body. My love for him was cut off, because I invented him and could not bear the reality, and because he loves his wife. Judith went off with a newspaperman, the worst of all, a fearful chattering creature, and Antony and I went to Montparnasse for a drink. We had orangeades at the Select. I left dear Antony and came home.

This morning to my dentist, who finished the job. My jaw aches, he says this will continue several days. I think he will make his bill reasonable. I could hardly let him touch me, but stood staunch and tried not to show my horrible fear.

I took toys to the children, and books, which Mamotchka is to hide until Christmas. I said goodbye to my little Kay, he clinging to my neck and kissing me passionately a thousand times. He does not really mind my going. Then I packed, very neatly, then met Hero at the Deux Magots, where we

---

[109]For "The Photograph" see November 14, 1929. "The Vicar's Pants" is a fragmented and rather incoherent story about a variety of characters including colliers, painters, two sisters, and a vicar who have all slept with the same "lady," going about their day-to-day activities.
[110]The Cluny Museum is the National Museum of Medieval Arts, located in the Latin Quarter.
[111]A *fine* is a term (now rare) for French brandy.

had a last talk, she bringing me my typewriter. Her heart was full of love for me, I told her I would make her yellow with envy by my letters. She gave me money to give to people in St. Tropez for the Noel. Then rushing to my hotel I ran into Judith. I felt so ashamed, she kissed me and said she loved me, very shyly, and I wanted to throw bricks at myself. At the Gare de Lyon dinner with Agamemnon and Wendy, an excellent meal with the best Chablis.[112] I became drunk. I just made the train. I was full of wine and felt light and cheerful. But when I saw Agamemnon's face, and in the train Wendy said something stupid and he said, "You are a fool," I felt I should not go. I do not think I ought to stay for that. I must not be mixed up in this, if he is unhappy enough he can go to the Muirs or Kurn. I do not feel I ought to be in this, I do not want to help alienate him from Wendy. But his face, he came running back to shake my hand, and shook it hard, not as he is accustomed, and his eyes were dead.

---

[112]The Gare de Lyon is a major train station in Paris.

Section 2

St. Tropez

December 18, 1929–February 15, 1930

Coleman took the train from Paris to St. Raphael in the south of France, arriving the following day. She was met at the station by a chauffeur who drove her to St. Tropez, where she had arranged to stay at the home of the Sandstroms, friends of Goldman with whom she had lived during her earlier sojourn on the Riviera. The property was being cared for by a man named Dante and his wife. In her two months here, Coleman penned dozens of sonnets and began work on a dramatic poem. She also contemplated the end of her marriage while becoming preoccupied with a nineteen-year-old local named Philippe, whom she dubbed "the Fisher Boy," and with whom she had had a sexual relationship during her 1928 visit.

December 18

There were two French fairies in my compartment, and one of them went out for the night, and I could stretch full length. I could not sleep, my jaw ached, and I thought of many things. When I saw the sun coming up over the hills I could not keep lying down. At St. Raphael I got off, excited. There was Lutz, the chauffeur, bronzed face, brilliant teeth. My bags into the car, and off. A cold wind, and the sun coming in and out. He said the weather had been like spring, this was the first cold day. The ride to St. Tropez turning rapidly around the curves, now the open sea, cold and harsh this afternoon in the wind. At St. Maxime, when I saw my little town across the bay, my heart dropped. Turned at La Feux, now the home stretch. I saw that the palm trees which had been killed by the ice last year were growing new. Into the town and up past the *Couvent*, around *La Tourelle*, along the Chemin St. Antoine, up the hill to the Sandstroms.'[1] I worrying now about my box of books, and about money.[2] On top of the hill I got out, Dante came out to take my bags. He said he could not *donner à manger*, that depressed me, and the mistral, I stood alone in my cold room among my bags.[3]

Then a fire in the grate for me, and my bags unpacked. A letter from Father with a check. A letter from Don, my little brother who is dying. My father says he cannot leave him even for a day.

I sent the check to Hero to cash, because the exchange in Paris is better, and told her to send 500 francs to Mamotchka for herself and the children. In order to get this off at once, so that Mamotchka would have it before Christmas, I went down to the village in the dark. I was dead tired, I could hardly walk. I could see nothing, I stumbled my way down the Chemin St. Antoine, past Hero's gate (my heart beating at that), and so to the village. I mailed the letter at the *gare*. Then I went to the Wagon and got something to eat.[4] I was greeted enthusiastically there. There are no *étrangères* here at the moment.[5] Walked home again, the stars out and the moon coming up red. I thought of the first time I walked this road, in May, 1928, with Hero. How beautiful it was, under the moon as now, only it was summer, and warm, all the trees green and the air loaded with odor of fields and gardens. Now it was cold, the trees and vineyards bare, but the stars were there, and the moon, and there was the water beyond, and the lights of ships. On top of the hill I stood and looked at the little town below, the ships, the *Phare*, the hills beyond, the sea.[6] I came in the back way and saw Dante's wife and their baby, then into my warm room, the fire burning in the grate. I attached my lamp and thought, "How happy I am—there my books on the shelf, there my pictures, and here the fire and the lamp." The pictures I put up were the *Baptism* of Piero Francesca, Mantegna's *Crucifixion*, The *Avignon Pieta*, which I am growing more and more to love.[7] To bed early, under warm sheets, happy to be alone.

December 19

I woke early, the sun streaming in. Out the window the hills, and the sky blue as indigo, heavy with golden clouds. Mme. S.[andstrom] came in to build

---

[1] *Couvent*: convent; *La tourelle*: turret.
[2] Coleman had stored the books she had brought with her during her first visit to St. Tropez at Goldman's house.
[3] "He could not give me anything to eat."
[4] Local restaurant.
[5] *étrangères*: foreigners.
[6] *Phare*: lighthouse.
[7] The *Avignon Pieta* has been ascribed to Enguerrand Charonton (circa 1460).

my fire. I talked cheerfully to her. I said, "Thank you for that wide desk, you remembered how I liked it." They are leaving for Paris shortly, they will *faire la bombe* with Hero for the Noel.[8] Dante will be in charge. I had it all worked out, my meals, I would eat in the village at midday and make my suppers in my room. So much the better, that much more privacy. I took a hot bath, which she made for me, then out I went with Hero's keys.

    I took the great key and opened Hero's gate. Here I was again, in this garden, shut in and tiny, like an English garden. I was back now in these soft places where I had been before, the places I had loved. I went into the house. There in my little room was my box of books. It filled me with intense joy, the symbol of my being alone. No place will ever be so dear to me as this.

    I came home and wrote to Hero and to Antony, telling them how happy I was. I sent postcards to Karen. I will write to Agamemnon and to Hippocra, I will write to Don and my father. Then I will begin my own writing. I will write every morning until noon, then go down to eat, then walk till four. Then home to read, eating my supper in my room, reading into the night. I will get up as early as I can and write from then until noon. This day I went into Bailli's and the Madame greeted me with joy.[9] She promised to *me faire un prix* if I would come every day—I will thus get a good fat meal for ten francs.[10] The meal was excellent—this is the only *bonne cuisine* in St. Tropez—hors d'oeuvres, crisp fish, meat and vegetables, salad, cheese, fruit[11] This costs fifteen francs but there is no one here and she will do well to entice me for ten. I then went into the shops, and in each one I was greeted as a friend long parted from. I did not go to the *Phare*, because I am still very tired. I must get some sleep again.

    My fire still burning, I went to sleep, reading the life of Poussin.[12] When I awoke I was filled with happiness again. I cannot believe I am here, and I cannot wait for the day. I ate cheese and bread and butter, with bananas. I can fix supper myself, sometimes eggs, sometimes cooking apricots. I brought Hero's flashlight, in case I have to go to the village after dark to mail a letter. I brought her stoves and pots. I will get my books tomorrow. I have not had time to think today, I am too excited at being here. The most excitement is the thought that I am ALONE. There is not one human being I have to consider. There is not one responsibility I have to endure. I can give myself up to myself as I have never done before. I shall read, I shall read, I shall write a little. And most of all, I shall think.

---

[8]*faire la bombe for Noel*: go all out with a party at Christmas.
[9]Local restaurant.
[10]"She promised to give me a fixed price."
[11]*Bonne cuisine*: good food.
[12]Coleman was reading *Memoirs of the Life of Nicholas Poussin* (1820) by Maria Callcott (1785–1842).

The thought of David is vague now. I will not take anyone else until I can have him, but I do not care how long I have to wait for him as long as I am here.

December 20

Today the *patronne* of the café that used to be the Commerce made much of my return, and offered me a porte. I must say it was pleasant, sitting there in the sun, looking out on the port and the hills beyond. I wish I could eat here every day instead of Bailli's cold restaurant. Coming home I thought I passed the fisher boy, but I pretended not to see him, and when I came out of Bailli's I was sure he [was] waiting there at the end of the street. When I got to the Chemin St. Antoine I heard him call, "Aymeellee" and I looked and saw him. I was cordial to him, but I told him I had come to work and could not play as I had done before. He looked so crestfallen that I was sorry. His hand was bound up, he is working in the factory and hurt it, now he has three weeks of "assurance." He goes around in a romantic haze, a beautiful little liar. His father abuses him and he has had no mother. I will be sweet to him, but I cannot see anyone.

December 21

Last night I tore up my old manuscripts, all the trash I wrote the summer of 1928, the book I began, and the bad parts of "The Wasted Earth." I kept only the revised form of this, "Ruth," "The Bell of La Miséricorde" and the "Lysias." Of stories I kept only those already published, "Interlude," "The Wren's Nest," "The Fugitives" and "Dry Leaves"—besides "The Visit" and "Pensions," a thing I may yet throw out.[13] Now for a new beginning, with concentration the aim. The pith, the essence.

---

[13]Her story "Interlude," noted earlier, is a taboo-breaking account of childbirth in which the protagonist screams and swears profusely during labour, and then rejects her newborn son. Autobiographical, the story anticipates her novel *The Shutter of Snow*. "The Wren's Nest" (published in *transition*, Summer 1928) is a surreal narrative about a woman who lives in the country with her parents, leaves for the city for a failed visit to her husband/lover, and then returns to the country to surround herself with nature. "Dry Leaves" (published in *transition*, February 1929) is another surreal story about a sextette singing to a girl/woman Myra in the countryside on one day; Myra goes to the local marketplace on the next day. "The Fugitives," also noted earlier, was published in the November 1929 issue of *This Quarter*. "The Visit" (extant) and "Pensions" (not extant) were unpublished. The three poems were not published. "The Bell of La Miséricorde" (the bell of mercy) is about a mother who buries and mourns for her son. "Ruth" is based on the Old Testament Book of Ruth, and depicts the sexual desire of Boaz for Ruth.

Today I read ten chapters of *Don Quixote*.[14] This gave me an intense pleasure, one I longed to share with Karen. It is a glowing tale. I have read no better prose than this except Shakespeare in his comic parts, and Rabelais.

I am so happy, sitting here by my grate, which burns orange underneath the balls of coal. I have all my books, I could not be more happy. I will have suffering, I am ready for it, I will not run away from it. But I am happy now, I cannot help that.

December 22

Today the mistral blows violent, there is no sun and it is cold. I do not go from my room. Dante's wife makes me a fire.

I finished destroying manuscripts today. I have them all in shape now. I am going to write a dramatic poem. I have the whole plan in my head. I do not know when I will be ready to do the life and death of Jesus, but I am not ready now. That will be a dramatic poem instead of a narrative. I will not begin writing until I have written my diary up to date (a terrible job, going by notes I made in Paris), and gotten my letters done.

The principal thing I have to do is to get rid of FEAR. I have been terrified of people until I know them. Until now I thought it was funny. Now I see it must be stopped. I am terribly afraid at night. The least sound fills me with foreboding, I imagine every sound and every object to be something terrible. My dreams are full of fears. A woman has so much more to be afraid of than a man. No wonder I love getting drunk, the least exhilaration puts all this out. But I used to wonder why, when I was tight, my relations with people turned out so successfully. It was because I didn't give a damn. When one is afraid one gets nothing from anyone. The reason I get on with people I love is that I am no longer afraid.

All this means nothing to me now. I don't need people now. But I am gregarious, I will need them. And as longs as that is so, I must learn to handle them. I am afraid of servants, people in shops, all who wait on me in postoffices or in omnibuses. I gave Dante 20 francs so as not to have to be afraid of him. I am frightened out of my skin by Dr. Bruno.[15] What I should have done was to have gone to his office again and at the first sign of nonsense gotten up and told him off. But I did not dare, instead I would not go. I wish I could get mad quietly. Control is the thing I must have. No one has ever been anything who did not have that. This is one of the things for which I most profoundly admire Hero.

---

[14]Miguel de Cervantes' (1547–1616) epic novel (1605, 1615).

[15]Coleman did not elaborate on her fear. Recall that on December 9, 1929, she commented: "gynocologists are such swine."

I read what I have written here and it makes me laugh. "I will write a dramatic poem." Well, there is no harm in trying to do it. There has got to be a beginning, and my poetry is better than I am. But to read what I have written here makes me despair. I have the unfortunate habit of quoting a good deal from good writing. It shows up my own. My prose style is impossible. I don't know what to do. I think prose has got to be simplified, as Cézanne did with painting. We must get back to the primitive. Writing has gotten out of bounds. More than any other art it has deteriorated. We must have strong, vigorous, short sentences. The prolix Victorian manner still influences all of us. It is abominable. We must have simplicity, directness, vigor. Homer, Rabelais, Dante, Shakespeare, Chaucer and the Bible are the best models. Then I should say Cervantes.

December 23

Last night I began to read Dante in Italian.[16] I read first the English, then the Italian out loud, so repeating until I could read the Italian alone. I read the whole first canto of the *Inferno*. I was pleased to find that I could do this so easily. I will accompany this with excursions into the Rapid Italian Course which I have.[17]

One thing I am determined upon for my child, and I have taken the first step—and that is that he shall be familiar with the best painting, the best music and the best poetry that has been created. He can learn to know the painting and the music now, and later the poetry, when he knows English well enough, and his understanding is ready for it.

When I was in the Select with Agamemnon there was an American girl talking near. I said to him, "When I realize that [it] is from this I have come, I begin to think I have talent." He said, "You must always compare yourself with your equals." I know this very well. I should not have to have much confidence to compare myself with these prattling flappers.

The principal thing I have got to do is this. I have to <u>find the mean between writing clearly and imitatively, and writing obscurely and in my own manner</u>. I got an enormous amount out of my contact with *transition* and the Surrealistes. Before that I had written only imitatively, nothing in the least distinguished. Through this influence I learned the extent of my imaginative powers. I learned to express myself with complete freedom. I learned to

---

[16]Dante Alighieri's (1265–1321) *Divine Comedy* (1308–1321) consists of the *Inferno, Purgatorio,* and *Paradiso.* Coleman was reading publisher J. M. Dent's Everyman Library edition of the *Inferno* which had the Italian version on one side, and the English on the other.
[17]*The Rapid Italian Course* was also published by Dent.

throw off the chains of other people's ideas. Now the problem is to discipline these imaginative powers. At first I discipline them so much that again I write like others. But it will come. I have only to practise, to write, to prune, to write. The best will not come soon.

December 24

The country is beautiful beyond words to tell. I walked all around the town, up the streets and down. I got a porte at L'Escale and saw the young man Hippocra was so fond of.[18] Madame said they were expecting Madame Colette and Monsieur de Segonzac tonight.[19] He is the French painter who said last year when I passed, "*Voilà une femme qui a quelque chose en elle.*" When Nora, the female painter, told me this, I said, "*Il a raison.*" [20]

The last time my heart moved for Karen was last summer, when I was reading him "Venus and Adonis" in the bathtub.[21] He began to look at me as he did before we knew each other. I thought it was in love, then suddenly he said something which showed him to be thinking about the sensuality of the story. He loves me in a sexual way, quite right, but I cannot return it. I must be looked at in passion for my soul. Damned inconvenient, and Agamemnon says it is not right.

Reading "The Ecstasy" of Donne's at the Muirs,' and their talking about it. [22] I was recalling today. I began to think, to see if I could remember ever having had such an ecstasy with any person. I think I did with Karen, early years, but then I demanded little. I cannot think of anyone but Hippocra with whom I have been on such a plane, and no sex in that. I think of David's face, it comes before me every now and then. I must have the combination of sex and romantic passion, respect of the mind. It is not fair to dear Karen that he has me for wife. I have said it to him but he says he wants it anyway. He says, "I like it, and that is all that matters." "But," I said, "You should have a wife who is sexual." He said, "But you are so interesting. 'Time cannot wither, nor custom stale,'" he said, "'Your infinite variety.' I can get sex other places." [23] This is not right, and simply means that he is making the best of it. I do not think he knows I do not love him sexually, I think he thinks I put all my sex

---

[18] This man is unidentified. Sonia Himmel ("Hippocra") had been here with Coleman in 1928.
[19] André Dunoyer de Segonzac (1884–1974), French painter and graphic artist, was the neighbour of "Colette" (Sidonie-Gabrielle Colette) (1873–1954), famous French novelist, short-story writer, dramatist, and journalist.
[20] "Here is a woman with something about her"; "He is right."
[21] Shakespeare's 1593 poem about sex and love.
[22] John Donne's 1633 poem about the fusion of lovers' souls.
[23] From Shakespeare's *Antony and Cleopatra*. General Enobarbus declares of Cleopatra, "Age cannot wither her, nor custom stale/Her infinite variety" (II, ii).

into my writing. So far he has been right. I have never been able to sustain sexual passion for anybody.

December 25

This is the best Christmas Day I have ever had. Not one Merry Christmas, not one card. Not the slightest nonsense. The weather was horrible, grey and drizzle. The weather has more effect on my state of mind than any thing in life. I went down to Bailli's and instead of shouting Merry Christmas at me she said, "*Quel temps exécrable.*" Then she said "*déplorable*" and "*inouï.*"[24] There was a swell Christmas dinner and nobody to eat it. This makes two Christmas dinners I have had. Last night I ate in state at the old Commerce. I have never eaten such a dinner. There were ten courses. I had Cap d'Or and ate for four hours all alone. It was very pleasant. Next to me sat Colette and de Segonzac. She talked the whole time without stopping, most amusingly. I liked her, she has a sharp small face, with a thin childish mouth. Her hair sticks out and her eyes glare. She is a woman of character and no doubt of intelligence. I have never read anything she has written, but she might write well. Her mouth, the under lip drawn in, shows passion. She has no doubt been through a great deal.[25] I did not like him at all, flabby and the remains of good looks, gone stale because there was nothing to support it. I talked a long time to the madam, round with a little perched nose.

Today after lunch I walked a bit in the drizzly wind. I saw my fisher boy as I was going to the boats. I went up to him and asked him how his hand was. We walked about and he came up the *chemin* with me to the gate. He said he could never be *camarade* with me. I said, "Why?" and he said, "*Je vous aime trop.*"[26] I am interested to find out what he means by that.

I had a desire to begin my dramatic poem in Paris, but I did not do so because I was afraid I would then chafe against doing Hero's mss. Now I must read *Othello* again and think about jealousy. I will want to write soon.

This morning I had a letter from my father. He said that Don was much weaker, that he hardly talked at all, and when he did it was scarcely audible.

---

[24]"What a wretched time"; "deplorable"; "unheard-of." Cap d'Or is a French wine.
[25]Colette was reputedly locked in a room by her first husband, Henri Gauthier-Villars (Monsieur Willy) and forced to write fiction, which she did, publishing four novels (the Claudine series) between 1900 and 1903. She divorced him in 1906, and married Henri de Jouvenal des Ursins in 1912, going on to have a publicized affair with her stepson, Bertrand de Jouvenal, which led to her second divorce in 1924. She also earned notoriety as a member of the coterie of lesbians in attendance at Natalie Clifford Barney's famous Left Bank salon. For Barney, see September 2, 1932.
[26]He could never be her "friend" because, "I like you too much."

He said, "He complains of pains in his throat and stomach. The doctor says the disease is working its way to these parts." I put down the letter and cried. He has nothing to want to live for, yet he clings to what he has like despair. When he ran out of my room in New York, when Karen was away and I repulsed him. I loved my little brother, I understood his abnormality. He loved me, he loved me because I was the best and the kindest woman he had known, and he loved me for my tenderness to him. When I knew he cared for my body I was afraid. I knew just enough not to be shocked, but not enough not to fear. I told him to go away, and he went out of the house and I never saw him again. He has never had a fair start, he was handicapped from my mother.[27] He is one of those desperate creatures who ought never to have been born. He is as unfit for life as a broken chick. It is well that it is he who is to die, and not another whose going would cause more sorrow. I do not suppose anyone ever loved him except me. I was a light, and he reached out to it with both his hands.

I think of Mantegna a great deal.[28] It is geniuses like this who stir me—the great sweep, the largest out of life. I do not like small and pretty persons of talent. I want the great flare of genius, genius of the highest order that has been in the world. I want Giotto and Mantegna, Dante and Michael Angelo, Shakespeare, Milton and Homer, Bach and Beethoven. I want enormous energies, devastating intellects, imaginations that have no limits, passion of the eternal sweep of earth.

December 26

I had a letter from Hippocra. She is not happy. I am waiting for her to come.[29] There is nothing I cannot share with her. I want to tell her, I do not want to write it.

I love the character of my son. He is strong, he is intense, sensitive as a leaf, his mind cuts into things. I do not know if he has any concentration. I do not know if his passion will be scattered. If he can keep it whole he will be something.

Just now I can think of nothing but writing because I have found myself. I have been thwarted for so long. When I am sufficiently sure of my genius, and when its results are worth reading, I will turn to life. I am sure of this.

---

[27] For more on Coleman's mother, see the introduction. Coleman has not elaborated on this episode.
[28] Coleman had been reading Maud Cruttwell's *Andrea Mantegna* (1901) about the Italian Renaissance painter (c. 1431-1506).
[29] Coleman would meet up with Sonia Himmel in February 1930, when they would travel together through Italy.

I wish I had never seen [Judith]. Her sweet sensitive face attracted me, her lovely body condensed my homosexual feelings, which had been growing less and less vague. They began at first in dreams. You cannot avoid these things, I cannot. They come in dreams to torment me anyway. I resolved to settle this, and after two years of it I told Karen I was going to do something about it. I had got so that I could think of nothing but women. I was more excited about Judith sexually than I had been over any man. This frightened me. I thought, "Can it be I am homosexual?" But I thought, "Whatever I am, that shall I be."

It turned out that it was very beautiful, it was exactly what I wanted and what I had imagined. Things never are what one imagines. When they are they are finished. It is because they are not that one keeps on.

Instead of liking men less I have wanted them more. I have never wanted any woman since that time, not her either. It has been hard on her, she does not know me, and I cannot explain. If she were more intelligent, if this had been Hippocra instead, there could have been good from it. But she has made me despise her, innocently she has done it, simply by provoking first my anger, then my sympathy.

The important thing for me is to remember that I am a woman. Even if my genius is as great as the greatest woman poet who ever lived, it will be a feminine genius. I am half and half, that is why Agamemnon calls me a little boy. People who are not discerning think I am one or the other, whichever side they see. I am both. But I am a woman, I have breasts and legs.

December 28

Last night I began my dramatic poem. The story I wrote in Antwerp (it is the plot of that) has made me suspicious of my writing.[30] Whether it is good or not, it is unlike anything I have ever done. I was carried away to the extent of 260 lines, a whole scene. It came so easily, without the slightest effort, from the first line, that I suspect it. But this I attribute to the fact that it is blank verse, which is easier than prose. After the restraints I have had to endure in the Spenserian stanza, and in sonnets, as well as that thrice-plagued fourth line rhyming of the "Lysias" poem, this is bliss. I am not sure whether this is poetry or not, it is not lofty. But it is damned good characterization. There is no nonsense in it, perhaps not enough. But in a scene in a newspaper office

---

[30]Recall her entry for November 14, 1929, in which she noted of this unidentified narrative, "I said that I had written a third of a story in Antwerp and had stopped because it seemed so good and I knew it could not be as good as it seemed to me then, so I wanted to wait until I had gotten cold about it."

there is not opportunity for poetic flights.[31] I will have a chance for those when I have the main characters involved in their conflicts.

Wrote to the Chief, and a note to Stallybrass to ask him when my book is coming out.[32] I thought it well to jog them up. A postcard from Antony and Judith on which Antony wrote, "Solitude is a form of masturbation." He is jealous of me. I wish I could see him. A letter from Hero bewailing her troubles. She cannot get on with her book. She devoted considerable space to a description of the Christmas dinner she gave the Sandstroms. There is no cook like Hero. She said in this letter that Agamemnon had come to see her. He must be desperate, he has to lean on someone. I wish I could do something for him. I am no good for a friend.

I had my hair waved, I could no longer stand its ugliness. When I was dining at L'Escale Christmas Eve and saw the attention that was being given to Colette and de Segonzac I felt small. When I found the same attention being given to me I was surprised. This is utter nonsense, I am always this way. I have not had enough respect in my life, and by Jesus Christ, for the years that remain to me I am going to have as much of it as I can get.

Sunday December 29

My fisher boy came out to the lighthouse. We went walking over back of the *Citadelle* and I finally got him to talking, by clever measures.[33] I found by manipulating him properly that he could be frank, and it appears that he was not inexperienced in the society of *étrangères* when he first saw me. Three years ago it seems a Frenchwoman made much of him, and used to take him out in the country in her car. Her husband would invite him to drink, not knowing of these expeditions. Thus did my child become versed in mundane ways. I then beguiled him into telling me what he did last summer. He had the other day affirmed that he had done nothing but pine for me, had not stirred from his home. It appears he learned even more of the ways of the world last summer. There were three Lesbians here and it seems they were very im-moral. My child and two of his friends spent much time with them, all drinks paid. He said he had never had such a good time. I said, "Why did you tell me last year that I was the first *étrangère* you had ever known?" He said, "*Je me disais, 'Elle sera fachée si je lui dis que j'ai connu l'autre.*"[34] His logic is impeccable, and he will go far.

---

[31]The poem was likely based on her experiences at the *Tribune*.
[32]The Chief was Coleman's Uncle Charlie. William Swan Stallybrass (1885–1931), senior managing director of Routledge, was publishing her novel *The Shutter of Snow* in England.
[33]The *Citadelle*, an ancient citadel (now a museum) sits on La Colline des Moulins (Mill Hill) in St. Tropez.
[34]"I said to myself, 'She will be angry if I tell her I have known others.'"

December 30

A beautiful letter from Karen. He said he admired me because I choose deliberately to work. It was a lovely letter. He said he had just finished reading the life of Van Gogh, and that I had all his strength with none of his weaknesses.[35] Karen has a lovely spirit. I wonder if it is not unique for a poet to have someone like that. I am fortunate in him and in my father. Without them my life would be different.

December 31

I wrote a letter to the mistress of Kay's kindergarten and sent her some of his drawings to spur her on.[36] I had a letter from Mamotchka describing the Noel. It was very exciting.

Kay's birthday will be the sixth, on which day he starts in school. I have found my gravures in Hero's house and have selected three for him. He knows them, they used to be on my walls when we first came to Paris. They are photographs of Rodin's statues—one of the *Age of Bronze*, one of *Eve*, and the *Poet and the Muse*. I think he will like to have these.

January 1, 1930

I sat on the ledge of my window in the sun, reading Dante. The hills hold in the sky, they surround the fields and give no rest. It is broad here, sweeping wide. It is large, not confined like Hero's garden. I thought of David. Below the child of Dante staggered. When he began to cry I thought of little Kay crying in New York. He used to cry all the time. I cannot bear to think of him then. I was a little insane because of him. My darling little child, you could not have been happy.

January 2

I worked today on my dramatic poem. I have never written in this manner, this is a change. I work slowly.

---

[35] Coleman did not specify which biography her husband was reading, but it may have been either *Van Gogh: a biographical study* by Julius Meier-Graefe, translated by John Holroyd Reece (1922); or *Van Gogh* by Paul Colin, translated by Beatrice Moggridge (1926).
[36] Recall her entry for December 14, 1929: John had behaved badly during his pre-school interview, and Coleman worried that he would not be welcomed when he officially began classes the following week.

It is all planned, I am working out the characters. Elizabeth the struggle between ambition (will) and physical love. This is the struggle of the woman who is an artist, this is the theme. David is the struggle between pride and love, and Philip between uncontrolled passion and the getting of what he wants.[37] He is not a drunkard because he cannot help it, there is no struggle there. He has no pride. He is a coward, while David is courageous. I think it will not end as I thought, I thought Philip would kill her, but he obviously is too much of a coward even to kill himself. I think David will kill Philip on account of Elizabeth, then he will kill himself. She will be left alone. She has gained her ambition but in doing it she has given them both up.[38]

I found two letters from Karen written last spring. They made me unhappy. He wanted me so. He wanted my body. I do not know what I am to do. I love Karen so deeply that just to see him gives me intense joy. When I first knew Karen he was an armchair philosopher. He used to jot ideas down on scraps of paper. If it had not been for me he would never have left advertising to go into psychology, and if it had not been for me he would never have left psychology to go into advertising.[39] I have hammered at him that he must get out of advertising. He says he wants to stay in business. I am profiting from his desire to make money, but I do not think it is right. I do not think it is right, either, that I should sacrifice genius to something he may not have at all. But it is too late for me to sacrifice my genius for anything. It has lifted its head too high, I will never let anything keep it now from getting all the way out.

January 3

Today I walked a little with my fisher boy. I was sitting on the *phare*, reading Storr's beastly translation of *Oedipus Rex* (I want to see how Sophocles managed character) and he came along.[40] His face is dark and handsome, his eyes especially. I looked at him very hard and decided he was a young girl. His *copin* is a sweet young fellow, that shows what he likes.[41] They have always been friends. His *copin* is shy and has not as much of the world in him as this one. He will of course never be content to remain my friend. He is only doing it now because he thinks I will change my mind.

---

[37]Coleman seems to be conflating the real and the imagined here, for recall that "David" was also her pseudonym for Philip Jordan; and Philippe was her fisher-boy.
[38]The themes of passion, murder, and suicide anticipate those of her second novel, "The Tygon."
[39]In 1927 Deak Coleman had co-authored the book *Psychology: A Simplification*.
[40]Francis Storr's (1839–1919) translation of *Oedipus Rex* was published in 1913.
[41]*Copin*: friend.

I had a letter today from Stallybrass, saying that the Viking Press would undertake my book, and so they would go to print at once.[42]

January 5

Women are never simple. From early years they have to think about catching men. They are more social than men because their life has depended on the development of their social instincts. They chatter because it is their stock in trade. A woman has to get twice as much confidence as a man if she wants to do anything because no one expects it of her. It is like being born a Jew, one has to do everything better before it is recognized. A woman of talent is apt to fall into the bog of thinking what she does is good because no woman has done it before her, instead of comparing herself to the best poets or painters who have lived, who were men. A woman has got twice the trouble a man has to get rid of conventions. She must get rid of false notions about sex and yet keep her integrity. A woman of talent, more than another woman, is sensitive to crudity, yet whenever a woman is "free," and known to be so, it is expected of her that she will be crude; Whereas she cannot bear this.

A woman has handicaps in getting to know life that a man does not have. She cannot know a man without sex, unless she is unattractive, and women of talent are apt to be attractive. I have wondered about this. Does a man ever get to know a woman without sex? I do not think so, unless he is a homosexual. I think sex is, at first, the only way to know anyone. Then one learns to tell from observation. But to lay the foundations of knowledge sex is absolutely necessary.

January 6

Today is the birthday of my adorable. I sent him a telegram. He begins at school, and God grant it marches. Six years ago today I was not very well. And on my birthday I was carried to the State Hospital, Karen holding me in his arms in the car.[43] I weighed 95 pounds, and I remember opening my eyes in the car and feeling myself in his arms. I wrote two sonnets to Karen, I worked over them a good deal but cannot tell what they are.

My fisher boy is what I want. I am learning things from him which I would not have got any other way. He is not a nuisance, he is tender and sweet and appreciates being with me, but he does not intrude. The fisher boy wants sex,

---

[42]Viking, now a division of Penguin, was the New York publishing house founded in 1925.
[43]Rochester State Hospital in New York State. John was born on January 6, Coleman on January 22.

but I find that when he has that he asks no more. He has a beautiful strong body, but I do not love that body. God damn it, I wish I <u>could</u> love someone's body.

January 7

I think constantly of Karen. Karen is identified with my genius, more than anyone else, even Agamemnon. If it had not been for Karen I do not think I would have written one poem. I stopped when I was seventeen, and I do not think I would have gone back if I had married someone else. We have endless things in common, we are always amiable together, we do not irritate each other. It is only this beastly sex, I cannot love him sexually as I did. It is done.

I worked an enormous amount on my play. I wrote 250 lines. The only thing to do is to write it, and not be so afraid of it. I feel as if I were putting out in to the Arctic Ocean.[44]

January 9

Letter from Mamotchka that He had been "good" at school. I was terribly excited when I opened the letter, and immensely relieved. I immediately wrote him and told him how much I loved him for it. She says that *tout* was *à merveille*.[45]

Information is facts, knowledge is facts in relation to each other and to a scheme. I have been reading *The Sacred Wood*. There is no book of criticism so perfect, except the *Poetics*.[46]

The essay "Tradition and the Individual Talent" contains some of the most profound statements on art and artists that have ever been uttered. He says in the introduction that in ages like the present the artist uses up all of his energies in fighting the public. This is only true of artists who have not got a strong talent. I think Eliot is a very unhappy man, he has not done what he wanted to do. He wants to write great poetry, and knows how it should be done, and he cannot. He speaks of the "flood of poetasters" in the reign of Elizabeth, a good point. The flood now may be presaging, for all we know,

---

[44]She went on to discuss the fact that certain people, such as Holms, would never realize their talent, whereas others such as Muir and Virgil Geddes would, simply because of their perseverance and because they had adjusted their genius to their living. While discussing Holms in this passage Coleman wrote of him and Guggenheim: "Now Wendy is pregnant again, and he tried to settle it by not thinking about it. She has had two abortions in this year and cannot keep on with it."

[45]"All was wonderful."

[46]T. S. Eliot's *The Sacred Wood: Essays on Poetry and Criticism* (1920). Coleman was most inspired by the essay "Tradition and the Individual Talent," first serialized in *The Egoist* in 1917. Aristotle's *Poetics* (350 BC).

a great age. This is the first book of criticism I ever read. Agamemnon lent it to me the summer of 1928 and I was at once struck with it.

January 10

Wrote my father something which will no doubt please him. Said that I believed national differences were the root of art, and that I was American in every fibre and would never try to go against it. This must have amazed him also. One of the things the matter with Eliot, he is an American and he has made himself into an Englishman.[47] It can't be done after ten years of age, I doubt. I am sure Eliot is an unhappy man, he is neither fish nor fowl. It rained all day today. I did not move from this room. I went over my "Lysias" poem to get it into shape for Father, that is to say I intended to mark the parts he could understand. I found it was not a bad poem at all, once the nonsense was struck out. I wrote a letter to Virgil Geddes and told him at last how glad I was about his plays.[48] I meant what I said, he is an unusual person. I can make him talk because people feel at home with me. That is I suppose a good thing although I hate it. I would prefer to be respected and feared. I console myself with the thought that no doubt everyone thought Shakespeare was just like themselves.

In letter to Muir I said: Agamemnon is not growing, a light has gone out. Agamemnon's situation, must have Kurn to lean on, cannot stand alone. Can think alone but cannot face life alone. Must have Wendy because needs sex and cannot get it other ways. Why people write, three reasons—rivalry with dead or living poets; desire for immortality; desire to make pleasing world for self instead of this one. I said Agamemnon had none of these desires. I said it was desperately sad and I urged him to write to him.

---

[47]Having moved from his native U.S. to England in 1914, Eliot entered the Church of England and became a British citizen in 1927.

[48]Geddes was a member of the experimental theatre company the Provincetown Playhouse, one that formed loosely in Provincetown, Massachusetts, in 1915, and moved to Greenwich Village, New York, in 1916. His play *The Earth Between*, which opened in March 1929, featured soon-to-be-Hollywood great Bette Davis in her acting debut. On a different note, Emma Goldman had attended the premier there of *The Athenian Women* (April 1918, by Playhouse founder George Cram Cook) with her friend Mary Eleanor Fitzgerald ("Fitzie"), who had been the secretary for Goldman's *Mother Earth* and who went on to become the managing director for the theatre company. Several people mentioned in Coleman's diary were affiliated with the Players, including Guggenheim's ex-husband Laurence Vail and Djuna Barnes.

January 12

I have made endless notes on little pieces of paper on the third act of *Othello*, and I will never get to copying them here. I have also made desultory notes on Dante, and a good deal on John Donne. I jot these things down, then this diary gets bogged up, then I have to go on with the day I decide to begin again and gradually work the part undone into the back. It is a mess and frequently makes me say the same thing twice. I hate like hell writing this, yet I am certain it is good for me. It keeps me from reading too much for one thing, because I don't want the nuisance of putting down what I think of what I read. That means I think more about what I do read. It is the damndest nuisance in the world right now, because I want only to write sonnets.

January 14

I do nothing but write sonnets. They are in the drawer, on the table, in the bed, in the waste basket. Sunday I sent 6 to Karen to astonish him. Short words are good for a whole line, or else a whole line with long words that flow easily, like "impediment" or "alteration." I have made a list of things I want to say and I will say them all in sonnets.

It is significant that I am writing these sonnets on scrap paper which is the backs of the sheets on which my "novel" was written. It takes about three sheets to make a sonnet. Sometimes I turn and read the backs and it makes me tear my hair.

My book was dedicated to my father, when I have a volume of short poems I will give that to Karen, "Lysias" to Hippocra, and my first dramatic poem to Agamemnon.[49] By that time I am certain I shall be dead.

January 15

I have to make myself write in this damned diary now, as well as do my Dante. I don't want to do anything but sonnets. The Dante is worth taking time off the sonnets, but this diary bores me terribly and I find it an awful chore. I am determined to keep it up because it helps me to concentrate on my thoughts, besides, I want to keep this record of my development. I am determined that someone who knows poetry and can write it shall leave behind what he has thought about the mechanics of it, a poet who has to give battle with the 20th century.

---

[49]In her entry for April 3, 1930 (F. 628, not transcribed), Coleman described receiving the proofs of the first three pages: "The Shutter of Snow, by Emily Holmes Coleman, London, George Routledge and Sons, Ltd. Then the dedication To My Father."

Arthur Waley told me about a conversation he had in college with Rupert Brooke.[50] He said that R.B. wrote a sonnet which he considered a great sonnet, and A.W. told him the sonnet form was dead. Rupert Brooke said, "It is not dead, it is just waiting for a man with sufficient genius to give it life again." Karen said the same thing to me once. Agamemnon said he was not sure, he thought it possible that the sonnet form was finished as far as this age is concerned. He is absolutely wrong.

I say I do not care for posterity, but I certainly care that my spirit shall remain in my poems after I am dead. And furthermore I care deeply that poets which follow me shall be inspired by me, as I have been by those ahead of me. I would like some poet who has not yet found himself to be able to pick up a letter of mine and get the start from it that I have got from those letters of Keats.[51] We are a brotherhood, living and dead, and we must hold out our hands to those who will come as well as to those who are gone. I feel myself to be a tongue saying in my own way what they all have said before. I feel I am in the vanguard, as Chaucer was in English poetry. I think I am in the vanguard of what may come in two hundred years.

The reason I think I must rush and write down every good thought I have now is that I am unaccustomed to thinking. I seem to imagine that if I don't get them on paper at once they will evaporate. Of course if they are any good they will recur again and again until they are a part of me. I notice though that whenever I take to writing, I stop my diary, which means that just when I ought to be recording what I think I am not doing it. Last summer I wrote nothing in my diary. So I am determined that of these exciting days I will leave some record besides the sonnets.

I must learn to divide myself, that is going to be my problem. I can do amazing things alone, without responsibilities or distractions. I have got to learn how to carry this into a life of responsibility and distraction. Of course I can do it. I did my book in Paris, with Karen there unoccupied all day, and in Antwerp I wrote much, playing with Panurge and Karen every evening. But I never get this intensity. I have got to get it.

My tendency has been to believe every word Agamemnon said, and Eliot. These are the only people alive who have such an influence. I often wonder what Eliot would think of my poetry and I don't know.

---

[50] English poet Rupert Brooke (1887–1915) had entered King's College at Cambridge University in 1906, Waley in 1907.
[51] Coleman had been reading editions such as *Letters of John Keats to his family and friends* (1891), ed. Sidney Colvin, or *The Letters of John Keats*, the complete revised edition (1895), edited by H. Buxton Forman, Reeves, and Turner.

I came to my skeptical ideas of God by myself, in an Episcopal school where no one dreamed of atheism.[52] My father helped me some without meaning to. It finished in college. As soon as my logical mind took hold of the idea that the Bible was annotated by those who copied it, and that Christianity was not the first religion to cherish the dogma of Virgin birth and the divinity of the Leader—There is much that is sensible in the Catholic Church. The practise of "retreat"—that is exactly what I am doing now. If anyone who pretends to think, imagines that he can do it in this modern world without once getting out of it he is misled.

It is not possible to be more happy than I am. I sing, I sing within. I do not have to do ONE thing I don't want to do, except write in this blasted diary.

Father made it possible for me to be here. I will never forget that.

When I think of the horror of the two weeks Kay was in London it makes me unhappy.[53] I just could not adjust myself, neither could Kay. It was a horror from beginning to end. Karen said, "I can't stand it any more." I love him so, it breaks my heart when these things are. Going back on the boat he was particularly sweet, so that I wouldn't give evil reports to Mamotchka. He put his coat over my legs so I would not be cold in the early morning train. He is an angel when he wants to be. Of course I said nothing to Mamotchka. But later I told her we could never try THAT again.

January 16

Now I have a cablegram from my father that my little brother is dead. . . . I wrote my father there is nothing to be said about Don that I have not already said. It is a life that is better out, better for him, and better for the rest. It is only joy one should have that he is gone now before his life grew any more tragic than it was. I am thankful that at last my father's long vigil is over.

January 17

Letter from Mamotchka saying that perhaps Kay has the whooping cough. She says if he has it is not dangerous. He has never had anything in his life but the grippe and I know he has got to go through with diseases. My poor little darling boy, I will have to see how this goes. If it goes badly I shall go back to Paris. It is true that I give up my child for my writing, but I would

---

[52]Coleman began attending St. Mary's on Mount St. Gabriel, a high Episcopalian boarding school, in 1906. For more on her childhood education, see the introduction.
[53]The summer of 1929. She recalled "the horror" in her entry for November 11, 1929, as well.

certainly give up my writing temporarily if he were sick. It may be that he has not got it.

This afternoon I sat at L'Escale and watched the port. I saw the *copin* of my fisher boy go by, limping. I asked him to have a drink, he was bashful but he came. He is a sweet thing, young, sensitive and impressionable. He is sweeter than Philippe but not so interesting.[54] As it is I am afraid he thinks I have a *béguin* for him.[55] Everyone in L'Escale looked with pop eyes when I got up and asked him to come. I had a simple feeling of sympathy for him but of course none of these imbeciles would ever understand that. He said he would like to take me out in his boat, he can row though he cannot stand up long, so I said I would go tomorrow if it is calm.

I am absorbed in thoughts of language and what we are to do. It is obvious that language is "dead," that is to say poetical language. But the way out is not through Joyce. The writers in New York have only begun to feel it.[56] But it is not through writing nonsense that this revolt is going to carry us back to poetry. It is through making new ways of seeing things serve our intelligence. There has got to be first the rebellion, then the discipline. None of these people know what discipline is, such discipline as I have been submitting my mind and my writing to these last sixteen months. Most of them have no talent at all, but there are some who if a stronger spirit should show them the way I am convinced would produce something living. I am sure that Djuna Barnes might.[57] If this idea of revolt is not governed by a first-rate intellect it is liable to run away with the poet. I haven't gotten anywhere yet, but I have at least come to grips with the problem. I can see even in these sonnets, which I feel to be a great advance on anything else I have done, that the language is not my own, not living yet. I can't yet get my own language out unless I do it in form that is ungoverned.

---

[54]Philippe was her "fisher boy," named here for the first time.

[55]"Crush."

[56]Coleman did not elaborate on who she included in this "New York" group, but perhaps she meant writers like Virgil Geddes (see January 10, 1929) who were working in Greenwich Village. She went on in this entry to make what would be the first reference to Djuna Barnes (see note below), whom Coleman had recently met in Paris.

[57]Djuna Barnes (1892–1982), who would become one of Coleman's closest friends, was an American journalist, novelist, short-story writer, and playwright—the Provincetown Players had performed three of her plays during its 1919–1920 season. In 1921 she left her native New York to go to Paris on assignment for *McCall's*, a trip in part funded by Guggenheim at the request of their mutual friend Leon Fleischman. In New York, Barnes had at one time been the lover of Laurence Vail, and had met Guggenheim through him there, but the women's intense, long-term relationship did not begin until they reconnected in Paris.

January 18

I have been thinking about Joyce's new book.[58] Agamemnon says he is sacrificing himself, that someone had to do this. I suppose he means someone had to call attention to the fact that language has gotten all out of hand as an instrument for saying something new. It is so clogged up with clichés and so much has been written that there is nothing to do but break it up. Muir says Joyce is unbalanced, he says in *Ulysses* even one traces the early symptoms.[59] This I believe to be nonsense, and the easy way out. I don't get this new work, but I have always had a conviction that it was significant in some way. I cannot believe that the author of the *Portrait of the Artist* and of *Ulysses* can be mentally unbalanced. They always say that of everyone who does something astonishing. For poetry I do not believe Joyce is any help so I do not try to read him. He is certainly not a poet, although he has a golden command of language. But he doesn't see things as a poet sees them, he sees them like a novelist. I think *Ulysses* has revolutionized the novel, it can never be the same after that. But whether I read Joyce or not I am full of understanding for his temperament and I shall watch him with interest and shall never cast a stone at him. Arthur Waley said he was not even intelligent, he said his "amazing" erudition was really very limited. What the hell does that matter? No one can say he is not intelligent. The grave charge against him is Lysander's charge, that he is a laboratory artist. Now *this* I feel to be a desperate thing.

I was to have met Philippe tonight and he did not come. It was exasperating. I waited out in the lane, the moon breaking through, the landscape still. I listened for sounds. It was divine, walking between the walls. The vines smelled richly. The deuce with him, I was very mad.

January 20

Saw Fisher Boy and he would not speak to me. Now I know he must be angry because I went out in the boat with his *copin*. In this goddamned town that is how things go. I would have told him, thought nothing of it, but evidently someone else did first, that was why he did not come Saturday beneath the moon. I dare say it looked queer when reported—I leaping from my seat on

---

[58]Joyce's *Finnegan's Wake*. Although it was not published in book form until 1939, much of it was serialized in *transition* from 1927 as "Work in Progress," often alongside Coleman's own work.
[59]Joyce's *Ulysses* (1922) was first serialized in *The Little Review* between 1918 and 1922; *A Portrait of the Artist as a Young Man* (1916) was first serialized in *The Egoist* between 1914 and 1915.

terrasse of L'Escale and inviting *Copin* for drink, then next afternoon going boating with him. I am too impulsive. No one would believe I felt sorry for him. I cannot conceive of anyone's thinking of him sexually. Now how shall I fix it with Philippe, I shall write him a note and command him to meet me at the *porte extérieure à 9 heures du soir*.[60] I shall tell him he is an ass, but I shall nevertheless not do further things to annoy him, because I haven't the time anyway to do them.

January 21

I passed Philippe on the port, I said, "*Bon Jour*, Philippe," sweetly, he was walking ahead. He turned transfixed and finally replied something. I walked sedately on, then he passed by Bailli's, but I was eating and did not go out to speak to him. I sent him a little note to meet me tomorrow night. Letter from Mamotchka worried me. Kay has the whooping cough, and while he is not ill I began to think I ought to go to Paris. He has better care from her than he could get in the most endowed of hospitals, and certainly than he could get from me. I found another *Zig et Puce* for him. If I don't go I will write him every day and send him a book every week. The only point in my going would be for him to realize I am concerned when he is sick. This way will be better. I should not go, there is no purpose, only sentiment. I shall use every cent I have for him and for the enlarging of Mamotchka's apartment. I could never get those stairs out of my mind, but it will help a good deal if there are three extra rooms. If these things hurt Kay, as Karen says, they would be worth considering. They hurt instead Mamotchka. She is a glorious woman. God has sent me Karen, my father and her. He seems to conspire that I shall have freedom in which to write. It is a conspiracy, aided by my strong will (ha ha).

Wrote to Dr. Hélie of American Hospital to go and see Kay at once.

Great discovery, I can do nothing else until I have finished it. It was forbidden for the present, but nevertheless I did. *Moby Dick*, the first American novel that was not a copper plate of the English! There is all of America in this, it gives me feeling for my country I never got from that ass-brained Whitman.[61] This is America—vast, strong, fumbling, gloriously vivid, marvellously true! It sweeps, in its best parts, with a tremendous passion.

---

[60]"Meet me at the outer door at nine o'clock tonight."
[61]*Moby Dick; or, The Whale* (1851), Herman Melville's masterpiece. Walt Whitman (1819–1892), American poet.

One could go through it with a pruning knife and make a work of art out of it. The good parts are so good and the bad parts so unnecessary to the whole.

January 22

Today is my birthday. I finished the *Inferno*, as I had planned.

Saw Fisher Boy sitting on a tartane in the water.[62] As I went by he turned and gave me a radiant smile, so I suppose that meant he got my note and would come. He has only an hour at noon. I was thinking of what Goethe wrote in his diary on his thirtieth birthday. It impressed me deeply when I read it in Lewes. I must look it up again. Before I do so, I will put down myself, and do it quickly:

Aged 31. I will give myself until 32 to be writing consistently good lyrics, I will give myself until 35 to write a good dramatic poem. I have already begun to think. My house is in order. I know whom I love and whom I do not love, what books I want to read, what I want to write. I am ready for the suffering which I know has got to come, and will meet it and not turn from it. It must be suffering that comes from passion, it must be sexual love. In this year I have had a renaissance, my garden was first plowed then weeded and now the seeds are sprouting. I have to make poetry live again, and that by putting new combinations into the old forms, the revolt disciplined.

January 23

I looked through some of Poe's essays last night, to see what *he* was.[63] God in his heavens; there is no use counting on anything here. He may have had genius, but it was a damned poor genius.

I suddenly saw it was 9–20 last night and rushed out to the gate. Fisher Boy was not there. I think he might have waited 20 minutes (I waited half an hour for him), but perhaps he did not come at all. I do not understand this, and have not got time to bother with it. I shall pay no more attention to him, and if he does not make some move to see me he is out of luck. And so, it might be added, am I.

Three telegrams this morning, birthday ones from my father and the Chief, and from Karen, one from Mamotchka telling me not to come to Paris as Kay was very well. This last an intense relief. Wrote endlessly long letters to my father and to Karen.

---

[62] Mediterranean fishing boat.
[63] Coleman may have been reading the 4-volume *The Works of Edgar Allan Poe* (1884); volume 1 contains a section entitled *Poems and Essays*, while volume 3 consists of his *Tales*.

January 27[64]

I thought, "Why has no one written about the feeling for a child?" (I have thought this before). It is obviously because there has not been a good woman poet who had had a child. Nor, I believe, have there been bad women poets who were mothers. Naturally a man cannot do this, his feeling at best is the slop of Coventry Patmore.[65] I thought By the Lord my feeling for my child is of terrific intensity, why do I not get this out? It proved to be the breaking of a bottle-up neck of the sea. I could not stop. I wrote 9 in one evening.[66]

Reading Hero's ms., finished it. Shall write her and give her great encouragement, she deserves it bless her heart. Worked for an hour on her drain and got it to working after the floods. What floods we did have, awful. Did not leave the house yesterday, ate cheese.

Saw Fisher Boy today, he turned his head. I pondered a long time and finally decided he must have come the other night, and thought I had arranged this trick purposely to spite him for his not coming the first time. So I decided I would write to him again, for I cannot go down there evenings, and he has no time at noon. The weekend it poured, no chance to see him.

---

[64] I have not transcribed the entries for the last three days. During this time Coleman noted, for instance, that the Sandstroms had returned from Paris and their visit with Goldman, and had brought back her manuscript for Coleman to edit further (January 24); and she worked on her sonnets (January 25).

[65] Coventry Patmore (1823–1896), English poet. His famous poem "The Angel in the House" (1854) helped to define the stereotype of Victorian femininity in its affirmation that women find fulfillment through marriage and their confinement to the private, domestic sphere of home and hearth.

[66] Coleman's archive contains many of these sonnets, each one titled "To My Son" (numbers 34, 35, 37, 38, 39, 42, 43, 44, 45, 48). Consider the first half of # 38, for example:

> The hour I felt you leap in my cold womb—
> Life I had made, now active, now alert
> To push its pattern through, to do me hurt
> Even to the end, when passing from the gloom
> Within my walls it burst into the light—
> That hour was sacred in my almanac. (F. 1465)

Just over one month later, Coleman described writing a sonnet to her son: "It is like a love poem, no one would think one could feel so about a child. I thought in the middle, 'I could write the title—to David [Philip Jordan]—but if I tried to write a poem to David it would not come out so intense.' It is evident that my feeling for my child is deeper and more intense than for any other person" (March 2, 1930, F. 626, not transcribed).

February 2[67]

At last two letters from my father. One of them was written the day after my brother's death. He was deeply affected, at least he thought he was—the emotional strain made him snap a little. His letter moved me, I wept and began to curse myself for being coldblooded. He described the last minutes of my brother's life, said he was unconscious for several hours, then suddenly opened his eyes wide and smiled. Father cried to him but there was no reply. He was dead. I know that if I had seen that it would have finished me, and I wish I had been there, I needed to see it.

My blood boils when I think of Philippe—I would like to drown him. What an ungodly pleasure it would give me to tell him what a sluggish livered creature he is.

I wonder if a woman can ever know enough about men to write drama unless she sleeps with most of the ones she knows. I wonder why Hippocra and I are not Lesbian, I suppose because we are neither of us Lesbians. There is sex in it of course, but we are both really normal, and do not want to monkey with our relationship. We can experiment on others. When I think of the fate that befell my one experience I am glad it was not Hippocra.[68]

I haven't an ounce of energy. Some strange fever has got hold on me, I sweat it out, then it comes back.

February 7[69]

Wrote to Judith and copied sonnets for her. Went to village and ate large meal at Bailli's, felt excellent. Leaving village heard my name called, looked and there was Philippe. His dark eyes are beautiful and his proud look held me as usual. He admitted to me that he had been very angry because I had gone in the *bateau* with his *copin*. What a fool I was. He says the *copin* told him I had made love with him and that I was angry with him (Philippe). It appears he has cooled down now, and willing to inquire why. Of course I never so much as touched his *copin's* hand, which I averred to him. He wanted me to meet him tomorrow afternoon. I said I would.

---

[67] During the past few days (in entries not transcribed), Coleman had been ill with the grippe, a milder form, she believed, of the influenza she had had the previous year.

[68] In her entry for February 26, 1930 (F. 626, not transcribed), Coleman wrote of her conversation with Himmel: "We said it had been well that no sex was in our relationship, or something might have been destroyed. I wanted it last year, partly because I thought she did, and she prevented, an instinct made her. She was right and I was relieved."

[69] On Feburary 4, Judith, who was in St. Paul de Vence in Provence, came to stay with Coleman during her convalescence, departing on the 6th.

February 8

This heavenly Saturday afternoon spent with Fisher Boy, walking in the lane. He was so sweet. The sun was brilliant. We wanted to go to Hero's, but the gardener was there. He showed considerable feeling. I said, "I think I have been very patient with you," and he came back at once, "Well, I certainly have with you—*ça, c'est sur*." I was taken aback, it had not occurred to me that he thought I was a problem. He has a hold on me, this child—I have always thought there was passion in him, and gradually it comes out. At the very end I angered him. I am not yet sure what it was—I hurt his pride in accidental banter—I was stupid. He grew very angry and flung away. He said severe things to me, and would not let me touch his arm. He said it was finished now, this was for good and all. I could have his *copin*. I laughed at first because I thought he was joking. He cannot know how ridiculous his words were. I cannot conceive of his *copin* except as if he were Kay. He stalked away, up the lane. I did not say a word, I stood watching him go. I guess it just won't be a go.

February 9

Nothing goes any more, it is killed. My mind does not work, I don't want to write, I am restless and disturbed. A note from Antony asking if he could come down from Geneva at the end of next week. How I would love to see him, a human being I can actually talk to. I sent a note to Philippe begging him not to be angry with me, that I was sorry I had offended him. He will probably take some days to get over his rage, so that it is not politic to send it so soon, but I thought I could do that much.

So sweet, pressing my cheek hot against Fisher Boy's in the lane. He has got some kind of a physical hold on me, *ça c'est sur*.

February 10

Furious wind, all day, rain. I ate eggs by the fire. Read my journal. Do not think much of it but it is better than last year. Want to make love to Philippe and can't.

February 11

Today is my father's birthday and he is reading the sonnet I sent him and looking at the gravure of the Anseide *Madonna*. Today I got my first proofs from Routledge. It was 32 pages. I found they had made only one mistake. I wanted to change multitudes of things, I wanted to rewrite the book. It is childish, immature. What shall I do? I can do nothing. It will have to go. I am not pleased with it.

A letter from my father, happy to be home again.[70] A most interesting letter from Virgil Geddes. I was amazed. I did not know he was so articulate. He says good things. He says, "I very rarely write to people. It is not easy for me to ramble and appear casual, and I have a fear of saying things between the lines, thus putting myself in the position of being too readily understood in relation to things I had no intention of saying, and also of being embarrassed should I later learn what I had unconsciously said." This is honest, and like him. He says he would not attempt a drama in verse, but that I might do something with it. He says he is inclined to believe mine will turn out to be a poem rather than a play. I wonder if that is so. It is exactly what I am afraid of. He says it does not matter so long as it is beautiful and entertaining— "entertaining in the higher sense where one is not merely diverted to laughter or unnecessarily depressed, but rides upon a kind of revealing ecstasy, neither mental nor physical in the definitive sense." This is good, but it does not matter. I want to write a drama, not a poem. I put it in poetical form for it [is] easier for me to ennoble the types in this way. He speaks of one's self-respect being at the bottom of one's talent.

I must have life, it is just as important to me as art. As a matter of fact, art is far more important to me now, I fancy, than it will be later. I think that in two or three years that will be a side issue.

February 12

Last night I went to the village, moon high, skies clear. At sunset extremely heavy clouds, gold and salmon. I could not find Philippe and came home soon.

Read carefully for the last time the proofs. Found that if one concentrates on it my book has merit. It is naive and immature, that strikes me at once. Yet one has to read it—there is such an intensity. It is vivid, very honest. It is original. I will allow only the best to reject it.

February 13

Looked out window for postman and saw Antony standing below. Rushed down to see him. He was beautiful, and so glad to see me. Intoxicated by sunshine and hills. We talked rapidly, he had wine with him. Mailman came,

---

[70] Her father had just returned to Hartford, Connecticut, from California, following the death of his son.

more proofs, beautiful letter from wife of Father's dear friend.[71] Could not read it because Antony talked. He said he loved this coast and this town more than any he had ever seen. He said, "You do not read your proofs," I said, "Not now." He said he did not want to see my book except entire, and not with me there. He said he had read an extraordinary poem by Laura Riding at the beginning of a book by Graves.[72] I must look into this. Agamemnon too says she can write. I have only seen nonsense of hers in *transition*. He looked through all my books, I thought, O if this would only keep up, but it won't. I knew that in a few hours poetry would not dare to lift its head, so I talked fast. There was too much to say, outdoors we went, he saying I should wear red sweater but not red beret. "There are so few people one likes," he said. I said, "I lied to you in the Select, I am terribly fond of you," I said, "And sexually too." He smiled sideways, felt better, but his pride would admit nothing. Said he had no interest in me sexually, both of us then relieved and could go on. Down the lane, first the sky (he mad about that) and into Hero's gate. "What is this? What is this?" I said, "Where I lived last year." "What, with that old bitch." I laughed, I used to be furious. Went into house and showed him. He was not impressed, liked much better my room on the hill.

After lunch we went to L'Escale where Antony took a huge fancy to the lady in charge, my round friend with the pug nose. We ate dinner, and drank, and Antony became tight as a drum. Finally we left there and he had all of St. Tropez to operate in. First he went to the railroad station and climbed on top of a train, then he tried to break into a first class carriage to spend the night. Then he chased cats, whirling. He decided to break arc lights later, then fell into an enormous puddle. I got him part way home by wiles, but he suddenly dived in under a hedge and said he would spend the night there. It was sheltered from the rain and wind. I wanted to go to bed, and managed after half an hour to drag him out of that. He was much disgusted when he found it was not in a field. I got him up to Hero's, persuaded him that he could not have a hot bath, and left him with a candle.

---

[71]The letter was from Mrs. Kremer, wife of Charles S. Kremer who was one of the directors of the Hartford Fire Insurance Company, where Coleman's father worked.
[72]Laura (Riding) Jackson (1901–91), American writer and critic. Living in Greenwich Village, she was invited in 1925 by Robert Graves (1895–1985, English novelist, classical scholar, poet, and critic) to England to collaborate on what would become *A Survey of Modernist Poetry* (1927), and then to travel with him and his wife, Nancy Nicholson (1899–1977, English painter), to Egypt. Though they formed a *ménage-à-trois*, Riding and Graves would move alone to Mallorca in 1929. She published poems in *transition* in 1928 (as did Coleman), as well as collections of poetry and criticism, and with Graves founded the Seizin Press (1927–39) and the journal *Epilogue* (1935–37). Riding left Graves in 1939.

February 14

Woke up early and did some writing. Was in the middle of a letter to Karen when Antony came in, chipper and lovely. I had a sweet letter from Karen and a little picture of him sitting between his piano and a window in his bathrobe on a Sunday morning. I loved the picture, it almost made me weep.

Antony and I had a most wonderful day. Our friendship grew into something important this day. He wanted to see my sonnets, I showed him some. After that it was different. He had never believed I could do anything. It *is* hard to believe. We talked of T.S. Eliot and Cezanne.

I went over my proofs after he left, and found the book moving, though ordinary in places.

February 15

The circus is in town. In the morning I went over to Hero's house to see if Antony had locked up everything, and found his old shoes, a bottle of wine, cigarettes. I straightened up Hero's room. I felt happy to be alone again, I love this privacy. Now I could think of my friendship with Antony. It is sealed at last, nothing can break it now. I foresaw this, but he was afraid even when he came that he might never want it. He has no faith, I have.

In the afternoon I went into the tent where the lions and tigers were.[73] They were feeding them. In order to attract the crowd they pretend to take the food away so that the lions roar. It made me sick. They can't leave them in peace even when they eat. I was angry and could hardly keep from sticking the man in the back. One lion I looked at a long time. It cannot be that any creation can have the majesty of gaze of such a beast and not actually *be* majestic. I mean have more strength and power in him, spiritual power, than a man. I looked at his eyes, but they were afraid. Majesty is not afraid. But such a face, the lifting of the head. Like Samson Agonistes, that was all I could think.[74] They have no room in the cages. I cannot bear it, it is wicked.

I saw Philippe and thought "Now I will speak to him. I don't care whether he is angry or not, this is too silly." I went up to him and said, "I would like to talk to you." It was in a tent of horses and he was perhaps disturbed by the close presence of others. He said, "What?" without smiling. I said, "Did you

---

[73] This episode may have contributed to Coleman's decision to feature lions and tigers in her novel "The Tygon."

[74] Coleman had been reading *Samson Agonistes* (1671), Milton's blank-verse tragedy about the biblical figure; she would also write her own sonnets "Samson Agonistes" and "Samson to Delilah" (published in Putnam's *New Review*) as well as a 3-act dramatic poem "The Death of Samson."

get my letter?" he said, "No, perhaps my brother got it," coldly. I said, "I sent you one." I said, "Why are you angry? I am sorry." He looked embarrassed and said, "Go away," very rudely. I said, "This is not nice of you, you are ungracious," he looked at me like someone who is trapped, then said, "*Allez, marche!*"[75] I could not stick this, my blood boiled. I was calm. I said quietly, without anger, "You are going to regret this. I say no more, but just remember that you will regret." I went away with dignity. I was most unhappy.

In the lane I became perfectly calm, no tears. He loves me, of course, and thinks I am a wanton woman who has played him for a fool. I hate this. But the more I think of it the more I see that nothing can ever be done. It is well that he stop knowing me because it would always be the same thing. I doubt if an acquaintance of years would change his opinion. I am genuinely fond of him, and understand him. Things like this are disquieting, they are the price one pays for freedom and intelligence.

---

[75] "Go, walk."

Part II

Section 1

Gloucestershire

August 9–August 25, 1932

The entry for February 15, 1930, is the last one that remains from St. Tropez. The diary opens again on February 24, from the Italian coastal town of Pieve Ligure. Coleman had met up with her American friend Sonia Himmel, and the two travelled to places such as Florence, Arezzo, Siena, Perugia, and Assisi.[1] From February 24 until April 13, the diary was kept almost daily, but there are a few instances where the entries break off into fragments, indicating that the record is not fully intact. This portion of the 1930 diary traces Coleman's obsessive study of the art and architecture of Florence and its environs as she literally dashed from one gallery, museum, and church to the next. I have not transcribed this segment, a decision inspired by Coleman herself, who acknowledged that in it she was "Just enumerating the Renaissance" and concluded: "Don't think it has much value except as an inventory of the 15th century."[2]

There are, however, aspects of the journal that bear notice. Coleman despaired that she may not be "a dramatic poet at all," and seems to have stopped working on her play.[3] But she underscored that her life abroad had cultivated her talent: "First, transition. That was my liberation. Then Agamemnon, that was the beginning of order. Now this—what is this? I don't know yet."[4] Within a short time she found "this"—her own poetic voice—as she exclaimed:

---

[1] In Italy, Coleman had given Himmel her diary to read: "Hippocra has been plowing through my diary. There is no other way for her to know me, I cannot express it to her" (February 27, 1930, F. 626); "Hippocra reading my diary. It was the only way. There was too much to tell her. She read it avidly, the part in St. Tropez" (February 28, 1930, F. 626).
[2] August 9, 1932, F. 629; August 11, 1932, F. 629.
[3] March 8, 1930, F. 628.
[4] March 12, 1930, F. 628.

I think something has happened. I do not dare to believe it. I think sonnet no. 67, which I wrote this afternoon, is a complete thing. I think it is absolutely my own, concentrated, and valuable. I have never felt this before, though I have been deceived in other ways about my writing. I felt it was the voice of God, and for the first time. I felt that the unspeakable had been said at last. The sonnet is this:

> *Great judge who sit upon my last despair*
> *And sentence to oblivion my soul,*
> *Whose final thundering words my body roll*
> *Into its long decay, in which my share*
> *Of the eternal feud is done: no line repair*
> *Of your hard judgment, for in this new role*
> *Silence and darkness will my faith console,*
> *So that what lived will be content to spare.*
> *And if the height of earthly paradise*
> *Where I have foundered in immortal tears*
> *Be then exchanged for peace, I hold that price*
> *Worth the succession of uncounted years*
> *When nameless and disrobed I will suffice*
> *To crust the surface of new hemispheres.*

I see places where concentration is lacking, it is not perfection. But I still think it have [sic] done what I have been working for, and that once done it is going to be easier and easier. I was afraid I was going to die without accomplishing it. I have known that it was in me to do it.[5]

This creative self-discovery came at the moment when she had been distancing herself from Holms, as she told Himmel: "I said he had meant infinite things to me, but that I could go on very well without him. He got me out of the transition-*Joyce* haze, and that might have taken a much longer time. But once out, I was bound to proceed as I have done."[6] Further, Coleman continued to correct her *Shutter of Snow* proofs and anticipated the book's publication in May. Coleman also organized all the poems she had been writing: "Went out this afternoon and bought a little book to put my sonnets in. The good sonnet I have at last done has made me think about getting them all together. I must have lost some of them, they are all over, on scraps here and there, some held

---

[5]March 24, 1930, F. 628.
[6]April 10, 1930, F. 628. She compared her novel *The Shutter of Snow* to the work of Lawrence and Joyce: "I think my book has many of his [Lawrence's] faults. Though I was not influenced by him, but by Joyce" (April 13, 1930, F. 628).

with elastics, two of them torn in two. I collected them and arranged them in order, then began to type them, beginning with 67 and going back."[7] These efforts illuminate how Coleman sought early on to archive her own manuscripts, ensuring that not only her St. Tropez poems but also hundreds of others, as well as the diary itself, would be carefully ordered and preserved.

In addition to her work, Coleman wrote endlessly about the men in her life. She penned a letter to her ever-supportive husband, "telling him what I have grown to be like since I left him, and asking him to try to understand me and not expect me to be a wife."[8] When he informed her that he had fallen in love with someone else she felt relieved of the burden of worrying that he would be lonely.[9] Meanwhile, at the circus in St. Tropez—where she had quarreled with Philippe[10]—Coleman had met the painter Peter Luling, with whom she had a sexual relationship, as she explained: "it was a natural event—I had been alone for two months."[11] However, it was Philip Jordan ("David") she wanted. In response to his cooling letters, she grew increasingly desperate to have him fall in love with her, though a tryst never materialized. Examining the kind of man who attracted her, Coleman reflected on past lovers: "I wanted to know them. I took it for sex," but Himmel urged her to "give up everything for love, and accept nothing less," warning her "that playing with sex was adolescent and could not suffice for a person of maturity."[12]

Another young man who concerned Coleman was her son, a source for much emotional tension as she struggled to balance her artistic and maternal interests. She wrote, "I cannot bear to be away from him, yet I cannot live with him, yet I miss him so strongly." And she expanded, "I love this child, nothing touches me so deeply. I thought about him all the time, and dreamed about him." She was also keen to emphasize of Madame Donn "that her three years' work could never be undone," a point reinforcing Coleman's respect for and dependence on her son's foster mother.[13]

The diary breaks off after her entry for April 13, 1930, written in Florence. Although it is possible that she continued with it for a brief period, she took a lengthy hiatus from diary writing: the next extant diary, dated August 9, 1932, opens with the heading "BEGINNING." In May 1930, after travelling with Himmel in Italy, Coleman went to Paris for two weeks to see her son,

---

[7] March 25, 1930, F. 628.
[8] March 23, 1930, F. 628.
[9] April 3, 1930, F. 628.
[10] See her entry for February 15, 1930, F. 626.
[11] March 8, 1930, F. 628. Luling was an American who had been educated at Eton and Oxford; he was married to novelist Sylvia Thompson.
[12] March 29, 1930, F. 628.
[13] March 6, 1930, F. 628; March 24, 1930, F. 628; April 4, 1930, F. 628.

and then on to Antwerp to be with Deak, where she lived with him more or less (taking time out for jaunts to Italy, Wales, and France) until February 1931, at which point she ended her marriage; as noted in the introduction, they remained on good terms and divorced in May 1932.

When in London in 1929, Coleman had met (Sir) Samuel "Peter" Hoare, an official of the Home Office in London who had literary aspirations—he had, for instance, published a few literary reviews for the magazine The Calendar *at the same time Holms was contributing to it.*[14] *An epistolary flirtation developed into a relationship over the next two years, but with Coleman hoping for a more sustained physical commitment than Hoare was willing to offer, she began a passionate and ultimately violent and doomed love affair with the Italian Lelletto Bianchetti while in Assisi in April 1931, and then moved with him to Rome. Describing their union in a letter to Holms, she exclaimed: "I have fallen in love with someone, for his body," and she went on to describe how she was now growing fascinated with his mind.*[15] *Having been with the twenty-seven year old aspiring writer and Italian translator for just two months, and with difficulty communicating—they spoke to each other largely in French—she described to Holms her feelings for Bianchetti: "I cannot tell you how I love this person, it is terrible—and the pain to express it is terrible." She painted a troubling portrait of their dynamics:*

> *In our relationship, as it is now, I must give in—I must be good to him, even if something is his fault. I am not used to this—but my character needs it. He wants me to be everything he likes, this is natural—but his methods of achieving this are marvelous. My feelings are constantly lacerated—I did not know I had so many superficial feelings, nor did I know so much vanity was in me. He has a terrible intensity, a controlled intensity—I love it so. I am happy if he is angry, if only I can see this. I have got what I want, I have got the artist and the man in one.*[16]

During the period of their involvement, Bianchetti was working on some short stories and translating Joyce's A Portrait of the Artist as a Young Man *into Italian.*[17] *Coleman and Bianchetti were invited, expenses paid, to*

---

[14]Hoare's reviews include "Poetry and the Absolute: Rimbaud" (Vol. 1, No. 4, June 1925); "The Market Place and the Cave" (Vol. 3, No. 1, April 1926); and "Paul Valéry" (Vol. 3, No. 3, October 1926).
[15]Undated letter, F. 1668.
[16]June 19, 1931, F.1668.
[17]Coleman reported to her father that when she and Bianchetti were in Paris in October 1931, they had met Joyce at an art exhibit and that Joyce delighted in speaking Italian to him (October

spend the summer of 1931 with Guggenheim and Holms at Guggenheim's rented villa, Bettiri Baita, near St. Jean de Luz on the coast of south-western France; Coleman had spent the previous summer with them there as well. Together off and on throughout 1931, Coleman left Bianchetti at the beginning of 1932, for he had proven to be an emotionally and physically abusive lover. Coleman registered the trauma she sustained in this relationship in her second novel, "The Tygon."[18] Here, Bianchetti, renamed Donato, cheats on, lies to, and hits Frieda, Coleman's counterpart. Frieda describes Donato as the devil and as her master, yet the man she desperately loves and is terrified will abandon her.

In discussing the book, Coleman often affirmed the autobiographical underpinnings of the characters. Her fictionalized ending, however, in which Frieda is driven to insanity by her sexual jealousy, kills Donato, and then commits suicide, suggests a symbolic rendering of Coleman's shattered psyche. In 1936, upon finishing what would be only the first version, she informed her father that the book "deals with the tragedy of love"; more pointedly, "It's all about sex" although "not much like the ordinary novel on that theme. It really gets to the spiritual heart of that vital spring of all our beings." Further, she revealed "that 'true love' can go wrong; and wreck the people who felt it—as John and Dorothy; 'intense love' cannot be satisfied, because it is made for another sphere, a more heavenly region. It is not adapted to the exigencies of this life."[19]

Coleman spent several months in Paris in the fall of 1931 and in the first part of 1932, visiting with her son as well as Holms and Guggenheim, staying at the Hotel Des Écoles at 15, rue Delambre and Guggenheim's flat at 55, avenue Reille, both in the 14e arrondissement. She then moved to London in April, settling at 61 Albert Bridge Road in Battersea. She had turned her attentions back to Hoare, so that the diary records her growing obsession with her hopes for sexual and emotional renewal through him. As for Bianchetti, both during their relationship and in the months following their separation, he was dependent on Coleman's—and through her, Guggenheim's—financial support, and the theme of an impoverished but leeching ex-lover plagues Coleman in the next diary.

In July, Coleman had gone with Himmel to Bourton Far Hill Farm in Moreton-in-Marsh in the Cotswolds, Gloucestershire, run by the Rightons; Guggenheim, John Holms, and Dorothy Holms were staying nearby. In August, Coleman and Himmel moved six miles down the way to a

---

30, 1931).
[18]For more on this novel, see the introduction.
[19]July 12, 1936, F. 1597.

guest house owned by Mrs. Dowdeswell, where the diary opens. Note that Coleman no longer uses pseudonyms so that, for example, "Hippocra" is now Sonia Himmel; "Agamemnon" is John Holms; "Wendy" is Peggy Guggenheim; "Karen" is Deak Coleman.

Cutsdean, Temple Guiting, Cheltenham, Gloucestershire, care of Mrs. Dowdeswell.

BEGINNING

August 9, 1932

Today sitting in the garden saw a young thrush who came up very close. Picked part of a worm, then ran from it. Wiped his beak on the ground. Then cuddled down on the grass, so that I could see how downy he was, and sat as if in nest, with his mouth half open.

Read my diary of 1929–30, and enjoyed the first part. The part in Florence dull. The beginning is awfully funny. When I in was in Paris (November, 1929) beginning to know Holms, it was interesting. But as soon as I got out from under his eye it begins to thicken up.

The St. Tropez part of this diary is missing, it must be in Antwerp. I was reading with excitement, anticipating the fisher boy. Suddenly it stopped. All that part was excellent. As soon as I got to Florence I got heavy—Sonia's admiring my "development" and both of us taking in the Renaissance.

White bird have seen twice, exactly like a gull. Wonder what the devil it is. Have been reading with keen enjoyment W.H. Hudson's *A Shepherd's Life*.[20]

Very interesting to see in the diary how I came to be friends with Holms. The first one would give all the early parts.[21] Thought the diary would be dull, but only the part in Firenze was. Very busy then with Art; Sex was also being considered.

I'll probably go to Temple Guiting tomorrow evening, to see if there is a letter from Peter, who is unfortunately not my lover.[22]

---

[20]William Henry Hudson (1841–1922), Argentinian-born American novelist and naturalist who moved to England in 1869. Coleman would read a number of his works, including *Birds and Man* (1901), *Land's End: A Naturalist's Impressions of West Cornwall* (1908), and *A Shepherd's Life: Impressions of the South Wiltshire Downs* (1910).
[21]See her entry for December 7, 1932: this early diary was presumably in Sonia's care; however, as Coleman went on to describe, when she got it back she burned it.
[22]Temple Guiting is another Cotswold village. (Sir) Samuel "Peter" Hoare (1896–1976) was a Scotsman educated at Inverness Royal Academy and Aberdeen University, who after serving with the Cameron Highlanders during WWI was appointed in 1920 to London's Home Office, the government department responsible for passports and immigration, drugs, police, and

Reading the first part of my diary gave me a spur, but the Firenze part has taken the heart out of me. It is just too awful, soggy like dough. Why do I get that way? I'm probably doing it again and don't know it. The excitements of solitude.

I was Goethe first in the diary, then Shakespeare, and later Dante. I had been Milton. I said that Goethe had a better mind.

I want to get past thinking of that, past those willful tender recollections. When I wrote that diary I was a fool. I love Peter. I'm quite sure I want him. If he knew anything at all, anything <u>at all</u>, he'd know this.

There's nothing in the diary about my first letter to him, which I wrote then in Firenze.[23] It must have come at the end. I stopped that diary because I thought I was writing out of vanity. Thank God something stopped it.

Very pathetic in the diary the struggle to write one sonnet. She <u>ought</u> to succeed! In the first part what a character comes out—so vital and full of guts. Judith said to me, "All you care about is Goethe and Coleridge." She was right, and it was a bit hard on her. All that about Antony. I'd forgotten that! If Peter only could understand this. Reading the diary I don't know why <u>anybody</u> should understand it. I don't think Peter had better see it.

How unutterably boring the parts about Firenze were. I can't help thinking that there ought to have been <u>one</u> observation that showed some insight. Nothing at all. Just enumerating the Renaissance.

August 10

Finished *A Shepherd's Life*. I must get more books like this.

Letter from Peggy saying she had got books and discs and art books were not there. I controlled myself as well as I could and wrote to Bianchetti.[24] I can't every minute think of him as a beaten dog I mustn't kick. I am so damned angry about these books. Whatever I think I'll just let him know he's got to respect my books. I didn't say anything about having given him gramophone, typewriter, and half of my French books. This recalling to life gratitude doesn't get far. He's

---

counter-terrorism. During his eminent career, among other things he served as the private secretary to Sir Herbert Samuel, and was Assistant Under-Secretary of State from 1948–1961 and the Head of the International Division from 1950–1961. He was made a CB in 1949, knighted in 1957, and appointed a KBE in 1970. After he admitted to disliking the name Samuel, he asked Coleman to "invent a name for me," which she did, to which he replied, "I have no objection to Peter" (letters F.176, November 29, 1930; December 9, 1930). Coleman's use of "Peter" would also distinguish him from Samuel John Gurney Hoare Templewood, 1st Vicount (1880–1959), British statesman. Emily and Deak met Hoare through mutual friends at J. Walter Thompson.
[23]Coleman was referring to when she was in Florence in early 1930.
[24]Coleman feared that Bianchetti had pawned her books, which she had stored at Guggenheim's place in Paris.

heard too much of it. Everyone has. Thinking of my diary again, it is evident that I need contact with life, if being alone brings forth such dough as this. It's like waddling in a mire. No lights, no mirage ahead. Nothing <u>ever</u> but gloom.

Letter yesterday from Peter Neagoe asking for photograph for anthology *Americans Abroad*.[25] Thought how pleased Father would be, and others in America. Felt like a fool autographing a photograph.

Have been very troubled about letter to Bianchetti, meditating another one, when this has had its effect, in which I will say what I loved in him. When I think of him I CAN NOT think of what a hard little cock he was, but always remember that sweet naive smile. I think of kissing the side of his head, his lovely soft hair.

Looked at myself in the glass for a time, and simply cannot make out what I really look like. Tried to think, "What would you think of such a face if you met it?" but could not. When I laugh I'm handsome, but when you see yourself close you see only the yellow skin.

Was so moved in journal at the writing of that sonnet.[26] I loved that child for wanting so much to write a good sonnet. But here I am, and what am I to do? I don't seem to have anything to say.

August 11

I should tear up this part on Firenze except that it means something to Sonia for what it recalls. Don't think it has much value except as an inventory of the 15th century. The first part of the diary—Paris and coming to St. Tropez—really moved me.

We talked today about our children, and I said how I am jealous of Madame Donn.[27]

---

[25]Peter Neagoe (1881–1960), dadaist and surrealist novelist and short story writer. Born in Romania, he emigrated to the U.S. in 1901, and in 1911 married the Lithuanian painter Anna Frankeul in New York. Moving to Paris after WWI, he worked as assistant editor of the periodical *New Review* (1931). His anthology *Americans Abroad* (1932) features brief autobiographies and signed photographs, followed by poems, stories, and commentaries, by a veritable who's who of the period such as Coleman, Djuna Barnes, Kay Boyle, e. e. Cummings, John Dos Passos, Emma Goldman, Ernest Hemingway, Eugene Jolas, Ezra Pound, Laura Riding, Gertrude Stein, and William Carlos Williams. Coleman submitted two poems to the work, "The Shepherd's Face" and "The Vision."

[26]The sonnet is the one she wrote in Florence on March 24, 1930.

[27]Himmel's two sons were Irving and Tony; Tony was staying at the Donns' with John.

August 12

We went walking to Temple Guiting, and no letters. The postman was coming out of the gate and said, "None for you." We were quite surprised as were not aware that he knew us.

I told her something about my book, and said I don't know how to do the father because I want him to be a mixed bad and good character, and all I can imagine is one who is good.[28] I said I don't want to draw someone I know. I said, "How I should like to put myself in a book or story as I was when I wrote that diary. What a chance for comedy, and I have that genius." Pitiful, all my wasted talents, I could be Goethe, I could be Zeno.[29] And here I sit, and rot.

Read a little Jung last night.[30]

August 13

Letter from Peggy asking us to come immediately to Hayford Hall, Buckfastleigh, Devon.[31] Wrote Sonia too. Thought she was so happy to have us come, then realized it was having Sindbad, and the good weather.[32] She wrote with such enthusiasm. I think she likes being in England, in Hayford Hall. Djuna is there. Went into Sonia's room excited, and thought about leaving here.

Last night identified birds we had seen on walk as fieldfares. Sun set in plum-coloured clouds. Two great clouds like dragons fighting in the sky, away from the sunset.

On the walk (which was to Temple Guiting again—and without success) talked about Binachetti, because I had letter from him.

He lies to me, about everything, that is the worst. Would like to know now if he is well, and would like to arrange for him to see doctor, but do not dare

---

[28] This book is an early draft of "The Tygon."

[29] Zeno is the eponymous protagonist in Italo Svevo's *La Conscienza di Zeno* (1923), translated as *The Confessions of Zeno* by Beryl de Zoete (1930). Svevo was the pseudonym of Ettore Schmitz (1861–1928), Italian novelist. Noted for its modernist experimentation, the novel is the "autobiography" written by Zeno for his Freudian analyst in order to uncover the roots of his addiction to nicotine. James Joyce, who had been Svevo's English tutor at the Bertliz School in Trieste in 1907, was an early champion of the work.

[30] Jung's *Psychology of the Unconscious: A Study of the Transformations and Symbolisms of the Libido* (1918).

[31] Guggenheim rented the manor house Hayford Hall for the summer and fall of 1932 and 1933. For more on the dynamics of the group there, see *Hayford Hall: Hangovers, Erotics, and Modernist Aesthetics*, edited by Podnieks and Chait.

[32] Guggenheim's son, Sindbad, who lived mainly with his father, Laurence Vail, was visiting.

inquire, as he would use it as a handle. Also is bound to think Peter is responsible for me.

Read Dorothy Wordsworth, lovely about the water spreading under the breeze.[33] I did not notice this before. Came to part about her freezing that night, not daring to get a blanket for fear of waking William. He wore himself out, did himself harm, and made himself ill with poetic regularity, but poor Dorothy had to make the beds and copy his articles. This is of course the basis of women's troubles. <u>They love doing this.</u>

Was full of Bianchetti when I arrived home, and wanted to write a great deal to him, but thought better of it. Every time I do this it makes trouble. Will wait to hear from him about the books. Then will write him a more decent letter. If he's pawned the books, will say nothing.

Yet I feel such tenderness for him. He must wonder how I have become so hard. Must think it is Peter's influence. He <u>knew</u> how tender I was, but he never felt my strength. Yet I am ashamed of this strength, and get no satisfaction from it, except that I can keep my money.

Sunday, August 14

Raining; [Mrs. Dowdeswell] gave us rotten hazelnuts. Sonia says she's not going to Peggy's. Doesn't want to face all that right now. Dreamed had several toothbrushes, all with handles broken. Wandering about in strange landscapes, uneasy. Stealing small picture frames from department store.

Last night walked to Temple Guiting again, no post on Saturdays. Saw a kestrel in distance, "wind-hovering." Could not get near it. Talked about mediums, discovered Sonia is psychic.

When we got home tried several stunts, making me do something unconsciously, which did not work. I suggested table tipping.[34] Got a small table, put the light low, sat still. She thought it was a joke, never having done it. Soon she began to feel a curious heaviness in her legs, as if glued to the floor, then she felt like stone. At the same time I felt something strong in the table coming up against my fingers. Distinctly felt this, frightened both of us. We put up the light

---

[33] Having never married, Dorothy Wordsworth (1771–1855) lived with her brother William (and later with him and his wife, Mary Hutchinson), for her adult life. Her journals first appeared in the posthumously published 2-volume *The Journals of Dorothy Wordsworth* (1897) which includes, among other autobiographical writings, *The Alfoxden Journal* (1798) (kept while she and William were in Somerset) and *The Grasmere Journals* (1800–1803) (kept while in Grasmere in the Lake District).
[34] Coleman was likely inspired by *The Confessions of Zeno* which she was reading, for there is a table tipping scene, which she quoted later in this entry (not transcribed). Coleman had also practiced table tipping when she lived in Rochester.

and talked about it, then tried it again. This only happened twice. Did not move the table. I felt nothing except in my hands, which had curious electric feeling, then felt the table pushing them, as if the wood were cracking and splitting to come up. She felt not only this but sensation in her legs and abdomen, could not get her breath. She was astonished, as has never done anything with this power.

We are going to try it again tonight.

She told me how boring I am when we were walking, said I drive her mad, going over and over something. I said I knew I could not listen to people, that nothing could change that, unless I am deeply interested. Talked about Djuna, and I tried to give her character; "Warm, bitter, sentimental."

I told her of my passion for Garbo, and illustrated how Garbo walks (wearily, like a hen turkey), and her voice.[35] Told her I would go at any time to see any play she was in anywhere. Sonia astonished (she has never seen her), laughed heartily. Told about Sunday paper which arrived in St. Jean de Luz and how P[eggy]. and I wrenched it from John. John said this was American mass feeling. Had life story of Greta in it, wonderful statements. I said the fact that 4 million, 999 thousand females thought as I did not disturb my pleasure.

We talked about *Zeno*, which I think is the best modern book I have ever read. I don't know why. Tells more truth perhaps. Hasn't imagination of Joyce or Lawrence. But it's a long book and out of 400 pages, 300 are first rate.

August 19

I lost my diary in London in my pocketbook, as much of it as I had written there, and I will not write that again now, but hope to have it turn up.[36] Reading the beginning of *Women in Love* yesterday, Lawrence, could not endure it.[37]

This poor bewildered mind ranging about. He explains so much because he is so bewildered. He dresses his women in costumes to forget what they are like inside. I think he has had a very bad influence on our generation. I detect this kind of writing in even journalism. He writes about men like a schoolgirl.

Wednesday I went to see Phyllis and told her about *Zeno*.[38] Her mother came in and Phyllis said, "This is my friend whose book you read," and her mother said very sweetly, "I couldn't have got through it if it hadn't been your friend."[39]

---

[35] Greta Garbo (1905–90), Swedish Hollywood film star.
[36] Between August 14 and 19, Coleman had gone to London to be with Hoare.
[37] *Women in Love* is Lawrence's controversial 1920 novel detailing the sexual and emotional relationships of sisters Ursula and Gudrun Brangwen with their respective partners, Rupert Birkin and Gerard Crich, in Beldover, a coal-mining town in England.
[38] Phyllis Jones (previously the "Redhead").
[39] The "book" was Coleman's novel *The Shutter of Snow*.

Went to cinema with Phyllis to see Jack Hurlburt as a policeman.[40] I didn't think it was very funny. There was a scene where he was directing traffic and two men with a long ladder went across. Then (it was suffocatingly hot) we went and lay under a tree in St. James Park.[41]

Then I met Peter and we went and drank at the Monico, talking about policewomen, whom I saw in the Underground at Piccadilly trying to stop whores.[42] He said Sonia was like wax, and Phyllis too, but Peggy had character. I said, "You have at least learned what men of the world are like" (in the Home Office) and he said he didn't want to know that; I said, "What do you want to do?" and he said, "Die."

Peter told me something that impressed me deeply, that he did when he was young in London. He forced himself to go with a prostitute, because he had never had woman [sic].

I left my bag in a taxi, with my passport and two pounds and my fountain pen. Had books in my arms, and was kissing Peter and did not notice the bag.

Yesterday morning, August 18th, he came to my room across the street and gave me a pound to pay my bill, since my bag was lost.[43] I tried to talk to him about Lawrence, whom I was reading, but he squinted up his eyes and could not stand it. I met him at one and he had his bag and a taxi, and we went to the train, getting sandwiches and plums in the station.[44] It was hotter than I can possibly describe. We argued about Lawrence in the train, because he will not admit anything, having discovered Lawrence for himself years ago.

When we got to Moreton we put the bicycle on the back of a taxi and came here, by way of Stow. Peter said the house was lovely, and we lay under the locust tree.

---

[40]Jack Hurlburt (1892–1978), English comedic actor, played a policeman in the 1932 film *Jack's the Boy*.

[41]Park in London's Westminster, close to Buckingham Palace and Whitehall, the government buildings where Hoare worked for the Home Office.

[42]The Monico Restaurant, now demolished, was located on Shaftesbury Avenue, Westminster. Piccadilly is a station stop in the Underground, or the London subway system.

[43]Hoare was renting rooms at 66 Oakley Street, Chelsea; he would make a more permanent move to 7 Oakley Street. Coleman rented a room across the road from Hoare, at 105 Oakley, and would later move into number 7, living in rooms above Hoare. As described by the Oakley Street Residents' Association: http://www.oakleystreet.org.uk, "Oakley Street was opened up in the 1850s. Lined with Victorian stuccoed residential terraces, it provides a route from the famous shopping area along Kings Road, Chelsea, to the River Thames Embankment and the splendid Albert suspension Bridge (1874)." Chelsea, now an upscale neighbourhood with expensive shops, was in Coleman's day a centre of artistic, intellectual, and bohemian activity.

[44]Coleman and Hoare took the train from London to Moreton, in Gloucestershire, en route to Cutsdean.

In the evening looking at Wyndham Lewis' drawings I saw that they had obscene suggestions, and showed him an unmistakable one of a woman leaning down over a phallus, and he denied it.[45] And he kept on denying this and imagining other things until I was quite angry and burst out venomously against him, saying that it was all of a piece with his sneering about Freud, and that in his smug little world we should have nothing against what the common man believed. This made him furious and he swore at me. And the rest of that evening he would not return to his sweet good nature, but made references to what I had said. I kissed his hand and went to bed.

Saturday, August 20

Yesterday we walked to Ford, through the fields, to the pub.[46] I sent a telegram to John [Holms] that I was coming next week.[47] Think he is disturbed because he thinks Hoare is going to prevent my seeing him. Said I was coming alone, and Peter going to Scotland.[48]

Wednesday, August 24

Peter has looked into Jung and brought forth this: "The return to the real world with erotic impression of officers singing the night watch." [49] He laughed very hard, then shut up the book and said, "Balls" and "Shit." But he keeps on reading it. I said, "Why do you read it?" He said "Because of the interest of reading on sexual matters." He says it's bad because people who get soaked with this kind of stuff transfer their interest from their immediate impressions to the analysis of them, and so lose the habit of immediate impressions. He says it can be all right in the hands of a good mind.

Peter says he feels like a phallic symbol.

---

[45]Wyndham Lewis (1882–1957), Canadian-born English writer, painter, and critic, associated with the avant-garde movement Vorticism. The term was coined by fellow avant-garde figure Ezra Pound in the little magazine which Lewis edited, *Blast*, of which there were only two issues (1914, 1915). Lewis' play *Enemy of the Stars* was included in the 1914 issue, and a new version with four illustrations by Lewis was published in 1932.
[46]Ford is another town in the borough of Cheltenham, Glouchestire.
[47]Coleman accepted Guggenheim's invitation to visit Hayford Hall.
[48]Hoare had relatives in Scotland and much to Coleman's chagrin he often went there to visit them rather than taking trips with her.
[49]As Coleman had been doing earlier in the month, Hoare read from Jung's *Psychology of the Unconscious*, specifically, Section III, "The Hymn of Creation."

This morning received photographs from Deak of himself, and wife on the sands.[50] Wife has fixed French smile, teeth in lips drawn back; Deak handsome and looking vulgar. Sonia said he was not standing straight as he used, and was heavier. These did not move me, as the sight of Deak has always done, because of his letter, which was not written to me at all but to a sort of collective audience observing Deak and spouse.

I told Sonia of what Eric said when I told him about our divorce, [he] listened attentively, then said, "I see; Deak retains poignant memories of you and is glad to have a fat girl to sleep with."[51]

P[eter]. said last night when Sonia was explaining about reading an Italian weekly (she wrote Peter that an Italian weekly had fallen into her hands recently and that she had suffered so much; and he read it meekly) and how the intellectuals suffered under Mussolini — that nineteenth century liberalism was finished, and that this was an age of order.[52] He said one had to accept that, that industrialism was the cause of this — so much organization needed to run it that personal liberty had gone by the board.

We talked about modern people who say they hate every aspect of industrialism, and want the simple life, then take every advantage of it, and love airplanes, and cities. I am not like this. Quite satisfied with the pot in our backhouse.

Sonia washed her hair and came running out with it sticking up and flying. I said, "She looks like an ourang-outan" and she was offended and I told her how Holms said his mouth looked like a balloon and mine looked like a zeppelin. I said to Holms, "What do our mouths betray?" He said, "Mine betrays a lot of evil things, but yours betrays nothing but melancholy lust." S. and Peter nearly died laughing at this. S. said, "That IS funny."

I can't write honestly about Peter because I want to marry him.

Peter told me a little about his childhood, and how he thought everything connected with sex was ugly, and love was something he could know, and none of the rest could have.

Said he wanted to have known me when I was twenty, so he could have formed me, or rather I accused him of this. He doesn't care for my talent, and would prefer me not to have it. This frightens me sometimes. But I'm not much afraid. I need to be loved much more.

---

[50]Henriette Louise Jamme, Deak's second wife.
[51]Eric Siepmann, formerly "Antony."
[52]Benito Mussolini (1883–1945), Italian Prime Minister (1922–1943) with the National Fascist Party.

Thursday, August 25

Last night Peter and I walked up to the top of that hill going to Stanway, and saw the sunset.[53] The sky was very thick with separated clouds, something like yesterday, a sea of yellow and blue. We saw real mountains in the distance. Coming home the sky had changed again, was softer, and the space larger between the clouds. Talked about Wyndham Lewis' article on Joyce, which hit the nail on the head so often that I wondered what was left.[54] Peter says *Ulysses* will live as a literary phenomenon. But if a book is all pastiche, how can it live? It must have some organic life, of its own.

Want to read *Ulysses* again, and get this settled for myself—how much is Joyce a virtuoso? Believe everything Lewis says, but yet there must be something left. But don't know why I feel this, or if it is a residue from my former adoration. What I adored then was not *Ulysses* but the feeling of freedom it gave me.

---

[53] Stanway is in the borough of Tewkesbury, Gloucestershire.
[54] Lewis' article "An analysis of the mind of James Joyce," which focuses on *Ulysses*, was published in Lewis' collection *Time and Western Man* (1927).

Section 2

Devonshire

August 26–September 9, 1932

As the diary continues, Coleman prepared to leave Gloucestershire to visit Peggy Guggenheim at the Hayford Hall estate in Devonshire. Sonia Himmel had passed on the invitation, while Peter Hoare would come down from London for the weekends. During this time Coleman's relationship with Guggenheim became increasingly strained as Guggenheim resented—as much as she facilitated—Coleman's proximity to John Holms. Djuna Barnes, another guest, had come to the baronial manor to work on the manuscript of her novel Nightwood. *Within the heavily sexualized, liquored, and literary atmosphere of the place, Barnes and Coleman were at first reluctant to become friends and supporters of each other's works.*

Friday, August 26

Yesterday afternoon we started to walk to the farm, by way of Toddington, and as we passed there I showed the two walnut trees to Peter and he crushed one of the leaves to make it smell, but it did not smell of walnut.[1] Farther on we saw a little bird sitting on a stone fence, and stalked him, got very close to him, hiding in the grass. It was a winchat. It had a white streak over its eye, barred back, and white spot on wing, breast soft and salmon-coloured.

Sonia went off alone, and Peter and I quarreled—the first time since he came. I could not stand it because he has not made love to me.

I went up and talked with Sonia after tea, and she said she had felt for a long time that Peter did not really want me physically. It went through me like a sword when she said it. I talked to him before we went to bed, and wept, and

---
[1] Scar House farm, where she went last year with Himmel.

he was miserable. I came right out with this, and he said it was not that, that he felt that easily enough. He cannot let himself go if he is not in love. We had a miserable evening, and went to bed sad, and did not sleep. I had horrible dreams all the night of Bianchetti, that I was kind to him, and he aloof. Then he saw that I had money in an envelope, and tried to get it.

The day was grey, a dull heavy mist, and we got up early and got our suitcases down, and Mr. Wiggett came to take Sonia and Peter in the car to Moreton. I am waiting now for him to return, and take me to Cheltenham.

I feel so sad at leaving, and could not bear to part from Sonia. I know that when I get to Devonshire I shall be happy, I shall see John [Holms], and there will be that new country, and the birds. And I know that Peter is coming there.

Just then I was given a telegram, a cable from my father, saying he will land in Plymouth on September 8th![2]

I went to Cheltenham in "Charlie's" car, and sat in the station looking at a movie magazine. It was dirty, and the noise of the trains got terribly on my nerves. I got in the train, which was occupied by a bitchy dark woman with two unpleasant little girls. Changed at Bristol, a horrible city. The country did not move me till we got to Exeter, a rather pleasant town, then after that we went along the sea. I saw hundreds of gulls in the mud. Saw what looked like terns. Along the shore of the sea, dreadful people bathing. Rocky headlands, but full of people, no loneliness. Teignmouth, then I got nervous, thought I was in wrong train. I did not know Newton Abbott was so near the sea.

John met me, coming down the stairs with a vague wandering look, Sindbad with him. Was not moved seeing Sindbad, is too ordinary, like a comic strip boy. Peggy and Djuna in the car. Peggy pretty, Djuna with scarlet lips and perched hat. We went to Torquay to do errands, wretched common resort, only the people were English and looked funny.[3] John sat at a table picking something out of his pocketbook, I saw a letter of mine there, and though I knew it was one I had written Peggy I began to feel excitement— "What if he ever kept a letter of mine like that?" Later John and I had a drink in a great dark musty room of a hotel pub.

Peggy's birthday and I bought her a novelty pin-cushion which was rather a flop. The noise of automobiles and the crowds made me feel sick. Djuna talks through her nose like a sea-horn. I didn't know what to say to her, but finally talked about candy.

---

[2]Plymouth, in the southwest of England (Devonshire), is a major Atlantic port.
[3]Torquay, a resort town on the English Channel, is part of the "English Riviera."

Then we came home, a long drive up through narrow roads overshadowed with ferns. John drove so fast I was sick, and had to talk to them. Then I saw moors, something like Clun Forest.[4] Began to feel pleasant again. We turned into the drive, and stopped before the house. The house is low and white, in Tudor style, surrounded by enormous beeches, and evergreens. A brook runs through the gardens, making a fall at the side of the house.

Pegeen came running out, and I was moved to see her, and hugged her, crying out to her. She stood and looked at me in pleased surprise. Entering the house found great ugly comic living room, like raftered barn. My bedroom shaped like an L, a heavenly shape, the corner with a chair, opening casement windows, the evergreens, a stretch of lawn, and the sound of the brook falling. A lovely little wooden desk, very inconvenient. Low ceiling, yellow walls, the room is lovely.

Living room full of ancestral portraits, generals.

John made a tour of the grounds. The beeches covered with lichen, mountain ash here grows like hawthorn. Tennis court and swimming pool, the latter pleasant and rustic. Grounds have been designed by someone most sympathetic. Half of it is wild and half laid out like Italian garden, but not so formal. Great beeches all covered with moss, every twig. Beyond this semiformal garden the moor.

In the evening Peggy vicious, said at dinner I had written imbecilic letter. This made me wild, having suspected it. Controlled myself, however, thinking, "I'll know another time." When she and Djuna went to bed I burst out and said, "I can't stand Djuna's stupidity or Peggy's malice." John talked patiently, trying to make me see them as they exist, not in a dream.

I said, "I don't know why you live with her." John said I couldn't see anything outside myself.

I said, "I don't call that love," referring to my letter. I had said in it that I knew Peggy would sacrifice for him. John said, "She can't stand it in those terms, you have to write her in her own terms. It is imbecilic." I said, "Then let that be understood: her terms are not my terms." He said, "Peggy would like to have me write, but she only thinks of me as a man." "Very well," I said, "Then let her stop cursing you for not writing." "That doesn't mean anything," he said. "I don't think that's love," I said. He said there are different kinds of love, I said, "Yes, and different degrees."

Lady Into Fox—we started on that, and he said that I could not appreciate that kind of writing; that it did not matter that there was no phrase or

---

[4]Clun Forest is a mountainous region in the county of Shropshire, West Midlands, England. The "moors" are the parklands of Dartmoor, in the county of Devonshire.

paragraph in the book that one could remember, it was the sequence of events that showed the genius.[5]

When we went upstairs, about half past one, I shut my door, then heard screams from Peggy's room. I heard, "You dirty little bitch, you falsify everything. You lie and lie, like a serpent." He kept on talking and talking, and she did not reply, after the screams died down. He said he could not stand her malice and venom.

I knew she had accused him when he came up, and probably had said it was later than it was, and nagged him, and he had hit her. This was a clearing of the air, putting his woman in her place. Tomorrow she would be humane. I thought about John, saying one thing to me, then going in his room and bursting out, and understood of course his pride. I read in bed, a vilely written book called *Wild Nature's Ways* by a man named Kearton, who evidently thinks nothing of putting wooden eggs in nests and spends most of his time telling you how his legs ache.[6]

Saturday, August 27

Maid brought me in a package from Peter, containing a book of Hudson's, *Birds and Man*, typewriter ribbon, and a compact. The compact was to replace the one I lost in my bag, and was emblazoned with a lady's face. I was afraid Sonia chose it. I was moved because Peter had thought of this. Also my money. Since my bag was never recovered, and Father is coming, I will keep the money this time.[7]

But I awoke before this, and looking out my window saw the evergreens, and the reeds, and heard the water rushing. The sun came through in gold bars on the grass. I got right up and bathed and took my opera glasses, and went out of the house.

I stood in the trees back of the house and heard the rooks cawing, hundreds of them above. Then I heard a lovely piercing little song, and saw a robin. He was sitting on a reed. They have thick necks, their heads coming to the neck flat like a German's, round behind, then straight. I went out on the moor.

---

[5] Coleman and Holms discussed *Lady into Fox* (1922), about a man who discovers his wife has turned into a fox. It is the first novel by Bloomsbury Group member David Garnett (1892–1981), English writer, publisher, and critic.
[6] *Wild Nature's Ways* (1903) is by Richard Kearton (1862–1928), English natural history writer and innovator of bird photography.
[7] As indicated throughout the diary, Coleman regularly gave money to those—like Bianchetti—in need.

I was straight away in ecstasy, the dew on the pale heather, and the smell, and the morning sun.

I then sent a wire to my father, saying I would meet him in Plymouth, and bring him here for a day. I will then go somewhere else in Devonshire with him, and we can go to Cornwall. I shall thus be here only two weeks, and I want to enjoy it intensely while I can. The moor gave me that feeling of ecstasy, which comes less and less, and when it does come takes one's heart in a vise of fear.

Wrote to Peter and told him about my father, and asked him to come here soon, and poured out to him whatever I had seen. I wanted him suddenly then, and did not want John [Holms]. I wrote Deak an endless letter, all about our son, and practical doings. I shan't be able to see Johnny now before he goes to school. I feel bewildered, there is so much, and I wanted to see my child.

They all went to pony races, which from what I heard afterwards must have been worth seeing, and I stayed at home and read Hudson's *Land's End*, which John found here.

Tea in the living room, taught the children how to play card tricks. At dinner we got talking about *Zeno*, and John shouted me down, screwing up his face the way he does when he gets impatient, and I got fearfully excited and shouted at him, because I had just read the book. He said something which was not true, a matter of fact. Then seeing Peggy and Djuna bored, I got angry, and kept on talking, more and more excited. Peggy said, "Djuna thinks you're both mad," and that set me off. "I don't care what Djuna thinks." Got into a fearful nervous state, then suddenly saw myself, excited and trembling, and knew that in any minute I might take up a glass and crash it. I held myself, about to weep, kept thinking, "What on earth is all this?" I did not say any more, and remained quiet afterwards in the living room while they were drinking coffee. Finally, when quite calm, joined discussion about the theater, then we got on Dostoyevsky. Djuna had told me to read the *Brothers Karamazov*.[8]

Then Djuna got up and said she was going to bed, and I said, "What's that for?" and she said she was tired, etc., so to make her stay I said, "You're a writer, aren't you? Don't you like to talk about books?" This did not produce the effect I desired, since she believes talking about books to be a pastime of those who do not write. P[eggy]. supported this, instancing John. P[eggy]. said John was a washout, and Djuna agreed. I ought to think this is funny, instead it irritates me.

---

[8]Coleman, Barnes, and Holms talked not only about Dostoyevsky but also about Tolstoy, and playwrights Eugene O'Neill (1888–1953) and Henrik Ibsen (1828–1906).

When they went to bed I burst forth on John, saying, "For two days I have wanted to hit both of them over the head with a cleaver." I listened to what he said.

He said that I did not understand anyone but my own type, that Djuna had no power of analysis, or logical reasoning, and had built up reserves against this knowledge, and hence was bored when books were talked about if they were analyzed. John said Djuna was more sympathetic to him in some ways than I, in spite of stupidity, because she has a developed taste, while mine is still being formed. Like when I came into this living room I experienced horror, while Djuna saw General Prendergast.[9] Said I was just as comic in the country in my way as she is, my tremendous excitement over birds.

I said that I could endure Djuna's quips because I felt there was goodness beneath, but Peggy's malice I simply could not face; he said that temperamentally I had more in common with Peggy.

I said, "What does Djuna think of me?" He said, "She thinks you're mad, and very young, but she thinks you have a talent—not a very large one—and she thinks a talent should be respected." I said, "What does she think of my mind?" He said she might admire it in a vague way, but not practically—i.e., would have no respect for my judgment.

He said Djuna was very conceited, and could not write without thinking she was a very great genius. Said this was due to very great inferiority complex underneath.

Robin now singing out in the reeds, and I must stop this, which has worn me out, and go and look at birds. I know what I feel about nature. The ecstasy that Wordsworth had was a <u>memory</u>; mine is a living thing.

Sunday, August 28

Took a long walk over the moor, the children, Djuna, Peggy, John. The heather sweet and beautiful, we lay down in it. Walked over and up to hut circles, of stone.

At dinner I told John about Hoare, why I was angry with him, and why went to London. They were much disturbed, and John said, "I'm really afraid he's not the right one." Djuna said I ought to avoid him as if he were the plague.

All agreed that it does not sound as though things could come right.

---

[9]Guggenheim rented Hayford Hall from Arthur and Margaret Prendergast, who owned the estate from 1912–56; Arthur's father, Sir Henry Prendergast, had been a general in Burma (see Podnieks and Chait, *Hayford Hall*, 25–26). Recall Coleman's description of the livingroom as being "full of ancestral portraits, generals" (August 26, 1932).

John was so disturbed that it cast a deep gloom over me. He said, "I'm afraid, even if you did fall in love, that he might have a brief renascence, and then turn into a dried up little old bachelor." I said, "That is what I fear; and if that is so, what am I going to do?" They said I was in love with him, but I denied it. John said, "You have put too much pains and patience into it to be able to give it up." Talking about Hoare gave such an impression of him. I said to Peggy, "Remember what he is like. Djuna, not knowing him, thought he was the fiend. Sweet, gentle little Peter, who would not hurt anyone. Peggy said, "What would he be like with Djuna?" He would treat her so well that she would think he admired her, then he would say to me, "That awful woman." Djuna said she wanted men to be polite. I was cast down by this, and terrified.

I said to Djuna, "You think women are noble creatures, put upon," and Peggy said she certainly thought she was.

Djuna said she could not stand a man who was not weaker than she, I the opposite. She said men could not stand it if you were superior to them, John said men loved Dorothy, then ran from her in fear. He said men were afraid of Dorothy because of her intensity. Said men fell in love with Kay because of her vitality, that Hoare and Alex Small were this type, who loved a woman for her vitality and not for her body, but would die for this as if it were the body.[10] Said I was partly like Dorothy and part like Kay, but he was lying, he thinks I am like Kay.

I said to Djuna, "Why do you hate men?" to make her laugh and perhaps answer it, and she said she did not, etc. Much later in the evening, when we were talking about something else, one of us disagreed with her about some man and she said, off her guard, "But, my dear, I hold no brief for men, I'd just as soon stick one of them with a poker as another." Djuna said she woke up laughing at my efforts to keep her from going to bed last night. As a last resort I hurled at her, earnestly, "Introvert."

Then we kept on drinking, and got very drunk, and talked about Djuna's writing. I said, "You have something to say, and don't say it." She said there was so much of Dan Mahoney in her book.[11] I said, "*Ryder* had no courage,

---

[10] Kay Boyle (1902–92) was an American expatriate novelist, poet, short story writer, translator, editor, and political activist whose early work was published, like Coleman's, in little magazines like *This Quarter* and *transition*. Having met Laurence Vail in 1928 when he was married to Guggenheim, Boyle later became Vail's second wife (1932–43) (Guggenheim was her matron of honour); the couple had three children. Note this first reference to Alex Small, formerly "Lysander."

[11] Daniel A. Mahoney (late 1880s–1959) was an Irish-American who, though not a qualified doctor, sometimes practiced as one on the Left Bank, especially performing abortions. Barnes' book referred to by Coleman is *Nightwood*, which Barnes was working on while at Hayford

you were afraid. I may have written an idiotic letter, but what I said was truth."[12] (Wrote her a wild letter 3 years ago, about *Ryder*.) I said, "What are you writing about Dan Mahoney for, he doesn't concern you, you should write about Thelma."[13] She said she had written about Thelma in this book, and wept every time she read it, and could not face Thelma's reading it. John and I said, "Do you think Emily Brontë thought what someone would think?" Djuna said Emily Brontë was like God, like Shakespeare and the Bible, and I got pretty mad, and said, "That's Americans; they must put on a pedestal [*sic*]." John said, "That isn't the way to talk to Djuna," but it was the truth. She kept saying, "No one can ever approach Emily Brontë," I said, "For God's sake, why not?" Djuna said she was more conceited about her work than I could imagine, I told her she did not think enough of herself. She said, "I think only two women have written books worth reading, Emily Brontë and myself." I said, "Even at that, you don't think enough of yourself."

Americans do not know what genius is, they talk about themselves in this way, yet expect nothing of themselves. I said, "I think as much of Emily Brontë as you do, yet I know that if I live I will write something just as good. What about Dorothy Wordsworth?" I said, "And other women? Do you think they had no talent? This one happened to get it out. You and I can get ours out as she could not." But this isn't the end of the problem: if a woman with Djuna's natural talent wants men weaker than herself it means she is not a woman. But Djuna is a woman, that's the curse of it, completely, through and through.

Then I got mad at something John said and rushed upstairs to bed, listened at the door, but heard no word of me. They got talking about *Ryder*, and I could not bear it, so after about 15 minutes went back down again. Then she got up and went upstairs to get *Ryder*, to read it. I cannot be read to, whether Shakespeare, Donne or Dante, and went sound asleep. John took it away from her, and read some. He was in a stiff pickle, she loves the book so, and will not hear one word. She read a lot, I didn't hear it, then John said one part moved him. She was very tight indeed (before this she had wept a little—about Thelma—and I had squeezed her hand and almost wept myself.)

Hall (published 1936). Mahoney was the basis for one of the novel's protagonists, the transvestite Matthew O'Connor, who falsely assumed the title of Doctor.

[12]*Ryder* (1928) is Barnes' Elizabethan *sui generis* satire of a patriarchal family. Correspondence from Coleman to Barnes in the Djuna Barnes Papers, Special Collections, University of Maryland Libraries begins in April 1934, and thus the "wild letter" referenced here is not extant.

[13]Thelma Ellen Wood (1901–70), American expatriate silverpoint artist, was the lover of Barnes from 1921–28, at which point Wood left her for the wealthy Henriette McCrea Metcalf (1888–1981). Barnes continued to carry a torch for Wood, depicting their intense relationship in *Nightwood*: Wood is cast as protagonist Robin Vote; Metcalf as the "Squatter" Jenny Petherbridge.

She cared so much what John thinks, it all came out. She pretends to despise him. At the end she wept and clung to John.

I came up and went into Peggy's room, Peggy sitting up in bed reading, furious. John came in and sat on the bed cheerfully, talking about Djuna. Peggy did not notice him. It was four o'clock. He said, "I couldn't bear it, it was so pathetic." She said, "You're pathetic" and began reading again. He told the whole story, and said, "I felt so sorry for her. She read me the part about Charles.[14] She was in love with that boy. It is vile writing. I felt so sorry for her I wept, and she thought I was moved by the writing, and clung to me. I kissed her. I didn't know what to do."

"You seemed to know what to do," said Peggy.

She kept on reading and wouldn't notice him and he, feeling cheerful, kept on talking. Peggy said she had listened at the door when she came up, and had heard things about herself. She said, "There was nothing bad." John said, "Look how melancholy she is." I wondered how she had heard nothing bad, since Djuna said she was ugly, and that John was a pimp.

Monday, August 29

Wakened by the maid, feeling horrible, about eight o'clock, with letters.[15] Madame Donn telling me how my child fought with Sonia's.

John and Djuna came in my room, both with dreadful hangovers. They kept pacing up and down on different sides. Djuna crawled along. She said she had been a fool, and asked me everything she did, and said, "What did you think of my book?" I said, "I didn't hear one word of it, I can't be read to. And you wouldn't let me take it." I said, "We made you get the book, you didn't force it on us." She said, "I generally do."

When she went out, to get a prairie oyster, John said rapidly that for two weeks before I came they had not been able to speak, since she wanted him to make her gay, and he could not come out of himself.[16] He said when left alone, each would get up and leave, out of embarrassment. He said, "She

---

[14]Charles Henri Ford (1908/9, or 1913 as he claimed-2002), American writer, photographer, filmmaker, and editor of avant-garde journals such as *Blues: A Magazine of New Rhythms*, subtitled *A Bisexual Bimonthly* (1929) and the surrealist *View* (1940–47). Barnes began a relationship with him in Greenwich Village in spring 1931 (she was 39, he was 21); it would last, with interruptions, until 1933. Barnes wrote a first version of *Nightwood* followed by a second version in many drafts, and in the original had written about Ford.

[15]Guggenheim had brought with her to the estate her own maid, Madeleine; cook, Marie; and nanny, Doris.

[16]A prairie oyster is a drink composed of raw egg yolk, Worcestershire sauce, and other seasonings taken to alleviate a hangover.

didn't want to come here, didn't think it was beautiful, she wants a social life, and be amused. She groused perpetually when she came." John said she lives alone in that flat and does not see a soul, when coming away wanted something like going to the Lido.[17] John said, "I am in the soup, since she told Peggy this morning, 'John was RAVING about my book.'" I told him how she had said to me that she wanted a man weaker than herself, and he said, "That's the dreadful thing about women artists. They have to be admired." (Since, of course, they are not sure of themselves.) I told him how I had been that way, right up until meeting Hoare. When Hoare did not like my poems I didn't care. I had previously had no interest in a man who didn't. He said, "That's what makes me think you may not write." I sat up in bed excited and said, "I've thought of this a great deal; and I know that I have to be a woman. But I think the other part will sometime push through again. Then I'll be left with nothing."

Djuna came to see me again, and talked, eating a pear, then said later "I'm going to shoot my pear" (feeling sick), and John thought that was a slang expression for vomiting. (He did not know she had eaten a pear.)

It rained all day, and I saw the rain and the trees, and felt quite content, here in bed. I was menstruating, and did not want to get up, it gave me a plausible excuse. All day I've been sitting here, reading Hudson (*Birds and Man*) and seeing the rain. When John was in here he saw a pied wagtail out on the grass, near the stream.

This morning John said I drove him to talking the other night, when he wanted to go to bed, absolutely drove him with questions, then when he began to answer them I went to sleep. I said, "To tell you the truth I don't live on anything now but passionate sexual hope." Djuna said, "What?" and John said, "That's bad." "I read all the time now," I said, "To keep my mind occupied.

John said Djuna needed love, just as I do, and it made him unhappy. He likes her very much. He said she has never been emotionally honest about anything. Her courage is wonderful, in life, but in her art she's a coward. She just sits at home and pours it out. He said he had got very bored before I came, because she will tell long stories, beginning, "I know I'm stupid," but the moral always is that she's a noble woman.

Djuna came in to see me at tea-time, and I had been asleep and could not get my mind focused. She said, "Do you want this Hoare?" and I said I had fallen in love with him before. She said "Do you think you can fall in love

---

[17]Barnes had been living in her apartment at 9, rue St.-Romain, on the Left Bank. The Lido is the strip of land separating Venice from the Adriatic Sea, famous for its beach and hotels such as the Grand Hotel Excelsior and the Grand Hotel des Bains.

with the same person twice?" then I said very seriously, in a ponderous earnest way, "I was in love all my life, like a child. And last year I fell in love for the first time, as a woman does. Now I can't feel anything." She looked uneasy and went out.

Tuesday, August 30

Last night we had an English dinner, steak and kidney pie, hard boiled potatoes, boiled cabbage, and Welsh rabbit. Horrible. I got up for dinner, and played Voi Che Sapete and the slow movement from the Surprise Symphony before dinner.[18] Walked around the room getting a kick from these.

 After dinner John said that if he felt about his father as I do about mine he would not be able to be with him for three weeks without telling him the truth about my life. This touched me right on the core. "If your sister lived with a man she wasn't married to," I said, "Your father would disown her, with all sorts of gestures. And he might be hurt a little in his heart. But if my father knew this about me," I said, "He would kill himself."[19]

 John said he couldn't help thinking that if I told him the truth there would be terrible suffering for a little, and that then he would accept it. I said he had already accepted everything that had come to him, but nothing like this had ever existed even in his faintest imagination, and that he was incapable of coping with it. Admitted my feeling for him was neurotic, and that if I were to follow my own convenience I would come right out with it, and let the chips fall. Find it most uncomfortable to talk to him, or write to him, on this dishonest plane. Told John how I lied to him in Naples about Bianchetti, and what a terror it put me in. Said if my father knew a little about the world, knew that people in an emotional crisis have got to lie, whatever their natural character, I might dare to tell him the truth. I said I should have begun telling him the truth when I was first married, when I first began to have ideas away from his. I remember how I went to him, when I had first known Deak, and said, "What's this? What you've taught me about life isn't true," and he was furiously angry and said, "Any young man that talks to a woman about sex before he married her is a cad," and got so excited that I could tell him nothing more. I half believed him then, I was afraid it was so, and I could not resist him, as I could now, with consciousness of right behind me. And as I loved Deak, I went over to what Deak believed, and hated my father.

---

[18]"Voi Che Sapete" is from Mozart's opera *The Marriage of Figaro* (1786). The "Surprise Symphony" is Haydn's Symphony No. 94 (1792).
[19]Coleman was not living with Hoare; rather, her statement reflects the promiscuous lifestyle she had been leading since coming to Europe.

I did not love my father for a long time after I was married. The relation we have now began after he first came to Europe. Even the first time he came, in 1928, I didn't love him; it began the second time, the summer in London.[20] Then my old feeling came back to me. I knew enough about life by then to understand him again.

Peggy and Djuna went to bed, and John stayed up a while, and got talking excitedly.

While John was talking, and I listening, Peggy came down. I had felt such a bond with him, like (though much less in intensity) the night in St. Jean de Luz when I read his sister's poem. He stopped, and Peggy sat down in front of the fire. She looked so small and pathetic that I could not hate her, as I used to do. We talked about Djuna to her, and I asked about Thelma. Peggy said Thelma made her think of pale, dead flesh, but Djuna thought her paleness was of life. John said the obvious thing about Thelma was sexual vitality, but that other people had told him she was just a strapping, fucking wench.

John said that Djuna did not even know what "public school" meant in England, and thought he was just a little upstart who wanted Peggy's money. "She loves this kind of thing, this house, and what it stands for, but she doesn't know this was my life before." I laughed inside at this, he <u>cannot</u> get away from that.

Peggy would not go to bed, came down to annoy John. He wanted to go, and she sat there, with a candle. I said this was like her fussing for three years about marrying him, then when he wanted to, she refused.

We talked about Djuna's lack of subtlety, that is why she can't get *Zeno*, and also why she does not know Peggy's wit. I said I could not laugh at Djuna's kind of wit, except rarely, not laugh with all my soul, whereas Peggy makes me feel delighted through and through. Peggy is witty because she isn't trying, she has the gift, and does not think of any audience. Djuna has the gift but is always talking to an audience. And as she does not distinguish in people, her imaginary audience is not a subtle one. Peggy is not subtle consciously.

John said that Djuna thought Thelma was the great sexual treat of the world.

In the morning I had a wire from Father, and a note from Bianchetti. He is back in Paris, and I think he has left his room in Brussels, unpaid, and all his things there. I have this <u>always</u> on my mind. It is like a stone that never leaves my breast.

In the morning I went out in the gardens here, which seem more lovely to me every day.

I went up on the moor with John and Sindbad, who were riding. Breaking out of the trees suddenly, there was the full sky, sweeping blue in the bright sun. The heavy clouds were suspended above the horizon. The moor glittered

---

[20]In 1929.

under the drops of dew. I lay down in the heather, and smelled the earth, and smelled the heavenly dew. I shall never forget that burst of sky, coming out of the dark trees, which surround the house, as though God were revealed suddenly in the sun.

I got on John's horse after he was through, and walked about, but could not get him to trot, and if I could, it would be painful for me, since I have not ridden for so long. I did not have on breeches, and my bare thighs worried me, since the groom was looking at them, and I knew John was nervous, being in England.

In the afternoon we went in the car to a cove some distance from here. Reached a farm, then all got out and began to walk down. Could see cliffs, and the sea, about a mile. When we got to the sea found the cove full of people. It was such a heavenly spot, and John had taken so much trouble finding it. The children undressed to bathe, and John and I went to climb a cliff.

Picked some wild thyme coming home, and kept smelling it. Held Pegeen in my lap, and felt her hair against my lips, and wished for a baby again, holding her when she fell asleep.

Wednesday, August 31

The sun is shining through the trees outside my window, on the reeds in the water below. This is the most beautiful place I have ever been in.

Last night Peggy and I had a terrible quarrel, and I don't know what I'm going to do. She does not want me to remain. She lay there lying by the fire and thought up things to say. She thought of enough to say to me so that I don't know just where to move next.

Apparently it began because I said it was too bad she interrupted John last night, but I was friendly, and said it in a friendly way, a propos of something she had said. The when I saw she was angry I retreated, and said I did not blame her for wanting John to come to bed.

But it was too late now, and much truth came out, some of which was that she had not wanted me to come.

John talked a long while to her, he said she wanted trouble, and was not contented till she'd made it. He said people acted from a multitude of motives, but she selected one, and made out that was all. She said she wanted me to leave.

I said, "Why did you invite me here?" She said, "For Djuna." I said, "How did you dare invite me, when you knew I'd have to go?" She said I couldn't get a man of my own and hung around hers. I said, "I was happy where I was. Why did you ask me here?" John was much excited and said that Peggy was fond of me, and knew it, and that now she wanted to make trouble. I said, "What do you think of yourself for not replying to my letter from London, in which I apologized with all the feeling a human being could for hurting you?" I said I had thrown the bottle at her for what I suffered last winter.[21] I said my so-called imbecilic letter had been written in the conception that she had an unselfish feeling for John. I said, "I know you haven't now; and I shan't write that way again." She said she didn't care so much for me since I had written these letters. She said she couldn't be friends with me.

I said I could never be friends with her, as I was with Sonia, but I was very fond of her. She said she didn't want me as a friend, that I was too egotistical and besides had nothing in common with her. John said we had a great deal in common, that everyone hated some things in people they liked.

So this went on, I saying very little in the course of time, but boiling. She said John had no friend but me, and needed me to make any contacts, and I "had better have him." John said he needed me to make contacts with Americans, this was true.

I suddenly came upstairs, when they put on some music. John played 127, to calm me down, and played something else I love.[22] I heard it through the door. I went to sleep on the bed, feeling miserable. Peggy had gotten amiable again, before I went away, and had said, "I apologize for ordering you out of my house." I didn't say anything.

John said, "I don't see how women can do that—hysterics and say what they don't mean—then forget it the next minute." I said, "I meant everything I said."

I can't go away from here because Father is coming to Plymouth, and I'd have nowhere to go. I want to go today. I want to get out of this, and let John manage it as he may.

I went out in the garden, and lay down on the grass.

I came to lunch, but did not speak to anyone, and then came to my room. I did not want to sulk, but could not speak. When I went to the bathroom I heard Peggy shouting up through the door: "It's gone on for four years, and I've had enough of it." John was protesting in reply.

I feel as if I could stab Peggy through the heart when she looks at me with hate. It's because I fear her, she has a heart like rock. She is untouchable in that mood, and being terrified I want to kill her.

---

[21]Coleman was likely referring to what she had "suffered" in her relationship with Bianchetti. This bottle throwing incident is unrecorded until this entry.
[22]Beethoven's string quartet No. 12 in E flat major, Opus 127.

She pretends she does not like me, because it's easier. Our relation is so complicated with love and hate that it's easier for her to pretend it's hate. I am just as stupid because I pretend all the time it's love.

Went out on the moor, walked up to the scraggly beech trees, all blown one way, where I went the first morning, and saw the plovers.

At dinner I sat feeling sorry for myself. Didn't speak to anyone the whole meal. When John asked me before dinner if I had gone out on the moor I almost wept in replying.

Spectacle of me sitting solemn and about to burst into tears in the midst of Peggy's and Djuna's witticisms.

Drank a great deal of wine, and after dinner could not face going upstairs alone again, so sat by the fire, and read Hudson. Very shortly was in a sort of coma, reading, did not know others were there. Finally, almost asleep, went up to bed.

Thursday, September 1

This morning I got a letter from Peter, and I read it and wept violently into the bed.

I had said in my letter that I was no longer going to destroy what he was trying to build. I knew this was stupid as soon as I had sent it. I write things like this in a coma of hopeful lying. He set me right about that.

Peggy came suddenly into my room, and said she was sorry for what she said, and that they did not want me to sit like a stone all day. I said, "I can't stay here if you don't want me; I'd have gone yesterday." She put her arms around me, and I proceeded to weep.

John came in and the conversation turned on their marrying. Peggy said she wouldn't do it because if she did she'd feel she was lost.

John said Djuna was a stupid woman who liked to feel that women were abused. I explained my letter from Moreton, which had so enraged Peggy. She said she wanted me to keep out of her life with John. I said, "How can I, when you drag me in?" She did not know that the letter was written because I was afraid she thought I did not know she appreciated John. What she feels about John I don't know—mainly jealousy for that part of him which she can't share.

I said to John, "It's largely your fault; she thinks of me as an appendage of you. You could destroy that notion." John threw up his hands and said, "All the illusions that I could destroy!" He said that Peggy told him the same about me.

Then we talked about them, because John said, "Think of the things she says to me," and I said, "That doesn't concern me; you love each other, and must know where you stand." "We don't love each other," said Peggy. John said he did not know why she kept saying this. She said, "Because we have no right kind of a life." He said, "Then do let's marry and have it." She said she wouldn't dream of it.

I said, "Why?" and she said she did not dare. She said, "I'm interested in children and you're interested in intellectual things." He quite rightly said Balls to that.

The truth is that Peggy is <u>afraid</u> to marry him. She wanted it for so long, and made his life a hell. Now that's over, she can have it if she wants it. And that attained, she has begun to think, "What will it really be?" and is afraid.

I told Peggy I understood her as I never did in St. Jean de Luz. (She said, "We've always fought; why do you take it seriously now?"). I said I only cared for John then.

I'll never forget what jealousy is.[23] I have learned that as I have never learned anything in my life. I may never have that again; if I live with Hoare I'll never have it. But those few months, that horror and agony. I'll never forget the murder feeling, stronger than the love. I had to keep this out of the love, keep them apart, and still. Or I'd have killed him, I didn't love him wholly, and wanted to kill him.

If I have loved him enough, I wouldn't have felt like that. The body was all I had, and the love of the body is the devil.

Friday, September 2

At lunch talking about the dance the night before. Madeleine and Doris were the belles.[24]

Talking about the black dog, who farts. Peggy said she could not have him in the dining room. John said he should think he would work it off dashing about the moor, but Djuna said that just shook him up for the house. "He effervesces at lunch." She said he was the wind-working wonder of Dartmoor. Peggy said he got more and more intimate with you, you couldn't give him an inch. She said to Djuna, "He'll suddenly appear in your nightgown." While Djuna was talking the dog came and lay down and put his head on her leg, and then when Peggy began he got up and stood with his head near her face, and began to shake his ears, which made him smell. She said, "Good God!" and rang for him to be taken out; then at dinner when we mentioned him again, he farted.

---

[23]Coleman was recalling the bitter jealousy she felt during her relationship with Bianchetti.
[24]Guggenheim's maid, Madeleine, and nanny, Doris, had attended a local dance.

Liver and crisp bacon for dinner and peas. I do eat so much. I was helping myself freely, saying, "I don't want to be a pig." Peggy said, "What are you going to do instead?" and we all laughed, and she didn't know why.

Began talking to Djuna about the famous letter I sent her in 1929, and I said all of it was true.[25] We had been talking about Chaucer. She described meeting me at the Deux Magots and said I asked her if she didn't pace the floor and think about Keats. I denied this, but John said, "That was your state of mind." We read the handwriting of several of Djuna's friends, one horrible one, Natalie Barney; and Victor Cunard's very unsympathetic.[26] Djuna's own was the best. Then we talked about men beating women and Djuna got off a lot of balls. First she says she wants men to be gallant, and recalls the troubadours, then busts out in a 20th century yowl. We talked about the sizes of men's penises in an embarrassed sort of way. Djuna spoke of her father in a very vulgar way and terrified me.[27]

Then they clamoured for the diary, since it was raining, and we had had tea, and the children had messed up the floor with cooking utensils. Peggy was bored and wanted me to read the diary. So I got it, thinking it would not go off well, and began reading it. The one written in Paris in 1929. "Goethe is I and I am he. He had a better mind, and a better education." From this opening sentence, until I stopped exhausted, at time for dinner, they sat and roared, and screamed, and howled with laughter, they doubled up and shrieked, until I was worn and Peggy had to go to the lavatory,

---

[25]This letter is not extant.

[26]Natalie Clifford Barney (1876–1972), poet, novelist, and playwright, was a wealthy American expatriate who in 1909 established at her Left Bank house on 20, rue Jacob, what would become one of the most famous and enduring salons of the century. Designed especially to support a Sapphic as well as modernist culture, the salon attracted artistic and intellectual figures such as Barnes, Guggenheim, Mina Loy, Janet Flanner, Gertrude Stein, Alice B. Toklas, T. S. Eliot, James Joyce, Nancy Cunard, Colette, Ford Madox Ford, Jean Cocteau, Sylvia Beach, F. Scott and Zelda Fitzgerald, Hart Crane, among countless others. Victor Cunard (1898–1960) was a correspondent for the *London Times* in Venice. Barnes biographer Phillip Herring describes how Cunard helped Barnes prior to her coming to Devon: "Barnes's decision to leave Paris for Hayford Hall was precipitated by a frightening attack of asthma at 5:00 A.M., which, as described to Natalie Barney, caused her hair to stand on end and her heart to pound in her chest. She took a taxi to her friend Victor Cunard, who got her coffee, held her hand, and sent his servant for their medical friend Dan Mahoney. Apparently the attack was not serious, but Guggenheim suggested that Barnes pack a bag and go with her to England" (191). Cunard was the cousin of Nancy Cunard (1896–1965), daughter of Sir Bache Cunard, heir to the Cunard shipping line. She was a poet, founded the Hours Press (in 1927 in Reanville, outside Paris), and became a political activist especially engaged in civil rights issues and in championing literature by Black writers.

[27]For Barnes' complex relationship with her father, see Coleman's entry for June 12, 1936, and accompanying notes.

because it had made her bowels work. I did not read all of it, only the comic parts.

I have never seen people laugh so much. I laughed so hard myself that I ached sitting in my chair. I read them more after dinner, and finally had to close for the night. Djuna went to bed before I stopped. She said it reminded her of Harry Kemp.[28]

Peggy was sitting knitting a green shirt for Sindbad's lamb, and when the parts came in about her she would throw up the knitting needles and open her mouth and show all her teeth and scream. John sat doubled up on the lounge, and he would hug himself with his arms and roll about the couch. Djuna sat and laughed as if it pained her face. God knows what she thought of me for this. John said there was far too much of this in her when she was young, and she had never admitted it.

I stopped reading it, because I got tired, and we had to go to bed. John said that some of these sentences were as good as anything he had ever heard in his life. I was much piqued by their interest, but I laughed so hard myself that I didn't get much chance to reflect on whether it was really good.

Peggy kept hoping for digs, and yet it came out that I was very fond of her then. In one place I got so complimentary that she actually looked embarrassed. The funniest parts could not be quoted out of their context; it was the character which was created in the diary, such a funny one. Like Shelley gone completely mad. This poor girl, whom I had made love to, hanging about, miserable, and I "cheering" her by telling her for God's sake to get in another state of mind, and offering her some of my books.[29]

When I read the part about Peggy meeting Eric Siepmann, that raucous evening, and John's conversation, and Peggy's hoarse remarks; "She got these opinions from John and he smiled fatuously while she uttered them";[30] I thought they would split their sides.

I didn't read any of the parts about Dorothy. When it got to the evening John came back from London, I stopped.[31] Naturally, Peggy wanted to see this, but I didn't want Djuna to hear it. I didn't want Peggy to see it either as I was afraid it would stir her up again.

The refrain that month seemed to be that Agamemnon was ruled by women, and that I had to snatch what pearls I could. Peggy said he came out badly in this, he really does, he looks like a dreadfully smug and

---

[28]Sometimes referred to as the "tramp poet," Harry Kemp (1883–1960) was an American poet and playwright who worked with the Provincetown Players.
[29]Percy Bysshe Shelley (1792-1822), English Romantic poet. "This poor girl" was "Judith."
[30]See her entry for November 9, 1929.
[31]See her entries for December 5 and 6, 1929.

conceited moralist. That's because I made him seem that way. I said, "If Peggy had written a diary then we'd have heard a different story." Peggy said she came out magnificently, it set her up a good deal, though she was disappointed there weren't a few malicious cracks. I said that when John came it didn't thrill me like a man, it was like seeing a long-wanted book on the shelf.

John looked thoughtful during some of this, and embarrassed; I think it made him feel ridiculous. Every <u>single</u> word he had said for a month taken down, and all of them moral and admonitory. But I loved this so, the whole diary breathes my passion for what I got from him.

Know how to get on with Djuna, play up to her a little, make her think she knows something. She thinks I'm quite mad. "Goofy, but interesting." She also thinks I'm sweet.

John told Peggy I was more fond of her than Djuna, which is naturally true, but Peggy likes the "female alliance." I have never had such a queer connection with anybody; neither of us says a word, and we don't get along so much of the time. But it's emotional, so that what each of us says hurts. I'm really afraid of her, for I can't tell what she feels.

John's life is such a vacuous pursuit of peace, he can't find it, and is so restless. His only anchor is Peggy, and if she breaks off from him I don't know what he'll do.

Saturday, September 3

Talking at lunch about the English maids, who can't stay out after ten o'clock and have to report within ten minutes after they come in at night.[32] P[eggy]. said it was lucky John didn't have to report ten minutes after <u>he</u> came in. To-do about Djuna interviewing Lady Astor, someone cabled her from America to do it, Djuna sat trying to think of telegrams, looking more and more like a small bull-dog.[33] She could not think of a thing. We all assisted, Holms pretending to know, getting American journalism and English manners

---

[32]In a paragraph from her September 2, 1932 entry (F. 629, not transcribed), Coleman noted that in addition to Guggenheim's French maid, the guests at Hayford Hall were served by "Ena, the Devon maid" who reported to "Jessie," both of whom worked for the estate's owner, Mrs. Prendergast.

[33]Nancy Witcher Astor, Viscountess Astor (1879–1964), American-born British politician and hostess. On December 1, 1919, she became the first woman to win a seat in the British Parliament. In London in 1926, Goldman had sought her help as Goldman worked to aid political prisoners, especially women, in Russia. Barnes, who supported herself through her journalism, had an established reputation as an interviewer. For details on this aspect of her career see chapter 4 in Herring's biography, as well as *Interviews*, edited by Alyce Barry (1985).

112 Section 2

inextricably confused. I began to read *Lorenzo in Taos*, a dreadful book on D.H. Lawrence.[34]

Asked Djuna what Mabel Dodge Sterne, the author of this book, was like, since she knew her in New York.[35] Djuna said she was very arty when art was on, and brainy when the brains were on, and that now she supposed she was very Indian.[36] "She knew just whom to talk to," said Djuna, "And what to say. Look at pictures and have a brief ecstasy."

In the evening we got rather tight and talked about John. Djuna really believes she is more intelligent than he. I was gasping.

Djuna said a little truth, goaded by me. She was sitting on the couch. Peggy was by John. Peggy said, "What do I care what his genius is, it does me no good? He doesn't use it." She said my diary had shown him up. I said, "It isn't that he's an encyclopedia, it's the sense of life he gives one." Peggy said, "He gives me a sense of death." Djuna said he did her too.

I said, "I can understand Peggy, since she lives with him, but how can you, a creative person, not see what is in John?" He was embarrassed and bored and kept trying to change the conversation, not that he didn't want to talk about himself (which was manna to him) but because he knew he appeared like such a fool to Djuna. He said, "That's the truth, for Djuna," but I was puzzled, and kept probing her. I said, "Do you really mean to say you don't distinguish between John and Courtenay Lemon?" (Her husband.)[37] She said, "They're just the same." I said, "Good God!" and John laughed very hard and said, "Well, there you are." When driven to it finally he told Djuna that it was bad in her that she couldn't stand criticism of her writing, and also that she couldn't write about herself. He told her, very gently, that she was far too unconscious of herself.

Djuna spoke rather heatedly of John's having no talent, and this roused me to shout, "How do you speak with such authority when you haven't read

---

[34]*Lorenzo in Taos* (1932) is by Mabel (Dodge Sterne) Luhan (1879–1962), American patron, journalist, and author. It is her account of the time in the early 1920s when D. H. Lawrence and wife, Frieda von Richthofen Lawrence (1879–1956), lived on her New Mexico ranch, Los Gallos, and includes letters to Luhan from D. H. Lawrence. Frieda's memoir of Lawrence, *Not I, But the Wind*, was published in 1934.

[35]In 1914, Barnes had taken some of her paintings to show at Luhan's salon at 23 Fifth Avenue in Greenwich Village. Emma Goldman had also attended the salon that year.

[36]After Mabel Dodge Sterne married a Pueblo Indian, Antonio (Tony) Luhan, in 1923, she took up Indian causes such as land reform, and she supported artists—such as Lawrence—who promoted the Taos region and Indian culture.

[37]Between 1917 and 1919, Barnes lived in Greenwich Village with Courtenay Lemon, a socialist intellectual, philosopher, and journalist, whom she considered her common-law husband.

a word he's written?" I said, "Do you know what people in London thought of him?"

John with three women fighting about him, an ideal moment for him, except that both P[eggy]. and Djuna thought he was a fool. P. admitted that he had "cleared up her ideas." She said, "He's told me a lot of things I want to know, but my he tries to pile a lot on that I don't want." She said she went to sleep when she first knew him. Djuna said, "I was glad to see he hadn't got you buffaloed." I said, "Go to it! Damn the men, they're all beasts!"

Djuna said it bored her always to discuss John and Peggy's affairs. I said, "I encourage them." She said I would like to talk to Natalie Barney. I said, "That horror. Good God!" Djuna said she was one of her best friends. I said, "It's definitely something bad in you that you call a woman like that one of your best friends." "What's the matter with her?" "She's a giddy gadder," I said. "She's false, through and through." John said it took a certain kind of talent to be able to play up to so many different sophisticated kinds of groups as Natalie Barney did. I said to Djuna, "You're so true. How can you endure such people as friends?"

It was all very comic, I in my best infuriated baby style, and Djuna really roused. John enjoyed himself.

P[eggy]. said John was the most intelligent man she knew, but that he had no talent. Djuna said she had met several men with the same brains.

John said our friends are those who think as much of us as we do ourselves. He said I was the only friend he had made in the last 10 years. I wouldn't talk to him, except this minute, because I hate so having to take scraps of him— just like Mable Dodge Luhan. I sat and read and he finally went to bed. He was wandering about, explaining how he loves to get tight and feel gay, and how much he wants a man. I've heard this so much I didn't listen.

I think he made love to Peggy because today she was quite changed. That's what the trouble is. He was a lover before he became a ghost.

Continuing with the to-do about Lady Astor. Djuna finally got her on the telephone and L.A. was at the hospital, seeing some dear one operated. Think Dj. has given it up. Felt sorry for her since she needs this money. I said to John, "I don't see how Peggy can have begun to give her money and then stop."[38] He said Peggy was giving her more. This made me feel better. I wanted to talk about my father and Hoare, Peggy wanted to talk about

---

[38] Guggenheim had been giving Barnes forty dollars a month; Coleman consistently pressured Guggenheim to continue her financial support of Barnes, which she did, though often begrudgingly.

Peggy Deutchbein, and Djuna wanted to talk about Victor Cunard[39] John had to give assistance on cables and letters, and correct Peggy's letter to Peggy Deutchbein. A good morning for him.

After we had got Lady Astor settled, Dj. went down to Buckfastleigh with Doris to mail the letter, and J. and P. and the children went out on the moor. Third day of rain. I wouldn't go. John stood on the hearth-stone and urged me to go, P. very sweet in red and yellow, looking efficient. John stood and explained to me that my brain was in a fog because I never went outdoors. Dj. said, "If only we could lay it to that." John was determined to get me out. I said I preferred to go alone to the moor. He said my whole life was wrong because I sat and sat.

Djuna thinks, according to John, that I am the most naïve person she has ever met, and have no brains.

Talking about people reading letters, since I left all mine down here last night, and then came down in the morning and said to Djuna, "Here are all my letters; I bet Peggy read them." Dj. was shocked, but I said, "Why not? She'd admit it." John said he wouldn't read any ordinary letter lying about because he wouldn't be interested, I said I would read any letter if I thought it had something about me in it. I said to Peggy, "If I'd been in your place I'd have never rested till I'd read those letters of Dorothy."[40] She said, "And I've never rested since."

I prattled to amuse them, getting tired of this. P. and J. came back from the moor worn out in fact so much that I said, "They must have made love on the moor." P. said, "My dear, the bog," and J. said, "The children." They sat after dinner, dead, and Dj. began to read *Lorenzo in Taos*. She could not stand the talk about it. But she was bored, then began to read Blake, I showed her the *Gates of Paradise*.[41] I kept rattling on, making audacious statements. Peggy trying to inquire into my sex life with Hoare. Djuna asked what Hoare looked like and Peggy said, "He looks like a little Jewish tailor." She said, "Now tell me exactly what Hoare thinks of me, so I'll know how to behave with him." She said she had a *béguin* for him at first, but didn't want him now since she had found out he wasn't a Jew.[42] I said I had made him lose his hair.

---

[39]Peggy (Marguerite Loeb David Deutschbein Waldman) was Guggenheim's best friend from childhood. Guggenheim refers to her as simply "Peggy" in her memoir: "I don't know what else to call her throughout this book, for she changed her name so often" (40).
[40]Letters sent by Holms' wife, Dorothy, to John after he had moved in with Guggenheim.
[41]Blake's *For Children: The Gates of Paradise* (1793) is a series of Blake's etchings with captions depicting the development of human beings from birth to death. In 1820, he expanded the work slightly and changed the title to *For the Sexes: The Gates of Paradise*.
[42]*Béguin*: infatuation

I told Peggy yesterday that I was going to follow her to bed every single night, and not sit up with John. So I did this, and came in their room afterwards and P. said now she understood, I was going to follow her to <u>bed</u>, and so get John!

She was half naked, and I stood looking at her, and said, "You shouldn't let yourself get fat; your beauty is in thinness." She said, "What do you mean? Am I fat now?" I said, "No, but there are some people who can't take on a couple of pounds." She said, "And there are some who could take off a couple of pounds, I suppose you mean." This is an example of her kind of wit, she plays on words, and at the moment it is amusing, often not repeatable.

Played "This Day Christ Was Born" alone in the room with John.[43] It was so beautiful, making the rafters ring. How I love this record! Took it and put it separately, as it's no longer published, and I don't want it damaged. Then played Peter's Mozart trio.[44] I want so much to be alone with John, not to talk, but just to <u>be</u> with him, to feel his natural presence.[45]

Monday, September 5

In the afternoon we all went over the moor in the automobile, to Princetown, where we had tea in a hotel, and came home. The prison was not depressing[46]; because I had imagined it alone and desolate in the midst of the moor. This does not mean that it would not be horrible.

Talking about women making up, I said how funny P[eggy]. and Dj. looked to me when I got off the train. Said women should not make up in the country. They said I would look much better if I did. Peggy said, "You look like the Ancient Mariner, weatherbeaten."[47] This went to my heart, and I made up after we got home, exclamations from Dj. and P. John didn't like it.

We talked about Gerhardi, and tried to get John to invite him, so Djuna could have someone to vent her spleen on.[48] It appears he hates intellectual

---

[43]"This Day Christ Was Born" (1611), composed by William Byrd (c.1539–1623), one of the greatest composers of the Elizabethan age.
[44]Coleman did not specify which of Mozart's trio sonatas she was listening to.
[45]Coleman has blackened out the next 5 ½ lines.
[46]The prison in Dartmoor's Princetown was built by French prisoners of war in 1806 and became a maximum security prison in 1850. One of Britain's most well known prisons, it is referenced in Sir Conan Doyle's *The Hound of the Baskervilles* (1901–1902). Doyle's crime novel takes place on Dartmoor, and the novel's Baskerville Hall may in fact be Hayford Hall, as suggested to Podnieks by the Hall's current owners, the Dunstans.
[47]The protagonist in Coleridge's "The Rime of the Ancient Mariner" (1978).
[48]William Alexander Gerhardi (1895–1977)—he changed the spelling to Gerhardie in the early 1970s—a close friend of Holms, was born in St. Petersburg, Russia, of English parents. After moving to England to attend Oxford University, he became a scholar of the Russian playwright

women. But John said he would be too polite to reveal it. Djuna telling about the Duchess of Marlborough, whom she could not get hold of to interview, nor no one else.[49] Then suddenly went to the palace, and walked in the front door. The Duchess (American) came down the hall and Dj. stayed there the whole day. At lunch Dj. said to the Duke, whom she said was a horrible little man: "Do you know anything about politics?"

P[eggy]. and I discussing in the car how we would arrange about Father. John is nervous about talking to him. I said he didn't want to see any of them I could keep him with me. P. showed me the rooms, and we decided to put Father and Peter next to Doris, Father would have a shower. I wanted to give Father this room, it's so lovely, but it's right next to J. and P. Peggy said, "But like this you can't sleep with Hoare." I said I did not intend to consider that.

In the evening we had a real set-to, which I started. Got annoyed at Djuna's thinking I exist in John's shadow, and said John was far fonder of me than Peggy realized. This provoked all kinds of trouble, which I later smoothed over. Admitted nothing was gained by talking like a fool. But truth got into the air then, after I apologized to Peggy. Dj. said I was nothing but a baby, and I said, "What do you think I think of you?" She said, "Come on, let's have it," and looked at me with an expression of a doe, so that my heart sank within me. I said, "I can't attack Djuna, she's too vulnerable." But she said, "Come on!" so I said, "I don't think you're entirely honest." "Why?" so I told her that she pretended to think little of herself, and she really thought she was noble. She spiked my guns by admitting this, but when I brought up an instance, she dug herself in at once. (She had said to me, "That's the kind of a sap I am," because she would go to work to support Thelma.) I said, "You don't think you're a sap." A good of talk on this [sic], and then down to the real topics. Her writing, and the fact that she won't write about herself.

She sat there looking splendid, speaking vigorously, then shouting, "Give me another glass of wine!" She can't argue any better than a dog can. But she's got so damned much pride that she can stick to anything. She said Emily Brontë did not write from talent but from something else. I said, "Yes, genius." She said it was "something else, the heart, something queer within." I said,

---

and short-story writer Anton Chekhov (1860–1904), as well as a novelist, perhaps best known for *The Polyglots* (1925).

[49] American-born Gladys Deacon (1881–1977) became the 9th Duchess of Marlborough in 1921, when she became the 2nd wife of the 9th Duke of Marlborough, Charles Richard John Spencer Churchill. The palace which Coleman went on to mention is Blenheim Palace, near Woodstock, Oxfordshire, declared a World Heritage site in 1987. Queen Anne had had it built for John Churchill, 1st Duke of Marlborough.

"That's genius. It's honest." Dj. said no one else could write like that, and I said, "That's how you give yourself away." She won't admit the least thing.

She admitted that she didn't think as much of her earlier stories as she pretended to.[50] John said they could not be criticized for anything but their point of view. He said if you accepted that point of view, which he considered a false one, you could only say that the stories were excellently done.

She sailed into John for his manner, which she said was offensive, and said he behaved like God come down for the weekend. John said, "<u>What</u> a weekend!"

I said, "Why do you think Bianchetti a skunk for taking money from me, and you think nothing of Thelma's doing it from you, when you had to <u>earn</u> the money?" "Because Thelma is a GIRL!" she shouted, and went on with that. She twisted herself all up. There was no possible rapport on this.

Great deal of talk about my feeling about John, and they both said if he wanted me to fall in love with him I would do so. I went into explanations with Peggy about my reactions to men before and after living with Bianchetti. John said Peggy had not realized I was really in love with Bianchetti, for the first time in my life. He told her she had been cruel. She said she realized it now. I lied till my tongue was thick about John. He said the same thing, only he believes it.

I said, "American women have no pride, and Djuna has so much. That's why I respect her." I told her what I thought of *Ryder*. I haven't read her stories, but I remembered *Ryder* well enough, since I had lived in it for three months three years ago. I said, "*Ryder* isn't honest, You pretend it's not serious, when it is." She said some balls about its being both serious and comic, and I said, "A work of art has to be written from a consistent point of view." I told her what is the truth, i.e., that she was afraid when she wrote *Ryder*, and wanted to hide what she really felt. I told her she was afraid of everyone. She insisted that she wrote "only for herself."

She said I only admired things of the intellect and that she didn't think that brains were necessary in creating, only the heart. Etc. I said I knew all this. She gave as an example of my caring only for the intellect the fact that I liked John. I said, "Then why don't I admire Arthur Waley?" I said I liked John mainly for the zest he has for life; and for his understanding of life.

She gets John so completely wrong, I can't fathom this out, unless it's because he makes her feel inferior. I said, "You think I'm a baby about life; it's true. But I think you're a baby about your writing." I said I could stand any criticism of anything I wrote. She hedged a good deal on this.

---

[50]Barnes' stories, along with poems, were collected in *A Book* (1923), revised and retitled *A Night Among the Horses* (1929).

She admitted most of it, but thinks, I think, that I don't really care about my writing.

This morning three letters from Father, full of excitement at coming. Says, "Even if Peggy asks, I don't want to stay there and meet a lot of people." He wants to go to the farm.[51]

Last night, just as things were getting really warm, and exciting, John went out to get some more wine. And Peggy lifted up her voice and began to yowl like a little dog. Djuna, hearing this, said she must go to bed, and did, and Peggy went after her (John meanwhile downstairs in the wine cellar) and I came up too. Peggy got into bed, and I waited for John, hoping that he would get Djuna. But he was angry with Peggy, for disturbing everything. I said it wasn't Peggy's fault, since both she and I had promised Djuna not to let her drink too much, because she is so ill.[52] But it wasn't that, it was Peggy's heartlessness in breaking up the conversation. She is a sly little edition of Mrs. Muir. I went to bed very annoyed with her. John said it was so good for Djuna to hear a little truth, and say a little. Peggy doesn't care about this, all she wants is bed, and her man in with her. It's just like Frieda Lawrence.

I have to keep in a tactful relation to Peggy and can't endure it. I like her, and would like to know her alone, separate from John. I'd prefer John to be living with someone I didn't like.

John says of course I do, everyone wants life to be easy for them.

I was pretty mad last night, only eleven-thirty, and everything going so strong. Peggy was bored and was glad to have it end. She doesn't want people to talk about genius. I don't blame her for that, but she's such a little shrew, turning up her nose screaming. Reading Hudson's *Land's End*, and thought of the first time I saw that, in October, 1926, after ten days across the Atlantic.[53] How I woke up, early in the morning, and heard the stewards calling out "Land in sight," and I rushed up on the deck, and in the heavy mist I saw the end of England. Everything was dark, and covered with gray and mist; but it seemed to me as if my life were beginning then.

Thinking a good deal of Peter now. Djuna said last night, "Think of a whole life with him." I said, "That's just exactly what I don't dare think of: I want it so much." I said that if Hoare looked like a Jewish tailor and I looked like the Ancient Mariner it was no wonder Djuna thought it should not go on.

---

[51]Burton Far Hill Farm, where Coleman had been before coming to Hayford Hall.
[52]For more on her illness, see note on Victor Cunard for the September 2, 1932 entry.
[53]*Land's End: A Naturalist's Impressions of West Cornwall* (1908) is by W. H. Hudson. Geographically, Land's End is the most western tip of England.

When Djuna sees Hoare she will have a shock, for we have said so many contradictory things. And what she will really see is a sweet little person, with a charming smile.

I told Djuna that since I had come to know her I thought far more of her than of anything she had written; and could not understand why she hadn't the guts to write about herself.

Tuesday, September 6

I am getting fond of Djuna, but it is wearing. I long for Hoare to come. The third rainy day.

At lunch we all read the backs of Sindbad's cigarette cards, which were a series of famous Beaus, and were very funny.[54] Alcibiades and Julius Caesar were among the number, and Narcissus! I got so interested reading, forgot to eat. Told John how I loved the bust of Julius Caesar in the British Museum, always moved by it, the wonderful beautiful mouth, and noble eyes and forehead. I said, "That's the only man in the past I'd have liked to have known." Djuna said, "Ah, Emily, I can just see you, tormenting Julius Caesar!" We played the "geography game" after lunch with the children, and I got the booby prize every time. Peggy said to Sindbad, after we were reading, "Let's play the Guggenheim game; do you know that?" He said, "What's that? Swindling people?" We laughed ourselves sick over this.

John said it was easier for me to read my diary because I didn't know it was funny except to them, I told him I had lied, I knew it was really funny, and should be published. I said it was extreme honesty which enabled me to read a diary like that in front of Djuna, honesty given to me by grace. John said Kay Boyle thought a good deal of my talent, was really excited about it. I pretended to think of this as a huge joke.

Djuna did not like hearing that Kay Boyle was excited about my talent.

John said the Scotch women did nothing but fuck, and were very sweet about it. Gave us a tender picture of Scotland in the spring, every bush occupied.

Talking about mouths, Dj. said she did not like mine. Told her about zeppelins and balloons. John said, "If you're going to have a mouth, why not

---

[54]Cigarette cards, first introduced by tobacco companies in the United States in 1875 and essentially discontinued during WWII, were trade cards designed to both protect the cigarettes with their hard backs and advertise the cigarettes themselves. Put out in a number of series ranging from baseball players, butterflies, and actresses, to Boy Scout and Girl Guides, Gardening Hints, and Lucky Charms, they early on became collector's items. Coleman's "Beaus" are part of the series of 50 cards by the Player's cigarette company entitled "Dandies."

have a sensual one? Not a tight one." We told Djuna hers was sensual. Her mouth is Irish, a sensual prig.

In the evening we talked about table tipping and Djuna said her grandmother used to go into trances and speak in the voices of those who were dead.[55] She used also to levitate objects. John waxed excited on this, saying that the sooner all this was cleared up and made a part of the body of scientific knowledge, the better. I said it was all connected, Blake's visions, etc.[56]

Djuna and Peggy recounting their early days in New York, Peggy pregnant, rushing about with Mina Loy's lamps on her stomach, Djuna in capes and canes.[57] Peggy used to invite people to tea and ask them how many cakes they ate. She gave Djuna some darned underwear.

This morning the rain poured down, driven about in clouds, but suddenly there was a break in the rain and the blue sky was seen, the broken clouds rushing across the sky. I could see the sun on the edge of one of them, a bright line of gold, with the sun hidden. Now it is pouring as before, the green trees are thick in it.

Peggy says, "Does Hoare think I am malicious 24 hours a day?" I said, "I wish he could see you with your children." She is very sweet with them, and her face is so full of love for Sindbad.

I am flattered because Dj. seems to care what I think but the truth is she cares what everybody thinks. I told her I didn't care what she thought when I go away from her. John said there was no use my <u>explaining</u> myself to Djuna, one's character is found out through living. He said we both lived in a dream world, hers of people, and mine inhuman. Djuna said she couldn't write her life because she couldn't walk over people, that if she had been a man she could do it. I said I <u>could</u> do it.

---

[55]Djuna's paternal grandmother was Zadel Turner Barnes (1841–1917). In addition to being a medium, she was also a journalist and writer of poems and stories.

[56]Blake began to have visions when he was a child; as an adult, he translated these into the complex personal mythology which informed so much of his poetry and art. Coleman would become increasingly fascinated with issues of spiritualism as she tried to reconcile the transcendent powers of God and the human imagination, as well as spiritual and physical, unconscious and conscious, forces.

[57]In her memoir, Guggenheim recounts that Loy "had just created a new, or old, form of *papier collé*—flower cut-outs which she framed in beautiful old Louis Philippe frames she bought in the flea market." Guggenheim offered to sell these on her trip to the States in March 1925, while pregnant with Pegeen, recounting: "I went all over New York carrying them on my fast-growing stomach" (60). It was later that year that Loy turned to making lamp shades. Guggenheim, having returned to Europe for the birth of Pegeen in August, set up a shop for Loy in Paris, in the Rue du Colisée, and helped to sell the shades; she also took "fifty or so" of them with her to sell on her 1927 trip to New York (71).

Can't even write in this diary, am not inspired. But I want dreadfully to write a poem.

Thursday, September 8

The skies bursting with rain, a roaring wind. Telephoned Plymouth to find out when Father's boat gets in, six o'clock tonight. I ache in every muscle, from the riding yesterday.

Yesterday I wore Sonia's boots and a pair of flannel trowsers of John, and went riding. The day was clear and brilliant, the thick clouds over the horizon, after rain. I have never seen the moor so beautiful. I had a slow grey pony at first, but could not make him move, and later changed with Sindbad, who was on Ginger. It was all new and very exciting to me, just being on a horse; it will take some time to ride. But I loved it! The moor swept out, in brown and purple, undulating beyond us. It seemed like mountain country. There was a brisk wind, and the sky. John had a new horse, a really lively one. Peggy in her riding habit, looking neat and frightened. We rode for about two hours. It is a lovely feeling, galloping across a moor in a wind.

Letters from Deak, Hoare and Phyllis. Hoare said he would come Friday or Saturday. Phyllis has got a job, secretary to Basil Rathbone.[58] In her letter she tried to be witty. She will have a legacy of 50,000 dollars when a female relatives dies, now aged 50 and supposed to have cancer. I told this to Peggy as fifty thousand pounds. Deak is going to take Johnny and Rostik to Antwerp.[59]

In the afternoon we went to Newton Abbot to the races.[60] Saw several steeplechases.

How beautiful they are when they take the jump. The sky so lovely, but the racecourse was foul. John won some money. Djuna looking polite and bored.

In the evening we told jokes, everyone weary from the riding. I told some nigger ones, made John split with laughter. Peggy told one awfully good one, about a woman who hated her husband, and when he died, and she saw him laid out stiff before her, put his arms akimbo and said, "That's more like it." Did not think Djuna's were very good. Djuna went to bed and P. would not retire, being angry with John because he stayed up late the night before.

---

[58] Basil Rathbone (1892–1967), British stage and screen actor. He is perhaps best known for playing Sherlock Holmes in fourteen movies such as *The Adventures of Sherlock Holmes* and *The Hound of the Baskervilles* (1939).
[59] For a brief holiday.
[60] The Newton Abbot Racecourse in Devon remains one of the most famous jumping racecourses in England.

J. went to bed and left P. sitting by the fire. She went and slept alone. This was because the night before last Dj. and J. and I sat up till two, drinking, but Dj. was nervous the whole time, and kept saying, "I must go to bed; Peggy will ask me if I love this man." John said all the time, "Nonsense; Peggy doesn't mind. I've arranged it with her." It appears the following morning however before P. could say one word he told her she was pea-brained, and that his friends wondered why he lived with her.

Tuesday night it <u>was</u> amusing, P. went to bed, and we persuaded Dj. to remain up, and she drank a little, then got very tight, and began to attack John. She had my book of Renaissance Poetry, which she would read, pretending that absorbed her. Then she would intersperse a dig at John, while reading aloud the poetry. I laughed and laughed. I egged them on. John was quite tight, and wanted to say some truth. But he didn't get very far. The gist of their sentiments seemed to be that each thought the other was poor and miserable. They were amiable. Djuna said, "I used to hate your guts, but now I think you're sweet." "What do you think he is?" I said. She said, "He's a poor little reed growing by the side of the river. So am I, but his reed is more gnawed than mine." "And much taller," said John. "How taller?" she cried, "Busy old fool, unruly son!"[61] John tried to get her to bring her book down and let him read it, but she wouldn't, because, she said, he thought too much of himself. While he was out getting wine I engaged Dj. on an account of her life, which was terrible. John came back and got melancholy, partly because he can't listen to people's lives and partly because his stomach began to turn. He was sick later.

Friday, September 9

Went to Plymouth yesterday and got Father, and brought him here. He looks well, much better than I had hoped.

We didn't get home till nine o'clock, a cold windy drive back, the stars wonderful over the green lanes. Father got warm before the fire, and we had some dinner. After dinner he got on very well talking to them, I keeping the conversation as lively as possible. Peggy said, "Do you like Emily's friends?" which rather disconcerted him.

Last night took Father upstairs to my room, and he got talking about the stock market and I fell asleep. I am going to give him this room. I couldn't decide because I don't like being next to Hoare. But when I saw that sweet man I couldn't bear not to give him this lovely room.

The first day is difficult, we get on better as time goes on.

---

[61] Opening lines from John Donne's "The Sun Rising": "Busy old fool, unruly Sun,/ Why dost thou thus,/Through windows, and through curtains, call on us?"

Thinking a good deal about Peter, and when I think of him sitting in this house it gives me a pleasant thrill. Want especially for him to see John and Peggy in their home. He thinks P. is a wild cocktail chaser. She said on the boat, "O I wish Hoare didn't hate me!"[62] I told her once he thought she was malicious. She loves Hoare, and wants him to admire her. On the boat going over to the breakwater Peggy was worrying about what to say to my father, and was very sweet. "Must remember my manners again," she said, and rehearsed speeches. "Were you seasick? Did you have pleasant table companions?" When he did arrive she was natural and lively.[63]

---

[62] Coleman, Guggenheim, and Holms had taken the tender out to the breakwater to meet Coleman's father's ship, the *Paris*.
[63] The diary temporarily breaks off at this point.

Section 3

Gloucestershire

September 23–October 9, 1932

After Hayford Hall, Coleman returned to Bourton Far Hill Farm with her father. The diary picks up again just before Mr. Holmes went back to the United States at the end of September, with Coleman reflecting on their time together. She then turned her attentions to Peter Hoare, who had again come from London to vacation with her, but sexual anxieties spoiled the reunion and, when he left, she was filled with despair. A surprise visit to the farm by John Holms revived her, and she soon decided to accompany him to London so that she could salvage her relationship with Hoare.

BOURTON FAR HILL FARM

Friday, September 23, 1932

Rain and mist. I read *Two Years Before the Mast*, and thought how much better Melville.[1] Sent a wire to the hotel in Cheltenham to have them send my bag which I left in the taxi yesterday.[2] This being the second time in one month I was pretty mad. There was no passport in this, since I haven't got one. But there was a twenty dollar bill and three pounds. I had bought a new fountain pen too yesterday, and that was in it. After worrying all the day I got a wire that they had sent it.

---

[1] *Two Years Before the Mast*, by Richard Henry Dana, Jr. (1815–1882), American sailor, writer, and lawyer. Based on his own seaman's diary, it was published in 1840, and in 1859 he added a new last chapter.
[2] Cheltenham is a spa town on the edge of the Cotswolds, Gloucestershire. Recall her entry for August 19, 1932.

Father and I got rather testy over the bag, and his stick, which was also left, and he went out for a walk. I showed him *The Lion and the Fox*.[3]

Rains and is very dreary, and I feel depressed, though Father and I had a very good talk late last night. I told him I had been supporting Bianchetti. He said Djuna would never get a fine clean young husband.

Late afternoon, cleared, in the west. Thinking of the horse I am going to have tomorrow.

Saturday, October 1

Father has gone, and I miss him, and feel closer to him than ever before. I went to Plymouth with him, and put him on the ship. It took a very long time, and the tender rocked away in the wind, in the dark; and the great ship glittered above it.

The night before Father left we had quite a row about Djuna! He doesn't seem to think much of her.

The night before this we talked about Deak a good deal, and I told Father how good he had been to me, and couldn't bear thinking of it. I felt horribly depressed, thinking of what Deak did to keep me. It made me almost sick. I couldn't get it out of my mind.

Coming back in the train I of course was depressed thinking of every little thing I could have done for Father.

In the train a very young woman had a baby of eighteen months, and it squalled like anything, whenever it was balked, and I longed to say to her, "Go to it and smack him." I love babies so much! Yes, and when they yell I want to pound them. Why don't I remember that when I see the little devils? Thought all the time of writing to Dr. Pierson and asking her if it was safe to have another baby.[4]

Father saying he was out of place at Hayford Hall, and how he hated Djuna, and said she wanted to make a game of him. I got all in a stew about this, I was so surprised. He doesn't know that a person like Djuna can have kind feelings towards him. He seemed to like John and Peggy so much, but I suppose he didn't criticize them because they were my friends. J[ohn]. and P[eggy]. thought Father was so happy, and they think he enjoyed Djuna. He probably did enjoy her society more than he remembers, or wishes to

---

[3]Wyndham Lewis' *The Lion and the Fox: The Role of the Hero in the Plays of Shakespeare* (1927). John Holms had reviewed this work in the April–July 1927 issue of *The Calendar of Modern Letters*. His main criticisms of the work were that Lewis consistently contradicts himself and that he presents "personal preoccupations . . . as objective critical interpretation."

[4]Dr. Pierson attended to Coleman after her postpartum depression sent her to the Rochester State Hospital.

recollect, but time his inferiority complex thinking it over later [*sic*], made him consider that she had been making him ridiculous. She shouldn't have called him Poppa!

Tuesday, October 4

I finished an endlessly long letter to Sonia Sunday morning, then wrote to Father. Kept thinking about Peter, and was very anxious. Wrote to Mr. Harvey.[5] Peter came a little ahead of time, the dog was barking, and before I could see out to the gate I heard his step and he walked in. We were very excited to see each other.

We had dinner immediately, chicken and apple sponge, then I took him to see my horse, and let Billy out. Peter said his legs were odd. Then Peter and I went walking, around where Father and I went, the lower way to Hinchwick. We walked along and it began to rain, and we ran up the hill and sat under a beech. Peter telling me about the letters of D.H. Lawrence, which have been published.[6]

We came home without going to Hinchwick as the sky was threatening, though there were little patches of blue in the grey. We had tea, then sat before the fire.

Peter had looked me worrying [*sic*], then he said, "What are you going to do? How are you going to live?" I did not answer, and felt love and desire rising in me; he sat with that intent look, his mouth half smiling. It came to my lips to say, "I want to marry you," and I sat with my heart almost stopped, as if I couldn't say it; but finally I said, "I want to be married." Peter turned half away and said, "You mean you want to be married to anyone." I did not answer.

Then this intense moment passed, and we began to quarrel.

It is with extreme difficulty that I write about Peter, and when I do, he comes out a rather sophisticated, somewhat hard individual, who has got me under his thumb; this being of course what a large part of me would like.

We talked a long time, and as it got time to go to bed I became more and more miserable, for I saw that I had allowed the wrong thing to happen. He did not come to my room. And I lay in bed and gave myself up to the most passionate weeping. I felt as if would divide in two, I cried so violently. I didn't want to go to his room. And yet the memory of those nights at Hayford Hall kept coming to me, when he had wanted me so much. I knew I had to

---

[5]Mr. Harvey was the principal of John's school.
[6]*The Letters of D. H. Lawrence* (1932) were edited and introduced by Aldous Huxley (1894–1963), English writer and intellectual.

swallow my pride, or I wouldn't have him. I went shivering to his room, and his head was on the edge of the bed, and he said, "Couldn't you sleep?" so tenderly. In a moment I had thrown my arms around his head, and I shivered and shivered, and I didn't want to cry. But his tenderness upset me. I got into the bed, soft and warm next to him, and we were close to each other. It was not a release, because he was going away, and I had only apprehension when I thought of the next day. It was not lovely, as in Devonshire, but only a little comforting.

I told him, before we went to bed, that he had no right to make love to me as he had done in Devonshire, and then decide that it was wrong. I told him that it was too late. He denied this strenuously, but I knew that it was true.

I went back to my bed in the early morning, and went to sleep at last, but woke up very early, and lay thinking of him. I got up and ate breakfast with him, which was silent, then when it was time to go I could not keep back the tears, and this moved him, and he was very tender.

Lying in bed last night, before I went to Peter I felt in such despair, not only for myself, which seemed very little; but I thought of Dorothy [Holms], and of my father's marriage, and of Deak; and it seemed as though I were feeling the sorrow and despair of the whole world. But in the morning, after Peter left, the clouds began to clear, and the sun came breaking through. And I thought I would go riding. I read the *Man in the Zoo* first, which rather amused me, and then went out to catch the horse.[7]

Took a hot bath after supper, and read *Sons and Lovers*, which is at least not as affected as some of the later ones, and which really held me, as far as I read.[8]

Friday, October 7

When Father was here I would look at his face and try to see it as if I'd had no connection with it, but never could. It was always the face of one whom I had loved all my life. Every feeling I ever had, from earliest recollection, is bound up in that face; and the wonder to me is that I've ever had any life at all, apart from it. I was thinking the same thing when reading *Sons and Lovers*. If the parent is as close to you as Paul's mother was to him (closer than Father ever could have been to me), I don't see how one ever gets out. And even if one does, that is there, always, governing the will, determining what we shall believe, and feel.

---

[7]*A Man in the Zoo* (1924), a novel by David Garnett.
[8]*Sons and Lovers* (1913), the novel by D. H. Lawrence, features an intense relationship between protagonist Paul Morel and his mother.

I can see very well where Peter has gotten some of his sexual ideas. The sexual parts of Lawrence make me almost vomit. Only an unsatisfied Puritan virgin can write like this. I was looking at *Women in Love* again, and trying to read it. It's the most <u>unspeakable</u> drivel one could possibly imagine. It's really the worst book I have ever read. Peter told me to read the chapter called "Excurse," which I did, since he said it contained a very good quarrel, but he didn't say what else it contained.[9] It's obscene! Page after page about her feeling the life in the back of his thighs—it's ludicrous! One feels one could take this man (Lawrence) and mangle him. How CAN people write like this?

"It was a perfect passing away for both of them, and at the same time the most intolerable accession into being, the marvellous fulness of immediate gratification, overwhelming, outflooding from the source of the deepest life-force, the darkest, deepest, strangest life-source of the human body, at the back and base of the loins." Reading this last night made me roar with laughter, but I went to bed and had an orgasm in a dream, so I suppose he can be said to have been successful.

I got a letter from Peter, which made me want to burn his heart out. If it were not for the horse, I would leave here, go to France, and let him wait for me. But since I have the horse I am not, after all, going to suffer so much, and can do without these tears. But I've been waiting for him all the week. And nothing but his sister has ever kept his weekends full. So lo and behold, here is his sister again.[10] He can't come now. He says he can't "be mean" to his sister, since she only comes to London once a year!

Sunday, October 9

I was sitting here, feeling perfectly wretched, when in walked John Holms.[11] I simply could not believe it.

We went to Moreton to dinner, to the Redesdale Arms, since Mrs. Righton wasn't prepared for dinner, and we had wine and talked. He had been with Hoare. I wouldn't admit anything I felt for Hoare, and said sardonic things, but finally, at three a.m., I did tell him. I had never admitted anything. I was so glad to see Holms that I couldn't think of anything else at first, as it was a

---

[9]"Excurse" is the 23rd chapter. The quarrel is between lovers Ursula Brangwen and Rupert Birkin, who eventually resolve their differences and go on to explore their passion in the manner quoted by Coleman.

[10]Coleman had written to Hoare, asking him to come to the farm for another week. He had responded that he might be able to do so; however, he had to back out to host his sister who was visiting from Scotland.

[11]Holms and Guggenheim had had a mild quarrel, and Guggenheim had gone back to Paris.

prayer's being answered (a prayer I had not even dreamed to pray). Then that wore off and I was in gloom again, intensified by him.

He tried to get me to think of writing again, but I wouldn't, I said I could write at any time if I felt like it (unlike him), but <u>don't want</u> to write now, since I have nothing to say. He said that lyric poetry was written by people who had nothing to say, and I should do that, but I said no, I did not want to.

Dear old Holms, setting everything right. I do love him. Was altogether a joy, until late, when he got tight and began repeating, and I got sleepy, since by that time I had decided to go back to London with him and nothing else mattered.

John said that the chief reason Peter feels the way he does is that I don't envisage the future enough. I said I envisaged it much more than he knew. I told him, passionately, that I wanted a home of my own, and a child. This depressed him.

John said I could probably not have another child, and I said I would even risk insanity again to have one; but he said no one who loved me could tolerate that. The truth is I might have no trouble at all, as Doctor Pierson told me, since that came from excessive pain (not taking gas oxygen), and an infection. I didn't take gas oxygen to save Deak money, neither of us dreaming that it would be such a horror to give birth. I said if I couldn't have another child, I would adopt one; and that I was fully determined to take John from Madame Donn. I told him how I would do it, little by little, and always let him visit them; and the responsibility of their support I would divide between myself and Deak.

Thinking of seeing Peter now; and all the world seems to be of no account; if only I see his face.

Section 4

London

October 11–October 29, 1932

Returning to London with Holms, who was en route to Paris to be with Guggenheim, Coleman continued her challenging relationship with Hoare while a resurgent Bianchetti frustrated her with his requests for money. Against this backdrop of emotional and sexual stresses, Coleman immersed herself in the cultural offerings of the city, going to restaurants, department stores, galleries, and films; socializing with literary figures like Edwin Muir and Arthur Waley; and trying to begin a book about her childhood.

105, OAKLEY STREET, CHELSEA

Tuesday, October 11

Sunday afternoon John and I went for a little walk before leaving [Bourton Far Hill Farm], to take one last look at the autumn.

When I shut the gate behind us at the farm, I knew that for a very long time, perhaps for ever, I should not see these lovely scenes again. Yet I was so full of the change in my life that I could not think of this, and only wanted the motor to go. But later, on the ugly road to London, passing over flats, and seeing row on row of houses all alike, I felt a horror of this life, of grim terror and death, and could not think of going to it. I wanted to shield myself from it, and never bear a part in such misery, and squalor.

It was raining as we came to London, and the city did not oppress me, in fact I felt resigned to it, and at least it was a city, and whole, and had existed a long time like this. It wasn't a succession of vulgar trials, like the suburbs we had just passed through. We came to 7, Oakley Street, but could get no answer to Peter's bell, though we saw his light, and went around to the Six Bells pub and telephoned.[1] He had his sister there; but when he came to the door I saw him as I remembered him, long ago, when I came to his rooms to see him, opening the door happy, and seeming to receive you into his very heart. His sister was timid, and not knowing us, and being afraid too, she talked conventionally, and it was embarrassing. We went to dinner to a Hungarian restaurant in Greek street, and talked in a desultory way, Holms going on to Hoare, as he does, and I trying to make his sister feel at home.[2]

We took her home after dinner, and Holms came for a little while to Peter's.

When John had gone I could not look at Peter, sitting in his chair. I knew he was looking at me, with what thoughts I did not know, though I felt strange with him, and silent. He looked at me so long, with such concentrated feeling, that I could not tell what he was thinking, but came suddenly to him, and put my head in his breast. We were like this for a long time.

I went back to my room across the street, and in the morning thought of him, and could see into his flat, where Mrs. Stafford was washing.[3] But I couldn't see him. I saw two other men come out of his house, and thought of Peter, and wondered what I wanted him to be.

John came at eleven, and did not want to go to Crowborough.[4] He was miserable without Peggy, and has a cold.

John and I went to the galleries where Wyndham Lewis has got some portraits, but they were disillusioningly dull—I had not expected that.[5]

These portraits were surprising because they were conventional, and banal, and were each someone who was in the public eye, and I did not know Lewis was like this. It was like the "trying to get on" of the most insignificant dauber in the social arts, and must mean that he is desperate for recognition.

We then went to an exhibition of modern English, which was a confusion to me, and I was glad Holms was there to talk to me.[6] I didn't like any of them; but could not distinguish between those who had a little talent, and those who were just poseurs. Said for instance that Gilbert Spencer (or Stanley) should

---

[1] The Six Bells Pub is in King's Road, Chelsea.
[2] In Soho, Greek Street is famous for its pubs and restaurants.
[3] Hoare's housekeeper.
[4] Holms and Coleman had arranged to visit the Muirs, who lived in Crowborough, just south of London. However, Holms found out they had moved to 7 Downshire Hill, Hampstead; he and Coleman put off their visit until the evening, as she went on to recount.
[5] Lewis' black and white sketches, *Thirty Personalities,* of figures such as Noel Coward, James Joyce, J. B. Priestly, and Rebecca West, were on exhibit at London's Lefevre Galleries.
[6] The London Group 30th Exhibition, October 10–28, 1932, at the New Burlington Galleries, offered modern painting and sculpture from artists such as Stanley Spencer, Vanessa Bell, and Cedric Morris. Formed in 1913, The London Group was an exhibiting society of English artists.

never put brush to paper, while Vanessa Bell, though worthless, was born to be a painter. There was one landscape of Cedric Morris, with barns, and a gate, which had a curious composition, not in the least successful, but which, after John had talked enough about it, I felt had a genuine original feeling.

We went to Hampstead, and found the street very easily, Downshire Hill, and it was an old house, quite battered. John wasn't sure this was the house, and looked through the letterbox and saw a sideboard in the back, and said he couldn't say why, but it must be Muir. Then he saw Edwin's coat and Willa's hat. "Oh, I know those clothes," he said. "I've seen them many years." We opened the door, which was ajar, for there was no reply to knocking, or ringing, and saw Gavin coming down the stairs, but he would not look at us. Then John walked in, and Edwin was there. He was so glad to see him.

The house was being renovated, they had only been in it four days. They were very tired. John was delighted with the rooms, which had great eighteenth century windows which looked out on a large ash tree. The house had been lived in for twenty years by an old woman who threw mutton chop bones on top of the wardrobe. They were all decaying there when the Muirs came. She also threw oyster shells outside in the garden.

Edwin was very discouraged about his book, and said he would not write any more, and was terribly depressed.[7] The book has only been out three weeks. But it has had stupid reviews, and very little notice. John and I brought a breeze of sanity to his troubles. John said, "Reviews, yes, if I were writing I should feel as you do. But when you mention names—James Agate and L.A.G. Strong!![8] You don't expect people like that to know anything about it do you?" Muir was ashamed that he had cared what these people think. But he remained depressed.

John got started talking to Muir, and they were happy, but they're shy, and their relationship, so intense for so many years, has through Willa become very difficult. She was exhausted from the house. We didn't go out to dinner, but had supper there, cold bacon and beef, and tomatoes and cheese, excellent. Muir got a little tight, and vomited afterwards, Willa casting herself down on the floor with a rag and rubbing the nap of the carpet in powerful sweeps, saying in rhythm, "He should have done it in the fire."

John drove me to my door, then sat there and tried to make me go to Paris (mildly) because he didn't want to drive alone, but I couldn't go now.[9] I held his finger and felt very loving towards him, and didn't want him to go.

---

[7] *Six Poems* (1932).
[8] James Agate (1877–1947), critic (mainly drama) for the London *Sunday Times*. Leonard Alfred George Strong (1896–1958), novelist, poet, and reviewer for the London *Spectator*.
[9] Holms was on his way to join Guggenheim.

From my window I saw Peter go into his flat, and move about in it, a dark figure, going in and out of the kitchen and living room, then he turned out the lights, and went forward to his bedroom. His life, hidden there, going away from me, I did not understand, and he moved about like someone I had never known.

Wednesday, October 12

Yesterday I went out and walked up King's Road looking in all the shops, which seemed new and fascinating to me because I had been in the country. I met Peter at Piccadilly Circus; but not before I had almost bought a hat. I did buy a pair of moccasins, blue, for the bedroom. We went to lunch at Castano's; and had spaghetti alla Bolognese.[10]

Peter took me to the door of the theater where the film *Grand Hotel* is playing, but I could not get in, and went back outside and looked at pictures of Greta Garbo, who is so beautiful, and the fat wooden faced John Barrymore.[11] Like a wooden surprised doll with a brush stuck on his mouth. And Joan Crawford, who has an American good look, but she is crude, and some others in the film, Lionel Barrymore, and Wallace Beery. Now why do I look at Greta and love her; it isn't only that I want to be like that. Her sweet compromising mouth, understanding of love—I'm sure she feels it. I came away from this and went into the News cinema, where I sat through an hour of absolute boredom, so that I don't see how they get people in a second time; except a *Silly Symphony*, by Walt Disney, *The Ugly Duckling*, one of the sweetest animated cartoons I have ever seen, really funny, making one almost weep for pleasure.[12] If people like this, why don't others make ones like them? Some people laughed very much.

I telephoned Phyllis, and met her at half past five (after buying a hat), and she was very pretty indeed, in new clothes. We went to Ridgways to tea, and told each other all our news.[13]

---

[10]King's Road is a fashionable street in Chelsea. Piccadilly Circus, a circular drive, is the hub of London's West End. Castano's is an Italian restaurant in Greek Street.

[11]The 1932 film, which won the Academy Award for Best Picture, features an all-star cast including Garbo, John Barrymore, Lionel Barrymore, Joan Crawford, Wallace Beery, Jean Hersholt, and Lewis Stone.

[12]News cinemas were theatres dedicated to showing newsreels or short documentaries highlighting the top news stories of the day, though the newsreels were also shown as the precursor to feature films in regular movie theatres. This form of news dissemination was popular until displaced by the television in the 1950s. *Silly Symphonies* was the series of 75 animated shorts by Disney Productions made from 1929–1939.

[13]Ridgways was a tea house selling its eponymous, famous brand of tea.

Thursday, October 13

I have the room I am going to live in now, which is almost human, looking out on the roofs of some old houses.[14] I am higher than the tops of trees that are in the back. They look pretty meagre and yellow; one of them a black poplar. I can see the four factory chimneys of the Electric Light and Power Company, which I saw, at a different angle, from my room last year in Battersea.[15] This room is painted in grey; and the bed-cover and curtains are of a dank unnatural green. The house is like an institution, breakfast up at half-past eight, trays all alike, rooms done at ten. Rules for the telephone; not banging the door. I thus feel at home, and can stay here.

Went to a cinema called *Bring'Em Back Alive* about the African jungle, half of it faked, but a thrilling fight between a tiger and a water buffalo.[16]

I met Peter at seven and we sat in Monico's drinking sherries and got very "intense" with each other, and it was horrible. I couldn't stop. Then we went to the Escargot to dine, and got rather tight and got on better.[17] We aren't natural together; and for the present it would be better for us not to be too much alone. Each is worrying what the other thinks, and there is such a strain that it's impossible. But Mercurey loosened us up, and when in the taxi afterward Peter held me to him my blood was soon on fire. We went to Gossy's afterwards, and Peter played his flute, Norman accompanying on the piano.[18]

We went to Peter's flat, and he made love to me. I completely forgot myself, and wanted him so much. I came away terrified of what would happen the next day. I determined not to see him, or talk to him.

I have been happy this morning for the first time in several months, except at Buckfastleigh.

Reading Catherine Carswell, which has proved to be a much better book than I expected.[19] She has a real understanding of Lawrence, though of course

---

[14]105 Oakley Street.

[15]Coleman had been living at 61 Albert Bridge Road. This road, which overlooks Battersea Park, is the continuation of Oakley Street on the south side of the Thames.

[16]This popular 1932 documentary style film starring the American Frank Buck is based on Buck's bestselling book of the same name about his adventures as a trapper in the Malayan jungle.

[17]L'Escargot is one of the most famous and fashionable restaurants in Greek Street, Soho. They drank Mercurey, a red wine from Burgundy.

[18]"Gossy" (Gosshawk) had been at the J. Walter Thompson office in London with Deak. She married (Sir) Norman Brook (1902–1967) who, having joined the Home Office in 1925, served in 1932 as the private secretary to Sir Herbert Samuel—the job Hoare had the year before. Brook became Deputy Secretary to the War Cabinet in 1942. It was through this couple that Emily and Deak met Hoare in 1929.

[19]Catherine Carswell (1879–1946), Scottish biographer, novelist, and literary journalist. Coleman was reading her newest study, *The Savage Pilgrimage: a Narrative of D. H. Lawrence*

it's too worshipful. The character that comes out of this book is <u>so</u> sympathetic to me, and every letter of Lawrence that I see, and every <u>expository</u> word he writes about his beliefs, makes him dear to me, in the deepest way, so that I am happy that he lived, and that our generation had one man like that.

I stayed in bed in the morning. I telephoned Colonel Egerton and arranged to go there this evening. Then I telephoned Peter to go with me, and he invited me to dinner, but said he would not go. Heavenly round bright sun, a dead orange, over the chimneys, and a street piano playing.

Saturday, October 15

Last night got a letter from Peggy enclosing one from Bianchetti, and her reply. I was in two minds about this; sick with mortification and disgust, and horrified with pity. He wrote her to give him money. She said she would give him a ticket to Italy, but could not aid him to remain in France, in view of his circumstances, which she said she knew.[20]

The letter from Bianchetti was disgusting, abasing himself, in a sickening way, before Peggy who hates him.

I dined with Peter Thursday night, and we did not go to the Egertons', as I felt rotten. We played about together, talking about Lawrence, and I felt very happy. We didn't say a word about the night. I came home feeling wretched with a cough, and stayed in bed all yesterday, reading Lawrence's *Letters*. I was very moved by them. Peter telephoned that he had got tickets for *Grand Hotel*—a film with many stars—and I got out of bed to go. It was the most horrible film I ever saw, duller and more vulgar, and more inept, than any I'd seen before. Greta Garbo was <u>unrecognizable</u>.

We came away from this so disgusted that Peter couldn't talk about Americans, and I felt <u>humiliated</u> that such a film as this could come from America—a film heralded as this has been, with the best criticism behind it. It wasn't that it wasn't proper; it was all too proper. It was crude, and obvious, not one little <u>spark</u> of life throughout, everything shouted and splashed, and "atmosphere" six inches thick. As for Garbo, she twittered about like a mechanical bird on a broomstick, and made such faces and gestures that I thought she was going to vomit when she rang the telephone, so that when emotion came there was nothing left to do. Words are inadequate to describe how ridiculous she made herself. Her face, so mobile, and so exquisitely beautiful in its expressions, was transformed into

---

(1932). Coleman was also reading *The Letters of D. H. Lawrence* (1932) edited by Aldous Huxley.

[20] In her following entry for October 18 (not transcribed) Coleman explained: "He can't go back to Italy because his suitcases are in Belgium. He was put out of Belgium in August for not having a card of identity. He owes several debts in Paris."

writhings of horror, laid on for the soda fountain shaker and the plumber, for whom all of this play was written, so it seemed.

Lawrence's letters really excite me. <u>He really knew what life is</u>. I can't bear this, finding it out now, when he's dead, and after so many of his books have infuriated me.

Sunday, October 16

It's six years today since I set sail for Europe. I didn't know what that would be, and never dreamed it. Nor did I know even when the boat was approaching land, and I saw in the grey morning the Cornwall coast, a memory which is more intense than any in my life before. That boat brought me to another country—to life, and the apples of the inward goal. The fruit of the life of the imagination, which when our vegetable bodies are removed we can see with the inward eye.

Wednesday, October 19

As I was leaving the house yesterday another letter from Peggy. In this she enclosed two from Bianchetti, one absolutely desperate, about his clothes. He would not go back to Italy without his things. The humiliation of appearing before his family as a beggar, he would not accept; he said he would rather die. In another he suggested in a crude managing way that she go to Brussels and get them. Of course when people are desperate they will do, and have to do, anything. But that particular style of Bianchetti belongs too much to his natural character to be supported. At any rate she sent him 500 francs (before receiving my telegram), to get his things in Belgium and his overcoat and passport out of the hotel in the rue Delambre; and a ticket to Assisi. She had already given him 100 francs from me, to eat. I now think he must be gone.

I went out to meet Peter, and went with him to Peter Jones' to get a lamp and table.[21] We sat in the A.B.C., because I only wanted tea, and made jokes at each other.[22] I went with him to Westminster in the Underground, and felt very near to him.

Friday, October 21

Today had lunch with Arthur Waley, telephoned him because of being annoyed with Peter. He asked me to have lunch. Met him at the British Museum. Before he came I looked at Gray's "Elegy," in Gray's handwriting,

---

[21] Peter Jones remains a fashionable department store in Sloane Square, Chelsea.
[22] "ABC" was the familiar term for the many London tea rooms run by the Aerated Bread Co. Ltd., a bread and flour company.

very peaceful, and "Hyperion."[23] Went into the Poetry Bookshop and asked for *The Shutter of Snow*, which they said they did not have but could get.[24]

I did not recognize Arthur Waley because he looked so thin, and is always smaller than I imagine, and had on a bowler hat and great checked trowsers, like a monkey dressed up for church. At first we didn't know what to say, but got talking finally. I looked at his face, which is an <u>excellent</u> face, except that the mouth's too small. His eyes are very kind. His face is beautiful, with high cheekbones, everything finely cut. But his eyes aren't alive. He's a very <u>good</u> man; but I don't like what comes out of his mouth. This perhaps because he feels inferior. He told me about Yeats; and about Edward Garnett; and about T.S. Eliot. It was tiresome at the time. But they all talk like this. I myself talked the most <u>awful</u> balderdash. I told the truth about D.H. Lawrence. The rest of the time I laughed at him. He has an ironic sense. He said Edith Sitwell lives in Paris now. I said I wanted to meet Francis Birrell, which he said he would immediately arrange.[25] I don't know why I want to meet Francis Birrell. I told some yarn about it. I told no end of lies. We got on very well talking about *Zeno*. Miss de Zoete is in town, which I didn't know, and I will see her.

I can't get on with people like Arthur Waley. What they really want is sham. He said Wyndham Lewis had said he was a shoddy Buddha, but that isn't true. The only thing that <u>isn't</u> sham about him is his Japanese.[26]

Yesterday Phyllis came and we had tea together. She went to a spiritualist meeting where the same spirit was claimed by two people. One man was in rapport with it first. Then suddenly a woman said, "That's <u>my</u> son!" Phyllis said the man was truly dismayed at being "robbed of his spirit." She told me also about going to the Eiffel Tower with some country friends, who didn't know where to go in London, and she suggested that, because Augustus John went there.[27] They had once met Augustus John. Then lo and behold he was

---

[23]Thomas Gray (1716–1771), English poet. The manuscript of his most famous poem, "Elegy Written in a Country Churchyard" (ca. 1742–1750), is housed in the British Museum, as is the manuscript of "Hyperion" (1820), a fragment of an epic poem by Keats.

[24]The Poetry Bookshop in Bloomsbury was established in 1913 by poet Harold Edward Monro (1879–1932) to publish and sell poetry and to be the site of poetry-readings.

[25](Dame) Edith Sitwell (1887-1964), British poet. Francis Birrell (1889–1935), writer and translator. After WWI he started a bookshop with David Garnett, called Birrell and Garnett, first located at 19 Taviton Street and then at 30 Gerrard Street, London.

[26]Waley, who is still one of the most respected Asian scholars in the world, translated such Japanese works as *The No Plays of Japan* (1921) and *The Tale of Genji* (1925–33).

[27]The Eiffel Tower restaurant, on 1 Percy Street, was especially popular with London's Bohemian artists, many of whose works—such as Wyndham Lewis'—adorned the walls. Its proprietor was an Austrian named Rudolph Stulik. It remains as the renamed The White Tower. Augustus John (1878–1961), Welsh painter, draughtsman, and Bohemian figure.

there, and bowed to them going out, which set their hearts aflame. Whereupon old Stulik came rushing up and said, "I 'ope you arrr not o-fended, Meesterr John is verrry near-sighted, and always bows to everybody, so as not to make a mistake." That finished THAT evening.

I wrote to Peggy today. She wants me to come to Paris right away. I'm going to go as soon as I have the money. I want dreadfully to see my child, and am thinking of every scheme for getting him here at Christmas.

Phyllis very amusing telling about the Rathbones (to whom she was, and perhaps is, secretary). Basil Rathbone struts down the stairs singing, and dashes up to his wife, upon whose lips he prints a very stagey kiss.[28] What a viper in their bosom Phyllis. And they think she just looks up at them with her adoring eyes. I was annoyed with her because she didn't tell me she had talked for 15 minutes with Gertrude Lawrence, when the wife of Basil was out.[29] How I should have loved that, and thought about it, and chersihed it! Phyllis has to be poked into life.

Saturday, October 22

Peter very funny last night, because he wants me to know Bloomsbury (partly for the excitement he gets himself), and yet he can't bear for me to get on with them. He said that he partly hated me and partly felt as if someone had handed him an ugly little baby, and he didn't want to drop it on the ground and kill it. I said that he was a fish and that no woman who wasn't (a) half mad and (b) sexually unsound, could ever tolerate him.

Last night I had the pip, or curse, and lay down on his bed, and he brought me gin, and we lay there and thought up spicy things to say to each other.

Sunday, October 23

I made up my mind, this afternoon (Saturday) that I would not allow Peter to kiss me, or touch me, until we are married. If we are not married, he shan't kiss me again. I've had enough of my weakness, and his meandering. It's humiliating; I've had enough.

Tuesday, October 25

More letters from Peggy, more begging letters to her from Bianchetti, finally he telephoned her and got 200 francs more, then left. I sent him ten dollars

---

[28]Rathbone's second wife was Ouida Bergère (1886–1974), an American actress and screenwriter who after marrying Rathbone became his business manager.
[29]Gertrude Lawrence (1898–1952) was an English actress who starred in musicals in London's East End and New York's Broadway theatre districts.

today, for November. Peggy gave him 950 francs, outside of my 100, and the ticket, and it will take four months to pay it back. I paid back my 100 and sent her ten dollars for him yesterday. He will resist having this taken out of his money, but resistances will be in vain.[30]

Wednesday, October 26

I sent a note to Miss de Zoete, to ask her to come to tea, or have me come there. Gossy called and asked me to come and play poker, since Eardley Knollys is with them.[31] Peter called and said to come to dinner, that he was too busy to go to lunch.

Began a book yesterday, about my childhood, which I pretended to Peter to have begun two weeks ago.[32]

Met Peter last night under Piccadilly Circus, after watching prostitutes in action (my favourite pastime) with policewoman looking on the other side, and we went to the Ivy, by a sudden intra-taxi decision, and we spent a lot of money, having oysters, whitebait, pheasant, celery, meringue glace and Stilton, with Stein wine and brandy.[33] It was heavenly good. I got a little tight but preserved my fidelity to my resolves, and then we went to a non-stop variety at the Pavilion.[34]

Then we came home, after having spent nine shillings on the seats, and two-and-six for a taxi, Peter exhausted, I supplied this. I didn't care. Went upstairs and I felt very queer, having been worrying about Peter. He lit the fire, and I was very sweet with him, he pleasant and distant yet I thought pleased. I told him what I had made up my mind [sic]. I think it startled him. He of course said it was the right thing to do.

Letter from Bianchetti, which I read in the toilet room of the Ivy, but it contained no fresh worries, only that he was leaving. He does not wish to be left without money, and will probably be annoyed when he finds he is only to have ten dollars a month for some time. There was also a very sweet letter from Father.

---

[30] Coleman had set up a support system whereby she sent Bianchetti a set sum of money each month. In order to pay back Guggenhehim for Guggenheim's lump payments to him, Coleman was going to take the money out of what she would have sent to Bianchetti each month.

[31] Knollys, a friend of Gossy and Norman Brook, was the private secretary to Lord Hambleden (for Hambleden, see entry for April 21, 1936).

[32] This manuscript was never completed, but it may be the source for "The Story of My Childhood," the first of two drafts in her archive dated January 3, 1963 (F. 1075).

[33] The Ivy is a restaurant, still in operation, in the theatre district at 1 West Street. It remains a popular site for opening-night parties.

[34] The London Pavilion Music Hall, in Piccadilly Circus.

Saturday, October 29

Yesterday I wrote all the morning, my book, wrote the whole first chapter, until we left California.[35] I don't know what to make of the style, which is not what I had planned. I thought the part about my mother going insane would be very hard to do, but it wasn't, because it didn't touch me. And my father didn't mean enough to me then for it to have touched me through him, even if I had known what he was feeling. I didn't know she was insane until a long time afterwards.

I want to get this out as it <u>really lies</u> in my unconscious, and God, but it is a heavy task to do! I don't know why I'm so oppressed, it's God's hell to get this out. Thursday I wrote Peggy a very long letter which made me laugh so much I hated to send it away. I had lunch with Peter.

Then I went home and Phyllis came, and we sat and talked, she putting two white silk patches on my underwear. I took her out to tea. I suddenly decided to write Deak to send me the papers I should have to have to get married, and wrote for them. But he won't send them for a while. I didn't mention Peter and I think Deak won't send me them because he'll fear I am going to make some error. I want to have these papers; if suddenly Peter and I should get married, if papers had to be sent for it would spoil everything.

The *Times Lit. Sup.* leading articles are really comic, like a great old steam-engine getting into move. Read their article on Emma's book, which made me want to write to her, and felt ashamed that I haven't done it.[36] If she didn't have plenty of admirers I would of course always write to her. I wrote Peggy honestly about my child, I never got it out before. The truth is, I don't want to see him now, because to see him I should have to be with Madame Donn, and I can't bear it. I want him entirely to myself, and in the best conditions. I prefer to wait until Christmas to see him. Even if his face comes before me fifty times a day, and his hair, I'll wait.

---

[35] For more on Coleman's early life, see the introduction.
[36] Emma Goldman's 2-volume autobiography, *Living My Life*, which Coleman had helped to edit, was reviewed in the Thursday, October 27, 1932 issue of the London *Times Literary Supplement*. The review noted that "Emotions of pity, of admiration, of indignation and astonishment are aroused; but the most lasting impression is one of profound sadness." The critic went on to position Goldman as an "ironic spectacle" of "a woman who has lived all her life in fierce publicity and who has given up almost every human tie for social ends (no matter how wrong-headed), remembered, not for her public work at all but for her passionate friendships and personal loyalties, her 'bourgeois sentimentality' and her never-failing compassion for the poor, the imprisoned and the helpless."

Section 5

Paris

November 30–December 23, 1932

In November, Coleman travelled to Paris to see her son, then aged eight, as well as Guggenheim and Holms. John was living with the Donns at 26 avenue Jules-Coutant, Ivry-sur-Seine, but Coleman took him back and forth from there to where she was staying—Guggenheim's apartment at 55, avenue Reille, in the south of Paris on the Left Bank. John enjoyed an active social life with his mother and with Guggenheim's seven-year-old daughter, Pegeen. Coleman, Holms, and Guggenheim, who often slept in the same bed when together, spent much of their time frequenting trendy cafés and clubs, drinking all night with friends like Giorgio and Helen Joyce, James Joyce's son and daughter-in-law. Barnes was also living in Paris and was often in attendance, joined by her ex-lover Thelma Wood who was visiting from New York. Though Wood aroused Coleman, it was Hoare, back in London, who remained at the forefront of her longings. Preoccupied with sex, the friends nonetheless devoted hours to discussing literature, especially their own work.

The only extant entry for the month of November is the one below.

Wednesday, November 30

When I woke up yesterday morning I pulled back the heavy curtains in this room and saw the sun, and felt happy. I sat up in bed and typed for some time. Peggy played the Brahms trio, which is really lovely. She and John engaged in mild altercations about lending Muir money. John said whatever he did with his money Peggy objected, even if he saved it.

Then came time to go and get Johnny, and I got into the bus. How inestimably depressing Paris is, the little cafés with awnings, and the little food shops. It all looked horrible. When I saw Johnny he did not show surprise but kissed me formally in front of Mr. Harvey, then when we got outside he began to chatter and did not stop for an hour. I listened to him, and felt very lonely and wondered how I was ever going to get him.

Mr. Harvey was distant with me, but I melted him down a little. I think this is because we have not paid enough attention to John's schooling. The school is full and he can afford to dispense with pupils now whose parents lift them in and out the way I've done with John. This disturbed me most of the afternoon.

We came here and Johnny set to work to "compose" an essay on his thoughts on the approach of Christmas. Johnny had supper with Pegeen, I sat looking at his strange face. Then got him in bed, and we dined, then went out to meet M. Lugon, Peggy's agent from Pramousquier, who is here to help her settle the business of her house, a lady having forged checks to pay for it.[1] We saw a dull film called *House Divided* which I saw in London with Norman and Gossy. John laughed at it. We saw one funny comedy. Then we went to the Boeuf sur le Toit, and the jazz and fast people put me in a trance.[2] Peggy talked animatedly to M. Lugon about money, and John [Holms] felt rather lonesome. I drank a great huge *fine* and felt sick. I thought about Peter, his dear body—could not forget it.

Helen and Giorgio Joyce joined us, with some friends, and I made Giorgio drink enough to want to dance.[3] He hopped about delighted. Then we went to Brick Top's in Montmartre, another boite, and danced and ate eggs.[4] I felt quite sick. M. Lugon was so proper and sweet, I kept feeling he was out of it, and talked to him, then he went downstairs, in the Boeuf, and did not reappear, and we thought he had been ill. John went down to see. They came back later. M. Lugon bid us goodbye outside the Boeuf. I said to John, "You weren't nice to him." I said, "Why didn't you ask him to come with us?" John

---

[1] The children were supervised by Doris, Guggenheim's nanny. Pramousquier, on the French Riviera, is where Guggenheim had lived for a time with her first husband, Laurence Vail. For details on the "business" referred to here, see the entry for December 14, 1932.
[2] *A House Divided*, directed by William Wyler, stars Marjorie Main and Walter Huston. The Boeuf sur le Toit was a small restaurant nightclub (a boîte) on the rue Boissy d'Anglas, on the Right Bank. In 1941, it moved to 34 de la rue du Colisée.
[3] Helen Kastor Fleischman was an old friend of Guggenheim from New York. She married Giorgio Joyce, son of James Joyce and Nora Barnacle, on December 10, 1930.
[4] Ada Beatrice Queen Victoria Louise Virginia Smith (1894–1984) went by the name Bricktop because of her red hair. An American who rose to fame as a jazz singer in Harlem, she opened her eponymous club Chez Bricktop in Paris (1924–1961) at 66, rue Pigalle in Montmartre, where she also sang and danced, becoming one of the most famous performers of the era, with her club attracting a massive international clientele. Montmartre (in the 18th arrondissement on the Right Bank) was and is like Montparnasse a major artistic hub of Paris. Montmartre was especially associated with African-American expatriates.

said, "My dear Emily, if you'd seen him downstairs in the Boeuf with his tart sitting on his knee."

I felt considerably cast down and foolish. He went back to the Boeuf, and really enjoyed himself. He comes from Lavandou.[5] He hadn't been in Paris for three years. He has a wife and children and is terribly sweet. I shall never again take pity on Frenchmen.

Coming through the fog on the way home the lights were beautiful. When we got here little John heard us, and thinking it was morning came stumbling up the stairs with his clothes. I said, "Good heavens, do you know what time it is?" As a matter of fact, it was twenty-five minutes to five. He insisted on staying, and wouldn't believe I was just going to bed. I persuaded him to go back to bed. I was extremely sick in the night. Johnny came in about seven, and I got up and got him ready for school. Doris took him in the car. Then I went back to sleep. Johnny returned before lunch, said he had been given a half holiday. Peggy and I didn't believe it.

He is wearing his new suit, which is too large for him. He is drawing a picture now. I said I was going to have him come in an airplane.[6] He is singing now. I'm awfully glad to be with him. The feeling it gives me to see him is strange, and I can't analyze it, it isn't just maternal, but has an element of fear.

I'm still so confused I can't think, I don't want to see so many people. I really love Peggy. When she came into the café I was happy to see her face. John [Holms] I love much more than I ever think about. Just now I don't need him.

I don't want anything but Peter, but I will want my child, and must not stay away from him. It's all confusion now because I really want Peter, <u>and nothing else</u>.

Friday, December 2

Lunch, John [Holms] eating as if dead, played the Harp quartet of Beethoven, some of it lovely. I played Mozart symphony no. 34 and Bach English Suite.

Johnny came running in at three o'clock, with brilliant colour, and we played Corinthian bagatelle and he got 2 francs.[7] We all went to get Pegeen, Peggy and I got out and looked at Mrs. Jolas' school, she crying to different people and showing Montessori extravagances.[8] As we were entering the school Johnny took hold of my coat and said quickly, "I like better a school

---

[5]Lavandou is in the south of France, on the Riviera.
[6]Coleman was referring to bringing him over to London for Christmas.
[7]Corinthian bagatelle is a form of tabletop billiards.
[8]Maria McDonald Jolas (1893–1987), American expatriate to France. In addition to founding the little magazine *transition* with her husband, Eugene Jolas, she ran a Montessori bilingual day school in the Paris suburb of Neuilly which Guggenheim's daughter attended.

where they're strict and beat you if you don't know your lessons." This vindicated exactly what John said. Then when he saw that we were only visiting the school he enjoyed it. Peggy arranged for the Jolases to come to dinner.

At home we all played Corinthian bagatelle and John got a score of 1020 without getting the balls back. We put them to bed, I put on Peggy's black lace dress. Johnny said, "What are you?" Then the Neagoes came, and Djuna and Thelma.[9] I was at once exceedingly attracted to Thelma. When they left had a bitter discussion with John about it, who was feeling contentious and was really insufferable. He was as much attracted to her as I was, but pretended to pass it off saying he knew just what she would be like etc., and went on repeating in the dullest way that ten years ago he would have loved fucking her. Now he knew that there was nothing exciting beyond that. He repeated it 40 times. I said, "I'm not in the same state you are in, I'm sexually starved, and she excited me. I was occupied all the time in thinking if I would have slept with her." He said, "You would of course." "I don't think I would," I said.

I understood so much of Djuna's misery. This woman is really attractive. I said, "What gave one the feeling that she lives for sex?" He said the way her eyes were set, and said her face was coarse (which I couldn't see), and said she was made for fucking. I said, "But she has a damnably sweet and unaffected manner, something straightforward about her which, in someone with such a handsome face is most exciting physically." If I had met her at another time I'd have taken pains to see her again. But as it was I was too divided, my vanity and curiosity were stimulated (I felt she was slightly attracted to me) but I couldn't think of even a woman sexually now (I wasn't sure, if I had been tight), and everything was complicated by Djuna anyway, who loves her so much.

I've never seen a more attractive woman. Even on the stage, they don't often have such a compelling face as that. She makes one want to make love. But it isn't in obvious ways, that's what is moving. She <u>seems</u> to be interested only in what is going on. One feels that underneath that reserve there is a tremendous power. John says the power is worth nothing, but I'd like to feel it. I think one would learn something. She hardly opened her mouth the whole evening, her reticence and shyness of course adding to the charm of her handsome face and bent-down head.

Little Johnny couldn't sleep, all the noise coming through the dumb waiter, and came upstairs dressed, and I had to rush him up to John and Peggy's room. When the Neagoes left I put him in my bed. This morning got him

---

[9]Though Wood had moved to New York in 1928 where she lived with Metcalf, she made occasional visits to Paris over the next several years.

ready for school and heard him say the 1 1/2 table. His ears are set like Deak's, very low down.

Annie Neagoe got tight and was full of Jewish life and put life into Peter [Neagoe]. We ragged him about his anthology and playing up to people like Caresse Crosby.[10] I told Peggy the only thing that holds you to him (because he seems so sweet and admits so much, then goes right on being the editor) is that Annie says he claps his hands for joy when he knows he's going to see John and Peggy, and can't work that day. Anne made an atrocious drawing of me. Peter made another of Djuna. Djuna put one or two truthful lines in which gave it a resemblance.

Next to Thelma (that name!) Djuna appears, to the ordinary eye, unattractive. But she has so much life in her face that the other hasn't got. I couldn't talk to Djuna, because the people were there. There's a vacuum in her head.

Feel like a photographic plate which has had several pictures taken on it, when it should have had only one. I <u>ought</u> to shut out everything except Peter [Hoare]; and I dare say I will, one day. I can't shut out the child, and <u>ought</u> not to shut out John [Holms], because God knows what is going on in him now. I sit fighting him.

He puts up every barrier, to keep you from pitying him, or even sympathizing with him. I know he hasn't the least idea how much I love him. I can't show it, and his habits of conversation irritate me more since I have been with Peter. But I had resolved not to let that interfere.

I shouldn't see John now. They are coming to London for several months after Christmas, and I encouraged them with all my heart. I'm very fond of Peggy.

Saturday, December 3

I talked with Peggy yesterday morning, said a few things I thought of John. She said, "I notice a change in you whenever you've been away from John." I said, "Yes, he can't bear any woman to develop any traits he hasn't fostered." When he came Peggy told him, changing everything I said. She dashed about the room removing objects that people had set down.

P. lay on the couch and wanted to stir up some excitement. When she accused John of wanting to make women like himself he was playing

---

[10]"Caresse" (Mary Phelps) Crosby (1892–1970), American poet, editor, and memoirist. In 1922 she married Harry Crosby (1898–1929), writer and assistant editor of *transition*. In 1927 they set up their own imprint in Paris, The Black Sun Press, which Caresse ran alone for thirty years following Harry's suicide in 1929. The press published authors such as Kay Boyle, James Joyce, D. H. Lawrence, Ernest Hemingway, among others. The anthology is Neagoe's *Americans Abroad*.

Corinthian billiards and said, "Yes, I must be about my father's business." There has been a good deal of talking over the telephone to the insurance agent because John ran into a funeral procession one morning when he was drunk. He doesn't remember it.

I read *Lady Chatterley's Lover* all the afternoon.[11] Finished it at midnight. Skipped all the intellectual conversations. When I began it I kept telling John how dull and vulgar it was, like any cheap novelist. I was bored with it until they made love. Then it suddenly became sensible. But this didn't last long. The end was hilarious. I read parts of it to J. and P. They put anemones in each other's navels.

Monday, December 5

Took Johnny and Pegeen out walking in the Park Montsouris.[12] I saw where Johnny used to play, it gave me an unpleasant nostalgic feeling, like dreams of him when he was a baby.

Chicken for dinner. After dinner I took Johnny to the Porte d'Orléans and we went in the metro to the Porte d'Italie where I put him in the tram.[13] Left Johnny sitting in the tram looking sad; I banged on the window and his face lit up. He went to a party at Madame Donn's of Rostique's classmates. Wrote a letter to M.D. about his cough, a note from her this morning says it is all gone.

I've been reading Kay Boyle's book, *Year Before Last* all afternoon.[14] It's the shoddiest shit. John says Americans write like this because they're barbarians, they've got the talent but not an ounce of honesty. It takes civilization to be emotionally honest, evidently. Last night P[eggy]. and J[ohn]. and I went to dinner at Prunier's—I ate oysters and dressed crab, then afterwards to the Boeuf, where Peggy got very tight and talked to John about his failings, so funny I laughed terrifically. Then we went to the Coupole, and she threw her pocketbook at him. It landed quietly on the floor. When we came home she suddenly got really angry with him, because he said she was stupid about the keys to the garage, and she got into my bed and said she wouldn't sleep with him. She got into a frenzy and talked about the abortion and said she had had it because he was an inhuman man and she couldn't live with him, or bear children by him, that he stifled all

---

[11]Lawrence's novel, first published in Italy in 1928, was banned for obscenity until 1959 (U.S.) and 1960 (U.K).

[12]Montsouris Park is lined on one of its four sides by avenue Reille, Guggenheim's street.

[13]The Porte d'Orléans (which is near Montsouris Park) and the Porte d'Italie are both subway and tram stations in Paris. Coleman was sending John back to the Donns in Ivry.

[14]Boyle's 1932 novel, set on the French Riviera, is about a woman who leaves her husband for another man.

her womanly feelings.[15] He was very much hurt by what she said. She later felt better but he was angry. She wouldn't go upstairs, so he got in the bed too, and we slept that way the rest of the night. I like being near to John as it seemed to relieve a sort of strain; and I felt natural with him today.

I thought of Peter all the time and missed him horribly. Being near to John did not excite me, but only made me wish for Hoare. How I longed for him, his soft round stomach to put my face in, and longed to feel his hands touch me. We did not get up for lunch but had it in bed upstairs in their room, in a sweet atmosphere of peace. Now I feel happy with them for the first time. I read sentences from Kay Boyle's book out loud and made them roar with laughter. The book is absolutely beyond belief, it's so false. There isn't one honest word in it. And yet there you are, she's such a nice human woman, with decent human feelings: how can she do it?

The Jolases are coming to dinner tonight, P[eggy]. tried to get the Roger Vitracs too, but they couldn't come.[16] John said he could not cope with Mr. and Mrs. J[olas]. and was going to a prize fight, but I said he could not do it. He said the last time he saw Mrs. J[olas]. was at the Joyces' for Thanksgiving dinner, and she wanted to sing and Jolas said, "No, there are sneerers here." So John thought that for once he would give her what she wanted, and when she sang he told her it was wonderful, and he had never liked her before.

Little P. feeling happy today too, purged of her furies. They seem to love each other, and it's a pleasure to be with them.

Tuesday, December 6

Letter from Emma recently got Peggy mad again, and she says she will never see her. I don't believe Emma was ever fond of her.[17]

Johnny came rushing home late, from the dentist. I could hardly wait to see him. We played balloon; and he drew pictures. I love to sit writing, and have him drawing near. We put him to bed upstairs. He and John were feeling each other's muscles.

---

[15]See her entry for December 14, 1929, in which Coleman noted that Guggenheim was pregnant again. That pregnancy was aborted, and may be what Guggenheim was referring to here.

[16]Roger Vitrac (1899–1952), French surrealist poet and dramatist noted for plays such as *Les Mystères de l'amour* (1927, with Antonin Artaud). At this time he was with Kathleen "Kitty" Cannell (1891–1974), American dancer and actor in the Provincetown Playhouse, and dance and fashion journalist in Paris.

[17]Biographer Mary Dearborn traces the tension that had been developing between Goldman and Guggenheim: Guggenheim felt slighted by Goldman's only mild thanks to her in Goldman's "In Appreciation" in her 1931 autobiography, while Goldman felt frustrated in feeling financially indebted to Guggenheim (83–85).

Then the Jolases came. Peggy wore her white evening dress, and I wore red. Hers is a beauty, fitting very close, with fullness just at the legs, and puff sleeves. Mine is the one I got in Rome. Mrs. Jolas is the most dreadful woman I have ever seen. Jolas was sweet, I kept looking at him and thinking, "Fat though he is, and ass that he may be, I see why I liked him." Generally I can't literally think why I liked people in 1927. He began to adore John, and I loved this, I was so astonished, but Mrs. Jolas (and Peggy a little) did everything in her power to keep them from talking. But they struggled nobly on, John borne up by countless combats with Willa [Muir]. Jolas loved John more and more, and wanted to talk to him, and when he got tight he said so. Maria wanted to go home. I bore the brunt of entertaining her. I held her amber beads.

Jolas loved the music, we played the Brahms trio, then the harp and flute concerto, then a part of the quartet in G, also Elizabeth Schumann (Her voice is perfect.) Mrs. Jolas trilled notes now and then and cried out joyfully. She said the slow movement from the G quartet was sugary. John drove them home, in the hope of getting Jolas to stay out, since they were both tight; but I think Maria held him. John came home late, after Johnny and I were in bed, and muttered in the chair for half an hour.

When I went up to get Johnny he was naked, and I got the bathrobe on him and made him walk downstairs. When he saw my bed he came to life. He was so sweet, snuggling down in it. He slept late this morning, and Doris had to waken us both. I did love him, and dressed him kissing him.

Wednesday, December 7

Feel happy and settled here now.

Johnny came home. Comes in with fiery cheeks. Finished Kay's book—what a worthless throwing about of fine words. I can't see her now. She's really like this. Excellent descriptive parts, but no soul, and no comprehension not even of the simplest thing. All showing off, we are wonderful, abase the world. Idea of self as noble gentlewoman. Very funny. Not a sentence that can't be read aloud and make you laugh.

I tried to read *The Shutter of Snow*, but it bored me because I know it too well. Some parts of this are exactly like Kay Boyle.

Took out the manuscript of my present book and decided to copy it.[18] But the parts where I feel excitement are not done right. Worked at it till John and Peggy went to bed.

---

[18]In her entry for December 10, 1932, Coleman offered more detail about this manuscript. Recall too that on October 26, 1932, she mentioned starting a book about her childhood. Later, in her entry for June 10, 1934, she referred to beginning her "book" in the fall 1933, and this

John told us that once he got them outside Jolas collapsed, and Mrs. J. longed to stay up. John said she wanted to find out what this curious young man is like. He could not get rid of her. I didn't realize till that night how much Jolas is like Neagoe and Muir—the same wives too.

Today my old journal came, from Sonia, and I tried to find some interesting parts for Peggy.[19] There weren't any. It's extraordinary that this should come the day after I read Kay Boyle. Shoddy American womanhood. It made me sick. I took out a little poem I wrote in New York, which rather moved me, and one or two others, and the Proust quotations, and went down and fed the entire thick manuscript to the flames in the house furnace. It gave me a slight pang.

In the 1928 diary it was first like Kay and Jolas, and *transition* imitators; then, after I met John, it was like Mabel Dodge Luhan. I said to Peggy, "You mustn't think it was just because I met John that I changed. I was longing for someone who could think, and would have found it in London anyway." I said that I hated anyone who was anything like what I was three years ago. Peggy said, "I hate anyone who is anything like what I am now." Mrs. Jolas said that Muir's book *Transition* came out <u>after</u> the magazine.[20]

If Peter wrote me a word of affection I would go.

Thursday, December 8

John said I shouldn't have thrown away my diary, that one should keep all records. I couldn't keep it. I copied my book and changed some parts. The best parts not right yet.

Thelma and Djuna for dinner, I got tight and couldn't think of anything but Peter. I want to go back Tuesday. Thelma became a little intellectual, not offensive, but one felt she should think of sex. Djuna's hair all mussy and she looked old. Thelma pretty stupid when she opens her mouth. They went out with them, I stayed home. I don't want Thelma, and was even bored with looking at her. Djuna really sweet but I haven't the time to think of it.

---

book would become "The Tygon." In another entry, for October 28, 1937, she noted that she took some material from the childhood book and used it in "The Tygon"—for example, the character Frieda's mother breaking a window, Frieda's mother's insanity, and her father singing to her.

[19] As Coleman went on to indicate, this was a diary kept in 1928, and is presumably her first volume as there is no mention of an earlier one. Sonia Himmel had been reading it in the U.S.
[20] In fact, Muir's *Transition: Essays on Contemporary Literature* was published by the Hogarth Press in 1926, and the magazine *transition* in 1927.

152 Section 5

Thelma really pretty tiresomely sentimental. Loves Jung and Keyserling.[21] I wouldn't go down to the toilet with her.

John asked me why I didn't write of my early married life, and said that was often when one's emotions were at the highest peak. The truth is my emotions have never been at the highest peak, or anywhere near it. The nearest was when I was with Bianchetti in Rome. I've always expected to write about that.

Saturday, December 10

Gave my book to John to read. He thought it was very simple and honest. But I told him at the beginning that I had not done several of the emotional parts as I intended to do them. He thought the end of the first chapter very good, the breaking of the window; and the part about the song my father wrote. He said I was a fool if I tore it up. Peggy read it also.

I began Ernest Hemingway's *Death in the Afternoon*, and the tone of it did disgust me[22]; but I kept reading it because of the subject.

John decided suddenly to go to the Austrian Tyrol at Christmas with the children; spent most of the evening trying to get Peggy enthusiastic. We all slept together.[23] We got to laughing because Dorothy said John's breath used to be like milk and now was foul. I said it was true, John said Pegeen said it was like cacas.

Got Johnny off to school in the cold, his breakfast in a thermos bottle because the maids don't get up early today. It was so cold. He didn't mind exchanging the airplane for the Austrian Alps in snow.

Monday, December 12

In the afternoon Johnny went in the car with John and me to the American Express, where he hoped to get travel booklets, but was again thwarted, as there were none. We took him to the Café Flore, where he had lemonade and roast beef.

In the evening we phoned Peter to find out about Austria, and if he would go, but he was out. I was reading Hemingway, but John and Peggy said they had to go to Helen Joyce's, as it was her wedding anniversary, and they had hurt her feelings too often. I couldn't bear to go. I went finally to please John.

---

[21]Hermann Graf Keyserling (1880–1946), German philosopher.
[22]Hemingway's novel *Death in the Afternoon* (1932) glamourizes bullfighting.
[23]In her entry for December 13, 1932 (not transcribed), Coleman would again note of the trio, "We all slept together again, but though it makes us like each other and promotes intimacy, John and I talk, and no one gets to sleep. He sits between us and drinks, and Peggy complains. I talked violently in my sleep. Feel like writing."

When I got there, there were Blums, Jolases and some other woman.[24] I liked Frank Blum, because she is Jewish and has such a defiant face, which means nothing since she is under her husband's thumb. We talked college days a little, which interested me very much, but I was afraid John would hear. Then we got Mrs. Jolas to sing. She sang with Giorgio. He has a most heavenly voice. He doesn't care anything about it at all. They sang some nice duets. Everyone put on different expressions during the singing.

The Blums went, and John kept passing around the drinks, Peggy having incapacitated Giorgio. She told him his marriage had been unsuitable. Jolas got ferocious for a minute. John kept him calmed down with drinks. Helen sat draping velvet over her body and pulling down Giorgio's head. She drank a great deal and said a few words about Svevo.

Giorgio said his uncle's preface was quite satisfactory but I said it wasn't, but didn't go beyond that because I was glad to have him come out and say something.[25] He said Svevo was a nice old man. Blum told before leaving a story in which John was a sort of indecisive hero. Jolas began suddenly to agree violently with John. When we got home I finished the Hemingway book.

The next morning I went upstairs to see John. He said Hemingway's excitement about the ring came from his not having any of the real excitement inside. The book makes you sick. I finished it because I love bullfighting. But it's a rotten book for an artist to write.

"Brave bulls," "brave men"—what is the use of intelligence? Let's all wallow in the gore. Let's be brave men and fuck and kill.

I phoned Peter about eleven o'clock. I could hear his voice as clearly as if he were in Paris. He thought I was speaking in London. He said he hadn't intended to go ski-ing.

When we came home Saturday night there was Johnny in my bed. John said, "I can't believe that funny little thing came out of Emily's loins."

I took the children to see Harold Lloyd in *Movie Crazy* at the Champs Élysées Theater. Tickets cost twenty-five francs. It made me laugh because the children laughed so hard. Brought them back in the metro. Johnny showed off and Pegeen followed him adoringly with her eyes. We later learned that in the morning he had been poking at her drawers. I was shocked at it, but J. and P. said not to say anything. However, I was embarrassed. He asked

---

[24]The Blums are unidentified.
[25]Giorgio's uncle was Stanislaus Joyce (1884–1955), English-language teacher in Italy and scholar. According to James Joyce biographer Richard Ellmann, when James Joyce declined (to the consternation of Livia Schmitz) to write a preface for Schmitz's (Svevo's) *Senilità* (1898), the novel Putnam was bringing out in England entitled *As A Man Grows Older* (1932), "a compromise was finally worked out by which Stanislaus Joyce wrote the introduction to detail his brother's reaction to Schmitz's books" (635–36).

me in the afternoon—"Are you glad of me?" They played hide and seek at night. Doris made the supper. Johnny spoke to Peter over the telephone and said, "Is it night where you are?" He said, "Will you come with us?" When he answered the telephone for Peggy he said, "*Qu'est-ce-qui se passe?*" thinking that was the way to reply.[26] Then we went out and met Alec Ponisovsky and his brother-in-law Paul Léon at a Russian restaurant.[27] It was so deadly dull at first that we over-drank ourselves in vodka, then it was the liveliest time I've had since Father and Djuna combatted at Hayford Hall.

M. Léon took a great interest in me, and I told him my name was Mrs. Simpson. Later I said it was Mrs. Pinkwhip. He wanted to win my favours, and this became a pivot for witticisms on the part of all present, including M. Léon himself. He would spit, blow and stutter in my face with passion, then put his arm around John, then attack Peggy for misbehaviour in Piccadilly Circus, where she frightened him five years ago by demanding if he loved her. The conversation was extremely lively; M. Léon jumped about like a chimpanzee. Alec sat devastated and bored, but lifted his head from time to time to make a comment. We had borsch, and pancakes with ice cream and caviar. We drank a great deal. M. Léon was quite indelicate.

We sat in the Russian bistro till midnight, and laughed so hard that we could not get up to go at first. We went to a Russian boîte, the Poisson d'Or, where Mr. Pinkwhip immediately forgot his passion on seeing a boy he knew who played the guitar. I can't remember what we said, except that M. Léon was telling seriously about his refusal to tell Joyce what whore was in Russian, and John said, "Oh, I shouldn't be so playful with Joyce, Paul." Most of the jokes turned on indecent allusions. I said I could understand that an American woman would be fascinated by this sophisticated subtle European. He would say, "Now let's DO it, Mrs. Pinkwhip."

At the boîte gipsies played guitars and sang, with real gusto. Most of the people there were Russian, and came in strong for the chorus. Never have seen such a lively boîte. Pinkwhip and Alec vied to sit next to the boy, who was a large-mouthed black imbecile. John kept talking about how much the singers enjoyed singing until I could have strangled him. One gipsy woman gave me a great kick. Alec and Paul, followed by John, handed out ten-franc notes like hot cakes. A very handsome woman was talking to a man, and

---

[26]"What's happening?"
[27]Alec Ponisovsky was a friend of Giorgio Joyce, and was currently teaching Russian to James Joyce. He had been briefly engaged to James Joyce's daughter, Lucia, in March 1932. His brother-in-law, Paul Leopold Léon, also a Russian émigré, had settled in Paris in 1921 and was now working as a secretary to James Joyce. Léon had first moved to London in 1918, where Guggenheim had known him. Léon's wife was a writer for the Paris edition of the *New York Herald Tribune,* publishing under the name of Lucie Noël.

John said she was a high class whore and I wouldn't believe it. The gipsy woman sang in a deep loud throaty gutteral. John pretty angry with Peggy because she didn't enjoy herself. If you sit and look at anything in a boîte John thinks you're bored. But I think Peggy didn't like the spreading about of the ten franc notes. She said at dinner she wished I bring 50 trunks and stay in her living room. John drove home like dynamite. I just loathed him. He was absolutely desperate. He was so drunk he couldn't see, and intended to kill us. If we had hit anything I'd have leaped out and stamped on his head.

He took the car out alone later and smashed it. The children went to school in the bus.

Wrote to the housekeeper in London and sent money to keep my room for a fortnight. I can't give it up, Peggy wanted me to have Phyllis pack my things and keep them. But I won't do it. Peggy and I went down town in the bus, she all the way asking my opinion of what she should do about John. When we came home I attacked John for driving like that and said P. was right. He said he wouldn't be so drunk if he could go to the country or get out of Paris. He didn't get hurt in the accident; but as Peggy says, that will come. He is in a desperate condition.

Wednesday, December 14

I wrote to Bianchetti all the afternoon, very painful and tiresome business; Peggy was out and I talked to John and complained. I said I wished everyone in the world was dead except himself, and Hoare and Johnny. I wrote also to my brother John; that was just as difficult.

Peggy has gotten embroiled with an American lady of who [sic] *sans aucune fortune personelle a trompé tout le monde dans la région de Pramousquier.*[28] She bought Peggy's house without paying for it and built all over it, and has done the same with other houses. Peggy had a letter today from her neighbor in Pramousquier who feels Peggy is responsible.

Djuna came to dinner, without Thelma. She is very unhappy. I didn't have much sympathy. It turned out that Peggy read my letters to her. She got tight and told it, to give herself a purge. I said I had known it. I was pretty disgusted, particularly with myself, for enjoying writing those letters so much.[29] Peggy is a little shit. She thinks it's all right if she's confessed it.

---

[28]"Without any private fortune deceived everyone in Pramousquier"
[29]In her December 5, 1932 entry, Coleman had noted of Guggenheim: "She has thrown away all my letters, sad for my vanity" (portion not transcribed).

Djuna showed us a letter from Charles [Henri Ford], such a sweet letter. I never dreamed he was as nice as that letter. Such a nasty little poseur, and underneath this sweet ingenuosness. Djuna obviously brings out what's best in him.

How to take Djuna is beyond me. She can't feel anything without being in, or thinking of a crowd—John says this is not entirely so. I don't feel anything when someone like Djuna goes on—I just can't. Every word she says is dramatic, said for a reply. She can't help it. Peggy sits there flapping open and shut her jaws in agreement. She wriggles her ears at Djuna. I prefer Djuna. She goes on about Thelma, what a shit she is, that is, expecting you to say so. Thelma came back to Djuna needing her protection, but would not admit it, and tried to resuscitate their old relation, and it hasn't worked. She attacks Djuna for loving Charles. Dj. says Charles never meant anything to her really, but Thelma is everything. She sat there crying out her heart, very sad, underneath I knew it. But the words just didn't mean anything.

Last night after they took Djuna home John sat and talked to me. He was furious. I was sitting up in bed, and I answered him. He said it was melancholy to talk to me any more. It's true that since I've been here I've done nothing but attack John. Hoare has made me conscious of how much he influences me, and I try to keep my end up by contradicting everything. He kissed me on top of the head before retiring. I felt very much torn. I have believed lately that I must get away from John. He's the only person in the world who believes in my genius.

Peggy playing scherzo of the first symphony.[30] Djuna cares so much what people think. There seems to be almost never that moment in her when you don't really care about anything but the truth—the way Peggy is. Yet it is there. She left her book for them to read, I tried to read some [of] it.[31] John found a part that was quite wonderful. Gave you a sudden quick feeling of fear for Djuna.

Thursday, December 15

I felt rather bad because I hadn't been more understanding of Djuna. It was stupid of me. Can't endure the amount of sham in her. I felt this way all yesterday, knew perfectly well that no matter how much sham, there was something absolutely true in her. This came out yesterday, when John read her book. There were some sentences that were the absolute truth, come right out

---

[30] They were listening to Beethoven.
[31] The manuscript that would become *Nightwood*.

of genius. There was one about jealousy.[32] Another wonderful one, watching the loved one waking up—"the smile of the hyena as she left that company."[33] This gave me the most intense excitement. There were others too. Most of the book is sentimental shit of the worst kind (Thelma and Fitzie), then these sudden wonderful truths.[34] I haven't read it yet, but John read aloud some of the best things. Then he read 70 pages so bad that he didn't think he'd ever see Djuna again. I told him it was his bounden duty to talk to her about the best and worst parts of her book.

Another fine part in Djuna's book was about women acrobats, and another of a tiger passing in a circus.[35] I have such a feeling for Djuna now, as if we had some deep bond I've never felt before. Especially because of the sentence, "when she left that company." I wonder if she has the least idea what it means. I love her for that. I want to see her now. John said he always knew she had it in her. You certainly couldn't know it from *Ryder*.

Friday, December 16

Johnny made quite a to-do about going to school last night, but I said he must go. This morning he was really upset about it. I insisted, and dressed him,

---

[32] In the chapter "Watchman, What of the Night?" Dr. O'Connor tells Nora Flood, who has been abandoned by her lover Robin Vote, "The heart of the jealous knows the best and the most satisfying love, that of the other's bed, where the rival perfects the lover's imperfections" (*Nightwood* 76).

[33] In the "Watchman" chapter, O'Connor explains to Vote: "'For the lover, it is the night into which his beloved goes,' he said, 'that destroys his heart; he wakes her suddenly, only to look the hyena in the face that is her smile, as she leaves that company'" (75).

[34] A good friend of Barnes, American Mary Eleanor "Fitzi" Fitzgerald (1877–1955) had been the business manager of the Provincetown Players, and like Coleman she had worked as secretary to Emma Goldman.

[35] In the novel's first chapter, "Bow Down," the narrator describes protagonist Felix Volkbein: "Early in life Felix had insinuated himself into the pageantry of the circus and the theatre. In some way they linked his emotions to the higher and unattainable pageantry of Kings and Queens. The more amiable actresses of Prague, Vienna, Hungary, Germany, France and Italy, the acrobats and sword-swallowers, had at one time or another allowed him their dressing rooms—sham salons in which he aped his heart" (10). Later in the novel, in the chapter "Night Watch," Nora Flood and Robin Vote meet at a circus, in front of the lions: "The great cage for the lions had been set up, and the lions were walking up and out of their small strong boxes into the arena. Ponderous and furred they came, their tails laid down across the floor, dragging and heavy, making the air seem full of withheld strength. Then as one powerful lioness came to the turn of the bars, exactly opposite the girl [Robin], she turned her furious great head with its yellow eyes afire and went down, her paws thrust through the bars and, as she regarded the girl, as if a river were falling behind impassable heat, her eyes flowed in tears that never reached the surface" (49).

then he began to cry. He had an "architecture" exam, and didn't have the notes, and said he wouldn't be able to write anything, and would be rapped on the hands with an iron ruler. This froze my blood. I told him not to go.

Madame Picabia came for lunch and grinned about the table.[36] Peggy in a great rush over business developments. Has located the forging American. Johnny much shocked over photographs of Sindbad naked. I began Muir's book, *The Three Brothers*, but it's very dull.[37] They all have lumps in their throats.

I dreamed about Johnny this morning, that he kept touching me, and I didn't want it, and he insisted, and I could hardly resist.

Received from Kay Boyle this morning copy of *Year Before Last* in the Caresse Crosby editions, marked, "To Emily, in appreciation of her book."[38] Very embarrassing.

Saturday, December 17

Talked to Peter a long time in the telephone, last night. He has agreed to go with us. After talking with him I felt terribly depressed. I shall see him Friday.

Johnny home all day because of the examination. I almost decided to take him to school in England. John talked me out of it because I haven't a proper place to keep him in, said I would communicate my tense state of mind, etc., and he would not be in normal conditions. Peggy took Johnny out with her shopping. Went to the Donns' for dinner, Johnny and I walked all the way over to the rue Patay. It was dark, and very damp, almost a fog, the only time of day I like in Paris; with people hurrying home in the streets. We looked in all the little shop windows along the rue d'Alesia and rue Tolbiac.

John says he is a happy child, and since he likes his teacher, I should not do anything, except speak to the Head Master about his English. John says I get morbid about him and he would get odd if he lived with me as things are now.

Djuna was here when I got back from the Donns.' John had been talking to her about her book for an hour. I didn't say anything until the very end; then I spoke enthusiastically about the best parts. She was quite happy, no matter what John said, so he said a great deal. She didn't mind; she knew he knew the best. They thought this was difficult to understand. Djuna got tight at the end, sat like a hen looking sideways at John, as if he were a cracker she would

---

[36] Gabrielle Picabia, wife of French impressionist cum avant-garde painter Francis Picabia (1878–1953).
[37] *The Three Brothers* (1931), a historical novel.
[38] Boyle's novel was first published by Faber, and then by Crosby's Black Sun Press, both in 1932.

like to eat. I laughed so much. "What are you sitting there for in your useless passion?" she said to me.

She doesn't know the good from the bad in her book, has no consciousness of herself. But very pleased that we had recognized. I was alive and sitting up the whole time. She didn't want to go home and when she left with John she wanted to stay out. Peggy made him promise not to stay.

Djuna is worried about money; and got tight enough to talk about it, Peggy sitting resisting. I don't know how she can do it.

The whole point is she won't give up Thelma, that is won't stop loving her; because she likes it; she's morbid and likes it. John said, "Do you want to be a woman or an artist? Make up your mind. It's a good thing to be a woman; but don't write." She said, "What do you think you are?" "A moral teacher," says John. Then he said, "Good writing is good living," and became covered with shame. They took it seriously. Djuna made Peggy write it in a book. I said, "Don't you think Djuna's getting fond of John now?" and she said, "I wouldn't touch John with a ten-foot pole." Peggy said, "You wouldn't have to," meaning that his pole was more than ten feet. Djuna said John should come to tea with Natalie Barney. John said, "I never read such an awful burst-up of shit," referring to one of N.B.'s books. She said, "You smug little red melon of a Shakespeare."

Djuna enjoyed herself immensely. She read aloud a great deal but nobody could listen.

Monday, December 19

Last night we went out with Djuna and Thelma, met them Café Flore, Djuna just had letter from T.R. Smith, Liveright, about her book.[39] Most intelligent letter I ever saw from an American publisher. But he wants her to write the book over. She had had her cry and was feeling gay. Thelma sat like a doughy cat. We went to the Viking, where John made me mad and I threw wine on him. He says he can't say one word to me. Wine went also on a gentleman behind, which was very humiliating. John got up and apologized. He was so angry at first he couldn't think; and they said I should apologize. I was afraid to do it. We went to the Poisson d'Or but would not give out tips. Peggy and

---

[39] T. R. Smith was an editor at the American publishing house Boni & Liveright, which had published Barnes' short-story collection *A Book* (1923), revised in 1929 as *A Night Among the Horses,* and *Ryder* (1928). Smith wanted the manuscript completely revised and although Barnes continued rewriting the book, she began to solicit it elsewhere. After many rejections it was eventually brought out by Faber & Faber in 1936. See Cheryl J. Plumb's introduction to *Djuna Barnes Nightwood: The Original Version and Related Drafts* (vii–xxvi).

Djuna in animated conversation about her book. Thelma got me between her legs and said I was the servant of art.

We went to Florence's, in Montmartre, where J[ohn]. and P[eggy]. got in a deep personal confab.[40] Djuna wept. I sat comforting Djuna. Thelma went up to another table, where negroes were, and sat down. Djuna was humiliated. John got her out by dancing with her. Poor Djuna said, "That's her sex appeal." I suddenly saw why Thelma has come back. When we met them at the Flore, Djuna looked pretty and lively, Thelma like an old greyhound. Peggy arranged to lend Djuna some money. Djuna said, "Don't you care for John?" and Peggy said, "I don't care even for an old siphon, that squirts straight at you." I kept thinking of Johnny. He has gone to Ivry. We took him out there, he has a cold, and I want it taken care of.

Very long letter from Bianchetti this morning. He found *Pinocchio* for John, a cheap copy. I sent him 50 francs for Christmas the other day.

Emma is in town. I must see her. Tomorrow a concert at Johnny's school. He is home today, in Ivry, to get over his cold.

This morning a letter from Father with two hundred dollars in it. He seems to want to spare it. I intended to send back twenty if he sent me fifty extra, now with this I don't know what to do. Bless his heart. I do need it. I put away fifty at once and did not acknowledge the existence of it, for I need it desperately in London, and do not intend to spend it on winter sports. I gave Madame Donn two hundred francs. Three hundred for the children, from Father. I gave the children fifty each. I pay my room, and Deak (the school), and Bianchetti, and what he owes Peggy. What is left I'll spend on ski-ing kit—which I don't want to spend. Fifty each, Doris, Marie and Madeleine.[41] I sent ten shillings to the Righton children, and 10 to the maids in Oakley St.

Ski-ing suit for Johnny, for me, boots and mittens. Horrible expense. I want also to pay Johnny's fare to Austria.

J[ohn]. and P[eggy]. have gone out to find out where we are going. Peggy is leaving tonight for Nice, to get Sindbad.[42] Sent Gossy and Norman a Christmas card, and sent also to Mr. Harvey and Mr. Matthews.[43] On Mr. Harvey's I put, "With every good wish and thanks for all you have done

---

[40]Chez Florence was the Montmartre boîte located at 61, rue Blanche, named for its main attraction: Harlem dancing and singing sensation Florence Embry Jones (1892–1932), considered the "first" African-American woman of the Paris jazz scene.
[41]Guggenheim's staff; Marie was Guggenheim's cook.
[42]Sindbad was living in Nice with his father, Laurence Vail, and his new step-mother, Kay Boyle.
[43]Mr. Matthews was a teacher at John's school.

for John"—I wanted to put—"Take this, you dirty old shit, and stuff it up your dried up old ass."

Christmas isn't really so bad when you've got a little money.

Tuesday, December 20

Johnny has the grippe, fever, in bed, and I am going there this afternoon to be with him, and release Madame Donn. Poor little devil—just before Christmas. Deak writes this morning to say he and Louise will take Christmas excursion train and spend 24 hours in Paris; very upsetting, as we can't possibly delay. We have to leave Friday night. Even if Johnny is prevented from going, by the grippe, I don't want to see Deak now. I have to think of Peter first.

I was going to take Johnny to the school concert today, but now cannot, and intended to talk to Mr. Harvey. So I wrote him a letter instead, which surprised me by its intelligence. Last night John gave me a long lecture, because I was reading Muir's book and did not know it was a historical novel.[44] I thought galleys could have existed in Muir's childhood. John said it was fascinating. He branched from this to other subjects relating to my deficiencies. His chief complaint is that I have become quite dumb. He says he can't conduct a rational conversation with me any more and that it is melancholy. He says my brain is clouded with the fumes of sexual desire. I said, "John doesn't want me to fuck." "On the contrary," he said, "There's nothing you need more. It might clear up your head."

He said, "I no longer fight with you. I'm just sad." I said I was a medium, and resented being so; and continually absorbed what he thought. He said I have got so used to fighting with Hoare, which is necessary, since that is a sexual fight, that I think I have to fight with him too, which is unnecessary. Peggy woke up and said, "What are you getting off, you old gas-bag?"

John said Thelma looked like a polyp; then he said she was like a stuffed mushroom. I did think she was like an amoeba, feeling about with stumps.

Wednesday, December 21

Peggy arrived this morning with Sindbad. Great commotion, have not yet got reservations. John has spent two days telegraphing Austria.

I spent two afternoons with Johnny, in Ivry, keeping him in bed. Last night he got up for supper, and they had their tree. Monsieur Donn got tight and was very sweet. I brought them vodka. I brought stars and trappings for the

---

[44] *The Three Brothers.*

tree; they had a lot. It was a very gay tree, a real Russian tree, overloaded, and brilliant with candles. Little Johnny sat in a red sweater.

I brought him tangerines, and *Zig et Puce*. He likes to read the most dreadful muck. I gave him inhalations every hour. He looked so sweet, under the towel, breathing in 150 times.

When I came home Neagoe was here. He had *Americans Abroad*. WHAT a gallery. Nothing of the slightest sense in it.

Last night I fell asleep while John was drinking, and talking to me about himself. I was so disgusted. When he went upstairs I kissed him, and held him very hard. Half of me needs Hoare; but half of me absolutely needs John, and cannot live without him. The woman part is so unsatisfied now that it's all I can think of.

Johnny wasn't really very sick. I remembered when he was two years old, and had the abcess in his ear. I used to love him when he was sick because it was the only time he was quiet.

Friday, December 23

Went out to Ivry and stayed a while with Johnny. He wanted me to see Emma so he could get a present. He said, "Tell her what a good guy I am." Djuna and Thelma and Mme. Picabia and some German for dinner. The German telephoned Austria for us. She screamed German into the telephone. Thelma cornered me and expanded. I was very nervous.

I thought of nothing all day but Peter's coming and am in a very nervous state. We don't know yet where we are going. Djuna suggested Lake Placid.

This morning it is bright and cold. Peter is coming tonight.

Part III

Section 1

London and Devonshire
March 22–July 24, 1933

The group, including Guggenheim, Holms, Coleman, Hoare, and the three children, went to Gargallen, Austria, for their ski holiday at the end of 1932. Coleman then returned to London with Hoare, but she did not take up her diary again until March 22, 1933. She made only two entries before stopping, and then resumed it briefly in July when she once again vacationed at Guggenheim's Hayford Hall estate, in company with Djuna Barnes as well as her new acquaintance Antonia White, the English novelist, translator, and diarist who would become one of her best, life-long friends. During this period Coleman grew profoundly depressed as she confronted the reality that her partnership with Hoare was untenable. At Hayford Hall her dark mood added to her often antagonistic attitude towards her hosts and other guests, but the comfort she received from her friends there, coupled with the ceaseless sexual banter and innuendo of their conversations and actions, diverted her and allowed her to recover her balance.

34, GREAT JAMES STREET[1]

Wednesday, March 22, 1933

Telephoned Mrs. Carswell and arranged to have her meet Antonia White.[2]

---

[1] Great James Street is in Camden, near Bloomsbury.
[2] Catherine Carswell (see earlier note). Coleman had met Eirine Botting, who went by her pen name Antonia (Tony) White (1899–1980) in early 1933, at a party given by Wyn Henderson. Guggenheim had known Henderson, and had become her neighbor when she and Holms moved to Trevor Square in London's tony Knightsbridge in 1933. A typographer, Henderson worked for presses such as Caresse Crosby's Black Sun Press and Nancy Cunard's The Hours Press.

I don't want to write a diary of events, partly because it's not interesting—but if I should write the kind of diary I like—it wouldn't be interesting either. I want to find out what is in me.

I'd like to write a poem about Holms.

I think Peter is important to me in my earthly life, and John is important to me in the heavenly life. I feel so sad all the time, I'm hardly ever happy now. I wake up in a fury of depression, but shake it off quickly enough—but how much of this is age and how much the beginning to understanding life I don't yet know. Djuna said the only time she was ever happy was writing, and I should think this would be the truth.

Read Antonia White's description in *Life and Letters*, and didn't know just what to make of it, because it's so like mine.[3] Like me with the life left out.

March 23

I feel insufferably depressed about this world. There is not one thing in it except love, and I can't have it. Somehow that—and the heavenly part—seem not to have any connection. That is in itself the proof that I love the wrong person. I think that if we were together, passion might change him—.

HAYFORD HALL, July 21, 1933

I felt very depressed, because Antonia has gone.[4] Djuna dressed up in evening clothes and they asked me to do it too. I said I felt more like killing someone.

After she moved to Bloomsbury, Henderson had influenced her lover, the publisher Desmond Harmsworth, to take on White's first novel, *Frost in May*, which was published in the summer of 1933 (Dunn 150). In this autobiographical story, Nanda Grey, White's persona, tries to come to terms with her artistic sensibilities within the confines of a Catholic boarding school. In 1906, when White was a child, her father, Cecil Botting, suddenly converted his family to Catholicism. In 1926, White renounced her religion but by 1940 she would once again become a practicing Catholic.

[3]Coleman was likely reading White's short story "The House of Clouds," which was published in volume V, number 28 (1930) of *Life and Letters*, a monthly periodical founded and edited by literary journalist and Bloomsbury member Desmond MacCarthy (from 1928–1933). The "description" Coleman referred to is an italicized preface written by MacCarthy in which he notes, for instance, that White's story "has psychological as well as literary value and a certain beauty; for it is as clear a record of 'fantasies' and emotions during temporary insanity as the patient could offer after recovery." The story is a fictionalized account of White's breakdown at the end of 1922, when she was institutionalized in the Bethlem Royal Hospital for ten months. The similarities between White's and Coleman's breakdowns and subsequent literary treatments of them are remarkable.

[4]White had spent a week at the Devon estate. This Hayford Hall diary begins here, *in medias res*.

At dinner they talked, and I said to Peggy, "I may die soon. I want you to know I'm very fond of you." I felt myself about to weep. I picked up a glass and dashed it on the floor. I said to Peggy, "I couldn't help it, I'm sorry." I thereupon took up two more glasses and smashed them and rushed out of the room.

I saw it all very plainly, what sort of a person I am. There can't be any life with Peter. I felt a sort of relief. Djuna came upstairs afterwards and said, "Come down, we all love you. Why did you do it?" I felt like a solid stone. I said, "I can't come down."

I heard John through the door saying, "He won't marry her because he knows it wouldn't work." I thought he was talking about Antonia and Earnshaw Smith.[5] Later, I heard him say, "I'm very fond of her," and thought he was talking about me. It was Antonia. Peggy suspected I was listening and came through on the other side but I heard her in time. Later she came in my room when I was lying on the bed and told me to get undressed, and opened the window.

Thinking about what Elsa Freitag-Loringhoven wrote: "True death is wealth tremendous, but it must be earned with life; that is why still I live."[6]—the only time I have ever seen that written.

I don't think about dying, but I think of getting out of this life, through despair. I haven't faced the genuine thought of dying. I don't think I ever would face it; if I died I think I would do it quickly without facing it, through cowardice because I didn't want to think.

I miss little Antonia because she distracted me. Djuna depresses me, with her dishonesty. Even if I got at Djuna, what good would it do me? She can still pat me on the head and say, "Poor baby" as at 55 avenue Reille.[7] Suffering hasn't taught her anything.

She's reading Antonia's book. Trying to like it but doesn't really think much of it. Tony dazzled by Djuna's outpour. Djuna gave her the *Ladies*

---

[5]Eric Earnshaw Smith was an English senior civil servant who had become Antonia White's second husband in 1925. After two years, the marriage was annulled for lack of consummation—Smith was gay—but the two remained close friends.

[6]Baroness Elsa von Freytag-Loringhoven (1874–1927), German-born poet and artist, circulating within cities like Berlin, New York, and Paris, was known as both "the first American dada" and "the mother of Dada" (Gammel 4). Despite the financial and emotional assistance she received from an artistic community that included Guggenheim and Barnes, she battled poverty and poor mental health throughout her life. She died from asphyxiation by gas—likely suicide—in her Paris flat on December 14, 1927. See *Barnoness Elsa: Gender, Dada, and Everyday Modernity, A Cultural Biography*, by Irene Gammel. Excerpts (including the line here quoted by Coleman) from some of the letters she wrote to Barnes in 1924 were printed in the February 1928 issue of *transition*, introduced by Barnes herself.

[7]Guggenheim's Paris address.

Almanac.[8] They sat gulling each other, Djuna lapping and little Tony grooming her. Brushing down her long hair and biting at her feet. She went away in a daze. Djuna gave her *Ryder* to read, but no one knows what Tony thought of it. They munched away together, a proper feast for Tony, and a further satisfied appetite for Djuna, who doesn't get this here.

Tony asked Peggy how she would take her death. "Very absentmindedly," Peggy said. Djuna lusts for flattery to feed her ill opinion of herself, Tony wants it to make her feel in the swim. Djuna would die without flattery, but Tony would go prattling right along. She talks as well as any woman I have ever met.

Djuna is too like me, but she's shoddy and has more guts.

Sunday, July 23

Djuna got tight at dinner, and since her hair had been washed she looked very pretty. She said to Peggy, "You said I didn't like you." Peggy said for her to say what she liked. "Come on, cutie; come on, red-cock." In the drawing room Djuna said she wanted to explain herself. Peggy said, "I'm so rich you can't approach me." Then we got serious. Peggy was attacked for being treacherous. Djuna started that, mildly. I was ferocious. Dj. said I had no sense of humour about myself. John said neither had Blake or Emily Brontë or Dante which I thought was more than was necessary. She talked a great deal about Dan.[9] John said she didn't understand that he was evil. He gave her an abortion then went through all her letters.

I said, "How can anyone have such a gift of God and absolutely no brains to operate with it?" She said I talked too much, then she said, "You think Antonia's talent is only a little less important than mine." This because at tea-time I tried to have an abstract conversation with her.

She went on about her talent till John said, "The best parts of your book are another world from Antonia." I said, "I know that, but she doesn't realize that she should do something about the bad parts, which are more extensive." John said, "You won't make her realize by bellowing." Peggy got very mad and exploded entirely. She blew up like a little steam pump and puffed when she was finished. What she said was exactly what she had said to me on former occasions, viz, "You live in a world of romantic lies." This she said to Djuna. To me she said, "You speak more truth than anyone I know except myself."

---

[8] Barnes' *Ladies Almanack* (1928) is about the Paris lesbian community.
[9] In June 1933, Barnes had become pregnant by Jean Oberlé, a French painter. Daniel A. Mahoney gave her an abortion in Paris, after which she travelled to Hayford Hall to recover.

I got very angry about Peggy's having talked about Hoare and me to Mary Reynolds, which I knew had taken place.[10] She said John did the same. I said to Djuna, "Just understand them thoroughly; they'll help you, but they'll have their fun."

Djuna began to get very loving with John. She began, "I chucked him under the chin the other day and he started back as though he had been shot." The truth is John hasn't liked Djuna much this time. But tonight her hair was thick and very red, and she was loving. "This looks like a rape," said Peggy. She had been asleep on the couch. Djuna threw herself on John and kept hugging him. Peggy said, "He'll assert his lump." Then she made a comprehensive survey of her person and said, "It's all right." She said, "If you rise, the dollar will fall." Djuna said he had no technique. John said his technique was so varied he must get another bottle. Djuna said to Peggy, "What a help-mate."

She flung herself on him perpetually, kissing him. She looked very pretty with her hair falling down. She kept twirling and untwirling a handkerchief. John told her she had written the best things of any woman in the last 50 years. She kissed him passionately on the neck.

Then she began to pound Peggy in the bottom and Peggy shrieked, "My God, how this woman hates me" and Djuna kept pounding her, then she began to pound me. She hadn't hit me four times before I had an orgasm. Djuna was very loving and very tender, and thought everyone was tight but herself. She wanted to help them all up to bed. She pounded and massaged me thoroughly. John turned down the lights and left us. I tried to hear something at the door but couldn't.

I was very angry with John because when I asked Peggy to tell me something in which I deceived myself he wouldn't let her—I felt such a fury with him, for a great many accumulated things, that I felt like killing him. I have such repressed passion in relation to John that I would hate to have it ever get out.

Djuna said to me, "Don't ever give up, inside yourself," meaning don't give up the feeling you have for the one you love. I don't know exactly what she meant. I was thinking it would be a matter of will, whether I gave Hoare up or not; I could keep to it, and perhaps live in the feeling I have had, without

---

[10]Mary Reynolds (1891–1950) was a well-to-do American expatriate bookbinder and advocate of avant-garde art. Her salon at 14, rue Hallé in Montparnasse was frequented by guests such as Guggenheim, Marcel Duchamp, Samuel Beckett, James Joyce, and Mina Loy. She had been involved with Laurence Vail at the same time he was seeing Guggenheim in New York, but the women became close friends after Vail introduced them to each other. She became the mistress of Duchamp in the 1920s, a relationship that lasted almost three decades. In May 1931, Reynolds had accompanied Guggenheim and Holms to Italy where they visited with Coleman.

ever seeing him. I could get out of it, if I made up my mind. It's <u>concentration</u>, more than living, that makes something out of emotion. Djuna hasn't lived with Thelma for five years.

She is so false with Peggy because of the money, that's her temperament, she couldn't take the money knowing what Peggy is like, so she won't admit it to herself, which I found out this afternoon. Just as she doesn't know what Dan is like, her whole book, and she's only found out now he is a shit. John was trying to make her see she must forgive him. She reads Dostoyevsky, intensely, but doesn't understand a word of it. She hasn't the faintest capacity to reason from one thing to another, hence can never free her mind, or unfreeze the falsity into which her emotions are set. She is much more gifted than I, I think—I used to have facility, but not like that, hers is much more varied. But I can't see how <u>any</u> artist can write more than a few scattered lines worth while if she can't free herself <u>intellectually</u> of wrong ideas.

July 24

Latest remarks of Djuna and Peggy: Peggy didn't want Sindbad to fetch a pair of scissors. John said, "He's ten years old, and can't bring a pair of scissors." Peggy said, "You're thirty-five, and can't bring anything." Djuna said the second ancestor from the left resembled me.[11] "He's got that wild luscious roving look." When she was reading something she wrote to Antonia, Peggy looked at her fixedly for some time and said, "Why have you got that tense baby look?" P. said, "When you're reading your works you always look like a baby wanting its bottle." This was hard. Last night Dj. said J. and P. were rough and worldly. John said, "One of the reasons I have very little charm is that I'm deaf." I said, "I hate it when Mary Reynolds squeezes up her eyes at you, as if she were going to squeeze puss out of them." Dj. said, "That's not even true." I said P. resembled a water lizard, J. said, "Yes, they slip rustling out of your arms." He said a photograph of Djuna looked like Albert.[12] She said, "Like the gnawed side of a cliff." I said, "Djuna, I can't help feeling that you could say just one word to me and it would put me straight. What do you think I need?" Peggy said, "A straight-jacket." Djuna said, "Lydia Pinkham's Vegetable Compound."[13]

The garden is so beautiful here that I love to lie in it, in the sun, and watch the little willow wrens tapping in the evergreens, upside down. I thought I

---

[11]Guggenheim describes the central hall of Hayford Hall accordingly: "The walls were covered with the usual ancestral portraits, shipbuilders from the Clyde" (*Out of This Century* 113).
[12]Albert was Guggenheim's butler, whom she brought from their residence in London.
[13]Lydia Estes Pinkham (1819–1883) developed this herbal tonic to ease pain during menstruation and menopause.

heard a brown wren yesterday. The trees are full of tiny little birds, all singing. What a heavenly place this is.

I've been very disgusted by reading the diary I wrote in October and November, 1932. I'd like to burn it except it would be healthier to keep it to remind me of what I can be like—and probably am like three-quarters of the time. Since I don't write anything but diaries it's the only way I can see myself.

Reading that diary disgusted me so, I said to John: "Why must I be always a middle class college girl?" He laughed so hard it gave him away. He suggested I should try to write something else besides diaries. I told P[eggy]. she could not know what I was like inside, an elephant trying to sit down on a dime—is just what I am like. If I were nothing but a middle class college girl I would have it settled; unfortunately I've got poetic genius.

Djuna didn't believe we had affection for her, and John sat down on a stool in front of the fire and began to simper, "Djuna" and look foolishly up and down, and P. screamed, "He's trying to show affection." Then Djuna said, "I really think he is," but she could not help laughing. I said he looked like Robin.[14] He did look like an innocent little dog.

Johnny broke a window of the hut and got in and took a boat belonging to one of Mrs. Prendergast's children.[15] She sent a policeman up here and Johnny lied to him. He wouldn't admit the lie. We found out he had done it.[16]

---

[14]Robin was Guggenheim's Sealyham dog; in August 1934, he would eventually be given a "wife," another Sealyham named Borotra.
[15]See August 27, 1932, note for Prendergasts.
[16]The diary for this period ends here.

Section 2

Yorkshire
June 8–July 3, 1934

Following the period in Devonshire there is a one year break in the diary, between July 1933 and June 1934. The gap is at least in part explained by the fact that on January 19, 1934, John Holms died suddenly. In her memoir, Guggenheim describes what would be his fateful fall from his horse while at Hayford Hall in 1933: "One afternoon in late August we went horseback riding in a typical Dartmoor rain. The rain wasn't bad enough to be uncomfortable but it was enough to cloud over John's glasses. Half-blinded, he allowed Katie, his horse, to stumble into a rabbit hole and throw him. His wrist was entirely dislocated" (121). Holms underwent countless treatments of massage to relieve the pain, but to no end, and it was finally decided that he needed surgery. Guggenheim and Holms had moved from their avenue Reille address in Paris to a house at 12 Woburn Square in Bloomsbury, and Coleman arranged for the operation to take place there. Tragically, Holms showed up for his operation hung over from a night of drinking, and he suffered a heart attack on the operating table. Upon his death, Coleman was sent for immediately and, as Guggenheim narrates: "For years I had told Emily that if John were to die, I would never see her again. Now I was only too happy to allow her to give up her own life and stay with me. She slept in our room and we talked about John for nearly two months and that saved me. I can't think of anything else that would have been better" (126). The impact of his death on Coleman is revealed in her diary, which she took up several months later.

In the spring of 1934, Coleman had returned to Hartford to see her father; he likely accompanied her back to Europe for they vacationed together in May at Scar House Farm in Hubberholme, Yorkshire. The diary begins again on June 8, 1934, with Coleman still in Hubberholme after her father's departure. She had changed residences and was now at a guest house owned

174 Section 2

or run by the Veritys, a local family who lived beside the Vicar and his wife, Mrs. Costobadie. As the diary opens, we learn that Coleman's relationship with Hoare continued to be strained, and she felt that if she stayed away from him for a while he would appreciate her all the more when she returned to London. In the meantime, she had become enamoured with a young journalist for the Yorkshire Post *named Iverach McDonald; he would go on to garner an international reputation as Foreign Editor for* The Times *of London (1952–1965). McDonald, who was staying at a nearby farm with his father, McDonald senior, was engaged to a woman in Leeds named Gwendoline (Gwenda) but he was attracted to Coleman, inspired by her knowledge of and passion for poetry. McDonald not only distracted her from Hoare but also served as a source of healing as she reminisced to him about Holms.*

Hubberholme proved to be an intense period in her literary development for she worked on her new novel, "The Tygon"; began the long poem dedicated to Holms called "The Cremation"; and contemplated the composition of the diary itself.

JOURNAL OF HUBBERHOLME

June 8, 1934

I went to see sheep shearing today, <u>June 8</u>, at a neighbouring farm. The ewes leapt after they were sheared, held by the horn to be marked (with tar)—like kittens, in the air. Mr. McDonald likes the shearing as he likes all things of farm-life, but he romanticizes farm life a bit, and I tried to say that coming away afterwards—I said what I thought everyone knew, that farm life is finished[1]; and it gives me only pain to see these people working; like Paradise gone. He is so extraordinarily innocent, and though he passionately loves natural things he hasn't suffered enough to know anything and never will. He is so sweet that it moves me; gentle, and really GOOD. His face is beautiful, with a sort of radiance.

Sunday, June 10

I went up on the moor yesterday, above the house: the first time I have been on the moors. The ground was spongey, like Dartmoor, but dry, and covered with grass instead of heather. I looked in the long grass incessantly, to find

---

[1] Iverach McDonald (1908–2006).

a nest. As soon as I got to the top of the pasture a curlew arose, and made a terrible wail.

Lay in the fields in the heat looking at the sky, and feeling heavenly. There was a small ash, with young leaves, flinging out its arms against the sky, pale green on the tender blue of the sky. I won't be as happy as this for years to come.

I go happily along the road thinking of things to put in my journal. If I think of five words of ordinary sense I'm so surprised I want to write them down. I wonder what John would think of me. I try to keep my balance, and not fall into the spiritual masturbation which John said I occupied my mind with in the country. I'm so happy now that it's incredible; even the knowledge that it must end in three weeks doesn't upset it. When I think of Peter I'm fortified. But last fall I felt fortified, when I began my book; lying in the tub, at 105 Oakley Street, in the mornings, I felt invincible.[2] I thought, "Nothing can make me suffer now." That lasted 4 months, and then I went into the worst suffering I ever had.[3]

Perhaps this is the same thing. If I can prolong this, by staying away from Peter, nothing will prevent my seeing him. If I can foretell the future, I will stay here until the 6th of July, without writing him; then, when I see him in London he will be upset. I will go to Hampshire, he will come there for a weekend, we will make love, and different results will follow than always, not so quickly as that.[4] If I keep away from him successfully, we will go away in September. But after that I shall go to America, which will decide it; for when I return from America I'm going to be with Sonia, somewhere in Europe, until spring.

The thought that I won't be in London again until next spring is refreshing. I'VE HAD ENOUGH OF IT.

Wednesday, June 12

McDonald talked with me for a long time about his relations with his fiancée. What little I know about sex seems to be of great benefit to him. As he walked along the road, speaking intensely of her, he seemed so lovely, so untouched by everything that makes me sick in the world, that I felt very drawn to him. There is something angelic in his nature; not that he isn't human—and

---

[2]"The Tygon." Coleman had moved from 35 Great James Street back to her old address at 105 Oakley Street.
[3]The "suffering" was the death of John Holms in January 1934.
[4]Guggenheim was spending the summer at a farm house called Warblington Castle, in Havant, Hampshire. Coleman would go there in July.

almost silly, in many ways, he is so unconscious of evil—but that beauty and goodness had found a dwelling place in him. He "kindles" as you talk to him. Last night we walked down the highroad and I told him about John Donne. The excitement I get from giving out in this way, whatever I know, to someone who takes to it so eagerly, and in whom it goes on working afterwards—someone so young and so anxious—is terrific, and I try not to be carried away by it, remembering that I have been starved for poetry, and starved for joy. I suppose I could fall in love with him, in a kind of way, but I don't feel in the least like it—but feel suspended in a sort of temporary joy—this lovely creature, and the sweet country around me.

It was a good hot day yesterday, hot and oppressive, the heat sinking on every leaf. I love the feeling of a real hot day beginning, the locusts in America, the skylarks here. I was sitting on the island, in the shade of trees, reading Eliot (Peter's *The Use of Poetry and the Use of Criticism*) when I heard a chick-chick I recognize, and there, across the stream, in the stone wall, was a wren with moss in her beak.[5] At last, now, the very thing I wanted, to see a wren building her nest.

I told McD. a little about Peter—describing John's eyes I spoke of Peter's—John's benevolent, like a god, and Peter's snapping with suppressed life. McD. showed me a picture of Henry Moore, the sculptor, in the paper, Grigson's friend.[6] He had a sullen look. I found the package of reviews of my book, read them, and felt quite set up.[7] McDonald wants to read them. I want him too, to think well of me, but it's embarrassing to give them to him. Have been telling him about London, and the way people in Bloomsbury behave. We were talking about the Creed, and I said I believed all of it—he said, "How could I?" and we began to go over it. When it came to, "conceived by the Holy Ghost" he said I didn't believe that and I said—"I believe everyone is conceived by the Holy Ghost." When we were talking the other night I said that he might have complete happiness, with Gwenda, but that the more sensitive one was, the less one could expect happiness, because one wanted so much.[8] He thought about that all night, he said, and wrote it to her, and is still thinking about it. I said I knew, at least, that I could not have it on this earth.

---

[5] T. S. Eliot's *The Use of Poetry and the Use of Criticism: Studies in the Relation of Criticism to Poetry in England* (1933).

[6] Henry Moore (1898–1986), English sculptor. Geoffrey Grigson (1905–1985), writer and editor who founded and edited the little magazine *New Verse* (1933–39).

[7] For reviews of *The Shutter of Snow* see the introduction.

[8] Gwenda (d. 1993) and Iverach were married in 1935, and are survived by their two children: a son and daughter.

Friday, June 15

Looked at the dedication in Muir's book, "To the memory of John Ferrar Holms, 1897–1934."[9] I never know that John is dead until I see something like that—until I hear someone say, "Poor Holms is dead," as Peter did once, or Peggy says, "since John died." I don't believe it otherwise, he is still living in me, and I think of him whenever I am alone. But "1897–1934" makes John's death more real than anything I have yet seen, as though the final seal were set on his life, as though now, like all the others dead, he were numbered with that throng. That passage, at any rate, that we know as "life," now is ended. Instead of taking death too seriously, I tend to think it not serious enough—it seems only a part of the whole—I'm sure John looks now and sees things we do in relation to what we were before we were born, and will be after. Not, as we see ourselves, only in relation to our mortal life.

I think of John climbing La Rhune with me—how lovely he was that day—when I was in love with him.[10] One can't get that spiritual tension without love. At least I cannot. It is of course the female, which I think doesn't exist, but which brings sex into it, every time. I was so sexless when I was in love with John—that I never thought of him consciously in a sexual way, but it must have been there. I didn't know what he was feeling that October day—now I can't forget it; now he's dead.

Remembering how he said it was wrong to burn up my diary in Peggy's house in December, 1932. It was the one I wrote in St. Tropez the summer of 1928. I couldn't stand having it exist, with so much falsity in it. It had the record of my first meeting with John in it. But it was all so false, I couldn't stand it. John said one should never burn a record, whatever its nonsense. I know now that that is so, because in thinking of the present diary I wonder if I won't want to tear it up some day—but am determined not to because of the joy it records.

Saturday, June 16

When I got up it began to be very hot. Yesterday was such a lovely day, from morning to night—McDonald's last day—in which we crowded so much intense pleasure—that I could not bear today to dawn fair and hot.

---

[9]The dedication is in Muir's *Variations on a Time Theme* (1934). Muir had also dedicated an earlier volume of poetry *Chorus of the Newly Dead* (1926) "To John Holms."

[10]This episode of climbing La Rhune, part of the Pyrenees mountains dividing France and Spain, occurred when Coleman had first met him in 1928.

I thought how lovely it would be to see him naked, his beautiful straight body, rising up to his lovely head, and his proof of manhood rising (I don't know what THAT would look like). I thought how sweet it would be to go bathing with him, and to touch our bodies, and to talk about poetry, and see the birds, and see the light on the hills, and sleep in each other's arms. I can imagine a sort of inhuman existence with him, in which I might, for a little time, be very happy—but it could not endure—he doesn't know enough, and never could, to keep me interested on this earth.

Wednesday, June 20

Reading Eliot in bed again—all this talk, talk, talk about poetry does get tiresome. Eliot hedges and fumbles, fudges about like an old owl. Then suddenly he says something illuminating, as if he had got tired. "I would hardly say"—"it cannot be certain but that"—"I would not willingly go beyond"—"we shall not know what not to expect." Really it seems as though the man had got into a bog, and couldn't get out except through some terrific effort of the will. He makes these superhuman efforts every 20 pages; then a little light begins to dawn.

Poetry to me is the revelation, through people of various KINDS of sensibility (the poets), of particles of the Divine Harmony which exists in the world, and always will exist, and to which most people have, through the progress of civilization, become blind. In great ages what is told people is true. We are in an age of change, when science is taken literally, and used as a goal instead of as a means to another goal; that is why people don't believe in anything, and can't believe in anything.

I started reading "Peter Bell" again (Eliot has his worth if he can lead you to that).[11] Here I am, as happy as anyone could possibly be, thinking about poetry, feeling the Eternal Hand touching my mind, as though I could go on forever. And I know that one gesture of a man I love could throw it absolutely to the winds—making me into nothing more than a common woman who loved her husband. And that could go on for years. I am perched precariously on a watershed of love and poetry. To fall down either side would give me the most intense delight; in either I would be fulfilling my highest function. This is what it means to be a poet and a woman. I can write about it calmly now; but the division in my nature which makes this state of being possible is very near to death.

---

[11] Wordsworth's poem "Peter Bell" (written 1798, published 1819) deals with the salvation of the dissolute potter Bell. Eliot wrote about the poem in his chapter "Wordsworth and Coleridge" in his *Use of Poetry* book.

Thursday, June 21

What is Eliot's value—I've almost finished the book. I can't read much, I think so much, and write so much in this journal. Eliot has a great deal of value. He and Joyce and Lawrence are the three strong spirits of this time.

This book does make me sad, for I remember with what joy I read the *Sacred Wood*, the first book of criticism I ever read. The TRUTH was in that, sweet enthusiasm, and love for beauty—and honesty and brilliant penetration. Only he never says enough. Always it will be said of Eliot—He didn't say enough!

> "And nature, through a world of death
> Breathes into him a second breath,
> More searching than the breath of spring."[12]

I had copied this in the front of Wordsworth before. Now it struck me, I have had that second breath breathed into me.

I often feel that life (amongst people) is like working in a laboratory; solitude is the preparation for that. It's so hard, to go into the world again, and fight; it's so heavenly to be alone, close with God.

I know I'll never know anything if I don't live in the world. I am not a saint. I am an artist and the world is my stuff—unfortunately.

I had a card from Deak, about Johnny. It seems so absolutely wrong, writing back and forth about a child. We should be together, with the child. I know this, but two wrongs (marrying Deak, and staying with him) do not make one right. Very well, then, REMEMBER that—never, never forget it. If ever you are disposed to take any female liberties with love.

I must try to make some fusion between the two halves of my nature; nothing could be more split in two. My two halves don't know each other; each despises the other; fears the other. The artist part of me loathes the female—it seems to stand for every weakness. The feminine hates the artist because it thwarts its functioning.

Saturday, June 23

I spent almost the whole day writing a poem called "The Cremation," finished it by night—but saw before going to bed that only 6 verses were good.[13] I started it with a burial because I didn't want to use the literal facts, then couldn't get going on that. I found that the actual facts of cremation excited

---

[12] Wordsworth's "Peter Bell."
[13] "The Cremation" is Coleman's poetic tribute to John Holms, who had been cremated on January 21, 1934.

me. This was interesting—probably means that I need something <u>new</u> to get going—especially something horrible. The <u>image of cremation</u> brought out the best verse. This ought to be a really good poem—I feel it so strongly—and have <u>concentrated</u> upon it, and what it implies, so long. Beginning with the death, the mourning, then into what follows, the imagination, the <u>future</u>. I think 6 verses are really intense. I want to change it today—it's the future I don't get right. I haven't got the fear into it. The verses are beautiful—

> Will he roam like the fish
> In the waters of the lake
> Or frozen like an otter breathe in ice?
> Will he in stretches of eternal snows
> Lie on the face of summer, like the rose?
> Will he in trees be one of a thousand steep
> In regions of rock and pine, will his soul sleep
> In marble or in fire

but the way I have them in the poem doesn't get the effect of intensity—but lets it down. I realized last night that I must have verses about <u>before birth</u>—I've only suggested it in the end—that must be the theme of the last part. I am delighted with this poem; I couldn't sleep.

I spoke too soon about old Eliot—he outdid himself in the last two chapters, especially the chapter entitled "The Modern Mind."[14] His brain really got to functioning. It was delightful—interesting, instructive, stimulating and important—that is, I think these two chapters will be read in the future. I have marked up Peter's book so much I'll have to buy him another one.

He thinks a great deal of the criticism of Mr. I.A. Richards—I think this is because Richards is learned in fields in which Eliot would like to be—psychology.[15] I can't think why he should take Richards' statements so seriously—they reveal that he hasn't the slightest atom of poetic understanding. Eliot criticizes Richards' "system" for making people understand poetry. Nothing could be more indicative of the state into which poetry has fallen through industrialism and popular education, than this "system," which Eliot criticizes quite seriously, and doesn't seem to realize that its existence is a joke.

---

[14]"The Modern Mind" and the "Conclusion" are the last two chapters in Eliot's *The Use of Poetry*.

[15]Ivor Armstrong Richards (1893–1979), English critic and poet. His main texts include *Principles of Literary Criticism* (1924), *Science and Poetry* (1926), and *Practical Criticism: A Study of Literary Judgement* (1929), in which he helped to pioneer a system for literary analysis based on close textual readings.

When I saw Eliot in London the day he read his poems in St. Martin-in-the-Fields, I felt very sorry for him.[16] From where I sat he looked worn; and when he read his poems he put much feeling in them. For the first time I liked his poems: but not because they were poetry. It was because they were such an honest record (honest for the most part) of despair; they should have been a creation out of despair; they were just a record. But I pitied him.

I spent the afternoon aiding Mrs. Costobadie with her children. I held the baby for some time.[17] It made me remember when Johnny was 2–4, a deadly time of my life. I told her her eldest (3) will get steadily worse until he is 6.

Thursday, June 28

The hours are crammed with things to do—I had to get letters written—and I don't want to do anything but finish the poem, "The Cremation." I have to help Mrs. Costobadie because it's indecent not to. And now McDonald is coming tomorrow (with fiancée and sister), for the weekend, and I shan't get anything done while he is here—and then I have to go back to London.

Phyllis wrote me rapturously about the Russian Ballet, making me eager to go back.[18] Otherwise I wouldn't go back until John comes.[19] But I want to go to the Ballet all next week, now that I see Phyllis' letters and the program, which Peggy sent me. Peggy sent me a long letter, full of news. I keep thinking of her when I read "In ashes his white thighs"—I'm sure that will make her cry. She loved him in that way—and it was thinking of her feeling that made those lines. She told me once she couldn't bear to think John couldn't fuck any more. It gave me a jolt.

Tuesday, July 3

It is a lovely hot day, with the sheep buzzing over the way, as they are still shearing, and the ashes murmuring. It is the same kind of day it was the morning after I arrived. I wish I were not going from it.

I don't want to leave this sweet spot, where I have been happy. I've been happy here, for four weeks, as almost I've never been happy before. I've had almost Paradise. To leave it, to go from this beauty into black London—I don't think I can do it. I don't want to see Peter, and have alternate thrills of

---

[16] St. Martin-in-the-Fields Church overlooks Trafalgar Square in London.
[17] Coleman would become the godmother of the baby girl.
[18] The De Basil Ballets Russes performed at the Royal Opera House at Covent Garden from 19 June to 11 August, 1934.
[19] Her son, John, would be visiting her from France shortly.

joy (invented) and nights of melancholy. They are invented because I believe he loves me. I feel very bitterly towards him.

I shan't keep a journal any more. It is an awful nuisance. I can't keep one casually, and keeping a full one means writing half the day—and thinking perpetually what you are going to say in it. It makes me think, and makes me observe, but I'm tired of such an intense devotion to it. It means I can't get anything else done. But I'm glad I kept one in Hubberholme. I'll read it sometimes, when I'm low, and far away from this stream, and church, and beautiful blue-green moors.

Section 3

London
July 5–September 1, 1934

Coleman returned to London refreshed by the Yorkshire countryside and ready to tackle Hoare yet again. She was not long in the city, though. Her son, John, arrived from France and they joined guests like Antonia White and Phyllis Jones vacationing at Guggenheim's new country estate, a farmhouse called Warblington Castle in Hampstead, where the playful and erotic dynamics of Hayford Hall were reenacted. Hoare came for his requisite visit of a few days, during which time he and Coleman rekindled their sexual relationship. Guggenheim's new lover, Douglas Garman, was also there. An English poet and British Communist Party member who had edited The Calendar of Modern Letters *(March 1925–July 1927) with Edgell Rickword, Garman was working for his brother-in-law, Ernest Wishart, who owned the avant-garde publishing house Wishart and Co. Guggenheim had met Garman through Holms in 1932 and they became involved after Holms died.*

Following the Hampstead holiday John Coleman went home to France, once again making the journey across the English Channel alone, while Coleman went back to London. She grew increasingly concerned that White was becoming suicidal as her third husband, (Sir) Tom Hopkinson, the English journalist, novelist, short story writer, and editor of The Picture Post, *was having an affair. At the same time, Coleman had recommitted herself to her novel and prepared to send a completed draft to White for her much-valued critique. Coleman had also discovered George Barker, the bisexual English poet and novelist who was fifteen years her junior; she fell in love first with his provocative writings and then with the man himself.*

LONDON

Thursday, July 5

It seems so noisy here, such a hell of a commotion! It is a bright hot sunny morning. It was very hot in the train. I read Hudson most of the way down, *Adventures Among Birds*.[1] I was delighted with it—the best of his books I've read. There are some wonderful passages in it, about the song of birds. What a pleasure to have Hudson, to keep the country with me!

As we came through Huntingdonshire, the evening light was on the landscape, and almost everything was beautiful; even the factory chimneys did not look so grim. I was reading Hudson—wonderful paragraphs, here and there, with the very breath of nature in them when I saw a sign "11 miles to London." I gave a jump, rushed into the lavatory and washed some of the cinders off; powdered my nose, and put my hat on. When I got into the station I had to find a porter, but finally he pulled the two bags out, and the typewriter, and my enormous books, and I got out on to the platform. And then I saw Peter coming along, looking quite brisk.

I was never so glad to see him, or he to see me. We kept looking at each other in pleasure. I got into the car and he drove me out into the streets. London, in the late afternoon sun, looked very sweet. I was frightened of the motorcycles, and the confusion. He drove me down to Chelsea, where I got a room.[2] We then went to Queen's restaurant in Sloane Square.

Peter drove me home. I didn't ask him to come upstairs as I was very tired. Today I had a gruelling day in the heat, trying to get rooms, as Isabel can't keep me but one night. She was almost in tears. I found rooms in Oakley Street, wired Deak to know if John could be sent on Monday instead of Sunday. I went in Phyllis' room and kissed her and talked to her for hours.

I couldn't sleep, and was up at six o'clock and dressed and reading when Isabel came in.

I met Peter and we tried to get seats for the Ballet, at considerable trouble and cost, everything being sold. We dined at the Escargot in Greek Street, a very nice dinner, with Riesling and sherry, got tight at once.

We sat very near the stage. The first was *Lac Des Cygnes*, with lovely music by Tchaikovsky.[3]

---

[1] W. H. Hudson's *Adventures Among Birds* (1913).
[2] Coleman spent the night at 105 Oakley Street, known as Shelley House. Operated by a woman named Isabel, the guest house was also home to Phyllis Jones. Coleman soon after moved to rooms at 73 Oakley Street (in what is now the Oakley Hotel) but she would be back at 105 in August.
[3] On Thursday, July 5, the program of the Ballets Russes, which Coleman described in some detail (not transcribed) included three ballets: *Le Lac des Cygnes* (*Swan Lake*), music by Peter

We walked disconsolately from Covent Garden to Piccadilly, where we took a bus, but had to get off at Hyde Park Corner. We took a taxi here. I said, "Wouldn't you like to come in?" and Peter said, yawning, that he was tired, and <u>genuinely meant it</u>. I went into the house frantic. I almost cried, in terror, "You'll <u>DRIVE</u> ME INTO THE ARMS OF SOMEONE ELSE!"

I made up my mind to tell him I want to make love with McDonald. I'm so DAMNED TIRED of saying the right thing to Peter, of doing this to make him do that, pretending this to make him think that. If he's so stubborn, let him go his way.

It's his <u>SLACKNESS</u> that drives me to lunacy. It wasn't that he was trying to control himself; he genuinely didn't WANT to come in—he was tired. It's my fault for letting things get to such a point. Thank God, thank God every moment that goes by, that at last—at last—I have a means of MOVING him.

Saturday, July 7

Phyllis and I went shopping; I bought a dust blue sports dress, very chic (2 pounds), navy blue and white buckskin shoes (16s.), and a white hat. I look awfully funny in hats, with my hair short. Phyllis said I was getting thin. I looked in the mirror and felt like a great big piece of raw beef. She and I went to Peggy's in Hampstead; the children flew at me, and I was ashamed of the fact that I never think of them.[4] Peggy didn't know I was coming; she gave a cry when she saw me.

She was extremely witty about the place we are going to. She said it was an old farmhouse with a Tudor tower; a glorified nursery; a horrible spot. She said I would leave it immediately. She said there was no room. "Anybody can ask anybody they want," said Peggy, "If they'll sleep with them." She talked a good deal about Dorothy and said she was coming. She asked Phyllis if she minded having Dorothy and Phyllis said "I can't bear her." "That's the trouble," said Peggy. "No one can bear anyone." The children were all yelling, and Phyllis was bandaging them. The name of the place is Warblington Castle, Havant, Hants, but Peggy says it is not a castle.[5] She said, "It has a moat but it only goes half way round." On a previous occasion she

---

Tchaikovsky (1840–1893), and starring, as the Queen of the Swans, Alexandra Danilova. This was followed by *Choreartium*, music by Johannes Brahms (1833–1897) and starring Léonide Massine, dancer and choreographer. The final ballet, *Petrouchka*, with music by Igor Stravinsky, also starred Massine, as well as Tamara Toumanova.

[4]After Holms died, Guggenheim had moved from Woburn Square to a house in Hampstead. Sindbad had come from Austria, where he was living with his father, to stay with his mother for the summer.

[5]The remains of Warblington Castle, in Hampshire, are a tourist attraction today.

was discussing with Phyllis how much she should get for taking care of the children, and Phyllis said she wouldn't take anything, as she would be kept— better than she kept herself. "But you must keep the children better than they keep themselves," said Peggy. I can't remember all that things she said, only that Phyllis and I were shouting with laughter most of the afternoon. I helped pack things into the car. It is insufferable the way Peggy lives. But she looked so sweet yesterday, and pitiful. She melts my heart, and, for John's sake, I would do anything for her.

I met Peter at the Home Office. He was ravished when I came in the room, all in new clothes. We drove to Gossy's, had dinner, then went to the Albert Hall to a Pageant of Parliament, which was terrible.[6] Had drinks at Gossy's afterwards. I told Norman I would not be in London for a very long time, and Peter heard me, and his face changed. So when we got to where I am staying now I told him I was going away to America, and then away with Sonia, and that then it would be spring and I would go to the country. He looked absolutely wretched.

I had a telegram from Deak saying John was arriving tomorrow morning. When Peter heard that he laughed, because I didn't want him to come until Monday. I was angry; it meant we could not go away for the weekend. Peter realized that; he didn't mind. Deak is accustomed to my wanting John ahead of time rather than later and sent him earlier.[7]

I went over to Phyllis' this morning and got her off; Peggy arriving at half-past ten in the car, with the children. I feel a little guilty at letting Phyllis go down there alone.

I'm going to lunch with Peter now, it's Saturday. I feel full of joy, for I'm going to see him now for two whole days. How I've looked forward to Saturday these past two years. I remember once Peter said that Saturday and Sunday were to him like other days, Sunday worse. How different that was from me. For two whole years I've counted every Saturday; I've counted the days in between and ticked them off, waiting. I've had such shocks, on one or two occasions, when he's gone somewhere. We've been together so much. I can't believe that such an intense companionship, for such a long period, can be nothing. I said to him last night, "I've really loved you; for about four years."

I thought afterwards in bed, "Yes, but Bianchetti was in those four years." I told Peter that if I liked someone else, it would be wicked. I told him I

---

[6] The Royal Albert Hall, opened in 1871 in Knightsbridge, continues to serve as one of London's most important venues for the performing arts. *The Pageant of Parliament* was a concert series.

[7] As he did with his mother, John visited with his father for brief periods of time.

probably was wicked; he said that was nonsense, etc., but I have a dreadful feeling about myself now.

I said to Phyllis, "I think it isn't going to be so bad in Hampshire." She said, "It will be a nightmare." She and I may share a room together, which I shouldn't mind, as she is so sensitive, and being in the country, with children, will mean we won't get any privacy anyway. I hope fervently, and hopelessly, for a large room of my own, such as I had in Hayford Hall, of heavenly memory. But from what Peggy says I'm not likely to get it. But I'm going to try to be a little more human; a little less selfish, if possible. I like having John in my room, when there's space. The lovely room I had, for two summers, at Hayford Hall—with its sweet L shape, and its outlook on the torrent, and the trees in the rain!

Sunday, July 8

I got up early, no buses about, London clear and cool on a Sunday morning, with not a person in the streets. Went in a taxi to Liverpool Street, where I arrived at 8 o'clock, and the train wasn't due until 8–38.[8] At 8–30 I went to the track and there [John] was, sitting there on his suitcase, which had a long sabre attached to it. He looked so sweet, and was so full of excitement. We got into a taxi and drove to Oakley Street. I have a very nice large double room at the top of a house (No. 73), and <u>at the back</u>. He could think of nothing but the sabre, which he had persuaded Deak to buy as he was leaving Antwerp. I asked him what he did on the boat. He said he went to bed very early, "but got up at 12 o'clock to have a lemonade." We went over to Battersea Park, and looked at the English Garden, which was thick with flowers—the arbours covered with wild roses, and pinks, mignonette, and all sorts of sweet smelling flowers.[9] We waited for Peter along the river. When John's bag was unpacked he said, "Now what are we going to do?" I was worried, and he said, "Can we go to Woolworth's? Can I go to a swimming pool? Can we go the cinema?" I had forgotten that it was Sunday! I hadn't so much as got him a kite to fly in the park. He said, "Oh never mind I can get a ticket to ride in the trams." When Peter arrived and suggested going to the Zoo at Whipsnade, I embraced him.[10]

---

[8] Liverpool Street Train Station. She had gone to pick up John, who had travelled alone by train and boat from Antwerp.

[9] Battersea Park is in Battersea, on the south bank of the Thames, across from Coleman's neighborhood of Chelsea.

[10] The Whipsnade Park Zoo is a branch of the London Zoo, North West of London in Bedfordshire.

Tuesday, July 10

John and I went to Covent Garden, where I got the tickets, for last night and tonight.[11] Then we went to the Chelsea Baths.[12] He wants me now to see that he can dive—"just to prove to you that I'm not a swine." When I saw him, standing nervously on the springboard, his face red, his nervous hands leaping up to his face, I had such a feeling of love and protection for him—the poor sad dear little boy. I wondered how I could have had him, knowing nothing. He's so intense, and loves life so. He dived several times, very well, but got cold and I had to make him go in. We played Pease Porridge Hot until half past six. I gave him half a crown for his supper at Hetty's and made him promise to go to bed at 8 o'clock, after taking a little walk in the Park.[13]

I met Peter at seven and we went to Simpson's—a place I love—and had roast mutton and currant jelly.[14] Peter says I think violence is passion. He said I was like one of those torches they use, to peel off girders. "As might be expected, their power is nothing but air." "And what are you like?" I said. He said he was like a very small Price's night light, which went on burning forever. He ate a good dinner, and sat looking very sweetly at me. We sat by the window looking down upon the Strand. I sputtered a good deal, and jabbered. We got to the Ballet early. The first moment I got into a comfortable position an exuberant spinster pinched me and asked me not to lean forward.

When I got home there were peanuts arranged in a pile, with a note saying, "Please eat these before you go to bed." He was asleep on top of the covers. Going down Regent Street he said, "I think Mussolini is the smartest man I know, except naturally our family." He was describing to Peter how a crocodile ate up a man in a cinema he saw (*Tarzan*) and he said, "He tossed him off just like a vulgar spaghetti." He looked very sweet in the bed. When he wakes up in the morning his little face is shining with excitement. He's very companionable. We are going to Havant tomorrow.

---

[11]On Monday, July 9, Coleman and Hoare saw the Ballets Russes perform *Cotillon* (*The Dance*), *Union Pacific*, and *Le Beau Danube* (*The Beautiful Danube*). They returned the next night with John and saw *Jeux D'Enfants* (*Children's Games*), *La Concurrence* (*The Competition*), and *L'Oiseau De Feu* (*The Fire-Bird*).

[12]The Chelsea Baths, opened in 1907, included two swimming pools.

[13]Hetty's was a local tearoom.

[14]Simpson's-in-the-Strand, opened in 1828, remains one of the most impressive restaurants in London for its classic British cuisine.

Wednesday, July 11[15]

I am waiting for Peter to come and take us to the train, with 6 suitcases, 1 typewriter, 2 boxes, a tennis racket and a sabre, and 2 coats and some odds and ends. The black poplar outside has very large summery leaves. I showed John my blue evening dress for him to admire, which is a ravishing thing, with a filmy train, and he said, "I do hope you don't get egg on it." The moment he woke up he began to talk about the Ballet. He said, "I think it was quite good." He said, "Don't they get tired to hell?" Peter enjoyed it immensely too.

I had a long chat with Arthur Waley and Miss de Zoete between the acts—I had not seen them for 2 years. She looked so pleasant, and he looked awfully sympathetic. Five years ago I was afraid of them, four years ago I admired them, in 1932 I thought they were dreadful. Such sweet natural pleasant people—I must be crazy that I can't see that easily. While I was talking to them Charles Henri Ford came up and screamed, "Emily HONEY!" I couldn't get rid of him. I saw that he was with Tchelitchew, and I said, "Ask him to take you away."[16]

Thursday, July 12

Peter got us into the train, which was a very small one, and said goodbye. I held his hand until the train pulled it away. I tried to make John sleep on the seat. John Holms' large book of poetry, which I always take with me, and which is too big to go into a suitcase, was put in the rack, and it fell on my head during the journey, frightening me terribly. It was very hot. It was a slow train, for which I was glad. I cannot, cannot get my bearings. They were there at the station, and were scandalized at the luggage. When we got to the place I couldn't believe my eyes; Peggy had said it was terrible. It is a sweet old 18th century farmhouse, with a garden, about a mile from Havant, across the road from a farm, with a beautiful high-backed wooden church near it, with a little tower. In front of the garden are the remains of Warblington Castle, a tall thick brick Tudor tower. There are great elms around the moat. The house is ravishing—simple, the dining room the pleasantest one they have had yet. It has a great wide 18th century window, perfect in proportions, looking out upon the garden. Comparison was of course made with Hayford Hall, which

---

[15]This is the second of two separate entries that Coleman dated "Wednesday, July 11." In the first one, not transcribed here, Coleman described the three previously noted ballets that she, John, and Hoare attended.

[16]Ford, who had been Barnes' lover, was now partnered with the Russian painter Pavel Tchelitchew (1898–1957).

was a very different place. Hayford Hall was a dream place, a lovely, heavenly poetic garden, a Paradise, far from nowhere, deep in the trees beneath the moor. Nothing could ever be like that again. My room at Hayford Hall was part of that Paradise, the only room there that was beautiful. It was a place for dreaming, and being happy. This place is not like that at all—the house is far nicer, more comfortable, and more agreeable, and the place more wide open and sunny—just the place for a practical summer, with children, and society. I never could stand people at Hayford Hall.

I got my 6 suitcases unpacked, and felt like a human being, with lots of space, and room for John.

We went swimming, we drove down to the sea, low tide, I went in wading. The sky was lovely, a wide sweep, silver and green. Two old English ladies went paddling with their drawers on; carrying parasols. Peggy was very witty the whole day. I want so much to remember what she says; her wit delights me. I am slowly thawing out.

Phyllis greeted us at the gate with a radiant face. She told me she had never been so happy. She likes Garman, and says Peggy is wonderful.[17] She is efficient with the children.[18] She loves her room. I needn't have worried. Garman very much in possession, happy, and a fool. They wanted me to wire for Peter, but I didn't think he would want to come down immediately; I don't know how he will take Garman; Phyllis will bore him. I am determined to be goodnatured this summer, and I'm not sure if I could be if he were here—too much shutting of the eyes has to be done to make me goodnatured.

After dinner we got very tight, and I acted the fool to please Garman. He insists on being serious. I loved Peggy, felt absolutely drawn to her, talking about Donne's "Ecstasy," which Garman WOULD discuss, knowing nothing about it. But there was a general relaxation eventually, and everyone said very funny things. I can't remember them—except that I kept wandering around the room, and Garman said, "What are you doing, going about here like an ebb tide?" I got into excellent form, as I used to do with John [Holms].

Going to bed, I looked out the window, and saw the tower black against the night, and the great high elms were black. I suddenly thought of John—and all these people, so trivial here, so silly, only Peggy who keeps hard in her heart that little remnant. I loved Peggy and knew she was thinking of John. It began to rain and we ran out on the lawn. The grass smelled deliciously. I sat

---

[17] Douglas Garman (1903–1969).
[18] In addition to Pegeen and Sindbad, there were other children visiting, including Coleman's son; Garman's daughter, Debbie (through his first marriage, to Jean Sophie Hewitt); and Garman's niece, Kitty Epstein, one of the three illegitimate children of American sculptor (Sir) Jacob Epstein (1880-1959) and Garman's sister Kathleen (Lady Epstein)(1901-1979)—the couple, together since 1921, married in 1955.

down and wrote a card to McDonald, and tore it up, and sent another in the morning.

John leaped out of bed and said, "I'm in the country!" and climbed the feudal tower. He's done nothing else. Phyllis worries me; it angers me because she wants me always to be silly. But she appreciated Peggy's wit; with her and me for audience Peggy is inspired. I cannot remember it to record it, which I want very much to do, since when I did three years ago it provided us with delighted mirth later to read it, Peggy as much as anyone. It is a kind of surrealist wit, utterly removed from actuality, solid madness, and doesn't remember easily.

Now we are going to the train to meet Tony.[19]

Friday, July 13

Everything very happy. Children equable, and Peggy saintly. Phyllis responsible and rather fussy. Garman fluttering. John told the children that when I wrote anything, "the text was composed of conseCUtive x-es."[20] We met Tony. She seemed distraite, so we had her telephone Earnshaw Smith. He couldn't come. Tony phoned him but he was in Birmingham. They all want Peter, but he has written to say he had to go to Cambridge.[21]

Peggy and I drove to the station to get Tony; it was raining and Tony looked as if it was all too much for her. On the way Peggy got out of the car backwards. A bus came by. I said, "My dear, I thought that bus went over your heels." She said, "Maybe it did." Later I told that to Phyllis and Peggy said, "I can't tell because I've changed my shoes."

Tony recounting Wyn Henderson's entrance (at last) into Bloomsbury Inner Circles. Julian Bell took her to a club.[22] They all went in a *char-à-banc*. Tony said, "They all changed tarts for supper." Tony and Garman

---

[19] Antonia White.
[20] One way Coleman edited her writing, including her diary, was to cross out words or sentences with consecutive XXXXXXs. Her diary is also replete with consecutive ZZZZZZZs.
[21] Much to Coleman's annoyance, Hoare spent many weekends in Cambridge visiting one of his sisters, Agnes Dorothy Mackenize Hoare (1901–1987). Dorothy Hoare (who married J. M. de Navarro in 1940) was an Assistant Lecturer in Anglo-Saxon at Cambridge University. Her books include *The Works of Morris and of Yeats in Relation to Early Saga Literature* (1937) based on her doctoral thesis of the mid-1920s, and *Some Studies in the Modern Novel* (1938). Here and elsewhere I am indebted to Dr. Onora O'Neill, former principal of Newnham College, Cambridge, as well as Elizabeth Leedham-Green, Assistant Keeper of the Archives of Cambridge, for their assistance in identifying various Cambridge women.
[22] Julian Bell (1908–1937) was the son of painters Vanessa Bell (Virginia Woolf's older sister) and Clive Bell. A *"Char-à-banc"* or "carriage with wooden bench" was a horse drawn carriage or motor car.

engaged in genuine English conversation about families. They said, "Not THE Russells."[23]

In the evening I made them go walking, and I went to bed with Barker's book.[24] I was very keen about it. It's almost impossible for me to read here. I am quite happy, in a vulgar way. Things from Barker (*Alanna Autumnal*)—:

(He is very young—20—and full of himself, and silly and self-conscious. But he has the real thing.)

"And as the malformations and dirty crags and wounds of the divinely planned countryside are done by some underground devil, this is spoken upwards to you from an unplumbable negation of the self. My senses barely manage to receive imprints; my mind cannot: God knows where my imagination now moves."

The beginning has meat in it, though it isn't right; and "unplumbable" etc. is silly. But the next! I long and long for John. I simply cannot endure it that I can't talk to him, when I see good writing.

"O shame on the male in me that could tolerate such a faint conventional sensation to forego the terror of emancipation!"—This is not expressed right, but the kernel is right. Leave out the word conventional. Even then the rhythm's not right.

It reminds me of the Baroness Von Freitag-Loringhoven. I wonder if he's read her. I think it's just the rhythms. His rhythms are good. It's the same kind of madness. I love the man.

"Death and only death can impart personal value to me, the value I ache to possess." I want very much to know the young man, and see if he knows what that means. Peggy lent me this book. She heard it talked about. I read her some of the passages.

He is better than any of the young men like Auden.[25]

Little Robin, that sweet little dog, they have allowed to get eczema, which upsets me very much. Today Garman drove to get his niece and daughter;

---

[23]The Russells are a prominent British line, including philosopher Bertrand Russell (1872–1970) with whom White had an erotic though unconsummated relationship in the late 1920s (see Dunn 103–104).

[24]George Barker (1913–1991). Coleman was reading his novella *Alanna Autumnal* (1933), a story about an obsessive and destructive incestual passion between a brother and sister. As Coleman went on to mention, the book was published by Guggenheim's lover Garman, who worked for the Wishart house.

[25]In addition to W(ystan) H(ugh) Auden (1907–1973), English poet, dramatist, critic, and editor, the "young men" Coleman referred to include poets Cecil Day-Lewis (1904–1972), Louis MacNeice (1907–1963), and Sir Stephen Spender (1909–1995). Considered the up and coming poets of the 1930s, they were grouped under the nickname the "Pylon School," referring to the left-wing, industrial themes and images of their work.

the niece is Epstein's illegitimate child. Now there are 3 girls, and Johnny played with them.

I do not mind Garman since I see it doesn't touch (hasn't yet) [Peggy's] and my relation with John. John, being dead, is with us, Garman is the skin. I have been social with him, but I cannot talk to him. How I would love to have McDonald here—for my sake, nobody else would want him. Tony very fat, in shorts, lunging at the racquet. Tony is intelligent, very social, makes gaffs. She hasn't a pretty face. I treat her with affection. I just long for McDonald.

I long for McDonald to talk with, and to sleep with Peter. Reading in Barker about her breasts was just too much for me.[26] If Peter comes here I shan't resist him; I shall go to his room and be with him—be with him—oh, I must be in bed with him, I cannot stand it. I thought of touching my breasts for hours.

I must write, I must write my poem. "In ashes his white thighs." (Peggy wants to see it. I can't show it to her.) Barker is very like the Baroness. Phyllis, her mouth open, her great legs gawking, in the doorway. Playing tennis her bosoms stood right out. How I envied them! Peggy is horrible with the children. She says Jewish and desperate things in front of them. I took her to task, and she was shocked to think of it. She says, "Tony's had four husbands" in front of Sindbad.[27] Both her children have been brought up, by her and Laurence, to think of sex, and falling in love, until it's dreadful. Garman is endurable now because he's happy.

Saturday, July 14

This place is not beautiful. I'm beginning to feel it now. I must get a new typewriter ribbon and try to write my book. Last night a row, a real peacherino. Tony would keep raking Garman for having been rude to her 7 months ago. I said, "English people take rudeness seriously." That angered her. She said I made myself the centre of everything. Peggy said, "She's lucky if she can." Tony and Garman promoted England. Garman was angry with Tony

---

[26]In Part II, Section 5 of *Alanna Autumnal*, protagonist Alanna longs for her brother, Edward: "And I am starving, not only for him, but for his kiss and caress of these breasts. . . . His obsession of my breasts, which he can caress and possessively kiss, and with his hands he tells what his mouth is unable to tell, and I with my breasts understand what in my ears I cannot understand."

[27]White had three, not four, husbands: Reggie Green-Wilkinson (from 1921–1923), Eric Earnshaw Smith (from 1925–1927), and (Sir) Henry Tom Hopkinson (from 1930–1938). Her first two marriages were annulled for lack of consummation: Green-Wilkinson was an impotent alcoholic and Smith, as noted, was gay. For more on Hopkinson, see the entry and note for August 16, 1934.

and then with me. I leaped up from the table, knocking a wine glass accidentally into Garman's lap and screamed for him not to tempt me! I went out of the room, and then P. came in laughing like hell and threw her arms around me. Garman came in and we shook hands gracefully. Garman said, "You were tempting ME. I might kill you. Someone will." I said, "They have." Peggy said to Tony, "I like those two little snails on your breasts; which one is enjoying himself the most?" Tony giggled away the evening. We all said whom we liked, some said they liked men, some women. Peggy said, "I met someone I liked the other day—I forget which sex it was." Tony very large and with a bitter smile wafted her cigarette and spoke feelingly. She admitted she wanted to sleep with Garman. Before that we had a lot of nonsense, Garman pulling me out through the window, and Phyllis leaping gracefully, and Tony lunging. Garman went upstairs to try to get Peggy, who had gone to bed. He leaned over her and tried to persuade her to come down, <u>as John used to do</u>. Earlier in the evening Peggy said, "Garman would be like [a] fly to sleep with; he'd come to life again to annoy you." Garman tried to get me to quote from Barker's *Alanna Autumnal*. I won't talk about it to him so he thinks I don't appreciate it. He said, "Come on, now quote one line." I said, "Damn it all, I'm 35, why should I quote other people?" Peggy said that was the best line of the evening.

Sunday, Monday, Tuesday, July 15, 16, 17

Went riding with Garman. The country isn't beautiful. But it's heavenly to be on a horse.

The next time Garman and Peggy and I went together. I saw little P. on the horse, looking bewildered, and I said, "Don't you want my horse?" She didn't respond, then I thought of John. My eyes filled with tears. Suddenly I thought of the moors, the wondrous beauty of them, us dashing out from Hayford Hall on to the moors. John jumping and galloping madly down the hill, which led to his death.

Played a great deal of tennis, preparing for a tournament which Tony organized. I talked with Tony about her husbands. With middle class English women you have to be extra polite—like whores. She hates me because I talk so much. I can't keep up a polite conversation—get bored—tell the truth—that starts something. Some people love me for it, others don't.

Very witty conversation going on the whole time, which I simply cannot remember—getting old. I long for a dictaphone in the livingroom. Tony is witty, Peggy's ga-ga comments are perfection, Phyllis makes dry rejoinders. I am naïve in my best way and Garman says a good thing in the general heat.

If Djuna were here, to add her especial poetic flavour, it would be something marvellous. Tony very much impressed with everything, though we drive her crazy.

<u>Tony</u> (impressed): How very many literary figgers we all know!

<u>Peggy</u> (after an embarrassed silence): They're all figgers.

Peggy said, "I've got to get a vet for the dog and Sindbad." She wants to hear about London. Tony engaged in an intellectual conversation with Garman about the Catholic Church, and was happy. I said that when I read St. Teresa I said, "This is the life for me! Thinks of nothing but herself from morning till night!" Peggy seized me in her arms and said she had forgotten what I was like.

Tony telling at dinner about one of her husbands' young women, who has a wooden leg.[28] She was blown up in a munitions explosion, during the war, and has been plated since, and is very successful with men. I asked Tony where she was plated, Tony said she had seen a map once but couldn't remember. Said her leg had a spring inside which she got wound up every year at the hospital, then it went so fast she couldn't keep up with it.

Tony very tiresome, hates me, wants to be quiet. Peggy said, "She'd like to like you, but can't." Tony told me all her family problems, I got interested. I got worried, because she might be going mad. Phyllis said, "<u>Adorable</u> as you are, Tony's had enough of you." We went swimming, in the heat, and cooled off. Johnny covered us all up in sand.

Wednesday, July 18

The downstairs windows in the house are lovely; in the drawing room the one looking out on the lane has creepers drooping about it, and the garden one has pink hollyhocks at the door, with the sun shining on them. The dining room window is absolutely beautiful. It is such a charming house. The country is flat, and uninteresting.

Peggy was sorting out things in her desk, yesterday afternoon, and I came by, and saw several photographs of John. I was taken unawares, and I could not keep from weeping. We wept together. She said I had no idea how happy she was to have me again. We talked about John a great deal.

---

[28] Mabel Lethbridge, writer of the autobiographies *Against the Tide*, *Fortune Grass*, and *Homeward Bound*. Working in a munitions factory during WWI, she was the only survivor of an explosion caused by a faulty shell. She was a one-time lover of Rudolph "Silas" Glossop (1902- 1993), an English mining engineer. Though Glossop had fathered Antonia White's elder daughter, Susan Chitty (b. 1929), he and White were never married. Glossop would become involved with Djuna Barnes in 1937.

I phoned Peter at eight o'clock, and could hear the phone ringing in Chelsea. He wasn't in. Somewhat later they rang me. I talked to him for about ten minutes. It was a terrifying conversation, about his coming. I was completely unstrung. I sat at the table and talked in a desperate way about Peter. Peggy was frightened and said she did not know what I would do.

After telephoning Peter I felt absolutely desperate, as if I might kill myself, or kill him. I forgot completely the existence of Johnny, it was wiped out. Then suddenly he came into the room, with Sindbad, they had been "duck-hunting" together. When he came in I began to cry, seeing him again, whom I had forgotten, my joy, and delight, and comfort—I do not dare to take comfort in him.

Tony departed, we all drew new breaths. But Dorothy Holms is coming. Peter and Garman are coming Saturday, I said Dorothy Holms must have men.[29] So Peggy phoned her to come Saturday instead. I am going to make love to Peter, whatever I feel, whatever my pride. I must do it, I must do something to break this. I am so starved for romantic love that if I don't do something to move Peter I will make some terrible mistake.

Thursday, July 19

It is six months today since the day John died. I have never ceased to think about him. When I was in Yorkshire he was in every feeling I had. Now I am vegetating, in a tiresome state, thinking of children. He seems quite far from me. Peggy and I talked about him.

Johnny said, "You look so funny when your gray hairs stick like that in your head." Peggy and I drove to South Harting to get Garman's mother and the 2 little girls.

Lunch full of lobster, which the children couldn't have, conventional conversation with Mrs. G[arman]., trying to cover up Peggy's bricks. Peggy looks at her like a future mother-in-law. I disgusted got away, am writing now. I want to write my book, do nothing, am disgusted. No word from McDonald, that's why I wrote him. I didn't know how to write him. Realize how different I am now, just a dry mother. I don't know why he hasn't written. How horrible is life, how terrible, fearsome, muddled, wicked and dreadful. What can I do? I cannot, cannot live without love. Peter knows it, knows it—why? Oh how tired I am, how I long to lie down in a green pasture, beside still waters.

---

[29]Garman, along with his daughter and niece, lived with his mother, Marjorie Frances McGill Garman, in South Harting, Sussex. Guggenheim had rented Warblington Castle so as to be near to Garman, who worked at his writing and editing at home. He came to stay with Guggenheim on the weekends.

Wednesday, July 25

Peggy talking about her guests; does not seem to know who she has asked; trying to think of who is coming which weekend. Got very mixed up. "Maybe they'll come after we go."

After the rain the sun shone on the hollyhocks. The boys went off for a picnic, taking tea. In the evening charming conversation between D[orothy]. and Peggy. P. said, "I called Clothilde (her sister-in-law) a whore."[30] Dorothy was shocked. P. said, "I had to call her something; I didn't know what to say." They talked about Laurence [Vail] in the same way. "Of course you were in love with him?" Peggy: "No, I just wanted fucking." Dorothy must think P. was in love with Laurence, because then she can think she was in love with John.

I slept with Peggy again, and Johnny came in, offended. "Why don't you sleep with me? I wake up and you aren't there. You belong to me." I said, "Do you think I have no other friend but you?" John: "I'm not your friend. I'm your result." I said, "What would you do if I married?" He said, "You can't; you're too old." I said, "What about Peter?" He said, "He doesn't want to." I said, "What would you do if I had a little baby?" Johnny said, "I'd sock him." He said, "You look so funny, with your grey hairs, and your nose is all twisted." I said, "What does my mouth look like?" He thought a minute then said, "A rugby balloon." He said, "Your teeth look like piano tusks." I said, "Damn it all, who do you think is beautiful?" He said, "Deaky." I got offended and said, "I am considered a goodlooking woman." Yesterday he said, "Your bottom looks like Norfolk and Suffolk." Everyone said, "What does he mean?" He said, "The map; where Harwich is." I said, "You realize that you are considered the image of me."

Letter from Peter saying he had tickets. I wired him to meet us at Waterloo at 6.[31]

Last night I told Dorothy that I asked Hoare if he wished really he had never known me. I said he said yes. Peggy: "You can't say such things to Hoare. It's putting sugar in his mouth." I never heard a better description of Hoare's character.

---

[30] Clotilde Vail, a blues singer who had been, according to Guggenheim, a thorn in her marriage to Laurence Vail (*Out of This Century* 149).
[31] Coleman had asked Hoare, who had come to Warblington for the weekend, to get tickets for the ballet. She and John went to London for the performance and then returned to Havant. The evening program for the Ballets Russes on Wednesday, July 25, at the Royal Opera House, included *Cotillon* (The Dance), *Le Tricorne* (The Three-Cornered Hat), and *Les Présages* (Destiny).

He wrote a letter to Peggy this morning saying "I am exhausted but grateful." I read it first; but when Peggy read it she shrieked with joy. "I shall write—Dear Sir—What exhausted you has nothing to do with me." Her mind runs on one subject and keeps to that always. She likes me to sleep with her because it makes Garman jealous.

Saturday, July 28

Peggy is so clumsy about money, because it is so important to her. They all went to the Morrises for tea and swimming.[32] I stayed here and wrote a very long letter to Muir. I wrote in great detail about all his poems.

Peter phoned he would be here at teatime. I went on a bird walk with Johnny.

Peter arrived about five. After he had been here a while it was discovered that he was leaving on Monday. I didn't want to hear more. I had understood he was coming for a week. I thought, "This is my life, constantly continuing, one step forward, two steps backward; forever cheating, lying, and pretending not to care; no love; no joy; whatever physical joy there is ruined by the prospect of the next catastrophe. What a lovely life! I've chosen it! I want it! I need it! Otherwise my soul will rot in hell, and I will lie in the gutter of female slime." God has chosen to purify me with this suffering.

Sunday, July 29

We took all the children to the cinema last evening, in the town of Havant. There was a wild west and a detective film. Flossy [Pegeen] kept saying, "Momma, are those the bad people?" The detective film was very complicated.[33] At the end a coloured portrait of George V. was flashed on the screen. Johnny shouted, "What's that?" and while they were playing God Save the King, he realized, and said, "Don't tell Peter." Peter said the picture looked exactly like an omelette. I went to my own bed, I felt frozen.

Before going to bed Peggy gave me a lecture about Johnny; said he was too intimate with me, and treated me impudently. I didn't pay any attention,

---

[32]Ira and Edita Morris and their son, Ivan, were Guggenheim's American neighbors at Warblington Castle. Ira and Edita were aspiring writers; Ira (nephew of Guggenheim's aunt Irene Guggenheim) had contributed to Garman's *Calendar of Modern Letters*, and had been included in Neagoe's *Americans Abroad*, alongside Coleman.

[33]They saw the 1933 film called *Private Detective No. 62* starring William Powell and Margaret Lindsay.

because I knew she was jealous because my relation with Johnny is so different from hers and Sindbad's. But when she had gone Peter said, "Don't always search for people's motives, but think—'Is what they say right or wrong?'" He said she was quite right. He said I treated Johnny like an equal and then expected implicit obedience out of him, and he couldn't reconcile the two different personalities. I said he was obedient, and I never allowed him to bother other people: he admitted that. I said I didn't want him to respect me. Peggy said it was dreadful because I told Johnny to behave one way in front of people and another when we were alone. But he understands this. I said living in England I had to make some (outward) concessions to what English people think about children, which I don't believe in. I have this understanding with Johnny. I told him he must not make a noise when Tony was around, or talk too much, or insult me. I don't care if he insults me when alone, if it's not insolent. Peggy thinks this is shocking. I told Peter she thought that, because Sindbad is too simple to have such relations with. She said I showed too much emotion to Johnny, and encouraged his possessiveness (shouting all day MEEmi, which nearly drove everyone crazy)—much worse when Peter is here.[34] I said I was casual with him, compared to what I felt. I said a woman couldn't help concentrating all her emotions on a child when she was thwarted from doing so with her husband.

I also said, "I've paid for giving him to Madame Donn" and Peter said, "What do you mean, you've paid; you're very lucky. You don't want him all the time. You NEED a certain amount of liberty." I was glad to have that bubble exploded.

Pegeen made pictures in the afternoon, out of the pasting things I brought her; lovely ones. She cut out little pieces of coloured paper. She pinned them on the wall, like an exhibition, and we all bought them. She made about a dozen, and there wasn't one that wasn't beautiful.

I came to Peter's bed; we were happy.

Monday, July 30

I stayed all night with Peter, and we were so happy. I wonder he can hold himself back, the next time. We are so well suited sexually, his slow dog-like sensuality, not frightening, like the cat; he takes me casually, and loves it so.[35]

We played tennis all the morning.

---

[34] Coleman's friends often called her "Mimi."
[35] The next 2 sentences have been XXXXXd out. Hoare stayed with Coleman until Tuesday morning, at which point he returned to London.

Thursday, August 2

I thought: I'm so fond of comments on other people's weaknesses; let's have a few on myself. I tried several. (1) Emily in a loud voice, roaring and giggling, her mouth open to show her back teeth, turning with eyes ashine the conversation upon herself; taking the reins, looking apprehensively about, bounds forward on her hobby. (2) Little Emily, barging about in the obscure sea of the intellect, having stepped off proudly from the shore; sees a raft containing the sacred words; mounts it and puts to the wind. (3) Sitting in a trance-like voice explaining to Peggy how to meet the English; to Phyllis the moral values of what she has done; to Sonia, her fallacies; looking shocked and dazed at their defections. (4) Emily picking her nose with the left small finger of her right hand, scratching her leg with the other, bellows poetical revelations. (5) Looking fondly at her son, sees the resemblance, smirks contentment; when the conversation turns on him, sparkles with a more than human smugness. (6) Emily kissing her son with loud smacks urges him to greater and greater heights of daring. (7) With bulbous female pretensions covering her flat breasts, sees man looking at her leg, falls into ecstasy.

I now feel I'm getting into art. (8) Emily, the light of God coming into her eyes, explains what Holms has meant. (9) Emily, frowning in contempt of those who are beyond the soul, announces Holms' intent; screaming because she is opposed, she falls back desperately upon his sentences; failing, she trembles, shudders, and smiles a change of front.

This I did by imagining different people thinking of me. i.e. As follows: (1) Tony, (2) Peter, (3) Peggy, (4) Djuna, (5) Peggy, (6) Peggy, (7) John, (8)[36] (9) Hugh Kingsmill.[37]

Friday, August 3

Peggy said she wanted to see no people, just the few she knew. Why should one go to parties? Only one reason, to find a man. She and Garman have a healthy relation; no flattery, at least on his part.

---

[36]Coleman has blackened out the name here.
[37]Hugh Kingsmill Lunn (1889–1949), English anthologist, biographer, novelist, and literary critic, was a writer and literary editor of the *New Statesman*, to which John Holms had contributed. He had met Holms while they were prisoners of war, and they had remained close friends (see Muir 177). His anthology *The Worst of Love* (1931) is a collection, as he states in its introduction, "from our literature in the last few centuries" of "numerous specimens of bad writing about love." His study of Dickens, *The Sentimental Journey: a Life of Charles Dickens*, was published by Wishart in 1934.

When we went driving in the evening (all over Hampshire) we stopped for petrol. Garman said, "Six and eight?" "Five and eight," the man said. Garman said to Peggy, "When you do it in your head . . . four times—" "Do it in his head," said Peggy, "It's cheaper."

We played cards with the children in the afternoon, a game called Rockaway, like dominoes. I got tight before dinner, on sherry, and played with them, which they liked. Riding in the night, we saw an owl sitting on a post. Peggy played a Brahms concerto, which was very lush.

Peggy got another sentimental letter from Djuna. They are terrible. Hardly one word of truth in them. Djuna must hate Peggy, by this time, since all must be revealed (how Peggy did not want her in her trouble)[38]; yet she goes on pretending just the same. Djuna only tells the truth about—about what? I don't know. Some truth comes out of her, in conversation, when she's very drunk. It can't be done in writing. Probably some of the things about Thelma are true. All these gifts—of the first order—and false, false! Like Faulkner.

I got out two old letters of Djuna, and prepare to answer them.

Monday, August 6[39]

Johnny woke up this morning and the first thing he said was, "Which one of those people do you abhor the most?" A good beginning to a day. When I got downstairs, after having made up (for the company), Sindbad said, "Oh you look different. You haven't got the same old worn face." Hoare beat Garman [at tennis] 7–5, 7–5, a great event, because Garman is the champion. I sat out on the ladder freezing, to watch them. When it was over Garman was terribly shy and I kept in; but when Sindbad came in and heard it he threw himself on Hoare and kissed him and said, "O what a great guy!" A green finch was singing sweetly in the scarlet runners while we were playing tennis.

I went in Peter's bed. When he came up, he made love to me in a frenzied way, not like he's ever made love before.

---

[38] The "trouble" Coleman mentioned is likely Barnes' abortion in June 1933.
[39] On Sunday, Coleman had taken the train to London to meet Hoare. They then drove in his new car back to Havant, where they were greeted by a fresh contingent of guests: the Loebs (Guggenheim's cousin Willard Loeb, his wife, Mary, and their two daughters); and the Wisharts (Ernest Wishart was, as earlier noted, Garman's brother-in-law who married Garman's youngest sister, Lorna, when she was just sixteen). Garman's seven sisters, who were well known in Bloomsbury society, are the subject of *The Rare and The Beautiful: The Art, Loves, and Lives of the Garman Sisters* by Cressida Connolly.

Wednesday, August 8

Peter and Garman talked about Wyndham Lewis at breakfast; Garman, who used to know him well, in a fairly dignified way. I wanted to know him, and read his works (parts of them). I tried to play "There is a tavern in the town" and other songs, and Phyllis and I sang, for the children's benefit. We then sang hymns, and Peter sang the bass. Phyllis played the hymns; but she didn't play well enough to get going. Peggy sewed while this was going on.

Peggy said, "I feel Hoare will stay indefinitely, if we're careful." She said, "Hoare will never go, if I keep on sewing."

Johnny said to me as I was getting into my blue evening dress—"Garman is Peggy's third husband. I wonder who will be the fourth."[40] I was considerably shocked. I told him Peggy had had a very unhappy life; we must want her to be happy. I thought, "I'll tell her that, the next time she talks in front of the children." She hasn't the faintest imagination about what children think; no decency about what to say in front of them. I've had bitter quarrels with her on this. Next time I'll just tell her what he said.

Went riding again, with Mrs. Pearce.[41]

Sunday, August 12

Stupid day, this not my life, must get to London and do something. Missed Peter terribly yesterday.[42] Everything ga-ga, rain, children playing ping-pong, getting marshmellow and honey on the furniture, played poker and I lost and pretended it wasn't really for money. Went to the farm and smelled the cows again. A man said, "Excuse me, miss, but do you like these quarters?"

Milton braying about, babbles about the publishing business, Wishart has arrived, very dull like a doormat, sits chewing a pipe and eating out inferiority complex.[43] Says nothing. Milton burbles and bibbles, babbles and pips. The publishing business is Milton's donkey field, around which he runs. The publishing business is Garman's Waterloo.[44] God how they talk. Wishart doesn't.

---

[40]Though Guggenheim was never married to Holms or Garman, she referred to herself as a "wife" with them. She was married to her second husband, German dada and surrealist artist Max Ernst, from 1941–1946.

[41]Mrs. Pearce, a former policewoman, and her husband lived on a nearby farm. Guggenheim's guests took riding lessons from them on horses such as Punch, Tony, and Pixie.

[42]Hoare had, as usual, visited for the weekend only.

[43]Milton Waldman, a publisher, had been married to Guggenheim's younger sister, Hazel. He later married Peggy David Deutschbein, Peggy Guggenheim's oldest friend, who had accompanied him to Havant.

[44]The Battle of Waterloo (June 18, 1815) in Belgium marked the defeat of French Emperor Napolean Bonaparte by British/Prussian forces. The term "Waterloo" has since come to mean

He plays poker and gets sulkier and sulkier. Milton babbles about the way to play poker, the label on the wine, full of the joy of life, burbling and palavering. I long to pull him, but Peggy his wife prevents it.[45]

Watched Wishart and Peggy play tennis against Garman and Milton. Wishart is a terrifying man. Moves like a rag doll. Has a heart of lead. Garman looked almost handsome, fighting like a fallen king. I have a warm feeling for him, when I see him with these people. There's something decent in him. Milton jumping about the tennis court like a great calf looking for the udder, bawling.

Garman read *The Shutter of Snow*. He didn't want to read it because I didn't appreciate his poems.[46] He said the first two-thirds was better than the last. I said the first quarter. He said it was a short story turned into a novel. I packed, an awful business. Johnny tried to be helpful. The children absolutely wild. Wishart won Sindbad's ping-pong tournament! Peggy drove me to the train, and on the platform she looked at me in that lost child way, which I cannot stand. She said, "I feel every time we part we're getting farther away from the life we lived—with John." I said, "That life goes on inside just the same." She said this last weekend made her feel that more and more. I said, "I'm getting really fond of Garman. I don't know what I have in common with him except you." She said, "That's enough."

She looks at me with fear and bewilderment in her face, her mouth slightly open. She feels like that all the time but conceals it—she is always bewildered and trying to "cope with" the future. When it comes out in her face it's too pathetic to be endured. Dorothy wrote her a letter about a dream she had of Peggy walking along a wall in some foreign country, weeping.

Johnny and I played cards in the train. The Downs were lovely. The country is still covered with willow herb. We got into London with all our suitcases, and there was no porter. It was dark and we were in the last car, and when finally a porter came he didn't have a trolley and had to go back for it. We stood on the platform of Waterloo Station, in the late evening, London dark and enormous around us. I put Johnny to bed as soon as we arrived at Oakley Street. Then I sat by the window, in the dark.

I had a strange feeling, as though I were not there, and all those people going back to their homes, did not exist in the street. They went backwards and forwards, doing their business, but I didn't think it was their business, or their homes. It was dark, and lights had come on, and there were noises in the streets around; a sort of peace came over me, a deep sort of melancholy,

---

a significant defeat.
[45] "To pull" is to seduce.
[46] In addition to editing *The Calendar of Modern Letters*, Garman wrote poems, some of which had been published in the June 1925 issue of *The Calendar*.

204   Section 3

not misery, but a kind of acceptance of things I recognized—this world was not false, but true, perhaps forever going on like that, somewhere, at some time, every movement, every gesture, continuing along the street, from home to home; from the people who passed silently, to me. I wondered what that feeling meant. I thought, "This is living; it is knowing." I sat suspended on the window sill, seeing Peter's dark windows across the street, hearing the Sunday evening sounds. It was beautiful, almost like a vision. I have not had that heavenly moment in just that way. I was sad, very sad, and knew all truth, for a minute.

Peter telephoned, from some place near Cambridge and said his car had broken down. I had been watching to see him come in. [47]

Tuesday, August 14

Johnny left yesterday morning. I missed him all day. I got a telegram from Monsieur Donn at 9 o'clock that he had arrived.

Peter came with us to the train. Johnny went to Woolworth's and got himself some writing pads before he left. I left him sitting in the train looking rather frightened. It is his 10th trip across the Channel by himself, I worried all day.

I went to the Hamburg-American Line to see about steamers. One leaves Sept. 28th and one October 5th.[48] I decided to go 1st class, as I think if I don't Johnny will be too restricted. After seeing Johnny off we went into Westminster Cathedral.

I made up my mind to go home after leaving Peter and write. It was like taking a cold plunge; but I did it. I began copying chapter I, with carbons.[49] I know I can write the book, such as it is, such as I am—now. Writing means breaking off from life, and I hate it. It nearly killed me to get going. Peter said I should read Yeats' *The Tower*, which I have (Peggy gave me John's new copy).[50] I read it after I had copied out two chapters. (I can't go on with the book till I get the first part right.)

I went to his flat for dinner. He drank a good deal and talked about himself. He played the last act of the *Valkyrie* after dinner, but I was too sleepy

---

[47]As earlier noted, at some point in August Coleman had moved from 73 to 105 Oakley Street, both of which were across the road from Hoare, a long-time resident of number 7 Oakley.
[48]Coleman, John, and Phyllis Jones would sail to New York on October 5.
[49]"The Tygon."
[50]Yeats' *The Tower* (1928) includes, among other poems, "The Tower," "Leda and the Swan," and "Meditations in Time of Civil War."

to pay attention to it. Then he played Palestrina to wake me up, and I awoke immediately and listened to it.[51]

Peter said Joyce had given up perfection, Lawrence thought it lay in the instincts, and Eliot was despairing about it. He talked a lot about sex. I listened to him. I said that once John told me love and lust ought to be identified—and were in Dorothy—then last year he said they would get farther and farther apart, of necessity. I think they ARE apart, sex IS evil, one knows it, in itself it is a waste of time. <u>But through it (in love) one finds the truth. A woman cannot know ecstasy any other way.</u> There is no marriage in heaven; there is no necessity for it. Here marriage is necessary—<u>to purge love of sex</u>.

Peter was very insulting, as usual when he feels he is loving me. He said, "How bored I get when I see that little female mind turning round and round." "I can't stand your personality; I only like your body."—etc. He seemed quite madly in love with me. He said I was a poor little chicken. He does love the female body so; he aches for it. He can't think of anything else. He said, "I would love to be a woman—a black frump, quaking with desire." He was mad with desire, and kept saying, "I'm not in love with you. I can't bear you—only your thighs." He thinks I've made his relation with me all wrong by insisting upon sex before he was ready for it (and keeps talking about Lawrence and how he felt about that). He began sexual relations with me by kissing me like a demon in Paris, in 1930; but I made it serious. I love him so much!

Standing against Peter, as I was finally going, I saw my reflection in the glass. And at last I thought I was attractive, a sight so rare. My short hair was falling over my brow, and I had a sort of pixie smile, instead of that sullen look, that damned pigheaded look, like a grouchy cow. My eyes were lit up and my nose tilted. I looked very like Johnny. I could not bear to leave my sweet Peter, and he hated it, and clung to me, saying, "I shall renounce all this tomorrow."

I am probably a mystic; and certainly a barbarian; and a fanatic. My instincts are so violent that there is no danger of my not following them. There is much more danger of my not <u>knowing</u> anything. My Peter, my sweet Peter, looking at me fiercely, and thinking how he hates me, gives me life!

——The Leda poem is much better than I thought (when John showed it to me). I've changed since John died, my lovely John, about whom every day I think, for one moment, as if I were praying—"What is he doing now?"

I didn't listen to the *Valkyrie*, but Peter said he loved it, and that the *Ring* was the greatest single achievement of the 19th century, and that Wagner was a vulgar necromancer. I met him for lunch and he began criticizing me as

---

[51]*Valkyrie* (1856) is the second of four operas in Wagner's *Ring* cycle. Giovanni Pierluigi da Palestrina was an Italian Renaissance composer.

soon as he saw me, telling me I resembled a lay preacher, and a spinster going for the laundry, &c. I had on my plain blue hat that turns straight up from my face, and a long blue coat, with epaulettes, and thought I looked fetching; he said I resembled one of the elder pupils of an orphanage.

When I came back I saw Phyllis. She was depressed at leaving Warblington, while I was glad. It's not my life. I was so sleepy I couldn't work, and couldn't go to sleep; instead I read a movie magazine with intimate details of the lives of Jean Harlow, Joan Crawford, Katharine Hepburn and Mae West. These are American cinema stars, all women. None of them can act, and 2 are just ordinary American girls, with that ceaseless energy, push—push—no one knows where we're going but let's get on. The other 2 have Personality. I'm interested in them. Why is it that only the women in America are interesting? John said because they were pioneers. The world is changing. Women are changing. It shows itself first in a new country. Then what is this change leading to?

Wednesday, August 15

I finished copying the first three chapters of my book. Was a little bored at the scenery in chapter 2, but got interested in the battle between Donato and his father.[52] The father a little Dostoyevskian. At any rate, I enjoyed it. I did this yesterday, by forcing myself, with a terrific effort of will. I haven't the faintest desire to write. I was thinking of Peter all afternoon and want nothing but to make love.

Peter came at 9 o'clock. I was docile at first, sewing; but he got into literature and I expressed myself. I was afraid it had spoiled the evening. I was on the edge of weeping. He told me about some critical essays his sister had written about E.M. Forster and Virginia Woolf; I.A. Richards had criticized them, and recommended them to Eliot, but Eliot didn't take them.[53] Peter said his sister's perceptions were so acute—but she had no idea of criticizing; she accepted authors she liked, like a little girl; but she missed nothing in them. I told Peter he never thought about good and evil—i.e., either morally, for one's life, or philosophically—the nature of evil. I got interested and saw him looking frightened. I wanted so desperately to make love to him that I tried every trick—stopped talking, looked miserable, clung to him, finally went to bed, and he sat on the bed,

---

[52]In "The Tygon," the character Donato is based on Coleman's lover Bianchetti. The protagonist, Frieda, resembles Coleman.

[53]In the late 1920s Dorothy Hoare was working on critical essays on E. M. Forster (1879–1970), as well as on Woolf, Lawrence, Hardy, Conrad, Joyce, and Mansfield. They were praised by her colleague I. A. Richards, who likely suggested Eliot publish them either as a book with Faber & Faber, where Eliot was a director, or as separate articles in *The Criterion*, the little magazine Eliot edited from 1922–1939. The material was eventually published as the book *Some Studies in the Modern Novel* (Chatto & Windus 1938).

and I went to sleep on his shoulder. He hates me so when I'm opinionated; yet the breath of his mind comes from my love of literature.

Thursday, August 16

I went on copying my book; chapters 1–3 are final.

The man and the woman don't seem alive. The father only is alive. Perhaps my conception of the man and the woman is not settled. What a mess this book will be. I don't want to write it at all. It just bores me stiff to think about it. What I want to do—there is only one reason I am writing it aside from making money and getting fame. I want the excitement of dramatic feeling. I suppose I can get it with grinding at the beginning.

I had lunch with Tony, who telephoned me. She sat in her jolly way and told me tragic things. She tried to commit suicide with Tom.[54] He is in love with Mrs. Grigson. As she went on, I heard the coldness, the icy deliberate indifference with which Deak received my hysteria in 1925. I wondered if it was the same thing—I said, "Are you sure he doesn't think you've been unjust to him?" She knew that all right. She thinks it will all blow over.

Tony must be almost repellent to Tom, and I don't think he would have slept with her at the beginning if she hadn't been intelligent. I wonder if she seduced him. I don't know. But I know she isn't a physical type for him, if she is for anybody. Mrs. Grigson resembles me a little; last year Tom would have done anything I said. Tony's fate—just now—depends on whether Mrs. Grigson wants him or not. I don't think she could want anybody. But even if this blows over the day will come when some woman will want Tom, and if so, Tony will lose him.

She sits talking, as Phyllis said, in a social way, to such a point that you can't believe the things she says are real. But they are real. Tony is not a tragic woman, and this life doesn't suit her—but there she is—she's violent, and could go out of her head—and die. She's taken a room at Earnshaw Smith's (her second husband) to work.[55]

---

[54] (Sir) Henry Tom Hopkinson (1905–1990). Towards the end of her marriage to him, in the summer of 1934, White discovered he was having an affair, the news of which drove her to attempt suicide: on vacation with Hopkinson in Brittany, she tried to fling herself from the window of their hotel room into the ocean (see Dunn 166–67). She later translated this event into her short story "The Moment of Truth" (*Horizon*, June 1941). Hopkinson's mistress was Frances (Galt) Grigson (d. 1937 from tuberculosis). She was the American wife of Geoffrey Grigson (1905–1985), English poet and critic, and together they founded the magazine *New Verse*, which he also edited (1933–1939).

[55] White and Hopkinson were living at 18 Cecil Court, Westminster; Smith was at 55 Paultons Square, Chelsea.

Friday, August 17

I met Peter for lunch. We went to Hamleys to get a birthday present for Pegeen.[56] Peter loved the toys. Writing the card I said, "From Emily and Peter Hoare" to see what he would say, and pretended it was a mistake. He was frantic. I wrote another "From Emily Coleman and Peter Hoare" and he didn't like that. He said Kay Boyle and Laurence Vail would see it. He wanted me to send it alone. This I refused to do. I said, "Who cares about your affairs?" and shut him up for the moment.[57] We went to Queen's Hall to get tickets for the Prom Concert, Mozart.[58] He said, "I would just like to smash you in the face," hungrily.

I left Peter and went to get some jodhpurs. A young man took the measurements. It was horrible. I should have taken Phyllis with me. It gave me the most dreadful feelings about England: a very proper young man who was the soul of politeness, so that I felt sure, took the measurements in such a way that I was trembling with fear and horror; and could not do anything. I kept thinking about it all the afternoon. I was so frightened. One should never have riding breeches measured without a woman. It shocked me so I haven't got over it. It is horrible to have someone do that to one. It's like being raped, in the war. A strange man, who seems to be decent, does such things. It is deadly primitive fear I feel—it is close to a dreadful experience—it could easily be a horrible experience, that one would never forget. I felt helpless, and terror-stricken, I thought it would never end. I could not go out, because he did not seem to be doing anything wrong. I think now I should have gone out, anyway.

Monday, August 20

I wrote a great deal, or rather am rewriting—the parts I don't like of chapters 1–9. The dance hall chapter was a nuisance. I now have chapters 1–9 finished. I'm going to send them to Tony. I still have to go over 25 more pages. But I can't go forward until I have the rest finished. Character of Donato now much

---

[56] Hamleys is a famous toy shop in Regent Street.
[57] Boyle, at this point married to Guggenheim's ex-husband, Vail, had earlier been involved with Hoare.
[58] Bombed during WWII, Queen's Hall at Langham Place had been, as London's main concert venue, the site of the annual Promenade Concerts or "Proms" (from mid-July to mid-September), conducted since they began in 1895 by Sir Henry Wood (1864–1944). On Thursday, 16 August, 1934, Coleman saw Wood conduct pieces by Mozart as well as by Franz Joseph Haydn, Eugene Goossens, Nikolai Medtner, and Engelbert Humperdinck. The Henry Wood Promenade Concerts are performed today at the Royal Albert Hall.

clearer, as soon as I got him in his home. Am very excited at the thought of what is to be written.

The manual labour of going over a book, with carbons, is terrible.

Tuesday, August 21

Finished getting ready chapters 1–10 to send to Tony, and wrote her—a mild innocent letter, invoking her criticism. I wonder what she will say about it. I should think she would say (A) that it is good, (B) that it isn't clear what the woman is, etc. (C) she can't tell by 9 chapters. I don't know what she will say.

Letter from Peggy saying, "I am so glad you are writing your book. I wish so much that your talent could take wing. It will give you so much that Hoare omits." We are going down there this weekend.

Friday, August 24

I was so pleased with chapter XIV that I went downstairs and showed it to Phyllis.[59] She seemed to be moved by it. "I forget that you can do something like this," she said. She said it could not be changed. She said it was terribly moving. I told her I enjoyed the prospect of having my gifts recognized, that no one knew I could write, and I could write, and people might patronize me less if that was known.

I love my book! It seems different from the one I began last October, and different from the one I was doing in Woburn Square. I told Phyllis it was easy to write like chapter 14 (if that is good); that flew out. I hardly changed anything. But to write what human beings say to each other in moments of emotion is not easy.

I am doing XV as it comes, studying Donato's character, he seems to be turning out a Puritan! I am going to tea with Tony today and she is going to talk about my book, which will delight me, whatever she says—I have never talked to her about my writing.

Saturday, August 25

Lunched with Peter at Ridgways.

I met Phyllis and she went with me to get the jodhpurs fitted. Peter says it's absolute nonsense for me to get into such a state. The man didn't dare do anything. Phyllis said he had a horrid face. I never looked at his face.

---

[59]Coleman has added in pen, in brackets, "finally ch. 29."

Then I went to Tony. I asked her right away about Tom and she didn't want to talk about it, and it appears she had a kind of crisis. He <u>had</u> been sleeping with Mrs. Grigson. I knew it. He seems only to have done it once. You can't believe them. I think she is mad from enraged vanity, and inferiority complex—which she always has, morbidity, and now it's justified.

She then launched into my book, and was very enthusiastic about it. She had marked down 4 pages of notes and criticisms. They were all small but very well sustained, and I agreed with practically everything. I was delighted with her reactions. I felt I had been keeping it in a cellar and now it was out in the air. She has a real sense of style, and never missed any subtleties. A reader like Tony is worth a fortune to the author, if he can get her reactions in process of constructing the book—because she is on the ground, earthy (sees from the outside)—not a poet—yet is intelligent and subtle enough to get everything, especially the human things.

I was thinking in bed this morning that perhaps I ought to lay the scene in America, and have them both Americans. I hate writing about foreigners, and a foreign country. I took it that way because it happened that way; then I had to make her German because I don't want myself in it.[60]

There was a terrible thing in *The Evening Standard*, a long letter from a girl who gassed herself, after trying to commit suicide with her lover.[61] I could hardly read it. Even Peter was upset by it. It was evident that they were very much in love. She said, "We tried to cut the main artery of each other." It gave me the feeling of one person. The man killed himself with a shotgun, next to her; she was to take it, and die. But she could not stand his death agonies. She went mad, and wandered all night, going back to him, and holding his hand, when he was dead. She got a room finally in Pimlico with a gas ring, and gassed herself. The letter was read at the inquest.

Ingleby Oddie, the coroner. <u>He sat on John's body</u>.[62]

Wednesday, August 29

Peter does not want to take me on his holiday. I am worrying him terribly; he would like to go with me to France; but he is afraid of the consequences. We walked around in Mayfair, near Piccadilly, for half an hour. "What good would it do us to go away for a month? You are going to America because

---

[60]Frieda is German, Donato Italian. Despite this comment, Coleman often acknowledged the autobiographical elements of the story.
[61]One of the headlines on the front page of *The Evening Standard* for Friday, August 24, reads: "Elsie Walsingham's Last Letter Tells How Lover [Peter Dawson] died."
[62]As Holms had died as the result of a heart attack during surgery, there had been an autopsy and inquest, at which the surgeons were cleared of any malpractice.

our relation is wrong. Isn't it going to make it worse if we stay together like that beforehand?" I said, "You have no right not to try to do something that might make it better." He went away, finally. He said he would come to see me in the evening. I felt better, and went and bought some clothes. I had tea and went to a news reel.

I came home and talked to Phyllis. I told her how much I longed for death, even if I were happy; the joy I would feel if I knew I were to die tomorrow. I told her I could never kill myself, not because of the wickedness to my father—the only human being who would suffer—but because "to him that hath shall be given"—and I am one of those who have.[63] I would fear death if I took my life. I told Phyllis that with every atom of my conscious being I <u>knew</u> there was a harmony, and that we can be one with it. I told her about John—(I never cease to think of him) how he is not dead. "I mention him in a casual way as if he were not dead. No doubt even Peggy thinks I'm callous. It's because he's not dead to me. Every word he ever said I remember. I never forget a single thing he said."

Saturday, September 1

I phoned Peter and met him to go over to get his car; he had had it looked over.[64] He was in a miserable state. He said he was not going abroad.

I woke up early and could not sleep, and came in Phyllis' room and cried. I got dressed early and went over to Peter's. He was up. I had tea with him, and talked about his sister's articles again; as we had last night. Then I asked him if he wouldn't go to the A[utomobile]. A[ssociation]. before going to the office, and arrange about the boat, and he said: "You're trying to force me to go, to suit your own ends, when I don't want to go." At this I burst into tears, and could not stop crying. He was so distressed, and kept stroking me saying, "Poor baby; you want someone to take care of you!" and looked as if he would die. He said, "I'll do anything you want. I'll do anything." He said, "I'll take you." He got up and telephoned the A.A. and made all the arrangements; arranged to get off Tuesday.

Now he has given in, and it will be so important to us, so important! I <u>believed</u> in it, I know that if we could be together this way, for a month, it would give us a chance to see if we could be happy. I <u>know</u> that when we do go Peter will be happy with me—I will <u>make</u> happiness between us.[65]

---

[63] Matthew 25: 29.

[64] Hoare had begun to give in to Coleman's desire to go abroad for his annual holiday; he had had his photograph taken for a special driving license and had taken his car in for a checkup.

[65] Coleman had added by hand: "What will that month mean? What will that happiness be? We will most likely fight."

Part IV

Section 1

London

January 16–March 13, 1936

Coleman vacationed with Hoare in France and Spain in September 1934, and then in October she sailed to New York with her son and Phyllis Jones.[1] *John stayed mainly with Coleman's Aunt Lett in Rochester while Coleman travelled, visiting with her father at his home in Hartford; with Sonia Himmel in and around Boston; and with Barnes who, after being at Hayford Hall in the summer of 1933, had returned to New York and was living in Washington Square in Greenwich Village. Here, in early 1935, Coleman began the editing work for Barnes that would result in the publication of* Nightwood. *Coleman returned to England in the summer, which she spent at Guggenheim's newest abode, Yew Tree Cottage in Hurst, Petersfield, East Hampshire. After another trip to Spain in September 1935, she was back at 105 Oakley Street before taking up rooms at 7 Oakley, in the same building as Hoare, which was where she was settled when she resumed her diary in January 1936.*

During this London period Coleman spent an increasing amount of time with White, whose mental health remained delicate though she had a new love interest: Eric Siepmann, the "Antony" in the earlier diary with whom Coleman had been involved. Guggenheim was having difficulties with Garman, in large part due to their profound class differences. Coleman had, meanwhile, intensified her relationship with Barker. Having learned from their mutual friend Muir that she and Guggenheim admired his work, and always strapped for money, Barker had telephoned Coleman in the summer of 1935 likely looking for patronage, which he soon received from the two women. Barker was married to Jessica Woodward (with whom he would

---

[1] There are only a few entries for this period, from November 18–December 9, and because the narrative is incomplete I have not transcribed them.

have three children) and living in Plush, Piddletrenthide, Dorset, in a cottage called "The Butts," though he made frequent trips to London. Coleman obsessed about having sex with him: she thought she may be in love with him; and she also wanted to seek revenge on Hoare for his tortuous, ongoing refusal to make love with her. Fearing the onset of "madness," she became especially focused in the diary on analyzing her sexual identity in light of her previous lesbian experience, what she called her "mania" for Hoare, and her fear that Barker was predominantly homosexual.

Artistically, as with the previous section, Coleman was coming to life again as a writer and was still eager to produce. She continued to develop "The Cremation" and had begun another long poem, "Melville on the Land," inspired by her reading of Moby Dick. And yet, determined as she was, her troubling writer's block and lack of inspiration threatened her literary intentions. Ironically, she was devoting herself to the literary career of Barnes, making it a personal mission to secure a contract for Nightwood from T. S. Eliot at Faber & Faber. After Coleman received a letter from Eliot expressing interest in the manuscript she, along with Guggenheim, arranged to bring Barnes from New York to London in order to advance the book's publication.

7 OAKLEY STREET, LONDON

Thursday, January 16, 1936

I worked all day on "The Cremation." I love the verse beginning "Will he roam like the fish in the waters of the lake?" which seems as good as anything I've written, and moved me. I was so happy with Peter yesterday at the Chinese exhibition (at which I behaved like a spoiled child), and at tea, and going up Charing Cross Rd. afterwards, in the cold, seeing Barker's poems poised high above the others in some bookshop, and looking for a pub Peter had been to with Norman.[2] And then, as ever, finding it to be a good one, happily drinking for hours, going to Josef's, looking at my Peter who rends my heart in pieces when I see his black head, ending at the Café Royal afterwards, where Peter imitated two fairies in front of us who were talking about actors.[3] I love him, fight with him, don't think I could live without him, should think he could easily live without me as I behave. Thinking about Barker today, I can never make love with him, I should think he would have to be cunning to

---

[2] The Chinese Exhibition, at Burlington House, featured Chinese art from Chou to Ch'ing, from 1000 B.C. to A.D. 1800. Barker's *Poems* was published in 1935 by Faber & Faber.
[3] Josef's was Josef Sheekey's fish and seafood restaurant in Covent Garden. The Café Royal, in Regent's Street, was frequented by artists and intellectuals.

get me to; I'll egg him on and then retire; cannot do it, I think. Do not WANT any person's body except Peter's. Must I live without it?

Thinking about Johnny, going down in the bus he confessed he looked at the tank the night before Christmas. He came over in frozen cold, went back in a terrible wind.[4] My darling! Can't think he will ever be anything to me—so full of his own life and I of mine. We'll touch, like spirits. I want to make "The Cremation" something wonderful.

Frightened to death of Barker's being homosexual, nothing will work. I only want him in the mind. I am afraid (a) of the thought of not seeing Hoare, of (b) ever giving up this flat (c) that B. and I will tear each other's souls out (d) that he will forget me (e) that I will enjoy making love to him before Hoare gives in (f) that Hoare will never give in. I could kill myself (a) if I am torn between the two (b) if Hoare doesn't give in—what shall I do? Can't write Djuna as she's had too much.

Sent Melville poem Tuesday to Muir and gave Tony a copy, which she likes. She's going to Cornwall.

When I read "Will he roam like the fish in the waters of the lake" (which I wrote in Yorkshire in June 1934) I wept the other day, seeing a vision. If one could have such moments often. I do not think my beliefs do me any good whatever. All day I have been restless, miserable, thinking of Hoare and Barker. Am determined tonight to endure Hoare again—his not making love to me. (After carefully sending a letter to Barker yesterday in which I said not to hesitate to ask for a loan of money if he ever needed to come to London.) Been writing poetry all day, alternating with making candy. I eat the candy nervously, go out to pee, sit, lie down, stoke the fire, write a little. Nothing on my book, as might be imagined. But have thought about it, have got Heidi properly conceived, so that Part III can go on; when that's done I can rewrite Pt. LV.[5]

Friday, January 17

While Peter and I were talking Tom telephoned in a sepulchral voice asked me about Siepmann.[6] Really I felt sorry for the man for the first time. Tony leaves for Cornwall today. His voice trembled, in a clergyman's way; I knew he was feeling badly. What he wants to know is, does Siepmann know Tony could go mad? (He does indeed know and is terrified of it.)

---

[4]John had come from France to see his mother over Christmas.
[5]In "The Tygon," the character of Heidi is Frieda's sister, who betrays her by having an affair with Donato. Coleman had initially based Heidi on Guggenheim.
[6]Tom Hopkinson, White's third husband. Although White was planning to meet Eric Siepmann at his cottage in Cornwall, he sent her a telegram asking her not to.

Can't give up the thought that I don't really want Barker, even if he wants me; do not want anyone but Peter; am going into this because I can't stand my life with Peter and Barker is the first person I've met who could take me out of it. Can't endure the vision of making love to him, or anyone, except Peter, who has the most deadly sexual attraction. I don't forget however the way I felt when Barker read St. Augustine and vanity and excitement would move me no doubt to make some move towards him; he being really lustful would settle the rest.[7]

This morning a little card from the *New Statesman*, etc.[8] I like your poem very much and hope to be able to print it, though it is rather long for this paper—Raymond Mortimer—which gave me satisfaction though I think he is trying to explain away the fact that they won't print it.

Very good for me to keep a diary now, relieves the strain on Djuna and keeps me occupied, when I was wandering about restlessly from the kitchen to here putting down a few lines of poetry now and then.

Tony came to see me; she is not going to Cornwall.

I told her details of my only Lesbian "affair" which rocked her with mirth. In the end she rather regarded me as a gay blade; looked admiringly, and a trifle apprehensively. She got onto Siepmann every time, as women do. I got onto Barker and Hoare whenever I could. I told her I felt like St. Augustine, that I was wicked, had been wicked, and that all my life should be a penance. Peter coming to dinner, have got a tiny cold chicken which I am trying not to eat before he comes. Gave Tony tea and honey. Tom will want Tony passionately, as soon as she gets Siepmann. Will she get him? She thinks not. Tony said I had done penance for 4 years. I said not enough: all my life. Very interesting thing, talking about sex, I said "Sex is evil; it is the fall of man" etc., and she said yes, but the way we go through with it is our only salvation (which I've thought); then I said, "Good people are attracted sexually by evil"—but then it occurred to me that evil people are attracted sexually by good. That's the other half, the half I had not thought of. Why is this—<u>sex is the longing for completion</u>.

I love my Peter, want to see him, long for him. When I was in bed with him it was never what I hoped. Slowly he has been giving way. The other evening when he caressed my face it felt as if he were wearing through the bone. My darling, how I love him, my sweet mate and companion. If only I can make him let go and not let him go myself.

---

[7]St. Augustine of Hippo's (354–430) *Confessions* recounts his conversion to Christianity.
[8]Coleman submitted her "Melville" poem to (Charles) Raymond (Bell) Mortimer (1895–1980), English literary and art critic who edited the *New Statesman* from 1935–1947. The poem would be published in the Friday, March 13, 1936, Spring Books Supplement alongside, for instance, Auden's "Poem" as well as book reviews by Huxley, Rose Macaulay, and Peter Quennell.

Saturday, January 18

We went to see *Sous Les Toits de Paris* last night, coming home in the snow.[9] It was an excellent picture, with a sulky, vicious, pathetic woman in it who gave me great thought. I want my woman to be like this, in a civilized form.[10] Peter enjoyed the picture very much. Some of it was terribly funny; we sat through it all again.

Our relation is so intense and always keyed up because of the sex suppression.

Dreamed queerly about Eliot the night before last; that I was caressing him, knowing all the time that he was famous, and he was packing a bag, telling me he had to commute all the way from Harvard, and how he hated America.[11] At the cinema, every time any love-making happened, thought of Barker, thought of him in bed, planned out all sorts of anticipated scenes. I won't see him for months, and when we do meet I don't think I shall make any advances to him at all. Do I really want him? If so, keep him off as long as I can. His having given himself away (as he thinks, unimportantly) I have all the cards: Because I know what he feels and what I feel now; and he only knows what he feels. I can be cunning as a cat; all I've learned from Hoare will be used on him. I shall go ruthlessly on, because I've made up my mind, at least to make him fall in love with me (which will do him only good). Nothing less than this will break Hoare's will. Nothing less than this, however, can break us up, either. If Barker falls in love with me I don't see how in the whole world I can ever resist him.

In other words, I am digging my grave. I've been sitting in a grave, so it seems, now for 37 years; I might as well have a deep one.

Hoare's sparkling eyes, like no one's, the suppressed life in them. He is in no way as near to me as Barker is (as a poet). As a human being I think he is ever so much nearer. I am such a goof, I could live on poetry. Barker said to me, "Have you no use for me at all except as a writer?" He meant it in an impersonal way. I said, "In your odd way you know a lot about human beings." He didn't like that. He wants me to think him perfect, wants the upper hand in everything (like McDonald, they are all the same these homosexual he-men). I wish I knew what he was like—he seems to me to be in flux. He says one thing one moment and contradicts it later; has no idea where he is

---

[9] *Sous Les Toits de Paris* (*Under the Roofs of Paris*) is the 1930 Franco-German film about the tragic love story of an impoverished singer, directed by René Clair, starring Albert Préjean and Pola Illéry.
[10] Coleman's "woman" is Frieda, protagonist of "The Tygon."
[11] T. S. Eliot had been an undergraduate and graduate student at Harvard.

going. But such a darling he is, the only respect-worthy and companionable person I've met in London except Tony.

Monday, January 20

Just sent wire to Sonia, as I called the U.S. Lines and am told the boat train gets in at 3 a.m. Wednesday morning. Am eager to see her.

A day in the country yesterday at the Stansburys,' who have rented a house near where Shaw lives, a sweet low-ceilinged rambling old house.[12] It was two years since John died. I did not think of him at all, in this atmosphere, it being possibly one of the two or three days since he died on which I have not thought of him. The night before had received a stinking letter from Peggy, saying I must stop telling her what to do with her money, to which I replied, with consideration (though in the next mail) a scorcher. Not the thing to do on the anniversary of John's death, but for many reasons thought it absolutely advisable. We spent this day hearing funny American songs ("Ida the Wayward Sturgeon"), the "Prune", etc., dancing—which I instigated, and enjoyed—mock ballet dancing, listening to Beethoven (Norman going through the whole *Moonlight Sonata* very well) eating excellent food, etc. I giggling and egotistic, trying to suppress it; agreeing with everybody; until the King's illness came up and then I got very gloomy.[13] The death of Kind George marks the passing of all that is decent and civilized in the modern world, the beginning of (necessary) Communism—none of them would understand—all the life I love—the end of life. He and the Queen have been for 25 years a stable symbol of the old, and have represented it as nowhere else could it be so represented.[14] I really cannot bear it when the King is dead.

Wednesday, January 22

My 37th birthday. Peter and I waited up for Sonia till 3 a.m.—she arrived at 5. I had a letter from Barker saying he may come to London next week.

Sonia came, we talked till 7, she looking sprightly. I wrote Barker as soon as Peter went to bed. Said I would like him to come, tone casual enough to keep him away, almost. Tony here in the morning—more letters from Siepmann, even better (extremely odd he writes pretentious letters to me),

---

[12]George Bernard Shaw (1856–1950) lived in the village of Ayot St. Lawrence, in Hertfordshire, from 1906 until his death. Helen Stansbury and her husband, Harold, were friends of Coleman and Hoare, and Gossy and Norman Brook.
[13]King George V (1865–1936).
[14]George V married Victoria Mary, daughter of the Duke of Teck, in 1893. On May 6, 1935, celebrations were held by an adoring public to honour his twenty-five years at the throne.

really interesting, Tony in love, trying to keep her head. E. Smith came to tea Saturday, talked about Tony. Tom sees Frances every week, says they have not slept together.

The night before last I was out with Peter, saw *Top Hat*, with wonderful tap dancing by Fred Astaire—provoked thoughts of heaven in me—that can be a heaven—anything can, perfectly and freely done.[15] Then the posters about the King began. "The King's condition shows diminishing strength." Felt very sad, then saw at eleven the next posters, "The King is dying." Went to Buckingham Palace where official bulletin had been posted, great crowds and cars. Then to Home Office to see if there was any news. Walking along the Mall felt very close to Peter.[16]

At H[ome].O[ffice]. policeman got news that the King was dead.[17] Very depressed, dreamed and was sad waking up depressed. England quite different, the poor King dead, strength slowly gone; King Edward the Eighth impossible.

Sunday, January 26

The most exciting thing that has happened in years, I think, was the reception on Wednesday of a letter from Eliot in which he shows great interest in Djuna's book.[18] I carry it around and read it to myself at intervals. It is just one year since I started trying to do something about that book, and the

---

[15]*Top Hat* is the 1935 musical hit starring Fred Astaire and Ginger Rogers.
[16]The Mall, fashionable promenade leading to Buckingham Palace.
[17]The King had died at Sandringham House, Norfolk, where the Royal Family had gone for Christmas. His body was brought back to London on January 23 where it lay in state at Westminster Hall; it was then taken to Windsor on January 28 and buried in St. George's Chapel. King George was succeeded by his eldest son, Edward VIII.
[18]In July 1935, Coleman had sent to Eliot (a director at Faber & Faber), via Edwin Muir, excerpts of the novel *Nightwood* she had helped Barnes to edit when they had been together in New York earlier that year. Coleman then wrote two letters to Eliot in October 1935, asking for an interview so that she could convince him to publish the manuscript (see Plumb xx–xxi). The second letter in the Coleman archive (October 31, 1935, F. 13) contains lengthy quotations from the novel. The letter begins accordingly: "Dear Mr. Eliot; I have your letter, in reply to mine about Miss Barnes' book. If you believe, from the excerpts you have seen, that the book would compare unfavourably with the work of Miss Kay Boyle, it would seem almost futile to send you the manuscript. However, it may be that I don't fully understand what you mean. Perhaps I misinterpret statements which you have made in your own writing, or, more possibly, that the excerpts, by themselves, do not form enough of a connection to bring out what seems to me the extraordinary value of Miss Barnes' book. But I should think that for anyone preoccupied with the problems of evil and suffering this would be a document which points the way to the things we most want to know."

obstacles have been terrific. He and another director want to publish the book; it only remains to convince the chairman, Faber, who has been away.[19] But Eliot says "Should the decision be adverse I shall continue to be interested in the possibility of getting someone to publish the book." I am afraid of this Chairman; he is without doubt a hard-headed business-man. So I don't dare write Djuna, yet. I shall write her about it, and not send the letter till I hear, which, according to Eliot, should be in a few days.

This letter reflects great credit on Eliot, too, considering life, and his life, and everything one knows; it shows he is not dead. I love him for the letter. Peter delighted, astonished at the letter. How it does set me up as far as he is concerned. But Djuna, Djuna! It will change her whole life. I simply cannot believe it. It's like one's feeling after a long illness.

Read some of Djuna's letters to Sonia; she read some of *Janus*.[20] "The Cremation" has to have almost all I have written lately thrown out.

Monday, January 27

I have been waiting to hear from Barker, starting at the sound of the telephone. Have been writing to Djuna, to tell her about Eliot—do not send it till I heard the definite decision of Faber's. I wish I would see her when she reads the letter. I had a letter from her in which she said a lovely thing about Thelma (Robin). How she spent the afternoon with her love Neagoe, and in the evening Thelma came and stayed with Djuna the night, in the other bed, and Djuna lay awake looking at her[21] She said, "She was only the stuffed skin of my love, and yet the only reality."

Sonia reading John [Holms]'s letters all day.

Thursday, January 30

The King's funeral was a terrible thing, depressing, gloomy, every artifice brought to make one suffer (successfully too). I read and read about it. Tom Hopkinson called me up the other night and in his clergyman's voice said how he loved my poem about Moby Dick. Siepmann has been in town seeing Tony. I am very glad he has.

---

[19]Geoffrey Faber (1889–1961), publisher, poet, and scholar; the other director is Frank Morley (1898–1980), American expatriate.
[20]*Janus*, published in 1935, brings together two of Barker's prose pieces, titled respectively "The Bacchant" and "The Documents of a Death."
[21]Barnes' affair with Peter Neagoe lasted from 1934 to 1936.

I am waiting for Barker, frantic—he did not come till Wednesday—then he was very sweet—terrified of him because he wanted to make love to me again, but gave no sign—I withdrew inside. Told Sonia after he had gone he is wicked. He read poems. Read Marvell's "Garden." What a poem; He had a poem of his own which was good in parts. Do not feel much from his poetry, on the whole; feel his talents only. Read him "The Cremation," he really excited by it—I discovered a page I did the other day and had not seen since was good—towards the end. The end not quite right—one word. Told Barker to finish it; he couldn't. He liked all the <u>best</u> parts. We were very close—I excited—talking—telling him life and <u>honesty</u> made that poem possible. Showed him Eliot's letter about Djuna—he partially pleased—said I should be stabilized by E's recognition of my criticism. I had to say, "Poof, do you think I need that?" not very tactful.

He left—"dashed"—which he does when hard-pressed by me—in relief. Will see him today. Barker left his poem "Ode to Man" 3/4 of which he has copied for me. Some of it heavenly—young of course—not all realized—but the real thing pressing through. A marvel of technical excellence, heavenly sounds, rhymes, words—passion perfectly expressed sometimes. Some wonderful things like

> Naked in the streets wander the prostitutes
> Pushing the downward boughs of prohibited
> Fruit food apart with sore bosoms, observing
> The fruit fall and rot on the hard ground,
> Whose bruises on the beautiful aluminium
> Limbs, by gold brutes grasped, shape palatable fruits.

I am sitting waiting for him to telephone. He was angry when he went, because I talked about "Ash Wednesday" in a way he didn't like. Barker is in love with Eliot—will not hear any truth about him, except at rare moments when he doesn't know he's conscious.[22] I think so much of Eliot, I respect his integrity to such a degree, that B. ought to know what I think of him. However in youth it is all adoration, or nothing. Not that he hasn't an independence of his own.

He phoned rather late and postponed seeing me, as he was going to see Eliot.

---

[22]"Ash Wednesday," Eliot's 1930 poem. Eliot, Barker's publisher, had made Barker his protégé of sorts, offering him support and encouragement with his poetry. As quoted in Fraser's biography of Barker, in June 1934, "Eliot was soon carrying Barker's poems around London in the inside pocket of his jacket and showing them to friends. Barker was, he wrote two years later, 'one of the very small number of young poets whose work I consider important'" (65).

Friday, January 31

Barker came. He read the whole of the "Ode to Man." Sonia was in raptures. I was thinking of him the whole time he was reading it. The latter part is even better; he is sending it to me. It is noble, and wonderful.

I was relieved when he went—he made me suffer so by not coming in the afternoon when I had waited for him. I really cannot endure the thought of this starting again. I was not alone with him this time except Wednesday at lunch, very personal he was indeed then, and an hour after that when I was reading him "The Cremation," when I was so near him it hurt even to think of it, and would not make one move. I can't think of it—know the end—waiting—Peter suffering—agony—Peter and I happy a little (or is that possible before I have grown so in love with Barker it will not be possible?)—then, the end. Sonia says he has suffered so much for his wife, not being able to give her things. She was ill. *Alanna* shows this, and the end of "The Bacchant" of course.[23]

He was pleased that we loved his poem. I gave him Yeats' "Leda and the Swan" to read. He liked that. He said, "O by the way Yeats wrote me a letter saying I was good and these other poets were not."[24] I said, "Did you ever? Why didn't you tell me?" "My dear woman there's a lot I don't tell you." Very childish.

I found out why he telephoned me last summer, what I have wondered. He had been told by Muir that Peggy and I liked *Alanna*.

Sonia and I discussing Barker like harpies—the poor boy if he knew what women were really like could never stand them. Tony came for dinner very lively looking at me in odd ways which betokened things I can't fathom; (a) cattiness; (b) bewilderment. Siepmann has been very good to her.

Tony suggested the side of me which is 22 might not be as attractive to Barker as the side which is 40. Since I've seen Barker's poem he might be any age. It is the most wonderful poem to be written in a hundred years; and the best ever written by a young man of his age. He has wonderful genius—which may go to almost any limits—if one could believe, in this day, that genius could flower.

---

[23] The eponymous protagonist of *Alanna Autumnal* winds up dying, abandoned by her husband, while her brother, who loves her, is condemned to a life in death without her. In the novella "The Bacchant," noted earlier, the male narrator similarly seems to go mad when Ruth, the young girl he loves, dies of a weak heart.

[24] At twenty-two years of age, Barker was the youngest contributor to Yeats' 1936 anthology, *The Oxford Book of Modern Verse 1892–1935*.

Tuesday, February 4

Reading Gertrude Stein's *Autobiography of Toklas*; terribly amusing. We went to Eliot's play, *Murder in the Cathedral*.[25] I was very ill during it, vomited continually; do not know why.

Saturday, February 8

Yesterday I asked Peter to lunch with me. I began to cry and said, "You won't leave me?" He melted entirely, and kept trying to touch my hand. He said, "What is the matter?" in loving melting tones. I cried and said, "I made love to Barker."

He drew back, saying shakily, "You have done?" I nodded. I didn't look at him after that, but looked away in determination.

We walked down the street. I had to go to the National Gallery, to meet Sonia. This was the best way, I thought, to make him think I had done it before I do do it; to make one desperate effort to make him save himself (and me) before it is too late. He walked with me to the National Gallery, but never said one word. I watched him walking down Trafalgar Square, down through the columns, through the people, until he was lost as a dot in Whitehall.[26] I went inside and felt so desperately sorry for him. He will never know he loves me until he suffers. He will not suffer as long as he thinks he has me.

But I felt pretty sick, and as though I never wanted to see Barker again. I sat for a long time waiting for Sonia.

We stayed out late, going to the Chinese Restaurant in Soho. I phoned Peggy, found she had been in London again without seeing me.[27] Misinterpreted my letter. Very miserable, said she had felt all the time like leaving Garman. Wrote to her today to get her to come before Sonia goes. Lovely sweet letter from Johnny; warms my heart, always makes me fear.

G. Stein's book really wonderful. Had no idea she was like that, real gusto and innocence, and sly humour; joy of life. Would like at last to know her.

---

[25] Stein's *Autobiography of Alice B. Toklas* (1933) frustrates distinctions between fiction and autobiography. In February 1936, Eliot's play *Murder in the Cathedral* (1935) was performed at the Mercury Theatre, a small church hall in Notting Hill Gate converted to a theatre and dance school in 1927.

[26] Whitehall is a street in London's borough of Westminster which contains many government offices; it runs south from Trafalgar Square, site of the National Gallery. Hoare was taking this street back to the Home Office where he worked.

[27] Guggenheim, who was having difficulties in her relationship with Garman, had come up to London with him from Yew Tree Cottage. She kept a flat in the city, in the Adelphi quarter, which she and Garman shared with Phyllis Jones.

The afternoon I spent with her was too stupid to get it.[28] Sonia reading my book. Don't feel I can ever see Barker.

Thursday, February 13

Writing this Thursday, as if before. But a great deal has happened. Sunday night I heard Peter come in, about ten. I went down Monday morning, after a horrid night.[29] He was sitting at breakfast. I walked in. I said, "What right have you to treat me this way?" We had some conversation. I gave him a great many home truths, saved up for years: this was the moment. I drove home my misery—his cowardice. I went out saying "What has happened is your fault." Peggy came Monday—it was bitter cold, with a wind. Peggy wouldn't talk about Garman, but Sonia was ever so glad to see her: "her Jewish sister." We lunched uptown with Peggy Tuesday, at the Quo Vadis in Dean Street.[30] I asked Peggy about Garman, we talked, she sounded desperate, I worried to death. I thought she was going to leave him; and thought perhaps she should. I said, "Let me have tea with him tomorrow and talk to him." Called me up as soon as she got home to say she was all right, that was nonsense, we would all have tea with Garman.

We went to Hetty's to dinner as early as possible, so I could knock at Hoare's door before Mrs. Stafford left. She let me in and I, under pretense of getting a book for Sonia (who was leaving on the morrow) came in upon him. He was sitting rather hunched-up in his big chair, sideways, looking desperate. I simply could not stand it. I made a move towards him and said, "Oh, Peter darling!" whereupon he knocked me away. He said, "Get away from me, you bitch!" I was terribly happy, but I did not show it. I said, "Why do you call me that?" and he kept saying, "You did it behind my back!" I said, "I did not, I warned you, I warned you for four months." He glared at me, and looked wretched, and I thought I had better tell him the truth, but was afraid to, unless I could get him to make some admission. I said, "Then you were fond of me. You did consider yourself my lover—though you never made love?" I said, looking for the book, "Anyone would think you were my husband." I was glowing inside. Then he said, "What I can't stand is the way you had him to dinner in my flat and then slept with him." I said at once, "I never slept with him." He pretended not to hear this. But soon he said, "What do you mean, you didn't sleep with him?" I said, "I never said I slept with

---

[28]Coleman did not elaborate on this earlier experience, possibly described in the diary she destroyed.
[29]Coleman was now living at 7 Oakley Street in the same building as Hoare.
[30]The Quo Vadis remains open at 26–29 Dean Street, Soho.

him." He relented in his face enough at this so that I began to make jokes about his character; and he began to laugh.

I went up to get Sonia, fearing she had gone to bed. We were very gay and happy and Hoare no doubt felt as if he had risen from the grave. At 1 o'clock we started to go and I thought, "Here's where everything snaps back again—the old habits." But after saying goodbye to Sonia, he seized me. I was saying goodnight to him affectionately, prepared to retire. He seized me, and seemed possessed. He was never like that before. I did feel some of the gates had been broken. I went upstairs and waited for him, and he came to my bed, and we lay naked in each other's arms, after five months of agony.[31]

Friday, February 14

I sat all day yesterday alone, after bathing and cleaning, happy to be alone and quiet, and trusting Peter for the future. He said, the night I gave in, "We will not make any plans, but just make love when we want, for a while," which is all I have ever wanted. I feel Paradise approaching, my first reaction is I cannot stand it—I have not the right to have spiritual and material happiness on this earth—as others have not—O God I have had enough suffering. My dream in the whole world (a woman who wants as much as anyone could want)—to marry Peter, to have this flat and have a cottage in the country—to write the sort of thing I've been meditating for years (I've already done that, "The Cremation")—every wish satisfied—it won't last, one or the other of us will die now (who wished for that so ardently for so many years). If these things happen—if I do marry Peter and then, the final wish, have Johnny with me most of the time, then I must think a great deal of other people.

Sunday, February 16

I wonder when the day of my death will come. That day, that lovely day, when my life passes out of this loathsome life-on-earth! It would give me heart to know. I am sure that some change occurs, on another plane. One does not go on suffering like this forever. I wonder if I will have Peter in another life? If I stick to him I will. The most terrible night, full of foreboding dreams, my throat clutched in misery. I have got up, but everything is black and without life or harmony. It is because Peter has gone back on me. Surely I should have had the intelligence to know that this would happen again. What a fool I

---

[31] The following day, Coleman went with Guggenheim and Jones to see Mrs. Hoyle, a fortune teller they had been to two years before. Hoyle informed Coleman that she would marry Hoare "soon." Himmel left London shortly after to continue on her travels.

am. I must suffer now for being a fool. Changes in life do not come so easily. But I'm in despair, the blackest doubt—I don't believe Peter will ever love me whole-heartedly—he is incapable of it. I thought I was free of the love for Barker—I felt so safe and so happy. I am not free—I have got to go through with it. I've got to go through with all that hell. Oh if I could endure unto death, if I could resist Barker and endure! In <u>some</u> life Peter could love me. What shall I do, I feel poisoned, as if I could not go on.

I waited for him all Saturday afternoon. Tony did not come, as invited, and Phyllis came very late (by my clock, which was an hour fast.)

Peter came finally, and I was very quiet, feeling sick and like death. Phyllis went, and finally I said to Peter, "Are you going back on me again?" etc., and "If you are, it's finished," etc. He seemed very troubled, said he didn't know, seemed sweet and understanding. But after dinner I lost control of myself and went into an hysterical fit—such as he has never seen—when in despair at his saying he "felt friction" between us after we had slept together (I have heard it so often) I leaped out of the chair, to put on my shoes and go upstairs, and feeling that this was the very end, and all our dreams gone tottering, and Barker encroaching upon me (the poor boy)—I hurled the shoes on the floor, jumped up and down in absolutely uncontrollable frenzies. He was frightened half out of his wits (I have never done this, in five years)—in a wild and shaking voice he commanded me to be quiet, "You silly little fool" he cried taking my wrists, but he was terrified out of his skin. I flung myself on the couch sobbing and lay there for some time. He was very kind to me, and good, and understanding. I thought it must have been fatal to lose such control, but I think it made him realize my suffering. I should have gone upstairs then, but I could not go, longing for him to be with me, and we talked and talked, and I said so much to make him realize what his nature is. His horrible nature, he doesn't believe in one thing, not in life, nor in death, nor in love, he believes and can believe nothing—God has done him in. So the only hope is Barker—that terrifying thought—that frightening witness of the life I fear. I hope, I pray God, I may not weaken with Barker—but make Hoare suffer as much as he can.

Monday, February 17

A very nice letter from Muir, about the whale poem. He said the most wonderful things: yet it didn't mean anything to me. I am in the very depths of despair. I want to die—I just feel I can't go on with it. I think of death with expectancy, and joy. I can't kill myself. I wish I had no one who would care if I did (my father); and that I believed it would be an end to this misery. I am absolutely convinced that one has to face <u>everything</u> in death. I have got to master this, become master of it, so it no longer kills me—in which way I'll have got beyond death.

I wrote a letter to Barker the other day. I will send it this morning. I will help him to come to London, and take him to *Romeo and Juliet*, etc.—how horrible! I didn't want to do that. I'll take him to *Figaro*.[32] I'll take the money to do it with which I should pay my debts.

What is there in me so female that I am scared out of my bloody wits at the <u>suggestion</u> that I might have to live alone. I write this wonderful poetry and have not the energy of a rabbit. I shall tell Barker the truth and throw myself (without his knowing it) on his care.

Yesterday I stayed on the couch, feeling sick, and when Peter had not come by half-past one I rushed downstairs, found his door wide open and rushed into his arms, weeping miserably. This is the sort of thing I do, then he took care of me all day, making me tea and supper like an angel, then I felt secure. We were like saints together until late, when after drinking a great deal of sherry he talked about the Home Office. And I tried to get him to make love to me, and he would not. It doesn't work to wait until he does it himself— he'll never move. Then I flew into a frenzy, and told him it was over, and I <u>would</u> make love with Barker.

Peter went into the kitchen and wept last night. He is tortured beyond belief. I am afraid of going quite mad sometimes, I feel such despair, and such a hatred of him, for poisoning our lives, which might have been happy. My suffering is more alive than it has been for months. The fact that I can write a diary is some relief.

But I wait for death—I think of death, with the most loving thoughts.

Tuesday, February 18

Very quiet last night with Peter. He came to dinner—I gave him dinner of steak, spinach, baked potatoes, Camembert and apples, and the same nice old creamed onion soup. I made sardonic references infrequently, which he took as his due, but was very pleasant. Tony was here in the afternoon; glad to see her. Told Tony I wanted to meet the Connolly who writes such good reviews for the *New Statesman*.[33] Copied "The Cremation" straight through, adding a

---

[32]*Romeo and Juliet* and *Figaro* were ballets being performed at London's Sadler's Wells Theatre in the spring of 1936.
[33]Cyril Connolly (1903–1974), British author, literary editor and journalist. Coleman was referring to his "New Novels" column in the *New Statesman and Nation*.

verse I made then; was very pleased copying it. Read it over in the evening and didn't seem to feel it. Peter read Muir's letter, pretending it didn't praise me. It said my poem had more original genius in it than any modern poem he had seen, and made the modern poetry seem thin and unimportant to him; but Peter ignored this.

Wednesday, February 19

Thinking about "The Cremation" and working on it. Tony phoned in distress to find out where Dr. Connor lived, as she could not get Phyllis.[34] I said, "Is it for you?" She hesitated, then blurted out, "Elspeth is dying!" A friend of hers—she went to Dr. Connor, naturally did not tell her mother, is now unconscious, had three blood transfusions last night, will die tonight. It filled my mouth with hatred. I feel I can't do justice to this in my book.[35] Tony wanted to ask Dr. Connor what he did to her. I said he wouldn't say, I was certain; does not answer the telephone. She said, "It's wicked!" I said, "Yet he's the life-saver of every woman in London." (He charges nothing at all, if the woman can't pay.) This horrible business, which I have never had—may at any minute have—now. The dreadful thing I nursed Phyllis through. I felt very weak. Telephoned Tony this morning but she had gone. I suppose the girl is dead. Dr. Connor has been in prison. He is an odd man, I think he really wants to help women. I suppose a death a year compensates for the hundreds he saves. It is the most monstrous wickedness.

Gossy and Norman came to dinner with Peter, dull, normal evening, only broken by Mozart's quintet and my abnormal coughing. They're going to have "Jack" MacDougall to dinner (Chatto & Windus) and have me, and if he spurs me on to finish my book it will be a good thing.[36]

Worked on my book most of the day, adding to Part IV. Do not know if it is good; put in Peter's and my late paradise. After this shall write short poems for a time. Letter from Deak suggesting I take Johnny to Switzerland for the summer—got me all upset.

---

[34] Dr. Connor was an illegal abortionist. Elspeth Glossop was the sister of Silas Glossop (lover of White and father of her daughter Susan). Barnes, who had an abortion by Dan Mahoney in 1933, named the abortionist in *Nightwood* Dr. O'Connor.

[35] "The Tygon" inscribes autobiographical elements beyond those involving Coleman's relationship with Bianchetti and Hoare. There is an episode, for instance, in which Frieda tries to find a doctor to perform an abortion, and when she is unsuccessful, takes "medicine" to induce one herself.

[36] Allan Ross ("Jack") MacDougall (1893-1956) was an American editor at Chatto & Windus, and was also a close friend of Barnes and Eric Siepmann.

Thursday, February 20

Tony came in late last night. The girl died. "What did they do to her?" (It was not Dr. C[onnor]., it developed.) "That girl was butchered" were the facts Tony presented. "What did her face look like?" "That girl was poisoned." Then she went on—"Just as she was to have been so happy." Tony has to go to the inquest and it appears the girl made a statement, while conscious, to the hospital authorities and to the police, naming Doctor Connor. I said, "This is indecent—a man like that—who saves women's lives." "Yes but if he sends her to someone who butchers her." I didn't know what to say. Phyllis and I agreed that we would never mention Dr. C[onnor].'s name if anything ever happened to any one. He will get into trouble. He's been in it before, and got out. I said to Tony—"You should _not_ say anything to make it worse." I had been thinking of the girl all day, and envying her. Sweet letter from Peggy this morning, very well written and very adult—very sweet—she is coming Friday.

Wrote Deak and said would be delighted to take Johnny to Austrian mountains for the summer, not Switzerland. It's an idea of Deak's, thinking Johnny is thin, that he needs mountain air. Nothing would please me better than three months with Johnny in Austria.

Coughed badly all night and Peter came to see me in the morning, avoiding my gaze; urged me to take care of myself. Gave me the Glyndebourne program—heavenly.[37]

Friday, February 21

Worked all day on "The Cremation," typed it all through, with 2 carbons, for Edwin Muir, Castlelea, The Scores, St. Andrews, Fife, Scotland; and for Miss Djuna Barnes, 111 Waverly Place, NY City. Last for Barker, Plush, Piddletrenthide, Dorset. Did not send that one. Do not know if it is good. This is now complete, at least for the time being. Wrote all day never noticed a minute. Stayed on couch. Cold much better. Dined with Peter last night. Burst into tears near his ankles. He does everything he can think of for me—discussed Mozart, Glyndebourne—he will get tickets for *Magic Flute*, *Don Giovanni* and *Cosi Fan Tutte*.

---

[37] Glyndebourne Festival Opera was founded in 1934, in Glyndebourne, Lewes, East Sussex. It featured five operas of Mozart in its 1936 season (May 29-July 5): *Cosi Fan Tutte, The Abduction from the Seraglio, The Magic Flute, Don Giovanni,* and *The Marriage of Figaro.* They were all conducted by Fritz Busch, with Hans Oppenheim sharing in the production of *The Magic Flute.*

Peter said, "Those dear little half-formed breasts" last Thursday night, and it keeps ringing in my ears as he touched them—his sensuality is exciting—and I feel absolutely desperate, now he has aroused me—when I look at him—this hell will get worse and worse; his giving in hasn't made it better.

Sunday, February 23

We got a few things out clear last night. Peter came home at lunch, and I was asleep, being still ill. I made him a poached egg and he ate a grape-fruit, and some tea and cake. I got him to come on the couch and read his paper, and I went to sleep lying beside him—<u>in such peace and paradise!</u> I felt so happy, and imagined a life where I could go to sleep peacefully every night, with him. But after about an hour, when he finished his paper he got up, I suppose lest he should feel physical desire. He made tea. I suddenly asked if I could read him "The Cremation." He looked frightened and gazed about for escape. I said, "Please let me. You are a pig." He finally gave in, seeing there was no exit. He said, "You don't read well." I said, "I do, if I know the poem and have a sympathetic audience." I read it all through. I never liked it so well. I was terribly moved by it.

He liked it very well. He took it and began to criticize it, and we had an hour, really a good hour, during which I felt nearer to him, poetically, than I ever have.

Yesterday had a letter from Barker who wants to come to London. He wanted his check—I got very worried, sent him five pounds at once, and will get out tomorrow to cash the check, Peggy sent—I wonder if he is very low. In the evening got a letter from Father saying he had received a thousand dollar a year raise, he was so happy! Said he was going to divide it between his broker, Aunt Eunice and me. I felt guilty, thinking of how sweet he is. I wish I could support him in his declining years; perhaps I'll have the money from my book. I ought to write another book if only for this. If I get twenty dollars a month more it will settle my debts with Peggy and enable me to do something for Barker and more for Mme. Donn. I felt at first I ought to ask Father to give my share to my brother—as indeed he ought to have more—but feel I ought to take it as it will enable me to help Barker, far more important—and Peggy may let him down in the autumn and I have got to be ready, with Sonia, to step into the breach. At first felt I ought to let my aunt have half of my share as she only gets $100 a month and God knows how she lives on it, in society. But the wisest thing is to accept it, as I can turn it to better uses—they can get on, and it's not important; whereas Barker's support is terribly important. I told him instead of taking him to *R[omeo]. and J[uliet]*. I would give him the money. I was wondering where I was going to get the money to do it anyway. Did not send him "The Cremation" as I want to go over it in light of Peter's criticisms.

Read "Ode on Intimations of Immortality" to see if I can get any new thoughts or feelings from it.[38] Think really "The Cremation" is Better. This sounds terribly presumptuous but I do really think it is the truth.

Have decided to have Frieda have a child in Part IV. Her having a child is not only the natural event following on their new love, but it will convince (taking so much time to tell) the reader of their peace and happiness, which I need as a preliminary introduction here for their greater tragedy. It will make the tragedy so much greater, the inevitable tragedy of his not loving her sexually, when it comes.

I very haughty about Tony's commonplace reverting to type when Elspeth died, which was of course disgusting to the observer. But what about the American-college girl aspects of my character? Revealed in letters and old diaries, which make me sick to read.

"The Cremation." Peter said the first verses, narrative, were beautiful. But he did not like the last verse at all, which Barker liked so much. Did not like "Flashes about him the worm" which B. loved. I said his opinion was excellent, though literal at times, and I would consider it fully, and was very thankful to have it. I wanted Barker's, Muir's and Djuna's—and wish I could get Eliot's too—before making the poem final. May take another 6 months on it. It is, up to the present moment, in one sense, my life-work. It says all I have thought or meditated upon about death for 20 years.

Monday, February 24

Last night we made love. We suddenly did. I felt very intensely indeed and pounded Peter's head, it was such a relief, after the misery. He was not well, and thought he was getting the flu—I took his temperature twice but it was normal. But this morning he had 100, he is staying in bed. The Dragon watches over him, but she has to go at one o'clock.[39]

Peggy came today, says she has left Garman. Do not think she can continue it. But should not be with him. Read her "The Cremation."

Peggy plans to stay up in London all this week—I don't know if she can do it. She claims to be able to stand alone and may be able to now. She said (what I thought was wise) that she knew she would never be able to live with John's drinking, should he come back again. Her honesty and directness and

---

[38] Wordsworth's poem "Ode: Intimations of Immortality from Recollections of Early Childhood" (published 1807).
[39] Mrs. Stafford, the housekeeper.

intelligent facing of the most dreadful facts between herself and Garman are incredible, and such a contrast to Tony's romanticisms. Yet I wonder if Peggy's fatalism does not come from her inability to imagine or believe in anything; a bad thing. I don't understand what she is—her honesty, coupled with imagination, would make her a great artist. I don't really see how a woman <u>can</u> face the truth so consistently and not be an artist. She said I gave her the courage to live, because I believe in her. We skated thinly on the subject of Djuna and money. She must have hurt Djuna, for Dj. has not replied to her letter re her coming to England. She has not replied to mine about Eliot. I got a horrible feeling she had committed suicide. I don't think she could have, or someone would have written us. I'm afraid she might have been in a state to do it, until she got my letter about Eliot; but perhaps that wouldn't save her. I don't believe of course anything like that has happened.

Wednesday, February 26

Peter not very well yesterday, still in bed. Peggy came to my place to spend the night.[40] Phyllis came. We all went to Queen's to dinner. Tony came in the evening. "Your rawhide bag is so lovely. Just the sort of thing I'd expect you to have." Peggy said, "You must know me very well—it is not rawhide—it cost 5 shillings." Then Tony, later—"What a lovely scarf about your neck—I love grey with yellow!" "This—I use if for a dust-cloth." When Peggy walked into the room to meet Tony she said, "I feel I'm never smart enough for Tony," in a casual way, at which Tony threw up her hands and cried, "O Peggy must you do this to me?" Air was turgid with embarrassment for quite a while. Tony was then explained (by me) to have been to the funeral of this girl who died, and to be somewhat on edge. Peggy was tranquil and very nice to Tony. Tony was given the seat of honour. She held forth as the other night using the same words. Conversation got deeply into abortions, so much so that I went downstairs to see Peter. I told him what I could remember of what they said. Peggy tried to get Tony to talk about Proust but she talked instead about the Royal Family. Peggy remained for the night. In the morning she sent Djuna a letter saying she would support her for a year, and we sent a cable asking her to reply at once if she was all right. Peggy had already written Djuna she would help her come to England but was not anxious for her to come. I said she could stay with me—God knows how she (or I) would stand it. I would love having Djuna in England and so would Peggy, once she got settled here. Can't imagine her talking to Eliot, don't see how they could exchange 3 words. Peter said if people like Eliot and Djuna could communicate, books

---

[40]Garman had also come up to London, and Guggenheim did not want to be in their flat together.

would not need to be written. Gossy and cousin of her friend "Spadge's" (woman named Alex Sidney who is head of the X-ray department at "Bart's") came to tea.[41] Woman a sad very determined overworked person, who writes at night. She read the *S[hutter]. of S[now].* and wanted to meet me since she loves the book. Very sweet in a pathetic way; lots of persistent British character, not vital. In the middle of the conversation the phone rang and it was Tony, in a very agitated voice—"Oh Emily can I come to see you?" in a faint and agonized voice. I said "Of course—but there are people here." She groaned and seemed to wander. I said "I'll phone you in a half hour" and did so. She had gone out. Worried I called Tom, not in, later called and Tony was there, lying down, Tom's voice very soothing and deep with distress. I do not know if this is some nonsense, or if something terrible has happened.

Tony takes herself so seriously, and her husbands, and her ailments, that one doesn't know where one is at; she is capable also of going out of her head at any moment, and throwing herself out of the window. One has to be ready for whatever she does. I am living in a maelstrom—myself and Peggy and Phyllis and Djuna and Tony! Women—women. Peter will know what women are like. He says perhaps the police have been questioning her about Elspeth—as the inquest was adjourned for more evidence. I thought it had something to do with Tom and Frances. Tom sounded guilt-struck and soothing over the telephone.

Thursday, February 27

Got up, dressed, and went over to see Tony, to see what this all was. She looked horrible, all swollen and very wretched. I comforted her as well as I could. There was no apparent cause of her sudden giving way yesterday, phoning me. The real trouble is I think that Tom is starting another love affair, which T[ony]. takes seriously; that and all this death and inquest and funeral business—enough to set anyone off their head.[42] I tried to comfort her, especially to make her feel that she could call on me. Siepmann writes her he is

---

[41]"Spadge" is unidentified. "Bart's" is St. Bartholomew's Hospital in London's Smithfield.

[42]It is likely that the new woman in Hopkinson's life was Joan Geary. Hopkinson had several lovers, some of them serious. It was his affair with Frances Grigson (see earlier note) in 1934 that precipitated the end of White's marriage to him. His relations with Geary also threatened White, who often felt she wanted Hopkinson back. Though White told her diary in early 1937, "He is very sure that he loves Joan and wants to marry her" (I: 85), it was a woman named Gerti Deutsch whom he eventually wed in 1938. In 1951, White discovered he was having an affair with her analyst, Dorothy Kingsmill, widow of Hugh Kingsmill; he would divorce Deutch to marry her.

happy in Spain—she feels he's out of her life.[43] I told her he was not—but at any rate she needs someone more stable than that. She needs primarily SEX. But ought to have it with love, and some stability. In a very bad state, poor child.

Wrote to Sonia and to my sweet dear little Monkey-Face giving him admonishings M[adame].D[onn]. asked for. I wish I had him with me. He seems always when I think of him as a lovely green oasis in the bleak and endless Saharas.

Saturday, February 29

Yesterday Tony and Peter to lunch. Tony in splendid form describing herself teaching school when she was 16. She described her clothes. She wore a lace and tulle hat, her hair frizzed out in great lumps. She wore a tube-dress, one bought by a width, the width of the body. She wore high yellow top button boots. She put on lots of make-up. She was asked to leave the school, a boys' school. It was war-time and the boys called her "Sir."[44]

I then got the most terrible headache. I was ill, and vomitting, all afternoon, and evening. Peter worried. He made tea. He is better, but has a bad cough. At night I got a hand-written letter from Barker. He is very childish about his birthday. This letter had a bit of joy in it. He said he didn't know when his brother was coming.[45] He is unreal. I feel he only exists for me to send money to. Now, I thought, this is what Peggy feels about everyone.

A cablegram finally came from Djuna, that she is fairly well, and writing.

[Peter and I] looked at the book called *The First Time I* . . . containing contributions by HK, Gerhardi, Tony, etc.[46] Tony's is the only one with any

---

[43]Siepamann, a journalist, was in Spain reporting on the increasing threat of what would become the Spanish Civil War. He was staying at the villa La Felicidad in Torremolinos.

[44]As her biographer Dunn describes, White "taught Latin, French and Greek, but the classes were a riot and she had to negotiate the boys' good behaviour by agreeing to tell them ghost stories at half time, as long as they had done their work first . . . Antonia's liking of the masculine and her longing for a brother made her a collaborative and entertaining teacher for the twenty boys in her control. But she was asked to leave after two terms. The head of the school had visited the classroom during the second half of the lesson, when a ghost story was in full swing" (58).

[45]Barker's brother, Albert Gordon, a painter and poet, had been nicknamed "Kitten" as a boy and the name "Kit" stuck through adulthood. See Fraser.

[46]"*The First Time I* . . ." (1935) was illustrated and edited by Eleanor Theodora Benson (1906–1968), English author. "HK" is Hugh Kingsmill. Other contributors included Beverley Nichols, Betty Askwith, Evelyn Waugh, Rose Macaulay, Prince Leopold Lowenstein-Wertheim, P. G. Wodehouse, Dorea Stanhope, and Benson herself. White's piece is "The First Time I Went

life. Peter read some of it out loud. I laughed like anything. Intelligent review again of Cyril Connolly's in *N[ew] S[tatesman]*—want to meet him.[47]

Sunday, March 1

This is 12–30 Sunday morning, I have come in from the first social gathering I have been to since I left New York, the 1st in 10 months. I went at 6 to meet Mary Reynolds and Laurence and Kay—liked Kay, which I never did before, and after dinner went with Phyllis to Mary Reynolds,' where she is staying with Marcel (Duchamp)—Hotel Mont-Royal, a touch of America-in-London.[48] There was Wyn Henderson and Mann Ray and others.[49] Got stuck between 3 men, all bores, Marcel one of them—liked him better than before. The conversation not bad for social moment, but not having heard any for long time felt very odd in it. Was impressed with my vanity, want nothing but to have every man in the room come up to me thinking "Isn't she beautiful, or interesting" or preferably, "Wouldn't I like to have her in my bed!" I get a bit of it, now, but how long will it last, and what will I do then at social gatherings when no one notices me, I will be a pretty sight since my vanity is colossal. I don't know anyone else of equal value who is so vain. Tony isn't. Laurence quite dead. M. Reynolds what I always expect. She does not like Peggy and Peggy thinks she is her greatest friend. Everyone playing up of course but why should they not, what else can they do? Peggy's little honest true face so sweet in the midst of the rest. One should not look at one's dear friends when at a social gathering.

I wrote a long letter to Djuna, in reply to her long one of a month ago. She is a wonderful woman. She is one of the most remarkable women who ever lived, and Kay Boyle a nobody.

Monday, March 2

Got off such a long letter to Djuna yesterday. I wish I had the letters I write her; better things come out when you have some exact point to make than in

---

on Tour." Having joined the Academy of Dramatic Art in 1919, she went on tour in 1920 for six months with the cast of *The Private Secretary*, playing the small part of the ingénue, Eva.
[47]In his "New Novels" column for Saturday, February 29, Connolly reviewed the following: *The Marchesa and Other Stories* by K. Swinstead-Smith; *The Pumpkin Coach* by Louis Paul; *Family Curse* by John Hampson; *Jackets Green* by Patrick Mulloy; *Rococo Coffin* by Richard Blake Brown; and *This My Hand* by Christopher Caudwell.
[48]Recall that Reynolds was the mistress of Duchamp.
[49]Mann Ray (1890–1976), American dadaist and surrealist artist, was a close friend of Duchamp.

a diary. I keep a diary because things come clear to me; but I'd rather keep my letters to Djuna—much more becomes clear. We went to Norman and Gossy's at 3–30 to hear the King (the P. of Wales) broadcast.[50] His accent was less cockney than usual. There is something appealing about him—don't know if it's romance. He is simple, and sincere. I can't forget the way he looked in the procession following his father's coffin to Westminster, before the funeral. There is something in his face not in the family—peculiar. He looks wistful and far away. Of course this may be the family feeblemindedness, coming out in another form. When the BBC Orchestra played God Save the King I experienced emotion. We sat at N[orman]. and G[ossy].'s for 8 hours, not budging except to go in and eat supper, which Gossy and I prepared. I read Garnett's *No Love* which seemed at first to be good.[51] It wandered, and got pointless. I gave it up half-way through. I wondered why people like Garnett write. I suppose he just likes to push a pen; you can see he gets pleasure from simple, pointless narration. He is properly placed with his column in the *N[ew] S[tatesman]*.

A letter from Djuna this morning, which I was very glad to get. It is not a good one. She is like a little baby with Neagoe. Learning the early tricks. I think they belong together, now. But they will have to go through a lot before they know it. She says I am a martyr and she is a tired wise old lady with her great love past. The first is wrong, but the estimate of herself is right; except that she leaves out one thing—the life that is still in her. She says she has to go on living when zest is dead—this is true, but zest unfortunately is not dead—that's her horror. Neagoe will in time I think come after her. She feels nothing because she is tired—it is up to him to make the next move—she has done everything. She has to have him however and her having him (a good and simple person) is a good sign in her. She doesn't know the faintest thing about life or men. She only knows one thing, what is in her book (which she knows so damned well); but is again is something different and she's got to go through it with agony [sic].

Wrote Djuna again, very good things, about lying about evil. When we lie the evil is evil; but when we face it, recognize the truth, it turns to good. She lied for years pretending Thelma's evil was good, and her good evil. She got it right in this book [*Nightwood*]. As a result, we know wonderful things about evil we never have known.

---

[50]King Edward VIII (1894–1972) had been made Prince of Wales in 1911.
[51]David Garnett's novel *No Love* (1929). His column in the *New Statesman* was called "Books in General."

Went out after this, met the McDonalds accidentally in Ridgways while waiting for Peter—we lunched with them![52] McDonald so ill at ease (though always keeping his end up) that I was nearly mad. Peter amused and a trifle bored (at my conversation). I said, "What do you think of my pretty pigeons?" "You just want to vamp him." What I want to know is why I fell in love with him (which I did). Because we were in Hubberholme.

Went after this to Charlie Chaplin. He is a comic genius and no mistake, not gifted with enough brains to work out the stories of his own pictures, but the most perfect mime that ever could be discovered. He won't be bettered. He has artistry (natural) to the point of insanity. He is lovely. I prefer the Marx Brothers simply because they do burlesque, which I have a preference for. The Marx Brothers are in town and I would like to see them tonight![53]

Wednesday, March 4

I woke up, after peculiar dreams, of landscapes—how they haunt me—and ecstasy. I was lying back in someone's arms (unspecified) and they were making love to me ever so delicately; so that I thought, "This is touching—this is not making love." It nearly killed me to open my eyes, find this bed and this room (which I love). I could not get up, start this life. I had to get up finally, and stood by the window feeling like death. I saw Tony coming out to start the day.[54] No word from Barker, he is not coming evidently, so I will go to *Figaro* with Peter.[55]

Thursday, March 5

Last night, after returning from *Figaro*, I had a note from Barker, saying he would be up in London tomorrow or Saturday. I did not go to sleep for some time, and when I did I had the most intense dream of being with Barker. I cannot remember all the facts now, but I don't think I will ever forget the way I felt when I woke up from the dream—which I did, in the middle of the night. I felt absolutely then that this [was] my fate, and I accepted it. It was a revelation of Barker's soul, and life possible between us, an entirely sexual dream. But the spiritual feeling was so intense that it had got beyond life, and was in

---

[52]The now married Iverach and Gwenda McDonald had moved from Leeds to London.
[53]Coleman saw Chaplin's *Modern Times* (1936). The Marx Brothers' latest movie, *A Night at the Opera* (1935), was playing at the Empire theatre.
[54]Following her separation from Hopkinson, White had moved to Coleman's former address, 105 Oakley, across the street from Coleman and Hoare.
[55]Mozart's opera *The Marriage of Figaro* was performed at the Sadler's Wells Theatre on Wednesday, March 4, at 8 p.m.

240   Section I

a state where everything was accepted—premonitions of the future known. I've had this dream about Peter often, but it was not the dream, but the feeling I had in waking up from the dream which I remember. When I awoke in the morning I remembered it; but then my mind put another aspect on it: that it was a temptation I had to resist, my soul being tried. I think I had better begin to read St. Augustine now—to get strength. We went to *Figaro*, it was beautiful, it was really done with spirit—with new sets, and Audrey Mildmay as Susanna, which pushed them all to a higher standard. Joan Cross always has been the best Countess for me, and her singing lovely.[56] Again and again, in the choral parts, I felt that lifting of complete ecstasy. But what is the good of it—it's only a barbaric glimpse of something I know could exist, that I want, and it only tortures me, there in Sadler's Wells, with dreadful people about, hard seats, Aldous Huxley in the front row, *Figaro* not quite right, Cherubino dreadful, and the orchestra like a set of sacking.

Peter was extremely pleased with it all, looked at Aldous Huxley hard between the acts (who with wife had been to see him about something and who did not recognize him), very sprightly wife not at all like the Maria I had imagined from Lawrence's letters—I like Huxley's face having studied it on a Channel crossing last June for 2 hours.[57] Barker will be here tomorrow night, or the next night, and I will be lost. In bed I thought, "Which <u>do</u> you want? Years of this, safety, patience? Or the tragedy? Sometime getting the real life with Peter (in this life or another)? Or getting a superficial ecstasy and dying for it?"

I will try to do something to "The Cremation" now. Will try to read St. Augustine. Have not been able to read this winter or autumn—only Rilke because Tony put me up to it, having given it to me[58]; and *Janus* because I had

---

[56]*Figaro*, a continuation of *The Barber of Seville*, depicts the romantic complications between the Countess, Rosina; her husband, the Count, who loves Rosina's maid, Susanna, who is engaged to the valet, Figaro; and the page, Cherubino, who favors Rosina. Audrey Mildmay (1900–1953) and Joan Cross (1900–1993) were British sopranos.

[57]Maria (Nys) Huxley (1898–1955) and her husband divided their time between the south of France and London, and while Coleman did not explain the reason for the Huxleys' visit to Hoare perhaps it had to do with some aspect of their travelling—passport and immigration. Coleman would have seen Aldous Huxley when she crossed the Channel en route to vacationing in Prague in June 1935, while it is likely that Huxley was either coming from or going to Paris for a congress of international leftist writers (see Bedford 303). The Huxleys were close friends of D. H. Lawrence; Aldous Huxley edited and wrote the introduction to *The Letters of D. H. Lawrence* (1932).

[58]Coleman was referring to Rainer Maria Rilke's existential novel *The Notebooks of Malte Laurids Brigge* (1910, trans. 1930). White, who gave the work to Coleman, recorded in her own diary in October 1935: [*The Notebooks*] "has affected me profoundly.... The effect was

to to know Barker. Have read nothing else. Why don't I write my book—so much, so much to say—and I don't say any of it.

Friday, March 6

The day arrived now when, possibly, my life begins. Hell starts at any rate that is sure—how can I avoid it?

It is awful to feel this dreadful passion, but it is my fate; it can no more be got out of than a mole can swim or a duck can swoop like a hawk. I was born to feel this, and when I do, whatever the horror of it (like hell), like Francesca I know I belong here.[59] Djuna said "Perhaps hell is your home; poets generally know their home when they find it." Barker and I were born possibly to die together in a hell past our conceiving. I sit and wait for him—put coldcream on my face, walk up and down in front of the mirror. I pull my brain together to think whether he would want me in skirts or in trowsers.

I had a letter from Muir about "The Cremation" saying "You have begun on your own now, and I cannot teach you anything; you are bound to teach yourself. . . . I have been reading your poem about John, which has moved me so much both for its subject and as a poem that I cannot say anything at the moment about it. It is a very strange and wonderful utterance, and I do not know anyone else who could have written it. I know I could not. I shall write to you about it later; But I have no doubt at all about its high and quite extraordinary excellence . . . Have you considered sending it to Eliot?" etc. He sent me a page of line by line criticisms of the Whale poem which I was delighted to have. Have not looked them up yet, as I have lost interest in the poem, but must do so—and send a revised version to the *N[ew] S[tatesman]*—if they ever intend to publish it. . . . Lovely clouds over the roofs of the houses on the opposite side of the street; I lie in the bath and watch them sliding slowly across the horizon, and think of spring, and ecstasy; and lying on a moor hearing skylarks and smelling heather, one's heart fit to burst with rapture of nature getting into one's blood and bones.

Nothing heard from Barker and as Phyllis wanted to see the Marx Brothers with me, I went, with her and Peter.

---

so violent that I had to lie down at intervals while I was reading it; I was shaking as if in high fever" (Vol. 1, 56).

[59]Francesca and Paolo are the murdered adulterers condemned to Circle 2 (Canto 5) of hell in Dante's *Inferno*.

Sunday, March 8

Nothing seems real to me until I've written it down. I don't exist at all until I read what I've done. I don't know what I've done. I feel dazed and without a rudder. I didn't make love to Barker. I feel I will one day. I didn't want him physically. He wanted me.

Barker phoned in the afternoon (he came up the night before), and Peter was here. Peter left, and I saw him to the head of the stairs quite coldly. He said to Barker, "I'll see you later." When he had gone I asked Barker if he wanted to see the Marx Brothers and he was enchanted. I said we would go out to eat and then go there. I asked him all about his financial situation and learned dreadful things—that his dog had killed a sheep, five pounds he had to pay—that took half his next quarter's rent; he had his rates raised. I said, "I am absolutely going to help you." He was embarrassed and that didn't make it any better. He wanted to make love to me, and said I need not tell Hoare. He said he felt very sorry for him. I said "What if I should fall in love with you?" He said, "Nonsense, I'm not that sort. Women don't fall in love with me." He said a woman had fallen in love with him when he was 15. He touched me, held my bare arms, as if he would break them—really it was very terrifying. I did not give in. I wasn't tempted really. I was so in a dream. Now writing about it (I knew it would be) I am tempted much more than I was. I threw my arms around his neck and said I was fond of him and did not want to egg him on for nothing.

We went out (I did not feel I could stand another moment of his company—I was simply longing for Peter) and had dinner at the Chelsea Tea House. He observed that *Thunder Over Mexico*, the Eisenstein film, was on across the street.[60] He wanted to go to that. We sat together and we held hands in the darkness—I loved his sweet frankness; his cold preposterous manner drops like a mask.

I came in and mounted the stairs trying to think if I ought to go to Peter or not. I decided nothing made much difference now, so I knocked, and sat down and recounted to him the evening.

In the midst of this a letter came from M[adame] D[onn] about "un petit bouton" on Johnny's eyelid which may have to be "enlevered."[61] I must write

---

[60] Sergei Eisenstein (1898–1948), Soviet Russian film director and theorist, set out to make a film *Que Viva Mexico!* with the support of U.S. socialist author Upton Sinclair and his wife, Mary Sinclair. After travelling from the U.S.S.R. to Mexico, Eisenstein encountered problems with the Sinclairs and the production was shut down. The feature short *Thunder Over Mexico* was produced by the Sinclairs and Sol Lesser with no involvement from Eisenstein, who returned to Moscow.

[61] *Un petit bouton*: a small pimple; *enlever*: to remove.

Deak immediately. I never think of Johnny when I am confused about love. But he remains here, the one true thing in my life, that gives me joy and not sorrow. It is a thing contrary to the other, absolutely the opposite, involving such completely different spheres of one's being that it is hard to feel the two at once—it is well nigh impossible. I told Barker that he is a poet and that I am a woman who writes poetry. I was surprised at the pleasure with which he took this up. He said "I never expected to hear those words from your mouth." I thought about it afterwards, having said it to please him. It is of course true. My poetry may be better than his, but I am not a "poet." I am first of all a woman. I used to be first of all a poet, in 1928–31; since I became a "woman" I have written much less, and that with great difficulty—not with the abandon with which I used to write. What I wrote before was bad and this is good. That is what is odd.

I told Barker his being homosexual or not didn't mean much to me (perhaps it should), as I thought almost all people were in some form or other, and he seemed masculine to me. I feel sure he could find himself sexually in a woman.[62] It has not been possible because most women, as he said, haven't liked him—though when he gets success (and a few clothes) he will find himself surrounded. But he has got mixed up with me because we began with poetry.

I never really want the worldly life—could not for a moment be satisfied in it. <u>Tony almost could</u>. People think, as I told him, that I am their most intimate friend, and <u>I reveal my true self only in my poetry</u>. But that self, which is so like Barker, underneath, has commerce with him, and flies to the unknown. I have no image of God—God is the essence of energy and passion—nothing anthropomorphic to me. I remember when reading my grandfather's sermons, in the early morning in Hartford last May (with the birds singing, the American birds, so sweetly in the trees outside), the sermon on heaven, "We shall be satisfied." I never forgot that sermon.[63] It was a literal transcription of what I believe "heaven" to be—not harps and singing but <u>each person doing what he has wanted to do most in life</u>. But my grandfather believed in a personal God. I can't believe in any God except as He is revealed in the black poplar, the whitethroat, and the mountains of Spain; and, more truly and more inexplicably, in poetry, music, painting, every form of art—and MAN.

---

[62]In 1941, Barker would become involved with the Canadian expatriate writer Elizabeth Smart. Their intense relationship would span nearly two decades and produce four children, as well as Smart's autobiographical account of their affair, *By Grand Central Station I Sat Down and Wept* (1945).

[63]Coleman's grandfather, like her father named John Milton Holmes, was a Congregational Church minister whose publications include *The Pilgrim Temple-Builders* (1866) and *A Faithful Ministry: Sermons* (1872).

Monday, March 9

A dreadful night, full of terrifying dreams; absolute despair, in the morning, no recourse but suicide. I dreamed Baker was some other man, I told him he could come to my room; he came and at once gave me four shillings, which he said was "pay for his pleasure." I gave it back, gritting my teeth. I began to prepare the bed, which was very large. It was covered with rubbish, and things kept spilling on the bed-cover, which I was looking at, thus desecrated, with tears. Then he came at me with great callousness and cruelty—I said, "No! Not like that!"—I got on the other side of the bed, and he pursued me, but I got away and ran to another room where I got in, and locked the door.

I think, "I must not keep Barker off because when he goes I'll regret it,"—but how important is this, compared to the horror I feel when I think of Peter?

Nothing has happened; it is half-past four and he had not telephoned. He has returned to Dorset.

Hoare's hold on me is almost entirely sexual. Break that and there would be nothing left, I know that—the things I love in him not being as important to me as this sexual mania I have for him.

Wednesday, March 11

I think of myself, with a man, as wholly feminine; and this has misled me greatly in my understanding of Hoare. I do not know in the least what I am like sexually—that is the truth. The only genuine sexual feelings I have ever had were the Lesbian affair I had in 1929 (and what about that? how much it showed!), my brief life with Bianchetti, and my life with Hoare. In the Lesbian thing I behaved exactly like a man. I wanted the woman terribly sexually, took her, was bored with her afterwards. It was the first time I had felt sexual desire. I thought I was a Lesbian. But I kept on liking men, looking up to them, wanting their attention (vanity—but why did I not want women's attention?). It is not as simple as that. Barker thought he had solved his life too, by turning homosexual. There are some people who seem to be entirely homosexual. They want no one but their own sex. This IS a perversion, a turning of the truths of nature. Because if a woman is wholly feminine, as some Lesbians are, an ordinary man should satisfy them; they get the extra kick out of a woman because it's bad. It may be born in them, or acquired. If it's born in them (as M. Anderson, etc.) they are damned.[64] I don't know

---

[64] Margaret Anderson (1886–1973) was the founder and editor of the influential *Little Review*, first published out of Chicago in 1914. In 1916 Anderson's partner, Jane Heap (former lover of

enough about them to say; I should ask Djuna. The truths about sex have never been known. In Shakespeare's time, or the Greeks, homosexuality was accepted, <u>but never investigated</u>. We are beginning to know things now that have not been discovered. I'll get started writing to Djuna, and perhaps fascinating things will come out.

I went into Hatchard's before meeting Peter for lunch and bought The Nonesuch Donne, which I sent to Barker.[65] I am going also to send him some money—but shall not communicate with him. I promised him the money and will send it, though to do so means I shan't have enough clothes. I am so selfish it kills me to give money away when I have no clothes; but my <u>better</u> nature, (God) makes me do it. I sent him Donne for his birthday, which was the 26th of February. And he was 23! O Lord, 23! When I see that I think I'm mad. There is no doubt he's too young for me; but I'm afraid in his heart he's old. I'm very young in the heart, and unsophisticated.[66] I then bought myself a new pair of shoes with extreme pleasure (though not as great as sending him Donne). They are brogues, for the country. I then bought a new hat and some mules. I do not see how I am going to have any more clothes than that this spring. But Barker has no clothes at all. He doesn't lead the bourgeois life, so he is not ashamed. He has only one suit, which is filthy, the poor fellow.

Thursday, March 12

I went out to dinner with a woman called Alex Sidney, a sad Lesbian who loves *The Shutter of Snow*, I met her at Gossy's. When I came home there was a thin letter from Barker on the hall table. I came upstairs and opened it and read a note which said as plain as anything could say that he loved me. I couldn't get my breath—it was like in the taxi when I heard John was dead.[67] I sat down. It was one o'clock. I wrote him a letter. I didn't send it—it was all about Hoare— it was mad. I sent another one, saying I <u>would not</u> sleep with him (I have made up my mind again) but leaving no doubt that I felt something for him.

Barnes), came aboard as co-editor. They moved the magazine to New York in 1917 and then to Paris in 1922. After Anderson and Heap separated, Anderson stayed in Paris while Heap took the magazine back to New York. Anderson penned a 3-volume autobiography: *My Thirty Years' War* (1930), *The Fiery Fountains* (1951), and *The Strange Necessity* (1962).
[65]Hatchard's book store is located at 187 Piccadilly. The Nonesuch Press was founded in 1923 by Francis Meynell, Vera Mendel, and David Garnett to publish inexpensive but good quality books.
[66]Coleman was thirty-seven. She has added by hand some time later, "No!"
[67]Although Coleman did not keep a diary at the time of Holms' death, she recalled in her later entry (not transcribed) that Guggenheim's butler, Blisset, had telephoned her with the news and she had rushed via taxi to Guggenheim's side (December 13, 1937, F. 642).

I don't want to keep this diary any more—the things that are going to happen I dread writing down any more. The diary keeps things clear to me. I hate to write down the dreadful facts which are going to happen. Though I shall not make love to Barker, I shall fall more and more in love with him. I want to hold out as long as I possibly can against actually making love, the most vital step—the thing that will really break something between me and Hoare.

Friday, March 13

I read *Janus* all the afternoon the day before I got Barker's letter. That inflamed me. Phyllis came to dinner last night. I read Barker's letter over and over when I got in bed. I feel thus cut off from Peter, and it's hard to be civil to him. I have to remind myself that it is my fault. He came up this morning and was pleased to hear that the *N[ew] S[tatesman]* had printed my poem, taking up a whole page (Tony telephoned me).[68] I did not suggest he come down for the weekend—I don't want him to—I do want a little rest—and it will do him good also. He was hurt, but tried to be gay.

I'm going to Peggy's now—it seems like an event—I can't get started.[69] The first time I've left this flat since October 8th.

---

[68]"Melville on the Land."
[69]To Yew Tree Cottage.

Section 2

London and Petersfield

March 16–May 28, 1936

Over the next few months Coleman travelled back and forth between London and Guggenheim's Yew Tree Cottage in Petersfield. Though still together, Guggenheim and Garman were increasingly at odds with each other and Coleman was a welcome relief—and mediator—for her friend. Coleman's son went down to the cottage during one of his England trips, but their relationship was threatened when Coleman reverted to her earlier habit of hitting him when she found his behavior disagreeable. After he returned to the Donns in France Coleman continued to analyze her maternal feelings and identity. Romantically, Coleman remained off and on with Hoare while her intimacies with Barker took an especially wrong turn: Barker's admitted "religious complex" which compelled him to "help" people sent Coleman mixed and temporarily traumatizing signals.

As usual, the London episodes showcase her busy social life while introducing us to new acquaintances such as Chatto & Windus editor Jack MacDougall and New Statesman and Nation *columnist Cyril Connolly. Most significantly, as Coleman awaited the arrival of Barnes, she tirelessly advocated on behalf of* Nightwood *and was rewarded with an invitation by Eliot to the Faber offices to discuss the novel in person. Coleman met with Eliot as well as the other two directors of the firm, Frank Morley and Geoffrey Faber. The event marks a highlight in Coleman's contribution to modernist literary history while offering a unique portrait of Eliot in "action" at Faber's. In terms of her own career, Coleman finished another draft of her novel "The Tygon," and continued to expand her poetic oeuvre with one poem inspired by the poet Wordsworth and another on the biblical figures Samson and Delilah.*

Monday, March 16

I came down here [Petersfield] Friday in the train. The country, which I have not seen for nearly seven months, is refreshing and quieting. It's still winter, but the soft land is smoking, and some of the bare trees have buds. During the whole time I have been down here I have thought of nothing but Barker, reading his letter over literally a hundred times. I have been dreaming of him in paradise, unrelated to ordinary life.

Friday, March 20

The night before I left Peggy's there was a long discussion between her and Garman, with me arbitrating, and there she sat like a little gnome curled up on a pillow. I told him it was the most pathetic thing I ever heard of, her reading Proust alone all one winter.[1] He was ashamed and went out to call the dog. I said this because whenever a discussion comes up between them, with regard to their life, she is always to blame. I told her the next morning however—as we took a walk over the fields—that though he has all right on his side (since she should never have lived with him) and has made every possible move to adjust their unhappiness, (while she has fretted and complained and sulked until recently), nevertheless she was the one I cared about, and whose welfare was dear to me—and whose soul was like my soul. Garman's is not.

I took several walks that morning—it was warm. I felt every bud bursting, and every bird shouting. I left, with them, at 4–30; they left me at Waterloo, and I walked down to the bus, in a fog, feeling the utmost depression. The city might have been beautiful in the thick grey. I did not feel it. The whole world seemed to sink over me, as if I were drowning. I got to Chelsea, got into my flat—no letter from Barker. There were several other letters. I read them mechanically as I sat in my coat, waiting for the new-lighted fire to warm the room.

The next day I was very restless, finally Tony came to tea, I talked to her, she sat sometimes like a sly cat, sometimes guileless (as Dorothy said her lack of cynicism about life is incredible); Gossy called and asked me to bring glasses to her cocktail party. I went to the party, met Jack MacDougall of Chatto & Windus, did not talk about my book, out of shyness, but took care

---

[1] Having bought the cottage for herself and Garman in 1934, Guggenheim tells us in her memoir: "Soon after Garman moved into Yew Tree Cottage I made him give up his job as director of his brother-in-law's publishing firm. At the end of our garden he built himself a little one-room house in which to write. His health was bad and he needed a quiet life in the country with exercise and little drinking . . . He soon began to read Karl Marx's *Das Kapital* and was immersed in it for months. During this time I read Proust . . . Garman disapproved of my reading Proust. He wanted me to read Karl Marx (141–2).

to vamp him, with result of being asked to his cocktail party (over Chatto & Windus) the next day.[2]

Back and had dinner with [Peter] and his sister, whom I had not seen for 3 years, she is not at all prepossessing but has an evil smarming face (I thought—though Peter thinks I am going too far). I did not like the evening and we got rid of her at 10 after a lot of lying (she and Peter each going at it—"Would you like to go?" "I'd like to go but I'd rather not." "Are you sure now you don't want to go?") But as we went down the stairs to put her on the bus, I snatched a letter from Barker. I put it in my bag. All the way over to Gossy's I thought, "What can it be? What can it be?"

More of the same people, remainders, and pretty bad ones. I went into the lavatory and read the letter. At first I couldn't make anything out of it, except that he was coming to see me; and was <u>not frightened</u>. It was a very stilted and intellectual letter and was written of course to calm me down, the central theme being that I was dying, or would die, and he would bring me to life!

I wrote him 2 letters the next day. I went to MacDougall's cocktail party, and there met Cyril Connolly whom I have wanted to meet. He is a short wide man with a broad face, a smile like Beaverbrook, small bulbous forehead, beady smiling eyes, a flat nose turning up.[3] He is a very interesting man and I wanted to know him. He said, in the taxi going back, with Tony, "It is hard when you got prizes for years and then suddenly there you are, doing things in real life, and there are no more prizes." He is full of life. Knows and takes seriously all the *transition* and Paris racket. Kept his eye on me as he circulated. He is known and popular and very social and I expected to lose him. Jack MacDougall even nicer in his own place, a comment on him—a really sweet and loveable man. Eardley [Knollys] again, Gossy cornered him, he is better with her, really living. Norman standing like a man-at-arms in opera. Joan Souter-Robertson, whose painting rather common, adorned the walls.[4] Would make a nice Lesbian piece for the night. Tony came (on my invitation!). She likes attention from MEN, as does Gossy, and they did not appreciate my efforts. Not a very exciting party. Lovely top flat rather chic—in Chandos Street. MacDougall a school-mate of Siepmann.

Tony spent day with me before this, we talked—she had phoned me and I seemed low, so she came over, sweet little thing, but when she got here I

---

[2]MacDougall lived in a flat above the company, on Chandos Street, Westminster.
[3]William Maxwell Aitken Beaverbrook, 1st Baron (1879–1964), British statesman and newspaper magnate. He bought the *Daily Express* in 1916 and the *Evening Standard* in 1923; he started the *Sunday Express* in 1918.
[4]Joan Souter-Robertson (1903–1994), painter. She had been married to Frank Freeman, a miner and would-be painter who was the best friend of Silas Glossop, and had had an affair with White's husband Hopkinson. In 1936 Souter-Robertson married biologist Jacques Cocheme.

was calm and we talked all day, as Djuna and I used to do, over eggs. She is jealous of Barker, unfortunately and sometimes gives it away. She is going to Spain <u>with Siepmann's mother</u> to see Siepmann!

Peggy in a bad state all this time, phones me, went back to Petersfield without Garman, as he has to stay up, invited me to come down, or come with Hoare, or bring Barker—isn't she funny. I sent Barker a telegram asking him to come Sunday. I got a reply this morning that he would. I have been in nervous fits all day—phoned Phyllis and am going to the cinema with her tonight.

Wrote Peggy, to calm her, but <u>cannot</u> go down there with Barker—if Hoare is going to Cambridge with sister I can have him here. I don't <u>dare think</u> of it. I may make love to him.

Cannot get myself down to even writing letters, or reading—have not written in this for one week, and would let it go easily now if I didn't force myself to keep on writing a diary. It is very good for me, keeps my mind clear.

Peter looked so heavenly sweet one moment at Gossy's, listening with his head on one side to something being told. Gossy handsome at MacDougall's, in modish hat, Joan S-R sidling up smiling sideways at me—she is reading *The Shutter of Snow*—I see what it will be like to be lionized and I'll hate it—I am so vain I love the <u>idea</u> but the <u>fact</u> is awful, unless one can gain by it some person or thing of interest. Pictured Barker there, the "coming young man"—he would not stand it at all. I asked Connolly if he was a dark horse of the *New Statesman* and he said "No I am in the show-case." He said I would get 2 pounds 17 for my poem. I shall give it to Barker as soon as I get it. That seems a lot to me, but then I wrote a lot. C's face very baffling—full of life, deviltry, humour and refinement (in spite of his being fat and in a way as ugly as any man could be). His character I really can't tell. Said he had tried to read *Ryder* but stuck in it [*sic*]. Tony looked like a baggy velveteen virgin.

Sunday, March 22

I went with Tony to the Connollys.' They are really very decent people. His wife is American, Middle West, a nice, lazy, dark, heavy, good-natured woman, sympathetic to me because she's easy and has a Roman nose.[5] Connolly improves greatly upon knowledge. He is terribly alive, on the *qui vive*, nervous, reminds me in a vague way of Elliot Paul; but he's not a shit.[6] His face much nicer when you know him, really kind, sympathetic, not at

---

[5]Jean Connolly, née Bakewell (1910–1950), was the first of his three wives. She would later marry Guggenheim's ex-husband, Vail.

[6]*qui vive*: on the alert. Elliot Paul was the co-editor (with Eugene Jolas) of *transition* from April 1927 to the spring of 1928, and had been a colleague of Coleman's at the *Tribune*.

all devilish—disconcertingly honest. Has quite a temperament. Really well pleased with himself. Witty with me. Could not quite make out if he wants to sleep with me; got that feeling, as if he were making a long distance charge. But he passionately loves conversation and would forget everything for that; (for which I can't help loving him). He has written a little pornographic book which is to be published by the Obelisk Press—in Paris.[7] I got cachet with him because I know all the Paris Americans. He wants to meet Kay Boyle. Knows literature and the good, but likes people, especially Americans. I think he likes me very much and intends to see me. They live in Kings Road, in a large house, sitting room at the top, which I took to be a flat at first, until the man servant came in with messages. They have money but he earns what he can from the *New Statesman*. I told him I regarded Paris-American life with a jaundiced eye, having been taken in by it at first. I felt much older than Connolly in spite of his superior social sophistication, and knowledge of literature. He is quite unconscious and enjoys himself. Really likes Tony and appreciates her—as much as anyone can appreciate Tony who does not know her intimately (The more I see her the more I like her). We went to dinner at an Italian place in Kings Road after staying there for 3 hours, and I told her Barker was coming tomorrow and talked to her. She was so sweet to me, after starting out with her usual incomprehensible deadly look, which means she has not a man; and gave me dial to put me to sleep.[8] When she kissed me goodnight, in her room, I thought there was a Lesbian touch, almost evil, <u>she was working in the evil</u>. I came to bed, could not sleep with one dial, and took the other which she had thoughtfully given me. I then slept and woke with a feeling that all my life had come to an end. Rose and made tea and orange juice, Mrs. S[tafford]. not coming. I liked her not coming; this day was sacred to me alone. I made the fire myself, washed, brushed my hair, put everything on with a sort of vestal feeling.[9] I carpet-swept the flat, washed the woodwork, arranged everything, laid out the two boxes of 50 cigarettes I had the sense to get for Barker.

It is now eleven—I don't know when he is coming—I got terrified in the thought that he might let me down, do some trick.

I am sitting here waiting for Barker. It is a warm sunny afternoon (now about half past twelve) and people are walking up the street from the Park to go to dinner. A muffin man came ringing his bell; I did not dare to go down to him for fear of missing the phone. I made myself some porridge. A band

---

[7] Connolly's novel *The Rock Pool* (Paris 1936, London 1947) depicts the protagonist, Naylor, as he turns to dissolute ways while vacationing in a resort town in the south of France. The Obelisk Press was founded by Jack Kahane in 1931, largely for the purpose of publishing works that, especially due to their sexual content, had been or had the potential to be banned in England and the United States. Among its authors were Radclyffe Hall, Henry Miller, and Anaïs Nin.
[8] Dial is a brand name barbiturate or allobarbital.
[9] Coleman has circled "sort of vestal feeling."

was out in the street, playing jazz. I danced a Charleston to the jazz, looking at myself in the glass. I was thinking I was pretty. My heart is breathless; I pace the rooms. Cleaning the tables, and the kitchen, I could not stand it any longer. I thought of the gramophone. For the last ten minutes I have been hearing the *Surprise Symphony*.

I am going to play some more Mozart, and continue until the telephone rings, or the doorbell rings. I think I shall go mad, if he keeps me waiting. If he is not here by half-past one I shall faint, I think, or do something strange.

I am going mad now. It's two o'clock. I suppose he went first to his family, to have dinner.[10] Why did he not phone me as soon as he got in? I am afraid my letters agitated him—made him feel unsure. Perhaps he could not get an early train. Never again will I allow this to happen. He must tell me exactly when he is due to come, and come then. I cannot stand any more of this. It suddenly came over me (what an innocent I must be) that I could get drunk. I have no glasses; I lent them to Gossy. I poured out a soup-dishfull of the last bottle of Peggy's sherry. I drank it up. I feel queer now, sensual. Why didn't I think of that? I'm not accustomed to drinking, and depending on that as a stimulus. I shall keep on drinking till he comes. I shall be quite tight and then won't resist him. Before this I was reading Henry Handel Richardson's book *The Fortunes of Richard Mahony*—which Alex Sidney lent me.[11] It is excellent—in spite of Victorian novelistic style weaknesses—At any other time I wd be extremely interested in it. But I couldn't read. I have done the right thing by drinking—I am quite dead now—already (not having eaten); and dopey. I will do anything (that my will has first sanctioned).

Tony said last night that she was in that state of ecstasy (in which she was before going to the asylum) because she was mad—it was abnormal; she said the unhappiness she had been undergoing before that (Reggie, her first husband, unsatisfied sex, etc.) she was entirely unconscious of. Tony is in my world. She says her state was different from mine (which is conscious)—I have been <u>consciously</u> unhappy for five years. I am tight now because I can't strike the right words.[12] My thoughts seem to come reasonably; perhaps that

---

[10]Barker's family, including his father (George Barker senior, or Pa), mother (Marion Frances Taaffe, or Big Mumma), and Grandmother Taaffe were living at 19a Upper Addison Gardens in Holland Park, in the London district of Kensington and Chelsea (Fraser 47).

[11]Henry Handel Richardson, pseudonym for Ethel Florence Lindsay Richardson (1870–1946), Australian novelist and short-story writer. *The Fortunes of Richard Mahony* (1930) is the collected trilogy of the series of historical novels *Australia Felix* (1917), *The Way Home* (1925), and *Ultima Thule* (1929), which trace the story of Dr. Mahony and his wife, Mary, as his fortunes rise and fall, his mental health deteriorates, and he dies of gangrene.

[12]Note that she was typing this, as with most entries.

is an illusion. I am so tight now that when I close my eyes, which I do when I think of Barker's coming, I am dizzy. I told Tony last night that I feared I wd go mad. I felt so queer—as if I would burst. I wonder what tightness is— because I continually strike the wrong letter, yet when I see it I recognize it.

... The telephone just rang—I ran to it from the sofa, where I had been in a state of half-being. When I spoke there was no answer. "This is too much, this is too cruel!"

O Jesus Christ, how hellish life is—there is no limit to what one must suffer, through illusion. Barker telephoned me, I said, "When are you coming?" He said, "In ten minutes." He arrived, came up the stairs, when he got here I burst into tears saying, "I thought you weren't coming." He comforted me, so tenderly, he started to make love to me. I didn't want it, he was very tender—I didn't want the end. We talked, I talked about Hoare, he made it clear he loved his wife, said his relations with Carpenter were not serious[13]; he said, "You understand that I do not love you." I said, "Certainly"—we talked, I sitting smoothing his hair, looking at his face which seemed so beautiful to me. Then, suddenly, we made love—I was excited, wanted terribly to do it. After, he went and sat in a chair, and I lay on the couch, feeling so happy I could scarcely breathe. He sank back in the chair with his lips half open, listening to "This Day Christ Was Born," which I played for him.[14] I looked at him lying that way and did not like it. I thought, "He's only lust." But then he said he was in a dreadful state, and I thought he was going to say he loved me; he did not, he came and sat beside me and said "It is so long since I have made love to a woman." I said, "You don't like it?" He said: "No." I felt my bowels giving way. This is the end. I did not however show any sign. "Then why did you do it?' He went into a long explanation which I don't understand, saying he has a religious complex and thinks he must help people. I tried to pin him down by quoting from his letters; but could not get light on it. At first I couldn't stand it at all. I went into the kitchen thinking, "I am going to commit suicide now." I stood by the window. There is something unreal about him. I am so dazed I can't think it out, and bewildered—-my fate is turned upside down—what I think and feel about everyone. I have not made a mistake in judgment like this for so long. When I think back I realize he never thought of me until he was

---

[13]Maurice Carpenter, a poet, is described by Barker's biographer Fraser as "a serious-minded youth who had escaped from the petit-bourgeois respectability of Caterham, in Surrey, into the arms of the communist cause. He divided his attention between urgent political organization and—by his own account—unsuccessful attempts to find someone to go to bed with" (43). As "a habitué of the Barker household in the 1930s" (6), Carpenter often stayed with Barker and wife Jessica, and was close friends with Barker and Barker's younger brother, Kit.
[14]Early seventeenth-century carol by William Byrd.

here the last time—but his letters since then are difficult to explain—he admitted his last letter was preposterous—I told him I only paid attention to the fact that he was coming to London. (He wanted me to destroy his letters—I said I would destroy any he wished, but not the short one.) I said, "Why did you say, 'I was sick, because I wanted to see you again'?" He said he did feel that way. I think what happened is he thought he was a little in love with me, then made love and hated it—as homosexuals do, I suppose. I know nothing about homosexuals—he said I didn't. I said he was masculine <u>but he said I didn't know what that meant in a homosexual. I am up against something I know nothing of</u>, and I am damned lucky he was honest at the beginning, so that I will not be more hurt. I don't think we will ever make love again. What I had dreamed! My dreams were based on a <u>desire for love</u>, and ecstasy—<u>better what I have with Hoare than this illusion</u>. I am feeling sick and utterly done with life. After the terrible excitement of the last two weeks it is horrible. Of course I think of Peter with joy now. I almost burst into tears—"I have done this dreadful thing—a dreadful thing in my life—make love to another man, for the first time in four years—for no reason." If I did not have Hoare I should commit suicide. Whatever I do with Hoare now is loathsome—I have been hating him because I thought another really loved me, and would make sacrifices for me; now this has happened I am likely to throw myself on Peter in relief. <u>That I cannot do, it is too loathsome</u>.

Wednesday, April 1

I have not written for such a long time. I couldn't write. Things are quiet now. I have not heard from Barker since he left. I do not want to hear from him. I have been trying to pick up the pieces of life. I wrote Hoare a letter which said everything any mortal could say, of what was the matter between us. It made him angry. I did not get far. I had to make him feel that he had made me do this. He behaved, as one might expect, like an outraged husband. I have convinced him, now, that I want him—and that I did this, at a terrible risk, because I do want him. I sent him the letter and then left the house every night for three nights, not seeing him for four days—so that he might have time to think about it. In the letter I said that if he did not act now, he would lose everything. He finally replied, after three days. His letter said that I gave him no help in his human life. It was bitter, but it said, "I'm not sending you the letter I did write you. That was angry and cruel." I wanted to know what this other letter said.

He put me through a terrible week. I think it must have changed him. It has changed me.

In the meantime, driven by sheer misery and thwarted desire, I finished my book. I began working on Part IV a week ago, and continued at it for a fairly regularly increasing speed as I neared the last part. I wrote 9,000 words the last day. (Yesterday). I wrote almost all of Parts IV and V (the mountain chapter and one or two others had been written in America and here) in 5 days.[15] I can't believe the thing is finished. I really got inside the soul of Donato. I haven't looked at it since I finished it—there will be a lot of plucking to do later. I sent Gossy a telegram for fun saying "Finished my book." She replied, "Three cheers—clever Demi!" Peter, out with another sister, came up and we talked till after two. I can hardly stand up today. He and I had gone to *Rosmersholm* the night before and he was most illuminating on Ibsen.[16]

Beatrix Holms wrote D[orothy]. Holms asking in tones of great enthusiasm, if the E. Coleman who wrote the poem in the *N[ew] S[tatesman]* on Melville was me, and if so, she wished my address at once. A little enthusiasm about that poem is not amiss. I was given heart by this, and wrote to her, having had her address for some time. I intended to write her how much I loved "The Zodiac" when I read it this winter after John's letters, and send her "The Cremation," which Peggy wanted me to send her. I then went over the Melville poem in the *NS* and made some changes in it. I haven't had any passionate enthusiasm over Melville except Tony and Tom—and a little from Muir. It gives me life.

The first night I left Peter alone with the letter I saw the Connollys—drank with them at the Café Royal before their going to dinner—Connolly a queer little man, very odd and I think dreadful in some ways—why he fascinates me I don't know. I sent him *The Shutter of Snow* on his desire.

Peggy has not been up—I was to go down there Friday—wired her I could not. She wrote me a letter saying, "We are all going into eternal dangers." I've thought of John [Holms] a great deal and thought he was near me. Johnny coming tomorrow.

Saturday, April 4

Peaceful life now, with John drawing pictures on my desk all day long, reading old *New Yorkers* asking me "What is the joke of this?" and when I explain consulting it again and roaring with laughter.

---

[15] The "mountain chapter" is a surreal depiction of a desolate Frieda, devastated by Donato's infidelities, climbing a mountain in both literal and metaphorical terms; she recalls happier times with Donato but also registers suicidal feelings as well as a spiritual communion with the natural world.

[16] *A Cycle of Ibsen: A Doll's House, Hedda Gabler, Rosmersholm,* and *Master Builder* began at the Criterion Theatre on March 2, 1936.

John is now playing Mozart's piano Concerto in G. There will be a surprise for him at the end when he hears the movement I used to play to him in Antwerp. He took out *Americans Abroad* and kept reading their biographies. I would say, "Take it away!" when I would see a face. This amused him; he said, "What one do you like?" It did give me a turn to see some of those Paris panhandlers. How funny it was to hear Connolly praising them, and to be high in his opinion because I knew them!

Saturday, April 11 (Yew Tree Cottage)

I've been down here all the week, playing with the children, sleeping, walking in the woods—the life of an animal—and self-forgetfulness. I feel drugged. I had a letter from Barker which Hoare forwarded from London. Barker was in London. He said that two days after I last saw him he had blinded his brother in a fencing bout.[17] The right eye had just been removed; the other would probably be useless. I could not imagine how Barker would take such a happening. I could hardly visualize it. Yet whenever I was alone, in the woods would come up the awful picture. I imagined the bloody accident, the gory face. I wrote him a note. Of course I did not know what to say. I said I would be in London Tuesday. Afterwards Peggy said absolutely struck with horror, "The only thing one can do is to find out if they've had the best doctors." I knew she would help him. As soon as I begin to imagine Barker, I keep thinking he will kill himself. He loves this brother more than anyone.

I've been reading *The Fortunes of Richard Mahony*, by Henry Handel Richardson, the Australian woman who wrote *Maurice Guest*.[18]

P[eggy]. and G[arman]. happy. I think when I'm here I take P[eggy]'s mind off herself, which in turn takes some of the load off Garman. She read me a diary the other day which she wrote this winter, which was simple and

---

[17]As Barker's biographer describes, Barker (twenty-two) and Kit (nineteen), in the presence of Carpenter, were having a playful round of fencing at their parents' home in Upper Addison Gardens when the accident occurred. Kit was rushed to Hammersmith Hospital, where "they were told that there was no point in attempting to save the eye. The shattered glass from Kit's spectacles, embedded in the raw socket, put that out of the question. So George and Carpenter waited in the anteroom while the eyeball was surgically removed under local anaesthetic." According to Fraser, Barker, haunted by this tragedy throughout his life, "would never be able to make reparation" (76–77).

[18]*Maurice Guest* (1908) is Richardson's first novel. Set in Leipzig at the turn of the twentieth century and featuring protagonists Louise and lover Maurice Guest, it was controversial in its time for its explicit depiction of hetero- and homo-sexuality and sexual passion.

moving and extraordinarily interesting as a document, because of its honesty and simplicity. She is as absorbed in herself as any human being I ever saw. I do at times concentrate on the lives of others, though I'm so egotistical. Peggy really cannot, although she believes she ought to. She cannot think of another person's life. This characteristic, which she deplores and so does G, seems to me more than anything to reveal that she is in some curious way an artist; her diary substantiates it.

Easter Monday, April 13

Peter left this morning after a curious weekend. He arrived Saturday evening. I went and stayed with him. He looked at me in a frantic way. We made love. I at least was happy and in peace. It was last night, I left as he was tired and worried about getting to work in the morning. By doing this I seem to have broken the spell of what I did with Barker, at least for me—I can't answer for him. Last night there was a fierce argument between me and Garman because neither he nor Peggy had let Kingsmill know John's letters had been refused by Wishart[19]; G. gave himself away, looking like an evil ghost. Envy hatred and venom poured out of him.

Played the piano for Peter who liked this evidence of my having once been womanly.

He and I walked in the woods. The primroses are full out. I can't think of anything more beautiful in the whole flower world than a nest of primrose on the edge of a pasture in spring, with their spike-like leaves framing them and their soft faces turned with rain on them towards the leaves. I found a little dead black-cap the other day and Johnny buried it. He was naughty while Peter was here as usual partly asserting himself out of jealousy, and partly because I am more critical of his behaviour. It came to a head last night and I took him upstairs and beat him. It made me sick. I did not hurt him but made a spectacle of myself and was unjust. He did not understand but I explained it to him later. Violence is wrong for me, come what may, because it is my terrible weakness. John needed a good walloping, he gets impossible; but I do not think I should do it. A man might; my relation with him should not be backed by force and I only make a fool of myself (to me, and to him) when I beat him.

This book of HHR is like Thomas Hardy. The more I read it the more I think of the book. There are cats here, 3, one Siamese, which is savage, and

---

[19] Hugh Kingsmill, one of Holms' closest friends, had hoped to see Holms' letters published. Coleman related that Garman had used his influence with his brother-in-law's firm to get the manuscript rejected.

frightfully sensual. Thinking about writing my dramatic poem. Would like to write it about Samson & Delilah.[20]

I got very mad with Johnny because he not only wouldn't obey me but was saucy besides, and peevish, and I walloped him hard, after taking him upstairs. Utterly ruined our relation for a couple of days. I explained it to him, and he saw my reasons, but kept away from me (inside) and made me feel sick. I hope this is the end of any of this business. When he was little and used to drive me frantic I resorted to hitting him—it never worked and it made me ill and him callous. Madame Donn has changed all that. Now he and I are so happy together, so lovable in comradeship, so affectionate—I must never do this again.

Wednesday, April 15 [London].

Heard from Djuna, complications her family [*sic*], not enough money from Peggy, her Paris flat ruined, must retrieve it, etc., but she is coming.[21] I came up yesterday afternoon from Hurst, really to see Barker if he was in London. Left John behind, after he decided first to come then not to come. ("It's like two cakes being put in front of me.") He saw me to the bus. I promised to bring him two sixpenny Toblerones from London. I begged him not to stay, but he would, until the bus came. Thinking of him going in, God, how can I risk hurting his love for me, or his trust in me—is this sentimental?—He probably got over it in a moment.

Saw my flat, how I loved seeing it again, all clean and smelling paintish I don't know why. Met Peter for dinner, very cross, began by insulting Peggy, I stood it for a while, very gentle, finally got really mad, blew off, said "You keep to your friends and I'll keep to mine." But Peter took my outburst kindly, pulled himself together, was kind; so I responded. The rest of the evening was sweet. I said Djuna was coming. He said, "Keep her well locked and concealed will you? She's too creative for me." We made love, he was

---

[20]Recall that on February 15, 1930, Coleman was inspired by Milton's *Samson Agonistes*. Her archive contains the poems "Samson Agonistes" and "Samson to Delilah," and the dramatic poem "The Death of Samson." The biblical story of Samson and Delilah (Book of Judges 16) tells of how the Jewish Samson, blessed by God with unusual strength, was betrayed by the Philistine Delilah into revealing the source of that strength: his hair. After Delilah had his hair cut, he was imprisoned and blinded. When he was brought in to a temple to provide entertainment for a pagan ritual, he grabbed the two support pillars on either side of him and, having regained his strength since his hair had grown back, shoved the pillars and brought the temple down, killing himself and his enemies.
[21]Barnes had bought a flat at 9, rue Saint-Romain in Paris in 1927; it had been let to tenants when she returned to New York, who had subsequently trashed the place.

so sweet. I said, "I would rather stay with you, and learn to stand your revulsions, than go with someone else."

Had lunch with Phyllis, looked sweet, she said Garman said "The weekend was bloody." Barker came at 5, he read me some ballads and the "Ode on Immortality,"[22] we had a lovely afternoon, talking about his brother, the sight of whose other eye is going to be saved. And about poetry. He is rather low, feels like an ox who has been beaten too much, he said. He has not written anything good he says since the "Ode"[23] — how glad I am he knows this — I said it did not matter, one had fallow periods, etc. He said, "Yes but I'm supposed to be a professional writer." How I adore to read with him, talk to him, he's like an angel. He's so good looking, his face much better now after this suffering. I do adore him, he is fascinating—and poetry with him becomes a universe.

Sunday, April 19[24]

Johnny left. I feel very sad. I passed a bad night, waking and sleeping, in depression, waking up early, thinking of Johnny, Peter and Barker in a black whirl. He woke up sad and I cheered him up, had his breakfast ready and surprise peanut butter. Peter came up to say goodbye to him and gave him arf a crown. He had fun yesterday, his last day. He went to the movies, Mickey Mouse films and Laurel and Hardy, then returned here to find Phyllis and Gossy and Peter who had come to tea.

While John was at the cinema I read *Mahony* yesterday, and finally I broke down and wept, so great was the power of it as it progressed. . . . After writing that I finished *Mahony*. The tears have been streaming down my cheeks. I wondered what made me weep like that, a thing I have not done since I was a little girl — no book has made me weep with utter abandon as the last days of Richard Mahony have done. I couldn't think of the author (the greatest tribute any writer could possibly have) for a long time after finishing it. It is a very great book. Henry Handel Richardson, whoever she is, is a woman of great literary genius. And she is completely unknown, amongst those who ought to be praising her. The book is quite properly an epic — and written in our time! It is incredible that it's not better known.

---

[22] Wordsworth's "Ode: Intimations of Immortality."
[23] "Ode to Man."
[24] Coleman had incorrectly dated this entry April 20. The date continues to be one day ahead of itself until Coleman noticed it on Thursday, April 23. I have changed these dates to the correct ones. Coleman wrote an entry for Saturday, April 18 (not transcribed), in which she told of going back to Petersfield on the previous Thursday, and then back up to London on the Saturday with John.

Monday, April 20

Today I met Peggy at lunch, Phyllis, and the children.[25] Letter from Djuna soothing my feathers which were evidently rumpled when last I wrote her. She gets everything wrong—then I scream, scream loud enough to wake the dead; and frighten her. She's coming early in May. Am going to a party tonight with Peter. Shall wear my blue dress with train Peggy gave me 2 years ago, and I bought a silver crown for hair.

Barker says he can't communicate through letters and barely reads letters, but I think I've forced him to the point of reading one or two of mine. To undermine his self-interest would be a job. But I've got all the weapons—a whole armoury—I am so full of variety I dazzle myself—no wonder I'm in love with myself—I don't know anybody else so exciting. John was superior to me, and Djuna is my equal, if not my superior at certain points; but neither of them seem half so charming as my view of myself. Djuna is so much more witty and amusing, and better looking too; and dresses better. But not half so subtle or intelligent, or so happy-minded with the world. John told me my smile was irresistible, if I kept my mouth shut. That's where the joker is. My mouth is never shut. That's why Peter, who might adore me, hates me. The fact that I can sit and regard myself as though I were someone else I was in love with also shows how tedious I am and how humourless. I am now going to take dinner with Peter before dressing for the Sadler's Wells party.[26] I'll see if I can shut up for three hours. A woman who talks the whole time is one of the unpleasantest things on God's earth; and when I was at Peggy's I caught sight of myself in the mirror while I was at the piano playing with the children, my face all screwed up, loud and reckless, making a bellow, showing all my teeth. I've had to call halt several times with Barker: he doesn't like it at all when I hold forth. (He says "sh").

Tuesday, April 21

A letter from Madame Donn saying my sweet John arrived. Last night went with Peter to the Sadler's Wells party which was at the home of Lord

---

[25]Guggenheim's son and daughter.
[26]The Sadler's Wells Theatre is in the London neighbourhood of Finsbury. The *Daily Telegraph* published the following announcement on Monday, April 20, for the party Coleman attended: "Lady Hambleden's house in Belgrave-square will be the scene of to-night's party given by the Sadler's Wells Society in honour of the singers and dancers who, under Miss Lilian Baylis' guidance, are keeping the banner of national opera flying in Rosebery-avenue." Baylis was the theatre's manager. For the Hambledens, see the next note.

Hambleden, a peer whose father got his money be selling stationary.[27] I really looked beautiful, I was surprised at how lovely I looked. My blue dress, which Peggy had made for me at Nicolas in Mayfair, with a train, very low back and high bertha front, suits me—but it needed pressing, and I didn't know if it was in style or not being two years old and I never see anybody in evening dress, or know the fashions.[28] But this dress is so original that I presumed it would be all right. Whether it was or not I still don't know, as no one mentioned it, except Peter who got into a state of rapture late in the evening and thought everything I had on was exactly right. This was partly due to drink—when I came down he had been drinking sherry with Norman, we had some more, and some wine—excellent dinner by Mrs. Stafford of shepherds pie and spinach on toast. I wore a head-dress which I had just bought, of silver braided cloth, standing up like a coronet—my hair had been done, and really I looked decent. I creamed my face and made it up properly for once. I only look this way about once in two years. I had the long navy blue quilted silk evening coat I bought from Djuna—and the silver sandals I bought years ago, which still are not tarnished. I look better in evening dress than in anything, and yet I never wear it—and would have got out of this party if I hadn't the wisdom to know that Peter would love me, and probably enjoy himself. In the taxi he looked so attractive, I had to kiss him. Then we got there and he didn't have any change for the taxi, so that was settled by the driver promising to come to 7 Oakley Street tonight! I went up a terrific flight of stairs to take off my coat, got lost coming down and ran into the servants' quarters, where they were being gay, and stopped, saying, "Beg Pardon, Madam." Found Peter, Jack MacDougall was there, whom I like, and Norman and Gossy. Gossy introduced me to Robert Helpmann the head ballet dancer, a sweet little man, whom I had seen the other night and not liked very much—he is a very good dancer.[29] He danced with me. Peter frightfully lively, got a bit drunk, looking all over for Mrs. T.S. Eliot whom he wanted to show me.[30] He never found her. Joan Cross sang *Dove sono* not very well, then suddenly *Deh vieni* to make your heart

---

[27]William, third Viscount Hambleden (1903–1948), was a British peer whose family had formed the stationary company W. H. Smith. In 1928 he married Patricia Herbert (Lady Hambleden) (1904–1994) who, in 1937, became Lady of the Bedchamber to Queen Elizabeth, a position she held for more than fifty years.
[28]Nicolas Berthe Maison at 143 New Bond Street, Mayfair.
[29]Sir Robert Helpmann (1909–1986), an Australian dancer and choreographer, was in 1936 the head dancer of the Sadler's Wells Royal Ballet Company. Coleman had seen him perform at the Sadler's Wells Theatre on Saturday, April 18, 1936.
[30]Vivienne (Vivien) Haigh-Wood married Eliot in 1915. Eliot left her in 1933 and she was committed to a psychiatric hospital in 1938, though she remained his wife until she died there in 1947.

ache. Eddie Marsh was there and kept staring at me instead of listening to the treasurer Sir Reginald Rowe who was making a speech.[31] Peter kept coming back in to tell me he could not find Mrs. Eliot—he spent the greater part of the party looking for her. He watched me dancing with fond eyes. We left about half-past one when nearly everyone had gone. Lord Hambleden is nice; looks like a Cossack servant—Lady H. ravishing as we said goodbye.

Peter would not leave me but kept standing looking at me and commenting on how everything was all right, and I was really a simple girl, and liked to enjoy myself ("Peter, I've always told you I loved dancing—but when do I get a chance to do it?"). He would not go to bed and I said he should, and that I would come down and be with him. But he wouldn't have that, he made me come down with him, and undressed me, taking such an innocent interest in how my dress and slip etc. came off. When he is like this I adore him, but not sexually, I could not feel much—but I love him so that I was happy to be with him. We were together for a long time. Peter very like a little boy, the baby Mozart I love. The odd thing is that when he criticizes me I feel more for him sexually. When he is at my feet, accepting everything I am relieved for these periods, so rare; yet I am not moved with sexual desire for him.

Wednesday, April 22

Reading about Samson in the Bible yesterday to think about my long poem—did not wish to write a dramatic poem after all—felt like a narrative—after the long hard work on my book. A dramatic poem, just to think of it, the conciseness, the boiling down, a terrible amount of work—I wanted to rest. "Will write about Samson—I like him. Will make the scenery Spain." So I thought, and then thought—"What will I do about the meter?" I didn't know. A few lines came into my head and I wrote them down, so began the poem, and continued for 250 lines, got the plan of it, in 5 parts. It needed revising a bit, which I did—wrote the 250 lines in about 2 hours. The meter is loose, free verse, rhymed, interrhymed, internally rhymed, very little rhyming so far.

Phyllis came, to spend the night, soothing and restful. Peter came after dinner, very pleased with prominent account in *Eve[ning]. Standard* of Lady Hambleden's party and Mrs. Grenfell in the red shoes.[32] Phyllis entertained

---

[31]Sir Edward ("Eddie") Marsh (1872–1953), a civil servant who was also a patron of the arts, translator, and editor of the 5-volume *Georgian Poetry* (1912–1922). Sir Reginald Rowe (d. 1945), managing director of the Wells.
[32]On April 21, 1936, the *Evening Standard* reported on its society page: "New Evening Colours at a Party," and described "Many coloured frocks were worn at the party at Lady Hambleden's house in Belgrave-Square last night"; and "Mrs. Reginald Greenfell's [sic] crimson sandals

us to bursting with laughter over the people who write in to the *Daily Mirror*, all of which letters she has to answer. In her best form. (Sindbad said to Phyllis—"You look very attractive to the naked eye.") Phyllis says they even ring up to ask where Selfridges is[33]; and they say—"I've made a pair of cami-knickers which are too wide at the top; what shall I do?" Then they send them in, and ask the D[aily]. M[irror]. to fix them. They send in knitting, needles and all. It is incredible—they write in to different people, who run columns in the paper. Phyllis answers them all—it is her job. They even send presents, things they have made, to Barbara Back, beauty specialist, or some other columnist they admire. Phyllis told all this with detachment and humour. Peter and I got hysterics. A girl wrote in and asked what material she should make her knickers of—"something that would soak up the perspiration."

Have not looked at my poem today; think it needs polishing, smoothing.

Nothing heard from Barker yet—what a darling he is and how I love thinking of him.

Not a word from Tony since she departed—she must have landed at Gibraltar Easter Monday. She has waltzed into the blue. Phyllis and I were wondering about her and Siepmann.

I sat down and wrote two more pages of my Samson which I can see is a poem I might love—I also fixed some of it. I wrote his love words to Delilah (before he married her). It is beautiful, and comes out like water from a spring—my springs are full and only want the pen put to paper, or the fingers to the typewriter. How sweet it is, how soft, and easy after the anguish and bitter struggling of prose. I am a poet, and should stick to my medium; all the more so because it's so easy and what I write, since it's from more unconscious sources, is more astonishing.

Friday, April 24

I had a short and impersonal letter from Barker.

Johnny's letter is so sweet, so mature and yet so childish. When I got the letter I put it away quickly, not thinking about it, as I do whenever he seems extraordinary, a letter or a painting. I feel he can't belong to me—that I can't have him. I wish he lived with me, so that I saw him every day—just to see him for an hour or two—I don't like to think about it—his being away from me these years—I don't know him—and can't know him, like this—if he lived with me and went to school I could do all the writing I wanted—I want

---

matched exactly the crimson handkerchief worn at the neck of her sapphire blue brocaded dress." Joyce Irene Grenfell (1910-1979), English actress.

[33] A major department store in London.

him with me. When he's not with me I get used to it, and fill my life, which is so full; but I would rather it were filled more with him—it is a question of money and of his being happy—as John [Holms] said years ago when I tried to bring him to England, he should not be alone with me when he is this age— he's queer enough and I would make him queerer. He is used to France, and Madame Donn, and she is wonderful for him—a normal home atmosphere. He has Deak in Paris, whom he adores, and Deak is a wonderful parent, in his way.[34] It would be like taking the pins from under him to put him here in a school. Even if I had the money I might hesitate.

Wrote <u>560</u> lines on my poem yesterday—wrote for 6 or 7 hours! It comes out so easily, with a bit of guiding—like guiding a wild dashing horse, with sure reins, held for 10 years, cleverly. I am so pleased with it—wrote the most astonishing things, a vision of life like Rimbaud. Feel Rimbaud and Blake in some of me. This poem is surrealiste, I think. I went to sleep, exhausted, about half-past three, and had horrid dreams that the poem was no good.

Jack MacDougall telephoned yesterday and arranged for me to go to tea with him instead of coming here, as I had invited him. Dining tonight with Earnshaw Smith.

Barker says he is writing a "very exciting poem"—I hope it's true and that he <u>is</u> pleased with it.[35] He's coming up here next week, to get his brother.

Monday, April 27

On Friday came a letter from Eliot saying, "I really believe that we are now getting to a point at which something can be done about *Nightwood*. I shd like very much to see you and have a talk with you about the book and about Miss Barnes." I am to go to tea with him tomorrow. When the letter came I didn't open it for some minutes. I couldn't believe it when I did. I've been in excitement. I annoy Peter by telling him what I am going to say to Eliot. "I don't like your saying '*un homme qui sait se conduire*,' etc."[36] Peter gets wild. He tries to tell me what to say and what not to say. He doesn't trust me; thinks I am capable of making a complete fool of myself. I have several subjects in my mind—first of all, Djuna—on which, and her book, I can descant—and listen—as long as he pleases. Then, Barker. Then Milton and Tennyson. Then

---

[34] Deak Coleman (with his wife, Louise) had returned to the Paris office of J. Walter Thompson in 1935, where he oversaw European operations.

[35] The new work may be part of his long poem published under the final title *Calamiterror* in April 1937.

[36] *Un homme qui sait [bien] se conduire*: A man who knows how to conduct himself.

American writers. I would love to talk to him about his criticism. I wouldn't touch his poetry—too tender a subject. Barker says he is sympathetic and tolerant and I don't doubt he'll put me at my ease. I am afraid I'll forget what I know. I'm longing to go. I didn't dare cable Djuna the news because they haven't actually accepted it yet. I'll be able to cable her Tuesday I think. Peter said, "If they take it, it's a triumph." I said, "If I get on with him I'm going to have him meet you." Peter would like to meet Eliot. It's all very exciting—the WORLD—about which I know nothing and with which I have had very little commerce.

Friday went to tea with Jack MacDougall. He was sweet and lovable. A chi-chi flat up above Chatto & Windus, but he is lovable. I dined with Earnshaw Smith who was in a jittery state about Tony—about whom I was anxious to hear. The news is very unfortunate, my poor Tony—she got blood-poisoning as soon as she arrived, the curse of Spain—has been ill ever since—Siepmann about as much help as a tarantula. Cabling has been going on—a comic saga regarding Tom [Hopkinson]—E. Smith though is upset and miserable. He doesn't want her to come back if she can avoid it—yet—as it was her long looked for holiday. He is afraid she will go out of her head in Spain of course—that terror for him. I said Siepmann couldn't provide the emotional stimulus to make her do that. Had a pleasant tight evening with E. Smith, went to the Café Royal.

[Peter and I] walked in Battersea Park Saturday, and had tea at Hetty's, and were very happy, laughing like anything at the newspapers and reading the Mickey Mouse comic I got for Johnny. The trees are out and in the Park the tiny lime leaves were green. We watched cricket. When I left him Saturday night I came up here, and I finished my poem.

It has nearly 1,600 lines. I did all the part about the destruction of the pillars very rapidly. Wrote about 560 lines Friday, all day, till teatime. Wrote the whole thing in 5 days, incredible.

Think I will begin a poem about Wordsworth. Letter from Deak praising my Melville poem. Called E. Smith—he said Tom has gone to Malaga by air, to get Tony—if she's not well enough to come, he (Earnshaw Smith) is going down to be with her. This is awful—poor Tony—the end of her holiday. Everything she touches becomes dust. I wish she would come back. Nice letter from Louise. Deak gets an awful kick out of my poem's being published; also seems to like the poem. He put a good deal of faith and trouble into making me a poet.

Think I will make the Wordsworth poem in a sort of "Lycidas" rhythm.[37]

---

[37] Milton's 1638 elegy "Lycidas." Coleman later noted that her poem (extant) is called "The Old Man."

Tuesday, April 28th.

I have been excited because I'm going to meet Eliot—as usual, can't eat or sleep. Read over our correspondence; what a <u>very</u> good letter I wrote him the second time: righteous indignation caused it, and the love of Djuna's book.[38] The quotations made me long to see that book once more. Alex Sidney came last night, Peter met her, thought she was a "tough nurse"; she expanded well in his presence. They found they had been in Salonika at the same time—in 1918.[39] After she left P[eter]. and I discussed her, then I said "Let's rehearse Eliot"; which we did, Peter was exact, peering over his glasses and murmuring in a clerical tone. I told him he treated me like am imbecile and I couldn't talk to him; that E[liot]. would treat me as an equal and I would be intelligent. Peter has met Eliot—he came to Peter's office and spent some time asking him what to do about something.[40] I got frightened from Peter's rendering of Eliot, which I was certain was lifelike; thought I would not be able to cope with it. Remember two or three occasions (on meeting Peter at the Gourmet in 1930—meeting Arthur Waley at the B[ritish]. Museum—meeting Edmund Wilson) when I lost my tongue and couldn't speak.[41] When Peter began to speak in Eliot's voice I couldn't speak for laughter. I've never heard him talk but was sure he talks that way. I began a poem about Wordsworth's old age, in meter of "Ode on Immortality."

Working on my poem and counting the hours; I am so excited at meeting Eliot I don't know what to do. Have made a list of subjects I want to discuss with him; various points in Djuna's book, Barker's "Ode" (the beginning of which I don't think is good), Muir's poetry, American writers, Kay Boyle, Holms. Also Milton. I do hope he behaves in a somewhat personal way to me—Peter was very remote and abstract and polite—I will never think of a word if he goes on like that. I said men are always different with women, but I am afraid Eliot isn't. I saw him once at the Ballet with a young woman,

---

[38] See her entry for January 26, 1936.

[39] After the Allies established themselves at Salonika, Greece eventually joined their forces in 1917. A successful offensive was launched from Salonika in September 1918, when the Allies advanced along the north front to capture Bulgaria and Romania, and recover Serbia. Sidney had likely been a VON (Victoria Order of Nurses).

[40] Coleman did not elaborate. Eliot may have visited Hoare to discuss becoming a British citizen, which he did in November 1927; or to get assistance for travelling to the U.S. when he took up the position of Charles Eliot Norton professor at Harvard from 1932 to 1933 (see Ackroyd 165; 192).

[41] The Gourmet is a restaurant in Lisle St., just north of Leicester Square. Edmund Wilson (1895–1972), American writer and literary and social critic.

listening attentively to her—pleasant mirage.[42] It will be like talking to an equal, a pleasure I haven't had except with Holms. But if Eliot doesn't make me feel at ease, by establishing some sort of personal accord, I may not get anywhere, or enjoy the couple of hours I am looking forward to.

I am terrified, and am going in an hour now—to take the 19 bus and go to Bloomsbury.[43] Since there is likely to be time to talk about nothing but Djuna's book I ought to be quite free—since when I get that theme my tongue is usually loosed.

... My going to see Eliot was really very funny. It proves beyond anything what a baby I am. I went in the British Museum to get up courage. When I got to Faber & Faber's I was not only early, through miscalculation, but terribly frightened. In the lift going up I said to myself, "Think of eternity! None of this matters." As soon as I got in the tiny little room of Eliot (in which he has the mantlepiece covered with snapshots) everything, of course, changed. He was very affable, and what's more, is attractive. He has an odd face. He looks like a sea-lion. We had tea and American chocolate cake. I said, "This is very kind of you"—Djuna's book—he said, "It is my public duty." But our conversation was not on that plane. Most of the time we were laughing. We laughed about everything. I had a list (in my bag) of intense serious subjects. I was going to get down deep into Life and Lit. But we just laughed; he made rather good jokes about Barker and Djuna—what she might be like—about everything. He has the sweetest smile, and looked at me very hard and I did feel the personal interest which I needed to start me off. We just had a social and amusing and slightly intellectual conversation. I should like to see him again. We discussed Barker, but not his writing, O dear how serious I am. We discussed his private life, or rather Eliot wanted to know it. I didn't tell him much. He said, "He's a very peculiar fellow." He said he didn't think he would have guessed Djuna's book was written by a woman. I said indeed I would—then he qualified it and said he didn't think the Doctor seemed like a woman's creation.[44] I agreed. The problem was that the book might be taken up by the censor. I said I knew she would be amenable to small matters of omissions. Then Mr. Morley came in, a blue-eyed American boy,

---

[42]Possibly Emily Hale (1891–1969), a romantic interest from his early Harvard days, who annually visited Eliot in England during the 1930s and to whom Eliot was deeply attached. Eliot's biographer Peter Ackroyd states: "Certainly when she was in England [Eliot] would take her to meet his friends almost as if they were a recognizable couple" (229–230). Ackroyd also informs us that in the summer of 1934 (when Coleman frequented the ballet), Eliot's sister, Marian, as well as one of his nieces had come from the U.S. to visit Eliot (212).
[43]Faber & Faber was then located at 24 Russell Square.
[44]Barnes' character, the transvestite Doctor Matthew-Mighty-grain-of-salt-Dante-O'Connor.

very sweet.[45] He gave a sort of careful oration about how they had come to take it. They are going to show me the correspondence—or rather, the reports they made to Faber, who was against it rather. They got together like two enthusiastic American fellows. They seemed like business men. Eliot phoned Morley—"Come up. I want you to meet Mrs. Coleman." At the very end I tried to say something serious about the book, at which Eliot nodded his head—he of course is sensitive to everything. Mr. Morley said, "She HAS looked down the drain," looking off as if he were standing in a fairy-tale. Eliot sat listening while he talked. M[orley]. said they would make her a definite offer—it was just a question of how amenable she would be. Eliot says, "She apparently is a tiger who is eating out of Mrs. Coleman's hand." I got frightened at this, because Djuna cannot be said to eat out of my hand. But I guaranteed that she would be amenable about small omissions. They are really enthusiastic about the book. I went out directly and cabled Djuna, and phoned Peter. I gave Peter a verbatim account of my interview, as far as I was able, in the midst of his Home Office business—so long, I was cut off twice.

    I was only there an hour and we talked about Djuna and Barker the whole time; I would like to see him again to discuss other things—and especially to talk really about the book. I said I had never learned so much from any book—that I hated not to have it by me. He said, to my great joy, that he didn't think Nora seemed cut in half (Nora and Cathy).[46] Eliot gave me the impression of a man who has carefully schooled himself to be a business man, but is somewhere else. Morley really sweet, starry-eyed when he talked about the book. I expect to see them again, for they are going to show me their correspondence. As I was leaving I asked Eliot if he didn't think the first 2 verses of Barker's "Ode" were bad. He said, "What Ode?" That was a blow—I said, "The very long one you are publishing."[47] He said, "I shouldn't be surprised if any of it were bad—I don't remember it—we'll take that up." I got the idea he can't make Barker out—a very different picture from what Barker gives one—of him sitting in reverence before Eliot. Eliot does everything possible for him but thinks he's a queer fish. Think Eliot and Hoare would have everything in common. Came away, as always, thinking how simple and sweet Peter is compared to other people of intelligence. I made one gaff—when censorship was mentioned, said—"I have a great drag with the Home Office"—but of course the H.O. is powerless—if a lot of influential

---

[45]Frank Morley (1899–1985) was, along with Geoffrey Faber and Eliot, a director of the firm.
[46]Barnes' protagonist Nora Flood had in the earlier versions been two characters, Nora and Cathy.
[47]Barker's poem "Ode to Man" (Part I), which he had showed Coleman (January 30, 1936), would be published in the October 1936 issue of the quarterly *The Criterion* (Vol. xvi, No. lxii), which Eliot edited.

people complain, they are obliged to move. It sounded silly, and conceited (as usual) because I had been saying I thought Djuna would do what I suggested. As usual, I am the great wonder-mover, everything bows before me—in my mind. They want to bring it out in an expensive form, to get the right audience—this, also, with a view to its not being prosecuted. E[liot]. says the English are against Lesbianism particularly.[48] E[liot]. and M[orley]. like brothers, conspiring. E[liot]. lends himself to all kinds of worldly nonsense, of which he is not a part. His eyes deep and very moving, his smile wide, his face sad and miserable, hollow eyes, not a very good brow. He sounded like any intelligent intellectual—not as interesting as Arthur Waley—no sensation of individuality at all. Yet I like him, like his face, would like to know him. He said he could not read new poetry because it upset him if it was good and bothered him if it was bad. Did not mind prose.

I made no mention whatever of my own writing, I cannot, when they are so friendly—I will just have to give my book to Jack MacDougall for C[hatto]. and Windus. They said they could not bring Dj's book out till fall—I did want hers to come out before mine—as it was written first.[49] I should not think it would do either of us good to come out at the same moment.

Eliot said he should think Djuna would not write again—he felt the pressure so great in this as though she had written herself out. He said the book was not "sexual" at all, but "went beyond sex," which is of course very much the point.

Thursday, April 30

Jack MacD. asked me to dinner—I couldn't go as I had a date with Peter—met him at the Café Royal. Before he came I was watching [Jacob] Epstein (who sat next to me talking to a man) saying that a friend of his had poissonality. E[pstein]. looks childish, sensual, licking chops, full of life. Peter Quennell and beautiful wife (who is really lovely and rather sardonic) sat behind me amiably arguing.[50] Peter has got a car! A black Rover sports coupe. He paid more than 200 pounds for it. We dined at the Ivy. Peter horribly depressed, I not helpful, though I made an effort to be, the Ivy really poisonous with old whores and horrible old men, and hunchbacks. By the time we got home I

---

[48]Protagonists Nora Flood and Robin Vote are gay, as are some of the other characters. The banning of Radclyffe Hall's *The Well of Loneliness*, for example, underscores that the "English are against Lesbianism." See the introduction.
[49]Coleman's novel "The Tygon" was not finished at this point. MacDougall rejected a completed version for Chatto & Windus in 1937, Eliot for Fabers in 1938, and it remains unpublished.
[50]Sir Peter Quennell (1905–1993), English poet, biographer, editor, and historian. His second of five wives, Nancy, was an editor and compiler.

was feeling rotten about Peter. I said, "You can't stay in the Home Office." He said, "I've reached the menopause," and said all he needed was to adjust himself. I said it had proved impossible. I said "How could Lawrence be efficient in your job?" He loved me, he was happy all the way down Kings Road for this. I was really disturbed, now am suddenly convinced he must get out, it is doing him in, will kill him.

I wrote again to McDonald, and this morning he phoned and asked if he could come and see me this afternoon.[51] I phoned the Connollys and said I would come for an hour at 5. Peggy came for a short time, said I gave her the breath of life; I recounted everything. I had written her about Eliot. She was so pleased she did not know what to do. She had Higgins for the weekend, who was much annoyed because he'd heard that Eliot said Barker had the only genius in England since Joyce; he couldn't bear it.[52] Peggy extremely pleased because Garman said, "Fabers won't take the book and Eliot will come around to us with it.[53] Peggy wanted every detail, to spike Garman.

Friday, May 1

McDonald came about half-past two. I was so glad to see him, remembered our extraordinary past. He was pleased with my flat. He is so beautiful, so young, so full of life, so ignorant. He said he had thought of me sometimes for days on end. All this came about from my writing him. Before he left he told me that he had been in love with me.

A far cry from McDonald was Connolly, to whose house I went at five. He had an American called Prokosch there.[54] (Peter said he has written a good book, called *The Asiatics*). First, Mrs. C[onnolly]. was not there. Connolly, at whose face I gazed with more than human wonder, trying to ferret him out, provided me with much food for thought. Looking at him I registered— "Ugly, vicious, nostrils wide and open, vulgar, dirty face, criminal, amoral." Why all this came out I don't know—he was in a strange mood—was writing a long hand-written letter to Peter Quennell (his lover or would-be love I think) to justify something about his (C's) book, which was turned down by Faber with a letter saying its lack of moral tone was deplorable.[55] (I made a

---

[51]Coleman had remained in contact with him and his wife, Gwenda.
[52]Bertram Higgins, poet, had been assistant editor of *The Calendar of Modern Letters* (1925–1927), the periodical edited by Garman and Rickword, and to which Holms had contributed.
[53]That is, to Garman's brother-in-law's publishing house, Ernest Wishart.
[54]Frederic Prokosch (1906–1989) was an American whose bestselling novels of the 1930s—*The Asiatics* and *The Seven Who Fled*—focus on the landscape or geography of Asia.
[55]Connolly's *The Rock Pool* (published by Obelisk in 1936) would be published by Hamish Hamilton in 1947, and includes a preface to Quennell about the book's morality. Quennell

gaff of telling him about Djuna's book and Eliot, to impress him, and saw at once that it touched a tender spot, so immediately switched to his, and said I would ask Eliot about it etc.) He let me read the letter. He is of course a maniac—a paranoiac. He admitted he could not stand the least criticism. He showed me a long screed he has written for the *S[unday]. Times* about Eliot's poetry.[56] He never mentioned the *S[hutter]. of Snow*, which disturbed me a little—until I thought it may have been that he liked it as little as *Janus*. It may have been that he was so set on these other subjects that he forgot it. I told him how I felt about V. Woolf's *To the Lighthouse*, where she tells you for 300 pages how beautiful the mother is.[57] A propos of his saying he wanted to give an effect of a girl's being attractive. He made notes on this. I was very careful to say nothing that would put him off, but tried to intrigue him—and to make myself out a sophisticated critic and woman of the world. I was reading the letter to Quennell when Prokosch came in—C. hastily seized it. I didn't finish it. But I got a lot of light on Connolly. He is fascinating, mad as a hare, not my kind of madness, not serious, nor profound, a strange mix. The letter was explaining how he had got his amoral tone from Latin authors at school—perfectly serious. I wondered what Quennell would think of it. He obviously worships Q[uennell]. And of course I had made one gaff after another (if I wish to know him) before; in saying I could not bear Q's writing, or Mrs. Q's face, etc. (all inferiority complex on my part); and especially in representing myself as a *Wuthering Heights* sort of person, which terrifies him. I think the *S[hutter]. of Snow* was too much for him.

. . . This morning Peter came out (I did not see him last night). I told him Tony might be arriving today—he said, "O I've been so happy without Tony! Now it's all broken up." He is quite pleased at my having a "social" life. I sent Barker a telegram to Dorset to ask him if he wanted to go to *Figaro* tomorrow afternoon. It was returned as the house is closed. He is thus in London, up to God knows what wiles; he has not communicated with me. I sent him another telegram to his father's house. Am about to write Eliot, from whom I have not heard. . . . At this precise moment Barker telephoned.

Barker came at half-past two. He said a strange thing about Eliot—that he was beginning to like young men! I didn't believe it and indicated so, to Barker's annoyance. We had a lot of fun talking later about Eliot—I told him how Eliot

---

would write the introduction for the 1981 reprint by Oxford University Press. Connolly had befriended the younger Quennell when they were students together at Balliol College, Oxford, in the mid-1920s.

[56] Connolly's article, "A Major Poet, The Influence of Mr. Eliot," appeared on May 3, 1936. It was a glowing review of Eliot's *Collected Poems* 1909–1935.

[57] Virginia Woolf paid tribute to her mother, Julia Stephen, through the character Mrs. Ramsay.

and I had a free discussion of what stories of his (B's) we should believe. Barker read me a long poem he is writing, which has a wealth of imagery and some beautiful conceptions[58]; very little knowledge. He is pleased with it.

He showed me a poem by Lionel Johnson called "The Dark Angel."[59] He read it to me. He said it was one of the best poems he had ever seen. It excited me beyond description. I wanted to make a copy at once, but he let me have his copy. It had these lines in it—

Nor will thine envious heart allow
Delight untortured by desire.
And all the things of beauty burn
With flames of evil ecstasy.

It is very exciting. Barker's poem seems young after it, and not concerned with life at all.

I didn't show him anything of mine. He told me a great deal about his family, and about his marriage. His face was unpleasant today—coarse and obtuse—his profile lovely at one moment—his eyes which are beautiful, so limpid and ecstatic; but I didn't like his mouth and chin—which slowly, I'm beginning to realize (through accomplished intuition), shows what's bad in him. His nose seemed vulgar today. He skin is shiny and he doesn't give one a feeling of elegance, or delicacy.

I am just as inhuman as he is; I don't show it so much. Being a woman I am anxious to please. But even when he is reading poetry to me, the most heavenly moments I have known with a human person, I feel away—I wish he would stop. I want to read it alone. I sit there and smile and smile and am a villain, with smiling face. I want his affection, and friendship. But to gain it, I have to submerge myself, and it kills me. I want always, with people, to be alone, unless sex is going on; or unless poetry is being read (I sometimes get quite free then); or unless someone is being really witty. Of course I liked being with Eliot because of the excitement and the vanity, etc. For a woman who wants always to be alone I seem to see a good many people.

Sunday, May 3

Peter and I went out in his car to a lovely part of Kent which he went to while I was in America. His car runs smoothly, is beautiful, low bucket seats; marvellously comfortable.

---

[58]Possibly *Calamiterror*.
[59]Lionel Johnson (1867–1902), English poet and essayist.

I said that people like Hemingway and Eliot had to develop a special psychology towards the world because of everyone wanting to meet them. This referred to a letter I wrote Eliot, in reply to his, confirming the interview, about Djuna's book. I wrote him a very personal letter, thanking him and Morley for what they did—speaking of Barker and Djuna—and sending him the poem "The Dark Angel," about which I made some comments. Peter does not think the poem is good, does not think I should have sent it. I terribly nervous (as with Connolly) that Eliot might snub me. Told Peter how when I knew Hemingway I was careful not to give impression I wanted to see him much. But with Eliot—someone like that! Peter said I had every social right to treat him as I would if he were not famous, because our relation was begun on grounds whereon celebrity hunters do not meet him.

I had a cable from Djuna, very happy about the book.

Monday, May 4

In the morning I went down to see Peter and he was looking sweet and happy. He said he had been so happy at Kew, and yesterday.[60] He showed me the *Times* which told how the Emperor of Abyssinia had opened the palace to the people, who came in and looted, wore top hats and burnt down half the city; while the Emperor fled.[61]

Earnshaw Smith phoned me that Tony was back yesterday. I had written her a long letter, giving her all the news, which went to Tom's flat. I met her for lunch, looking pale. She has been very ill. She said Siepmann behaved very well. We talked for hours at lunch; she came back here. I made her lie down. I was very glad to see her. She says the Communist in Siepmann's book is himself. The book is extraordinary. I had no idea he had such talent. It is the best farce, in some ways, I've ever read.[62] He said the book was just to make money. It is a perfectly splendid farce on the movie industry.

---

[60]Coleman and Hoare had spent Saturday, May 2, walking in Kew Gardens (the Royal Botanic Gardens). One of the most famous gardens in England, Kew opened in 1759 in Richmond in the southwest of London.
[61]Haile Selassie (1891–1975) was the emperor of Ethiopia (Abyssinia) (1930–1974). Though he appealed to the League of Nations after Italy tried to invade the country in 1935, he received no help, and in 1936 was forced to flee as Italian forces occupied the capital of Addis Ababa. In 1941, with aid from Britain, he returned to Ethiopia and his throne.
[62]Siepmann's 1936 novel, *Waterloo in Wardour Street*, is a satire about the British film industry.

Tuesday, May 5

Last night I was reading the little poem of Vaughan, "The Revival." I know nothing of Vaughan.[63]

[Peter] came up with *New Verse* and another poetry magazine, *Contemporary Verse and Poetry*, a new one.[64] I looked at various things; he tried to get me to read a poem of Dylan Thomas. I can't, cannot, absorb these things. I have nothing to do with the poetry of my age. I read Barker's poetry because I know him. . . . . I read some of Barker's "Ode to Man" to Peter against Barker's wish (he wants no one to see it). I read my "Old Man" poem to Peter. It is perfectly awful. In 10 verses there are not more than 10 lines in it that are worth preserving. Peter was very nice about it, but told me what he didn't like. The opening he thought good. I'll write what good remains.

The Old Man

Sullen with the eye of ordinary use
    I now refuse
To gaze upon the opening flower
That in the dew once, in an hour
    Unprecedented, grew,
In a passion past recalling.

Older, in this garden, with a slow
    Decease, I've grown.
In my eye no longer glows
Passion, that was scaled within my tears.
Blind, behind me, in the rocks of fear,
The awful bodies of the unknown peer.

Centuries of heaven have shined
In the hollows of my mind

    The shame
Of death, knowing what the end will be.

---

[63]Coleman transcribed this poem, as well as Vaughn's "Son-Days" and Henry King's "Exequy."
[64]*New Verse* (1933–1939) was a little magazine founded and edited by Geoffrey Grigson. *Contemporary Poetry and Prose* (which Coleman here misnamed) was a magazine edited by Roger Roughton which had its first issue in May 1936. It included two poems—entitled "Two Poems" 1 and 2—by Welsh writer Dylan Thomas (1914–1953) as well as his short story "The Burning Baby."

Far from the beginning have been spent
Those powers which flooded once my life.
In the full knowledge of that power
Immortal I lived, as love and divine men grow.

The deep delight that was in the morning
   Winds, rising
In heavenly tempests without warning
Over the earth, and in their typhoon blew
The grass, the earth, the hyacinth without warning.

  The brush
Of snow upon mountain range
Brought to my spirit the tumult of loved change
   And I
Pure and delighted soul upon that sky
   Knew not
That in days not born I'd see
Death in each crevice, each abandoned tree.

Nothing remains of that. . . .
But shame, sorrow, guilty retreats.
   My being
Radiant with mystery has shed its grace . . .

This is all that remains. I threw out all the rest, which was mostly clichés. I have not got into the thing. I felt like throwing it into the fire. But I didn't. I thought, "I'll fix it." I felt I could do it. Peter must have been very disturbed by some of it. I kept calling it a "dirty" poem; but said I would "clean" it. It contains possibilities.

Thursday, May 7

Tony came. I gave her "The Cremation" which she read frequently, commented upon, and was delighted with. I let her lie down, then gave her supper, of scrambled eggs on toast and the rest of the Brie. Peter phoned and said he wanted to go to a good detective film called, *Crime Without Passion*, in Kings Road.[65] Tony left. There were 5 letters for me, from Djuna, Sonia, Peggy,

---

[65] The film is directed by Ben Hecht and stars Claude Rains.

Barker and my father. Djuna said she would be in Paris May 8th (today).[66] Barker's letter was horribly discomfiting. It asked for an advance of his last quarterly money from Peggy. It made me ill to read it—because I should have asked him how he was getting on when I saw him, instead of which, out of uneasiness (he is so proud) and the fact that I am low in money myself, I did not ask him. Due to his brother's illness and other things he has got very low in funds—a natural event and to be expected, on what the poor boy tries to live on. Peggy however, like all the rich, likes to support someone who accepts what she gives and never asks for more. She knows they always will ask for more. I felt sick. I knew this would happen—how could it not?—and I had no money and did not dare write to Peggy, although if I could see her and show her the letter she might be very sweet about it. What is galling is being in the power of people who have no right to be in power over you; what right has Peggy to have money and Barker not? Although she half feels this (a phenomenon for any person born with money), the other half is close wicked Jewish, careful of the disposal of every cent. To cope with this half is almost more than I can bear—I want to be violent. The truth is, if I keep to a sense of reality, Peggy is wonderful. I finally got Peter to promise he would not cash a check I gave him some time ago for money he lent me last summer—he had not cashed it yet—and wrote Barker a letter (how he must have hated writing me). I sent him ten pounds, and when I come back I'll talk to Peggy about making things easier for him until the end of the quarter.

Tuesday, May 12

I got a nice letter from Eliot last night, objecting strenuously to Djuna's book being called *The Anatomy of Night*. He knew the L. Johnson poem. He liked it of course. But did not write about it as if it were a living thing. He said, "The late A.E. Housman and Ezra Pound" agreed with him that it was "on the whole the most satisfactory" of Johnson's poems.[67] Really! But he did object hard to the title of Djuna's book, sign of life. He did not discuss Barker's poem. It was a pleasant letter. So I wrote him another, setting forth my view on *The Anatomy of Night* (saying that in any case Dj. would do what they wanted but I just wanted to protest). I asked him what he thought of Milton and put in a few things to jog him; I asked him what he thought of Kay Boyle—turned that into modern American writing, since he

---

[66]Note that Coleman has dated this entry May 7. Because she usually wrote up one day's events on the following day, she often conflated dates.
[67]Alfred Edward Housman (1859–1936), English poet and classical scholar.

evidently won't discuss anyone they publish. Asked him what he knew about H. H. Richardson. This letter was a long one. I hope he'll bear with me. I'd like principally to know him. His letter was however sweet. He said my portrait of Djuna was alarming and that he would look forward to seeing her with eagerness and trepidation.

I had a letter from Djuna, from Paris, this morning, as I was finishing mine to Eliot. It made everything else seem trivial. She is so happy about the book. She can't sleep, and had aching pains—"thinking—thinking—coming alive again—<u>wanting</u> to write again—imagine it!" I felt so happy about this I couldn't think of Eliot or myself, or Peter. Fancy this happening—fancy Djuna really coming to life, a new life, because her book is appreciated and will be published.

Wednesday, May 13

After spending all day dreaming and meditating and half sleeping, writing to Eliot and in my diary—I woke from a half sleep with the strangest feeling (I know this means some other life, I was in touch with)—I telephoned Peter to meet me at the Café Royal. He did, at 6–30. I showed him Eliot's letter—he was pleased with it—he went off into diatribes against me for not agreeing with E[liot]. about the title. I quoted my letter to E[liot]. as best I could. He said that I "had some sense and would give Eliot the impression that I was a moron." I said E[liot]. did not expect me to be a brilliant mind, but enjoyed the feminine intercourse. I told him various things I wrote Eliot. He said I was "female and trying to make a hit with him." I said I had not made it clear what I felt about Milton. Peter is always telling me what I think, and putting words in my mouth. I preserve my demeanor with difficulty. We drank 3 sherries. Peter Quennell was there looking like a tired clam. I left Peter and he went home to dinner, while I went to a movie called *These Three* containing Miriam Hopkins, Merle Oberon and a school.[68]

Letter from J[ack]. MacDougall praising *S[hutter]. of Snow*.

Peggy came and we drank sherry, [. . .] went to the Good Intent and drank of bottle of wine, by which time we were very tight, or I was. I showed her Barker's letter and said he was in London now trying to get the Durham University job (he phoned me this morning but I couldn't see him today—but he was so happy over getting Eliot and Herbert Read to write letters

---

[68]The film, an adaptation by Lillian Hellman of her play *The Children's Hour*, caused a stir for Hellman's filmic erasure of the protagonist's lesbianism.

recommending him), etc.[69] I said I thought Hoare ought to help him, as well as she and I. She told me about her money matters and the truth is she has very little left for herself, so that she has to hesitate even to buy a dress—due to giving $400 a month to Laurence [Vail] and $500 to Garman (house etc.) and $100 to Djuna, $150 to Dorothy, etc. I was ashamed that I had ever thought her mean.

Tony came for an hour this morning and told me Tom had improved the drowning story beyond all recognition—really drowned himself this time.[70] I am anxious to see it. She said he very nearly did drown the other Saturday, in his boat—she saw him directly after and he looked "melted down," as if some devil had gone from him. Very queer this—and Tom—who is not really interesting at all yet has this inhuman talent. She does not like my corresponding with Eliot. I got my poem back from R[aymond]. Mortimer saying he "liked it extremely" and advising me to send it to *New Writing*, *London Mercury* or the *Criterion*.[71] Tony said I should not be crushed. I want Eliot to see the poem, but do not dare to send it—wish Djuna would mention it. I said to Tony, "Wouldn't you think Barker would mention that poem to Eliot? He is so mean!" Tony said he was young and felt the whole poetic world was his own province, especially as far as females were concerned. She said I was unusually generous and could not understand envy. I said I envied every woman who was well dressed and goodlooking, but that in poetry I felt only the Communion of the Saints when I saw good writing. She said this was uncommon. She has not heard from Siepmann yet. J. MacDougall says Siepmann's book is not selling, which irritates me.

Wrote Djuna, on Peggy's advice, that she had better live in her apartment in Paris this first winter and see how it went; she is terrified of London. She is to come for the summer—which she will like; will get on with Garman I think. Very anxious to see Djuna; as she says we will talk for 24 hours

---

[69]Barker was applying to teach English at Durham University, Northumbria. As Coleman later noted on June 12, he did not get the position. He would, however, be successful in landing a job teaching English in Japan at Sendai University, in November 1939. He and his wife would stay there only until July 1940; concerned about the war, he wrote to his newest admirer, the wealthy, aspiring Canadian writer Elizabeth Smart, to provide him with two plane tickets to the United States which, with some help, she was able to do. Smart went to meet the Barkers in California, at which point she and George began what would become a nearly twenty-year long affair.

[70]Hopkinson spent years working on his story "I Have Been Drowned," about a man who risks his life to win a sailing regatta. Dedicated "To Antonia White," it was eventually published in the monthly paperback *Penguin New Writing* in January 1941.

[71]Coleman had sent Mortimer her "Cremation" poem early in the month, but he was now refusing it for the *New Statesman*.

without stopping. Going to be a bit difficult with Peggy—her inferiority complex—love of me—Djuna will not see this or understand (possibly will).

Thursday, May 14

Last night I dined with Peter in his flat; we awaited Phyllis who did not come. My Peter sat with bright eyes—I read him a copy I made of my last letter to Eliot, to amuse and shock him. He said my point on Milton was clear enough. I thought it wasn't. He agreed the letter was rather verbose. (I paid no attention to the style. I dread thinking that these diaries bear the same fault.) I said Eliot might not "rise" to any of these points, but there was no harm in trying to get him to.

Peter said it was outrageous the way I said "I'm taking too much of your time" (to Eliot) then went on asking more and more questions. We agreed that Eliot's poetry is rather thin. I said Muir was the only living poet who wrote in the world of poetry; that one day I wanted to talk to Eliot about Muir's poetry. I don't think he'll come out much about his contemporaries. But if I get to know him (a very long business no doubt—perhaps never) I might get a few honest words out of him. I don't know what my chances are of getting to know him. He's very reserved, his life all planned. Even if he came to admire my work he might not want to give much time to seeing me. He doesn't see Barker often; and if B[arker]. lived in London I don't think E[liot]. would be intimate with him. He's much more likely to respond to me on the social plane. But I am very interested in him; would really like to <u>know</u> him—not just see him.

Peter and I lunched at Peter Jones' new restaurant.[72] This was a gleam of another world. Suddenly we were surrounded by debutantes and handsome young women, coming to lunch. Peter nearly bugged his eyes out. We discussed the probable character of everyone who came in. I had bought Eliot's new essays for Barker.[73] A mannekin came in and walked up and down the lunch room with a sign 12 1/2 guineas, very uneasily as though saying, "Sorry—I have to do this"—smirking. I saw a nightgown for 12 shillings (before Peter came) I was dying for. I thought, "Barker" and didn't get it. This is the first time, almost, that I've stopped myself buying something I could afford because of feeling that I had no right to it.

I ought to look at my "Death of Samson" but cannot—I want to get more away from it . . . After writing that I immediately opened the poem. It is a remarkable poem, it is full of extraordinary feeling. The meter wants working

---

[72]The London department store.
[73]Eliot's *Essays, Ancient and Modern* was published by Faber & Faber in 1936.

over—I just poured it out. Wonderful, deep lines in it, of human suffering. I have got Peter and me in this somewhere!

The main thing is to get the poem out exactly as it is to go (its meaning, movement). Then polish up the form. The poem is moving. That's what I want—in simplicity, to show the evil of life, the good of death, the wicked, the strong, the meek.

Friday, May 15

Think vanity and childishness (fear, not wanting responsibility) are awful demons in me; no limit to them. My flying off the handle in Love is only vanity. My vanity is Colossal! Much worse than Barkers'—it is a personal vanity—a woman poet's. How distressing. I want to die.

Thinking of my sweet little Johnny, and every time I think of him I get a sharp feeling of joy.

Sunday, May 17

I could not wait to see Peter yesterday morning. I dressed and went down to see him. It is no use—whenever I think of going away for a little while, my heart gets icy. I was so impatient to see him I couldn't wait to hear him get out of the bath. I went down. I suggested we go to Kew and that we go to Cambridge to see his sister today.[74] He fell in readily with these suggestions.

I met Tony outside, and went and had a "cawfee" with her for about three hours. Tony—I love her and believe in her more and more; she has the gift of God—understands all knowledge and all mysteries—whether she writes or not she is one of the saints—with whom one can have communion. She is a woman of genius, as I've known since I read her diary (could not know from *Frost in May* or be sure from the "House of Clouds"). Of course I was confirmed in the knowledge by the 30 pages of the book she began a year ago.[75] We were so fascinated we did not know the time, and said "Let's have lunch now"—discovered it was five past two o'clock. I was to meet Peter at half past one. I was so happy with Tony I could have gone on forever. . . . I do hope Eliot writes to me—he is a skunk if he lets this poor little wandering knowledge-luster go unacknowledged. The poor man is busy.

---

[74]Dorothy Hoare. See entry and note for July 13, 1934.
[75]White's short story "The House of Clouds" was published in 1928; her novel *Frost in May* in 1933. Her new book, begun in 1935, is *The Lost Traveller*, which would become the second installment in her fictionalized autobiographical quartet. She suffered from long bouts of writer's block: it would not be published until 1950.

Peter was late, we got sandwiches, etc., and drove to Kew, he very despondent and complaining about his face, the car, etc., his health, etc. As soon as we got in Kew everything changed. He became peaceful.

Monday, May 18

Yesterday was full of lilacs and Cambridge dons and conversation that wore me down so that coming home in the car I had a back-ache. It was a strange day—quite out of my ordinary life. We went down to Cambridge to see Peter's sister, whom I liked more than ever, really loved, she is so enthusiastic and sweet little-girl lovable—though she has her own mind, so he says; she doesn't look it. I am just waiting for some man to take that plum. She is a lecturer in English at Cambridge and knows her subject; has excellent critical taste, and a sweet taste about everything.

We went to Barley a sweet village near Cambridge. We lunched at a student's tea-shop in Cambridge. We saw the "backs" of Trinity.[76] It is so peaceful here. The academic life seems to have more advantages than any other life; the hard work (now and then) is more than compensated for.

I have been to Cambridge before and am always delighted with it—there is no comparison between its charm and Oxford's. I should think people of a student type of mind would feel themselves, at times, almost in Paradise, if they don't mix up with the rivalries, etc., which could poison academic life. Someone with a permanent position there could have what we most desire in life—security among one's fellows, peace in which to do one's work; someone in these conditions, who was also married to a don she loved, could be in Paradise! I said Dorothy ought to be married, Peter agreed; some of these women are self-sufficient, but she is very feminine, and is sweet and I should think might be snapped up. We walked up and down the lanes of Cambridge, and along the Cam—the lilac, in behind Newnham, where she lives, was ravishing—I smelled it until there was no scent in me left—I smelled every one we came to.[77] It has a rich powerful sickish smell which brings back old dreams, revelations and lands one has forgotten.

We dined "in Hall," a terrifying performance; we sat on a dais, got up and helped ourselves to food, the students far below us quietly sitting in socks bare legs and jackets, some pretty—I am so near-sighted and I couldn't see half what I wanted to see. I sat next the Head, a casual female who was very

---

[76]The "backs" refers to the area of the Cambridge colleges, including Trinity, which back on to the River Cam.

[77]Founded in 1871, Newnham followed Girton College in admitting women to Cambridge.

sympathetic, blasé, spoke slowly and did not care, with a mannish smile.[78] Opposite were varying females of knowledge and parts—one who had written a book on some abstruse anthropological point, just out—a terrifying woman who lived alone in Africa with daggers behind her, brave and calm, getting her dope.[79] A bouncing minx had written another book.[80] I feel irreverent as I write this and all the time I was at supper I felt myself the young girl and was astonished to find I could converse with them. In point of fact I am four years older than Dorothy and the same age as several of them. Her book is scholarly and is called *The Fool in Literature*—I think. These came to coffee afterwards—I got on with the Head by discussing Higher Criticism of the Bible! I got on with minx by discussing Faber & Faber, her publishers. Peter was terrified at supper, as well he might be—it was sweet to see donnish heads turned towards a Man's Opinion—He did not catch on to his power. Dorothy is an excellent hostess who says little yet lets everyone expand—looked so different from the others—the essence of femininity—I wonder she has got so far on her own energy.

I was very tired at the end, and could hardly speak coming home (but continued to do so as I will to the grave). I didn't want to go to Peggy's today, hated the thought of it, the packing and arranging. But now it's done and I am about to go to the train, I am happy that I shall be in the country again.

Yew Tree Cottage, Hurst [May 19]

Coming down in the train, peace came to me. Peggy is happy now, she feels the spring in every muscle of her heart. As I write there is a wren singing his shrill metallic wirey song; full of heat and flies. I bought some espadrilles as soon as I got off the train. The weather has been ravishing; hot with a breeze—full sun, and clouds, trees waving. I immediately went down the

---

[78] One of Lytton Strachey's five sisters, Joan Pernel Strachey (1876–1951) was the Principal of Newnham (1923–1941).
[79] Dr. Onora O'Neill has identified the anthropologist to be Audrey Richards (1899–1984). In his essay on Richards in *Cambridge Women: Twelve Portraits* (ed. Shils and Blacker), Adam Kuper tells us she had been a student of Polish anthroplogist Dr. Bronislaw Malinowski (1884–1942) at the University of London, who advocated that anthropologists live within the culture they are studying. Richards was the first woman to heed his theory, going alone to Rhodesia (May 1930–July 1931; January 1933–July 1934) to investigate the Bemba tribe. Coleman referred to Richards' publication *Hunger and Work in a Savage Tribe: a Functional Study of Nutrition Among the Southern Bantu* (1932).
[80] O'Neill identified the minx as Enid Welsford (1892–1981), author of *The Fool, His Social and Literary History* (1935). Elsie Duncan-Jones, who wrote the entry on Welsford for *Cambridge Women*, notes that Welsford was so small that she had to have special clothes made; O'Neill added that she had to have built-up pedals designed for her car.

gulley and began looking for nests. I was so happy and then Garbage [Garman] came and they began to want me to play tennis. I didn't come for that but could do nothing. There is a young man here called Alec Ponisovsky, whom I used to know in Paris, a very old friend of Peggy's. I could not give myself away in front of him and so was trapped. I could have murdered Peggy who knows my hatred of tennis. She supported me feebly but I had to go. I behaved in what for me was decent style; but it struck them as fearfully bad manners. We had a discussion of manners at tea. I told Peggy she let me down—I can't expect Alec and certainly not Garbage to know me. I played the stinking game, getting a headache and moving about in a senseless manner. I said my manners were awful when I knew people. Garbage said—"It's surprising how quickly you get to know them." I could not help laughing. I said, "I never visit anyone because neither they nor I could stand the strain." (All life seems to have gone out with John dead.) I said I had beautiful manners all day at Cambridge and had a back-ache as the result.

Wednesday, May 20

We talked a good deal with Alec who is a sad disillusioned Russian with no mind but extremely sensitive and has a sense of reality if it's put in his mind; he was the lover of Peggy's sister Hazel.[81] He really appreciates Peggy, in a sort of idealistic way—but it's a pleasure to talk with someone who knows her extraordinary quality even if he idealizes her; the people I know tend to think her a joke, or a sad little girl; or just terrible.

Peggy has been divine, like a little angel. The first night I slept in Garbage's house, and awoke not knowing where I was with the birds flooding the gulley.[82] The sun was pouring through the early trees. Last night I slept with Peggy in her room. We talked all evening about Mr. Pinkwhip ([James] Joyce's friend, Léon, whom I named Pinkwhip that night in December 1932)—a Russian married to Alec's sister. Joyce adores him because he's a buffoon besides being extremely intelligent; a Dostoyevskian character.[83] Alec says he sleeps with Lucy (his wife) and thinks of Mrs. Pinkwhip. We joked like anything about Pinkwhip. But Joyce loves him. He has become his only friend. Alec says Mrs. J[oyce]. tries to keep him from drinking but Pinkwhip gets there first. He adores Joyce. He loves him for

---

[81] Ponisovsky had been the lover of Hazel Guggenheim for four years. She left him for Milton Waldman, who became her second husband.
[82] Recall that Garman had built a small one-room house at the end of the garden at Yew Tree Cottage where he could write.
[83] For details about the figures described here, see her entry for December 12, 1932.

the kick; does not tell other people. Pinkwhip's name is Paul Léon. Alec has an intense love of laughter, and life; he is dead in some ways; I remember in 1932 (the Pinkwhip evening) he never responded to anything; he was unhappy then about Joyce's daughter whom he was supposed to marry; and would not, through not having enough money—though I suspect it was because he loved Hazel; the year before that, when I was with Bianchetti he was very gay and used often, with his twin brother (now dead) [to] go out and make merry with John and Peggy, and B. and me. Alec always liked me and once when I danced with him he held me close; but of course, since I loved Bianchetti did not do anything. I felt very queer last night rehearsing all that gayety (which John used to bring out in me). I have become very dull since then. In some ways I am dead. I think so much about my soul I have no time for gayety. I thought, "How easily I could sleep with Alec, since he means nothing to me yet attracts me (I am afraid of Barker whom I could love), and Peter not know it; there he is, in the next room, I am starving for sex—no complications; yet I know I would not do it."

I am sexually miserable and want every man I see who will look at me and knowing the two things that frighten them—emotional intensity which I can't feel for anyone but Peter and so am safe—and not dressing chicly—I can get any man I want, except the ones who really must have a wealthy chic woman.

Thursday, May 21

I wrote to Barker last night to send him the rest of his quarter's money which Peggy generously advanced him; she is also going to give him 8 pounds extra so that he will have had two pounds a week, not 24 pounds a quarter.

As I sit here I look up on that field which is above the living room, now spluttered with buttercups, brilliant green, against the round blue edge of the sky. Talked to eager Peggy a good deal about Eliot and Djuna—said Djuna's book would create a sensation as great as *Ulysses*.[84]

On Friday, May 22, Coleman went up to London. Among the items she recorded over the next few days are the following: White had been ill from a hemorrhage caused by an infection of the cervix and needed an operation; Coleman took care of Barker's rent for July; Coleman and Hoare went out of town from Saturday afternoon until Sunday, and although he had made love to her on Saturday night he refused to do so again on Sunday evening. She returned to Guggenheim the following day in a depressed state.

---

[84]Joyce's *Ulysses*.

Wednesday, May 27

Reading *Jack Robinson* all day.[85] I think the most remarkable young book I have read to date—of modern books. Not the mad poetic gifts of Barker, but a much sounder grasp on life; a much higher intelligence behind it. It's hard to judge, as Gerald Brenan ("George Beaton") can't create character; yet he has a grasp of what character is. Barker hasn't the least. *Ulysses* is a freak book, very hard to judge. "Beaton" has not the original gifts of Joyce or Barker or Proust, but he has developed what he has in an amazing way. He has squeezed the last drop out of his talent. This is a change from moderns, who one always feels have never begun to realize what gifts they have: certainly not Joyce. It is not as good as Djuna's book—hers is the only one I can say is superior to it.

I like *Jack Robinson* because it is the normal life. I must write him, I wonder if he will answer me. I feel shy about writing people as Eliot has not answered my letter—two weeks—and I wonder if he really can regard me as I would some young and untalented person, who wanted my knowledge. I can't conceive of refusing anybody any spiritual thing; and do not believe that Eliot can. He must be very busy and hasn't the time.

Peggy and I looked at a depressing cottage in South Harting, I wanted a cottage for the summer—suddenly thought of it.

Thursday, May 28

I finished *Jack Robinson*. I wrote a letter to Gerald Brenan. Wrote to Sonia and Barker. Expect Djuna tomorrow or Saturday. Father coming in late August, on the airship Hindenburg. I don't know how safe this is—he is very expeditious to try it.[86]

I went in to see Peggy before packing. She is worried about Djuna's coming, that she won't be able to talk to her. She said, "If she's stupid, I can't

---

[85]*Jack Robinson: A Picaresque Novel* (1933) is about a protagonist reflecting on his life as an English boy who ran away from home. It was written by Edward Fitzgerald (Gerald) Brenan under the pseudonym George Beaton (1894–1987), a peripheral member of the Bloomsbury Group.

[86]In a letter sent to Barnes on August 26, 1936, Coleman reported: "Father was more excited over his zeppelin trip than anything in his life—developed 3 diseases before leaving, out of fear—got them all cured, frantically—is o.k. now. The quarters were very cramped—they left—and arrived—at night—a nuisance—so did not see enough of land—but he can't get over coming here in 2 days! I won't forget the zeppelin [moving] into the hangar out of the night and rain in Frankfurt that night—a monstrous giant, bigger than an ocean liner, being pulled quietly into home, exactly on time, after crossing half the world" (University of Maryland). The Hindenburg caught fire and was destroyed while trying to land in New Jersey on May 6, 1937; 35 of the 97 people on board died.

talk to her. I'm so stupid myself." Peggy said that she and I had a "perfect understanding" whether we spoke or not. I came up to London in a slow train, Peggy seeing me off—How many partings we have had—she and John [Holms] and I—in what strange stations! She looks always the same when I leave her; since 1934, like a child that has to face terror.

Section 3

London

May 29–June 12, 1936

Settling into London again, Coleman prepared to receive Barnes—en route from Paris—who was to reside temporarily with Coleman although she also went to Yew Tree Cottage to see her friend and patron Guggenheim. Nightwood was the topic de jour, fuelled by the fact that Barnes would have two meetings with Eliot; in reporting on these meetings, Coleman further revealed her role in editing and shaping the novel. However, tensions arose as Barnes wondered if Coleman had been too aggressive in making cuts to the manuscript, while Coleman rightly feared that, while Eliot was responsive to Barnes, he had no interest in maintaining a more personal, collegial correspondence with Coleman herself.

With Barnes back on the scene Coleman was eager to entertain her, as were White and Hoare, and the diary expands once again in Barnes' witty, stimulating, and sensual presence. Barnes provided Coleman with fresh doses of "surreal" dialogue, and Barnes, along with White, offered much valued critiques of Coleman's poetry and fiction. Barnes was further helpful in providing distraction for Coleman, who was still obsessively querying her sexual emotions for Barker while feeling an increasing sense of death at the hands of the lifeless Hoare.

Friday, May 29

Expecting to hear all day Djuna was coming. Tony dined with Peter last night, I did not come as I thought she would enjoy being alone with him. I came in about half-past ten. She told me today he had been saying my poetry was good and that I had developed!

I reread my last letter to Eliot, feeling sick because he has not answered, fearing I had been presumptuous; it was too long, but it was a sweet letter, and intelligent. The poor man is rushed to the eyes with work, but if he makes no reply at all I shall think he is pretty mean. Told Tony how Barker said, "I think Eliot is a major poet, and when I'm with a major poet I'm a bit stiff." She loves Barker and says his kind of loyalty ("In other words" I said, "He's genuine, you mean") is very rare nowadays.

But my Tony came off best today when I read her my Samson poem. I had a headache and was sick and did not want to read, but began it. We then sustained interruptions of Mrs. Stafford, who came to clean, forcing us to the street. We went to her room after lunch and I finished reading it. She thought the last third let down. I, who had been getting fearfully excited over the last, was astonished. We went over it, and I felt she was right. She picked out, infallibly, the good lines; thought the rest commonplace. She said the beginning (1st 2/3) was so wonderful it set a standard for the rest, which might be all right for someone else. She said I should give an idea of his physical blindness; also make the scene where they are mocking him—which is now ordinary—horrible. Greatly exhilarated by her comments.

She is all for its being a dramatic poem. She wants to see my book, poked me up terribly about it, said to give it to MacDougall, get it done at once, and send it to him. Said it would save my dignity (not to give it to Fabers) and besides they might refuse it because they are already going to publish Djuna's book which means losing money. Said she advised me strongly, since MacD. wants to see it, to finish it at once and send. I said I would not send it unless she criticized the end, the part she has not seen, written since she read it last summer.

Want to get the poem done properly now, am excited—Djuna coming tomorrow probably—Phyllis this evening. Djuna to meet Eliot next Tuesday.

Sunday, May 31

This is a miserable waking—I had a wretched afternoon and evening with Peter yesterday. Nothing that I believe about him seems to do any good, no hope for our relationship. He is really mad, much madder than we know—I see no hope of our ever coming together. There is no way out for me—except bearing it. He came, feeling ill and disgusted (what really gets me down is when he seems dead), was disagreeable to me, and carping (criticizing, in a nasty personal way, every word of mine, every look.) I did the best I could with him.

We had several drinks, and I became less violent (since I really want him); we went to dinner at Queen's. When we got home I said to Peter, "Let's make love. I'll wait for you upstairs," which is the only way I know of to get him to want to—to be calm and sweet, not excited or emotional (unless he is tight—and he won't get tight any more). He looked at me in that cowlike way he does. I hate, worse than poison, this cajoling him, it is absolutely the opposite of what excites me—God knows I have hardly ever been excited with him—I am always hoping for some joy that never comes—my nature is to be sought, and taken by a man. I loathe the memory of lecherous men who could not wait for me—but there is a life between that and having one you love never want you. (I am near crazy as I write, and think of Barker, wondering if I did give in to his attraction for me, if I could have a life with him worth living). I went upstairs and undressed, made my bed in the sitting room. (I had a note from Connolly as we came in, asking to see me, saying he had wanted me to come down and see them in the country—now they had returned). I went down after some time and found him sitting in his mackintosh reading the *New Statesman*. Feeling like hurting him, I said, "Don't come up if you really don't want to"—these horrible, humiliating, ignominious words, putting me in the position of a whore who is not wanted. I went out and to the bathroom, trying to keep quiet.

I went upstairs and to bed, and lay for some time despairing of my life, wondering what would come of this—for I know I have too much life to bear it. I had almost got to sleep, after what seemed hours, when he came in, in his bathrobe, and sat on the bed. <u>He sat there like a man who has come to be hung</u>. I patted him, rolling over sleepily away from him, saying, "Don't stay, if you don't want to." He sat there, and I knew that he was mad, stark mad, as he sat there, after 5 years of "loving" me, the changes that have taken place, the passion that has been expended—still he sat there, like an ox that has been taken to the ax. He did not go, but just sat on the bed. I got wild. I said, "Why, if you don't want me, should I be faithful to you? I have stood as much as I can endure. You don't want me. This is your proof of it. Now go, get out, get quickly out of here, before you drive me insane. Leave me alone, O leave me, to work out my fate as best I can. Don't blame me for what I do! Get out!" I said passionately as he still remained, like a fish caught in a net. "Get out of my life!" He went out quietly. I lay in unhappy dreams, in which Connolly was uneasily involved. I had miserable dreams all night. I woke up and knew he was stark raving mad, there was nothing to do.

Monday (Whit-Monday) June 1[1]

While I was sitting thinking "My last day alone for a while" Peter rang me up and said he was going to the country and would I come. I agreed, and

---
[1] Whit-Monday is a Bank Holiday in the United Kingdom.

we passed a sweet, amiable afternoon. He took me to a part of Surrey, near Leatherhead, above Dorking. It was Whit-Monday yet our walk was almost unmolested.

I worried more and more as the afternoon wore on because I was going to meet Djuna. Finally I said, "Will you go with me?" He said Certainly. I was worried at Djuna's coming, got into an increasing neurotic state.

We reached Victoria ahead of time. When Dj. got off the train she looked well. I was glad to see her. She embraced Peter and called him Darling. He was pleased and we put all her luggage in the car (she pleased with the car) and came here. Djuna and I did not quite know what to say to each other, I told her the first 3 days would be the hardest. Peter got whisky and made himself agreeable; he and Djuna got on.

Her paintings were unpacked and Peter fell in love with them, that is, was astonished at them.[2] They are quite wonderful, not like the paintings of anybody else, quite extraordinary. He had no idea she was so clever with the brush and kept looking at them, remarking on them. She has got a new one, of Scudder, better than all the rest, a corpse-like evil fellow, in cravat and bristling hair.[3] She has modelled the face beautifully. My picture looked strange as ever; it has a green cap now. Peter fascinated by it, how it resembles me, yet is not I. She has taken (as she did with Scudder I suppose) everything bad in my face—and how she instinctively knows it—and developed that, leaving out what is fine or sensitive or delicate; it is like a terrible undeveloped prize-fighter. Peter loves it, saying it shows American brutalized spirituality. When I told her Morley said, dreamily, "She's certainly looked down the drain!" she was offended.

[Peter] said after she went to bed that she was "sensible" and intelligent, and knew just where she was, was very feminine and attractive. She walked around in a lacy dressing gown, lay on the couch. He and I talked, about her and the pictures, for hours after she retired.

I couldn't sleep, felt so stimulated, the life Djuna has, though she feels old and tired, and is really ill from low blood-pressure—she is vital as earth. Tony coming to lunch with us. Peter taking her around London after lunch. Dj. and I talked all the morning, though she ill, after drinking a bit, talked about her book, Eliot, Neagoe, Peter, Peggy, Tony, etc. She gets inspired when she talks about Neagoe. "My little piece of Transylvanian sassafras, spitting in the prune keg." I was laughing. She loves an audience and anything starts her off.

---

[2] Barnes enjoyed painting portraits of people she knew.
[3] Phillip Herring notes that Barnes had begun seeing Scudder Middleton in 1934, at the same time that she was involved with Peter Neagoe. Middleton (1888–1959), an American poet, was an alcoholic who attracted her sexually because he looked like Thelma Wood (221). Herring also tells us that Barnes had begun a portrait of Coleman, titled "Madame Majeska," in either 1934 or 1935 (220).

She said, "We lose everything getting to know ourselves." Talked about life in Paris (she loves Paris and will probably live there), she can't—as I anticipated—talk to any of "the girls" there any more.[4] Got fed up with Dolly Wilde, who sounds tedious. A dope fiend who puts in the dope before your eyes. "She wears it as if it were a decoration." Natalie Barney devoted to her and doing nothing.

Tuesday, June 2

Tony came, full of woolly bedazzlement, her own term, at seeing Djuna again.

We made merry with my Hayford Hall diaries, looking for the meeting of Djuna and Tony. When I found it it was a gem.[5] It was so terrible Djuna had to walk out of the room. Djuna said all a man wants is to be left alone. She said the most contented sight in this life was the back of a man walking away from a woman.

Tom's name was mentioned and she said, "Do you remember how he used to fling his torso into the brook, thinking he was giving the brook a moment?' Tony was overcome with mirth at this. When asked what H.D. was like, Djuna said, "Well she <u>looks</u> like an explosion in a shingle factory." . . . everyone laughing at that she said, looking round, "She's very nice."[6]

Peter came and drove us, after some discussion to Surrey, where we showed Djuna the suburbs along the road, and the English country, and pubs. She said, "I'm so glad to be in Europe I could kiss the copings." We passed a girl with mops of long hair, Djuna said, "There's virginity with a stress." She said she couldn't imagine an English husband indulging in connubial bliss. She said, "I can't see them bending." Tony said, "Well they sway a little." Djuna said the trolley buses had trolleys to give them an antique look; she liked the taxis, said she wanted the high hip model. She said she had missed the boat entirely (we told her she should marry an English millionaire) because she couldn't "lie in the bush without a heart." She then got on to my hat which she liked from the front but objected to a ribbon hanging off behind. She said, "Boys that wear those don't pass the grade." And "you can't afford to accentuate that notion." She said Sonia was "a low-running smouldering Jewish trouble creeping up on you from the back."

---

[4]The "girls" are those who frequented Barney's lesbian salon in Paris like Solita Solano (1888-1975), American writer and long-time partner of *New Yorker* journalist Janet Flanner, and Margaret Anderson (Barnes letter to Coleman May 24, 1936, F. 17). Dorothy ("Dolly") Wilde (1895-1941), niece of Oscar Wilde, was a heroin addict and a lover of Barney's since 1927.
[5]This section of her 1933 diary is not extant.
[6]Hilda Doolittle (1886–1961), American imagist poet.

We had hilarity all the way to the village where we had tea. Tony and I were screaming with laughter. Peter sat driving with his smile from ear to ear which could not be seen from the back. At tea we were describing Siepmann to Djuna and she said he sounded as if he had "a little bit of badger blood." I tried to get Peter to give an imitation of Garman but he couldn't. I began imitating his voice and Djuna said, "Rather like a rook at nightfall—I see." We said he could be vindictive under certain conditions, Djuna said worrying, "I'll provide the conditions." We kept reassuring her. Peter said Garman "only got a little rancid." We looked at Djuna's passport photo. Peter said it resembled a benign Frenchwoman lecturing on theosophy and hypnotism—Djuna said my old passport photo looked as if I were "a girl convict let out to see the world." I told Djuna I had "got used" to Garman finally—she said, "It's the things we get used to that wear us down." I said Hayford Hall was heavenly, "so full of life, and congenial people—though couldn't get on with any of them." In the back of the car with Djuna I told her she was a joy to me, that it was wonderful to be in a party and be stimulated myself; since John died I had to give all the stimulation wherever I was. She said Peter was like a little black honey bear holding the pot—all the honey was gone and he was looking for it—and it was gone. I could not bear this—"It's true!" I said. Djuna said, "He's got something else in the pot" trying to change it. Peter said, one of the few times he spoke from his set joyful smile—"Djuna is a kindly magic grandmother, trying to put something in my pot." In the evening I said, when we were all making a noise—"What's in his pot now?" Djuna said, "Wasps." I told her she said at Hayford Hall that her mother thought her father was "Shelley on horseback" when she saw him. Djuna said "yes but he dismounted." She said Peter was my "little thermos bottle of love."

We had drinks at a pub, Djuna coming freezing into the pub, alone with Peter and saying loudly "I'll need my astrakhan drawers if I stay in this climate," and all the Whit-Monday inmates of the pub looking around surprised. Then we went on to Leatherhead where we had a very good dinner. I launched forth on Gerhardi's *Resurrection* and put up an intelligent and impassioned defence of it, against Peter and Djuna, answering them both at once.[7] Tony agreed with me but said little. She doesn't flower in this hothouse air, has to have a little quiet stream to herself. But she enjoys it, like a child at a banquet. Tony said that I "tried to walk in 2 dimensions," Djuna said I had that "staggering, stumbling, I-must-pipi look (you'll never know because you can't see yourself behind)—and she doesn't look as if she believed there

---

[7] Gerhardi(e)'s autobiographical novel *Resurrection* (1934) was dedicated "To the Memory of John Holms."

was a comfort station in the world either"—"Our little Buster, hurrying to perdition." This last referring to my hat.[8]

Tony told Djuna she dreamed about her, and Djuna asked for her smelling salts, and when Tony said she'd done it twice Djuna said, "This is collusion!" We got home about 11 and I made Djuna go to bed as her health is not good, to Peter's dismay, who seems never to get enough of her. She is a breath of God's light life and heaven. I didn't know at all how I needed her. Virtues come home to roost—I made Peggy bring her over, for Djuna's sake, and feel as if I couldn't let her leave the flat though I nearly died preparing for her. At dinner I told her how much I thought of *Man the Unknown*.[9] Peter adores Djuna and I feel this may change my life.

Djuna in bed, I made tea for Peter, Tony, and me downstairs and Tony and I talked about Djuna, Peter not contributing anything. He loves her. But doesn't like women to let go. Tony said she had never seen anything like her brilliance—that it was dazzling, and like no one she had ever seen or heard of. She said Djuna's wit gave her a sense of death underneath. I reminded Peter of what he had felt about the pictures. We agreed we had had the best day in many months—a really paean day, recalling—(I told Djuna this morning)—John and the life and gayety he gave us. I can't think when I have been so happy with four people, since Hayford Hall.

This morning I took Djuna in her tea and we started off as in New York, talking about Peter my love and Peter Neagoe.[10] I got her Hoare's electric iron and she washed and ironed.

I took her out to lunch (she dressed up in a tailored brown outfit, natty to the teeth) and we talked for some time more. I then put her in the taxi to send her to Eliot. I told her to ask for the American rights, and—if she could get it—an advance. As we walked in King's Road, me clutching her arm I said, "Think Djuna last winter walking along MacDougall Street if you'd thought that in one year you'd be walking in London to meet T.S. Eliot to get a contract for your book!"[11]

---

[8]The reference is to Joseph Frank "Buster" Keaton (1895–1966), the American slapstick actor and film director who created his own version of the porkpie hat (felt or straw with a flat top) for his films.

[9]Alexis Carrel (1873–1944) was a French doctor and author of the bestselling eugenicist-themed book *L'Homme, Cet Inconnu*, or *Man the Unknown* (1935).

[10]Coleman was referring to being with Barnes in New York in early 1935, when she had assisted Barnes with *Nightwood*.

[11]Steeped in literary and cultural history, MacDougall Street is one of the most famous streets in Greenwich Village.

Djuna hasn't returned yet, I am longing to hear what transpired, and Peter is coming to dinner to hear all of it from her own lips.

She is very physical about people, part of the animal that is so strong in her. People ought to be more like that. Tried to talk to her about what I feel of life and life eternal but she thinks I'm a little "befogged by my idea of a future life." I got her to try to explain what she sees when she says, "In the resurrection, when we come up looking backward, I shall see you only of all that company."[12] She sees this life, thinks that is only a feeling, does not believe it happens. She means her love for Thelma is eternal in this life.

Peter called up then, just an hour before I expected him, after I had been counting on it all day and got the food for dinner and was expecting to have a sweet evening, with Djuna talking about Eliot—to say that he couldn't come as his sister (India) phoned and he had to see her—If this isn't like him—letting me down eternally just at the moment when I'm feeling best. But possibly he called up late to hear about Djuna and Eliot (she has not come back yet—6–45).

Wednesday, June 3

Djuna came home from Eliot and said first of all (after a whiskey) she liked him, he was sweet. She liked his sad eyes and what I called his clown smile. A little later she said, "I don't know why, when you get educated, you have to act like an old bath cloth." Later, "I can't understand why they go so goddamned dead the minute they hit Dante." She was rather annoyed with me, in fact now I think of it she looked sad when she came in, and asked for a drink—that must have been it; because very shortly she produced the note I had attached to the ms., saying that if necessary, I should think the first and some later chapter could be omitted—(the chapters about Felix), which I, in a passion of worry (the part about Felix being dull and the whole thing unconnected with the book, and having found Eliot unwilling to read even the excerpts) had written.[13] It looked odd. I had forgotten about it and Djuna said I hadn't written her that; also there were places where I had obliterated certain phrases. I had written her all this, which was of course only done to get them to read it—I not intending to change anything without her permission, but she is so difficult about criticism and I hadn't had much time, being desperate

---

[12]In *Nightwood*'s chapter "Night Watch," Nora Flood watches her lover Robin Vote prepare to abandon her for the evening, yet again: "Half narcoticized by the sounds and the knowledge that this was in preparation for departure, Nora spoke to herself: 'In the resurrection, when we come up looking backward at each other, I shall know you only of all that company'" (52).

[13]In the novel, the faux Baron Felix Volkbein marries Robin Vote. After their son, Guido, is born disabled, Robin leaves Felix and takes up with Nora Flood.

anyway so I sent it in that way and had forgotten it. She had said when she saw these deletions, "That girl would take anything out with a meat-axe." I went up in smoke. I was touchy anyway about what Eliot thought of me, he not having answered my letter about Milton, et al. This was the limit. I almost wept, tried to restrain myself, said little, but indicated that I thought Djuna had let me down, after what I had done (the care I had taken), with Eliot. She flew off and repeated over and over that she had told him "how wonderful I had been," like a mowing machine, while I endeavoured to get SOME sense of what people think of each other into her head.

   It was rather sad and I felt sick, as it all could have been avoided had I remembered to tell her this. On beholding the mss. she then would not have screamed. But as usual, only her feeling mattered, not mine, and I gave it up, though she was terribly hurt and soon would be, I feared, sorry I had got the book published for her! But it all came out all right, we had dinner (steak) and she began reading the Night Chapter, rather tight and her mouth full of tacks, as at Hayford Hall; I knew almost every word of it and was so happy to hear it again (not having seen the mss. for 7 months), got lost completely in the wonderful meanings of the sleep and dream parts. Djuna was annoyed that Peter did not come, but by this time we were both in the ether and had forgotten him. He appeared about half-past ten, popping with eagerness and shame, and Djuna took a drink and started. She went over the whole ms and told us every word Eliot and Morley had said, page by page. She said Morley was "a great cabin trunk with nothing in it." She said when Eliot made one correction, "I'll take anything from you, Mr. Eliot." "What did he say?" "Oh he perked up like a hound's ear—it may be a rabbit, it may be a porcupine!" She said E[liot]. was "liberated in a horrifying way." They got on balls, testicles, and pubic hair. They were embarrassed and Djuna was vigilant. Djuna said he had that wise but lenient look when he corrected her spelling. "I said, 'Who can spell?' then I said, 'Eliot, I can tell from your face that you can spell.'" She forgot herself and called him Eliot. She said E[liot]. and M[orley]. behaved like "little boys in their first long pants shriven of their Faber & Faber history." In one place Eliot suggested "foreign diplomat" for "Danish minister." "Isn't that a bit stiff?" Djuna says. At one point where she says "mortadello" (which Peter at once corrected to "mortadella"), Eliot and Morley said, "What is that?" It had an obscene suggestion. "It's an Italian sausage," Djuna said. "I gathered," Djuna reports E[liot]. to have said, "That it was a sausage." At one point Eliot changed the word buggers to boys. Djuna said to me, "Imagine trying to wake Eliot up!" I said, "Yes, he's rather ascetic." "Looks as if his testicles had been tied in a Greek knot," said Djuna. "He looks as if slippery elm had gone through him for years, with early Greek phrases on it." At one point there was a discussion of whether bird's nest had the suggestion of pubic hair.

Peter was delighted with Eliot's handwriting on the margins, read them all; Djuna said she would cut them out and give them to him! He sat absolutely fascinated. Djuna told him off for not coming to our family party, her big night. He was awfully ashamed. All the things he will not take from Peggy and me (which make him uneasy), from big breezy Djuna he seems to delight in.

Before Peter came, and she began to read, I read her my two letters to Eliot, the first ones, and his two replies. She sat listening to the one which made him read it, in the sweet way she can listen (in NY) like a young girl, putting her whole mind on it. She loved the letter. She said it was genius.

Peggy came. Said Tony looked like "a whole shop-window moving forward." Djuna told how Annie N[eagoe]. calls her Djunia. Peggy said she would soon be calling her Senior.

Djuna very funny trying to get Hoare to tell when he was going away. She did this to help me, though she partly wanted to know, to know when she could see me. She got a little tight. Said of Eliot—"Do not commit a nuisance! (As though anyone would think of posting a bill)." Began—"Peter darling, when are you nesting?" "I'm nesting on china eggs," he said. "I'm unsettled on my clutch." She thought he meant his car. "Yes, I've noticed it." She said, "Come, tell us. You're very annoying, even as a friend, dear. We love you, but we want to have a life." He said, "Nothing on earth could stop you from having a life." She loved that, held his hand. He looked at his watch. "He keeps shooting his cuff" she said, "Give him Big Ben." Later, he was wandering around. "You shift about like a fog," she said. Speaking of my portrait she said, "You look like that when you're resisting the pull of gravity." He said, "It's like a shark." She said, "Emily is a little like a shark." Peter said, "She doesn't have to turn on her back to eat at any rate." He complained that the smaller picture looked dark and negroid at night. "What do you think YOU look like at night?" Djuna said.

She read her book out loud. Peter sat and loved it. It was a charming evening. I made her read some of it over again, and I read some of it, because she reads as if she had hot potatoes in her mouth. I was moved to the point of tears, by a phrase I had not noticed—"Shadow boxing, that the heart may be murdered."[14]

---

[14]In the chapter "Watchman, What of the Night?" Dr. O'Connor talks to Nora Flood: "'And do I know my Sodomites?' the doctor said unhappily, 'and what the heart goes bang up against if it loves one of them, especially if it's a woman loving one of them. What do they find then, that this lover has committed the unpardonable error of not being able to exist—and they come down with a dummy in their arms. God's last round, shadow boxing, that the heart may be murdered and swept into that still, quiet place where it can sit and say: 'Once I was, now I can rest'" (79).

She had this followed by an explanatory phrase, as she often does, and I begged her to eliminate it. Peter demurred. Djuna said, "No, she's marvellous about this sort of thing." She cut it out. I was terribly moved by passages I had known. Djuna reads abominably, she gets her teeth all in it and has no expression. She knows it; she never reads except when she's tight, and this accentuates a natural impediment. Peter really loved what she read. It was a great event.

Djuna and I went around in Chelsea. She loved the small 18th century houses. One studio was marked Pipsworth. She was going to marry that man and be Djuna Pipsworth, have that studio. I showed her Cheyne Row, Cheyne Walk, Church Street, Chelsea Church. We had tea in Battersea Park, under the limes there.

I read her my <u>last</u> letter to Eliot, in the morning. She nearly split with laughing. It seemed funny to me too. Read out loud, it was incredible. It just went on and on. "Patronizing Eliot!" said Djuna. She said I was wonderful. She said I should be put on a monument. She said she loved me. We screamed with laughter, picking out phrases. I said, "I suppose I got spoiled, writing to John about everything I wanted to know." Djuna said, "Yes, dear, but he wasn't working for Faber & Faber!" I realized Eliot would never answer it, felt like a fool. We read my Melville poem, Djuna said it was a "great poem." We went over it, changing some things. Djuna described Cecil Beaton[15]— "He's always starting up with a handkerchief."

I asked Connolly to tea, and Tony. Connolly and Djuna looked at each other like 2 dogs. Tony held forth in a literary way, doing very well. I showed Connolly Djuna's book, told him about it. He read parts, but we were talking and he couldn't see it; he likes personalities better than literature. He was afraid of the book—Tony thought. He spoke sincerely and well of the *S. of Snow*. I said, "Now darn it, you haven't mentioned it—what did you think?" He said he enjoyed on the first page, after a description of the hall, the calm statement, "the grating where we threw the plates."[16] Mrs. Belloc-Lowndes, sister of H. Belloc, wants to meet me.[17] An old lady in an 18th cent. house in Westminster, almost wears caps. Djuna's (grandmother) cup of tea. I will meet her and arrange her for Djuna. This lady loves the *S. of Snow*. Writes thrillers, knows everybody, aged 70 busting with life.

---

[15]Sir Cecil Walter Hardy Beaton (1904–1980), English stage and costume designer for film, theatre, opera, and ballet, as well as photographer, artist, and author.

[16]Coleman's novel opens with a description of the hall, and then the room, of the psychiatric hospital to which the protagonist has been committed: "There was nothing in the room but the bed and the chicken wire and high up on the wall the iron grating where she threw the plates" (Dalkey edn. 3).

[17]Marie Adelaide (Belloc) Lowndes (1868–1947), writer of popular fiction. Her brother, Hilaire Belloc (1870–1953), was a poet and author.

I liked Connolly enormously. He sat on the couch, I stood before the fire, Djuna in the big chair, Tony in the little squat one. Conversation was lively, interesting, original and agreeable. Peter was playing golf, Home Office handicap (this was Saturday). We had tickets reserved for [Chekhov's] *The Seagull*, but the conversation was so pleasant, things were so humming (never has this happened in my quarters since America), that I phoned and cancelled them, saying they should all stay for supper of bacon and eggs. C[onnolly]. had to go home—Tony was meeting Tom—so agreeing to meet afterwards we broke up, at 7–30. Peter came and we dined at Queen's. Took him to the Connollys' after. In the afternoon somebody said, "Cigarettes are a substitute for masturbation." Connolly said in a weak pleasant voice, "But why should people substitute anything for masturbation?"

We went there, it was frosty. Djuna sat like a rigid Venus, legs crossed, head cocked, with mannish hat, in center of room, did not get on. Tom came, wet and pulsating. Peter sat like a little lost codfish. I made perpetual conversation, shaking my bottom about, Connolly wandering restlessly and subversively. Mrs. C[onnolly]. amiable and doing nothing—she is an ideal hostess. Little Tony sat on the couch, quite tight, beaming radiantly in her dimples, smiling and taking up literature as she'd a mind to.

Tony alive and really sweet. I love her when tight—she was nicer than anyone—free, delightful, happy, and lively. I like Mrs. C. who is heavy and listless—. She is charming. Mispronounced Goethe, Quennell didn't know what she meant, corrected it, she said—"Well, Goethe then." (This was the next day (Sunday) when Tony and I were invited to lunch, to meet Quennell.) In the morning I talked to Djuna about Hoare; the phone rang—Deak! I arranged to meet him, hung up, and burst into tears.[18]

Went to lunch at the Connollys,' Quennell entered, high-set-up young man with thin wide mouth; sensitive turned out nose. He is either sweet or wretched. He is tall, moves about self-consciously, smiling, one shoulder wider than the other, rather chic, but fake. His face is tired. He is about 33. He is malicious, villainous (can be in his eyes); he is, when handled, lovable, trusting and lively. Full of life. Is intelligent, prejudiced, cold, vain to a point of insanity, horrible, at moments; lovable and gentle when at home. Very self-conscious, fearful. I mentioned *Zeno*—since he was so mean about Beryl de Zoete (buggery I fancy). He did not like it. I made myself objectionable by praising it. Tony told what I did about Djuna's book. I said, "I'm not English: it is just too bad if Eliot did not know a good book when he saw one." Everyone looked admiringly. Connolly loving me yet scared. I retrieved myself

---

[18]Coleman explained why later in the entry.

with Quennell by praising his review of Charles Morgan which I thought was a masterpiece.[19]

I came away, Connolly gave me his book the night before, "Emily from Cyril."[20] I hadn't read it yet. Took away Quennell's *Baudelaire* (looked at some short stories of his, but did not take any), George Beaton's first book (which is nonsense), and the *Tropic of Cancer*, by one Henry Miller, a terrifying American.[21] It contains talent. Djuna borrowed it, really, from C[onnolly], Saturday night. I promised to return all Thursday; asked me to lunch.

Came back to meet Deak and Djuna, encouraged Deak to get off one of his sagas; they burst with laughter. All dined together (after hearing some of *Figaro*—the heavenly joy of that!), Deak, Peter and Djuna got on. After they retired I went to see Peter. He made me mad, "sitting there taking everything for granted" (Phyllis' remark—as Djuna says—"that man acts as if he gave you a full sexual life every night")—I said, "I've got an idea. I think I'll have a platonic friendship with you, and a love affair with Barker." This made him frantic, he got up and said, "Get out of here!" I thought he was going to throw a cup at me.

In the morning I told him I was sorry, on the phone, said I said it deliberately to be shittish. He was sweet and forgiving. There is no point in doing things like this to him. Go away from him, don't see him, but when you do see him, be sweet. Or nothing.

Put Djuna on the train.[22] She was nervous about meeting Garman. Very glad to have the flat to myself, get sleep, re-orientate my life, and inner life again. She returning Thursday. Long to see her again. The problem will be solved by her living in London, near me. Can't have the cottage near Peggy. Lunched with Deak & Harman, sweet, bullet-headed, frightfully sensitive young Cambridge man who loves Deak.

I told Djuna I wept because Deak had been so good to me, and I did not want that, I wanted an intense, struggling life. The sight of Deak and his angelic magnanimous nature was too much for me; the absolute sweet tenderness of his feeling for me, which will always be and which he expresses

---

[19]Charles Morgan (1894–1958), English novelist, critic, and playwright, was the chief drama critic for *The Times* from 1926–1939. Quennell reviewed Morgan's novel *Sparkenbroke* (published by the Obelisk Press in 1936) in the column "New Novels" in the Saturday, April 4, 1936 issue of the *New Statesman and Nation*.
[20]*The Rock Pool*.
[21]Quennell's *Baudelaire and the Symbolists: Five Essays* (1929). Coleman had earlier read Beaton's *Jack Robinson* (1933). Henry Miller's (1891–1980) *Tropic of Cancer*, the sexually explicit autobiographical novel about a down and out writer, was published by the Obelisk Press in 1934 but was banned in the United States until 1961.
[22]Barnes was going to visit Guggenheim at Yew Tree Cottage.

in John now.[23] He is happy with his wife, and she is all I never was, and what he needs to make him contented—sexually materially and companionately; but his heart—whatever it was—his youth—was with me.

Thursday, June 11

I need to struggle, to live, being not only an artist but a woman and a saint— that is, I have saintly aspirations. I mean that the perfection of my character is more important to me than art; if they conflict, I will choose the former. I hate the evil in me—I recognize it, and perpetually strive to change it: this is certainly one of the conditions of sainthood; though my manners and behaviour might not convince the outside observer that such was so.

Friday, June 12

Djuna's 44th birthday. She didn't come yesterday instead I got a silly telegram from Garman rousing me from bed in the morning—I didn't know what it was all about and was irritated because my life is unpleasant. Read the beginning of the *Tropic of Cancer* published by the Obelisk Press in Paris (as Connolly's and Charles' [Morgan] books were), by one Henry Miller, an American whose face I had seen and not liked at all in *Americans Abroad* nor had I liked what he wrote about himself.[24] Did not read his story there, put off by the sensual glum look of his face—the boredom and bald rank mawkiness of it. But this book is another story—it is wonderful! I don't know what to think yet—have only read half. It is so true and so beautiful in parts, so radiant with happy life, bursting with Melville the Whale Life the Continents America and all the soul undeveloped of our continent. Here is the first. Djuna's is the first good book to come out of America (perhaps *The Enormous Room*—I know not the *S[hutter]. of S[now].*—if that's good)—but Djuna's is not American.[25] This book of H. Miller's is. I wonder what is coming—where

---

[23]Coleman has underlined this sentence by hand. She has also written at the bottom of the page: "I forget—forget—my life with Deak" ("forget" has been underlined twice).
[24]Miller, who had appeared alongside Coleman in the *Americans Abroad* anthology, wrote the following autobiographical entry: "Born in N. Y. City, 1891. No schooling. Was tailor, personnel director in large corporation, ranch-man in California, newspaperman, hobo and wanderer. Was a 6-day bike racer, a concert pianist, and in my spare time I practice saint-hood. Came to Paris to study vice." The story he included is "Mademoiselle." When Miller arrived in Paris in March 1930, he spent his first month in the same place Coleman had resided: Hôtel Saint-Germain on the rue Bonaparte.
[25]*The Enormous Room* (1922), autobiographical record of internment during WWI by American poet e. e. cummings (1894–1962).

it leads to. Excited me most terribly. It's an "obscene" book—nothing in it shocked me.

Went to see Connollys, they not in, had a terrible from the curse in the womb [sic], took a mouthful of gin at the C's unbeknownst to them, feeling rotten, read *Vogues*, left, staggering under 4 bottles of beer which I bought to prepare for tonight. Peggy phoned Djuna was not coming—I was pretty mad. She had a bad hangover—as I thought, they had been tight.

"So now I shall be alone with Barker" I thought trembling. Barker came, brown, looking sweet and very handsome. I had my arms around his neck, weeping violently. He made a little love to me. I could not respond, one inch, I felt nothing sexual. I felt, "I may begin to love him!" and it broke my heart, I was sick and felt the ground going from me and all the horror beginning of last fall—I became hysterical and broke away from him. He was so sweet, understands nothing, except that I'm miserable, was so patient. I made him dinner—I don't know what we talked about. The phone rang at 9—Tony, by appointment—I threw my arms around Barker's neck and pressed my face close to his—I felt so sorry for him because he has lost this beastly job—which he longed for—and his face is so beautiful, so good.[26] Tony came and looked sweet, in a crinoline brown striped gown with billows—I suppose she looked very silly—I suppose Phyllis would roar at her—honestly I thought she looked lovely in it—suited her style, she billowed in every direction, sitting in the center of it, suavely smoking. I love Tony—she came in feeling cross and Barker put his foot in it at once as usual. He said, "Why aren't you writing?" and then went on to add, "It's probably just laziness." This would I knew start Tony into probably screams of hysteria, and rightly, since it's a sore point with her, and why should it not be when she knows she has something real to say (suspects it—<u>I know</u> it—about her) and can't write and here are people popping all about her in creative and uncreative productions? I calmed this by silencing Barker and hinting he should have some tact, etc., she then went after him and said he only wanted to be praised. I laughed so hard it eased them both.

When [Barker] left I saw him to the hall and I kissed him, and looked at him. He thinks the worst thing is his rejection by the Durham authorities—his being without money. He will have 3 pounds a week now, I have promised it to him. I am giving him one pound, Peggy & Sonia I trust the other 2. He does not know who is giving it to him. I do not know the grinding drag of poverty.

Talking of St. Teresa, Tony said she was a gourmet for favours. I told Tony it was a temptation to me, the contemplative life (in a convent)—if I were not a writer (i.e. must know the world) I would ask for nothing but the beauty

---

[26] See her entry for May 13, 1936.

of the contemplative life, in the country, <u>entirely free</u> of the world. "It's the compromise that eats me," I said. "I want either to make love from morning till night for 5 years; or else retire to a convent; anything short of that is killing me." Tony looked alarmed, did not want me to inflame Barker. Barker loved Djuna's portrait of me.

Arthur Waley asked me to lunch—I am going now.

On the bus going to Arthur Waley thinking why the *Tropic of Cancer* is not obscene. <u>Not my life</u>—could not live that life—any more than I could live the life of Djuna's book: but it IS LIFE, is genuine. Nothing that is <u>real</u> is obscene. It is the foul mind of man makes it so. The most villainous scenes in Miller's book are observed naturally—even when one man observes another "fucking" it's natural—nothing extraneous, just the ordinary observation of the man whose zest for life is so great it includes everything. The word c-u-n-t is the one word in the whole world I really cannot stand pronouncing. But these things are habit—I couldn't stand "shit" before I came to England, nor "fuck" before I heard the innocent way Peggy uses it. The Americans in Paris talked this way—I've heard them enough. The bistro he talks about must be the one across from the *Tribune*—it must be the *Tribune* he worked on.[27] That life is natural—it's degraded, it's horrifying—to me now—but it IS life, genuine, real, more real than their life in America, in smug small towns and bourgeois liaisons. It's better for them to have whores and talk about cunts than for them to be lying Sunday school teachers and pay their debts; that's what these people once were. The *Tribune* and Paris is a <u>step</u>. It's <u>honesty, first</u>. <u>Cast off the old skin</u>. Hemingway, Faulkner, Kay Boyle have as much talent—but their standards are false. <u>This one has come through to honest values</u>. It's not the obscenity of Joyce; the convent masturbator.

Arthur Waley is beautiful, from the side, had not noticed it. His profile is strong and thoughtful, sensitive. Front face he is tight-lipped and his eyes are rather like Peter Quennell's—no they are better—they are burning eyes, burning with some kind of fire? He looked—as I've always thought—like a monkey. He is a darling. I got on with him better than ever.

Came home, Djuna here, bought her 17th century poetry for her birthday. She took it calmly. She said Peggy made queer remarks about money. If she

---

[27]Miller worked as a proof-reader of stock market reports on the *Tribune* from 1931–1932. The bistro is Gillotte's, across the street from the *Tribune* offices on rue Lamartine. In the novel, Gillotte's becomes Monsieur Paul's: "At Monsieur Paul's, the bistro across the way, there is a back room reserved for the newspapermen where we can eat on credit. It is a pleasant little room with sawdust on the floor and flies in season and out. When I say that it is reserved for the newspapermen I don't mean to imply that we eat in privacy; on the contrary, it means that we have the privilege of associating with the whores and pimps who form the more substantial element of Monsieur Paul's clientele" (139).

does it in front of me she'll test my friendship. Saw her Faber contract, seems to me unfair—I advised her to stick for the American rights. She has gone now, seeing Eliot—I asked her to please not get me further in wrong with him. She'll get it wrong, make some further ruin for me. I'll get nothing but shit for having slaved for this book—of that I'm mortally sure. Garman's already said to her, "Did you write any of the book yourself?" I said, "A few more cracks for this book and somebody's going to get killed." She was confused, loves me, is dazed by me, doesn't understand, wants to know me—I love her and in time we will make a good team. There's everything in her I admire, even brains if you can dig them out, and I will make sacrifices to know her—though I must say at this precise moment I don't feel like making sacrifices for anybody but myself. I would like to make love to Barker—for hours—for hours! I will read the *Tropic of Cancer* now, and finish it, before taking it over to Connolly.

I went to the Connollys' to a Surrealist cocktail party, met David Gascoyne and Humphrey Jennings, who were a relief after some of the pills I've had.[28] I liked them; got a little tight, took their addresses. Gascoyne likes Barker, is the first person I've met who speaks understandingly of him.[29] Eliot did not. Eliot is <u>very</u> conventional, even about geniuses. Djuna loves him, wants him; says his "organ is in the Church." Saw Peter Quennell at the party, he was very sweet to me.

I am in a madhouse. Peggy has left Garman, Tony is going into the hospital to be operated upon, Djuna does not know where she is or what to do; Phyllis is unhappy about Stephan.[30] And I—God knows what is happening to <u>me</u>, that little life that seems so colossal to me when I am alone; now it hardly seems to matter what happens to me. I am going up to Yorkshire on the 1st of July. Many things have gone on. I can't remember most of them. Peter took Djuna

---

[28]David Gascoyne (1916–2001) was considered something of a prodigy when his first volume of poems, *Roman Balcony and Other Poems* (1932), was published in England when he was only sixteen. His *A Short Survey of Surrealism* (1935) set him up as one of the chief propounders of the movement in Europe, as did his translations of many French surrealists. Humphrey Jennings (1907–1950), English poet, painter, and documentary film-maker, was one of the organizers of the 1936 Surrealist Exhibition in London and a founder of the Mass Observation project (1937). He died falling off a cliff on the Greek island of Poros while scouting for film locations.

[29]Barker's biographer Fraser reports that, "Throughout the autumn of 1936 both Barker and Gascoyne were frequent visitors to Oakley Street, at Coleman's flat and at White's. The closeness of the two addresses was later to give rise to the misnomer, the 'Oakley Street Poets'"; "Despite the lack of a shared artistic programme, however, the network of friendship persisted" with Coleman carrying a torch for Barker, White for Gascoyne (86–87).

[30]As previously noted, White had an infection of the cervix; Stephan was Phyllis Jones' married lover.

and me up to her ancestral home in Rutland.[31] If she were writing the diary something different would come out; it meant life to her. I enjoyed it as a country weekend. Little churches, churchyards, gardens, meadows, birds, old houses, hawthorn hedge-rows. She likes old towns because they are old; not because they're beautiful.

I read the *Tropic of Cancer* which is a terrible book, brutal, cruel, lovely; containing the most dreadful truths—from a shallow mind. It is ugly, but in the end, in spite of the horrible picture one sometimes gets of him, I would like this person: I could not help liking anyone who suffered so much from creation. More about it later—how I have read it I don't know, with no moment to breathe—talking to Djuna—so strange she is, so absolutely uncomprehending when I put anything in my language. Yet she sees everything. She called Hoare "that little indomitable Scotch rubber plant." He sings in the bath—that really stumps Djuna. "What with his voice and his Home Office, he's got his sex life solved." She said of me, "She talks in longhand and writes in shorthand and I can't understand either." She said, describing Connolly to Peggy: "an old lady knitting his jock-strap." (This terrified me). She said of Garman that he wasn't human, he was "a doll, that says Communism when you pinch its stomach."[32] She said, "I never did talk about my life much, till Emily got me corroded." We read Donne's "Ecstasy"—I read it to Peggy and Djuna, to show Peggy what Djuna had with Thelma. Djuna had not read the poem. She drives me crazy in human ways (as I drive others mad), but the look on her face when you read poetry to her makes up for life, death, and her internal jungle.

I told her yesterday I was dying—felt death in my bitterest inward love (for Hoare). Peter took us to Hampton Court. She said she wanted to live there, "could be Shakespeare if she could get a 6-month's lease on the place."[33] Peter said he couldn't stand it, that he would be depressed by it. She said, "I want to be alive, in the midst of death." Then looking at him, "Not dead, in the midst of life." This went home.

---

[31]Barnes' mother, Elizabeth Chappell (1862–1945), an aspiring poet, had been born in the East Midlands, England, in the county of Rutland (now Leicestershire), in the town of Oakham. Her home was called Flore House. Barnes would later use the house, fictionalized as "Burley Hall," in her autobiographical play *The Antiphon* (1958).

[32]A fervent member of the Communist Party, Garman had been working as a lecturer at the Marx Memorial Library and Workers School. As Guggenheim would later describe him, "Garman went around the country in a second-hand car he had bought for the purpose, giving lectures and trying to recruit new members" (*Out of This Century* 152).

[33]The group had gone to Surrey to visit Hampton Court, the palace of Henry VIII and later of William and Mary, during the week of June 15, 1936. Though this entry is dated Friday, June 12, Coleman used it to write up events that took place during the following week, as she made clear later in the entry: "this is the 17th)."

I told Djuna Hoare loved me more when I went away—could not stand it—etc., she said, "If you go away far enough maybe he'll get married to you." I said even if I knew foreign languages I wouldn't dare to criticize literature in them—Dj. said, "I'll write my next book in Swedish." Tony going into the hospital today. She is to be operated upon tomorrow afternoon. It is ostensibly a minor thing—I will not go into the gory female details which Dj. and Peggy love. This diary is the pattern of my life. If Djuna wrote it, it would be all Oakham, and Hampton Court, and her friends' madness, and her lack of privacy and what should she do with her life, and Eliot and her book. She saw him again. He said, "Mrs. Coleman seems to be a little tense." Very funny, I thought. You dear creature, some day you'll say Blake was a little tense too; made this statement to Peter and Djuna in Rutland, to their great embarrassment. If Peggy wrote it my darling little flower at this moment she doesn't know what it would be—she left Garman—for the night. Has really left him, in her heart.

Djuna told me yesterday morning (this is the 17th) all about her youth and adolescence—it is plain why she turned to a Lesbian love—sex was horrible to her—her father—a horror of the first water, what a terrible man—and she had to make love to his friend at 16 to please him, to start her off, supposed to marry him.[34] Violence, fights and horror were all she knew in her childhood, no one loving her except her grandmother—whom she passionately loved. Her father, when she was 16, behaved in a way so inconceivably wicked that one does not know why such persons are not wiped off the earth. He tried to make love to her—she was washing dishes—he came out and said, "Now you're 16 I've always wanted to know you then," [removed his organ from his trowsers] (I really can't see it).[35]

Djuna fled to the barn where she was found screaming by her mother who went after her father with a meat-axe. They lived with her father's mistress and her children, besides the 5 children of Djuna's mother.[36] There

---

[34]Barnes' father (1865–1934) was born in Massachusetts as Henry Aaron Budington, but as Barnes' biographer Herring indicates, he went by various names such as Harry, Harold, Wald, and Brian Eglinton Barnes. Herring describes him as "an itinerant musician, painter, and writer, who was content to be supported by his own mother's journalism while he fiddled and sowed his seed wherever a field was in want of a plowshare (xviii)." Herring suggests the "friend" was Charles Titus, who lived next door to the Barnes' Huntington, Long Island farm (268). Herring also draws attention to the likelihood that Djuna had a sexual relationship with her paternal grandmother, Zadel Barnes (see earlier note), for they slept together for years, and Zadel wrote her granddaughter sexually charged letters throughout her adolescence (54–55).
[35]Coleman has crossed out by hand the line "removed his organ from his trowsers" (though it remains legible) and the statement "(I really can't see it)" has been added by hand.
[36]Barnes' father married Elizabeth Chappell in 1889, and by 1897 his mistress, Fanny Faulkner (Mrs. Elizabeth F. Clark), moved in with him and the rest of the Barnes clan. Barnes and

was filth and violence for 18 years, then the law descended on him and he had to marry the mistress, which he did out of fear of going to prison. A fanatic of the <u>brain</u>, a horror past imagining, he had not the guts to face his beliefs (polygamy), and married "Fanny" (Kate Careless—in *Ryder*) and left Djuna's mother.

This diary is mixed-up, it is now Thursday, June 18th, and I have been to see Tony in the hospital, where she was taken yesterday, to await an operation today, in her womb.[37] She was violent yesterday on being taken in, did not like the room, which made her think of the asylum.[38] She wanted to leap out the window. Today she was better and I soon had her laughing like anything at a surgeon who came in like an undertaker and said, "Dr. Beaver will give you what you want. Dr. Beaver will give you anything," then retired. Tony said she hoped Dr. Beaver, whoever he was, did not realize what she really did want. She was reading *Maurice Guest* and got me excited about it—I looked at the beginning and could hardly bear not to take it now.

. . . Going into Peter's desolate flat, so empty, so precise, and yet disorderly, with the disorder of absolute death, <u>I wonder what I am doing in this galère. I wonder truly. How did I get in?—Through wrong motives, false designs</u>. I wanted truly to wake him up. It cannot be done—what I stand for is too horrifying to him, who wants security. Djuna said love, which should go through him like a cataract, goes through him with terrible, intense pain, as silver nitrate goes through the kidney. Peggy said he sang in the bath because one more night was over with, during which he had overcome sex. She said also it might be he sang because one more night was past in which I had not slept with someone else. . . .

I had tea with Gossy yesterday, gossiped, she told me about Glyndebourne. Peter and I are going there June 24, 25, 26th. If we were not going, I would break with him now, some kind of break. On whatever separation I make I will be crucified. <u>I am sick at heart—Djuna sustains me: I cannot exist alone</u>. Unless I could get up to Hubberholme, which I am going to do July 1st. When I have Johnny I will be able to live, better.

Faulkner had four children: Muriel, Duane, Buan, and Shiela, who died in infancy. Within the same time span (1890–1906), Barnes and Chappell had, in addition to Djuna, four sons: Thurn, Zendon, Saxon, and Shangar ("Charles"). Eventually Chappell moved out, taking her children to New York City in July 1912. She was divorced in November of that year, and the same month Harold Barnes married Faulkner. Barnes satirized Faulkner as "Kate Careless" in *Ryder* (Herring 28–41).
[37]Coleman has added above this line, in handwriting: "the thing women love most to talk about."
[38]Bethlem Royal Hospital.

Section 4

Glyndebourne, London, and Yorkshire
June 23–July 21, 1936

Coleman attended the Glyndebourne opera festival near Lewes, East Sussex, and then, after a brief return to London enjoyed a three-week sojourn in her beloved Hubberholme in Yorkshire. Accompanied by her son, she regained "strength and life and spiritual energy." She worked vigorously on her revisions to "The Tygon," in particular developing more fully the theme of sadism inspired by her taking stock of her liaisons with Hoare, Barker, and Bianchetti.

Tuesday, June 23

I am going to leave London tonight with Peter, en route for Glyndebourne, where we shall see, tomorrow, and two subsequent nights, *The Magic Flute*, *Cosi Fan Tutte* and *Don Giovanni*. I have lunched with Clutton-Brock.[1] He was sweet, tentative, gasping. He has invited me and Johnny to come to his 16th century country house.

   I went to see Tony in the hospital. Peggy and I had a sudden row in the corridor about whether or not I should tell Djuna that Peggy would never send her back to America. I flew off the handle and swore I'd never see Peggy; all was over between us if she did that. We nearly burst into tears. We went back in again to see Tony and she must have wondered what our expressions were about. Peggy brought her 2 dozen yellow roses—later she told me they were sixpence a dozen. Coming away she told me in the bus, after I had apologized, that her finances were in a bad state and that she worried about it; she gives so much money away that she has very little left. I almost wept,

---
[1] Alan Clutton-Brock (1904–1976), art critic and painter.

because I can't ever decide whether Peggy is a saint or the meanest person I ever met—and neither can she. She actually gives away 3/4 of her income, to a point where she is worried, sometimes, whether she has enough to buy herself a dress. The income tax, too, has taken a lot of money.

Tony much better—yesterday I gave her a long lecture on her behaviour—she thinks she is dirt under Tom's feet. I told her what Tom was. (I've never done this before.) She felt much better. She is coming out of the hospital next week, and going to Peggy's when she gets out. Djuna lovely, says "that girl is wonderful (me); she'll introduce you to your own mother and tell you you ought to get to know her; she'll read your works out loud and tell you you wrote them, don't understand them and should improve them." In the Good Intent as we were leaving I said, "Did I bring anything in here?" Djuna said, "Nothing but your crashing sensibility and the javelins in your pants, dear." She says I am (with Hoare) the wrong girl on the right track.[2]

I got off Tuesday night for Uckfield with Peter—a strange departure, since I couldn't pack, but kept talking to Djuna in a frantic way, she lying in bed. We got to Uckfield at one o'clock, after losing our way two or three times. It was horribly depressing—I slept in a tiny hard-bed room, in fact did not sleep.

Wednesday we went to Eastbourne, I feeling better at being away from London and Djuna (whom I love but when she is there I can't live in myself.)

We went to "Beachy Head" and Peter made me look down the perpendicular cliff, to the blue water, above which seagulls flew. We lay on the down afterwards. We were not happy. We got back so late we were nearly late for our first night at Glyndebourne, we dressed and got there just as the doors were closing—we saw the *Magic Flute*.

The next day it rained and I stayed in reading *Axel's Castle*, an extraordinary book. It is by Edmund Wilson and is the best book of modern evaluations I have yet read.[3]

Boiling hot, we drove about trying to find Blackboys.[4] But Peter squelched me for something, as usual, and I struck him. He dropped the wheel of the car and turned to me, narrowing his eyes in such hatred that I never saw it on any face. He lifted his fist. I broke into hysterical tears, cried for fifteen minutes.

---

[2]Coleman spent the next three pages retelling events of the past two weeks; at the beginning of these pages she has written in hand: "Repetitious."
[3]*Axel's Castle: A Study in the Imaginative Literature of 1870 to 1930* (1931) includes essays on "Symbolism," "W. B. Yeats," "Paul Valéry," "T. S. Eliot," "Marcel Proust," "James Joyce," "Gertrude Stein," and "Axel and Rimbaud."
[4]A village in East Sussex

I was frightened out of my wits. I only slapped him lightly on the face. But what is there, ready to boil up at me. I can't forget it. I had nightmares afterward. In the afternoon, when I was in the bath, I heard him outside the door. I had an image of him, lurking around doors to think of me. I think he is some kind of sexual maniac. I got this intuition suddenly.

I stuck to my determination not to make love with him, and was cold and even mean to him so that he did not expect it. *Cosi Fan Tutte* the second night. We ate sandwiches in the car. We saw Bernard Shaw all 3 nights, "very clean" as Phyllis says, all pink and beard and nimble, with a soft nose.

We went to *Don Giovanni* the third night.

We went into the gardens before the play, between the acts, and, in the dark, after it was over. I saw James Strachey and talked to him, making him overstay his dinner and bewildering him with comments on Elvira.[5] The gardens were ravishing, but Peter was far from me. He said, speaking of Hayford Hall—"Any ordinary English person would have thought it was revolting." I turned on him like a wolf; I said, "It was life, not death! Go and have your ordinary English person—that has nothing to do with that life!" I couldn't speak to him, that remark made me so ill.[6]

I am trying to get this diary up to date. There is no time to write it in London, nor could I when I was away. Djuna saw Eliot again. She said, "You know that great cloud of enveloping kindness, that goes straight through you, into the Church." She does nevertheless adore him. My situation is ambiguous now, though she says it is not nearly so much so as I think, since I have dwelt on it intensely, and E[liot]. probably (so she says) has only thought of it once or twice, scratching his head. I have annoyed him, I'm certain, also taken up much of his time. At the same time pride demands that he should recognize I am not an imbecile, and try to excuse it. If he saw my writing he might—but as it is he is likely to be severe. (I sent "The Cremation" to *The Criterion*, impersonally, at Dj.'s suggestion.)[7]

---

[5] James Strachey (1887–1967), psychoanalyst, was the youngest of the ten Strachey children. In 1920 he had gone to Vienna as both a pupil and a patient of Freud, and he became the general English translator and editor of Freud's 5-volume *Collected Papers* (1924–50) as well as of the 24 volume *The Standard Edition of the Complete Psychological Works of Sigmund Freud* (1953–74). Strachey was also an expert on classical music, and wrote for Glyndebourne's programmes. Elvira, a character in *Don Giovanni*, was played by Luise Helletsgruber.

[6] Coleman and Hoare made their way back to London over the next two days via Winchester, Farnham, and Aylesbury.

[7] The poem was never published in this magazine. Coleman's archive contains three drafts of the poem, including the one noted here, completed in 1936, as well as the last one dated "final April 5, 1956 (F. 1685). The poem was published posthumously, in the Catholic Worker Farm (Tivoli) poetry magazine *Wild Places* (Vol. II: Spring 1977).

Eliot said any of the people written about in Djuna's book, so far from complaining, ought to be proud of it; when she told him that the N.Y. publishers thought more of *Ryder*, he wheeled round and said, "They're crazy!" I am glad to note he thinks the same as I do about *Ryder*. It was inconceivable that he shouldn't—but I didn't know what he would tell Djuna. She now realizes dimly, I having dinned it into her for one year, and John before that, that *Ryder* is not good. She said to me, "I can't die; I haven't written anything." Extraordinary, from her, who thinks every one of her writings superb. But I said, "Anyone who has written that book need never write another line." She said, "Do you really think so?" I said to her—"This book is much better than I think" which amused her.

I went to see Tony. She was looking gay, having just got out of the hospital. But this was Tuesday. Monday I waited for a call from Barker, and got one about 12. I was in a dreadful pother, could hardly talk to him. He came at half-past three. When he came, we talked, and I put my head on his knees, after a long time. We sat like this, he on the couch, stroking my hair. He does not love me; he makes love very tenderly. I did not let him touch me—he did not try—but remained there for some time. I had fully made up my mind before I went away with Peter—I had chosen my course.

But when I was on the couch next to Barker I could not let him make love to me, but only wanted affection. He seemed perturbed and said, "You're in a very nervous state. You don't really want to make love." I said, "I think of it all the time." He said, "You mustn't think of it so much. I don't want it as much as all that." I said, "If you don't want it, that will settle it." He said, "I'm not in love with you." He said he was in love with his wife. I sat for a long time gazing out of the window. He asked me what I was thinking of, and I said, "I'm thinking it does not matter, one word of what we say. Whatever is going to happen, will happen—no words of ours will change it." He said, "I'm surprised to hear you say that." "You think I'm stupid then?" "No," he said, "Only a trifle obtuse." This irriated me, with the other (which I had called out of him). I told him David Gascoyne was physically attractive to me. When he wanted to touch me I almost wept and said, "I'm frightened!" He said I was a coward. I said it was because I knew what to fear.

He said something about money—which upset me very much—I getting the notion that he wanted to know me for money (Peggy's nightmare). I gave him in May and June every spare penny I had, and more; he has no idea of how much of a sacrifice it was. He thinks people who go to Glyndebourne have all kinds of resources. He is very sensitive about money, and proud; but at its best this relation is impossible.

I had lunch with Peter Tuesday and we went to the Surrealist Exhibition.[8] He put order in my soul where there had been some confusion. David [Gascoyne] was not there; I left him a note.

I went to dinner with Peter, where Phyllis came, and Peter was in extremely good form.

After Phyllis left I put my arms around Peter and said, "What is the matter with you?" He said, "I don't know." He did not touch me. I said to myself, "This was your last chance" and let him go.

The next morning Peter managed to get me to St. Pancras in time for the train, after a terrifying half hour—he was so late; then we found the train had left; they had told me the wrong time. We sat for an hour. I talked to him about HUBBERHOLME AND THE VERITES (the machine is out of order).[9]

When Peter put me in the train I felt desperate. I didn't look at him when the train left.

Thursday, July 2, Hubberholme

The ride up here is not beautiful, and gets worse, as the manufacturing fields are approached, until, when one gets to Leeds, it is horrible. I changed there, got into the Skipton train. The country begins to get a little better. At Skipton I found the Verities, and we began the 20-mile drive to Hubberholme; but I couldn't take it in at first. I had to shake myself and try to imagine I was there. Mr. Verity looked well, Mrs. V[erity]. seemed younger than I remembered her, her face sharper and more individual. The country got more and more peaceful.

I decided coming from Skipton that I was not going to leave here in one week. It was arranged that Johnny should come, and sleep on a mattress in my room: I wrote letters immediately arranging it—cancelled our weekend with Clutton-Brock, asked Phyllis if she would meet John and put him on the train for Skipton. Thus I can have 3 weeks here. It is positively incredible that I get

---

[8]The International Surrealist Exhibition was held from June 11 to July 4 at the New Burlington Galleries, London. It was organized by a committee which included Gascoyne, Jennings, Herbert Read, André Breton, Roland Penrose, and others. The Exhibition featured works by André Masson, Picasso, Brancusi, Max Ernst, Chirico, René Magritte, Miro, Yves Tanguy, Dali, and Giacometti. Peter Quennell reviewed the show in the June 20 issue of the *New Statesman and Nation*, noting that it offered works "from Picasso to collages of the most inept and tiresome sort."

[9]Recall she had stayed with the Veritys when she visited Hubberholme in June 1934. Her typewriter was broken.

so involved in London that I haven't been here for 2 years. I feel strength and life and spiritual energy, to renew the fight when I go back.

Do not want to write a great long diary here but try to get some CREATIVE work done, instead like a feeble woman of only thinking of my life. I HAVE imagination, why in Christ don't I use it?

When I went to see Tony in the morning the day before I left she entertained me with accounts of insects; she is reading Fabre.[10]

She said it was extraordinary that one who believed in eternal life should profit so little from it on the earth. I said, "You have no idea how it sustains me. You do not know how violent I am." I said to her, "Without that, I would have killed myself, in the spring of 1933, in 1934, last summer when I came back from America, many times last winter. I would have killed myself," I said, "Even realizing what it would do to my father." She nodded. "There is not one day," I said, "That I do not think of eternal life. It is all that makes me live." I feel of course like Elsa, the Baroness Von Freitag-Loringhoven: "True death is wealth tremendous; but it must be earned with life—that is why still I live."

I don't know if I recorded in this diary the morning I read from my excerpts from the Baroness' letters to Djuna, to Peggy and Djuna.[11] "I rise in the morning—I go to my death-trap." The wonderful things about the next world: "Whom shall I meet? I'll be a whirlwind. I'll be a gull." Djuna's art, as expressed in *Nightwood*, is far greater than anything the Baroness ever wrote— yet these few letters (among many worthless ones I'm told) are extraordinary in their mystical beauty; the imaginative horror of their suffering.

I keep thinking of Barker and making love to him, of his touching me on the couch. I can imagine the strength and curiosity of his touch; but I cannot endure it. I think of Peter's hand creeping up my leg, that used to send me into ecstasies of desire, which were never fulfilled; is that all over now? The tears rush to my eyes if I believe it. I sat looking at the moor which rises up from the garden, and read *Maurice Guest*, Tony allowed me to keep it, since I had no time to read it in London.

Saturday, July 4

Thinking of Djuna and her 2 remarks about the *S. of Snow*, which she'd been looking at when I was at Glyndebourne—"I see the cat the cat sees

---

[10]Jean Henri Fabre (1823–1915), French naturalist specializing in insects. His main work is *Souvenirs Entomologiques*, published in 10 volumes between 1879 and 1907. White was fluent in French, and would begin translating French novels in 1949.
[11]Coleman has not recorded such a time, but she did quote the same lines, above—"True death. . . ."—in her entry for July 21, 1933; see note for that entry.

me"—referring to the style; and "I laughed so when I read, 'I wrote the doctor 17 pages and she said it was enough.'"[12] I have been patient with Djuna. Also, when I said, "If I find I don't like my book when I'm up in Yorkshire"—she added rapidly, and hopefully—"You'll throw it all out?" This really is too much. I was so dazed at the time, between my miseries and the confusion of having a person in my flat, that I almost let it pass, saying only—"I'd as soon cut off my head."

I began reading my book last night, and read all of Part I. It is first-rate.

Read today Part II which is all right, but less objective. I don't see how this can be helped; you get more into the minds of the characters.

I sleep like a rock here—I am reborn! I have no worries, only in the distance. I feel peace, an eternity of quiet—I must do what work I can. But what weakness is in me that I didn't work in London, that I have no <u>internal</u> peace?

Saw a book of David Garnett's on the sofa downstairs—"To Gladys Verity from David Garnett" and thought, "Damn! Bloomsbury knows my place." I was angry and finally pleased. Lovely singing, like Schumann, on the radio—how much sweeter music is when it comes unannounced.

Everything in London is canned and settled beforehand—I can't abide such things. Music ought to appear suddenly, and one find out afterwards what it was. This is the amateur's view, the kind of pleasure I get. The trouble with me is I want paradise on earth—like Lawrence.

Sunday, July 5

I've been reading *Maurice Guest* all the morning; an incredible book. It is far more fascinating to me than *Richard Mahony*, possibly because it is about a woman: it deals with that terrible human thing—a woman's passion.

If there is ONE THING I want to do in my book (and it will be the first time it's ever been done) it is to show that a passionate woman is DEATH to a man who loves her, who is not equal to the strength of her emotion.

Monday, July 6

. . . Phyllis sent me a telegram (which I opened fearfully) saying she would be "delighted" to meet Johnny. Sweet Phyllis! He loves her so. He'll also be delighted.

---

[12]Protagonist Marthe Gail, who is institutionalized in a psychiatric hospital, has asked her doctor to transfer her "upstairs" where the patients are more "quiet" and enjoy greater privileges. As Coleman wrote in the novel, "Dr Brainerd told her to sit at her desk and write her all the reasons why she wanted to go upstairs and she wrote seventeen pages and Dr Brainerd said that was enough" (Dalkey 38).

But I can't think of anything except *Maurice Guest*. What fate possessed me to make this the only book I brought up with me except Muir's poems? I did not know it would have any bearing on my book. Sadism—do not know if this is brought out in my book—especially since it is only recently I have imagined what lies in Peter's and my relationship. "Four Years" (I haven't got the time element straight yet and won't do so until Tony has seen it all) is the embodiment of my relation with Bianchetti and Peter.[13] I am stimulated by the violent scenes in *Maurice Guest*, which have not taken place yet between me and Peter.

This book has made what I think will be an indelible impression on me. I haven't been influenced by any other book, outside of *Wuthering Heights*, except Djuna's.

Wednesday, July 8

Had a fine letter from Djuna about Dorothy—she called her a "clock telling the time without hands." John was her hands. I wrote her a very long letter. Was delighted to hear from her. I like getting away from my friends and hearing from them. Paradise would be to have them (Djuna, Tony, Peter, Peggy, Phyllis, etc.) up here, accessible whenever I wanted them! . . . It's heavenly to work hard, so that one forgets where one is—you think you are in the city—and then suddenly go out in the road. I go to bed at 10 every night. Heavenly.

. . . Djuna got 12 copies out of Faber (by Eliot), clever—he said he only got 6 when his books came out!

Saturday, July 11

I wrote Peter a little letter and said I wanted to come back and begin over again. I really can't do anything else.

I finished my book, at 6–30 p.m. today. Finished the writing of the extra parts. I was very happy when I reached the end of the book—happy in Frieda's death. It was over. I went outside, feeling ecstatically happy, for a half hour. I went down the road singing, to the island. Everything seemed intensified to me. The sun was out—it had been raining half the afternoon. I stood at the bridge and looked over into the whirlpool, as Frieda did.[14] Slight

---

[13]"Four Years" and also "Five Years" were Coleman's working titles for "The Tygon."
[14]Having killed Donato by knocking his head against a balustrade and throwing his body into the Tiber River, Frieda, we are told at the end of the novel, "looked down into the water. She saw her life, stretching out into seasons. One can resist with one's conscious mind. But in the

yellow flowers, on very long stems, are growing out of the cracks, beginning to blossom. I went in the garden, looking at the delphiniums, which look as though bees nested in them; the bedraggled sweet William; the almost finished day lilies. The roses are lovely. I want to put this garden in my book somewhere. Now that it's done, I'll be putting little bits in, here and there.

I sleep well here. Mrs. Verity comes in a quarter to nine with a cup of tea. It is so pleasant to hear her foot coming down the hall. Mr. Verity asked me to go to Skipton but I would not leave my book. Now Johnny is coming—another life. I'm longing to see him, dreading—as always—the first adjusting. Every time I've had him the last two years it has been harder to part with him than before.

I worked like a slave on my book, hardly doing anything else, for 12 hours, two days. I keep having ideas for it.

I am half a saint (wishing to be a saint) and half an artist. I am an artist. I am at last now successful in my writing. I mean I am writing what I want to write. It has taken me 10 years. The other part I am not successful in at all. I haven't even begun; have truly just made a beginning. It is only two years since I read the Gospels (in Woburn Square) and decided that that WAS the right life.

We went to Skipton Monday; I posted my book to Tony, feeling a great relief. John's train was half an hour late.

Wednesday, July 15

It rained most of the time. John fished, carrying maggots. We took a long walk and got soaked, sitting under trees—by Scar House Farm. He rode the pony, which suddenly lay down and rolled, and gave him a great surprise. He painted an ash, very good indeed. Sat down by the ghyll with his easel. I read the *Imitation of Christ* which is very boring.[15] What one wants is a book by some Christian who knows what the struggle is; not just preaching, out of air and books. (St. Augustine; I wish I had it here.) I had a long letter from

---

dream it comes. And suddenly in one's life one makes the gesture that ends in death in the dream. She climbed up on the balustrade. The water, cold and challenging, hardly seemed to exist. As in a trance she moved, got up on the parapet, looked down. He was there! He had sunk! She believed she could see him, pressing his face into the mud of the Tiber, the river that he loved. She would be alone, if she did not make the jump. She jumped. She struck the water. She flailed her arms, trying not to swim. She felt the water coming in, choking her. It slowly came, painfully invading her, until she was drowned."

[15]Thomas a Kempis (1380–1471), an Augustinian monk, was the author of Christian mystical books. His *De Imitatione Christi* (1426) was first translated from the Latin into English in 1556. Coleman was likely reading the 1925 London reprint of Richard Whytford's translation.

Djuna, whose flat is about to be sold in Paris, and she is off. She feels her life is hanging. A wonderful letter from Peggy. A letter from Gossy—she is having "piles" chopped off—horrible—Must write to her at once.

Today a letter from Father enclosing a clipping about Alexander Berkman. He committed suicide.[16] I felt very sorry for Emma; was glad I sent her a telegram (from Uckfield) on her birthday. I must write her now. She will feel utterly lost, without him. He was, in a sense, her whole life—all the past of it—and she mothered him and was—in her way—a wife to him. She will be dreadfully alone. I must write her.

I feel quite lost without my manuscript.

My imagination was terrifically stimulated by the strange foreign life in Rome with Bianchetti, I worked out that 10 chapters in that book are true—happened between me and Bianchetti. Heidi is completely made up—I started with Peggy but found such a good person as Peggy didn't work at all—had to make her up out of knowledge.[17]

John sleeps on a mattress at the foot of my bed, is so sweet. Has a rod Mr. Verity lent him. Mr. V. caught 4 trout, let John bring them in.

Thursday, July 16

I wrote some "Proverbs of Sainthood and the Imagination." I tried to get into concise form a few aphorisms I have learned. One is influenced by Blake's *Proverbs of Heaven and Hell*, and the Bible; it is hard to get one's own form. I see from this Notebook I had this idea 2 years ago—but did not write any. I thought possibly they were best expressed in poetry; but would like to make a little book of maxims, which could be published one day, when I'm dead.[18] I want to get into maxims the union of art and religion which I deeply feel.

John and I walked to Yockenthwaite by the road and back on the other side. Letter from Peter this morning, not saying much—he is writing another. Djuna going to Paris to sell her flat—has not gone yet; wrote wonderfully about Peter. She said, "The longer I know that charging imp of death the less I understand—his bright quick step on the stair—his shining eyes and his rocklike denial of life—saying he has no heart 'except for myself' . . . how anyone ever got into his arena is a mystery—in fact it's magnificent—Emily

---
[16]Suffering from the ongoing pain from a prostate condition as well as enduring financial worries, Berkman killed himself in Nice on June 28, 1936.
[17]Heidi is Frieda's sister, who has an affair with Donato.
[18]Coleman's archive contains a number of unpublished essays with titles such as "Art, Science and the Unknown," "Art, Science & Religion," and "Beyond Blake, Nietzsche" (F. 1007, 1008, 1010). Blake's *The Marriage of Heaven and Hell* contains a section "Proverbs of Hell."

got in—right inside the cage and there she stands cracking the whip at that little stone griffon, who however still sits in his corner, holding his dripping pound of fate—untamed!!!"

She said she saw my book going into 105 [Oakley St.] to Tony! Heard from Tony too—not well and disturbed about Tom in some way—I can't make out how—it's no good saying she doesn't love him because she's determined to spend her passion on him, and when a woman wants to do that, that is doom.

When I was walking with John back from Yockenthwaite I felt such a sympathy with him—he seems to feel what I do; we get on best in walking—or when I'm joking with him. When he is childish (like a savage) I am patient, but I don't love him so much—as I did not love him when he was aged 2 to 7 years, that awful period. I ought to read to him, and talk to him more about interesting things. I can't tell him too many <u>elementary</u> things; as soon as someone else has laid the ground I can tell him many things. I talk to him a lot about his painting, and painters, and things I have seen. I fear we shall get more and more intimate as we get older. I feel the hopelessness of communicating to anyone I love, as usual; and am happiest when he is sitting near me, or playing, occupied; which is the way I feel about everyone I love, except Peter. Him and him only I want to share, <u>really get through to</u>; to something beyond us.

Sunday, July 19

I was reading the diary I have written up here. It is terrible. I cannot stand my own writing—unless it is inspired. There is a cocky college girl flavour to it which positively nauseates me; I must be like that. I write too many words and explanations.

I can't get Barker out of my head—sex—sex—I think of nothing else—imagine myself kissing his head; I can't get beyond that. I don't imagine anything more—yet to imagine that thrills me. Barker's attitude to sex is so dangerous to me—he doesn't care—he only wants animal satisfaction—and will take it when he can get it; the opposite of Peter.

Tony's letter was self-conscious, self-pitying. It was a cry from the heart too. She is tedious when she gets on to her mental illness, self-dramatization. Such nonsense she gets from Carroll and Eric.[19] But she IS in a very bad way. I am aware of it. She might kill herself.... I'm not sure about what she wrote about my book—I wonder if it's being a novel (her form) does not frighten her—is it envy?[20] Unconsciously; is it envy, in life? I went over the book in

---

[19]Dr. Dennis Carroll, White's psychoanalyst from 1935 to 1938; Eric Earnshaw Smith.
[20]In her entry for Saturday, July 18, Coleman recorded that she had received "a long fine letter from Tony. [. . .] She thinks the book is chaotic, on the human plane—but is not sure, doubting

my mind last night, chapter by chapter, to see what she meant by its being "chaotic." It's true I can't do conversation.

Monday, July 20

The sun came out today. It was like the breaking of the arctic night. J[ohn]. and I walked on the hill above the road here. I told him about "socking" Mr. Hummel in 1927, at his request, to his intense satisfaction.[21]

Had tea at the Vicarage yesterday. Borrowed a book on Wm. Morris written by A. Clutton-Brock![22] (I don't think he likes it that I cursorily refused his invitation; I'll go there). J. and I played a horrid game of making squares. I looked at him as he lay asleep and did not dare to think of him. Already now I can't stand the thought of separating from him; what will it be in September?

Reading life of William Morris by A. Clutton-Brock, who may be my man's father. What a delightful respect-worthy man Morris was. I agree with everything he felt about the poor.[23] But I cannot interest myself in politics— have less aptitude for it than he had; and do not intend to waste my gifts of God on nonsense; I can help Barker. I can assist Djuna; do things for the Donns. I would help Tony if she didn't have E. Smith and Tom. I believe personal aid, to those one loves and respects, is the best way out of Communism. Next winter I won't have any money left over for clothes—or entertainments. And why should I? I get every single thing I need anyway, between Peter, Peggy and my father. I must use my own money to do for Barker.

Tuesday, July 21

If I had had a child any different from this one I wouldn't have got on with it at all. This boy is incredibly like me; even when he's a nuisance, with his fastidious tastes, and determined ways, it's my world—the world of the fine distinction, the absolute joy. He knows exactly what he wants; even though a baby—in so many ways he still is—he is led precisely by the most definite

---

her own reason. [. . .] I don't know if she's right or wrong, since she didn't say where she felt such. She may be right—I can't tell; she says she 'feels surer' with my poetry" (F. 637).
[21]Jack Hummel, Coleman's boss at the *Tribune*. See the introduction.
[22]Coleman's acquaintance Alan Clutton-Brock (noted earlier) was the son of Arthur Clutton-Brock (1868–1924), a critic for the *Times Literary Supplement* as well as author of studies like *William Morris: His Work and Influence* (1914). It was Alan who had invited her to his country house (see entry for June 23, 1936).
[23]William Morris (1834–1896), English designer, artist, writer, printer, and social reformer. He helped to found the Socialist League in 1884 and later joined the Hammersmith Socialist Society, offering up his house for meetings.

tastes. I can't help admiring and loving it; though it makes him difficult. He loves it so here; plays and fishes without company. He wants me with him; but if I read or write he lets me. He is incredibly sweet, and lovely, about the things I love. I am so lazy, and so unanxious to communicate with him, unless I can get off a monologue. I do fairly well though, being so full of life.[24]

---

[24]The diary breaks off here.

Part V

Section 1

London

November 14–December 31, 1936

After a visit from her father, during which they travelled in Europe, Coleman returned to London at the end of the summer. She began an affair with the then twenty-nine-year-old filmmaker Humphrey Jennings whom she had met, along with the poet David Gascoyne, the previous June. Jennings was married to Cicely Cooper — they had two daughters — and, according to biographer Kevin Jackson, the affair with Coleman was Jennings' first infidelity, though several more would follow, including with Guggenheim.[1] While Coleman did not keep her diary for this period, both White and Gascoyne recorded in their respective journals the romance between their friends. According to Gascoyne, for instance, "Antonia tells me that Humphrey and Emily are wildly in love with one another. She says that Emily's behaviour is positively wild with elation, and that she threw her hat over Waterloo Bridge."[2]

Coleman's diary reopens in November as the month-long liaison was coming to an emotionally disastrous end for Coleman. Rejected by Jennings, she had become mildly involved with her acquaintance Alan Clutton-Brock, but she lapsed into suicidal despair as she tried desperately to win Jennings back while also seeking to make amends to a cuckolded Hoare. The plot thickened as Guggenheim — on her last legs with Garman — and Jennings became interested in each other, to Coleman's horror. While contemplating Communism, the abdication of King Edward VIII, and psychoanalysis, Coleman was energized by the support she received from White and Barnes; Barnes's vital assistance with "The Tygon"; a visit from her son; and the promise of a new lover, the Welsh poet Dylan Thomas.

---

[1] Jackson 174–75.
[2] October 22, 1936 (quoted in Jackson 174).

LONDON, 1936

Saturday, November 14

Last night dinner [Alan] Clutton-Brock during which (tea, before) I kept him from mentioning marriage. He showed me a wonderful passage in *The Winter's Tale* about jealousy; I read from *Othello*—the other more agreeable to him, though he loved what I read—he is disgusted with life—not enough. Arthur [Waley] there, did not appreciate *Nightwood*, I almost said, "The *S. of Snow* is as far as you can go."

I phoned Humphrey several times, always engaged, a line I was given to get him. Finally had to phone him from Clutton's, he pretty mad—has a nerve to mind my seeing Clutton considering he has pretended to abandon me. Clutton looks like a spontaneous carp. Arthur almost handsome, except eyes, which shift, like an old woman, with malice; says excellent things. "What does E.M. Forster look like?" He says, "A disappearing milkman."

Graham-Bell (a young calf) there, went to a ball afterwards.[3] Clutton-Brock tight and quite funny, like "Spotty" Strachey.[4] London Group Ball.[5] Horrible pictures on the walls. G-B. tried to kiss me in the stairs (lovable boy, but mawkish), I said, "I DONT KISS PEOPLE IN THE STAIRS."

Humphrey coming to lunch with me and Djuna and Tony.

I was very ill last night after I came back from the ball, lay in bed in absolute despair again, kicking (literally) and crying. I went down to Peter's bed, God knows what I did that for, but did not really try him, the darling, because I knew I was a skunk. I said to Djuna in the morning (when we were going over my book)—"It is horrible to come down to every thing you thought you had done away with in yourself." I am more of a baby than ever, cannot grow up, scream and yell (in private at least) if I can't have just what I want, when I want it.

Lunch, Humphrey frightfully nervous, rude, difficult, Tony patient, Djuna positively angelic. Djuna and I have been going over my book, most exciting, this morning. She very keen about it. She said it was almost impossible

---

[3] Graham Bell (1910–1943) was a painter with the Euston Road School (dedicated to realism, naturalism, and leftist ideology) as well as art journalist and author of *The Artist and His Public* (1939). He died while training with the Royal Air Force.

[4] The painter John or "Spotty" Strachey—so nicknamed because of his spots or acne—was the younger son of Lytton Strachey's brother Ralph.

[5] The London Group, established in London in 1913 and continuing to this day, was formed by a group of radical exhibiting artists seeking independence from the established Royal Academy. Members included Jacob Epstein, Wyndham Lewis, and Henry Moore, and Bloomsbury figures like Roger Fry, Duncan Grant, and Vanessa Bell.

to have a murder and suicide; I said "I'll have it if it takes me 5 years to do it." Humphrey does not look pleased because I have given my book to Djuna. After lunch which was partly amusing partly nervous we walked down to the river (which Djuna referred to as "the Thames, or whatever this is"). Came back here. Humphrey read a new "report" about the life of Byron, that he read me a part of the other day; it is incredible. Djuna and Tony enraptured by it.[6] It was strange and original. Djuna said something new in the world could be done by H[umphrey]., a new biography, photography, painting, poem—in this "book." He is an incredible fellow. Very pleased at our appreciation, kept looking at me. Tony excited and talking about it.

Tony had to go to tea with Logan Pearsall Smith—I said, "Why do you go to tea with that old bugger?"[7] Djuna said, "My God if you hint that the left back tail feather of Emily's pet pheasant isn't straight, she screams; then what she says about about people's friends [*sic*]." Tony said, "What would you think if someone said that when you went to see Clutton-Brock?" I said, "As far as I can see, that's what they do say." Humphrey enjoyed this. Phyllis came, I made brown bread toast in the fire. H[umphrey]. lay down, Djuna ironed, I played the gramophone, for the first time in months: played Mozart and Palestrina. H. sat up and began writing. He looked very sweet and kept looking at me. He was comradely all the afternoon. When he left he kissed me suddenly on the mouth, then went. Before he went he phoned his wife, which I didn't like and went in the kitchen to endure it.

Monday, November 16

All day Sunday Djuna and I did my book, she getting well into Part V. Humphrey did not even phone. We had the book spread out on the sitting room floor all day; she went out for lunch, brought me back a Hamburger sandwich. I dressed finally and we had tea in Peter's flat. He very odd, seeing the girls occupied all day. They went out for dinner, I stayed, was brought ham and beef sandwiches! I wrote a new short chapter while they were out. This is the first Sunday since I've known Humphrey (since that first lovely

---

[6] Jennings had been reading an edition of Thomas Moore's *Letters and Journals of Lord Byron*, with notices of his life (1830). Passionate about Byron, Jennings had painted the *Portrait of Lord Byron with Book* (1935) while his essay "The Boyhood of Byron," part of a larger planned work and which is likely what Coleman went on to refer to, was published in the December 1936 (No. 8) issue of *Contemporary Poetry and Prose*.

[7] Logan Pearsall Smith (1865–1946), born in the United States, settled in England where he became a literary critic, and especially famous for his writings on the English language (i.e., *English Idioms* (1923) and *Words and Idioms* (1925). White had known him for several years, having met him through her second husband, Earnshaw Smith.

326   Section 1

day in Kew) that I haven't had a desperate suicidal struggle.[8] Djuna made me go at my book, last week, the day after my last and dreadful row with Humphrey. I moaned so, she said, "Are you a writer? Or just a yelling female?" I got out the book, gingerly let her, with many fears, take Part I. From then we started.

New hat, a Juliet cap, with a rod like an acorn, is a great success. When Djuna saw it Friday night—I wore it at Peter's to show him—she would burst into roars—at my face.

Today worked all day on my book. She thinks the end is right. Found a lot of sloppy writing in Pt. V where I got bored. Peter sweet as turnips when the girls were reading.

Djuna said she didn't like the title, "Four Years." "Doesn't mean anything." I said, "Do think of a title." We thought of the Melville phrase—"As loving as leopardesses, as cunning as doves"—I said, "The Leopardess and the Dove."[9] She said that was arty, too long, no good. Then she said—"The Tigon."

We got so excited we didn't know what to do. It brought the whole book together, made the woman something (which she badly needed to be)—androgyne, devil, dove, beauty. The part I wrote about the tigons in the zoo last night I looked up again: perfect.[10] If I'd had the title in mind I couldn't have done it so subtly. Said I ought to give Djuna ten pounds. She said, "Now the account's squared."

Friday, November 20

Djuna has just gone, I am glad because I need to be quiet; yet how I miss her! I was to have gone with Humphrey to Peggy's for the weekend; I thought I would have him here tonight. Tomorrow it is three weeks since we made

---

[8]Drawing on Coleman's correspondence with Barnes in October and November, 1936, Herring notes that in mid-October, Coleman and Jennings took a walk in Kew Gardens where Coleman "announced her wish to marry him. As far as she was concerned, the matter was settled, but in the next month, when he kept putting her off, she quarreled with him, and the truth came out: he was already married and had two children. She wrote Barnes: 'The colossal brutality of his behaviour is beyond belief'" (232–233).
[9]Coleman slightly misquoted the line. In Melville's novella *Benito Cereno* (1856), the American Delano describes the African slave women aboard a Spanish ship as "unsophisticated as leopardesses, loving as doves."
[10]In chapter IV, Frieda and Donato recall visiting a zoo in Milan. Frieda describes, "Then we came upon the tygons. Tygons, animals rarely born, half lion and half tiger, one with stripes and one with mane," to which Donato adds, "They were united in love, surrounded by a crowd which was half curious. We were interested, feeling that something new was in the cage."

love. . . . I have been alone with him only twice since then—at lunch. When he phoned that he could not get away either tonight or tomorrow, that frenzy came over me, which will do me in. I am so desperate. I did not give any indication, except a pause, on the telephone . . . I was quite calm. I said, "Phone me if you are free tomorrow." Oh can I stand the dreadful grinding of this, getting him back again. If I can get him here alone just once—it is done. Then go away if you like—but get him to make love once. I have lost him, quite, he seems not quite lost, but something has happened—I've done it myself—he is finished with me. Only calm and waiting can get him back, and I have not had him here alone since the day we last made love (Saturday was that day, Sunday, by arrangement, I was with Peter, Monday we quarreled violently on the phone—that was I—I could not stand his manner—he came Monday and read Gray to Barker[11]—he tried to kiss me in the taxi—how little did I care how easily I lost him—I did not want to kiss him, we were quarreling—we went to the Group Theater cocktail party, at which Eliot spoke[12]—we quarreled the whole time—we left—we quarreled in the street—I in a frenzy said, "Go to the devil" and left him standing in the street; when I got home I was appalled. The next morning he phoned and came here—I was sweet and penitent. We would have made love then, Djuna was here. She came out. We got into a terrible discussion. I laid all my cards on the table (what a fool!)—told him what my nature was. <u>That</u> frightened him. . . . Nothing from him Friday, Saturday or Sunday. I in the throws of suicide, the end, it is no use.[13]

He has got me on the hip, in the ass, on the brain. I can not live without him now. He has done it. Then I wrecked it, and he backed out. I want Humphrey now for my life—if I lose him it will be because I am clumsy. It is he or death—I shall not cry, or think of sleeping potions: I shall fight for him—fight my own soul.

---

[11]Thomas Gray (1716–1771), English poet and classical scholar.

[12]London's experimental Group Theatre (1932–1939) was formed by Rupert Doone and Robert Medley. Those who wrote plays specifically for the company include W. H. Auden, Christopher Isherwood, Louis MacNeice, and Stephen Spender. Eliot's *Sweeney Agonistes* had premiered in November 1934 at the Group's location at Great Newport Street, and had been given another run in October 1935 (see Ackroyd 215–16).

[13]Coleman tried to update the diary on the last several days of their relationship, but she got the days confused, repeated herself, and tried to sort out the chronology: "Something wrong here—trying to get straight—he had lunch with Tony, Djuna and me on Saturday. I've written about this." She described how her erratic, possessive and violent nature turned him off, and their final fight in a street: "Too late, he would not come home, he would leave. I pled in the street, begged, wept, promised. Too late. When I went, he said 'Take care of yourself.' But now he was finished, he believed nothing more—he had made a mistake and must get out of it."

Monday, November 23

Just did my bank account and find I have six pounds between now and my next allowance (Dec. 7th), with 6–13–4 rent to pay. This is nice. I have economized like anything, and this is the result. It is more than I can do to take care of Barker. I have got to continue doing it. I will have to get some money somehow. . . . A very bleak day, as Djuna said,"You think you're at sea."

. . . Humphrey is a dreadful, horrible child. I am sure of one thing—that he is quite impossible for me to have any dealings with, if I want to preserve my sanity. He is quite mad, as I thought long ago; "love," being "in love"—whatever it was he felt when he pursued me so energetically—humanized him for that brief moment; perhaps "sex" will humanize him again. Christ, I can't endure the thought of making love with him, and going through this again afterwards, or some similar aftermath. He is fascinating, to a degree. He knows eternal truth. Yet, were I to make my life with him, as far as I can see now, I might as well cut my throat. I keep wondering what his wife has done—adapted, adapted; <u>no wonder</u> she didn't want to make love with him! He never has given her an orgasm. Himself, himself! No other thought. She must have found herself in mothering him, and in her children. He is incapable of a free, square, human relation. He treats me as if I were a painting. Actually said to me—"My nature is to paint, and paint—and then when I feel like it, I stop painting!" This ought to teach me: just remember that!

Think of suicide with exaltation—in moments of reason know I will be in hell for it. When I fall dependent on him I "give him the creeps"—he has said twice.

He doesn't say anything normal: when I said, once, "Do you mind fighting with me about art? Does is make you want me less physically?" he said, "When I'm putting you down in an argument I feel I'm making love to you sadistically." Really!

It was Thursday, October 8th or Wednesday the 7th that we met at Ridgways: the hour that started all this. He was fully and utterly deceiving in the first week or so. He has grown up a little, critically, since perhaps—humanly. He gets a vicious look, like a little dog when he's angry—not quite real; though I dare say the effects are real. I feel he's all theories—only comes down to earth when he's fucking—not much then, to be honest. When he tells me how to put on my lipstick I took him for a husband, when he makes love, a lover; no, a mistake, he's an angel or devil, but neither human thing.

A horrible thought came over me, rereading this—"No woman would ever stand this"—of course Peggy would—she said if I were not really in love with Humphrey she would "like a try at him"! I said, "Does he attract you sexually?" but she said, "No, it's that he's so fascinating." I said, "Well please don't." But thought no more about it. Now I think possibly he might fall for her. She would understand his work, and be more docile with him than I; to say nothing of being more attractive physically, I should think, to a man. This may be perfect nonsense. And would the money count—it might easily.

I am horrified at this thought of Peggy—like a dream at dawn. He has been faithful to his wife for eight years. Not looked at another woman as far as I know. They don't look at him. What I mean to him as a person scarcely exists. He wants an American who will be passionately worshipping him, understanding him, giving him violent sexual satisfaction: docile. Peggy. Also the money. What does money mean to him—a lot.

I am so afraid of further suffering that I dare not move.

. . . While I was writing that, Peter came, to take me out to dinner. I kept away from him. But he seemed to want me, and when I put my arms around his neck, as I so often do, he took hold of me. We were both a little tight from sherry. I began to think, as I have done these last three weeks—but thought, "Do what you feel—don't think." This time, <u>don't</u> think. Peter is your love. So I didn't. He was passionate: more so than he has ever been. I would not think of anything. . . . When we were lying together I felt peace, a coming together of chaos. . . .

Hurst (Peggy's)—December 1

Depressions past anything settled on me today. After the morning I could barely endure it. I came down here on the 4–50 train. Peggy met me and when I arrived here, the cottage looked so sweet, the country beautifully bare. In front of a large wood fire I was almost relieved. Garman talked to me a lot about Communism after dinner, till one. I said I would likely become one. I think I should do so to give myself something to do, and it is something I believe in. Garman was so elated—simple fellow—by my interest (we had a very good talk) that he wanted me to come to bed with him and Peggy! I had to say that I was really very unhappy—and wanted to be alone! In the morning he came at me, through the door, but I (longing for privacy and my own thoughts—though doomed) pretended to be asleep. I worked on my book all day. I thought of Humphrey whenever I wasn't working, it seemed to eat into my life. Can I get him out of my life? It torments me. It got worse and worse until by tea time I was in a suicidal state again. Felt the woods weighing down on me, the lovely sunny day was death to me and Peggy's happiness with Garman now, which has arrived late and with considerable sacrifice of her original nature, made me writhe with envy. I seem always to be envying Peggy!

How can I feel so intensely about someone I've known only (really) two months? I was as intense about Barker—no reason. I must have <u>all</u> my emotions centered on someone; I don't seem to care <u>who</u> it is. Does this mean I should take them less seriously? <u>If the suffering were less, yes; but it is not</u>.

December 3

Wrote two new chapters for my book—one ordinary, to give her a little background (in Spain), the other wonderful (the kittens and dreams). Finished last night at one o'clock going over the whole book after Djuna's corrections. Her corrections of style very good, and her noticing of the number of times I said "sex," "body," "soul," "immortal" and "feminine" was important. I threw out numberless lines from long conversations. When I see it in final typed form I shall do more. It shall not be said that these people talked themselves to death.

Djuna's great contribution was "The Tigon." It changed the book for me. I bore that title in mind as I went over it this time.

Letter from her this morning—terrible time with teeth—very happy because her book is taken by Harcourt, Brace in America![14] And Eliot is going to write a preface for it!

Felt better last night, and again today. Am frightened now to return to London! Wrote both Humphrey and Peter to make arrangements for meetings.... Finished the book now, for final typing. Hands of Phyllis tomorrow, or Saturday. When she's done it, one more reading, in fair unblacked-out form, to be sure. Will send copies to Tony and Djuna too, to have their last words.

Djuna's telling me when she with Thelma she didn't dare to sleep [sic]— tried to keep awake—because she couldn't stand the waking. Am getting like that. What must I do—knuckle down.

I was thinking in bed last night—my real joy here—that if I could <u>fasten</u> my mind upon the irreconcilable FACT that this earth is hell, we only have glimpses of paradise to "fertilize" us ("Joys impregnate"[15])—make us know what that other life is; if I could get that into my <u>blood and bones</u> (must it only be got in—to me—by suffering?), I could be happy. If I would not <u>expect to have heaven</u> here; <u>but take heaven, when it comes, as a promise</u>. The longing for it may be the subject of poetry; but not to be expected as experience.

I say to Peggy (Garman is in London) that I dread like poison becoming a Communist—as she does—because I know it isn't my forte to further a cause[16]; and whatever my enthusiasm might be momentarily aroused in me, I

---

[14]An abscessed tooth was causing Barnes pain. Her novel, for which she received 50 pounds advance, would be published in 1937, with the preface by Eliot. See Herring 233.
[15]"Joys impregnate. Sorrows bring forth" is a line from Blake's "Proverbs of Hell."
[16]Coleman had been reading the *Communist Manifesto*.

would want to defect after a moment. I might be willing to "fight" for Communism, were there a struggle like that in Spain, in England; I might even be got excited enough to want to go there and fight now. I fear hurting my father—he is unprepared as I've previously had no political interests (he thinks the Communists are his mortal enemies—and so they are); I fear being deported. That would kill me. G[arman]. said I could join under an assumed name. I want to be naturalized in time. I would rather have that accomplished first. As for my beliefs, I believe in Christ, to the limit; hence there is no other alternative. It is the only course open to anyone who loathes the social injustice.

The most intense excitement in the papers about the King and Mrs. S[impson].[17] It is all out at last. Garman wired P[eggy]. "Congratulations American success—see evening papers."

P[eggy]. went to Petersfield and got the *Evening Standard*. I wouldn't go, thinking it was all a hoax, or meant something else. When she drove in she honked, and there it all was all over the *Evening Standard*. Very stirring for us. I read her the details.

London, Saturday December 5

Last night I wrote Humphrey a letter settling everything between us. I had just begun to feel calm in Hurst, and coming back to London and phoning him, having him temporizing, made me quite wild again. I knew I could not stand it—that instead of seeing him Monday, as he suggested (having been "doubtful" about today wishing to work or sleep—and the same tomorrow) I must write him something which would put an end to future meetings. I cannot any longer go on with this; it will end in my suicide.[18]

We came up from Hurst yesterday morning—bringing two small kittens which I recklessly said I would take—in a box.[19] I wanted them to distract me: that and Communism!

---

[17]In December 1936, it was revealed that King Edward VIII was in love with the American Mrs. Wallis Warfield Simpson (1896–1986). Rumours that he would abdicate the throne so that they could marry sent the country into turmoil. Coleman would have read, for instance, in the *Evening Standard* on Thursday, December 3, "The King: Premier asks M.Ps not to question him yet." On Friday, December 4 it was reported: "If the King marries his wife must be the Queen/Govt. refuse to change constitutional law: Dominions stand by Mr. [Stanley] Baldwin"; "Mrs. Simpson goes by night to France"; and "Mr. Baldwin, the Prime Minister, made in the House of Commons this afternoon a statement explaining the position which has arisen between the King and his ministers as the result of the King's wish to marry Mrs. Ernest Simpson." The *Times* referred to the possible marriage as being "incompatible with the throne."

[18]Coleman reflected on this time in a later diary entry: "I was planning suicide, would almost get to the point of asking Tony, innocently, for the dial" (Jan 13, 1938, F. 641).

[19]She named them Mouse and Monster.

Wednesday, December 9

Saw Tony at lunch, a most hellish rainy cold day. I want to be "psychoanalyzed," have been thinking about it. I don't think I could stand the trip to Harley Street every day.[20] Yesterday, cold and rain, horrible. Tony interesting and illuminating, as usual. I have been "happy," actually lying in bed contented. Relief from prolonged pain. I know my relation with Peter can't bring me any joy. Tony said, "Don't think ahead the rest of your life, or even six months, think one month, cope with that." She always gives sensible advice, but can't follow it herself—like me.

Trying to read Barker's "Ode" and Tony's old diary of 1921.[21]

Friday, December 11

The King abdicated.[22] I was proud at first, then depressed. I stood, and walked up and down, before Parliament while they were waiting for his decision. I was moved when I read the simple statements of his resolve to renounce the throne; almost in tears. I met Peter and he was most unhappy—said the English had turfed out the only man they had had for years who might make a thing of the Monarchy. They don't want a King; they want a figure-head, to represent what they think they are—and when it's contrary, they won't have the man, preferring the symbol.[23] We went along Piccadilly to the D[uke]. of York's house where [there] was a rowdy crowd asking for the new King. The real King will broadcast tonight—I hope to go to Gossy's. It may be a triumph of "selfishness" (individuality) over "character," but it took some guts to resist the Prime Minister, the tradition and Queen Mary.[24] It is all a

---

[20] Harley Street, in Marleybone district, is still lined with the mansions which serve as the offices for medical specialists, including psychiatrists and psychoanalysts. Coleman would visit White's analyst, Dr. Dennis Carroll, on December 17, 1936.

[21] White began her diary in 1921, but in 1947 would burn the first two volumes.

[22] On Thursday, December 10, the headline of the *Evening Standard* read: "The King Abdicates / Duke of York Monarch." The paper noted that a message from King Edward VIII was read that day in the House of Commons by the Speaker: "After long and anxious consideration I have determined to renounce the throne to which I succeeded on the death of my father, and I am communicating this, my final and irrevocable decision." The page-two headline ran: "King to Premier: I am going to marry Mrs. Simpson: I am ready to go." Edward was succeeded by his younger brother, Albert Frederick Arthur George (1895–1952), Duke of York, who became King George VI. As the *Standard* reported on Friday, December 11, "The new king began his reign at 1:52 p.m., when Royal Assent to Abdication was pronounced."

[23] Coleman underlined by hand, "to represent what they think they are," and added above "preferring the symbol": "they're such liars."

[24] Mary (1867–1953), queen consort of George V and mother of Edward VIII and George VI.

fairy tale, made for females like Phyllis, Helen, Peggy and me. Peggy here for a few moments yesterday morning, reading newly bought newspapers. It is a triumph of British hypocrisy. Peter said the English had no guts any more. But I think they have guts to stick up so bloodily for their hypocrisy. Feudalism Victorianism and ancient truth will die hard here. They let their beloved George's heir go.

Phyllis is typing my book, <u>for the last time</u>. I haven't written the extra parts yet. Djuna still unhappy about her teeth. I think less and less of Humphrey. It's like a bad dream, slowly disappearing, and I come back to life.

Saturday, December 12

Peter came to dinner, which I cooked for him, the first in a very long time. We had smoked salmon, lamb chops with currant jelly and baked potatoes, endive-onion-beet and tomato salad, and Brie. We had a sick sort of Beaune which I got in Kings Road. Then we went to Norman and Gossy's (they were out) to hear the King's broadcast.[25]

Edward spoke in a distinct, rather high, deliberate voice, with his faint Cockney accent. He seemed to be releasing something. It must have been moving for him, for he was to leave Fort Belvedere immediately for Portsmouth, on a destroyer to put out from English shores forever.[26]

I shall never feel the same about the English; perhaps I've learned something. The calm way they let this happen. The Empire (trade, prosperity) the only personal thing that means anything to them. The only people I love are freaks. The freaks stood up for the King; but the great ranks of British stolidly received the news of the abdication. I wonder if Edward was not puzzled at the lack of feeling for him. Several of his sentences brought tears to my eyes. I am glad I heard it from his own lips (as he was speaking it). The words in the papers this morning seem dead. "My brother will have that matchless blessing, not bestowed on me" (he hesitated—the words are commonplace but he spoke them with feeling)—"a happy home and children." He said, "without the support, at my side, of the woman I love." It would have broken the hardest hearts. He said that she had, "Up to the last, tried to persuade him to take a different course." I wonder if this little broadcast can silence those dirty tongues.

---

[25]Edward's broadcast took place at 9 pm on December 11, from the Augusta Tower at Windsor Castle.
[26]Edward, who became the Duke of Windsor, left England for Austria. After her divorce from Ernest Aldrich Simpson became final on April 27, 1937, Wallis Warfield and the Duke would marry on June 3.

Sunday, December 13

The King said, "And so I lay down my burden." When he said, "God save the King!" at the end, it sounded almost forced. One wonders how intelligent he is; as much as an average stock-broker, I suppose. It is such a moving thing, his sailing away from England—He must have felt a great deal. They can't meet for five months, until Mrs. Simpson gets her decree. What the King has done is to be honest—unforgivable in England. What a figure he has become because he has done this. Had the guts to be himself, in a country where such a thing, for a king, is not only "unconstitutional," it is unheard of; to say the least, it is "bad taste." "He was always a bounder" they will say—the hypocrites who read the *Times*, the bishops, the political leaders, the social backbone. What lice.

Monday, December 14

I dreamed about Humphrey again—I was with my father—I can't remember that—but Humphrey came, and we were walking in a garden. I have the most compelling desire to see him, because of these dreams.

I phoned Tony and told her I must see her. I went to lunch with her—she was comforting. I am quite sick—quite mad again—back on the wheel—can't eat or think—don't move—can't think of anything but suicide. The sight of anything sweet makes me feel ill. An inertia seems to take hold of me, I can't leave this room, don't want to see anyone (except Peter). I phoned Humphrey, about 5 o'clock, but he was not there, had not been all day. I will get out and walk the streets.

I talked with Tony about being psycho-analyzed. I am going to have an "interview" with her analyst. If this happens I will have to ask Father to help me. If I could pay a pound a week—which I do not see how I could do unless Peggy helped me a little with Barker—that would help Father. Tony thinks I could get it done for 10/6 a time. That is very cheap.

Friday, December 18

I saw Tony's analyst yesterday, whom I really liked. It was a joke telling him what is the matter with me. There is something "wrong" with all people who have genius. You can't tell him that. "I am not adapted to this world—because I have genius. I am too violent for these parts, and too sensitive for the compromises one has to make to live." I appeared very vital, as always, and he thought I was in the bloom of health. I have no obsessions, no compulsive neuroses; I eat and sleep. I am just miserable because I've been crossed in love. It seems a silly thing to do to become psycho-analyzed. He seemed to think it could do me some good. He knows three men, he says, who would be excellent to handle my situation.

Peggy has been in a state, leaving Garman. She was quite wild day before yesterday. She stayed with me night before last. I think she's right, at long last. He gives all his time to Communism.

I want to read Dante—I feel the will which is lacking in me—can psychoanalysis do me good? Tony thinks I can be helped before things get worse; on the principle, I suppose, that every one should be.

. . . Just wrote 5 new pages for "The Tygon," on suffering, joy and suicide. They are to go in at different points.

Dr. Carroll asked me if I "ever felt deserted."[27]

Tuesday, December 22

Johnny is here, does not seem so affectionate as before; is just as sweet and considerate and lively.

John loves the kittens and plays incessantly with them, and is very lovable and argumentative about Communists and Fascists and very intelligent, repeating Deak's opinions, but being able to criticize life somewhat on his own account and people, whom he already knows—and has for years—far more than his father. I get angry when he begins with Deak's opinions, but am saying nothing.

Finished Tony's whole diary. Very exciting before she goes mad. Quite grown-up before the end of the diary. I can't realize people have whole lives which took place before I met them—She says the same thing about me; she was really grown-up when I met her. But she seems so un-disillusioned still. Today went with John to the Cameo Mickey Mouse program and saw the *Big Bad Wolf* again which is a good one. Bought a new orange-red wool dress with Peggy's money. I feel dopey and think of Jennings as one thinks of something heavenly, that is departing. I can't help thinking of him in that way. Went to Simpsons and Fortnum & Masons with Peter.[28] John and I saw Television.[29] Boring. One more mechanical device which is astonishing, and means nothing. He liked it because it was of some music-hall rapid-sketcher; he liked the sketches. He is lovely—I get on better and better with him. We had dinner alone together, Peter at some H[ome].O[ffice]. party. Mouse is in

---

[27]Coleman has heavily blackened out the line that follows this sentence.
[28]Simpsons of Piccadilly was a high-end clothing store for men, which opened in April 1936; Fortnum & Mason was a department store, also in Piccadilly.
[29]The BBC began its television broadcasting service from Alexandra Palace, North London, on November 2, 1936.

my bed, feels queer. Wondering what John [Holms] would have said about Humphrey debacle.

Sunday, December 27

We have had a nice Christmas, as homey and full of simple pleasures as if we were a family! Appalled by the thought of Christmas, but wanting to give Johnny a proper festival, I purchased a large tree and baubles, and got small things in King's Road. We decorated it Thursday afternoon, Christmas Eve. It was beautiful when we got it done. It is a delicate, snow-clad, glistening angel tree. Phyllis was here that day, and again Thursday [Friday], Christmas. I tried to remember what I did every Christmas since 1926. I don't think any of them were happy except the one I spent alone in St. Tropez. I had beat it from Paris on the 18th of December.

Last Christmas was fairly happy, and this one, really, very. I had a turkey which Peter and I roasted, and I made a flakey mince pie.

For the last two days Peter and John have done nothing but try to rig up a complicated pulley system for conveying the kittens back and forth in their basket. Eliot wrote a splendid preface for the American edition of Djuna's book.[30] My book will never affect anyone as much as that. I feel sick at all my relations with Eliot. Now that Djuna has the book published, and fame will come to her—now that she is supported by Peggy (P. has promised me, privately, she will not let Dj. down), I find I don't feel happy when any new honour comes to her. Envy rears its head. It is impossible for me to want others to have honour and happiness unless they are poor and miserable. (As far as Dj. goes, she is still that) and when I think about it I want her to have a great deal more honour. Actually, if her book were not appreciated in America I should be furious—it depends on which side of me is uppermost. But I just note, in passing, what the human heart is like.

Whenever I feel sad, or think of Jennings, I think of Peter and Johnny and seem to be able to bear it.

---

[30]Having acknowledged (without a nod to Coleman) that it took him, "with this book, some time to come to an appreciation of its meaning as a whole," Eliot emphasized: "What I would leave the reader prepared to find is the great achievement of a style, the beauty of phrasing, the brilliance of wit and characterization, and a quality of horror and doom very nearly related to that of Elizabethan tragedy" (xi, xvi). Coleman's feelings of envy towards Barnes may have been exacerbated by the fact that, despite Coleman's ceaseless—and collaborative—efforts to help with the book, Barnes dedicated it "To Peggy Guggenheim and John Ferrar Holms." Barnes eventually gave Coleman public credit for her support by dedicating her last book, *Creatures in an Alphabet* (1982), to the deceased (1974) Coleman.

Monday, December 28

I have just read Eliot's preface to Djuna's book again and liked it even better than before. When I see how Eliot loves the book, I become even more sick to think what he must wonder about what was cut out. If only Djuna had preserved what was cut out—nothing could vindicate me more. But she threw away the awful parts in New York. I am terribly afraid Eliot thinks something valuable has been omitted. If only he could have seen the book as it was when I first saw it. Perhaps he can see from *Ryder* what Djuna's weaknesses are. But the sort of sentimental balderdash we threw out in New York, about Robin, does not appear in *Ryder*.

I was phoned by "Ozzy," who asked, in a tone of delicate drunkenness, if I would come out and meet Dylan Thomas.[31] I went—to the 6 Bells—at 6—and there I met Dylan T., a round-eyed animal with a chuckling gutteral laugh, and a rosy personality. I was delighted with him. Ozzy was tight, in a helpless beatific state. We went from the 6 Bells to 2 Bloomsbury pubs, where I became tight, and sweet to a Welshman called Richard Hughes who thought in a simple way to sleep with me.[32] I met Bernard Spencer, a young man who wrote a poem full of feeling, in *New Verse*.[33] I kept telling him how much I liked the poem. He was flushed with pleasure and thought I had mixed him with Stephen Spender.[34] A Scotch Turk removed Dylan from our society, to preserve him for himself and posterity.[35]

When I came home a long note from Johnny informed me of his activities.

---

[31]"Ozzy" was Oswell Blakeston, pseudonym for Henry Joseph Hasslacher (1907–1985), a British poet, novelist, film theorist, and a filmmaker. In a letter to Barnes, Coleman wrote: "I forgot to tell you that Oswell Blakeston is the guy who introduced me to Dylan—the only good office he has done me, though I have known him for five years" (University of Maryland Archives, April 6, 1937). Thomas was close with Coleman's and White's friend Wyn Henderson, and he had been in attendance at the Surrealist Exhibition whose organizing committee included, among others, Gascoyne and Jennings.

[32]Richard Hughes (1900–1976), Welsh poet, dramatist, novelist, and short-story writer.

[33]Bernard Spencer (1909–1963), English poet. It is not clear which poem Coleman read, as she does not specify the issue, and Spencer contributed regularly to *New Verse*. However, she had earlier noted reading the April/May 1936 issue (when she first read Thomas), and this could have been where she discovered Spencer: his poems "A Thousand Killed" and "Suburb Factories" were published then.

[34]Spencer and Spender were both contributing writers to the magazine *Oxford Poetry* (created in 1910 and still in circulation today) and in 1930 had served as co-editors.

[35]Likely Norman Cameron (1905–1953), a Scottish poet who had contributed to *Oxford Poetry* from 1925–1928. He was a copywriter at J. Walter Thompson, Deak Coleman's company where, in January 1937, White would also land a job.

Tuesday, [December 29]

D. Thomas opened my heart by raving about the works of Tony. Beginning with *Frost in May*, the "House of Clouds," and now her poem, which has just come out he says in *Contemp. Pr. & Poetry*.[36] We discussed her writing enthusiastically. He wanted very much to meet her. Last night, when I went home to get J[ohn]'s dinner before going out again to the Bloomsbury pubs, I phoned Tony and told her. She was pleased, said she didn't believe it. Barker was with her but he dislikes D[ylan]. T[homas]. She couldn't come out. Today I lunched with her. Johnny came. He sat silent for some time, then said, "Say, don't you think I look like a son-of-a-gun in these pants?" It was the first time Tony had seen him in long trowsers. Said she, "Do you mean, do you look an extraordinary spectacle in those trowsers?" (When I asked him, afterwards, what he thought of Tony he said, "O she's a cute kid"). He went to the Olympia Fun Fair and spent all his money.[37]

I went to Tony's flat with her and at first was pleased with it.[38] Later everything became monotonous. I felt a great warmth of feeling for her and sat reading her <u>present</u> diary—which she permitted to my surprise and pleasure—looking for things about myself. (The real surprise was to find nothing!) I was thinking how good her diaries are, how honest she is, how intelligent, both about herself and others; she knows other's characters. There was a long thing about me and my book which was very sweet, and the criticisms were just.[39] I didn't learn anything, because I know my deficiencies so well. I hoped to find some new ailment. I read for hours, in front of the gas fire which gave a pleasant glow, eating chocolates. She wrote letters. David

---

[36] White's poem "Epitaph," about the death of Elspeth Glossop, was published in the December 1936 issue of *Contemporary Poetry and Prose*. White noted in her diary in November 1936: "N[ew] S[tatesman] rejected it 'too violent and emotional'; Jennings has got it into *Contemporary Poetry*. It is amusing to be called too violent and to appear for the first time in poetry among the revolutionary young" (Vol. 1, 80).

[37] Constructed in 1885, Olympia remains as a series of exhibition halls in West Kensington.

[38] After living at 105 Oakley, White had returned to the home she had shared with Hopkinson at 18 Cecil Court, though he had moved out (White *Diaries* Vol. 1, 11).

[39] White's "present" diary, a small, red, hardcover book, contains the years 1935–1936. Coleman was likely reading the entry for September 28, 1936, in which White noted, for instance: "I love Emily and am too much afraid of hurting her. Her book ["The Tygon"] is so very personal to her. She seems to want us and the world to judge it, not as a thing in itself but 'think what this woman must have been through to write it . . . ' I love a great deal of the book but I am not happy about it as a whole [. . .] The trouble is, in spite of herself, she grinds an axe in this book and explains, or rather protests her particular belief all the time. That Frieda should believe certain things is right. But that the writer should assume certain things are and can be no otherwise is wrong. The novel is not a pulpit. Tolstoy and Lawrence both invalidated their work by preaching . . ." (Vol. 1, 79).

Gascoyne came. I didn't fit with him. He had just seen D. Thomas. He spoke of Humphrey, who he said was "the life of the party" at a silly Surrealist gathering. I felt absolutely sick, ordered a taxi and left, envying Tony. I had a long letter from Deak about money which depressed me and which I had to answer.

Thursday, December 31

The sweetest letter from Father yesterday saying such dear things about my wanting to help Barker. I have had nothing but pain and criticism and acute discomfort, from the beginning, on this score (Deak was offensive on the subject too). I couldn't believe Father meant it. He said he wanted to be able to send me more money, so I could help people. I felt such love for him, for that statement; I couldn't believe it. I expected, when I finally admitted to him I was helping Barker—which I had to do over this psycho-analysis project— that he would say I "couldn't afford to do it," should look to my own needs, shouldn't sympathize with others when I wasn't earning my own money, etc—the words I have always heard from Peter.

Saw D[ylan]. T[homas]. again yesterday, went to 6 Bells and met him, he was looking adorable, sweet, sympathetic; how John [Holms] would love him. He has not great intelligence. But has instinctive knowledge of everything good. D.T. and I walked up and down Kings Road trying to find a drinking club. I had to leave him, to come back here, to be here when Helen Stansbury came—who wanted to see John.

I was happy walking up and down with Dylan, and talking—happy as I had been with Humphrey—carefree and joyful, as if drunk. I find that instead of withdrawing from life as a result of being hit on the head by Jennings, I am more eager for it than before. I am so anxious for a little real joy, I will do anything for it.

D.T. phoned me to come to 6 Bells at 9, I gave dinner to J[ohn]. and Peter, then went. When I got there I was horribly disappointed not to find D. there. Ozzy phoned later and wished me to come and see some friends of his in Beaufort St., I foolishly went.[40] The man was nice. Ozzy tight and very eloquent. Has some sense, is sweet, but no judgment of <u>any</u> kind—people or literature.

David [Gascoyne] said, when I asked if one could ever have Dylan in the home—"No, he behaves badly." "What does he do?" "Well," said David, thinking. "He frets." Dylan has a really noble sense of values of people, puts

---

[40]Beaufort St. is in Chelsea.

them all just right; yet he can get on with anyone. He said, "Don't be bored with <u>people</u>; possibly with what they <u>say</u>."

Dylan T. phoned this morning with sweet apologies and said he was so tight he slept through the Underground. I did not mind. If I don't expect people to do things I will be happy. He said, when I came yesterday, that my face was the same, he had been afraid it would have some hard lines in it. He said he wished he could live in London as we could do each other much good.[41]

---

[41]Thomas was living a nomadic existence, staying for periods of time with family, lovers, and friends, and in hotels, in England and Wales.

Section 2

London, Winchcombe, and Petersfield

June 10–October 5, 1937

The diary stops on December 31, 1936 (for what would be a five-month hiatus), shortly after which Coleman had a brief sexual relationship with Dylan Thomas. The gap in her recorded life is filled in by her correspondence with Barnes.[1] On January 18, 1937, for instance, Coleman explained her decision to take a break from the diary:

> I can't stop this letter without telling you a word about me, but honestly I don't even write my diary any more because I am so sick of <u>statements</u> about myself and my life. I want only to live, be allowed to live. This seems to be vouchsafed me at the moment. I am happy but intensely nervous. I don't trust anything, don't believe anything, don't count on any future. I am alive and not brooding however which I suppose is better than being dead and screaming. I shall write some poetry soon. The young man—who is Welsh—goes back to Wales soon to write his own poetry, which is damned good. He is the other shining light besides Barker. They each think the other is negligible. I do not write my feelings because I wish only to pray God that they be allowed to last.

She ended the letter, "I can't write more as it sounds so foolish. In 6 months if it's still going on I'll make a statement!"

In a letter on January 29, Coleman described Thomas: "He has however no sense of responsibility and is half mad. He has gone to Wales—I <u>put</u> him on the train and have regretted it of course, though he did lead me a pub-life while he was here like nothing you never heard of on earth. Yet he's so

---
[1] Letters quoted are from the Papers of Djuna Barnes, University of Maryland Archives and Manuscripts Department.

sweet. He protests undying love, and I think means it—would not let me out of his sight, without great pain, for 3 weeks, until I made him go." Comparing him to Jennings, she affirmed, "I think D.T. suits me better, if I can weather the absences (which I approve of, considering his London habits), physical unfaithfulness, which I'm sure to get, and utter irresponsibility with regard to life and death. Do you think I can stand this?"

Coleman was justified with her concerns. Like the younger Barker and Jennings, Thomas was fifteen years her junior. He had met the English dancer Caitlin MacNamara (1913–1994) at a pub in London in April 1936, and although she was the lover of Welsh artist Augustus John, she and Thomas became involved. At the time Thomas pursued Coleman, MacNamara was in Ireland. Coleman was aware of MacNamara, who would marry Thomas in July 1937, in Cornwall.

There are three extant letters from Thomas to Coleman in her archive—and published in The Love Letters of Dylan Thomas—which offer a glimpse into their romance. In the epistle dated January 28 and 29, sent from his parents' home in Cwmdonkin Drive, Swansea (for which she had "put him on the train," as noted to Barnes), Thomas began, "darling Emily dear, dear Emily darling, Emily Emily dear Emily," and went on to write: "I think of you so much. I think of us, and all the funny, nice things we've done, and all the nicer things we're going to do. I think of nice places and people, and, when I think of them, you're always there, always tall and death-mouthed and big-eyed and no-voiced, with a collegiate ribbon or a phallic hat. I think of us in pubs and clubs and cinemas and beds. I think I love you." He emphasized, "this evening, like a fallen cherub at my window facing the park, I'm writing to you, to Emily, to my darling, inaudible, scabious, American Emily. I love you." Of MacNamara, he confirmed: "Of course I shall sleep with her; she's bound up with me, just as you are; one day I shall marry her very much—(no money, quite drunk, no future, no faithfulness)—and that'll be a funny thing." In the same letter, the following day, he continued: "It's half past ten in the morning: are you asleep? I wish I was fast asleep by your side, very warm, dreaming about the milk-white birds of Eden and the blue goats of Gehenna; and I wish [. . .] that I was waking up by your side, turning round slowly to see your face in the first of the shining, snowy morning. I wish I was with you." He added, "Never care what people say, my darling: Peggy's 'He won't write,' & Antonia's 'He doesn't love you' and Norman's 'Beware, beware!' I shall always write to you, and always love you, & never hurt you purposely: never hurt you at all, you're a very rare and expensive animal, and Christ knows I'm a lucky little man to love you & have you loving me." After promising to see her when he returned to lecture at Oxford and Cambridge in February and March, he closed, "Let's do everything in the world—(though I know what we'll do, of course: just go to pubs and bed. And what could be lovelier, anyway? I'm always happy with you)."[2]

Coleman's relationship with Thomas was played out during the bitter disappointment of having her manuscript "The Tygon" rejected by Chatto & Windus, as she updated Barnes on February 6: "My book was returned today by MacDougall, who couldn't get it off his hands fast enough; it must have burnt him. He said it 'frightened and alarmed' him." This news, coupled with the repeated frustrations of trying to hold on to Hoare, led her to confess, "I hope I have the guts to keep alive." As she did with previous men, she regarded Thomas as her salvation, telling Barnes, "I, for one, am so down that I will stake all on this." By April 6, though, she confided, "I have completely lost trust in Dylan," and yet, "I think I'm in a good period now, even if I don't see or hear from Dylan for two months—I feel singularly above him, somehow—my calm doesn't seem to come from HIM but from some satisfaction I have got from having had the sex and the companionship I wanted so badly, <u>for two months</u>."

When the diary reopens in June, the romance with Thomas was over but she used the text to reflect on what had passed. Barnes meanwhile had taken up with Silas Glossop, White's ex-lover and father of White's elder daughter Susan; Guggenheim turned to Jennings; and Coleman resolved to stick with Hoare.

LONDON, June 10, 1937

I wish this day I could begin an honest life—a life with one person in it, and my work. I wish I would wake up in the morning with some purpose in my heart, and with no desire for "love," except that connected with Peter. I believe, and with less to go on than before, that Peter is my Fate. He loves me, in his insane, cowardly way. His love, founded on cowardice, letting me down whenever I want worldly support is more intense than anyone has ever felt for me, more understanding of me. If I were not so violent (what I most fear) I could give in to it, and repose in some peaceful, useful design—instead of chafing night and day, planning suicide.

I cannot get on with anyone but Peter (who for this reason by implication, must understand me), as the last six months have shown. I went with Dylan out of cowardice (it is no excuse to say that it was to prevent suicide)—I will do <u>anything</u> to avoid despair and honest suffering—I will not see it through—I have endured a great deal with Peter, but always, since 1933, with the hope to get out of it. It has become clear that I cannot get out. I tried 3 times. I am back where I began. I don't know if Peter is. I should try to win

---
[2]Letters from Thomas to Coleman (F. 556); published in *Love Letters* 35–41.

his confidence back, but that will be very hard. He will never really believe in me. How can anyone?

I must write—that is what I am here to do. I could do it if I could clear my mind. It is a schoolgirl malady, my malady. If I would live with the truth, I wouldn't need "love." By the truth I mean I must live with what I have of Peter, who has turned out to be the background of my life. <u>All I have ever done outside of him is wrong</u>; I have only done right in leaving others. If I would only write—clear my mind of desires, opiates. I cannot rid my heart of the conviction that romantic love lies around the corner. Though I know that happiness is impossible, and that I am too much of a freak ever to satisfy any man except Peter. He has endured me. I am grown into him. Nothing will make me know these things except ignominious failure. I am ashamed of my life with Dylan—the self-deceit, the opiate—the shirking of the responsibility of Peter.

I know I am not the sort of person who ought to have several "love affairs." It is not right for my soul. It won't do Djuna harm, because she has had her great love; and what she does now is not important. What I do now is <u>my life</u>; my monument of hope. I did not lie to myself quite so much with Dylan, having been ashamed of my self-deceit with Humphrey. But I lied. (More to him than to myself.) He was more honest with me than I was with him. I used him to quiet my terrors, more than he used me—for he can use anyone, and I only a few; so he believed it more. He believed me, that's what I did wrong. Whatever he did, he told me the truth.

I am a "danger to others and to myself," Djuna said, because, as I said, I could not know if I was in love for a very long time. I don't know what I have done to Dylan. Most people think he couldn't be harmed, but I am not sure what effect this reversal has had, or if he understood it. Humphrey has not been hurt in the least. "The world will destroy any man if he is strong enough," Dylan said. . . . I don't know the value of Dylan—he is superficial, I know; yet that is not all of it; he has a conscious soul. I don't know what I've done. I took the opportunity of leaving him because of Caitlin: but I'd have done it later.

I went down to see Peter last night and tried to make love with him, for the first time in 8 months.

Although Peter did not make love with me, I felt I belonged to him more than ever, and when I came back, at 2 o'clock, I found Djuna washing (she'd come back from seeing Silas).[3] I didn't say anything to her, but got into my bed. I realized how really strange is my relation with Peter; she thought I was either

---

[3] Barnes was back in London, staying with Coleman; in August she would move into her own flat, also in Chelsea, at 60 Old Church Street. Since her return, Barnes had become involved with Silas Glossop. White had introduced them, as she recorded in her own diary on May 25,

very happy because I had slept with Peter, or very unhappy because I hadn't. I woke today feeling more peaceful than I have since Dylan went with Caitlin.

There is no record of why Dylan and I broke up—I have neither kept a diary nor written to anyone. It was because I couldn't stand the falsity of our life. He was honest with me. I wasn't with him. I endured too much, because of losing Humphrey. Instead of applying that knowledge to Peter (I no longer needed it with him, I imagined) I used it with devastating falsity in living with Dylan. I don't know if I have the events right, since I tend to forget what other people do to torment me, and remember what I do to them.

I went with Dylan out of pure excitement and vanity. (I stayed with him out of fear, fear of committing suicide.) I did not lie to myself about Dylan's feeling for me, at any rate. But I counted on him, and on feelings which I simply did not have for him—counted on living with him. It is all muddled.

Wednesday, June 16

My trouble is that I have saintly desires, longings for perfection. I am religious. The thought of a convent is joy to me. But I can imagine too much of the envy, malice and wickedness in a convent. I would like to live in a community where one could never speak. I may end my days in this way.[4]

It can do my soul in, sleeping with people I do not love, in the hope of finding "love." The one I want does not want me.

Last day at Yew Tree Cottage, August[5]

I wanted to write last night in my diary because I felt an epoch in my life ending—with Humphrey's making love to Peggy.[6] I think it has come about.

1937: "Last night I had an unexpectedly delightful evening with Djuna, Emily and Silas.[. . .]. Apart from nervous anxiety that Djuna would be bored by Silas (he was obviously excited and delighted by her) and that Emily would be violent with him, it was an excellent party" (Vol. 1, 85). Barnes and Glossop's union lasted nearly a year, ending when Glossop lost sexual interest in her.

[4]Coleman's statement is prescient, for as noted in the introduction she spent over a decade on retreat at Stanbrook Abbey, and after joining the Catholic Worker Farm in Tivoli, New York, remained in Holy Poverty until her death in 1974.

[5]Coleman's diary is sporadic over the next two months. She wrote entries on Thursday, June 17 and Sunday, July 25, from London; and then August 6, from Guggenheim's Yew Tree Cottage, before this last undated one there.

[6]As her relationship with Garman had ended, Guggenheim was looking for something to do with her life. She decided to open an art gallery, and had asked Jennings to join her on the project. She recounts the weekend Jennings went down to Yew Tree: "Emily was there, and as she was finished with him, she offered him to me as though he were a sort of object she no

I feel a change in her life has come, which, because I love her so much, I have wanted to bring about. Peggy really needs him and will certainly suit him (as I knew even last autumn) far better than I.

I didn't know if it would happen before I went to America; but it has happened.[7] Largely through my making Peggy believe he wanted her. (I also told Humphrey he was a fool, that I didn't want him and Peggy did.) But it was rather hard for it to happen, with me here. They both being simple—and she needing him desperately in one way (she's in absolute despair about her life with G[arman].—knows it must end), and he needing a woman (an American woman, let's say, one who can appreciate him)—it happened.

I don't know what my future will be. I don't trust myself. But I'm going to write at any rate; since I've been down here my book has prospered.

London, August 21 (Returned from Yew Tree Cottage.)

I am determined to make my own fate, by will power, at least as long as I can. I do not know how much character I have. I seem to have none. Peter has been disagreeable to me since I came back; his attitude being that he has been cheated of life, by me it is sometimes implied, and can't have anything. Hence I am in his way and he is not sure he won't benefit by my going to America.

Djuna is looking for houses, to live with Silas—it was sweet to see her—she supports me and I feel there will be a wonderful friendship one day, when she is established in London. She can't think of writing now.

John has been sweet, fascinated by Djuna, anxious to make an impression on her. I have not had so much trouble with him as I've had this summer for nearly six years.

Since I have been back, in the two days I have spent in London, I have felt I didn't want Peter. I never had it so strong. I feel done with him. Instead, as a year ago, of wanting someone else to replace him, I want myself.

At the end of August, with a loan from Hoare Coleman realized a long-held dream when she purchased a cottage called Boxholme in Balls Cross,

---

longer required, and I went in his room and took him in the same spirit. He had strange ideas about pleasures in life, and one was to spend the weekend in a millionaire yacht club. He never achieved this ambition with me, since it was so far removed from my normal taste" (*Out of This Century* 159–60). The affair lasted only a short time before Guggenheim called it off, and although their collaboration on the gallery also fell through Guggenheim did go on to establish Guggenheim Jeune—what would be the first of several galleries for her. Located on Cork Street in London, it opened with a show by Jean Cocteau in January 1938.

[7]Coleman would sail for the United States at the beginning of October to visit her father, other relatives, and Sonia Himmel.

Petworth, West Sussex, which she took possession of the following month. From September 3 to 18, she vacationed with her son at Shetcombe House in Toddington, Winchcombe, Gloucestershire, a property run by the Rightons, who had owned Bourton Far Hill Farm where she had stayed in 1932. Hoare spent the first week with them before going alone to Scotland to see his family. They filled their days hiking, horseback riding, reading, and playing card games, and John honed his passion for photography with his new camera. I have transcribed only the last entry from this holiday period, as she prepared to return to London.

Saturday, September 18

We took the horses out, preparing to go to Dumbleton again, as we did the other day.

We are going to London, from Cheltenham, tomorrow, and will have another life; this life, here, far from everyone and with Mrs. Righton, and the daily gallop with the horses has been a good one.

Since my chief joys in life are (outside of art) birds, trees, flowers and horses, with a little study of my friends on the side, I may truly be able to accommodate myself to this damnable planet when I get in my cottage. I am going to ride as much as I possibly can. When I own a horse, and a cottage, then I shall be very nearly contented.

I feel a change of life coming—the beginning of my going to America. The summer is over, John is virtually gone back—in spirit I am sailing, to another realm, which is not my world. I shall be happy there, for I shall write in Hartford, and try to get on with Father, and make his life pleasanter; and shall see Sonia; and see Chief. I have never been unhappy except through a man; when I am alone, I am happy under any circumstances.

John and I played rummy, which we love. One of us always beats the other terribly, and it runs in days. He is full of sexy horse-play. His language is awful. His face is delicate, and feminine. He brushes his hair back with two fingers and says "Fuck it." He said the other night, while playing cards—"What is the thing a woman has broken when she's married?" I said, "A bellup." He went into stitches and wouldn't believe it. So finally I said, "I'll tell you what it really is—it's a hymen." At that he nearly collapsed with mirth. So since he wouldn't believe that I said it was a mogy. Then eventually I said I would tell him really—it was a horse-porse. He said he would find out by going out and shouting one of them in the hall, so he went to the door and cried, "Bellup!" "Really!" I said. "That's too much. We'll have to leave here." He looked interested and thought it was that, and eventually I got bored with his repetitions and said it really was hymen and I didn't want to hear any more. He doesn't believe me yet and there's no dictionary.

We have the same room (necessity) and are extremely modest, but he screams and shouts if I open the door and shrieks—"Go 'way, or I'll kick you in the cock!" Nothing will induce him to modify this language, since he's just learnt it; but I went to bed the same time he did the other night, and he undressed in the bathroom. When he came in I was in bed but I screamed, "Go 'way! Go 'way! Or I'll kick you in the cock." This brought him to tears of mirth; he hasn't said it since.

When I kiss him he says, "No raping." When I was writing last night about him he seemed suddenly to live. Nothing lives, for me, unless I've seen it written, or write about it. Life is the rough draft of art. There are several rough drafts, then the completed thing in a sentence. One more proof, for me, that the imagination is the reality, and fact the illusion.

Coleman returned to London but did not resume her diary until September 22, when she and her son were at Guggenheim's Yew Tree Cottage, which Barnes and White were also visiting. Coleman began, though, by writing about the few days spent in London before going to Petersfield. The diary is especially enlivened and lightened by the literary and erotic banter of Coleman, Guggenheim, Barnes, and White as they interacted in the city. The diary then shifts to the countryside, with Coleman preparing the garden of her cottage for planting. She was about to leave for her annual trip back to the United States to see her father, but she intended to move into the cottage permanently upon her return to England. The edited selection of the diary closes with the last entries recorded during this expatriate period, with Coleman aboard the SS. Westernland heading out to the open sea. Her mood was one of almost unprecedented gratitude and contentment.

YEW TREE COTTAGE, September 22

John very shy and remote with Djuna; because he loves her. I looked at Djuna's painting of me and was really horrified. Then looking at those marble-rolling eyes I said, "That girl is going to kill someone—if he doesn't kiss her first," glancing at the horrible thick sensual mouth. Djuna said it was superb, that remark.

I suffered horrors under a permanent wave hearing Mr. Harold's troubles of the home and life. I went to dinner, at Tony's, with her and Djuna. A memorable evening. We went into the sitting room, and nonsense [] got on— Djuna ranting, T. saluting.

[Tony] said she preferred her girl-friends to her boy friends, and Dj. said she did too, and I said so did I, except for John and Hoare. I said women meant something to each other they had not meant hitherto, but Tony said they probably did in the 18th century. Dj. drank and got tight and I started the truth telling by saying T. hadn't the faintest idea of what any man was; was not honest. Dj. and T. discussed Silas, fencing—very well—neither giving in. Dj. is a match for the little Borgia[8]; I am not. I think T. loves me more (if she loves anybody) for that reason. She hates Djuna now—as she has hated me, at times (for having men and for being "an aristocrat"—as she calls me, enviously); but she could never keep it up with me because I'm so open and ingenuous. D. however has a little Borgia in her own make-up and T. resents it. T. likes Dj. because she isn't an aristocrat, hence her deadly snobbery can't function (about which she's so honest; she's as honest as God, when put to it); she can feel comfortable. Also, Dj. was never a rival. Now, with Silas, she could put poison carefully in Dj.'s food. What's good is Dj. has seen this (aided by Silas' truthful accounts of their monstrous relation), and looks upon Tony with admiration. She came out with all of it—said "You're a bad, bad woman," sweetly, going now and then to pet Tony. She said, "You're good. Why don't you see it through, instead of trying to be a good woman?" "I daren't," said Tony. She was alive and interested, replied in that calm lively tone, possessing everything. (When I think of the pages I have pitied Tony in; she got me into her circle too—cats and all[9]). I said, "Yes, Tony, you've had everything. You've had Tom, Eric and Silas eating out of your hand, giving you everything, you've given nothing, just got benefits. Yet you think you're the little abandoned woman." "I am," she said. "You've got even the cats," Djuna said. "You're a bad little spider." "The flies have always managed to bite me hard before they got away," said Tony.

"Nonsense," said Djuna. "You don't care." "Do you really think there's no good in me?" said Tony. I watched her face like an eagle. I said, "You're greedy. Don't you think you've had enough?" She wavered, her face changed several times, then she said with an awful look, her eyes squeezing up, her mouth nasty—"Not as much as I want." Dj. and I roared at that. "Am I really so bad?" said T. to Djuna. "Not bad enough," said Dj. "You ought to be the real poisoner." "Yes, I haven't courage enough," says T. "I'm afraid no one will love me." Djuna went over, very tight, and began

---

[8] Lucrezia Borgia (1480–1519), Italian noblewoman whose reputation was mired in gossip that, among other things, she helped her family poison enemies, and she slept with her father and brother.
[9] White wrote two children's books about her cats, *Minka and Curdy* (1957) and *Living with Minka and Curdy* (1970).

embracing her, and Tony snuggled up to Djuna's bosom like a real little blonde woman, sensual, and suddenly I saw how a man can want her, which I never see; I see her intellectual and personal attractiveness, but never her sensual. Her mouth opened, dreamy and she was pretty, and natural. She had a voluptuous look. Djuna said, "You're a bad little woman." "Is Emily bad?" said Tony, snuggling. "Emily is good," said Djuna looking at me. "Emily is all good."

I felt happy, and realized how much I want that; I want to be a saint more than an artist. I am more interested in the perfection of my soul, through knowledge and control, than in the imaginative setting down of what I know.

Djuna said, "Look at that bad little hand." "I know my hands are bad," said Tony. She has beautiful, perfect little fingers, and keeps them set together. When she smokes, her hand is always set that way; a kind of grace, with devilish cunning. Djuna would say, as she got tight, "Look at that little hand!" I said, "Look at Tony's ears." They are like an embryo's, set liquid in the head. Her whole head is monstrous, like a devil's. Tony's eyes are cold, loveless. Her blonde hair and her rosebud smile, and dimple. She said, "I can't be myself; I'm afraid; no one would love me. I'd be a monster." "And a good one," said Djuna. She kept coming over and caressing her. She said she loved her and Tony was one of her pet passions. Tony took it all naturally, as if she was accustomed to hear every night the most dreadful truths about one's soul that anyone ever could utter. She said, "What do you think of Emily?" "Emily?" said Djuna and her bantering tone dropped and for one moment I saw the passion within her (ah if one could keep with that—only through love can one live with it)—"Emily—is the most precious possession I have in the world." Then she began pounding me at once, for I was lying on the couch—Djuna having by this time massaged Tony's head and neck for her headache, and I could not stand the sight of Tony being massaged since it is ecstasy to me. When T. got up I reposed and said in a tone which would vamp Djuna, "Do my vertebrae a little." Whenever Djuna gets tight she massages someone, showing her innate feminine, loving and nursing nature. "Does anyone ever do this to me?" she said, pounding me. Then she began to pound my bottom and said, "Look at it. What is anyone to do with that?" I said "What does my bottom show, Djuna?" She said, "It's what you know. Your shoulders are what you hope." We laughed hard at this. Djuna said, "Your bottom is what you've learned of life. It's enormous, and snooty. Your poor little shoulders are where you're frightened, and lost." God how good this was—I remembered—what I knew at that moment of her saying it I'd never forget—my lying in the bath this spring and her saying—"Brains and no breasts—you're damned!"

I had lunch with Phyllis the next day and was struck by the lovely beauty of her face; it is all goodness. I went to see Djuna for a few minutes before leaving—she was low with a hangover but in the sprightly manner of those who have been drunk the night before and are dying she went over each detail of the night with Tony, that she could remember. I refreshed her, being one of those maddening people who aren't drunk. Of course I miss something by not being drunk.

I met Peggy accidentally in Waterloo, not expecting to see her till the train. She said her life snapped back again. It had been madness. Going down in the train, with the children around us, she told me about Humphrey. She doesn't really want him. She wants Garman.[10] Whenever I see Peggy suddenly I know she means more to me than any woman I have ever known. I can talk better to Djuna. Not that Peggy ever bores me, but naturally, not being a writer, and my kind of writer, as Djuna is, I can't talk to her so well. But we have far more of an understanding of each other's heart natures and minds than Dj. and I have. Perhaps because of John, and the years I've known her; but also she's quick and alive where Dj. is slow & unadaptable. Perhaps age.

September 23 (Yew Tree Cottage)

Peggy drove me to my cottage yesterday. She was afraid she would not like it. So was I, until we slowed up near it, and I saw the box and the hedge. I knew that it was my right thing. I stood for a long time looking at it, possessing it. The dear little house, like a cottage with eyes, and there was Virginia creeper, brilliant scarlet, up the side. I stood feeling the garden and the soil, and the fruit trees, creep into me. I shall never know what nature means until I've got physically into it, with my own hands. Peggy was pensive, affected by my cottage. There is a ploughed field opposite, and I hate to be away from it at any time, the seasons change the soil so, and the aspect of the ground. I shall not see it for four months. I felt my new life beginning, "nearer to the truth," and Peggy did too; she got into it while I was there, and began to envy me. She said afterwards, "It makes me feel I should get a country cottage too"—a perfect Peggyism.

I went all though it, adapting myself and my furniture to it. I shall live in it as soon as I return from America, and give up the flat immediately.[11]

---

[10]Guggenheim would return to Garman briefly before the relationship officially ended.
[11]Coleman would never live permanently in her cottage. As noted in the introduction, although she returned to Europe in early 1938 following her American holiday, she was back in the United States by early June. Always eager to help Barker financially, she invited him and his

Coming back Peggy and I talked about Barker and how she feels about money. She is going to give Barker an equal sum with me, but hates to do it, not knowing how long it will keep up; and hates to give any more money to Djuna.

I saw two snapshots of Kay Boyle Pegeen had, that showed her to have life and character and decency.[12] Her nose is beaklike and her mouth small and full. She has a tolerant, childish look. I thought of Djuna in sun-bonnet, high-waisted checked gingham frock and her father's brogans, with long hand-made curls and a sheaf of poems, coming to New York from the farm and getting her poems accepted.[13]

John plays the gramophone all day, exactly as I used to do, rushing through to the next thing in a whirl of learning. He told Peggy he couldn't sleep for thinking of music. I showed most of my bulbs to Hall, the gardener, who said they were excellent.[14] I left them at the cottage, and will plant them with Peter I think. Thinking of how Tony never mentioned me in her diary—or rarely—when I was looking for the bad things she said. At a time when we saw each other nearly every day—and my diary was full of her. Hers was full of men!

Peggy said I was not honest about Barker, that I gave money to him because I had been in love with him—and expected her to do the same. I was angry—it is so untrue—I feel nothing for Barker except pity for his struggle—for sentimental reasons I would rather give money to Bianchetti; but I know Barker deserves it, is honest—while B[ianchetti]. is not. (I had

---

wife to live in it while she was away. An undated letter from Barker, though clearly sent at the time of their move to the cottage in May, expresses his gratitude: "First let me repeat that this cottage is the nearest thing I've met to a rural paradise—I had expected to find it a place of some charm after hearing how rhapsodic you could be about it but I think that you did not exaggerate. [. . .] I have already succeeded in feeling more at home here than I have ever felt anywhere before, and can understand your contortions of regret at having to leave it. But believe me the pleasure that Jessica and I derive and will derive from living here cannot be a wholly barren or one-way thing. [. . .] When I reflect how depressing and unpleasant my state might be except for the advent of this place and your knowledge of my life and its requirements then I begin to speculate on the possibility of all sorts of extraordinary contingencies such as the existence of providence and the 'meaning' of being" (Coleman archive F. 1–8). When it became clear that Coleman would not be returning to Europe, her father, who had signed a promissory note to Hoare, sold the property in the spring of 1939.

[12]Boyle, as Vail's wife, was Pegeen's stepmother.

[13]Herring similarly describes how, "One day, probably in the spring of 1913, clad in a calico dress and carrying a basket, and looking rather like a milk-maid gone astray, Djuna appeared at the *Brooklyn Daily Eagle*." After her parents' separation, Barnes had been taken to New York City by her mother in the summer of 1912. Her first work to appear in print, in *Harper's Weekly*, was a poem called "The Dreamer" (75).

[14]Hall was Guggenheim's gardener.

said that I thought we ought to sacrifice—feel it—when we gave.) But I economized all winter, giving up clothes and amusements, so that I could send this money regularly to Barker—and whenever Johnny came, Christmas and Easter, I felt it dreadfully; to say nothing of the constant <u>worry</u> (though I know if I get in the soup I will be rescued, but I don't <u>want</u> to get into the soup) about coming out all right; When Johnny came in July then I did get into the soup—I did get a few clothes for myself—for one instant I stopped denying myself—and I did go to Yorkshire with Johnny. The result was I overdrew my account, and Peggy rescued me; in one of the sweetest and most spontaneous gestures I've ever seen from her.

I think of the poor, with nothing, the suffering, and I think "I haven't had that—that grind—I've always had enough money—my wants are simple and I can satisfy them—I can spend three or four pounds now on my garden (which seems a fortune to Barker)—I can have the cottage. It all costs money. Have I any right to it, who have not earned it with labour? But," I think, "I have earned it with my suffering, with my passionate living to find the truth—I've done that. And I <u>will</u> write, and perhaps eventually earn money from it." I do not believe I have really the right to money, which is so needed by those in poverty. But I think, "Suppose Barker were told about my childhood—my mother insane, my childhood in a school where I could not call my soul my own, and was always unhappy, never understood; would he not think he had been fortunate, compared to me?" Once the garden is started properly, I shall spend very little money living.

An astonishingly good thing by Eliot in a *Criterion*—quoted by Matthiessen—"Very few people today have earned the right not to be a Communist."[15] I didn't know E[liot]. knew that. I was thinking of the Japanese bombing Canton—I am really frightened now. Ever since I saw the picture in the *News Chronicle* of shovelling the dead in Shanghai into a truck.[16] It is what war in Europe will be. Everybody knows it but no one dares

---

[15]Coleman had been reading *The Achievement of T. S. Eliot: An Essay on the Nature of Poetry* (1935) by Francis Otto Matthiessen. In the chapter "The sense of his own age," Matthiessen quotes Eliot on Joyce: "The Catholic paradox: society is for the salvation of the individual and the individual must be sacrificed to society. Communism is merely a heresy, but a heresy is better than nothing." Matthiessen, in a note, draws attention to Eliot's commentary in the April 1933 issue of *The Criterion*: "I would even say that, as it is the faith of the day, there are only a small number of people living who have achieved the right not to be communists."
[16]The Second Sino-Japanese War (July 7, 1937–September 9, 1945) was fought between the National Revolutionary Army for the Republic of China and the Imperial Japanese Army for the Empire of Japan. On Tuesday, September 14, 1937, the *News Chronicle* published a photograph of bodies on a truck, with a caption that read: "This is the closing scene from the Paramount Film news record of the bombing of Shanghai. Bodies of civilians killed and mangled in the

to think. It hangs over. It is bound to come before five or ten years are up. Hitler or Mussolini will force it. Suppose England should be allied—for her "interests" (which I care nothing for) with Hitler or Mussolini against Russia? What would I do? I am for England, my home, the people I love best; but what would I do if England fought the Communists? I couldn't keep out of it—I couldn't sit in my cottage, in my garden in peace, if Fascists were bombing the people I loved in London and Paris. What would I do? I would go to London and tend the wounded, do what I could, regardless of side. If England fought with Soviet Russia against Hitler and Mussolini, what would I do? One has to decide these things. I don't believe in war, would not be conscripted (if I were a man). I believe in passive resistance in my head but my passions would never let it happen. I would be embroiled—one has to <u>act in one's age</u>, whatever the eternal sentiments which one's heart and will entertain.

. . . We went to a cinema and saw an excellent comedy with Hulbert and Cicely Courtneidge.[17] Peggy and I shrieked with laughter. Very angry with Johnny, who is mean and superior again (he always is here) and I went and sat somewhere else at the cinema. I can just keep from striking him. I looked at him lying asleep and thought his nose is rather thick, for all its smallness. He did not look very pretty. He is too much for me now—he is too influenced by the prevalent modern idea that no one should ever <u>feel</u> anything; or does he get this from his growing pride, and admiration of Deak? He is also lovable, and tried to talk to me after the cinema, and this morning (sleeping in the same room with me because Garman is here) he adjusted the fallen quilt over me, to show that he is fond of me. But I preserved cold dignity; I don't know how to deal with him. I could stay away from my son[18]—I love him dearly and when we live intimately together I miss him awfully, when he leaves; but the life of the mind, which I can't share with him, is more important to me. He's happy and I can't dominate him. I don't need him.

And yet, always, he has been something to me, away or with me.[19] I wanted it. I loved it. Therefore I must put up with it. What infuriates me is when he despises me. I'm in love with him I suppose, and must have his esteem: it's the fight I have with Peter. And every fight lets me down in his esteem; as with Peter.

---

streets are being loaded by Red Cross workers on to a lorry for burial." On September 13, the Chinese had attacked Japanese marines who were occupying Shanghai.

[17]They possibly saw the musical comedy *Elstree Calling* (1930) starring English actress Cicely Courtneidge and her husband, Jack Hulbert.

[18]The word "indefinitely," still readable, follows "son," but Coleman has crossed it out by hand.

[19]There is a sentence, which follows, but Coleman has heavily blackened it out.

Saturday, September 25

Djuna spoke of the "sex-grin" of Silas, and said it was so happy, "as though he were eating his way through paradise"—which startled me, and upset me, and made me think that perhaps I have to know more about sex to write. This would reverse my plans for life, which are now based on writing. I came downstairs still angry with Johnny; but when I saw his rear heaving up from the floor, leaning on his elbows studying the album of the discs he was playing—those ridiculous gymnastic shorts with a large white handkerchief protruding from the infinitesimal pocket behind, and his glasses on, I felt sorry for the poor odd little mutt. Peggy and I discussed money again—how she feels about it—she said I could not possibly imagine how anyone felt who had that Jewish meanness—so that every penny saved was an irrational delight, and every pound spent a lunatic agony.

I began reading a Life of Hart Crane, and sat up at once and was electrified to know that America had produced a genius like this.[20] I never admired his poetry and since I didn't like him personally I was not in a position to know what I know now, from the facts of his life. I read the book until late at night, remembering how I met Hart Crane, in Paris, in 1928 or spring of 1929 and didn't like him because he pinched my bottom and wouldn't talk to me about poetry. I saw him again at a party where he was very quiet and drunk.

The city is monotonous, every day is the same. In the country every day is different. The environment of Oakley Street never changes. How can I have endured it there so long; one becomes apathetic—accepts the half-thing, for some other thing: I did it for Peter. How my life is to be changed now, in the country. Thinking while reading about H[art] C[rane] of being at Cambridge with Dylan—how those little squirts—except Andy—did not listen to what I said, and listened to Dylan.[21]

---

[20] *Hart Crane: The Life of an American Poet* (1937) by Philip Horton. As a gay and Christian poet who suffered from what he felt was his marginalization in society, and prone to ongoing alcoholism and depression, Crane (1899–1932) jumped to his death from the ship taking him from Mexico back to New York. He had been in Mexico from 1931–1932 on a Guggenheim Fellowship, established by Peggy Guggenheim's uncle Simon Guggenheim.

[21] In early March 1937, Coleman had accompanied Thomas to Cambridge where he lectured. She described their visit in a letter to Barnes: "We went down to Cambridge for the weekend, but remained 5 days, we had such a pleasant time, reading poetry incessantly, and drinking (I don't do much of this but I like to be with people who are drinking, as I used to do so often with John—and with Siepmann, and with Alex Small). The boys there never do any work. I got such a dose of poetry it will last for months. We stayed with some of the people to whom Dylan lectured before he came this last time" (March [undated] 1937, Djuna Barnes Papers).

Hart Crane went with J. Walter Thompson. Is there anyone on earth who hasn't had a connection with this company? What guts he had. He had a mind; that is what dazzles me, I didn't know any American (of talent) did have—except Barnes with <u>her</u> funny mind.

At this point in my reading of Hart Crane's biography the phone rang and G[arman]. came in to say I was wanted and as I was in bed—where I had retired at 9 instead of going up to Petersfield in the rain to hear G. speak[22]—I was angry, thinking it was Djuna who wanted chatting. Imagine my surprise when it was Inverness, and turned out to be Peter. It still seems odd, and untrue. He said he wanted to come back early, to plant things in my garden. I agreed to this. He sounded sad, and penitent, ill at ease.

Sunday, September 26

Johnny would not go to sleep but insisted on talking and trying to get me to talk about sex, which I wouldn't. I let him read in bed and said "Make out you're asleep." He is delighted with me when I drop the mother. G. spoke in the square and John went to hear him. I didn't, not wanting to be snatched from Hart Crane, but had to do a parcel of lying to Peggy to make up for it. I half lie and half tell her the truth (about my attitude to Garman). Today he had the day off—took it—and discussed gardens with me or rather took me about and discussed his.

Monday, September 27

The Hart Crane book is absorbing. I don't want to get famous: <u>you never can have your true life again</u>. I can't stand reading about his degeneration. If I had met him quietly somewhere (in Mexico) and had never heard of him, I'd have known what he was like. But he was so famous—Hart Crane![23] and then when I met him, he pinched my bottom. I can't read about it. It was much worse than John [Holms]. He lost pride, honour, everything. He lost all his inspiration. He died. And went on living. The only possible end was suicide, which he so madly wished. O what a life, what a horror. He finished it completely—he went through—to the end; the very end of hell. I love him, love him! The horror of his life, and death—which was the right end—the end he

---

[22] Garman was officially employed by the Communist Party to lecture on Communism. Though Garman had already begun an affair with a married Communist named "Paddy" (whom he would eventually marry), his relationship with Guggenheim took a few months to finally peter out.
[23] Coleman has added the exclamation by hand.

knew must come—which he courted. He was honest—true. Crane saw the filth of life, the post-war revelations. He saw the *Waste Land* through—he didn't go into the English Church and smirk. I have not been so stirred by any contemporary thing. The greatest contemporary influence on me was knowing John, and reading *Nightwood*. Then, Barker's writings moved me. But the life of this person, who is more my kind of person (as far as I can see) than either John [Holms] or Djuna—(certainly more than Barker). I shall never be the same after reading this.

What makes me love John [Coleman] is that he took 8 pictures of the cottage yesterday when I was worried. I wanted them taken and didn't have time. He just did it and never told me and really I love him so for it, I couldn't forget it.

SS. WESTERNLAND, October 4

We have just passed Eddystone Light.[24] The ship is a foreign ship upon a foreign ocean. It rocks and sways and passes. Its course is set westward, and through this interminable sea it plows on.

The seagulls swoop and glide above the side, with the sun shining through their wings. The sun glitters on the afternoon water. The water is a deep blue and the white ship plows through it. She sways a little but never wavers in her course. We have passed the little fishing boats of Cornwall. They rocked in our swell. I walked about the decks, after the sun had set, and every now and then the thought of my garden came to me like sudden memory when one is in love. I thought of all my friends, now rapidly passing in my wake. I am so happy, to be alone in my small cabin, with only the sea and my thoughts. The people are non-descript and don't have to be dealt with. I can never forget the last two days in my garden, with Peter and Phyllis. It was nearer to a happy life than I have ever been. Waiting in the hotel in Southampton, after Phyllis and Peter had gone, I made a diagram of my garden, and which beds would be in bloom when—to see what I shall get to complete it when I return. I am so happy that I feel it is not right to have it, because of the extreme poverty and misery of others. But I was born with a capacity for joy which has had very little chance. And I deserve this change from the suicidal misery which has been my state for years. I have expiated my crimes with Deak, I think; I have paid for them in never having any fulfillment with Peter.

But Peter was so sweet, all the day, taking me to the boat (buying Mothersill), stopping to see Warblington on the way.[25] The Queen Anne house gave

---
[24]The Eddystone Lighthouse is off the coast of Devon.
[25]Warblington Castle, where Coleman had vacationed with Guggenheim.

me pleasure, even more than I had felt when we lived in it; and the feudal tower. I told Peter he would write in the next world. He said, "O yes, take a little pen, have a little write." I said, "Yes, you will, but you will have to live your character first." He said, "Your conception of the next life is that you will have a lovely horse, that runs and runs!" I embraced him and said that was exactly what I did want in the next life, and in this life.

He and Phyllis planted a horse-shoe bed of bulbs entirely at their own discretion. We had two solid days of gardening, and it was pleasant. We had beer and sandwiches on the lawn, with Phyllis. (We went and met her at Haslemere.) As we were leaving the cottage for the last time I observed that Peter had opened the kitchen door; so that one could look through the house to the orchard. I hadn't realized that the cottage was built like that—so that with the kitchen door ajar and the front door open one looks through to the green orchard, the trees descending in the grass. The sight of it, standing on the garden path, upset my equilibrium, as if my cup were running over. I am afraid to have too much happiness. I think insanity is very close to that realm; I remembered it was for Tony. When I have been in love, and my love returned, it has made me very nearly mad. I want to think of the cottage in a quite ordinary way, and do the work necessary for it; for if I think of it my head begins to whirl because I am not used to the joy.

Tuesday, October 5

The sun glitters on the sea. I went all over the boat. The boat pitched and I went up to the bow and watched it go splintering, swaying, through the water.

Coleman Diary Entries Omitted

1929 (F. 625): Nov. 4, Nov. 24, Nov. 25, Nov. 29, Nov. 30, Dec. 3, Dec. 7, Dec. 8, Dec.10. (F. 626): Dec. 27.

1930 (F. 626): Jan. 4, Jan. 8, Second entry Jan. 9, Jan. 11, Jan. 13, Jan. 24, Jan. 25, Jan. 26, Jan. 28, Jan. 29, Feb. 1, Feb. 3, Feb. 4, Feb. 5, Feb. 6, Feb. 24, Feb. 25, Feb. 26, Feb. 27, Feb. 28, Mar. 1, Mar. 2, Mar. 3, Mar. 4. (F. 628): Mar. 5, Mar. 6, Mar. 7, Mar. 8, Mar. 9, Mar. 10, Mar. 11, Mar. 12, Mar. 13, Mar. 14, Mar. 15, Mar. 16, Mar. 17, Mar. 18, Mar. 19, Mar. 20, Mar. 21, Mar. 22, Mar. 23, Mar. 24, Mar. 25, Mar. 26, Mar. 27, Mar. 28, Mar. 29, Mar. 30, Mar. 31, Apr.1, Apr. 2, Apr. 3, Apr. 4, Apr. 5, Apr. 6, Apr. 7, Apr. 9, Apr. 10, Apr. 11, Apr. 12, Apr. 13.

1932 (F. 629): Aug. 21, Aug. 22, Aug. 23. (F. 630): Sept. 24, Sept. 26, Sept. 28, Sept. 29, Oct. 2, Oct. 6, Oct. 8, Oct. 18, Oct. 30. (F. 631): Dec. 1, Dec. 4, Dec.13.

1934 (F. 632): June 14, June 17, June 18, June 24, June 25, Second entry June 29, June 30, July 1, July 2, July 4. (F. 633): First entry July 11, July 20, July 21, July 22, July 23, July 24, July 27, July 31, Aug. 1, Aug. 4, Aug. 5, Aug. 7, Aug. 9, Aug. 10, Aug. 11, Aug. 18, Aug. 24, Aug. 27, Aug. 30, Aug. 31. (F. 634): Nov. 18, Nov. 20, Nov. 22, Nov. 24, Nov. 27, Nov. 28, Dec. 3, Dec. 9.

1936 (F. 635): Feb. 1, Feb. 9, Second entry Feb. 14, Feb. 15, Feb. 25, Mar. 1, Mar. 3, Mar. 7, Mar. 10, Mar. 21. (F. 636): Apr. 5, Apr. 18, Apr. 3, May 6 (dated March in error), May 17, May 23, May 25, May 26, May 30. (F. 637): July 9, July 18. (F. 638): Nov. 21, Nov. 22, Nov. 29, Nov. 30, Dec. 6, Dec. 7, Dec. 19, Dec. 20.

1937 (F. 639): June 17, June 25, Aug. 6, Aug. 23, Aug. 24, Sept. 3, Sept. 6, Sept. 8, Sept. 9, Sept. 12, Sept. 16, Sept. 17, Sept. 28.

Bibliography

Archival Sources

The Emily Holmes Coleman Papers. University of Delaware Library, Special Collections. Newark, Delaware.
Djuna Barnes Papers. The University of Maryland Libraries Special Collections. College Park, Maryland.
Manuscript Diaries and Letters of Antonia White. Chitty, Susan, Private Collection.
Letters of John Coleman. Coleman, Marie Claire, Private Collection.

Published Sources

Ackroyd, Peter. *T. S. Eliot*. London: Hamish Hamilton, 1984.
Barnes, Djuna. *Collected Poems with Notes Toward the Memoirs*. Ed. Phillip Herring and Osías Stutman. Madison: The University of Wisconsin Press, 2005.
Barnes, Djuna. *Nightwood*. In *Nightwood: The Original Version and Related Drafts*, edited by Cheryl J. Plumb, 1–139. Normal: Dalkey Archive Press, 1995.
Barry, Alyce, ed. *Interviews* by Djuna Barnes. Washington: Sun and Moon Press, 1985.
Beach, Sylvia. *Shakespeare and* Company. London: Faber and Faber, 1960.
Bell, Anne Olivier. "Editing Virginia Woolf's Diary." In *Editing Virginia Woolf: Interpreting the Modernist Text*, edited by James M. Haule and J. H. Stape, 11–24. New York: Palgrave, 2002.
Blodgett, Harriet. *Centuries of Female Days: Englishwomen's Private Diaries*, New Brunswick: Rutgers University Press, 1988.
Benstock, Shari. "Expatriate Modernism: Writing on the Cultural Rim." In *Women's Writing in Exile*, edited by Mary Lynn Broe and Angela Ingram, 19–40. Chapel Hill: University of Carolina Press, 1989.
———. *Women of the Left Bank*. Austin: University of Texas Press, 1986.

Boyce, Neith. *The Modern World of Neith Boyce : Autobiography and Diaries.* Edited by Carol DeBoer-Langworthy. Albuquerque : University of New Mexico Press, 2003.

Bradbury, Malcolm. "*The Calendar of Modern Letters*: A Review in Retrospect." *The London Magazine.* October 1961, Vol. 1, No. 7, 37–47.

Brittain, Vera. *Testament of Youth.* New York: The Macmillan Co., 1933.

Broe, Mary Lynn. "My Art Belongs to Daddy: Incest as Exile, The Textual Economics of Hayford Hall." In *Women's Writing in Exile,* edited by Mary Lynn Broe and Angela Ingram, 41–86. Chapel Hill: University of North Carolina Press, 1989.

Bunkers, Suzanne and Cynthia Huff, eds. *Inscribing the Daily.* Amherst: University of Massachusetts Press, 1996.

Butter, P. H. *Edwin Muir: Man and Poet.* Edinburgh: Oliver and Boyd, 1966.

Carpenter, Humphrey. *Geniuses Together: American Writers in Paris in the 1920s.* London: Unwin Hyman, 1987.

Carrington, Dora. *Carrington: Letters and Extracts from her Diaries.* Edited by David Garnett. London: J. Cape, 1970.

Chait, Sandra. "Site Also of Angst and Spiritual Search." In *Hayford Hall: Hangovers, Erotics, and Modernist Aesthetics,* edited by Elizabeth Podnieks and Sandra Chait, 150–169. Carbondale: Southern Illinois University Press, 2005.

Chitty, Susan. *Now to My Mother: A Very Personal Memoir of Antonia White.* London: Weidenfeld and Nicolson, 1985.

Coleman, Emily. *The Shutter of Snow.* Normal: Dalkey Archive Press, 1997.

Coleman, Loyd Ring, and Saxe Commins. *Psychology: A Simplification.* New York: Boni and Liveright, 1927.

Connolly, Cressida. *The Rare and The Beautiful: The Art, Loves, and Lives of the Garman Sisters.* New York: HarperCollins, 2004.

Crosby, Harry. *Shadows of the Sun: the Diaries of Harry Crosby.* Edited by Edward B. Germain. Santa Barbara: Black Sparrow Press, 1977.

Dearborn, Mary V. *Mistress of Modernism: The Life of Peggy Guggenheim.* Boston: Houghton Mifflin, 2004.

Dickinson, Emily. *The Complete Poems of Emily Dickinson.* Edited by Thomas H. Johnson Boston: Little, Brown and Co., 1960.

Dunbar-Nelson, Alice. *Give Us Each Day: the Diary of Alice Dunbar-Nelson.* Edited by Gloria T. Hull. New York: W. W. Norton, c1984.

Dunn, Jane. *Antonia White: A Life.* London: Jonathan Cape, 1998.

Eliot, T. S. Introduction. *Nightwood,* by Djuna Barnes. New York: New Directions, 1961. xi-xvi.

Ellmann, Richard. *James Joyce.* New York: Oxford University Press, 1982.

Falk, Candace. *Love, Anarchy, and Emma Goldman.* New Brunswick: Rutgers University Press, 1999.

Felber, Lynette. *Literary Liaisons: Auto/Biographical Appropriations in Modernist Women's Fiction.* DeKalb: Northern Illinois University Press, 2002.

Fitch, Noël Riley, ed. *In transition: A Paris Anthology.* New York: Doubleday, 1990.

Ford, Hugh. *Published in Paris: American and British Writers, Printers, and Publishers in Paris, 1920–1939*. New York: Macmillan, 1975.

Ford, Hugh, ed. *The Left Bank Revisited: Selections from the Paris Tribune 1917–1934*. University Park, The Pennsylvania State University Press, 1972.

Fothergill, Robert. *Private Chronicles: A Study of English Diaries*. London: Oxford University Press, 1974.

Fraser, Robert. *The Chameleon Poet: A Life of George Barker*. London: Jonathan Cape, 2001.

Gammel, Irene. *Barnoness Elsa: Gender, Dada, and Everyday Modernity, A Cultural Biography*. Cambridge: MIT, 2003.

Gannett, Cinthia. *Gender and the Journal: Diaries and Academic Discourse*. Albany: State University of New York Press, 1992.

Gascoyne, David. *Collected Journals 1936–42*. London: Skoob Books, 1991.

Geddes, Minna Besser. "Emily Holmes Coleman." *Dictionary of Literary Biography: American Writers in Paris, 1920–1939*. Detroit: Gale Research Co, 1980. Vol. 4.

Gerhardie, William. *Memoirs of a Polyglot*. New York: Knopf, 1931.

Gill, Anton. *Peggy Guggenheim: The Life of an Art Addict*. London: HarperCollins, 2001.

Goldman, Emma. *Living My Life*. 2 vols. New York: Dover, 1970.

Graves, Robert. *Goodbye To All That*. London: Cassell, 1966.

Guggenheim, Peggy. *Out of This Century: Confessions of an Art Addict*. London: Andre Deutsch, 1997.

Hanscombe, Gillian, and Virginia L. Smyers, *Writing for their Lives: The Modernist Women 1919–1940*. London: The Women's Press, 1987.

Hemingway, Ernest. *A Moveable Feast*. New York: C. Scribner's Sons, 1964.

Herring, Phillip. *Djuna: The Life and Work of Djuna Barnes*. New York: Viking, 1995.

Hogan, Rebecca. "Engendered Autobiographies: The Diary as a Feminine Form." In *Autobiography and Questions of Gender*, edited by Shirley Neuman, 95–107. London: Frank Cass, 1991.

Hopkinson, Lyndall P. *Nothing to Forgive: A Daughter's Life of Antonia White*. London: Chatto and Windus, 1988.

Isherwood, Christopher. *Christopher Isherwood Diaries: 1939–1960*. Edited by Katherine Bucknell. London: Methuen, 1996.

Jackson, Kevin. *Humphrey Jennings*. London: Picador, 2004.

James, Alice. *The Diary of Alice James*. Edited by Leon Edel. New York: Dodd, Mead, 1964.

Lamos, Colleen. "Queer Conjunctions in Modernism." In *Gender in Modernism: New Geographies, Complex Intersections*. Edited by Bonnie Kime Scott. Urbana: University of Illinois Press, 2007. 336–343.

Lee, Hermione. *Virginia Woolf*. London: Chatto and Windus, 1996.

Mansfield, Katherine. *Journal of Katherine Mansfield*. Edited by John Middleton Murry. London: Constable, 1954.

Marnham, Patrick. *Wild Mary: The Life of Mary Wesley.* London: Chatto & Windus, 2006.
Martinson, Deborah. *In the Presence of Audience: Diaries, Lives, Fiction.* Columbus: Ohio State University Press, 2003.
Matthews, William. "The Diary as Literature." In *The Diary of Samuel Pepys,* edited by Robert Latham and William Matthews. Vol. I: xcvii-cxiii. Berkeley: University of California Press, 1970.
McAlmon, Robert and Kay Boyle. *Being Geniuses Together: An Autobiography.* New York: Doubleday, 1968.
Miller, Henry. *The Tropic of Cancer.* New York: Random House, 1961.
Monk, Craig. *Writing the Lost Generation: Expatriate Autobiography and American Modernism.* Iowa City: University of Iowa Press, 2008.
Moritz, Theresa, and Albert Moritz. *The World's Most Dangerous Woman: A New Biography of Emma Goldman.* Vancouver: Subway Books, 2001.
Muir, Edwin. *An Autobiography.* London: The Hogarth Press, 1954.
Neagoe, Peter. *Americans Abroad.* Amsterdam: Servire Press, 1932.
Nicolls, Peter. *Modernisms: A Literary Guide.* Berkeley: University of California Press, 1995.
Nin, Anaïs. *The Diary of Anaïs Nin.* Edited by Gunther Stuhlmann. 7 vols. San Diego: The Swallow Press and Harcourt Brace Jovanovich, 1966–1980.
Olson Liesl. *Modernism and the Ordinary.* New York: Oxford University Press, 2009.
Partridge, Frances. *Memories.* London: V. Gollancz, 1981.
Plumb, Cheryl J. Introduction. *Djuna Barnes Nightwood, The Original Version and Related Drafts,* edited by Cheryl J. Plumb, vii-xxvi. Normal: Dalkey Archive Press, 1995.
Podnieks, Elizabeth. *Daily Modernism: The Literary Diaries of Virginia Woolf, Antonia White, Elizabeth Smart, and Anaïs Nin.* Montreal and Kingston: McGill-Queen's University Press, 2000.
Podnieks, Elizabeth, and Sandra Chait, eds. *Hayford Hall: Hangovers, Erotics, and Modernist Aesthetics.* Carbondale: Southern Illinois University Press, 2005.
Putnam, Samuel. *Paris Was Our Mistress: Memoirs of a Lost and Found Generation.* Carbondale: Southern Illinois University Press, 1970.
Rich, Adrienne. *On Lies, Secrets, and Silence: Selected Prose, 1966–1978.* New York: W. W. Norton & Co. 1979.
Rosenwald, Lawrence. *Emerson and the Art of the Diary.* New York: Oxford University Press, 1988.
Rosner, Victoria. *Modernism and the Architecture of Private Life.* New York: Columbia University Press, 2005.
Rubio, Mary, and Elizabeth Waterston, eds. *The Selected Journals of L. M. Montgomery.* Toronto: Oxford University Press, 1985.
Scott, Bonnie Kime. *The Women of 1928.* Vol. 1 of *Refiguring Modernism.* Bloomington: Indiana University Press, 1995.

———. ed. *The Gender in Modernism: New Geographies, Complex Intersections.* Urbana: University of Illinois Press, 2007.

———. ed. *The Gender of Modernism: A Critical Anthology.* Bloomington: Indiana University Press, 1990.

Shils, Edward, and Barmen Blacker, eds. *Cambridge Women: Twelve Portraits.* Cambridge: Cambridge University Press, 1996.

Siepmann, Mary. Introduction by Callil, Carmen and Mary Siepmann. *The Shutter of Snow.* By Emily Coleman. London: Virago Press, 1981.

Smart, Elizabeth. *Necessary Secrets: The Journals of Elizabeth Smart.* Edited by Alice Van Wart. Toronto: The Coach House Press, 1987.

———. *On the Side of the Angels: The Second Volume of the Journals of Elizabeth Smart.* Edited by Alice Van Wart. Hammersmith: HarperCollins, 1994.

Stein, Gertrude. *The Autobiography of Alice B. Toklas.* New York: Vintage Books, 1960.

Suleiman, Susan Rubin. *Subversive Intent: Gender, Politics, and the Avant-Garde.* Cambridge: Harvard University Press, 1990.

Thomas, Dylan. *The love letters of Dylan Thomas.* London: J. M. Dent, 2001

Tremlett, George. *Dylan Thomas: In the Mercy of his Means.* London: Constable, 1991.

Weber, Ronald. *News of Paris: American Journalists in the City of Light Between the Wars.* Chicago: Ivan R. Dee, 2006.

White, Antonia. *Diaries 1926–1957.* Edited by Susan Chitty. London: Constable, 1991. Vol. 1.

———. *Diaries 1958–1979.* Edited by Susan Chitty. London: Constable, 1992. Vol. 2.

———. *Frost in May.* Toronto: Lester and Orpen Dennys, 1981.

Woolf, Virginia. *The Diary of Virginia Woolf. 1915–1941* 5 vols. Edited by Anne Olivier Bell and Andrew McNeillie. London: Penguin, 1979–1985.

———. "Modern Fiction." In *The Common Reader*, Vol. I: 184–95. London: Hogarth Press, 1948.

———. *Moments of Being*: *Unpublished Autobiographical Writings.* Edited by Jeanne Schulkind. London: Chatto & Windus, 1976.

Index

ABC, 137
Abdication, King Edward VIII, 323, 331*n*17, 333
Abortion: Daniel A. Mahoney, 99*n*11, 168; discussion of, 234; Djuna Barnes, 168, 201*n*38; Elspeth Glossop, 230*n*34; Peggy Guggenheim, 41, 59*n*44, 148, 149*n*15; "The Tygon," 230*n*35.
Adventures Among Birds (Hudson), 184
Agate, James, 133
Alanna Autumnal (Barker), 192, 193*n*26, 194, 224*n*23
Alighieri, Dante, 50
Ambition, xxxix, 36, 57
American Hospital, 29, 31, 32, 37, 66
Americans: Cyril Connolly, 249; expatriates, xxxiv, 20*n*50, 27*n*71, 29*n*75, 99*n*10, 100*n*13, 109*n*26, 144*n*4, 145*n*8, 169*n*10, 222*n*19; genius, 100; *Grand Hotel*,134, 136; language, 302; living in reaction, 28; modernism, xi; "The Tygon," 210; writers, xxiii, 148.
Americans Abroad (1932), xxxi, 84, 162, 256, 300
Anderson, Margaret, 244
Architecture, 77

Art, xiii, xvii, xix, xxv–xxvii, 71, 77
Artists: female, xiii, xxv–xxvi, 102, 179; Left Bank, xxiii; patronage, xxvii, xxxi–xxxii.
"Ash Wednesday" (Eliot), 223
Astaire, Fred, 221
Astor, Nancy Witcher, 111–12, 113, 114
Auden, Wystan Hugh, 192
Austria, 152, 165
Autobiography of Alice B. Toklas (Stein), 225
Axel's Castle (Wilson), 308

"The Bacchant" (Barker), 224
Back, Barbara, 263
Bailli, 48, 52
Ballet, 184, 185*n*3, 188*n*11
Barker, George: *Alanna Autumnal*, 192, 193*n*26; "The Cremation," 233; Dylan Thomas, 338; Elizabeth Smart, 243*n*62; family, 252*n*10; feelings for, 248, 263, 284, 287, 289, 303*n*29, 312, 329–330; fencing accident, 256, 259; financial support of, xii, xxvi*n*53, 232, 236, 245, 250, 251, 276, 284, 301, 318, 328, 334, 339, 352, 353; homosexuality, 216, 243, 244; "Ode to Man," 223, 224;

368 Index

Peter Hoare and, 225, 228, 229, 242, 257, 299; poetry, 243; relationship with, xii, 183, 245–46, 260; resisting advances, xxxiii, 220, 260; sexual relationship, xxxvii, 247, 251–53, 301, 310, 317; struggle with feelings for, 216, 217, 218, 219, 223, 228, 239, 244, 245, 289; T. S. Eliot and, 223, 265, 267, 268, 271–72, 278, 279, 288; teaching position, 277–78; women as poets, 243; Yeats's 1936 anthology, 224n24.

Barnes, Djuna: Antonia White, 168, 349–50; career, 64n57; childhood, 305–6; Coleman's diary, xxxii, 110–11, 303–4; Coleman's father's opinion of, 126–27, 154; Coleman's letters, 109; Common-law husband, 112; Cyril Connolly, 297; Deak Coleman, 299; description of, 94, 156; Douglas Garman, 299; Duchess of Marlborough, 116; Elsa von Freytag-Loringhoven, 167n6; Emily Brontë, 100; Eric Siepmann, 292; financial support of, xxvi$n$53, xxvii, 159, 278, 355; flat in Paris, 316, 258; George Barker, 250; Henri Ford, 156; illness, 290; Jean Oberlé, 168n9; John Coleman, 348; John Holms, xxviii, 97–8, 102–3, 107, 112–13, 169, 171; Julius Caesar, 119; Kay Boyle, 119; Lady Astor interview, 111–12, 113–14; Logan Pearsall Smith, 325; men, 99, 107, 109, 113, 291; modernism, xii; motivation from, xxvii; Natalie Barney, 109, 159; New York, 120; *Nightwood*, xii, xxvii, xlii, 93, 99n11, 100n13, 101n11, 156n31, 159n39, 215, 216, 221n18, 230,236, 247, 264, 267–69, 277, 284, 287, 293–95, 312, 314, 324, 336–37, 357; opinion of, 94, 95, 98, 111, 113, 117, 156, 157, 168, 237, 260, 304; opinion of Coleman, 111, 170, 292; paintings, 290, 348; Peggy Guggenheim, 101, 160, 168, 170, 234–35, 258, 301, 307, 336; Peter Hoare, 99, 102, 114–15, 217, 258, 291–93, 304; Peter Neagoe, 238; Rudolph "Silas" Glossop, 346, 355; *Ryder*, 100, 117, 157–58, 310; Scudder Middleton, 290; sexuality, xxviii, 169, 350; *Shutter of Snow*,xl, 297, 312–13, 324; table tipping, 120; talent, 64, 102; Thelma Wood, 104, 146–47, 159, 170; Thomas Dylan, 344; "The Tygon," xl, 323–25, 326; writing, 166.

Barney, Natalie Clifford, 109, 159
Barrymore, John, 134
Battersea Park, 187, 265, 297
Baudelaire and the Symbolists: Five Essays (Quennell), 299
BBC, 335n29
BBC Orchestra, 238
Beachy Head, 308
Beaton, Cecil Walter Hardy, 297
Beaton, George, 285, 299
Beaufort Street, 339
Bell, Anne Olivier, xiv
Bell, Graham, 324
Bell, Julian, 191
"The Bell of La Miséricorde" (Coleman), 48
Bell, Vanessa, 132n6, 133, 191n22, 324n5
Benstock, Shari, xxiii, xxiv, xxvi, xxxiv;
Berkman, Alexander, 7n13, 316
Bianchetti, Lelletto: Coleman's father, 103, 126; emotions, 152; financial support, 94, 96n7, 117, 160, 352; James Joyce, 80n17; love affair, 80–81, 108n23, 284; requests for money, 104, 131, 136, 139–140; sadism, xxxvii, 307, 314, 316; "The Tygon," xxxii, 230n35.
Birrell, Francis Frederick Locker, 138

Birth trauma, xvi, 25*n*67, 32*n*86, 48*n*13
Bisexuality, xii, xiii, xxxiv, xxxv, 183.
    See also Sexuality
Blakeston, Oswell (Ozzy), 337, 339
Blake, William, 114, 120
Blodgett, Harriet, xviii, xix
Bloomsbury, 15, 139, 191, 267, 313
Bloomsbury Group, 15*n*39
Blum, Frank, 153
Bois, 40
Borgia, Lucrezia, 349
Bourton Far Hill Farm, 81, 125–30, 131, 347
Boxholme cottage, 346–47, 351–57
Boyle, Kay: career, 99*n*10; Coleman's fiction, xxxi, 119; Cyril Connolly, 251; Pegeen Vail, 352; Peter Hoare, 208; *The Shutter of Snow*, 150; standards, 302; *Year Before Last*, 148, 149, 158.
Brain tumor, xxxviii
Brenan, Gerald (George Beaton), 285
Brick Top, xxvii, 144
Bring 'Em Back Alive, 135
Broe, Mary Lynn, viii, xliii
Brontë, Emily, 100, 116
Brooke, Rupert, 62
Brook, Norman: career, 135*n*18; *House Divided*, 144; "Gossy" Gosshawk, 135*n*18, 140*n*31, 144, 220*n*12, 238, 249; King's broadcast, 238; with Peter Hoare, 230, 261; the Prune, 220.
Buchan, Frances, xvii

Caeser, Julius, 119
Café de Versailles, 22
Café Royal, 216, 255, 265, 269, 277
California, xi, xv, xvi
Cambridge, 280–82
Cameron, Norman, 337*n*35
Camp Pinecliffe, xxi, xxii
Carpenter, Maurice, 253
Carroll, Dennis, 317, 335

Carswell, Catherine, 135, 165
Catholicism, xxxvii, xxxviii, xxxix, 63, 195
Catholic Worker Farm, xxxviii, xliii, 309*n*7, 345*n*4
Cauterization, 31–32
Celibacy, xxxviii
Censorship, 267, 268
Chait, Sandra, viii, xliii
Champs-Élysées, 26, 40, 153
Chaplin, Charlie, 239
Chappell, Elizabeth, 304*n*31, 305*n*36
Charing Cross Road, 216
Chatto&Windus, 230, 247, 248–49, 343
Chelsea Baths, 188
Chelsea Tea House, 242
Chemin St. Antoine, 45, 46, 48
Chez Florence, 160
Childhood, Coleman's, xiv, 140, 141
Children, xv, xxiv, xxxiii, 11, 26, 37, 38, 68, 130
Chinese exhibition, 216
Circus, 73–74
Cliches, 65
Clun forest, 95
Clutton-Brock, Alan, 307, 311, 318, 323, 324
Coaney, Lucy Adams, x–xi, 141
Coleman, Deak (Karen): birthday, 24; Coleman's writing, 22, 56, 58, 61; courtship, xxi–xxiii; dining and dancing, 4; divorce, xxiii, xxv, 3, 80, 90, 126, 141; *Don Quixote*, 49; John Coleman, xxiii, xxiv–xxv, 15, 31, 63, 130, 179, 186, 230, 263–64, 335, 354; John Holms, 3; joins family in Europe, xxiv; marriage to Emily, xxiii–xxv, 10, 11, 31, 80, 299, 357; picture of, 73; poetry, 16, 32, 265; premarital sex, xxii, 32, 103; *Psychology: A Simplification*, xxiii*n*43; real name, xx*n*29; sexual relationship with, 26, 51, 57; sonnets, 58, 61.

Coleman, John (Kay) Milton Holmes: American Hospital, 37; anger with, 14–15, 56, 181, 257, 348, 354; Austrian alps, 152, 160, 161, 162, 231; broken window, 171; Christmas, 41, 161, 162, 336; crying, 56; desire to be with, 97, 161, 179, 225, 306; feelings for, 14, 16, 20–21, 31, 34, 63, 145, 150, 162, 181, 196, 217, 225, 242–43, 259, 280, 315, 335, 354; jealousy, 197, 199; living arrangements, 7*n*12, 66, 143, 158, 162, 199; Pegeen Vail, 148, 154; Peggy Guggenheim, 202; Phyllis Jones, 204*n*48; relationship with, 199; return to the Donns, 41*n*106, 204, 247; school, 143–44, 158, 161; sensitivity, 37; visits with, 22, 24, 26, 145, 148, 150, 193, 195, 198–99, 201, 203, 257, 338, 353; whooping cough, 63, 66, 67.

Coleman, Marie Claire, vii, xxxix*n*103

Colette, Sidonie-Gabrielle, 51, 52

Collected Poems with Notes Toward the Memoirs (Barnes), xlii

Commins, Saxe, xxiii*in*43

Communism: death of King George, 220; Douglas Garman, 183, 304, 329; Eric Siepmann, 273; fight for, 331; John Holmes, 335; personal aid and, 318; rise of, xiii, xxvii; T. S. Eliot, 353.

Confessions (St. Augustine of Hippo), 218*n*7

Connolly, Cyril: *Americans Abroad*, 256; career, xii, 229*n*33, 237*n*47, 251; description of, 247, 249, 255, 270–71, 298, 304; desire to meet, 229, 237; Djuna Barnes, 297; dreams of, 289; invitation from, 289; masturbation, 298; *New Statesman*, 250; *The Shutter of Snow*, 297; surrealist cocktail party, 303.

Connolly, Jean, 250

Conservatism, xxiii

Consumerism, xiii

Cooper, Cicely, 323

Cosi Fan Tutte, 231, 307, 309

Covent Garden, 185, 188

Crane, Hart, xxx, xxxiii, 355

Crawford, Joan, 134

"The Cremation" (Coleman): Antonia White, 275; Beatrix Holms. 255; completion of, 229–30; *Criterion*, 309; Edwin Muir, 241; George Barker, 223, 224; Peggy Guggenheim, 233; Peter Hoare, 232, 233; polished poems, xxxii; revising, 217, 233; writing, 174, 179–80, 181, 216, 227.

Criterion, 309

Crosby, Caresse (Mary Phelps), 147, 158

Cross, Joan, 240, 261

Cultural adventurists, xxiv

Daily Mirror, 263

Dante, 45, 46

"The Dark Angel" (Johnson), 272

Day, Dorothy, xxviii

Deacon, Gladys, 116*n*49

Dearborn, Mary, 41*n*107, 149*n*17

Death: "The Cremation," 233; facing, 167; of John Holms, 177; thoughts of, 210, 227, 228, 228, 229.

Death in the Afternoon (Hemingway), 152

"Death of Samson": Antonia White, 288; inspiration, 247, 258, 262; revising, 279–80; writing, 263, 265, 279–280.

Dentist, 14, 26, 34, 35

Depression, xvi, xxx, 126*n*4, 166, 248, 259, 329.*Seealso* Suicide

de Segonzac, André Dunoyer, xxviii, 51, 52, 55

Deutchbein, Peggy, 114

Deux Magots, 9*n*25, 14, 17, 42–43

Devonshire, 93–123, 166–69
De Zoete, Beryl, 12, 138, 140, 189, 298
Dial, 251
The Diary of Virginia Woolf, xlv
Diaries, traditional activity of, xviii–xix
Diary, Emily Coleman's: Antonia White, viii, xix, xi, xii; as archive of modernism, xii, xiii, xiv, xxiv, xxvi, xxvii, xxviii, xxxii, xlii, xliii; beginning of, xii; deprecation in, xxi; Djuna Barnes, xii, 110, 305; editing, vii, xiii, xliii–xlvi; financial freedom and, xxvi; John Holms, xxxi, xlvi, 245*n*67; as literary product, xvii, xviii; length of entries, xvii, xxxi, xlv; originality, xxxi; Peggy Guggenheim, xii, 110, 151; Phyllis Jones, xii, xliii; Sonia Himmel, 84, 77*n*1, 82*n*21, 151; themes and topics, xxxiv.
Disney, Walt, 134
Divorce, xxiii, xxv*n*52, 80
Don Giovanni, 307, 309
Donn, Nina (Mamotchka): financial support, xxv, xxvi*n*53, 46, 160, 232, 318; jealousy, 84, 141; John Coleman, xxiv–xxv, 7, 15, 38, 39, 46, 79, 143, 264; motherhood, xxiv, 247, 258.
Donne, John, 176
Don Quixote, 49
Doolittle, Hilda, 291
Dostoyevsky, Feodor, 6
Drama, 69
Dreiser, Theodore, xxvii
"Dry Leaves" (Coleman), 48
Duchamp, Marcel, 237

Ecstasy, 97, 98, 254
"Ecstasy" (Donne), 51, 190, 304
Eddystone Light, 357
Edward VIII, 221*n*17, 238*n*50, 331*n*17, 333–34

Egerton, Clement (Tommy), 8, 9
Egerton, Kay (Poplar), 8
Egotism, xxxiii
Eiffel Tower restaurant, 138–39
Eisenstein, Sergei, 242
Eliot, T. S.: Arthur Waley, 18; communism, 353; Cyril Connolly, 271; Djuna Barnes, 234, 309; Dorothy Hoare, 206; dreams of, 219; Emily Hale, 267*n*42; George Barker, 223, 267, 268, 271; influence on Coleman, 62; nationality, 60; *Nightwood,*xii, xxvii, 216, 221, 247, 264–68, 270, 276–77, 287, 293–96, 303, 305, 309, 314, 330, 336; Peter Hoare, 205, 277, 279; "Tradition and the Individual Talent," 59; unanswered letter to, 273, 277, 279, 280, 285, 288, 297; *The Use of Poetry and the Use of Criticism,* 176, 178, 179, 180; Vivienne Haigh-Wood, 261*n*30; women writers, xxxii.
Emily Coleman Papers, xl, xliii
Engagement, xx, xxii, xxxix
The Enormous Room (Cummings), 300
"Epitaph" (White), 338
Epstein, Jacob, 269
Eternal life, 312
Evening Standard, 210, 331
Evil, 176, 205, 218, 238
Expatriates, xiii, xxiv, xxvi, xxvii, xxxi, xxxiv, 3–4, 14*n*35, 20*n*50, 27*n*71, 29*n*75, 99*n*10, 100*n*13, 109*n*26, 144*n*4, 145*n*8, 169*n*10, 222*n*19

Faber & Faber, xii, 216, 267–68, 282, 295
Faber, Geoffrey, 222, 247
Fabre, Jean Henri, 312
A Farewell to Arms (Hemingway), 34–35
Fascists, 335
Fear, 49, 97

Female alliance, 111
Femininity, xxxiv, 37, 68n65, 244, 277, 282
Figaro, 239, 240
Films, xii, 22, 131, 134, 293
Finale of Seem (Lowenfels), 29
Finnegan's Wake (Joyce), xxx, 65
The First Time I . . . (Benson), 236
Fisher boy (Philippe): *copin*, 57, 64; friendship, 52; jealousy, 65, 66, 67, 68, 69–70, 73–74; need for solitude and, 48; preoccupation with, 45, 58–59, 70, 82; society of *etrangères*, 55.
Fitch, Noël Riley, xxx
Fitzgerald, Mary Eleanor (Fitzie), 157
Fleischman, Helen Kastor, (Helen Joyce), 144, 152
Florence, 77
Ford, Charles Henri, 101, 156, 189
Ford, Ford Madox, 30
Ford, Hugh, xxiv
The Fortunes of Richard Mahony (Richardson), 252, 256, 259
France, vii, ix, xi, 3
Freytag-Loringhoven, Elsa von, 167
Frick, Henry Clay, 7n13
Frost in May (White), xii, 166n2, 338
"The Fugitives" (Coleman), 17, 42
Futurism, xiv

Gannett, Cinthia, xviii
Garbo, Greta, 87, 134, 136–37
Garman, Douglas: *Alanna Autumnal*, 194; Antonia White, 193, 194; argument with, 194, 257; career, 183, 196n29, 248n1; children, 192-93; communism, 304, 329, 356; description of, 190, 193; fondness for, 203; getting used to, 292; John Holms and, 193, 257; Peggy Guggenheim, 194, 198, 201, 225, 226, 233–34, 248, 257, 303, 305, 323, 329, 335, 351; Peter Hoare, 292; poetry, 203; publishing, 202–3; riding with, 194; *The Shutter of Snow*, 203; tennis, 201, 203, 283; Wyndham Lewis, 202–3.
Garnett, David, 238, 313
Gascoyne, David, xxviii, xliii, 303, 310–311, 323, 338–39
Gates of Paradise (Blake), 114
Geary, Joan, 235n42
Geddes, Virgil, xxviii, xxxi, 30, 60, 71
Gender: advantages of, 20; artists, xl, 179; diaries, xviii–xix; expatriates, xxvi; issues, xiii, xl, 58; poetry, 243; pressures, xxxvii, xxxix; sex wars, xiii; women's troubles, 86.
Genius: adapting to world, 334–35; Americans, 100; avoidance of criticism, xxxix; Deak Coleman, 57; Edgar Allan Poe, 67; Edwin Muir, 13; Eric Siepmann, 6, 14; formation of, 11; George Henry Lewes, 5; John Holms, 28; *Lady into Fox*, 95–96; *Nightwood*, 157; preoccupation with, xvii, xix, xxix, 15; wasted, 85; woman of, 13, 53.
Genre blending, xiv, xvii–xviii, xxxviii, xli
George V, xxvii, 198, 220, 332n24
George VI, 332
Geraci, Joseph, vii, xliii–xliv
Gerhardi, William Alexander, 115
Gieseking, Walter, 24
Glossop, Elspeth, 230, 233, 235, 338n36
Glossop, Rudolph "Silas," 195n28, 343, 344, 346, 349, 355
Gloucestershire, 82–91, 125–30
Glyndebourne, 231, 307–8
Glyndebourne Festival Opera, 231n37
Goethe, Johann Wolfgang von, 5, 10
Goethe (Lewes), 5, 32
Goldman, Emma (Hero): admiration of, 49; Alexander Berkman, 316; anarchist, 7n13; autobiography, xxv, xxvii, 3, 20, 33, 52, 68, 141; Deux

Magots, 42; Dorothy Holms, 8; John Coleman, 162; John Holms, 28; letter from, 55; love for, 22; memories, 11; Mina Loy, 27, 29; Nancy Astor, 111*n*33; Peggy Guggenheim, 27, 28, 34, 149; Trianon, 39.

Gordon, Albert, 236*n*45

Gosshawk, "Gossy": description of, 250; EardleyKnollys, 140, 249; Glyndebourne, 306; *House Divided*, 144; Jack MacDougall, 230, 248–49; King's broadcast, 333; men, 249; Norman Brook, 135, 144, 160, 186, 230, 238, 249, 261, 333; piles, 316; Robert Helpmann, 261; "The Tygon," 255; visits with, 135, 186, 235.

Grand Hotel, 134

Graves, Robert, 72

Gray, Thomas, 137–38, 327

Great James Street, 165–66

Grigson, Frances (Galt), 207, 210, 235*n*42

Guggenheim, Peggy (Wendy): abortion, 41, 148–49; admiration for, 283; Antonia White, 191, 193, 194, 234, 296; art gallery, 345–46*n*6; Austria, 161, 165; autobiography, xii; Bettiri Baita, 80–81; character, 88; Coleman's cottage, 351; Coleman's diary, xii, xxv, 110, 151; Coleman's father, 123, 126; communism, 330–331; "The Cremation," 181, 193, 255; description of Emily Coleman, xxii, xxv; Djuna Barnes, 101, 104, 113–14, 118, 122, 156, 159, 160, 168, 169, 170, 201, 234, 258, 279, 285–86, 302, 307, 336; Dorothy Holms, 6, 21*n*56, 23, 35*n*94, 196; Douglas Garman, 183, 194 196–97, 201, 215, 225, 226, 233, 248, 250, 303, 329, 335; Emma Goldman, 7*n*13, 27, 28, 34, 149; encouragement from, xxv, 209; fatalism, 234; female alliance, 111; first meeting, xxv, 3, 7*n*13; fondness for, 26; George Barker, 256, 276, 284, 334, 352, 353; Gloucestershire, 93; Hayford Hall, 85, 93, 165; Helen Joyce, 143, 152; Humphrey Jennings, 326–27, 328–29, 345–46, 351; inferiority notion, 17; intellect, 16; John Coleman, 199; John Holms, xii, xxviii, xxi, xxxi,3, 4, 5*n*6, 8*n*17, 11, 13, 15*n*38, 16, 22, 25, 26, 35, 37, 41, 43, 60, 104, 106–7, 111, 117, 118, 143, 147, 148, 155, 159, 161, 173, 177, 190–191, 196, 203, 210, 255; language, 302; Laurence Vail, 39; Lelletto Bianchetti, 80–81, 83, 136, 137, 140, 160; love for, 145, 147, 167, 190; malice, 95, 96, 98; Mina Loy, 120; Mrs. Jolas' school, 145–46; *Nightwood*, 270; Paris, 143; patronage, xii, 198, 220, 232, 276, 353, 355; Paul Léon. 154; Peter Hoare, 99, 114, 116, 120, 167, 198, 202, 258, 306; Phyllis Jones, 190; quarrel with, 105–6; sale of house, 144, 155, 158; sexuality, xxxv–xxxvi; social gathering, 237; tennis, 283; "The Tygon," 316; vanity, 22, 25; Warblington Castle, 183, 185–86, 189, 196*n*29; witty conversation, xii, xxviii, 104, 115, 121, 190, 191; Wyn Henderson, 165*n*2; Yew Tree Cottage, 215, 247.

Haigh-Wood, Vivienne, 261*n*30
Hale, Emily, 266–67
Hall, Radclyffe, xxxv
Hambleden, William, 261, 262
Hamleys, 208
Hanscombe, Gillian, xxxiv
Happiness, 176
Hart Crane: The Life of an American Poet (Horton), 355, 356
Hasslacher, Henry Joseph, 337, 339

Hatchard's book store, 245
Hayford Hall, viii, xxxviii, xlii, xliii, 85, 93–123, 166–71, 309
Hayford Hall, Hangovers, Erotics, and Modernist Aesthetics, xliii
Helpmann, Robert, 261
Hemingway, Ernest, xxviii, xxxi, xlii, 34–35, 152
Henderson, Wyn, 165*n*2, 191–92, 237
Herbert, Patricia, 261*n*27
Hetty's, 188
Higgins, Bertram, 270
Himmel, Sonia Ginsberg, (Hippocra): Arizona visit, xxxviii; Boston, 215; Bourton Far Hill Farm, 81; career, 9*n*21; children, 84*n*27; Coleman's diary, 77*n*1, 82*n*21, 84, 151; Deak Coleman, 90; Djuna Barnes, 87, 291; George Barker, 220; Greta Garbo, 87; love, 79; Peggy Guggenheim, 85, 86, 226; Peter Hoare, 88, 90; prose, 19; psychic abilities, 86; relationship with, 51, 53, 69; *The Shutter of Snow*, 34*n*90; traveling in Italy, 77, 82; weaknesses, 200.
Hoare, Dorothy, 281–82
Hoare, Samuel "Peter": Alex Sidney, 266; Antonia White, 218, 271, 308; Austria, 152, 153, 165; Bloomsbury, 139; Boxholme, 346–47, 357; career, 82*n*22, 268–69; 270; Coleman's birthday, 220; Coleman's poetry, 102; "The Cremation," 232; Cyril Connolly, 270; "The Dark Angel," 273; "Death of Samson," 279–80; description of, 176; Djuna Barnes, 99, 102–3, 119, 169–70, 292, 296, 304, 306; Dorothy Hoare, 191*n*21, 281; Edward Muir's letter, 230; English, 333; *Figaro*, 239, 240; *The First Time I . . .*, 236; frustration with, 107, 125, 129, 134, 139, 165, 166, 174, 185, 191*n*21, 198, 228, 246, 332, 345, 346; George Barker, 217, 224, 225, 226, 228, 229, 242, 244, 247, 254, 259, 284, 288–89, 310, 312; Glyndebourne, 307, 309; good and evil, 206; *Grand Hotel*, 134; Hayford Hall, 93, 309; Humphrey Jennings, 323; impotence, xxiii, xxxvii, 93, 185, 216, 284, 287, 311; industrialism, 90; John Holms, 89, 98, 130, 161, 162, 176; longing for, 81, 83, 123, 127, 130, 143, 144, 145, 149, 151, 162, 193, 196, 205, 216, 218, 242, 250, 280, 343; marriage, xxxiv, xxxvii, 80, 90, 127, 141, 227; "The Old Man," 274; opinion of Coleman's friends, 88; Pegeen Vail's birthday present, 208; Peggy Guggenheim, 99, 114, 120, 123, 197, 199, 202; perfection, 205; platonic relationship, 139, 140; prostitute, 88; relationship with, xxiii, 131, 132, 135, 149, 188, 204, 205, 221, 257, 260, 326, 354; sadism, xxxviii; sexual relationship, xxiii, xxxvii, 129, 135, 183, 199, 201, 232, 257, 261, 329; T. S. Eliot, 222, 234–35, 264–65, 266, 268, 273, 277, 279, 295; tennis, 201; *Ulysses*, 91; vacation with, 186, 211, 215; *Valkyrie*, 204; vitality, 99; women, 235, 266.
Holmes, John Milton: Bourton Far Hill Farm, 125–26; Coleman's childhood, xv, xvi, xvii–xviii; Coleman's promiscuity, xxiii, 103–4; Coleman's thoughts of suicide, 211, 228; Don Holmes, 16, 22, 29, 46, 53, 63, 69; face, 128; financial support from, xxvi, xxvi*n*53, 56, 63, 160, 232; Hayford Hall, 116, 118, 122–23, 126; Hindenburg, 286; nationality, 60; *The Shutter of Snow*, 61; visits with, 29*n*76, 125, 173; wife, xv, 141.
Holmes, William (Don), xv, 16, 29, 52–3, 63, 69

Holms, Beatrix, 38*n*97, 255
Holms, Dorothy (Kurn): Antonia White, 248; intensity, 99; John Holms, 3, 8, 10, 11, 13, 21, 23, 26, 29, 34, 35, 36–7, 50, 81, 152, 205; Peggy Guggenheim, 35, 43, 114, 185, 196, 197, 203.
Holms, John Ferrar (Agamemnon): Austria, 165; *The Calendar of Modern Letters*, xxxi, 5*n*6, 126*n*3; career, 5*n*6; childhood, 38; Coleman's diary, xii, 82; Coleman's poetry, 15; "The Cremation," 174; Deak Coleman, 31, 51; death of, 173, 177, 183, 210*n*62, 245*n*67, 255; description of, 15*n*38; desires, 60; distancing from, 78, 82, 145, 147; Djuna Barnes, xxviii, 112; Dorothy Holms, 3, 8*n*17, 21, 34, 81; Edwin Muir, 5, 8, 11; Emma Goldman, 27, 28, 55; Eric Siepmann, 6, 13, 14; "The Fugitives," 17; genius, 11, 25, 28, 54; influence, xxxi, 28, 29, 62; John Coleman, 20–21, 264; language, 65; Laura Riding, 72; Laurence Vail, 39–40; Left Bank, 4; letters, 222; long talks with, 11, 12, 23; love for, 16; "Lysias" poem, 14; mouths, 90; Peggy Guggenheim, xxxi, 3, 13, 15, 25, 26, 35, 41, 60, 81, 93, 143, 144, 286; Peter Hoare, 89, 97, 125, 129–30, 132; philosophy, 18; prose, 19; return from Sweden, 8; returning to London with, 131; sensitive people, 17; sexuality, xxxvi; sonnets, 62; suffering, xl; superiority complex, 27–28; T. S. Eliot, 18; underdogs, 27; vanity, 22–23; "The Visit," 24; Walter Lowenfels, 29; war, 36–37; women, 13, 111.
Home Office in London, 80, 83*n*22, 88, 135*n*18, 221, 268–69
Homosexuality: Emily Coleman, xxxv, 244–45; George Barker, 217, 243, 254; Judith, 9*n*24, 54; prison camp, 36–7.
Hopkinson, Henry Tom: Antonia White, 183, 207, 235, 265, 308, 317, 349; Cyril Connolly, 298; Eric Siepmann, 217, 218; Frances Grigson, 210, 221; Joan Geary, 235*n*42; "I Have Been Drowned," 278; "Melville on the Land," 222, 255.
A House Divided, 144
"The House of Clouds" (White), 280
Housman, Alfred Edward, 276
"House of Clouds" (White), 338
Hubberholme, 173–82, 307–19
Hudson, William Henry, 82
Hughes, Richard, 337
Hume, Benita, 6*n*9
Hummel, Jack, xxiv*n*48, 318
Huxley, Aldous, 240
Huxley, Maria (Nys), 240

"I Have Been Drowned" (Hopkinson), 278
Imagism, xiv
Imitation of Christ (Kempis), 315
Immortality, 36
Impressionism, xiv
Incest, 305
Industrialism, 90
Inferiority complex, 23, 98, 127, 202, 210, 271, 279
Inferno (Dante), 50, 67
"Interlude" (Coleman), 32–33, 48
International Surrealist Exhibition, 311
The Ivy, xxvii, 140, 269

Jack Robinson: A Picaresque Novel (Fitzgerald), 285
Jackson, Laura (Riding), 72
Jamme, Henriette Louise, xxvi*n*52, 90
Janus (Barker), 222
Jennings, Humphrey: affair with, xxxvii, 323, 344; Alan Clutton-Brock, 325; David Gascoyne, 339; Djuna Barnes,

325; dreams of, 334; first meeting, 303; Peggy Guggenheim, 328, 343, 346, 351; rejection, 326–27, 328, 339; suicidal thoughts, 325–26, 329, 331; thoughts of, 334, 336.
John, Augustus, 138, 342
Johnson, Lionel, 272
Jolas, Eugene, xxviii, xxix–xxx, 18*n*45, 145*n*8, 149, 150
Jolas, Maria McDonald, xxvi, xxviii, 18*n*45, 145*n*8, 149, 150, 151, 153
Jones, Phyllis (Redhead): Basil Rathbone, 121, 139; beauty, 351; Boxholme, 357; career, xii, 9*n*24; Coleman's diary, xliii–xliv; *Daily Mirror*, 263; Dan Mahoney, 230; Douglas Garman, 259; inheritance, 121; jodhpurs, 208; John Coleman, 311, 313; "Lysias" poem, 14; New York, 215; Peter Hoare, 88, 299; Ridgways, 134; Russian Ballet, 181; *The Shutter of Snow*, 87; spiritualist, 138; Stephan, 303; "The Tygon," 209, 333; Warblington Castle, 183, 185–86, 191, 193, 194, 195, 202, 206; weaknesses, 200.
Jordan, Philip (David): career, 4, 9*n*25; description of, 10; desire for, 11, 16, 22, 29, 48, 51; love affair, 29, 48, 79.
Josef's, 216
Joyce, Giorgio, 143, 153
Joyce, Helen, 143, 153
Joyce, James: analysis of, xxviii, xxix, 6–7, 179; Ettore Schmitz, 85*n*29; influence of, 78*n*6; language, 64; meeting in Paris, 80–81; *transition*, xxx; Wyndham Lewis' article, 91.
Judith: cooling desire, 10, 16, 30, 42, 43; depression, 30, 110; desire to be a man, 20; love affair with, xxxv, 9, 54; "The Visit," 24.
Jung, Carl, 89
J. Walter Thompson, 3, 356

Keaton, Joseph Frank, 293
Kemp, Henry, 110
Kempis, Thomas a, 315*n*15
Kew Gardens, 273, 280, 281, 326
Kingsmill (Lunn), Hugh, 200, 257
Knollys, Eardley, 140, 249

L'Escargot, 135
Lac Des Cygnes, 184
La Coscienza di Zeno (Svevo), 85, 87, 97, 298
Ladies Almanac, 167–68
Lady into Fox (Garnett), 95–96
Lamos, Colleen, xxxv
Language, poetic, 65
Latin Quarter, 3
Lavandou, 145
Lawrence, D. H.: analysis of, xxviii, xxix; influence of, 78*n*6, 179; *Letters*,127, 136, 137; *Lorenzo in Taos*, 112; sensuousness, 21; *Sons and Lovers*, 128–29; *Women in Love*, 87, 88.
Lawrence, Gertrude, 139
"Leda and the Swan" (Yeats), 224
Left Bank, xiii, xxiv, xxvii, xxix, 3–4
Léon, Paul, 154, 284
Lesbianism, xiii, xxxiv–xxxv, 218, 244, 269
Les Halles, 25, 26, 40
Lethbridge, Mabel, 195
The Letters of D. H., Lawrence,127, 136, 137
Leucorrhea, 29, 30
Lewes, George Henry, 5*n*2
Lewis, Wyndham, 89, 91, 132, 138, 202
"Life and Death of Jesus Christ" (Coleman), 19, 49
The Lion and the Fox (Lewis), 126
Literary criticism, xl, 97
Literary network, xxxi
Living My Life (Goldman), xxvii, 7*n*13, 141

London Group, xxvii, 132*n*6, 324
London Pavilion, 140
Lorenzo in Taos (Sterne), 112
Louvre, 8, 37
Love, 59, 81, 95, 99, 178, 344, 345
Lowenfels, Walter, 29, 30
Lowndes, Marie Adelaide (Belloc), 297
Loy, Mina, 27, 29, 120
Ludwig, Emil, 5
Luhan, Mabel, 112*n*34, 112*n*36, 113
Luling, Peter, 79
"Lycidas" (Milton), 265
"Lysias" (Coleman), 14, 15, 16, 18, 48, 54, 60

MacCarthy, Desmond, 166*n*3
MacDougall, Allan Ross (Jack): career, 230*n*36; new acquaintance, 247; personality, 249, 261, 265; "The Tygon," 230, 248–49, 269, 343.
MacDougall Street, 293
MacNamara, Caitlin, 342
Madox, Ford, 30
Magic Flute, 307
"A Major Poet, The Influence of Mr. Eliot" (Connolly), 271
Mahoney, Daniel A, (Dr. Connor), 99–100, 168, 230
The Mall, 221
Man the Unknown (Carrel), 293
Marriage: Deak Coleman, xx*n*29, xxiii–xxv, 3, 79–80; expatriate American women, xxvi; Humphrey Jennings, 326*n*8; Peggy Guggenheim and John Holms, 108; Peter Hoare, 127, 139, 140; stereotypes, xxix, 68*n*65.
Marsh, Edward, 262
Marx Brothers, 239, 241
Masochism, 23
Matthews, William, xli
Maurice Guest (Richardson), 256, 306, 312, 313, 314
Maurin, Peter, xxxviii
McDonald, Gwenda, 239*n*52

McDonald, Iverach: chance meeting, 239; desire for, 177, 185, 193; farm life, 174; lack of response from, 196; personality, 175–76; relationship with, 174, 270; spirituality, 176.
McDougall, Jack, 277, 278, 288
McGreevy, Thomas, 30
Measure for Measure, 21
"Melville on the Land" (Coleman), xxxii, 216, 218*n*8, 228, 246, 255, 297
Men: attraction to, 24, 54, 117; defining herself, xx; diary traditions, xviii–xix; Djuna Barnes, 99, 100, 109, 113; modifying behavior, xxxiii, 58; need for attention, 244, 249; writing drama, 69.
Meynell, Vera Mendel, 36
Middleton, Scudder, 290
Mildmay, Audrey, 240
Miller, Henry, 299, 300, 302
Milton, John, 6, 10, 12, 202
Misogyny, xxxiii
Moby Dick, 66
"Modern Fiction" (Woolf), xiv
Modernism, xi, xii, xiii–xiv, xxiv, xxvi, xxvii, xxxii, xxxv, xxxvi, xxxvii*n*99, xlii
Monico Restaurant, 88
Monogamy, xxv, xxxiv, xxxvii
Montmartre, 144, 160
Mood swings, xvi, xxiv
Moore, Henry, 176
Moors, xxxvi, 95, 174, 182, 194
Morgan, Charles, 299
Morley, Frank, 247, 267–68, 295
Morris, Cedric, 133
Morris, Edita, 198
Morris, Ira, 198
Morris, William, 318
Mortimer, Raymond, 218, 278
Motherhood: concern for son, 79; expatriate women, xxxiv; limitations, xxiv; maternal feelings, 20–21;

modernist women, xxxvii*n*99; negotiating identities, 4; anger, 38, 354, 355; role of, xxxviii; writing and, 11.
Movie Crazy, 153
Mrs. Dalloway (Woolf), 33
Muir, Edwin: career, xii; "The Cremation," 241; D. H. Lawrence, 21; "The Ecstasy," 51; influence, 28; James Joyce, 65; John Holms, 5, 11, 13, 143, 177; love for, 8; "Melville on the Land," 228, 230, 255; poems, 198, 279; praise and commentary, xxxii; socializing with, 131, 133; stay with, 13; *The Three Brothers*, 158, 161.
Muir, Wilhelmina, 8, 13, 133, 150
Murder in the Cathedral (Eliot), 225

National Gallery, 8, 225
Nationality, art and, 60
Nature: enjoyment of, xxxvi, 48*n*13, 98, 184, 241, 351; spirituality and, xxxvi–xxxvii; truths of, 244.
Neagoe, Annie, 147
Neagoe, Peter: career, 84*n*25; *Americans Abroad*, xxxi, 84, 147, 162; Djuna Barnes, xxxi, 222, 238, 290, 293.
New Jersey, xv, xvi
New Statesman, 218, 241, 246
Newton Abbot Race course, 121
New Verse, 274
"New York" group, 64
Nicholls, Peter, xiii
Nightwood (Barnes): Arthur Waley, 324; Coleman advocating for, xii, xxvii, 216, 221*n*18; critique of, 156–57; Djuna Barnes, 93, 312; editing, 215; evil, 238; experimental texts, xii; influence, 357; title, 276–77; Thelma Wood, 100*n*13; T. S. Eliot, 216, 221, 247, 264–65, 287, 293.
No Love (Garnett), 238
The Nonesuch Press, 245*n*65

The Notebooks of MalteLauridsBrigge (Rilke), 240

Obelisk Press, 251
Oberlé, Jean, 168*n*9
"Ode on Immortality" (Wordsworth), 233, 259, 266
"Ode to Man" (Barker), 223, 224, 259, 268, 274
"Old Man" (Coleman), 274–75
Olympia, 338
Olympia Fun Fair, 338
Orlando (Woolf), 33
Othello, 33, 37, 61, 324
Out of This Century: Confessions of an Art Addict (Guggenheim), xlii, 5*n*6

The Pageant of Parliament, 186
Paris, xii, xxiv–xxv, xxvii, xxxvii, 7, 143–62
Pasdeloup Orchestra, 24
Patmore, Coventry, 68
Patriarchal culture, xix
Patrons, of modernism, xii, xxvi, xxvii
Paul, Elliot, xxix–xxx, 250–51
Pepys, Samuel, xli, xlii
Petersfield, 250
Philippe. *See* Fisher-boy
Philosophy, 18
"The Photograph" (Coleman), 21
Physical abuse, xxiv, 81, 96, 158, 247, 258
Picabia, Gabrielle, 158
Piccadilly, 88, 185, 332
Piccadilly Circus, 134, 154
Poe, Edgar Allan, 67
Poetics (Aristotle), 59
Poetry: American, 15; Arthur Waley, 12, 18; biblical references, xxxix, 11; body of work, xl; gender and, 243; inspiration through, 62, 178; James Joyce, 64; letters, xxi; suffering and, 12; *transition*, xi, xxix–xxx; voice, 77–78; writing, 67.

The Poetry Bookshop in Bloomsbury, 138
Polygamy, 306
Ponisovsky, Alec, 154, 283
The Possessed (Dostoevsky), 6
Postpartum depression, xvi, xxiii, xxx, 126*n*4
Pound, Ezra, xiv, xxxiii–xxxiv
Poverty, xxxviii, 301, 318, 353, 357
Power, desire for, 22
Pramousquier, 39, 144, 155
Primitivism, xiv
Private Detective No. 62, 199*n*33
Prokosch, Frederic, 270, 271
Promiscuous behavior, xxiii, 4
Prose, 19, 50
Proverbs of Heaven and Hell (Blake), 316
"Proverbs of Sainthood and the Imagination" (Coleman), 316
Prunier's, 25
Psychoanalysis, 335
Psychology, 180
Publication of diary, xi, xliii
Puerperal fever, 25*n*67
Putnam, Samuel, 30
Pylon School, 192*n*25

Queen's Hall at Langham Place, 208
"Queer Conjunctions in Modernism" (Lamos), xxxv
Quennell, Peter: career, 269*n*50; Café Royal, 269, 277; Cyril Connolly, 270, 271, 303; description of, 298.
Quo Vadis, 226

Rabelais, François, xxviii, 6–7, 30–31s
Rages, 30
Rathbone, Basil, 121, 139
Ray, Mann, 237
Rebellion, against organized society, xvi
Recognition, need for, 25
Religion. *See* Spirituality
Respect, 55

Resurrection (Gerhardie), 292
Reynolds, Mary, 169, 170, 237
Rich, Adrienne, xviii
Richards, Ivor Armstrong, 180, 206
Richardson, Henry Handel, 252*n*11, 256
Rickword, Edgell, 183
Riding, Laura, 72
Rivalry, writing and, 36, 60
Rochester State Hospital, xxiii, 17*n*43, 25*n*67, 58*n*43
The Rock Pool (Connolly), xii, 251, 270
Rowe, Reginald, 262
The Royal Albert Hall, 186
"Ruth" (Coleman), 48
Ryder (Barnes), xii, 100, 117, 310

The Sacred Wood (Eliot), 59, 179
Sadler's Wells Theatre, 260
Sampson, Harriet, 20
Sanitarium, xv–xvi
Scarborough, Jake, xxxviii
Schmitz, Ettore (Svevo), 85*n*29
School of Good Shepherd, xvi
Scott, Bonnie Kime, viii, xiii–xiv
Selassie, Haile, 273
Sex: before marriage, xxii; evil and, 205, 218; relationships and, 58, 79; struggle with ambition, xxxix, 57; wars, xiii.
Sexual abuse, 305–6
Sexuality: criticism and, 262; ecstasy and, 51–52; Emily Coleman, xxxiv–xxxv; emotional intensity, 26, 284; homosexuality, 54; identity, 4; lesbianism, xxxv, 216, 218, 244, 269; lovers, 80; modernism, xiii, xxxv–xxxvi, xlii; passionate women, 313; promiscuous behavior, xxiii, xxxiv; social networks, xii.
Shakespeare, 5–6, 28, 30
Shaw, George Bernard, 220, 309
Short stories, body of work, xl
The Shutter of Snow (Coleman): birth trauma, xvi; Djuna Barnes, 312–13;

introduction, xxii; proofs, 70–71, 72, 73; publication, xi, 4, 8; reissued, xliii; work in progress, xxx–xxxi.
Sidney, Alex, 235, 245, 252, 266
Siepmann, Eric (Antony): Antonia White, 215, 218, 220–21, 222, 224, 235–36, 236*n*43, 249, 250, 265, 273, 278; career, 6*n*9; Djuna Barnes, 292; Feodor Dostoyevsky, 6; John Holms, 13; Judith, 42; Luxembourg, 7; Peggy Guggenheim, 110; relationship with, xxxvi, 10, 11, 70, 72; self-confidence, 25; solitude, 55; Tom Hopkinson, 217.
Siepmann, Mary, xxii
Silly Symphonies, 134*n*12
Simpson's-in-the-Strand, 188
Simpsons of Piccadilly, 335
Simpson, Wallis Warfield, 331, 332*n*22, 333*n*26
Sino-Japanese war, 353*n*16
Sitwell, Edith, 138
Ski Holiday, Austria, 165
Small, Alex (Lysander), 5, 14, 24, 65, 99*n*10
Smart, Elizabeth, xlii, 243
Smith, Ada (Bricktop), xxvii, 144
Smith, Eric Earnshaw, 167, 191, 207, 264, 265, 273
Smith, Logan Pearsall, 325
Smith, T. R., 159
Smyers, Virginia, xxxiv
Social network, xii, xlv–xlvi, 303*n*29
Socialism, 7*n*13
Solitude, xxv, xxvi, xxxvii, xxxix, 9, 12, 47, 55, 83, 179
Sonnets, xxxli, 5, 48, 54, 58, 64, 68, 69, 73, 78, 61, 62
Sons and Lovers (Lawrence), 128
Sorbonne, xxiv, 3
Souter-Robertson, Joan, 249, 250
Spencer, Bernard, 337
Spencer, Gilbert, 132
Spender, Stephen, 192*n*25

Spirituality: beliefs, 330; biblical phrases, 11; Catholic Church, 63; convent, 345; the Creed, 176; grandfather's sermons, 243; precedence over sexual and worldly life, xxxix; religious poems, xl.
SS. Westernland, 348, 357–58
Stallybrass, William Swan, 55, 58
Stansbury, Helen and Harold, 220, 339
"The Stars" (Coleman), xvii
St. Augustine of Hippo, 218
Stereotypes, xix, xxxix, 26
Stevens, Wallace, xvi
St. Mary's on Mount-St. Gabriel, xvi, 63*n*52
St. Nicholas, xvii
"The Story of My Childhood" (Coleman), xiv, xv, 11*n*28
Strachey, James, 309
Strachey, Joan Pernel, 282*n*78
Strachey, John (Spotty), 324
Stream of consciousness, xiv
Strong, Leonard Alfred George, 133
St. Tropez, xxv, xxvi, xxxi, xxxv, xxxvii, 3, 45–74
Success, lack of, xxxix–xl
Suffering, 10, 11, 175
Suffrage movement, xiii
Suicide: Alexander Berkman, 316; Antonia White, 207; Djuna Barnes, 234; Dylan Thomas, 345; Elsie Walsingham, 210; George Barker, 244, 253; Humphrey Jennings, 327, 328, 331, 334; John Holms, 21; Peter Hoare, 254, 327, 343; "The Tygon," 81, 324–25, 335;
Superiority complex, 27
Surrealism: exhibition, 311; "The Fugitives," 17*n*43; "Lysias" poem, 18; modernism, xiii–xiv; Peter Neagoe, 84*n*25; *transition*, 18*n*45; "The Wren's Nest," 48*n*13; writers, xi, xiv, xxx.
Symbolism, xiv

Taboos, xiv, xxxiv, xxxv, 48*n*13
Temple Guiting, 82, 85, 86
Themes, xiv, xxxiv
These Three, 277
Thirty Personalities (Lewis), xxvii, 132*n*5
This Quarter, 4, 17*n*43, 42
Thomas, Dylan: Antonia White, 338; break up, 344; description of, 337; personality, 339, 340*n*41; poems, 274; pub crawling, xii; romance with, xxxvii, 323, 341–42, 343.
Thunder Over Mexico, 242
Times Literary Supplement, xxx–xxxi, 141*n*36, 318*n*22
Titus, Edward, xxxiii, 17, 30*n*79, 42
Tonny, Kristians, 20
Top Hat, 221
To the Lighthouse (Woolf), 271
The Tower (Yeats), 204
"Tradition and the Individual Talent" (Eliot), 59
Tragedy, writing, 33
transition, xi, xxix–xxx, 4, 18
Tribune, xxiv–xxv, xxvi, xxvi*n*53, xxvii, xxix, xxx, 5*n*4, 302
Tropic of Cancer (Miller), 302, 303, 304
Two Years Before the Mast (Dana), 125
"The Tygon" (Coleman): abortion, 230; Antonia White, 288; basis for, xxxii, xxxii*n*73, 73*n*73, 81; Coleman papers, xl; Djuna Barnes, 324, 330; Jack MacDougall, 269, 343; Phyllis Jones, 209; sadism, 307, 314, 314*n*13; setting, 210; spirituality, xxxvi; title, 326; tragedy, 230; writing, 150–151, 174, 204, 206, 207, 209, 217, 230, 255, 315, 335.
Typographical play, xiv

The Ugly Duckling (Disney), 134
Ulysses (Joyce), 65, 91, 285
Under the Roofs of Paris (Sous Les Toits de Paris), 219

Underdogs, 27
Urquhart, Thomas, 6

Vail, Clotilde, 197
Vail, Laurence: Djuna Barnes, 64*n*57; John Holms, 35, 39–40; Pegeen Vail, 27*n*71; Peggy Guggenheim, 3, 144*n*1, 278; Peter Hoare, 208.
Vail, Pegeen Guggenheim: birthday present, 208; detective film, 198; Devonshire, 95; John Coleman, 26–7, 31, 143, 144, 153–54; John Holms, 152; motherhood, 105; Mrs. Jolas' school, 145–46; Park Montsouris, 148; pictures, 199.
Vail, Sindbad: Coleman's face, 201; description of, 94, 199; duck hunting, 196; moors, 104; Peggy Guggenheim, 85, 119, 120; photograph of, 158; scissors, 170.
Valkyrie (Wagner), 204–5
Vanity, 22–23, 24, 237, 280
"The Vicar's Pants" (Coleman), 42
"The Visit" (Coleman), 24, 26, 48
Vitrac, Roger, 149*n*16

Waldman, Milton, 202*n*43
Waley, Arthur: description of, 138, 189, 302; James Joyce, 65; London, 9*n*24; poetry, 12, 18, 28; respect, 26; sonnets, 62.
Walsingham, Elsie, 210*n*61
War, 21*n*56, 36
Warblington Castle, 183, 185
"The Wasted Earth" (Coleman), 24*n*65, 48
Waterloo in Wardour Street (Siepmann), 273*n*62
Weaknesses, self-assessment, 200
Wellesley College, xx–xxi
The Well of Loneliness (Hall), xxxv
Welsford, Enid, 282*n*80
Wesley, Mary, 6*n*9
Whipsnade Park Zoo, 187

White, Antonia (Tony): abortion, 230; autobiography, xii; blood-poisoning, 265, 273; Coleman's diary, xii, xxxii, xxxvi; Coleman's lack of success, xxxix, xl; "The Cremation," 275; critiques, xxxii; Cyril Connolly, 250, 297, 298; "Death of Samson," 288; description of Emily, xi, xl, 10n26; Djuna Barnes, 290–91, 349–50; Dylan Thomas, 338–39; Earnshaw Smith, 167; Eric Siepmann, 215, 217n6, 218, 220–21, 222, 224; first meeting, 165; genius, 280; George Barker, 278, 288; Humphrey Jennings, 324–25; insects, 312; *Life and Letters*, 166; marriage, xxxvi; "Melville on the Land," 217; men, 249; mental illness, 252, 317–18; patronage, xxvii; Peggy Guggenheim, 234, 296; Peter Hoare, 271, 287, 290; psychoanalysis, 332, 334, 335; revision, 168; spirituality, 301–2; suicide, 183, 207; surgery, 284, 303, 305, 306, 307, 310; teaching school, 236, 236n44; Tom Hopkinson, 217, 235, 278, 308, 317; "The Tygon," 209; Warblington Castle, 191, 193, 194–95, 196; women, 349.
Whitehall, 225
Whitman, Walt, 66
Whit-Monday, 289–91
Whooping cough, 63–64, 66
Wild Nature's Ways (Kearton), 96
Wilde, Dorothy (Dolly), 291
Wishart, Ernest, 183, 201n39, 202, 203, 257
"The Woman of Samaria" (Coleman), 19
Women in Love (Lawrence), xxviii, 87, 129
Women of the Left Bank (Benstock), xxiii
Women's Writing in Exile (Broe), xliii
Wood, Henry, 208n58
Wood, Thelma Ellen: Coleman and, xxxvi, 100n13, 143, 146, 152, 159–60; Djuna Barnes, xii, 100, 104, 156, 159, 160, 170, 222, 294; financial support, 116; John Holms, 161.
Woodward, Jessica, 215–16
Woolf, Virginia, xiv, xxvii, xlii, xlv–xlvi, 33
Wordsworth, Dorothy, 86, 99
"The Wren's Nest" (Coleman), 48
Writers, women as, xxxiii–xxxiv
Writing, reasons for, 61
Wuthering Heights (Brontë), 314

Year Before Last (Boyle), 148, 158
Yeats, W. B., 204, 224
Yew Tree Cottage, 247, 256–58, 282–86, 345–46, 348–57
Yorkshire, 173–82

About the Editor

Elizabeth Podnieks is an Associate Professor in the Department of English and the Graduate Program in Communication and Culture at Ryerson University, Toronto, where she teaches and researches in the fields of modernism, life writing, mothering, and popular and celebrity culture. She is the author of *Daily Modernism: The Literary Diaries of Virginia Woolf, Antonia White, Elizabeth Smart, and Anaïs Nin* (McGill-Queen's University Press, 2000), and the co-editor of *Hayford Hall: Hangovers, Erotics, and Modernist Aesthetics* (Southern Illinois University Press, 2005). Podnieks has also guest edited two special issues of *a/b: Auto/Biography Studies*: "Private Life, Public Text: Women's Diary Literature" (Summer 2002), and "'New Biography' for a New Millennium" (Summer 2009). Moreover, she is the co-editor of *Textual Mothers, Maternal Texts: Motherhood in Contemporary Women's Literatures* (Wilfrid Laurier University Press, 2009) and the sole editor of the collection *Mediating Moms: Mothers in Popular Culture* (McGill-Queen's University Press, 2012).

PS3505.O2783 Z46